1997 World
Development
Indicators

World development indicators

Copyright 1997 by the International Bank
for Reconstruction and Development/THE WORLD BANK
1818 H Street, N.W., Washington, D.C. 20433, U.S.A.

This volume is a product of the staff of the Development Data Group of the World Bank's International Economics Department, and the judgments herein do not necessarily reflect the views of the World Bank's Board of Executive Directors or the countries they represent.

The World Bank does not guarantee the accuracy of the data included in this publication and accepts no responsibility whatsoever for any consequence of their use. The boundaries, colors, denominations, and other information shown on any map in this volume do not imply on the part of the World Bank any judgment on the legal status of any territory or the endorsement or acceptance of such boundaries.

The material in this publication is copyrighted. Requests for permission to reproduce portions of it should be sent to the Office of the Publisher at the address in the copyright notice above. The World Bank encourages dissemination of its work and will normally give permission promptly and, when reproduction is for noncommercial purposes, without asking a fee. Permission to photocopy portions for classroom use is granted through the Copyright Center, Inc., Suite 910, 222 Rosewood Drive, Danvers, Massachusetts 01923, U.S.A.

Questions and comments about this product? Please contact:

IEC Information Center, Development Data Group
The World Bank
1818 H Street, N.W., Washington, D.C. 20433, U.S.A.
Hotline: (800) 590 1906 or (202) 473 7824; fax (202) 522 1498.
Email: info@worldbank.org.
Website: http://www.worldbank.org or http://www.worldbank.org/html/iecdd/wdi.html.

ISBN 0-8213-3701-7

1997 | World Development Indicators

The World Bank

Foreword

We have redesigned the *World Development Indicators* to expand its coverage of development issues in a new, free-standing format, complemented by a comprehensive database on CD-ROM and a redesigned *World Bank Atlas*. This new family of products embodies many aspects of the change we are trying to bring about at the World Bank Group.

First, the selection of indicators reflects a broader, more integrated approach to development. The *World Development Indicators* starts from the premise that development is about the quality of life. It places people and poverty reduction first, at the center of the development agenda where they belong. In its five main sections it recognizes the interplay of a wide range of issues: human capital development, environmental sustainability, macroeconomic performance, private sector development, and the global links that influence the external environment for development.

Second, the new *World Development Indicators* is an excellent example of global partnership in creating and sharing knowledge and in making knowledge a major force for development—an area where I see the World Bank playing an increasingly important role. I would like to thank our partners in the United Nations family, the International Monetary Fund, the World Trade Organization, the OECD, the statistical offices of more than 200 economies, and countless others who have made this unique product possible. Throughout the volume we have acknowledged their contributions in order to guide researchers and others seeking information to the many sources on which it draws. And because the *World Development Indicators* draws on the Bank's own cross-country experience and sectoral knowledge, I am particularly pleased to note the important role of the new sectoral networks of Bank staff in the redesign. Their support and that of staff of the International Finance Corporation and the Multilateral Investment Guarantee Agency truly make the *World Development Indicators* a Bank Group product.

Third, the new *World Development Indicators* reflects the Bank Group's new emphasis on development impact and outcomes. I hope that the *World Development Indicators* will become the principal mechanism by which the world measures progress in reducing poverty and in enriching the lives of people everywhere. For this to happen, however, all of us—governments, international institutions, and the private sector—will have to pay far more attention to the coverage, timeliness, and quality of information about development policies and outcomes. The detailed technical notes that accompany each set of indicators show how much work still lies ahead.

Finally, the annual *World Development Indicators* is very much a work in progress. In the spirit of the new Bank, its redesign reflects extensive consultation with our clients. And knowing that it could be even richer and more comprehensive, we welcome your comments to assist us in making it even more powerful in serving our clients' needs.

James D. Wolfensohn
President
The World Bank Group

Acknowledgments

This book was prepared by a team led by K. Sarwar Lateef. The team consisted of Mehdi Akhlaghi, Aelim Chi, David Cieslikowski, Jihee Kim, Bertha Namfua, Saeed Ordoubadi, Sulekha Patel, Eric Swanson, K. M. Vijayalakshmi, Mildred Weiss, and Estela Zamora, working closely with other teams in the International Economics Department's Development Data Group. The CD-ROM development team included Mehdi Akhlaghi, Azita Amjadi, Elizabeth Crayford, Reza Farivari, Asieh Kehyari, Angelo Kostopoulos, and William Prince. Contributions were also made by staff from throughout the Development Economics Vice Presidency. The work was carried out under the management of Shaida Badiee and under the general direction of Masood Ahmed.

The choice of indicators and textual content was shaped by close consultation with and substantial contributions from staff in the four emerging thematic networks of the World Bank—Environmentally and Socially Sustainable Development; Finance, Private Sector, and Infrastructure; Human Development; and Poverty Reduction and Economic Management—and staff of the International Finance Corporation and the Multilateral Investment Guarantee Agency. T. N. Srinivasan, Paul Armington, and Michael Ward were also instrumental in helping shape the product and commented extensively on drafts of the book. In addition, we received substantial help, guidance, and data from our external partners. For individual acknowledgments of contributions to the book's content, please see the credits. For a listing of our key partners, see the *Partners* section.

Bruce Ross-Larson was the principal editor, and Peter Grundy, the art director. The cover and page design and the layout and desktopping were by the American Writing division of Communications Development Incorporated, with Grundy & Northedge of London. The External Affairs Vice Presidency oversaw publication and dissemination of the book.

Preface

Our goal in producing the *World Development Indicators* is to put useful information about the world in the hands of policymakers, development specialists, students, and the general public. This new volume—together with its companion publications, the *World Bank Atlas* and the *World Development Indicators* CD-ROM—has been totally redesigned, based on extensive consultation with partners inside and outside the World Bank and in close collaboration with the Bank's sector specialists and research staff. We have expanded the coverage of the *World Development Indicators* to provide an overview of the main themes of development that are the focus of the World Bank's work: the welfare of people, the use and preservation of the environment, the growth and structure of the economy, the complementary roles of states and markets, and the growing links between economies. Guiding our selection of indicators is a desire to present the most useful and interesting information available on trends in development. Over the coming years we expect the coverage to evolve and grow, reflecting emerging issues in the global economy and greater availability of data.

Previously published as an appendix to the *World Development Report,* the *World Development Indicators* now takes its place as the World Bank's principal statistical survey of world development. It contains most of the data previously published in the Bank's *World Tables* and *Social Indicators of Development.* Unlike the *World Tables*, which presented tables for each economy containing long time series of macroeconomic data, the *World Development Indicators* follows a cross-sectional format, with tables arranged topically.

Most tables show indicators for a recent year and an earlier year, covering 148 economies with populations of more than one million. Where possible, the indicators are in growth rates or shares. This format is designed to facilitate comparative analysis of important economic trends across countries and over time. For researchers who need time series of primary data, the *World Development Indicators* CD-ROM contains time series of all indicators available in the *World Development Indicators* database. And for those who want a brief overview of the world economy, the *World Bank Atlas* summarizes 34 current indicators for 209 economies in maps, graphs, and tables.

We have tried to ensure that the indicators are consistent with international standards and are reasonably comparable across economies and over time. But the state of international statistics is not good. Many statistical offices are underfunded, and their staffs undertrained. In some areas the importance of accurate measures of social and economic aggregates for policy formulation is not recognized—or worse, statistics are manipulated to support policy. It is not possible to correct for all possible sources of error, but where difficulties are known in collecting and reporting data, we have—in what is another new feature—provided warnings in general notes or in specific footnotes to the tables. When data have been found to be unreliable or to deviate seriously from accepted norms, they have been omitted. We have limited our selection of indicators to those that are available for most of the principal economies.

We welcome your suggestions and comments on these new products. Please write to us at World Bank headquarters or send us email at info@worldbank.org.

Masood Ahmed
Director
International Economics Department

Shaida Badiee
Senior Manager
Development Data Group

Contents

Contents

Acronyms and abbreviations

Technical terms

bbl	Barrel
btu	British thermal units
CCCN	Customs Cooperation Council Nomenclature
CFC	Chlorofluorocarbon
c.i.f.	Cost, insurance, and freight
CITES	Convention on International Trade in Endangered Species of Wild Flora and Fauna
CO₂	Carbon dioxide
COMTRADE	Commodity Trade database
CPI	Consumer price index
cu. m	Cubic meter
DHS	Demographic and Health Survey
DMTU	Dry metric ton unit
DPT	Diphtheria, pertussis, and tetanus
DRS	Debtor Reporting System
ESAF	Enhanced Structural Adjustment Facility
FDI	Foreign direct investment
f.o.b.	Free on board
FYR	Former Yugoslav Republic
G-5	France, Germany, Japan, United Kingdom, and United States
G-7	G-5 plus Canada and Italy
GDP	Gross domestic product
GEMS	Global Environment Monitoring System
GFS	Government Finance Statistics
GIS	Geographic information system
GNI	Gross national income
GNP	Gross national product
ha	Hectare
HIV	Human immunodeficiency virus
ICRG	International Country Risk Guide
ICSE	International Classification of Status in Employment
IFS	International Financial Statistics
ISCED	International Standard Classification of Education
ISIC	International Standard Industrial Classification
kg	Kilogram
km	Kilometer
kwh	Kilowatt-hour
M1	Narrow money (currency and demand deposits)
M2	Money plus quasi money
M3	Broad money or liquid liabilities
mmbtu	Millions of British thermal units
mt	Metric ton
MFA	Multifibre Arrangement
MUV	Manufactures unit value
NAFTA	North American Free Trade Agreement
NEAP	National environmental action plan
NGO	Nongovernmental organization
ODA	Official development assistance
P/E	Price-earnings ratio
PPP	Purchasing power parity
R&D	Research and development
SAF	Structural Adjustment Facility
SDR	Special drawing right
SITC	Standard International Trade Classification
SNA	U.N. System of National Accounts
SO₂	Sulfur dioxide
sq. km	Square kilometer
TFP	Total factor productivity
TRAINS	Trade Analysis and Information System
TSP	Triple superphosphate

Organizations

ADB	Asian Development Bank
AfDB	African Development Bank
APEC	Asia-Pacific Economic Cooperation
CDC	Centers for Disease Control and Prevention
CDIAC	Carbon Dioxide Information Analysis Center
CEC	Commission of the European Communities
DAC	Development Assistance Committee
EBRD	European Bank for Reconstruction and Development
EDF	European Development Fund
EFTA	European Free Trade Area
EIB	European Investment Bank
EU	European Union
EUROSTAT	Statistical Office of the European Communities
FAO	Food and Agriculture Organization
GATT	General Agreement on Tariffs and Trade
GEF	Global Environment Facility
IBRD	International Bank for Reconstruction and Development
ICCO	International Cocoa Organization
ICO	International Coffee Organization
ICP	International Comparison Programme
IDA	International Development Association
IDB	Inter-American Development Bank
IEA	International Energy Agency
IFC	International Finance Corporation
ILO	International Labour Organisation
IMF	International Monetary Fund
IRF	International Road Federation
ITU	International Telecommunication Union
IUCN	World Conservation Union
LME	London Metals Exchange
MIGA	Multilateral Investment Guarantee Agency
OECD	Organization for Economic Cooperation and Development
PAHO	Pan American Health Organization
U.N.	United Nations
UNAIDS	Joint United Nations Programme on HIV/AIDS
UNCED	United Nations Conference on Environment and Development
UNCTAD	United Nations Conference on Trade and Development
UNDP	United Nations Development Programme
UNECE	United Nations Economic Commission for Europe
UNEP	United Nations Environment Programme
UNESCO	United Nations Educational, Scientific, and Cultural Organization
UNFPA	United Nations Population Fund
UNICEF	United Nations Children's Fund
UNIDO	United Nations Industrial Development Organization
UNRISD	United Nations Research Institute for Social Development
UNSO	United Nations Statistical Office
WCMC	World Conservation Monitoring Centre
WFP	World Food Programme
WHO	World Health Organization
WTO	World Trade Organization
WWF	World Wide Fund for Nature

Partners

Defining, gathering, and disseminating international statistics is a collective effort of many people and organizations. The indicators presented in the *World Development Indicators* are the fruit of decades of work at many levels, from the field workers who have administered censuses and household surveys in every part of the world to the committees and working parties of the national and international statistical agencies that have developed the nomenclature, classifications, and standards that are fundamental to an international statistical system. Nongovernmental organizations and the private sector have also made important contributions, both in gathering primary data and in organizing and publishing their results. And academic researchers have played a crucial role in developing statistical methods and carrying on a continuing dialogue about the quality and interpretation of statistical indicators. What all these contributors have in common is a strong belief that accurate data, readily available, will improve the quality of public and private decisionmaking.

Statistical indicators are a classic example of a public good. Like all information, they are costly to collect, but once available in a convenient form, they can be shared widely at little additional cost and with no diminution of their value. Indeed, it is of benefit for all to have good information widely shared. One of the consequences of the public nature of statistical indicators, however, is that they are often taken for granted and the work of those who developed them goes unacknowledged. In the new *World Development Indicators* we want to take a first step toward correcting this situation by identifying the organizations that have contributed data directly to this volume. We recognize that such a list omits many others whose work is no less vital. In the future we hope to see our list of partners grow. In the meantime we wish to acknowledge our debt and gratitude to all those whose efforts have helped to build a base of comprehensive, quantitative information about the world and its people.

International agencies

Food and Agriculture Organization

The Food and Agriculture Organization (FAO) was founded in October 1945 with a mandate to raise nutrition levels and living standards, to improve agricultural productivity, and to better the condition of rural populations. Since its inception the FAO has worked to alleviate poverty and hunger by promoting agricultural development, improved nutrition, and the pursuit of food security—the access of all people at all times to the food they need for an active and healthy life. The organization provides direct development assistance; collects, analyzes, and disseminates information; offers policy and planning advice to governments; and serves as an international forum for debate on food and agricultural issues.

Statistical publications of the FAO include the *Production Yearbook*, *Trade Yearbook*, and *Fertilizer Yearbook*. The FAO makes much of its data available on diskette through its Agrostat PC system.

FAO publications can be ordered from national sales agents or directly from the FAO Distribution and Sales Section, Viale delle Terme di Caracalla, 00100 Rome, Italy. Website: http://www.fao.org/default.htm.

International Civil Aviation Organization

The International Civil Aviation Organization (ICAO), a specialized agency of the United Nations, was founded with the signing of the Convention on International Civil Aviation on December 7, 1944. It is responsible for establishing international standards and recommended practices and procedures for the technical, economic, and legal aspects of international civil aviation operations.

The ICAO promotes the adoption of safety measures, establishes visual and instrument flight rules for pilots and crews, develops aeronautical charts, coordinates aircraft radio frequencies, and sets uniform regulations for the operation of air services and customs procedures. The ICAO's membership consists of 185 countries.

To obtain ICAO publications contact ICAO, Document Sales Unit, 999 University Street, Montreal, Quebec H3C 5H7, Canada; telephone: (514) 954 8022; fax: (514) 954 6769; email: sales_unit@icao.org; Website: http://www.cam.org/~icao.

International Labour Organisation

The International Labour Organisation (ILO) is the United Nations specialized agency that seeks the promotion of social justice and internationally recognized human and labor rights. Founded in 1919, it is the only surviving major creation of the Treaty of Versailles, which brought the League of Nations into being. It became the first specialized agency of the United Nations in 1946. The ILO has a structure that is unique within the United Nations system, a tripartite structure that has workers and employers participating as equal partners with governments in the work of its governing organs. As part of its mandate, the ILO maintains an extensive statistical publication program. Its most comprehensive collection of labor force statistics is the *Yearbook of Labour Statistics.*

Publications can be ordered from the International Labour Office, 4 route des Morillons, CH-1211 Geneva 22, Switzerland, or from sales agents and major booksellers throughout the world and ILO offices in many countries. Fax: (41 22) 798 86 85; Website: http://www.unicc.org/ilo/index.html.

International Monetary Fund

The International Monetary Fund (IMF) was established at a conference held in Bretton Woods, New Hampshire, U.S.A., on July 1–22, 1944, a conference that also established the World Bank. The IMF came into official existence on December 27, 1945, when representatives of 29 countries signed its articles of agreement. The IMF commenced financial operations on March 1, 1947. It currently has 181 member countries.

The statutory purposes of the IMF are to promote international monetary cooperation, to facilitate the expansion and balanced growth of international trade, to promote exchange rate stability, to assist in the establishment of a multilateral system of payments, to make the general resources of the Fund temporarily available to its members under adequate safeguards, and to shorten the duration and lessen the degree of disequilibrium in the international balances of payments of members.

In furtherance of its purposes the IMF maintains an extensive program for the development and compilation of international statistics. The IMF is responsible for collecting and reporting statistics on international financial transactions and the balance of payments. In April 1996 it undertook an important initiative aimed at improving the quality of international statistics, establishing the Special Data Dissemination Standard (SDDS) to guide members that have or seek access to international capital markets in providing economic and financial data to the public.

Major statistical publications of the IMF include *International Financial Statistics, Balance of Payments Statistics Yearbook, Government Finance Statistics Yearbook,* and *Direction of Trade Statistics.*

For more information on IMF statistical publications contact International Monetary Fund, Publications Services, Catalog Orders, 700 19th Street, N.W., Washington, D.C. 20431, U.S.A.; telephone: (202) 623 7430; fax: (202) 623 7201; telex: RCA 248331 IMF UR; email: pubweb@imf.org; Website: http://www.imf.org; SDDS bulletin board: http://dsbb.imf.org.

International Telecommunication Union

Founded in Paris in 1865 as the International Telegraph Union, the International Telecommunication Union (ITU) took its present name in 1934 and became a specialized agency of the United Nations in 1947.

The ITU is an intergovernmental organization within which the public and private sectors cooperate for the development of telecommunications. The ITU adopts international regulations and treaties governing all terrestrial and space uses of the frequency spectrum and the use of the geostationary-satellite orbit. It also develops standards for the interconnection of telecommunications systems worldwide. The ITU fosters the development of telecommunications in developing countries by establishing medium-term development policies and strategies in consultation with other partners in the sector and providing specialized technical assistance in management, telecommunications policy, human resource management, research and development, technology choice and transfer, network installation and maintenance, and investment financing and resource mobilization.

The major statistical publication of the ITU is the *Telecommunications Yearbook*.

Publications can be ordered from ITU Sales and Marketing Service, Place des Nations, CH-1211 Geneva 20, Switzerland; telephone: (41 22) 730 6141 (English), (41 22) 730 6142 (French), and (41 22) 730 6143 (Spanish); fax: (41 22) 730 5194; email (Internet): sales.online@itu.ch and (X.400): S=sales; P=itu; A=400net; C=ch; telex: 421 000 uit ch; telegram: ITU GENEVE.

Organization for Economic Cooperation and Development

The Organization for Economic Cooperation and Development (OECD) was originally set up in 1948 as the Organization for European Economic Cooperation (OEEC) to administer Marshall Plan funding on the European side. In 1960, when the Marshall Plan had completed its task, the member countries agreed to bring in the United States and Canada to form an organization to coordinate policy among the Western industrial countries.

The OECD is the international organization of the industrialized, market economy countries. At OECD, representatives from member countries meet to exchange information and harmonize policy with a view to maximizing economic growth in member countries and helping nonmember countries develop more rapidly. The present members of the OECD are Australia, Austria, Belgium, Canada, the Czech Republic, Denmark, Finland, France, Germany, Greece, Hungary, Iceland, Ireland, Italy, Japan, the Republic of Korea, Luxembourg, Mexico, the Netherlands, New Zealand, Norway, Poland, Portugal, Spain, Sweden, Switzerland, Turkey, the United Kingdom, and the United States. Membership for the Slovak Republic is under consideration.

Associated with the OECD are several agencies or bodies that have their own governing statutes, including the International Energy Agency (IEA) and the Centre for Cooperation with the Economies in Transition.

To further its aims, the OECD has set up a number of specialized committees. One of these is the Development Assistance Committee (DAC), whose members have agreed to coordinate their policies on assistance to developing countries and economies in transition.

Major statistical publications of the OECD include *National Accounts of OECD Countries*, *Labour Force Statistics*, *Revenue Statistics of OECD Member Countries*, *International Direct Investment Statistics Yearbook*, *Basic Science and Technology Statistics*, *Industrial Structure Statistics*, and *Services: Statistics on International Transactions*.

The OECD operates five publications and information centers: in Bonn, Mexico D.F, Paris, Tokyo, and Washington, D.C. These centers promote OECD publications and documents nationally and make them available to a large public. The OECD designates a depository library in every country, usually the national library, and supplies it with free copies of publications and working documents.

For information on OECD publications contact OECD, 2, rue André-Pascal, 75775 Paris Cedex 16, France; telephone: (33 1) 45 24 82 00; fax: (33 1) 45 24 85 00; Websites: http://www.oecd.org and http://www.oecdwash.org.

The United Nations

The United Nations and its specialized agencies maintain a number of programs for the collection of international statistics, some of which are described elsewhere in this book. At United Nations headquarters the Statistics Division of the Department of Economic and Social Information and Policy Analysis provides a wide range of statistical outputs and services for producers and users of statistics worldwide. By increasing the global availability and use of official statistics, the division's work facilitates national and international policy formulation, implementation, and monitoring.

The Statistics Division publishes statistics in the fields of international trade, national accounts, demography and population, gender, industry, energy, environment, human settlements, and disability. Major statistical publications of the Statistics Division include the *International Trade Statistics Yearbook,* the *Yearbook of National Accounts*, and the *Monthly Bulletin of Statistics*, along with general statistics compendiums such as the *Statistical Yearbook* and *World Statistics Pocketbook.*

For publications contact the United Nations Sales Section, DC2-0853, New York, N.Y. 10017, U.S.A.; fax: (212) 963 3489; email: statistics@un.org; Website: http://www.un.org.

United Nations Children's Fund

The United Nations Children's Fund (UNICEF), the only organization of the United Nations dedicated exclusively to children, works with other United Nations bodies and with governments and nongovernmental organizations to improve children's lives in more than 140 developing countries through community-based services in primary health care, basic education, and safe water and sanitation. According to its mission statement, adopted in 1996, UNICEF "is guided by the Convention on the Rights of the Child and strives to establish children's rights as enduring ethical principles and international standards of behavior towards children."

Major publications of UNICEF include *The State of the World's Children* and *The Progress of Nations*. UNICEF publications are available through UNICEF field offices in developing countries and through UNICEF national committees in industrial countries. Many UNICEF publications are also available on the Internet.

For information on UNICEF publications contact UNICEF House, 3 United Nations Plaza, New York, N.Y. 10017, U.S.A.; telephone: (212) 326 7000; fax: (212) 888 7465; telex: RCA-239521; Website: http://www.unicef.org.

United Nations Conference on Trade and Development

The United Nations Conference on Trade and Development (UNCTAD) is the principal organ of the United Nations General Assembly in the field of trade and development. It was established as a permanent intergovernmental body in 1964 in Geneva with a view to accelerating economic growth and development, particularly in developing countries. UNCTAD discharges its mandate through policy analysis; intergovernmental deliberations, consensus building, and negotiation; monitoring, implementation, and follow-up; and technical cooperation. UNCTAD's 188 member governments aim to achieve steady, sustained growth in all countries and to accelerate the development of developing countries, so that all people can enjoy economic and social well-being.

UNCTAD has a major program of publications in trade and economic statistics, including the *Handbook of International Trade and Development Statistics.*

For information contact UNCTAD, Palais des Nations, CH-1211 Geneva 10, Switzerland; telephone: (41 22) 907 12 34 or 917 12 34; fax: (41 22) 907 00 57; telex: 42962; Website: http://www.unicc.org/unctad.

United Nations Educational, Scientific, and Cultural Organization

The United Nations Educational, Scientific, and Cultural Organization (UNESCO) is a specialized agency of the United Nations established in 1945 to promote aims set out in the United Nations charter: "to contribute to peace and security by promoting collaboration among nations through education, science, and culture in order to further universal respect for justice, for the rule of law, and for the human rights and fundamental freedoms . . . for the peoples of the world, without distinction of race, sex, language, or religion . . ."

The principal statistical publications of UNESCO are the *Statistical Yearbook*, *World Education Report* (biennial), and *Basic Education and Literacy: World Statistical Indicators*.

For publications contact UNESCO Publishing, Promotion, and Sales Division, 1, rue Miollis F, 75732 Paris Cedex 15, France; fax: (33 1) 45 68 57 41; email: c.laje@unesco.org; Website: http://www.unesco.org.

United Nations Environment Programme

The mandate of the United Nations Environment Programme (UNEP) is to provide leadership and encourage partnership in caring for the environment by inspiring, informing, and enabling nations and people to improve their quality of life without compromising that of future generations. The UNEP was established as the environmental conscience of the United Nations system and has been creating a basis for comprehensive consideration and coordinated action within the United Nations on the problems of the human environment.

UNEP publications include *Global Environment Outlook* and *Our Planet* (a bimonthly magazine).

For information contact UNEP, P.O. Box 30552, Nairobi, Kenya; telephone: (254 2) 62 1234 or 3292; fax: (254 2) 62 3927 or 3692; Website: http://unep.unep.no.

United Nations Industrial Development Organization

The United Nations Industrial Development Organization (UNIDO) was established in 1966 by the General Assembly to act as the central coordinating body for industrial activities within the United Nations system and to promote industrial development and cooperation at global, regional, national, and sectoral levels. In 1985 UNIDO became the sixteenth specialized agency of the United Nations. As the youngest such agency, it was given a mandate that recognizes the economic realities of industrial development in today's world. UNIDO's constitution calls for the organization to assist in development, scientific, and technological plans and programs for industrialization in the public, cooperative, and private sectors.

UNIDO's databases and information services include the Industrial Statistics Database (INDSTAT), Commodity Balance Statistics Database (COMBAL), Industrial Development Abstracts (IDA), and the International Referral System on Sources of Information. Among its publications is the *International Yearbook of Industrial Statistics*.

For information contact UNIDO Public Information Section, Vienna International Centre, P.O. Box 300, A-1400 Vienna, Austria; telephone: (43 1) 211 31 5021 or 5022; fax: (43 1) 209 2669; email: unido-pinfo@unido.org; Website: http://www.unido.org.

World Health Organization

The constitution of the World Health Organization (WHO) was adopted on July 22, 1946, by the International Health Conference, convened in New York by the Economic and Social Council. The WHO's objective is the attainment by all people of the highest possible level of health, defined as a state of complete physical, mental, and social well-being and not merely the absence of disease or infirmity.

In support of its main objective, the WHO carries out a wide range of functions, including coordinating international health work; helping governments strengthen health services; furnishing tech-

nical assistance and emergency aid; working for the prevention and control of disease; promoting improved nutrition, housing, sanitation, recreation, and economic and working conditions; promoting and coordinating biomedical and health services research; promoting improved standards of teaching and training in health and medical professions; establishing international standards for biological, pharmaceutical, and similar products; and standardizing diagnostic procedures.

The WHO publishes the *World Health Statistics Annual* and many other technical and statistical publications.

For publications contact Distribution and Sales (DSA), Division of Publishing, Language, and Library Services, World Health Organization Headquarters, CH-1211 Geneva 27, Switzerland; telephone: (41 22) 791 2476 or 2477; fax: (41 22) 791 4857; email: publications@who.ch; Website: http://www.who.ch.

World Trade Organization

The World Trade Organization (WTO), established on January 1, 1995, is the successor to the General Agreement on Tariffs and Trade (GATT). It is now the legal and institutional foundation of the multilateral trading system and embodies the results of the Uruguay Round trade negotiations concluded with the Marrakesh Declaration of April 15, 1994.

The essential functions of the WTO are administering and implementing the multilateral trade agreements that make up the WTO, serving as a forum for multilateral trade negotiations, seeking to resolve trade disputes, overseeing national trade policies, and cooperating with other international institutions involved in global economic policymaking.

The Statistics and Information Systems Divisions of the WTO compile statistics on world trade and maintain the Integrated Database, which contains the basic records of the outcome of the Uruguay Round. The *WTO Annual Report* includes a statistical appendix.

For publications contact World Trade Organization, Publications Services, Centre William Rappard, 154 rue de Lausanne, CH-1211 Geneva, Switzerland; telephone: (41 22) 739 5208 or 5308; fax: (41 22) 739 5458; email: publications@wto.org; Website: http://www.wto.org.

Private and nongovernmental organizations

Currency Data & Intelligence, Inc.

Currency Data & Intelligence, Inc. is a research and publishing firm that produces currency-related products and undertakes research for international agencies and universities worldwide. Its flagship product, the *World Currency Yearbook*, is the most comprehensive source of information on currency. It includes official and unofficial exchange rates and discussions of economic, social, and political issues that bear on the value of currencies in world markets. A second publication, the monthly newsletter *Global Currency Report*, covers devaluations and other critical developments in exchange rate restrictions and valuation and provides parallel market exchange rates.

For information contact Currency Data & Intelligence, Inc., 328 Flatbush Avenue, Suite 344, Brooklyn, N.Y. 11238, U.S.A.; telephone: (718) 230 7176; fax: (718) 230 1992; email: Curncydata@AOL.com.

Euromoney Publications PLC

Euromoney Publications PLC provides a wide range of financial, legal, and general business information. The monthly *Euromoney* magazine includes a semiannual rating of country creditworthiness.

For information contact Euromoney Publications PLC, Nestor House, Playhouse Yard, London EC4V 5EX, U.K.; telephone: (44 171) 779 8999; fax: (44 171) 779 8617; Website: http://www.euromoney.com.

Institutional Investor, Inc.

Institutional Investor magazine is published monthly by Institutional Investor, Inc., which develops country-by-country credit ratings every six months based on information provided by leading international banks.

For information contact Institutional Investor, Inc., 488 Madison Avenue, New York, N.Y. 10022, U.S.A.; telephone: (212) 224 3300.

International Road Federation

The International Road Federation (IRF) is a not-for-profit, nonpolitical service organization representing the views and interests of all road-related industries across the world. The IRF has more than 600 corporate and institutional members in approximately 100 countries around the world—companies, associations, research institutes, and administrations concerned with modernizing and developing road infrastructure. To encourage better road and transport systems worldwide, the IRF assists in the transfer and application of technology and management practices that will produce maximum economic and social returns from national road investments, through its consultative status with the United Nations and the OECD and its advisory capacity with the European Union.

The IRF publishes *World Road Statistics*.

For information contact International Road Federation, 63 rue de Lausanne, CH-1202 Geneva, Switzerland; telephone: (41 22) 731 71 50; fax: (41 22) 731 71 58; email: IRD@dial.eunet.ch; Website: http://www.eunet.ch/Customers/irf.

Moody's Investors Service

Moody's Investors Service is a global credit analysis and financial opinion firm. It provides the international investment community with globally consistent credit ratings on debt and other securities issued by North American state and regional government entities, by corporations worldwide, and by some sovereign issuers. It also publishes extensive financial data in both print and electronic form. Clients of Moody's Investors Service include investment banks, brokerage firms, insurance companies, public utilities, research libraries, manufacturers, and government agencies and departments.

Moody's publishes *Sovereign, Subnational and Sovereign-Guaranteed Issuers*.

For information contact Moody's Investors Service, 99 Church Street, New York, N.Y. 10007, U.S.A. Website: http://www.dnb-dc.com/moodys.html.

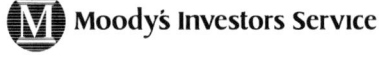

Political Risk Services

Political Risk Services is a global leader in political and economic risk forecasting and market analysis and has served international companies large and small for nearly 20 years. The data it contributed to this year's *World Development Indicators* come from the *International Country Risk Guide*, a monthly publication that monitors and rates political, financial, and economic risk in 130 countries. The guide's data series and commitment to independent and unbiased analysis make it the standard for any organization practicing effective risk management.

For information contact Political Risk Services, 6320 Fly Road, Suite 102, P.O. Box 248, East Syracuse, N.Y. 13057, U.S.A.; telephone: (315) 431 0511; fax: (315) 431 0200; email: custserv@polrisk.com.

Price Waterhouse

Price Waterhouse is one of the world's largest international organizations of accountants and consultants. Founded in 1849, it now consists of a network of 27 individual practice firms in 119 countries and territories. Staffed with knowledgeable professionals committed to client service, it is uniquely equipped to advise on matters relating to international operations, not only in individual countries but also on a regional or global basis.

For information contact Price Waterhouse World Firm Services BV, Inc., 1251 Avenue of the Americas, New York, N.Y. 10020, U.S.A.; telephone: (212) 819 5000; fax: (212) 790 6620; telex: 362196.

Standard and Poor's Rating Services

Standard and Poor's *Sovereign Ratings* provides issuer and local and foreign currency debt ratings for sovereign governments and for sovereign-supported and supranational issuers worldwide. Standard & Poor's Rating Services monitors the credit quality of $1.5 trillion worth of bonds and other financial instruments and offers investors global coverage of debt issuers. Standard & Poor's also has ratings on commercial paper, mutual funds, and the financial condition of insurance companies worldwide.

For information contact The McGraw-Hill Companies, Inc., Executive Offices, 1221 Avenue of the Americas, New York, N.Y. 10020, U.S.A.; subscriber services: (212) 208 1146; Website: http://www.ratings.standardpoor.com.

WORLD CONSERVATION MONITORING CENTRE

World Conservation Monitoring Centre

The World Conservation Monitoring Centre (WCMC) provides information services on the conservation and sustainable use of the world's living resources and helps others to develop information systems of their own. It works in close collaboration with a wide range of organizations and people to increase access to the information necessary for wise management of the world's living resources. Committed to the principle of data exchange with other centers and noncommercial users, the WCMC, whenever possible, places the data it manages in the public domain.

For information contact World Conservation Monitoring Centre, 219 Huntingdon Road, Cambridge CB3 0DL, U.K.; telephone: (44 12) 23 27 73 14; fax: (44 12) 23 27 71 36; Website: http://www.wcmc.org.uk.

World Resources Institute

The World Resources Institute is an independent center for policy research and technical assistance on global environmental and development issues. Because people are inspired by ideas, empowered by knowledge, and moved to change by greater understanding, the institute provides—and helps other institutions provide—objective information and practical proposals for policy and institutional change that will foster environmentally sound, socially equitable development. The institute's current areas of work include trade, forests, energy, economics, technology, biodiversity, human health, climate change, sustainable agriculture, resource and environmental information, and national strategies for environmental and resource management.

For information contact World Resources Institute, 1709 New York Avenue, N.W., Washington, D.C. 20006, U.S.A.; telephone: (202) 638 6300; fax: (202) 638 0036; telex 64414 WRIWASH; Website: http://www.wri.org.

Users guide

Principal sections

Section 1   World view

Section 2   People

Section 3   Environment

Section 4   Economy

Section 5   States and markets

Section 6   Global links

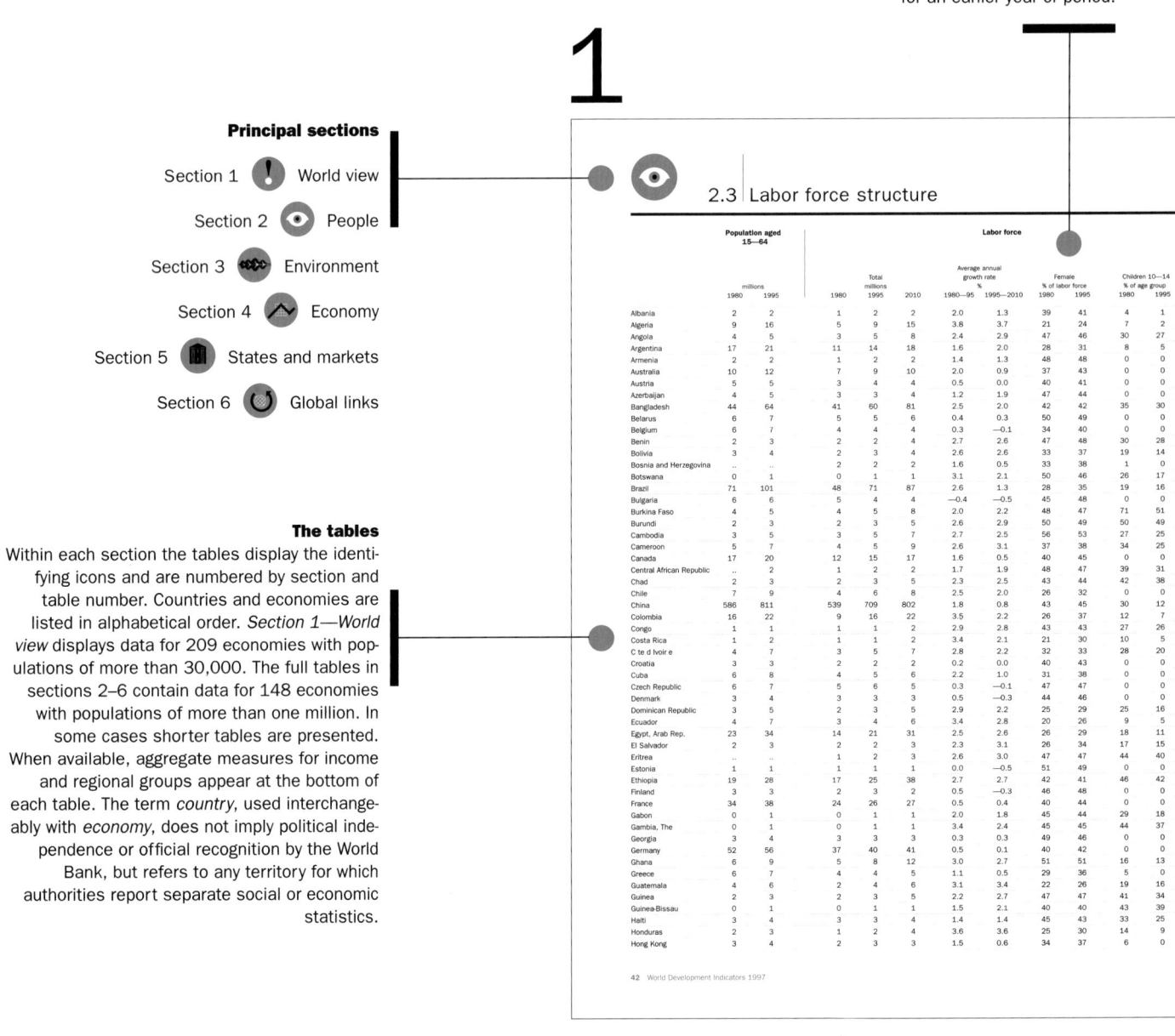

The tables

Within each section the tables display the identifying icons and are numbered by section and table number. Countries and economies are listed in alphabetical order. *Section 1—World view* displays data for 209 economies with populations of more than 30,000. The full tables in sections 2–6 contain data for 148 economies with populations of more than one million. In some cases shorter tables are presented. When available, aggregate measures for income and regional groups appear at the bottom of each table. The term *country*, used interchangeably with *economy*, does not imply political independence or official recognition by the World Bank, but refers to any territory for which authorities report separate social or economic statistics.

Statistics

Section 1—World view includes data for 209 economies (those with more than 30,000 people). Data in the remaining sections are presented for 148 economies (those with more than one million people whose governments disseminate data on a regular basis), plus Taiwan, China, in selected tables. Data are shown for economies as they were constituted in 1995, and historical data are revised to reflect current political arrangements. Throughout the tables, exceptions are noted.

Data for China do not include data for Taiwan, China, unless otherwise noted.

2

Labor force structure | 2.3

	Population aged 15—64 (millions)		Labor force — Total (millions)			Labor force — Average annual growth rate (%)		Labor force — Female (% of labor force)		Labor force — Children 10—14 (% of age group)	
	1980	1995	1980	1995	2010	1980—95	1995—2010	1980	1995	1980	1995
Hungary	7	7	5	5	5	−0.5	−0.3	43	44	0	0
India	394	562	300	398	518	1.9	1.7	34	32	21	14
Indonesia	83	120	59	89	123	2.8	2.2	35	40	13	10
Iran, Islamic Rep.	20	34	12	19	35	3.3	3.9	20	24	14	5
Iraq	7	11	4	5	9	2.8	3.6	17	18	11	3
Ireland	2	2	1	1	2	0.8	1.3	28	33	1	0
Israel	2	3	1	2	3	2.7	2.5	34	40	0	0
Italy	36	39	23	25	25	0.7	−0.1	33	38	2	0
Jamaica	1	2	1	1	2	2.0	1.6	46	46	0	0
Japan	79	87	57	66	67	1.0	0.1	38	41	0	0
Jordan	1	2	1	1	2	5.0	3.9	15	21	4	1
Kazakstan	9	10	7	8	9	0.9	1.0	48	47	0	0
Kenya	8	14	8	13	19	3.3	2.5	46	46	45	41
Korea, Dem. Rep.	10	16	8	12	15	2.8	1.5	45	45	3	0
Korea, Rep.	24	32	16	22	26	2.2	1.3	39	40	0	0
Kuwait	1	1	0	1	1	3.3	2.1	13	28	0	0
Kyrgyz Republic	2	3	2	2	3	1.5	1.8	48	47	0	0
Lao PDR	2	3	2	2	4	2.5	3.0	45	47	31	27
Latvia	2	2	1	1	1	−0.2	−0.6	51	50	0	0
Lebanon	2	2	1	1	2	3.3	2.7	23	28	5	0
Lesotho	1	1	1	1	1	2.3	2.4	38	37	28	22
Libya	2	3	1	2	3	3.3	3.5	18	21	9	0
Lithuania	2	2	2	2	2	0.4	−0.1	50	48	0	0
Macedonia, FYR	1	1	1	1	1	1.2	1.0	36	41	1	0
Madagascar	5	7	4	6	10	2.7	3.0	45	45	40	36
Malawi	3	5	3	5	7	2.8	2.4	51	49	45	35
Malaysia	8	12	5	8	12	2.8	2.7	34	37	8	3
Mali	3	5	3	5	8	2.4	2.9	47	46	61	55
Mauritania	1	1	1	1	2	2.2	2.5	45	44	30	24
Mauritius	1	1	0	0	1	2.1	1.3	26	32	5	3
Mexico	35	55	22	36	52	3.2	2.5	27	31	9	7
Moldova	3	3	2	2	2	0.2	0.5	38	42	3	0
Mongolia	1	1	1	1	2	3.0	2.5	46	46	4	2
Morocco	10	16	7	10	15	2.6	2.5	34	35	21	6
Mozambique	6	8	7	8	12	1.6	2.4	49	48	39	34
Myanmar	19	27	17	23	30	2.0	1.8	44	43	28	25
Namibia	1	1	0	1	1	2.4	2.5	40	41	34	22
Nepal	8	12	7	10	14	2.4	2.4	38	40	56	45
Netherlands	9	11	6	7	7	1.5	0.1	31	40	0	0
New Zealand	2	2	1	2	2	1.9	1.1	34	44	0	0
Nicaragua	1	2	1	2	3	3.3	3.6	29	36	19	14
Niger	3	4	3	4	7	3.0	3.2	45	44	48	45
Nigeria	38	58	30	44	67	2.7	2.8	36	36	29	26
Norway	3	3	2	2	2	0.9	0.3	40	46	0	0
Oman	1	1	0	1	1	4.0	4.6	7	15	6	1
Pakistan	44	70	29	46	77	3.1	3.4	23	26	23	18
Panama	1	2	1	1	1	2.9	2.1	30	34	6	4
Papua New Guinea	2	2	2	2	3	2.2	2.1	42	42	28	19
Paraguay	2	3	1	2	3	2.9	2.8	27	29	15	8
Peru	9	14	5	9	13	3.1	2.7	24	29	4	2
Philippines	27	40	19	28	41	2.7	2.5	35	37	14	8
Poland	19	26	19	19	21	0.3	0.4	45	46	0	0
Portugal	6	7	5	5	5	0.4	0.2	39	43	8	2
Puerto Rico	2	2	1	1	2	1.8	1.5	32	36	0	0
Romania	14	15	11	11	11	−0.1	0.1	46	44	0	0
Russian Federation	95	99	76	77	79	0.1	0.1	49	49	0	0

World Development Indicators 1997 43

Data are shown whenever possible for the individual countries formed from the former Czechoslovakia—the Czech Republic and the Slovak Republic.

Data are shown for Eritrea whenever possible; in most cases prior to 1992, however, it is covered in the data for Ethiopia.

Data shown for Germany refer to the unified Germany, unless otherwise noted.

Data shown for Jordan refer to the East Bank only, unless otherwise noted.

In 1991 the Union of Soviet Socialist Republics was formally dissolved into 15 countries (Armenia, Azerbaijan, Belarus, Estonia, Georgia, Kazakstan, Kyrgyz Republic, Latvia, Lithuania, Moldova, Russian Federation, Tajikistan, Turkmenistan, Ukraine, and Uzbekistan). Whenever possible, data are shown for the individual countries.

Data shown for the Republic of Yemen refer to that country from 1990 onward; data for previous years refer to the former People's Democratic Republic of Yemen and the former Yemen Arab Republic, unless otherwise noted.

Whenever possible, data are shown for the individual countries formed from the former Yugoslavia—Bosnia and Herzegovina, Croatia, the former Yugoslav Republic of Macedonia, Slovenia, and the Federal Republic of Yugoslavia. All references to the Federal Republic of Yugoslavia in the tables are to the Federal Republic of Yugoslavia (Serbia/Montenegro).

Additional information about the data is recorded in *Primary data documentation.* This section gives an overview of some of the national and international efforts to improve basic data collection and provides information on primary sources, census years, fiscal years, and other background. *Statistical methods* provides technical information on some of the general calculations and formulas used throughout the book.

Discrepancies in data presented in different editions of the *World Development Indicators* reflect not only updates by the countries, but also revisions to historical series and changes in methodology. **Readers are therefore advised not to compare data series between editions of the *World Development Indicators* or between different World Bank publications.** Consistent time-series data are available in the *World Development Indicators* CD-ROM.

Except where noted, growth rates are in real terms. (See *Statistical methods* for information on the methods used for calculating growth rates.) Data for some economic indicators for some economies are presented in fiscal years rather than calendar years; see *Primary data documentation.* All dollar figures are current U.S. dollars unless otherwise stated. The methods used for converting national currencies are described in *Statistical methods.*

The World Bank's classification of economies

For operational and analytical purposes the World Bank's main criterion for classifying economies is gross national product (GNP) per capita. Every country is classified as low income, middle income (subdivided into lower middle and upper middle), or high income. Consult the front cover flap to check a country's income classification. Note that classification by income does not necessarily reflect development status.

Because GNP per capita changes with time, the country composition of income groups may change from one edition to the next. Once the classification is fixed for an edition, all historical data presented are based on the same country grouping. The income-based country groups are defined using 1995 GNP per capita:

Low-income economies are those with a GNP per capita of $765 or less in 1995.
Middle-income economies are those with GNP per capita of more than $765 but less than $9,386. *Lower-middle-income* and *upper-middle-income economies* are divided at GNP per capita of $3,035.
High-income economies are those with a GNP per capita of $9,386 or more.

Aggregate measures for regions

The aggregate measures for regions refer only to low- and middle-income economies. The country composition of regions is based on the World Bank's analytical regions and may differ from common geographic usage. For regional classifications see the map on the inside back cover and the lists on the back cover flap.

Aggregate measures for income groups

The aggregate measures for income groups include the 209 economies shown in the summary tables of section 1 wherever data are available. To maintain consistency in the aggregate measures over time and between tables, missing data are imputed. Most aggregates are totals (designated by a *t*) or median values (*m*) or are weighted averages (*w*). Weighting may result in discrepancies between subgroup aggregates and overall totals. See *Statistical methods* for further details.

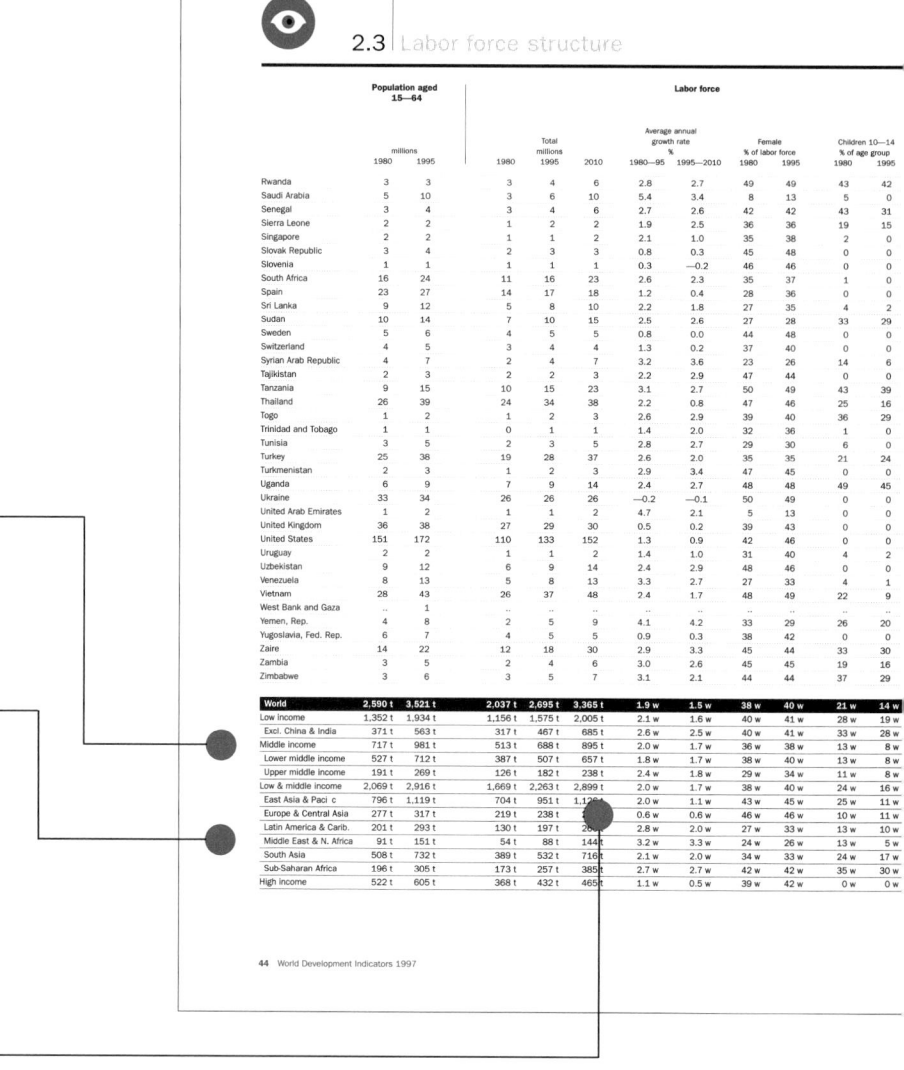

Footnotes

The most recent available data are presented for each of the indicators shown. Although international standards of coverage, definition, and classification apply to most statistics reported by countries and international agencies, there are inevitably differences in coverage, currentness, and quality. When there are competing sources of data, World Bank staff review the data to ensure that the most reliable are presented. Known deviations from standard definitions or breaks in comparability over time or across countries are noted in the tables. When available data are deemed to be too weak to provide reliable measures of levels and trends or do not adequately adhere to international standards, the data are not shown.

Commentary
For some tables brief discussions are included on the overall theme of the table, explaining why the indicators shown are useful for measuring development.

4

Labor force structure | 2.3

Definitions
Definitions provide short descriptions of the principal indicators in each table. These are necessarily brief and may omit some details.

Notes about the data
About the data provides a general discussion of international data standards, data collection methods, and sources of potential errors and inconsistencies. Readers are urged to take the time to read these notes to gain an understanding of the reliability and limitations of the data presented.

For a full discussion of data collection methods and definitions readers should consult the technical documentation provided by the original compilers cited in the *Data sources*.

Who is in the labor force?
The labor force includes both people who are currently employed and those who are unemployed. In practice, it is difficult to count the unemployed accurately, especially in developing countries. And it may be just as difficult to know who is fully employed.

According to the International Labour Organisation (ILO) definition, the unemployed are those "without work but available for and seeking work." Countries with unemployment insurance systems often base estimates of unemployment on those who file claims and thus certify that they are seeking work. But these systems do not count discouraged workers who have given up their job search because they believe that no employment opportunities exist or do not register as unemployed after their benefits have been exhausted. In developing economies rural women may not be counted as part of the labor force during seasons of low agricultural activity.

Some unemployment—often called "frictional unemployment"—occurs in all economies as a result of the normal operation of labor markets. At any time, some workers are temporarily unemployed—between jobs as employers look for the right workers and workers search for better jobs. In countries without unemployment insurance or other forms of social assistance, it may not be feasible to remain without work for a prolonged period. Instead, people find some form of work, often in informal or unrecorded activities.

Taking into account the underemployed— those engaged for only a few hours a week or employed in jobs requiring lower qualifications than they have—would yield a higher estimate of labor underutilization. Household surveys that examine unemployment and underemployment confirm that unemployment figures alone may seriously underestimate the underutilization of labor (table 2.3a).

Table 2.3a Unemployment and underemployment in three countries
percentage of the labor force

Country	Year	Un-employed	Dis-couraged workers	Under-employed
Ghana	1988–89	1.6	1.5	24.1
Ukraine	1994	0.4	..	14.5
Vietnam	1992–93	1.3	3.5	10.0

Source: World Bank 1995g.

About the data
Data on the labor force, or economically active population, are collected by the ILO from the latest census or survey of countries.

Despite the efforts of the ILO to encourage the use of international standards, labor force and employment and unemployment data are not fully comparable because of differences among economies, and sometimes within economies, in definitions (for example, daily or weekly rates) and coverage. Data comparability is also hampered by differences in methods of collection, classification, and tabulation. The reference period is another important source of differences: in some countries census data refer to the status of each person on the day of the census or survey or during a specific period before the inquiry date, while in others the data are recorded without reference to any period. And in some countries the statistics on labor force relate to people above a specific age, while in others there is no specific age provision. For a review of the problems relating to definitions, methods of collection, and classification of data on the labor force, see ILO (1990a) and the chapter notes in the ILO *Yearbook of Labour Statistics.*

The estimated population aged 15–64 typically provides a rough estimate of the economically active population. But in many developing economies children under 15 work full or part time. And in some high-income countries many workers postpone retirement past age 65.

Estimates of women in the labor force are not comparable internationally, because in many countries large numbers of women assist on farms or in other family enterprises without pay, and countries differ in the criteria used to determine the extent to which such workers are to be counted as part of the labor force.

Reliable estimates of child labor are hard to obtain. According to UNICEF's *The State of the World's Children 1997,* in many countries child labor is officially presumed not to exist, and so is not included in surveys or covered in official data. Data are also subject to underreporting because they do not include children engaged in agricultural or household activities with their families. Available statistics suggest that more boys than girls work, but the number of working girls is often underestimated because surveys do not include girls working as unregistered domestic help or those doing full-time household work in order to enable their parents to work outside the home.

Definitions
● **Population aged 15–64** is the number of people who could potentially be economically active, excluding children. ● **Total labor force** comprises people who meet the ILO definition of the economically active population: all people who supply labor for the production of goods and services during a specified period. It includes both the employed and the unemployed. While national practices vary in the treatment of such groups as the armed forces and seasonal or part-time workers, in general the labor force includes the armed forces, the unemployed, and first-time job-seekers, but excludes homemakers and other unpaid caregivers and workers in the informal sector. ● **Average annual growth rate** of the labor force is computed using the exponential endpoint method. See *Statistical methods* for more information. ● **Females as a percentage of the labor force** shows the extent to which women are active in the labor force. ● **Children 10–14 in the labor force** is the share of that age group that is active in the labor force.

Data sources
Labor force estimates are calculated by the World Bank's International Economics Department by applying sex-specific activity rates from the ILO database, *Estimates and Projections of the Economically Active Population, 1950–2010,* to the World Bank's population estimates to create a labor force series consistent with its population estimates. This procedure sometimes results in estimates of the absolute size of the labor force that differ slightly from those published by the ILO in its *Yearbook of Labour Statistics.*

World Development Indicators 1997 **45**

Data presentation conventions and symbols
The cutoff date for data is February 1, 1997.
The symbol .. means that data are not available or that aggregates cannot be calculated because of missing data in the year shown.
A blank means not applicable or that an aggregate is not analytically meaningful.
The numbers 0 and 0.0 mean zero or less than half the unit shown.
Billion is 1,000 million.
Trillion is 1,000 billion.
The symbol / in dates, as in 1990/91, means that the period of time, usually 12 months, straddles two calendar years and refers to a crop year, a survey year, or a fiscal year.
Figures in italics indicate data that are for years or periods other than those specified. Data for years that are more than three years from the range shown are footnoted.
Dollars are current U.S. dollars unless otherwise stated.

Sources
The World Bank collects development data from international organizations, government agencies, and other public and private organizations to improve its understanding of and advice on development issues ranging from health and education to privatization. These partners are identified in the *Data sources* section following each table, and key publications of the partners drawn on for the table are listed and sometimes displayed. For a description of the partners and information on their data publications see the *Partners* section.

Statistical methods

This section describes some of the statistical procedures used in preparing the *World Development Indicators*. It covers the methods employed for calculating regional and income group aggregates and for calculating growth rates, and it describes the World Bank's Atlas method for deriving the conversion factor used to estimate GNP and GNP per capita in U.S. dollars. Other statistical procedures and calculations are described in the *About the data* sections that follow each table.

Aggregation rules

Because of missing data, aggregations of data for groups of economies should be treated as approximations to unknown totals or average values. The regional and income group aggregates at the end of most of the tables are based on the largest available set of data, including the values for the 148 economies shown in the main tables, the smaller economies shown in tables 1.1, 1.2, and 1.3, and Taiwan, China. The aggregation rules are intended to yield estimates for a consistent set of economies from one time period to the next and for all indicators. However, small differences between the values of subgroup aggregates and overall totals and averages may occur because of the approximations used. In addition, discrepancies due to data reporting and accounting practices may cause differences in such theoretically identical aggregates as world exports and world imports.

How group aggregates in the *World Development Indicators* are calculated depends on the nature of the indicator. In group and world totals (indicated in the tables by t) missing data are imputed using a suitable proxy variable in a benchmark year, usually 1987. The imputed value is calculated so that it (or its proxy) bears the same relationship to the total of available data as it did in the benchmark year. Imputed values are not calculated if missing data account for more than one-third of the total in the benchmark year. Proxy variables are selected from a set of variables for which complete data are available for 1987. The variables used as proxies are GNP in U.S. dollars, GNP per capita in U.S. dollars, total population, exports and imports of goods and services in U.S. dollars, and value added in agriculture, industry, manufacturing, and services in local currency.

Aggregates of ratios are generally calculated as weighted averages of the ratios (indicated by w) using the value of the denominator or, in some cases, another indicator as a weight. The aggregate ratios are based on the available data, including data for economies not shown in the main tables. Missing values are assumed to have the same average value as the available data. If missing data account for approximately one-third of the total value of the weights in the benchmark year, no aggregate is calculated. In a few cases the aggregate ratio may be computed as the ratio of group totals after imputing values for missing data according to the rules for computing totals. Aggregates calculated as medians of the available data are indicated by m.

Aggregate growth rates are generally computed as the weighted averages of growth rates. In a few cases growth rates may be computed from time series of group totals (see the discussion below on methods of computing growth rates). Growth rates are not calculated if more than one-third of the observations in a period are missing.

Exceptions to the rules occur throughout the book. Depending on the judgment of World Bank analysts, the aggregates may be based on as little as 60 percent of the available data. In other cases, where missing or excluded values are judged to be small or irrelevant, aggregates are based only on the data shown in the tables.

Growth rates

Growth rates shown in the *World Development Indicators* are calculated as annual averages and represented as percentages. Except where noted, growth rates of values are computed from constant price or real value series. Three main methods are used to calculate growth rates: the least squares, the exponential endpoint, and the geometric endpoint. Rates of change from one period to the next are calculated as proportional changes from the earlier period. Note, however, that the annual changes in the speed of integration indicators in table 6.1 are not proportional growth rates but average annual differences.

Least-squares growth rate. Least-squares growth rates are used wherever there is a sufficiently long time series to permit a reliable calculation. If more than one-half of the observations in a period are missing, no growth rate is calculated.

The least-squares growth rate, r, is estimated by fitting a linear regression trend line to the logarithmic annual values of the variable in the relevant period. The regression equation takes the form

$$\log X_t = a + bt,$$

which is equivalent to the logarithmic transformation of the compound growth equation,

$$X_t = X_o (1 + r)^t .$$

In this equation X is the variable, t is time, and $a = \log X_o$ and $b = log (1 + r)$ are the parameters to be estimated. If b^* is the least-squares estimate of b, the average annual growth rate, r, is obtained as [antilog $(b^*) - 1$] and multiplied by 100 for expression as a percentage.

The calculated growth rate is an average rate that is representative of the available observations over the period. It does not necessarily match the actual growth rate between any two periods.

Exponential growth rate. The growth rate between two points in time for labor force and population indicators is calculated from the equation

$$r = \ln(pn/p_1)/n$$

where pn and p_1 are the last and first observations in the period, n is the number of years in the period, and ln is the natural logarithm operator.

This growth rate is based on a model of continuous, exponential growth between two points in time. It does not take into account the intermediate values of the series.

Geometric growth rate. The geometric growth rate is applicable to compound growth over discrete periods, such as the payment and reinvestment of interest or dividends. Although continuous growth, as modeled by the exponential growth rate, may be more realistic, most economic phenomena are measured only at intervals for which the compound growth model is appropriate. The average growth rate over n periods is calculated as

$$r = \exp\{[\ln(pn/p_1)]/n\} - 1.$$

World Bank Atlas method

In calculating GNP in U.S. dollars and GNP per capita for certain operational purposes, the World Bank uses a synthetic exchange rate commonly called the Atlas conversion factor. The purpose of this conversion factor is to reduce the impact of exchange rate fluctuations in the cross-country comparison of national incomes.

The Atlas conversion factor for any year is the average of a country's exchange rate (or alternative conversion factor) for that year and its exchange rates for the two preceding years, after adjustment for differences between the inflation rate in the country and the inflation rate in the G-5 countries (France, Germany, Japan, the United Kingdom, and the United States). The country's rate of inflation is measured by its GNP deflator. The inflation rate for G-5 countries is measured by changes in the deflator for the SDR (special drawing right, the International Monetary Fund's unit of account). The SDR deflator is calculated as a weighted average of the G-5 countries' GDP deflators in SDR terms. The weights are determined by the amount of each currency included in one SDR unit. Weights vary over time both because the IMF changes the composition of the SDR and because the SDR exchange rate for each currency changes. The SDR deflator is calculated in SDR terms first and then converted to U.S. dollars using the SDR to dollar Atlas conversion factor.

This three-year averaging smooths annual fluctuations in prices and exchange rates for each country. The Atlas conversion factor is applied to the country's GNP. The resulting GNP in U.S. dollars is divided by the midyear population for the latest of the three years to derive GNP per capita. When official exchange rates are deemed to be unreliable or unrepresentative of the effective exchange rate during a period, an alternative estimate of the exchange rate is used in the Atlas formula (see below).

The following formulas describe the computation of the Atlas conversion factor for year t:

$$e_t^* = \frac{1}{3}\left[e_{t-2}\left(\frac{p_t}{p_{t-2}} \Bigg/ \frac{p_t^{S\$}}{p_{t-2}^{S\$}}\right) + e_{t-1}\left(\frac{p_t}{p_{t-1}} \Bigg/ \frac{p_t^{S\$}}{p_{t-1}^{S\$}}\right) + e_t\right]$$

and for calculating GNP per capita in U.S. dollars for year t:

$$Y_t^\$ = (Y_t/N_t)/e_t^*,$$

where e_t^* is the Atlas conversion factor (national currency to the U.S. dollar) in year t, e_t is the average annual exchange rate (national currency to the U.S. dollar) for year t, p_t is the GNP deflator for year t, $p_t^{S\$}$ is the SDR deflator in U.S. dollar terms for year t, $Y_t^\$$ is the Atlas GNP in U.S. dollars in year t, Y_t is current GNP (local currency) for year t, and N_t is the midyear population for year t.

Alternative conversion factors

The World Bank systematically assesses the appropriateness of official exchange rates as conversion factors. An alternative conversion factor is used when the official exchange rate is judged to diverge by an exceptionally large margin from the rate effectively applied to domestic transactions of foreign currencies and traded products, the case for only a small number of countries (see *Primary data documentation*). Alternative conversion factors are used in the Atlas method and elsewhere in the *World Development Indicators* as single-year conversion factors.

Primary data documentation

The World Bank is not a primary data collection agency for most areas other than living standards surveys and debt. As a major user of socioeconomic data, however, the World Bank places particular emphasis on data documentation to inform users of data in economic analysis and policymaking. The tables in this section provide information on the sources, treatment, and currentness of the principal demographic, economic, and environmental indicators in the *World Development Indicators.*

Differences in the methods and conventions used by the primary data collectors—usually national statistical agencies, central banks, and customs services—may give rise to significant discrepancies over time both among and within countries. Delays in reporting data and the use of old surveys as the base for current estimates may severely compromise the quality of national data.

Although data quality is improving in some countries, many developing countries lack the resources to train and maintain the skilled staff and obtain the equipment needed to measure and report demographic, economic, and environmental trends in an accurate and timely way. The World Bank recognizes the need for reliable data to measure living standards, track and evaluate economic trends, and plan and monitor development projects. Thus, in concert with bilateral and other multilateral agencies, it has funded and participated in technical assistance projects to improve statistical organization and basic data methods, collection, and dissemination.

The World Bank is working at several levels to meet the challenge of improving the quality of the data that it collates and disseminates. At the country level the Bank is carrying out technical assistance, training, and survey activities—with a view to strengthening national capacity—in the following areas:

- Poverty assessments in most borrower member countries.
- Living standards measurement and other household and farm surveys with country partner statistical agencies.
- National accounts and inflation.
- Price and expenditure surveys for the International Comparison Programme.
- Statistical improvement projects in the economies of the former Soviet Union.
- External debt management.
- Environmental and economic accounting.

At the institutional level the World Bank undertook a major renewal program, forming a new unit, the Development Data Group, to concentrate on collecting, enhancing the quality of, and disseminating development indicators. New initiatives include:

- Improving documentation of data collected by the World Bank.
- Enhancing dialogue with primary data producers in the field and improving data partnerships within the Bank and with other agencies that are major data producers.
- Upgrading systems and technology to improve data collection and management and to disseminate data to a broader audience through CD-ROMs and the Internet.
- Strengthening partnerships with other multilateral agencies to improve coordination of statistical capacity building activities in developing countries.

Metadata for macroeconomic indicators

Economy	National currency	Fiscal year end	National accounts					Balance of payments and trade		Government finance
			Reporting period[a]	Base year	SNA price valuation	Alternative conversion factor	PPP survey year	Balance of Payments Manual in use	System of trade	Accounting concept
Albania	Albanian lek	Dec. 31	CY	1993	VAP			BPM5	G	
Algeria	Algerian dinar	Dec. 31	CY	1980	VAB			BPM5	S	
Angola	Angolan kwanza reajustado	Dec. 31	CY	1970	VAP			BPM5	S	
Argentina	Argentine peso	Dec. 31	CY	1986	VAP	1972–81		BPM5	S	C
Armenia	Armenian dram	Dec. 31	CY	1993	VAB	1990–95		BPM5		
Australia	Australian dollar	Jun. 30	CY	1989	VAP		1993	BPM5	G	C
Austria	Austrian schilling	Dec. 31	CY	1990	VAP		1993	BPM5	S	C
Azerbaijan	Azerbaijannian manat	Dec. 31	CY	1987	VAP	1990–95		BPM4		
Bangladesh	Bangladeshi taka	Jun. 30	FY	1985	VAP		1985	BPM4	G	
Belarus	Belarussian ruble	Dec. 31	CY	1990	VAB	1990–95	1993	BPM4		C
Belgium	Belgian franc	Dec. 31	CY	1985	VAP		1993	BPM5	S	C
Benin	CFA franc	Dec. 31	CY	1985	VAP		1985	BPM5	S	
Bolivia	Boliviano	Dec. 31	CY	1980	VAP	1974–85		BPM5	S	C
Bosnia and Herzegovina	Bosnian and Herzegovinian dinar	Dec. 31	CY	1987	VAP			BPM5		
Botswana	Botswana pula	Mar. 31	CY	1986	VAP		1985	BPM5	G	B
Brazil	Brazilian real	Dec. 31	CY	1980	VAB			BPM5	S	
Bulgaria	Bulgarian lev	Dec. 31	CY	1990	VAP	1991–95	1993	BPM5	G	C
Burkina Faso	CFA franc	Dec. 31	CY	1985	VAB			BPM5	S	C
Burundi	Burundi franc	Dec. 31	CY	1980	VAB			BPM5	S	
Cambodia	Cambodian riel	Dec. 31	CY	1960	VAP			BPM5	S	
Cameroon	CFA franc	Jun. 30	FY	1980	VAP		1985	BPM4	S	C
Canada	Canadian dollar	Mar. 31	CY	1986	VAB		1993	BPM5	G	C
Central African Republic	CFA franc	Dec. 31	CY	1987	VAB			BPM5	S	
Chad	CFA franc	Dec. 31	CY	1977	VAB			BPM5	S	C
Chile	Chilean peso	Dec. 31	CY	1986	VAP			BPM5	S	C
China	Chinese yuan	Dec. 31	CY	1990	VAP			BPM5	G	B
Colombia	Colombian peso	Dec. 31	CY	1975	VAP	1993–95		BPM5	S	C
Congo	CFA franc	Dec. 31	CY	1978	VAP		1985	BPM5	S	
Costa Rica	Costa Rican colón	Dec. 31	CY	1987	VAP			BPM5	S	C
Côte d'Ivoire	CFA franc	Dec. 31	CY	1986	VAB		1985	BPM5	S	C
Croatia	Croatian kuna	Dec. 31	CY	1994	VAB		1993	BPM5		C
Cuba	Cuban peso	Dec. 31	CY	..	..				S	
Czech Republic	Czech koruna	Dec. 31	CY	1984	VAP		1993	BPM5	G	C
Denmark	Danish krone	Dec. 31	CY	1980	VAB		1993	BPM5	G	C
Dominican Republic	Dominican peso	Dec. 31	CY	1970	VAP	1992–95		BPM5	G	C
Ecuador	Ecuadorian sucre	Dec. 31	CY	1975	VAP			BPM5	G	B
Egypt, Arab Rep.	Egyptian pound	Jun. 30	FY	1987	VAB		1985	BPM4		C
El Salvador	Salvadoran colón	Dec. 31	CY	1962	VAP	1990–95		BPM5	S	B
Eritrea	Ethiopian birr	Dec. 31	CY	1992	VAB			BPM4		
Estonia	Estonian kroon	Dec. 31	CY	1993	VAB	1990–95		BPM5		C
Ethiopia	Ethiopian birr	Jul. 7	FY	1981	VAB		1985	BPM4	G	B
Finland	Finnish markka	Dec. 31	CY	1990	VAB		1993	BPM5	G	C
France	French franc	Dec. 31	CY	1980	VAP		1993	BPM5	S	C
Gabon	CFA franc	Dec. 31	CY	1989	VAP			BPM5	S	B
Gambia, The	Gambian dalasi	Jun. 30	FY	1976	VAB			BPM5	G	B

Data sources and years

Economy	Latest population census	Latest household or demographic survey	Vital registration complete	Latest agricultural census	Latest industrial data	Latest water withdrawal data	Latest survey of scientists and engineers engaged in R&D	Latest survey of expenditure for R&D
Albania	1989		✓		1990	1970		
Algeria	1987	PAPCHILD, 1992			1993	1990		
Angola	1970					1987		
Argentina	1991			1988	1993	1976	1988	1992
Armenia	1989		✓		1991	1989		
Australia	1991		✓	1990	1992	1985	1990	1990
Austria	1991		✓	1990	1994	1991	1989	1989
Azerbaijan	1989		✓			1989		
Bangladesh	1991	DHS, 1994			1992	1987		
Belarus	1989		✓			1989	1992	1992
Belgium	1991		✓	1990	1994	1980	1990	1990
Benin	1992	WFS, 1981		1992	1981	1994	1989	1989
Bolivia	1992	DHS, 1994			1994	1987	1991	1991
Bosnia and Herzegovina	1991		✓		1991			
Botswana	1991	DHS, 1988			1994	1992		
Brazil	1991	DHS, 1991			1992	1990	1985	1985
Bulgaria	1992		✓		1994	1988	1992	1991
Burkina Faso	1985	SDA, 1995			1983	1992		
Burundi	1990				1991	1987	1989	1989
Cambodia	1962					1987		
Cameroon	1987	DHS, 1991			1994	1987		
Canada	1991		✓	1991	1994	1991	1991	1992
Central African Republic	1988	DHS, 1994–95			1992	1987		
Chad	1993					1987		
Chile	1992				1994	1975	1988	1992
China	1990	Population, 1995			1994	1980		
Colombia	1993	DHS, 1995		1988	1994	1987	1982	1982
Congo	1984				1988	1987	1984	1984
Costa Rica	1984	CDC, 1993	✓		1994	1970	1992	1986
Côte d'Ivoire	1988	DHS, 1994			1993	1986		
Croatia	1991		✓		1992		1992	1992
Cuba	1981		✓		1989	1975	1992	1992
Czech Republic	1991	CDC, 1993	✓		1991		1992	1992
Denmark	1991		✓	1989	1992	1990	1992	1992
Dominican Republic	1993	DHS, 1991			1985	1987		
Ecuador	1990	DHS, 1994			1994	1987	1990	1990
Egypt, Arab Rep.	1986	DHS, 1995	✓		1993	1992	1991	1991
El Salvador	1992	CDC, 1994			1994	1975	1992	1992
Eritrea	1984							
Estonia	1989		✓			1989		
Ethiopia	1994	Family and fertility, 1990		1989–92	1990	1987		
Finland	1990		✓		1994	1991	1991	1991
France	1990	Income, 1989	✓	1988	1994	1990	1991	1991
Gabon	1993				1982		1987	1986
Gambia, The	1993				1982	1982		

Primary data documentation

Metadata for macroeconomic indicators

Economy	National currency	Fiscal year end	National accounts					Balance of payments and trade		Government finance
			Reporting period[a]	Base year	SNA price valuation	Alternative conversion factor	PPP survey year	Balance of Payments Manual in use	System of trade	Accounting concept
Georgia	Georgian lari	Dec. 31	CY	1987	VAB	1990–95		BPM4		
Germany	Deutsche mark	Dec. 31	CY	1990	VAP		1993	BPM5	S	C
Ghana	Ghanaian cedi	Dec. 31	CY	1975	VAP	1994		BPM5	G	C
Greece	Greek drachma	Dec. 31	CY	1970	VAB		1993	BPM5	S	C
Guatemala	Guatemalan quetzal	Dec. 31	CY	1958	VAP			BPM5	S	B
Guinea	Guinean franc	Dec. 31	CY	1989	VAP			BPM5	S	C
Guinea-Bissau	Guinea-Bissau peso	Dec. 31	CY	1986	VAP	1972–86		BPM5	S	
Haiti	Haitian gourde	Sep. 30	FY	1976	VAP			BPM5	G	
Honduras	Honduran lempira	Dec. 31	CY	1978	VAB			BPM5	S	
Hong Kong	Hong Kong dollar	Dec. 31	CY	1990	VAB		1985	BPM4	G	
Hungary	Hungarian forint	Dec. 31	CY	1991	VAB		1993	BPM5	G	C
India	Indian rupee	Mar. 31	FY	1980	VAB		1985	BPM4	G	C
Indonesia	Indonesian rupiah	Mar. 31	CY	1993	VAP			BPM5	S	C
Iran, Islamic Rep.	Iranian rial	Mar. 20	FY	1982	VAB		1985	BPM5	S	C
Iraq	Iraqi dinar	Dec. 31	CY	1969	VAB				S	
Ireland	Irish pound	Dec. 31	CY	1985	VAB		1993	BPM5	G	C
Israel	Israeli new shekel	Dec. 31	CY	1990	VAB			BPM5	S	C
Italy	Italian lira	Dec. 31	CY	1985	VAP		1993	BPM5	S	C
Jamaica	Jamaica dollar	Dec. 31	CY	1986	VAP			BPM5	G	
Japan	Japanese yen	Mar. 31	CY	1985	VAP		1993	BPM5	G	C
Jordan	Jordan dinar	Dec. 31	CY	1990	VAB			BPM4	G	B
Kazakstan	Kazak tenge	Dec. 31	CY	1993	VAB	1990–95		BPM4		
Kenya	Kenya shilling	Jun. 30	CY	1982	VAB		1985	BPM5	G	B
Korea, Dem. Rep.	Democratic Republic of Korea won	Dec. 31	CY	1990	VAP			BPM5		
Korea, Rep.	Korean won	Dec. 31	CY	1990	VAP		1985	BPM5	S	C
Kuwait	Kuwaiti dinar	Jun. 30	CY	1984	VAP			BPM5	S	C
Kyrgyz Republic	Kyrgyz som	Dec. 31	CY	1987	VAB	1990–94		BPM4		
Lao PDR	Lao kip	Dec. 31	CY	1990	VAP			BPM5		
Latvia	Latvian lat	Dec. 31	CY	1993	VAB	1990–95		BPM5		C
Lebanon	Lebanese pound	Dec. 31	CY	1990	VAB			BPM4	G	
Lesotho	Lesotho loti	Mar. 31	CY	1980	VAB			BPM5	G	C
Libya	Libyan dinar	Dec. 31	CY	1975	VAB			BPM5	G	
Lithuania	Lithuanian litas	Dec. 31	CY	1992	VAB	1990–95		BPM5		C
Macedonia, FYR	Macedonian denar	Dec. 31	CY	1990	VAP					
Madagascar	Malagasi franc	Dec. 31	CY	1984	VAB		1985	BPM5	S	C
Malawi	Malawi kwacha	Mar. 31	CY	1978	VAB		1985	BPM5	G	B
Malaysia	Malaysian ringgit	Dec. 31	CY	1978	VAP			BPM5	G	C
Mali	CFA franc	Dec. 31	CY	1987	VAB		1985	BPM5	S	
Mauritania	Mauritanian ouguiya	Dec. 31	CY	1985	VAB			BPM5	S	
Mauritius	Mauritian rupee	Jun. 30	CY	1992	VAB		1985	BPM5	G	C
Mexico	Mexican peso	Dec. 31	CY	1980	VAP			BPM5	G	C
Moldova	Moldovan leu	Dec. 31	CY	1993	VAB	1990–93	1993	BPM5		
Mongolia	Mongolian tugrik	Dec. 31	CY	1986	VAB	1993		BPM5		C
Morocco	Moroccan dirham	Dec. 31	CY	1980	VAP		1985	BPM5	S	C
Mozambique	Mozambican meticai	Dec. 31	CY	1987	VAB			BPM5	S	

Data sources and years

Economy	Latest population census	Latest household or demographic survey	Vital registration complete	Latest agricultural census	Latest industrial data	Latest water withdrawal data	Latest survey of scientists and engineers engaged in R&D	Latest survey of expenditure for R&D
Georgia	1989		✓			1989		
Germany			✓		1993	1991	1989	1989
Ghana	1984	DHS, 1993			1987	1970		
Greece	1991		✓		1994	1980	1986	1986
Guatemala	1994	DHS, 1995			1990	1970	1988	1988
Guinea	1983	SDA, 1994–95		1989		1987	1984	1984
Guinea-Bissau	1991	SDA, 1991		1988		1991		
Haiti	1982	DHS, 1994–95				1987		
Honduras	1988	DHS, 1994		1993	1994	1992		
Hong Kong	1991		✓		1994			
Hungary	1990	Income, 1995	✓		1994	1991	1992	1992
India	1991	National family health, 1992–93		1986	1993	1975		
Indonesia	1990	DHS, 1994			1994	1987		
Iran, Islamic Rep.	1991	Demographic, 1995		1988	1993	1975		
Iraq	1987				1992	1970		
Ireland	1991		✓	1991	1994	1980	1988	1988
Israel	1983		✓		1993	1989		
Italy	1991		✓	1990	1991	1990	1990	1990
Jamaica	1991	LSMS, 1994	✓		1992	1975	1986	1986
Japan	1990		✓	1990	1994	1990		
Jordan	1994	DHS, 1990			1994	1975		
Kazakstan	1989		✓			1989		
Kenya	1989	DHS, 1993			1994	1990		
Korea, Dem. Rep.	1993					1987		
Korea, Rep.	1990					1992		
Kuwait	1985		✓		1993	1974		
Kyrgyz Republic	1989	LSMS, 1994	✓			1989		
Lao PDR	1985					1987		
Latvia	1989		✓			1989	1992	1992
Lebanon	1970					1975		
Lesotho	1986	DHS, 1991			1985	1987		
Libya	1984			1987	1989	1994	1980	1980
Lithuania	1989		✓			1989	1992	1992
Macedonia, FYR	1991		✓				1991	1991
Madagascar	1993	SDA, 1993			1988	1984	1989	1988
Malawi	1987	DHS, 1992				1994		
Malaysia	1991		✓			1975		
Mali	1987	DHS, 1987			1981	1987		
Mauritania	1988	PAPCHILD, 1990				1985		
Mauritius	1990	CDC, 1991	✓			1974	1992	1992
Mexico	1990	DHS, 1987				1991	1984	1984
Moldova	1989		✓			1989		
Mongolia	1989					1987		
Morocco	1994	DHS, 1995				1992		
Mozambique	1980					1992		

Primary data documentation

Metadata for macroeconomic indicators

Economy	National currency	Fiscal year end	National accounts					Balance of payments and trade		Government finance
			Reporting period[a]	Base year	SNA price valuation	Alternative conversion factor	PPP survey year	Balance of Payments Manual in use	System of trade	Accounting concept
Myanmar	Myanmar kyat	Mar. 31	FY	1985	VAP			BPM4	G	C
Namibia	Namibia dollar	Mar. 31	CY	1990	VAB			BPM5		C
Nepal	Nepalese rupee	Jul. 14	FY	1985	VAB			BPM4	G	C
Netherlands	Netherlands guilder	Dec. 31	CY	1990	VAP		1993	BPM5	S	C
New Zealand	New Zealand dollar	Jun. 30	CY	1982	VAP		1993	BPM5	G	B
Nicaragua	Nicaraguan gold cordoba	Dec. 31	CY	1980	VAP			BPM5	G	C
Niger	CFA franc	Dec. 31	CY	1987	VAP			BPM5	S	
Nigeria	Nigerian naira	Dec. 31	CY	1987	VAB	1992–95	1985	BPM5	G	
Norway	Norwegian krone	Dec. 31	CY	1990	VAP		1993	BPM5	G	C
Oman	Rial Omani	Dec. 31	CY	1978	VAP			BPM5	G	B
Pakistan	Pakistan rupee	Jun. 30	FY	1981	VAB		1985	BPM4	G	C
Panama	Panamanian balboa	Dec. 31	CY	1992	VAB			BPM5	S	C
Papua New Guinea	Papua New Guinea kina	Dec. 31	CY	1983	VAP			BPM5	G	B
Paraguay	Paraguayan guaraní	Dec. 31	CY	1982	VAP			BPM4	S	C
Peru	Peruvian new sol	Dec. 31	CY	1979	VAP	1987–91		BPM5	S	C
Philippines	Philippine peso	Dec. 31	CY	1985	VAP		1985	BPM5	G	B
Poland	Polish zloty	Dec. 31	CY	1990	VAP		1993	BPM5	G	C
Portugal	Portuguese escudo	Dec. 31	CY	1985	VAP		1993	BPM5	S	C
Puerto Rico	U.S. dollar	Dec. 31	CY	..						
Romania	Romanian leu	Dec. 31	CY	1993	VAB	1992	1993	BPM5	G	C
Russian Federation	Russian ruble	Dec. 31	CY	1993	VAB	1990–95	1993	BPM4		C
Rwanda	Rwanda franc	Dec. 31	CY	1985	VAB		1985	BPM5	G	C
Saudi Arabia	Saudi Arabian riyal	Hijri year	Hijri year	1970	VAP			BPM5	S	
Senegal	CFA franc	Dec. 31	CY	1987	VAP		1985	BPM5	S	
Sierra Leone	Sierra Leonean leone	Jun. 30	CY	1985	VAB		1985	BPM5	G	B
Singapore	Singapore dollar	Mar. 31	CY	1985	VAP			BPM5	G	C
Slovak Republic	Slovak koruna	Dec. 31	CY	1993	VAP		1993	BPM5		
Slovenia	Slovenian tolar	Dec. 31	CY	1992	VAB		1993	BPM5		
South Africa	South African rand	Mar. 31	CY	1990	VAB			BPM5		C
Spain	Spanish peseta	Dec. 31	CY	1996	VAP		1993	BPM5	S	C
Sri Lanka	Sri Lanka rupee	Dec. 31	CY	1982	VAB		1985	BPM5	G	C
Sudan	Sudanese pound	Jun. 30	FY	1982	VAB			BPM4	G	
Sweden	Swedish krona	Jun. 30	CY	1990	VAB		1993	BPM5	G	C
Switzerland	Swiss franc	Dec. 31	CY	1990	VAP		1993	BPM5	S	C
Syrian Arab Republic	Syrian pound	Dec. 31	CY	1985	VAP			BPM5	S	C
Tajikistan	Tajik ruble	Dec. 31	CY	1993	VAP	1990–94		BPM4		
Tanzania	Tanzania shilling	Jun. 30	FY	1992	VAB		1985	BPM5	G	
Thailand	Thai baht	Sep. 30	CY	1988	VAP		1985	BPM5	G	C
Togo	CFA franc	Dec. 31	CY	1978	VAP			BPM5	S	
Trinidad and Tobago	Trinidad and Tobago dollar	Dec. 31	CY	1985	VAB			BPM5	S	
Tunisia	Tunisian dinar	Dec. 31	CY	1990	VAP		1985	BPM5	G	C
Turkey	Turkish lira	Dec. 31	CY	1994	VAB		1993	BPM5	S	C
Turkmenistan	Turkmen manat	Dec. 31	CY	1987	VAP	1990–95		BPM4		
Uganda	Uganda shilling	June 30	FY	1991	VAB			BPM4	G	
Ukraine	Ukrainian hrivnya	Dec. 31	CY	1990	VAB	1990–95	1993	BPM5		

Data sources and years

Economy	Latest population census	Latest household or demographic survey	Vital registration complete	Latest agricultural census	Latest industrial data	Latest water withdrawal data	Latest survey of scientists and engineers engaged in R&D	Latest survey of expenditure for R&D
Myanmar	1983			1993		1987		
Namibia	1991	DHS, 1992				1991		
Nepal	1991			1992		1987		
Netherlands	1971		✓	1989		1991	1991	1991
New Zealand	1991		✓	1990	1992	1991	1990	1990
Nicaragua	1971	LSMS, 1993			1985	1975	1987	1987
Niger	1988	Household budget and consumption, 1993		1982	1988			
Nigeria	1991	Consumption expenditure, 1992		1990	1987	1987	1987	
Norway	1990		✓	1989	1994	1985	1991	1991
Oman	1993	Child health, 1989				1975		
Pakistan	1981	LSMS, 1991		1990		1975		
Panama	1990			1990		1975		
Papua New Guinea	1989				1989	1987		
Paraguay	1992	CDC, 1992		1991	1981	1987		
Peru	1993	LSMS, 1994				1987	1981	1984
Philippines	1990	DHS, 1993				1975		
Poland	1988		✓	1990		1991	1992	1992
Portugal	1991		✓	1989		1990	1990	1990
Puerto Rico	1990			1987				
Romania	1992	LSMS, 1995	✓			1994	1992	1992
Russian Federation	1989	LSMS, 1994	✓			1991	1991	1988
Rwanda	1991	DHS, 1992			1986	1993	1985	1985
Saudi Arabia	1992	Maternal and child health, 1993	✓		1989	1975		
Senegal	1988	DHS, 1992–93				1987	1981	1981
Sierra Leone	1985	SHEHEA, 1989–90			1993	1987		
Singapore	1990		✓			1975	1987	1987
Slovak Republic	1991		✓			1991		
Slovenia	1991		✓				1992	1992
South Africa	1991	LSMS, 1993				1990	1991	1991
Spain	1991		✓	1989	1994	1991	1990	1990
Sri Lanka	1993	DHS, 1993	✓			1970	1985	1984
Sudan	1993	DHS, 1989–90				1995		
Sweden	1990		✓			1991	1991	1991
Switzerland	1990		✓	1990		1991	1989	1989
Syrian Arab Republic	1981				1992	1976		
Tajikistan	1989		✓			1989		
Tanzania	1988	LSMS, 1993			1988	1994		
Thailand	1990	DHS, 1987		1988	1991	1987	1991	1991
Togo	1981	DHS, 1988			1984	1987		
Trinidad and Tobago	1990	DHS, 1987	✓			1975	1984	1984
Tunisia	1994					1990	1992	1992
Turkey	1990	Population and health, 1983		1991		1991	1991	1991
Turkmenistan	1989		✓			1989		
Uganda	1991	DHS, 1995		1991	1989	1970		
Ukraine	1991		✓			1989	1989	1989

Metadata for macroeconomic indicators

Economy	National currency	Fiscal year end	National accounts					Balance of payments and trade		Government finance
			Reporting period[a]	Base year	SNA price valuation	Alternative conversion factor	PPP survey year	Balance of Payments Manual in use	System of trade	Accounting concept
United Arab Emirates	U.A.E. dirham	Dec. 31	CY	1985	VAB			BPM4	G	B
United Kingdom	Pound sterling	Dec. 31	CY	1990	VAB		1993	BPM5	G	C
United States	U.S. dollar	Sep. 30	CY	1985	VAP		1993	BPM5	G	C
Uruguay	Uruguayan peso	Dec. 31	CY	1983	VAP			BPM5	S	C
Uzbekistan	Uzbek sum	Dec. 31	CY	1987	VAB	1990–95		BPM4		
Venezuela	Venezuelan bolívar	Dec. 31	CY	1984	VAP			BPM5	G	C
Vietnam	Vietnamese dong	Dec. 31	CY	1989	VAP			BPM4		
West Bank and Gaza	Israeli new shekel	Dec. 31	CY	..	VAP					
Yemen, Rep.	Yemen rial	Dec. 31	CY	1990	VAB	1990–95		BPM4	G	C
Yugoslavia, Fed. Rep.	Yugoslav new dinar	Dec. 31	CY	1984	VAP		1985		S	
Zaire	New zaïre	Dec. 31	CY	1987	VAP			BPM5	S	C
Zambia	Zambian kwacha	Dec. 31	CY	1977	VAP		1985	BPM5	G	C
Zimbabwe	Zimbabwe dollar	Jun. 30	CY	1980	VAB		1985	BPM5	G	C

Note: For explanation of the abbreviations used in the table see the notes. a. Also applies to balance of payments reporting.

Notes on metadata for macroeconomic indicators

● **Fiscal year end** is the date of the end of the fiscal year for the central government. Fiscal years for other levels of government and the reporting years for statistical surveys may differ, but if a country is designated as a fiscal year reporter in the following column, the date shown is the end of its national accounts reporting period. ● **Reporting period** for national accounts and balance of payments data is designated as either calendar year basis, (CY) or fiscal year (FY). Most economies report their national accounts and balance of payments data using calendar years, but a limited number use fiscal years, which straddle two calendar years. In the *World Development Indicators* fiscal year data are assigned to the calendar year that contains the larger share of the fiscal year: if a country's fiscal year ends before June 30, the data are shown in the earlier year of the fiscal period; if the fiscal year ends on or after June 30, the data are shown in the second year of the period. Note that Saudi Arabia follows a lunar year whose starting and ending dates change with respect to the solar year. Because the International Monetary Fund (IMF) reports most balance of payments data on a calendar year basis, balance of payments data for fiscal year reporters in the *World Development Indicators* are based on fiscal year estimates provided by World Bank operational staff. These estimates may differ from IMF data but allow consistent comparisons between national accounts and balance of payments data. ● **Base year** is the year used as the base period for constant price calculations in the country's national accounts. Price indexes derived from national accounts aggre-

gates, such as the GDP deflator, express the price level relative to prices in the base year. Constant price data reported in the World Bank are partially rebased to a common 1987 base year. See the notes to table 4.1 for further discussion. ● **SNA price valuation** shows whether value added in the national accounts is reported at basic or producers' prices (VAB) or at purchasers' prices (VAP). Purchasers' prices include the value of taxes levied on value added and collected from consumers and thus tend to overstate the actual value added in production. See the notes to table 4.2 for further discussion of national accounts valuation. ● **Alternative conversion factor** identifies the countries and years for which a World Bank—estimated conversion factor has been used in place of the official (IFS line rf) exchange rate. See *Statistical methods* for further discussion of the use of alternative conversion factors. ● **PPP survey year** refers to the latest available survey year for the International Comparison Programme's estimates of purchasing power parities (PPPs). See the notes to tables 4.14 and 5.5 for further details. ● **Balance of Payments Manual in use** refers to the classification system used for compiling and reporting data on balance of payments items in tables 4.21 and 4.22. BPM4 refers to the fourth edition of the IMF's *Balance of Payments Manual* (1977), and BPM5 to the fifth edition (1993). Since 1995 the IMF has adjusted all balance of payments data to BPM5 conventions, but some countries continue to report using the older system. ● **System of trade** refers to the general trade system (G) or the special trade system (S). For imports under the general trade system, both goods entering directly for domestic consumption and goods entered into customs storage are recorded, at the time of their

first arrival, as imports; under the special trade system, goods are recorded as imports when declared for domestic consumption whether at time of entry or on withdrawal from customs storage. Exports under the general system comprise outward-moving goods: (a) national goods wholly or partly produced in the country; (b) foreign goods, neither transformed nor declared for domestic consumption in the country, that move outward from customs storage; and (c) nationalized goods that have been declared from domestic consumption and move outward without having been transformed. Under the special system of trade, exports comprise categories (a) and (c). In some compilations categories (b) and (c) are classified as re-exports. Direct transit trade, consisting of goods entering or leaving for transport purposes only, is excluded from both import and export statistics. See the notes to tables 4.8 and 4.9 for further discussion. ● **Government finance accounting concept** describes the accounting basis for reporting central government financial data. For most countries government finance data have been consolidated (C) into one set of accounts capturing all fiscal activities of the central government. Budgetary central government accounts (B) exclude central government units. See the notes to table 4.16 for further details.

Data sources and years

Economy	Latest population census	Latest household or demographic survey	Vital registration complete	Latest agricultural census	Latest industrial data	Latest water withdrawal data	Latest survey of scientists and engineers engaged in R&D	Latest survey of expenditure for R&D
United Arab Emirates	1980				1985	1980		
United Kingdom	1991		✓	1993	1994	1991	1991	1991
United States	1990	Current population, 1994	✓	1987	1990	1990	1988	1988
Uruguay	1985			1990	1994	1965		
Uzbekistan	1989		✓			1989	1992	1992
Venezuela	1990	LSMS, 1993			1993	1970		
Vietnam	1989	Intercensal demographic, 1995				1992	1985	1985
West Bank and Gaza		Demographic, 1995						
Yemen, Rep.	1994	DHS, 1991–92				1987		
Yugoslavia, Fed. Rep.	1991		✓				1992	1992
Zaire	1984			1990		1990		
Zambia	1990	SDA, 1993		1990		1994		
Zimbabwe	1992	DHS, 1994				1987		

Note: For explanation of the abbreviations used in the table see the notes.

Notes on data sources and years

● **Latest population census** shows the most recent year in which a census was conducted. ● **Latest household or demographic survey** gives information on the surveys used in compiling household and demographic data presented in section 2. PAPCHILD is the Pan Arab Project for Child Development; DHS is Demographic and Health Survey; WFS is World Fertility Study; LSMS is Living Standards Measurement Study; SDA is Social Dimensions of Adjustment; CDC is Centers for Disease Control and Prevention; and SHEHEA is Survey of Household Expenditure and Household Economic Activities. ● **Vital registration complete** identifies countries judged to have complete registries of vital statistics (✓) by the United Nations Department of Economic and Social Information and Policy Analysis, Statistical Division, and reported in *Population and Vital Statistics Reports*. Countries with complete vital statistics registries may have more accurate and more timely demographic indicators. ● **Latest agricultural census** shows the most recent year in which an agricultural census was conducted and reported to the Food and Agriculture Organization. ● **Latest industrial data** refer to the most recent year for which manufacturing value added data at the three-digit level of the International Standard Industrial Classification (rev. 2 or rev. 3) are available in the UNIDO database. ● **Water withdrawal survey** refers to the most recent year for which data have been compiled from a variety of sources. See the notes to table 3.3 for more information. ● **Latest surveys of scientists and engineers engaged in R&D and expenditures on R&D** refer to the most recent year for which data are available from a data collection effort by UNESCO in science and technology and research and development (R&D). See the notes to table 5.13 for more information.

World view

1

No word might be used but what marks either number, weight or measure.
—Sir William Petty, 1676

The organization and coverage of the *World Development Indicators* reflect the priorities of an institution dedicated to promoting economic development. The focus is on people, the environment, the economy, the relative roles of states and markets, and the links between industrial and developing economies. But what is development? And how do we measure it?

Life's quality

Since the 17th century economists have viewed development as a means of improving standards of living and the quality of life in very broad terms. Sir William Petty, one of the first development economists, was interested not only in national income but also in such factors as "the Common Safety" and "each Man's particular Happiness" (cited in Sen 1988).

"Ultimately," Amartya Sen argues that "the assessment of development achieved cannot be a matter only of quantification of the means of that achievement. The concept of development has to take note of the actual achievements themselves" (1988, p. 15). These achievements—Sen labels them as "functionings"—include the length of life (life expectancy) and the "nature of life" and what people value as important to their well-being (nourishment, good health, clean air and water, the ability to move about freely).

True, these values differ greatly from individual to individual, reflecting different aspirations, conceptions, abilities, and tastes—and from society to society, reflecting culture and tradition. Yet there clearly are certain basic needs common to all mankind for food, health, shelter, and personal freedoms, which if met constitute development (Dasgupta 1993).

In measuring development, it helps to distinguish between indicators that measure the "constituents" of development (such outcomes as health and literacy) and those that measure its "determinants," the goods and services that produce development or well-being, such as food, shelter, safe drinking water, clean air, education, health care, and real national income (Dasgupta and Weale 1992). Partha Dasgupta and Martin Weale show a strong correlation between the rankings of 48 developing countries for GNP per capita (adjusted for purchasing power parity) and their rankings for five other indicators (life expectancy, infant mortality, adult literacy, political rights, and civil rights). This leads Dasgupta to observe that "recent suggestions that national income is a vastly misleading index are not borne out by this exercise. We can do better than merely rely on national income, but we wouldn't have been wildly off the mark as regards an ordinal comparison of countries had we relied exclusively on national income per head" (1993, p. 115).

Not the same for all

One reason to go beyond national income is to capture inequalities in access to resources. Life expectancy, infant mortality, and adult literacy measure outcomes, but they also say much about differential access to assets and income and about other pervasive forms of differentiation based on gender.

The causes of gender inequality, linked as they are to the decisions in households, are particularly complex. Regardless of how such decisions are made, they clearly are influenced by market signals and institutional and cultural norms that do not capture the full benefits to society of investing in women. Limited education and training, poor health and nutrition, and denied access to resources depress women's quality of life—and hinder economic efficiency and growth. This is disturbing, because women are agents of change, shaping the welfare of future generations.

Social and environmental sustainability

The environment can no longer be thought of as a source of free goods and services. Environmental values and costs should be included when measuring the quality of life. Although this is easier said than done, we cannot ignore the damage that people do to their environment or the damage done to themselves through environmental degradation. The poor often suffer the most. They cannot escape the polluted air in the streets of cities or from the open fires burning wood or dung in rural areas. They cannot protect themselves from contaminated water, and their farmlands are more likely to suffer from soil erosion. Development may be a cure for environmental ills—the rich can afford to maintain a healthy environment—but it is also associated with greater consumption of natural resources, particularly energy, and potentially destabilizing alterations in natural balances. The challenge for governments and citizens alike is to find development strategies that are sustainable at a local and a global level.

From farming to computer programming

The process of development is sometimes referred to as "structural transformation," the change in patterns of consumption, production, technology, foreign trade, and resource use. And the developed market economies have perhaps seen more profound change in this century than at any other time in human history (Drucker 1994).

At the beginning of the 20th century farmers constituted the largest single group in today's industrial economies. Today they make up no more than 5 percent of the workforce. Even blue-collar workers, who dominated the labor force of high-income economies in the 1950s, have retreated to proportions common at the beginning of the century.

East Asian economies are now experiencing a similar—possibly even faster—structural transformation. But they are at one extreme. At the other are many countries and parts of countries that remain untouched by major change.

Fueling the structural transformation is economic growth, the "expansion in productive resources and the increase in the efficiency of their use" (Syrquin 1988). This growth comes through increases in inputs and through technical change. A proxy for technical change is the growth of what is called total factor productivity (TFP)—that is, the contribution to economic growth by the increase in productivity of all factors combined—of such inputs as land, natural resources, and human and physical capital. In practice, however, it is difficult to disentangle technical change from the factors of production, because that change is embodied in labor (through education, training, and experience) and in capital (through the innovations embodied by machinery and equipment).

Developing countries nevertheless appear to experience slower TFP growth than do the industrial countries—and countries that grow faster typically enjoy faster TFP growth (World Bank 1991b).

A large number of cross-country studies of the post–World War II period throw light on the process of structural transformation (Syrquin 1988):

• Savings and investment tend to rise as a share of GDP during periods of rapid transformation. All the evidence points to strong correlations between growth rates and investment rates.

• Rapid agricultural growth has been generally associated with successful industrialization and sustained gains in overall output and productivity. Such growth usually reflects improvements in yield (output per unit of land) and is often associated with the use of modern inputs (fertilizers, agricultural machinery).

• While agriculture provides the initial stimulus for transformation, its importance declines with development. The share of agriculture in output and employment tends to fall with industrialization, but farm productivity outstrips the relatively inelastic demand for food. So, food prices fall relative to other consumer prices.

• In household budgets food's share declines with sustained progress, facilitating the diversification of spending and choices. Changes in the structure of demand therefore tend to drive changes in production.

• International trade is an important pathway for structural transformation, especially for small economies. Small economies have small domestic markets and must specialize—their share of trade (exports plus imports) in GDP is high. If they lack natural resources, they must develop competitive exports of manufactured goods and, increasingly, services. Large economies with large domestic markets may have a relatively smaller share of trade in GDP, but they are still likely to be important world traders. Production for domestic consumption provides them with a base for developing an efficiently sized and competitive export sector. For all economies, regardless of size, access to imports from world markets is important for sustaining efficient production processes and high levels of consumption.

The tables in this section provide an overview of the quality of life, gender differences, and economic structure in the 209 economies for which data are available. (In the rest of this book indicators are shown only for 148 economies whose populations exceed one million.) Following the tables is a set of charts that summarize key development trends shaping the world economy.

1.1 | The quality of life

	Population density	GNP per capita[a]		Poverty	Infant mortality rate		Total fertility rate		Adult illiteracy rate		Access to sanitation
	people per sq. km 1995	$ 1995	PPP[b] $ 1995	% of people living on less than $1 a day (PPP) 1981–95	per 1,000 live births 1970	1995	births per woman 1970	1995	% of people 15 and above Male 1995	Female 1995	% of population 1994–95
Afghanistan	36	..[c]	..	..	198	158	7.1	6.9	53	85	8
Albania	119	670	..	..	66	30	5.2	2.6	..	..	100
Algeria	12	1,600	5,300[d]	1.6	139	34	7.4	3.5	26	51	..
American Samoa	285	..[e]	..	..	..	..	..	..	..	..	..
Andorra	142	..[f]	..	..	..	..	..	..	..	..	..
Angola	9	410	1,310[d]	..	178	124	6.5	6.9	..	..	16
Antigua and Barbuda	157	..[e]	..	..	..	18	2.6	1.7	..	..	..
Argentina	13	8,030	8,310	..	52	22	3.1	2.7	4	4	89
Armenia[g]	133	730	2,260	..	..	16	3.2	1.8	..	..	..
Aruba	421	..[f]	..	..	..	..	..	..	..	..	..
Australia	2	18,720	18,940	..	18	6	2.9	1.9	..	..	90
Austria	97	26,890	21,250	..	26	6	2.3	1.5	..	..	100
Azerbaijan[g]	87	480	1,460	..	..	25	4.7	2.3	..	..	..
Bahamas, The	28	11,940	14,710[d]	..	35	15	3.5	2.0	2	2	98
Bahrain	836	7,840	13,400[d]	..	64	19	6.5	3.1	11	21	100
Bangladesh	920	240	1,380	..	140	79	7.0	3.5	51	74	30
Barbados	607	6,560	10,620[d]	..	38	13	3.0	1.8	2	3	..
Belarus[g]	50	2,070	4,220	..	..	13	2.4	1.4	..	..	100
Belgium	..	24,710	21,660	..	21	8	2.2	1.6	..	..	100
Belize	9	2,630	5,400[d]	..	..	36	6.9	3.9	..	..	57
Benin	49	370	1,760	..	155	95	6.9	6.0	51	74	22
Bermuda	1,260	..[f]	..	..	..	..	..	..	..	..	..
Bhutan	15	420	1,260[d]	..	..	..	..	..	44	72	22
Bolivia	7	800	2,540	7.1	153	69	6.5	4.5	10	24	44
Bosnia and Herzegovina	..	..[c]	..	..	..	..	..	..	..	..	..
Botswana	3	3,020	5,580	34.7	95	56	6.9	4.4	20	40	55
Brazil	19	3,640	5,400	28.7	95	44	5.0	2.4	17	17	73
Brunei	54	..[f]	..	..	57	9	5.6	2.9	7	17	..
Bulgaria	76	1,330	4,480	2.6	27	15	2.2	1.2	..	..	99
Burkina Faso	38	230	780[d]	..	141	99	7.0	6.7	71	91	14
Burundi	244	160	630[d]	..	138	98	6.8	6.5	51	78	48
Cambodia	57	270	..	..	161	108	5.8	4.7	20	47	..
Cameroon	29	650	2,110	..	126	56	5.8	5.7	25	48	40
Canada	3	19,380	21,130	..	19	6	2.3	1.7	..	..	85
Cape Verde	94	960	1,870[d]	..	86	46	7.0	4.0	19	36	24
Cayman Islands	127	..[f]	..	..	..	..	..	..	..	..	..
Central African Republic	5	340	1,070[d]	..	139	98	5.7	5.1	32	48	..
Chad	5	180	700[d]	..	171	117	6.0	5.9	38	65	32
Channel Islands	..	..[f]	..	..	19	7	2.0	1.7	..	..	..
Chile	19	4,160	9,520	15.0	77	12	4.0	2.3	5	5	71
China	129	620	2,920	29.4	69	34	5.8	1.9	10	27	..
Colombia	35	1,910	6,130	7.4	74	26	5.3	2.8	9	9	70
Comoros	224	470	1,320[d]	..	..	87	..	5.9	36	50	83
Congo	8	680	2,050	..	101	90	5.9	6.0	17	33	9
Costa Rica	67	2,610	5,850	18.9	62	13	4.9	2.8	5	5	99
Côte d'Ivoire	44	660	1,580	17.7	135	86	7.4	5.3	50	70	54
Croatia	85	3,250	..	..	..	16	..	1.5	..	..	68
Cuba	100	..[h]	..	..	39	9	3.8	1.7	4	5	66
Cyprus	79	..[f]	..	..	29	8	2.6	2.2	..	..	100
Czech Republic	134	3,870	9,770	3.1	21	8	1.9	1.3	..	..	..
Denmark	123	29,890	21,230	..	14	6	2.0	1.8	..	..	100
Djibouti	27	..[h]	..	..	159	108	6.6	5.8	40	67	..
Dominica	99	2,990	..	..	..	17	5.5	2.3	..	..	..
Dominican Republic	162	1,460	3,870	19.9	98	37	6.1	2.9	18	18	85
Ecuador	41	1,390	4,220	30.4	100	36	6.3	3.2	8	12	64

	Population density	GNP per capita[a]		Poverty	Infant mortality rate		Total fertility rate		Adult illiteracy rate		Access to sanitation
	people per sq. km 1995	$ 1995	PPP[b] $ 1995	% of people living on less than $1 a day (PPP) 1981–95	per 1,000 live births 1970	1995	births per woman 1970	1995	% of people 15 and above Male 1995	Female 1995	% of population 1994–95
Egypt, Arab Rep.	58	790	3,820	7.6	158	56	5.9	3.4	36	61	..
El Salvador	271	1,610	2,610	..	103	36	6.3	3.7	27	30	73
Equatorial Guinea	14	380	..	..	163	111	5.7	5.9	10	32	50
Eritrea	..	..[c]	..	..	..	..	..	..	..	..	..
Estonia[g]	35	2,860	4,220	6.0	20	14	2.2	1.3	..	..	..
Ethiopia	56	100	450	33.8	158	112	5.8	7.0	55	75	10
Faeroe Islands	32	..[f]	..	..	..	..	..	..	..	..	..
Fiji	42	2,440	5,780[d]	..	49	21	4.1	2.7	6	11	..
Finland	17	20,580	17,760	..	13	5	1.8	1.8	..	..	100
France	106	24,990	21,030	..	18	6	2.5	1.7	..	..	96
French Guiana	2	..[f]	..	..	44	..	..	..	..	..	..
French Polynesia	61	..[f]	..	..	..	17	5.6	3.0	..	..	..
Gabon	4	3,490	..	..	138	89	4.2	5.2	26	47	76
Gambia, The	111	320	930[d]	..	185	126	6.5	5.3	47	75	34
Georgia[g]	77	440	1,470	..	..	18	2.7	1.9	..	..	..
Germany	234	27,510	20,070	..	23	6	2.0	1.2	..	..	100
Ghana	75	390	1,990[d]	..	111	73	6.7	5.1	24	47	29
Greece	81	8,210	11,710	..	30	8	2.3	1.4	..	..	96
Greenland	0	..[f]	..	..	..	..	..	..	..	..	..
Grenada	268	2,980	..	..	..	..	..	..	..	..	..
Guadeloupe	253	..[e]	..	..	42	11	4.5	2.1	..	..	..
Guam	273	..[f]	..	..	22	9	4.7	2.7	..	..	..
Guatemala	98	1,340	3,340	53.3	100	44	6.5	4.7	38	51	71
Guinea	27	550	..	26.3	181	128	6.0	6.5	50	78	6
Guinea-Bissau	38	250	790[d]	87.0	185	136	5.9	6.0	32	58	20
Guyana	4	590	2,420[d]	..	80	60	5.4	2.4	1	3	90
Haiti	260	250	910[d]	..	141	72	6.0	4.4	52	58	24
Honduras	53	600	1,900	46.5	110	45	7.2	4.6	27	27	68
Hong Kong	6,252	22,990	22,950[i]	..	19	5	3.3	1.2	4	12	..
Hungary	111	4,120	6,410	0.7	36	11	2.0	1.6	..	..	94
Iceland	3	24,950	20,460	..	13	4	2.8	2.1	..	..	95
India	313	340	1,400	52.5	137	68	5.8	3.2	35	62	29
Indonesia	107	980	3,800	14.5	118	51	5.5	2.7	10	22	55
Iran, Islamic Rep.	39	..[h]	..	..	131	45	6.7	4.5	22	34	82
Iraq	46	..[h]	..	..	102	108	7.1	5.4	29	55	36
Ireland	52	14,710	15,680	..	20	6	3.9	1.9	..	..	100
Isle of Man	..	..[e]	..	..	..	..	..	..	..	..	..
Israel	268	15,920	16,490	..	25	8	3.8	2.4	..	..	70
Italy	195	19,020	19,870	..	30	7	2.4	1.2	..	..	100
Jamaica	233	1,510	3,540	4.7	43	13	5.3	2.4	19	11	74
Japan	333	39,640	22,110	..	13	4	2.1	1.5	..	..	85
Jordan	47	1,510	4,060[d]	2.5	..	31	..	4.8	7	21	30
Kazakstan[g]	6	1,330	3,010	..	..	27	3.4	2.3	..	..	..
Kenya	47	280	1,380	50.2	102	58	8.1	4.7	14	30	43
Kiribati	107	920	..	..	105	55	..	3.8	..	..	100
Korea, Dem. Rep.	198	..[h]	..	..	51	26	6.2	2.2	1	3	100
Korea, Rep.	454	9,700	11,450	..	46	10	4.3	1.8	1	3	100
Kuwait	93	17,390	23,790[d]	..	48	11	7.1	3.0	18	25	..
Kyrgyz Republic[g]	24	700	1,800	18.9	..	30	4.9	3.3	..	..	53
Lao PDR	21	350	..	..	146	90	6.2	6.5	31	56	30
Latvia[g]	41	2,270	3,370	..	21	16	1.9	1.3	..	..	..
Lebanon	391	2,660	..	..	50	32	5.4	2.8	5	10	..
Lesotho	65	770	1,780[d]	50.4	134	76	5.7	4.6	19	38	35
Liberia	29	..[c]	..	..	178	172	6.8	6.5	46	78	24
Libya	3	..[e]	..	..	122	61	7.5	6.1	12	37	..

	Population density	GNP per capita[a]		Poverty	Infant mortality rate		Total fertility rate		Adult illiteracy rate		Access to sanitation
				% of people living on less than $1 a day (PPP)	per 1,000 live births		births per woman		% of people 15 and above		% of population
	people per sq. km 1995	$ 1995	PPP[b] $ 1995	1981–95	1970	1995	1970	1995	Male 1995	Female 1995	1994–95
Liechtenstein	194	..[f]	..	..	..	..	..	..	..	..	..
Lithuania[g]	57	1,900	4,120	2.1	24	14	2.4	1.5	..	..	..
Luxembourg	..	41,210	37,930	..	25	6	2.0	1.7	..	..	100
Macao	20,750	..[f]	..	..	..	7	4.5	1.8	..	..	..
Macedonia, FYR	83	860	..	..	..	23	3.1	2.2	..	..	..
Madagascar	23	230	640	72.3	181	89	6.6	5.8	..	..	17
Malawi	104	170	750	..	193	133	7.8	6.6	28	58	63
Malaysia	61	3,890	9,020	5.6	45	12	5.5	3.4	11	22	94
Maldives	850	990	3,080[d]	..	127	52	7.0	6.6	7	7	40
Mali	8	250	550	..	204	123	7.1	6.8	61	77	44
Malta	1,163	..[e]	..	..	28	9	2.0	1.9	..	..	100
Marshall Islands	..	..[h]	..	..	..	..	..	..	..	..	..
Martinique	364	..[f]	..	..	38	7	4.4	2.0	..	..	..
Mauritania	2	460	1,540[d]	31.4	148	96	6.5	5.2	50	74	64
Mauritius	556	3,380	13,210	..	60	16	3.7	2.2	13	21	100
Mayotte	..	..[e]	..	..	..	..	..	..	..	..	..
Mexico	48	3,320	6,400	14.9	72	33	6.5	3.0	8	13	70
Micronesia, Fed. Sts.	..	..[h]	..	..	..	32	..	4.6	..	..	39
Moldova[g]	132	920	..	6.8	..	22	2.6	2.0	..	..	50
Monaco	..	..[f]	..	..	..	..	..	..	..	..	100
Mongolia	2	310	1,950[d]	..	102	55	5.8	3.4	..	..	..
Morocco	60	1,110	3,340	1.1	128	55	7.0	3.4	43	69	63
Mozambique	21	80	810[d]	..	171	113	6.5	6.2	42	77	23
Myanmar	69	..[c]	..	..	128	83	5.9	3.4	11	22	42
Namibia	2	2,000	4,150[d]	..	118	62	6.0	5.0	..	..	36
Nepal	157	200	1,170[d]	53.1	166	91	6.4	5.3	59	86	6
Netherlands	456	24,000	19,950	..	13	6	2.6	1.6	..	..	100
Netherlands Antilles	250	..[f]	..	..	24	11	2.9	2.1	..	..	..
New Caledonia	10	..[f]	..	..	..	15	4.3	2.5	..	..	..
New Zealand	13	14,340	16,360	..	17	7	3.2	2.1	..	..	..
Nicaragua	36	380	2,000[d]	43.8	106	46	6.9	4.1	35	33	..
Niger	7	220	750[d]	61.5	170	119	7.2	7.4	79	93	15
Nigeria	122	260	1,220	28.9	139	80	6.9	5.5	33	53	63
Northern Mariana Islands	..	..[f]	..	..	..	..	..	..	..	..	..
Norway	14	31,250	21,940	..	13	5	2.5	1.9	..	..	100
Oman	10	4,820	8,140[d]	..	119	18	8.4	7.0	..	..	72
Pakistan	169	460	2,230	11.6	142	90	7.0	5.2	50	76	30
Panama	35	2,750	5,980	25.6	47	23	5.2	2.7	9	10	87
Papua New Guinea	9	1,160	2,420[d]	..	112	64	6.1	4.8	19	37	26
Paraguay	12	1,690	3,650	..	55	41	6.0	4.0	7	9	30
Peru	19	2,310	3,770	49.4	108	47	6.0	3.1	6	17	47
Philippines	230	1,050	2,850	27.5	66	39	6.4	3.7	5	6	75
Poland	127	2,790	5,400	6.8	33	14	2.2	1.6	..	..	100
Portugal	108	9,740	12,670	..	56	7	2.8	1.4	..	..	100
Puerto Rico	420	..[e]	..	..	29	11	3.2	2.1	..	..	..
Qatar	59	11,600	17,690[d]	..	68	18	6.8	3.9	21	20	100
Réunion	3	..[f]	..	..	54	8	4.3	2.2	..	..	..
Romania	99	1,480	4,360	17.7	49	23	2.9	1.4	..	..	49
Russian Federation[g]	9	2,240	4,480	1.1	..	18	2.0	1.4	..	..	..
Rwanda	259	180	540	45.7	142	133	8.2	6.2	30	48	..
São Tomé and Principe	172	350	..	..	..	60	..	4.8	..	..	21
Saudi Arabia	9	7,040	..	..	119	21	7.3	6.2	29	50	86
Senegal	44	600	1,780	54.0	135	62	6.5	5.7	57	77	..
Seychelles	169	6,620	..	..	..	15	..	2.4	..	..	92
Sierra Leone	59	180	580	..	197	179	6.5	6.5	55	82	..

	Population density	GNP per capita[a]		Poverty	Infant mortality rate		Total fertility rate		Adult illiteracy rate		Access to sanitation
	people per sq. km 1995	$ 1995	PPP[b] $ 1995	% of people living on less than $1 a day (PPP) 1981–95	per 1,000 live births 1970	1995	births per woman 1970	1995	% of people 15 and above Male 1995	Female 1995	% of population 1994–95
Singapore	4,896	26,730	22,770 [d]	..	20	4	3.1	1.7	4	14	*100*
Slovak Republic	112	2,950	3,610	12.8	25	11	2.4	1.5	..	..	*51*
Slovenia	99	8,200	..	..	24	7	2.2	1.3	..	..	*90*
Solomon Islands	13	910	2,190 [d]	..	..	41	..	5.1	..	..	..
Somalia	14	..[c]	..	..	158	128	7.0	7.0	..	..	..
South Africa	34	3,160	5,030 [d]	23.7	79	50	5.7	3.9	18	18	46
Spain	78	13,580	14,520	..	28	7	2.8	1.2	..	..	*97*
Sri Lanka	280	700	3,250	4.0	53	16	4.3	2.3	7	13	66
St. Kitts and Nevis	114	5,170	9,410 [d]	..	..	31	*3.5*	2.4	..	..	..
St. Lucia	272	3,370	..	..	..	17	*5.5*	2.9	..	..	..
St. Vincent and the Grenadines	285	2,280	..	..	..	19	*5.0*	2.3	..	..	..
Sudan	11	..[c]	..	..	118	77	6.7	4.8	42	65	..
Suriname	3	880	2,250 [d]	..	53	33	5.6	2.6	5	9	*56*
Swaziland	55	1,170	2,880	..	139	69	6.5	4.6	22	24	*63*
Sweden	21	23,750	18,540	..	11	4	1.9	1.7	..	..	*100*
Switzerland	178	40,630	25,860	..	15	6	2.1	1.5	..	..	*100*
Syrian Arab Republic	77	1,120	5,320	..	96	32	7.7	4.8	14	44	*78*
Tajikistan[g]	42	340	920	..	..	42	6.8	4.2	..	..	*62*
Tanzania[j]	34	120	640	16.4	129	82	6.8	5.8	21	43	*86*
Thailand	114	2,740	7,540	0.1	73	35	5.5	1.8	4	8	*87*
Togo	75	310	1,130 [d]	..	134	88	6.6	6.4	33	63	20
Tonga	144	1,630	..	..	..	18	..	3.3	..	..	100
Trinidad and Tobago	251	3,770	8,610 [d]	..	52	13	3.6	2.1	1	3	*56*
Tunisia	58	1,820	5,000	3.9	121	39	6.4	2.9	21	45	*72*
Turkey	79	2,780	5,580	..	144	48	5.3	2.7	8	28	*94*
Turkmenistan[g]	10	920	..	4.9	..	46	6.3	3.8	..	..	*60*
Uganda	96	240	1,470 [d]	50.0	109	98	7.1	6.7	26	50	60
Ukraine[g]	89	1,630	2,400	..	22	15	2.0	1.5	..	..	*49*
United Arab Emirates	29	17,400	16,470 [d]	..	87	16	6.5	3.6	21	20	*95*
United Kingdom	242	18,700	19,260	..	19	6	2.4	1.7	..	..	*96*
United States	29	26,980	26,980	..	20	8	2.5	2.1	..	..	*85*
Uruguay	18	5,170	6,630	..	46	18	2.9	2.2	3	2	*82*
Uzbekistan[g]	55	970	2,370	..	..	30	5.7	3.7	..	..	*18*
Vanuatu	14	1,200	2,290 [d]	..	..	41	..	5.0	..	..	..
Venezuela	25	3,020	7,900	11.8	53	23	5.3	3.1	8	10	*55*
Vietnam	226	240	..	..	104	41	5.9	3.1	4	9	21
Virgin Islands (U.S.)	291	..[f]	..	..	..	19	5.3	2.4	..	..	..
West Bank and Gaza	..	..[h]	....	..	..	28	..	6.2	..	..	..
Western Samoa	59	1,120	2,030 [d]	..	..	22	6.7	4.2	..	..	..
Yemen, Rep.	29	260	..	..	186	100	7.7	7.4	..	..	*51*
Yugoslavia, Fed. Rep.	103	..[h]	..	..	53	18	2.4	1.9	..	..	*100*
Zaire	19	120	490 [d]	..	131	..	6.2	..	13	32	9
Zambia	12	400	930	84.6	106	109	6.8	5.7	14	29	42
Zimbabwe	28	540	2,030	41.0	96	55	7.7	3.8	10	20	*58*

a. Calculated using the World Bank Atlas method. b. PPP is purchasing power parity. See the notes following these tables. c. Estimated to be low income ($765 or less). d. The estimate is based on regression; others are extrapolated from the latest International Comparison Programme benchmark estimates. e. Upper middle income ($3,036 to $9,385). f. Estimated to be high income ($9,386 or more). g. Estimates for the economies of the former Soviet Union are preliminary, and their classification will be kept under review. h. Estimated to be lower middle income ($766 to $3,035). i. References to GNP relate to GDP. j. Data cover mainland Tanzania only.

1.2 | Gender dimensions of development

	Population sex ratio		Gross primary enrollment				Female labor force		Life expectancy at birth			
	women per 100 men		Male % of relevant age group		Female % of relevant age group		% of total		Male years		Female years	
	1970	1995	1970	1993	1970	1993	1970	1995	1970	1995	1970	1995
Afghanistan	95	96	47	46	8	16	7	35	37	44	37	45
Albania	98	95	109	95	102	97	40	41	66	70	69	76
Algeria	105	98	93	111	58	96	6	24	52	68	54	71
American Samoa	..	..	..	..	..	..	..	..	..	..	..	..
Andorra	..	..	..	..	..	..	..	..	..	..	..	..
Angola	104	103	98	..	53	..	47	46	36	45	39	48
Antigua and Barbuda	..	116	..	..	..	..	..	..	65	72	69	78
Argentina	99	104	105	108	106	107	25	31	64	69	70	76
Armenia	105	106	..	87	..	93	46	48	69	68	75	74
Aruba	..	..	..	..	..	..	..	..	..	..	..	..
Australia	98	99	115	108	115	107	31	43	68	74	75	80
Austria	112	107	104	103	103	103	38	41	67	74	74	80
Azerbaijan	106	104	..	91	..	87	45	44	64	66	72	75
Bahamas, The	102	99	..	100	..	103	40	46	63	70	69	77
Bahrain	86	77	114	109	84	112	5	19	60	71	64	75
Bangladesh	93	97	72	128	35	105	5	42	45	57	43	58
Barbados	113	106	103	..	101	..	40	46	66	73	71	78
Belarus	118	112	..	96	..	95	51	49	68	64	76	75
Belgium	104	104	103	99	104	100	30	40	68	73	75	80
Belize	102	100	..	111	..	107	19	22	57	73	61	76
Benin	103	105	51	88	22	44	49	48	43	49	45	52
Bermuda	..	..	..	..	..	..	..	..	..	..	..	..
Bhutan	99	128	11	..	1	..	40	..	..	..	..	..
Bolivia	103	102	91	..	62	..	32	37	44	59	48	62
Bosnia and Herzegovina	..	..	..	..	..	..	..	..	..	..	..	..
Botswana	115	107	63	113	67	120	53	46	50	50	54	53
Brazil	100	101	..	..	..	..	22	35	57	63	61	71
Brunei	94	92	..	111	..	104	20	34	66	73	68	78
Bulgaria	100	104	101	87	100	84	44	48	69	68	74	75
Burkina Faso	102	103	17	47	10	30	49	47	39	45	42	47
Burundi	108	103	42	76	20	63	51	50	42	45	45	48
Cambodia	100	108	35	..	26	..	49	53	41	52	44	54
Cameroon	103	101	103	..	75	..	37	38	43	55	46	58
Canada	100	102	101	106	100	104	32	45	69	76	76	82
Cape Verde	110	115	..	119	..	110	28	38	55	65	58	67
Cayman Islands	..	..	..	..	..	..	..	..	..	..	..	..
Central African Republic	109	106	88	92	41	..	49	47	40	46	45	51
Chad	104	102	52	80	17	38	42	44	37	47	40	50
Channel Islands	..	106	..	..	..	..	..	..	..	74	..	82
Chile	102	102	107	99	107	98	22	32	59	72	66	78
China	94	94	..	120	..	116	42	45	61	68	63	71
Colombia	101	100	107	118	110	120	23	37	59	67	63	73
Comoros	..	102	46	96	21	81	43	42	46	54	47	58
Congo	105	104	..	..	..	..	41	43	43	49	49	54
Costa Rica	98	98	110	106	109	105	18	30	65	74	69	79
Côte d'Ivoire	97	97	71	80	45	58	33	33	43	53	46	56
Croatia	107	105	..	..	..	..	38	43	..	70	..	78
Cuba	96	98	121	104	121	104	20	38	68	74	72	78
Cyprus	102	100	..	101	..	101	33	38	69	75	73	80
Czech Republic	107	105	..	99	..	100	46	47	..	70	..	77
Denmark	102	103	95	97	97	98	36	46	71	72	76	78
Djibouti	103	105	..	41	..	31	..	..	39	48	42	51
Dominica	..	100	..	..	..	..	..	..	..	71	..	75
Dominican Republic	97	97	100	95	100	99	22	29	57	68	61	73
Ecuador	99	99	99	124	95	122	16	26	57	67	60	72

	Population sex ratio		Gross primary enrollment				Female labor force		Life expectancy at birth			
	women per 100 men		Male % of relevant age group		Female % of relevant age group		% of total		Male years		Female years	
	1970	1995	1970	1993	1970	1993	1970	1995	1970	1995	1970	1995
Egypt, Arab Rep.	98	97	87	105	57	89	8	29	50	64	52	66
El Salvador	99	104	87	79	83	80	21	34	56	66	60	72
Equatorial Guinea	105	104	86	..	67	..	37	35	38	48	42	51
Eritrea	..	..	..	52	..	41	47	47	..	..	..	..
Estonia	119	112	..	84	..	83	51	49	66	65	74	76
Ethiopia	102	99	23	27	10	19	42	41	39	47	42	51
Faeroe Islands	..	..	..	..	..	..	..	..	..	..	..	..
Fiji	96	98	106	128	103	127	12	27	63	70	66	74
Finland	107	104	84	100	79	100	44	48	66	73	74	80
France	105	105	118	107	117	105	36	44	68	74	76	82
French Guiana	..	..	..	..	..	..	..	..	..	..	..	..
French Polynesia	95	96	..	127	..	123	..	..	..	67	..	73
Gabon	104	103	89	..	81	..	46	44	43	53	46	56
Gambia, The	103	102	34	84	15	61	45	45	35	45	38	48
Georgia	113	110	..	..	..	..	48	46	..	69	..	78
Germany	112	105	..	97	..	98	39	42	67	73	74	79
Ghana	102	101	73	83	54	70	51	51	48	57	51	61
Greece	105	103	108	..	106	..	26	36	70	75	74	81
Greenland	..	..	..	..	..	..	..	..	..	..	..	..
Grenada	..	107	..	..	..	..	..	..	..	..	..	..
Guadeloupe	104	105	..	..	..	..	38	45	64	72	70	79
Guam	77	90	..	..	..	..	..	..	..	70	..	76
Guatemala	97	98	62	89	51	78	12	26	51	63	54	68
Guinea	101	99	45	61	21	30	48	47	36	44	37	45
Guinea-Bissau	103	105	57	..	23	..	39	40	35	42	37	45
Guyana	101	101	100	98	96	98	20	33	58	61	62	67
Haiti	104	103	..	..	..	..	46	43	46	54	49	57
Honduras	99	98	87	111	87	112	14	30	51	64	55	69
Hong Kong	97	92	118	..	115	..	35	37	67	76	73	81
Hungary	106	108	98	95	97	95	40	44	67	66	73	74
Iceland	98	99	94	102	100	98	34	44	71	77	77	81
India	93	94	90	113	56	91	29	32	50	62	49	63
Indonesia	102	100	87	116	73	112	30	40	47	62	49	66
Iran, Islamic Rep.	98	96	93	109	52	101	13	24	55	68	54	69
Iraq	97	97	95	98	41	83	7	18	55	60	56	62
Ireland	99	100	107	103	106	103	26	33	69	74	73	79
Isle of Man	..	..	..	..	..	..	..	..	..	..	..	..
Israel	98	99	96	95	95	96	30	40	70	75	73	79
Italy	104	105	112	98	109	99	29	38	69	75	75	81
Jamaica	105	102	119	109	119	108	43	46	66	72	70	77
Japan	104	103	99	102	99	102	39	41	69	77	75	83
Jordan	95	92	..	94	..	95	6	21	..	69	..	72
Kazakstan	108	106	..	86	..	86	47	47	..	64	..	74
Kenya	100	101	67	92	48	91	45	46	48	57	52	60
Kiribati	..	95	..	..	..	..	..	..	..	56	..	61
Korea, Dem. Rep.	105	103	..	..	..	..	46	45	58	67	62	74
Korea, Rep.	99	99	104	100	103	102	32	40	58	68	62	76
Kuwait	76	77	101	..	76	..	8	28	64	74	68	79
Kyrgyz Republic	109	104	..	..	..	..	49	47	..	63	..	72
Lao PDR	98	103	66	123	40	92	45	47	39	51	42	54
Latvia	119	114	..	83	..	82	51	50	66	63	74	75
Lebanon	99	109	130	117	112	114	..	28	62	68	66	71
Lesotho	109	104	71	90	101	105	39	37	47	57	51	60
Liberia	99	98	75	..	36	..	38	39	45	46	48	46
Libya	91	92	..	110	..	110	19	21	50	63	53	67

	Population sex ratio		Gross primary enrollment				Female labor force		Life expectancy at birth			
	women per 100 men		Male % of relevant age group		Female % of relevant age group		% of total		Male years		Female years	
	1970	1995	1970	1993	1970	1993	1970	1995	1970	1995	1970	1995
Liechtenstein	..	..	..	..	..	..	..	..	..	..	..	..
Lithuania	113	111	..	95	..	90	49	48	67	63	75	75
Luxembourg	103	104	112	..	112	..	27	37	67	73	74	80
Macao	..	103	..	..	..	..	23	39	58	75	62	80
Macedonia, FYR	97	96	..	88	..	87	30	41	..	71	..	75
Madagascar	103	99	99	75	82	72	45	45	44	56	47	59
Malawi	108	103	..	84	..	77	51	49	40	43	41	44
Malaysia	98	98	91	93	84	93	31	37	60	69	63	74
Maldives	89	95	..	136	..	133	38	42	51	64	49	63
Mali	104	106	30	38	15	24	47	46	36	48	39	51
Malta	108	103	107	109	106	106	21	27	68	75	72	79
Marshall Islands	..	..	..	..	..	..	..	..	..	..	..	..
Martinique	104	105	..	..	..	..	38	47	66	73	71	80
Mauritania	103	102	20	76	8	62	47	44	41	51	44	54
Mauritius	100	101	94	107	93	106	20	32	60	68	65	75
Mayotte	..	..	..	..	..	..	..	..	..	..	..	..
Mexico	100	101	106	114	101	110	19	31	59	69	64	75
Micronesia, Fed. Sts.	89	95	..	..	..	..	30	..	..	63	..	66
Moldova	..	109	..	78	..	77	52	42	..	65	..	73
Monaco	..	..	..	..	..	..	..	..	..	..	..	..
Mongolia	101	98	..	..	..	..	46	46	52	64	54	66
Morocco	100	100	66	85	36	60	14	35	50	64	53	68
Mozambique	104	104	..	69	..	51	49	48	40	45	44	48
Myanmar	100	101	88	..	78	..	44	43	47	58	50	61
Namibia	104	101	..	134	..	138	39	41	47	55	49	57
Nepal	97	96	44	129	8	87	39	40	43	57	42	56
Netherlands	100	101	101	96	102	99	26	40	71	75	77	81
Netherlands Antilles	101	104	..	..	..	..	33	42	61	75	67	80
New Caledonia	93	97	..	125	..	124	..	..	..	71	..	75
New Zealand	100	100	111	102	109	101	29	44	69	73	75	79
Nicaragua	101	99	79	101	81	105	19	36	52	65	55	70
Niger	104	102	19	35	10	21	45	44	37	44	40	49
Nigeria	103	103	47	105	27	82	37	36	41	51	45	54
Northern Mariana Islands	..	..	..	..	..	..	..	..	..	..	..	..
Norway	101	101	85	99	94	99	29	46	71	75	77	81
Oman	98	89	6	87	1	82	6	15	46	68	49	73
Pakistan	93	92	57	80	22	49	9	26	50	62	49	64
Panama	96	97	101	..	97	..	25	34	64	71	67	76
Papua New Guinea	92	94	63	80	39	67	42	42	47	56	47	58
Paraguay	100	98	115	114	103	110	21	29	63	67	68	72
Peru	98	101	114	..	99	..	22	29	52	65	56	68
Philippines	99	99	..	..	..	..	33	37	56	64	59	68
Poland	106	104	103	98	99	97	45	46	67	67	74	76
Portugal	111	107	99	122	96	118	25	43	64	72	71	79
Puerto Rico	104	105	..	..	..	..	27	36	69	72	75	80
Qatar	54	60	111	92	86	87	4	12	59	70	63	75
Réunion	108	104	..	..	..	..	23	42	59	70	67	79
Romania	104	104	111	87	113	86	44	44	67	66	71	74
Russian Federation	120	112	..	107	..	107	51	49	..	58	..	72
Rwanda	102	102	76	78	60	76	49	49	43	38	46	40
São Tomé and Principe	..	102	..	..	..	..	..	..	..	66	..	72
Saudi Arabia	94	81	61	78	29	73	5	13	51	69	54	71
Senegal	100	100	51	67	32	50	42	42	42	49	44	51
Seychelles	..	95	..	..	..	..	..	..	..	69	..	76
Sierra Leone	104	104	40	..	27	..	36	36	33	35	36	38

	Population sex ratio		Gross primary enrollment				Female labor force		Life expectancy at birth			
	women per 100 men		Male % of relevant age group		Female % of relevant age group		% of total		Male years		Female years	
	1970	1995	1970	1993	1970	1993	1970	1995	1970	1995	1970	1995
Singapore	95	98	109	..	101	..	26	38	65	74	70	79
Slovak Republic	103	105	..	101	..	101	41	48	..	68	..	76
Slovenia	107	106	..	97	..	97	36	46	66	70	73	78
Solomon Islands	89	95	..	102	..	87	46	46	..	62	..	63
Somalia	102	101	17	..	5	..	44	43	39	47	42	50
South Africa	100	101	100	111	99	110	33	37	50	61	56	67
Spain	105	104	121	104	125	105	19	36	70	74	75	81
Sri Lanka	92	100	104	106	94	105	25	35	64	70	66	75
St. Kitts and Nevis	..	116	..	..	..	..	..	..	..	67	..	72
St. Lucia	..	110	..	..	..	..	..	..	61	68	64	73
St. Vincent and the Grenadines	..	102	..	..	..	..	..	..	62	69	64	76
Sudan	100	99	47	59	29	41	20	28	42	52	44	55
Suriname	100	104	129	..	122	..	22	31	62	66	66	73
Swaziland	103	103	91	123	83	116	33	37	44	57	48	61
Sweden	100	101	93	100	95	100	36	48	72	76	77	81
Switzerland	105	103	..	100	..	102	34	40	70	75	76	82
Syrian Arab Republic	95	97	95	111	59	99	12	26	54	66	57	71
Tajikistan	103	100	..	91	..	88	45	44	60	66	65	66
Tanzania	103	102	41	71	27	69	51	49	44	50	47	52
Thailand	101	100	86	*98*	79	*97*	48	46	56	67	61	72
Togo	104	102	98	122	44	81	39	40	43	49	46	52
Tonga	..	96	..	..	..	..	..	..	..	67	..	72
Trinidad and Tobago	103	104	106	94	107	94	30	36	63	70	68	75
Tunisia	102	98	121	123	79	113	13	30	54	68	55	70
Turkey	97	95	124	*107*	94	*98*	38	35	55	66	59	71
Turkmenistan	103	102	..	..	..	..	46	42	57	..	64	..
Uganda	102	103	46	99	30	83	48	48	49	44	51	44
Ukraine	121	114	..	87	..	87	51	49	66	64	74	74
United Arab Emirates	60	58	112	112	71	108	4	13	59	74	63	76
United Kingdom	106	104	104	*112*	104	*113*	36	43	69	74	75	79
United States	105	104	..	107	..	106	37	46	67	74	75	80
Uruguay	101	105	115	109	109	108	26	40	66	70	72	77
Uzbekistan	105	102	..	80	..	79	48	46	..	..	..	..
Vanuatu	93	88	..	*105*	..	*107*	..	..	..	63	..	65
Venezuela	97	98	94	*95*	94	*97*	21	33	63	70	68	75
Vietnam	106	103	..	..	..	..	48	49	54	65	57	70
Virgin Islands (U.S.)	..	106	..	..	..	..	..	..	..	72	..	79
West Bank and Gaza	..	98	..	..	..	..	..	..	..	..	..	..
Western Samoa	93	89	..	..	..	..	..	..	..	67	..	71
Yemen, Rep.	103	99	38	..	7	..	8	29	41	53	42	54
Yugoslavia, Fed. Rep.	102	101	108	*72*	103	*73*	36	42	66	70	70	75
Zaire	106	102	110	78	65	58	45	44	44	..	47	..
Zambia	102	102	99	109	80	99	45	45	45	45	48	46
Zimbabwe	101	100	81	123	66	114	44	44	49	56	52	58

1.3 | Structural transformation

	GNP per capita	Labor force in agriculture		Agriculture		Investment		Trade		Central government revenue		Money and quasi money (M2)	
	average annual % growth 1970–95	% 1970	1990	% of GDP 1970	1995	% of GDP 1970	1995	% of GDP 1970	1995	% of GDP 1980	1995	% of GDP 1980	1995
Afghanistan	..	66	52	..	..	5	..	22	..	..	..	27	..
Albania	..	66	55	..	56	..	16	..	52	..	23	..	47
Algeria	0.6	47	26	11	13	37	32	51	57	..	..	53	39
American Samoa	..	..	..	..	..	..	..	..	..	..	..	..	..
Andorra	..	..	..	..	..	..	..	..	..	..	..	..	..
Angola	..	78	75	..	12	..	27	..	132	..	..	..	..
Antigua and Barbuda	4.9	..	..	..	4	..	22	..	217	..	..	46	62
Argentina	−0.4	16	12	10	6	24	18	10	16	16	..	19	19
Armenia	−0.3	27	17	..	44	..	9	..	85	..	..	..	..
Aruba	..	..	..	..	..	..	..	..	..	..	..	..	51
Australia	1.4	8	5	6	3	27	23	29	40	22	25	36	61
Austria	2.2	15	8	7	2	30	27	61	77	35	36	73	90
Azerbaijan	..	35	31	..	27	..	16	..	66	..	..	..	9
Bahamas, The	1.7	7	5	..	..	..	..	..	..	20	16	30	53
Bahrain	−2.2	7	2	..	1	..	27	..	191	34	28	40	71
Bangladesh	1.5	81	64	55	31	11	17	21	37	11	..	18	36
Barbados	1.9	17	7	11	5	26	13	138	96	27	..	38	59
Belarus	..	35	20	..	13	..	25	..	..	..	..	..	10
Belgium	1.9	5	3	3	2	23	18	101	143	44	45	45	80
Belize	3.0	40	33	..	20	..	26	..	109	..	..	26	43
Benin	0.1	81	62	36	34	12	20	50	64	..	..	17	25
Bermuda	1.2	..	..	..	..	..	..	..	..	..	..	..	..
Bhutan	5.5	95	..	..	40	..	32	..	84	9	15	..	28
Bolivia	−0.7	55	47	20	..	24	15	49	47	..	18	16	45
Bosnia and Herzegovina	..	50	11	..	..	..	..	..	..	..	..	..	..
Botswana	7.3	80	46	33	5	42	25	86	101	34	57	28	26
Brazil	..	45	23	12	14	21	22	14	15	23	26	11	26
Brunei	..	13	2	..	3	..	..	..	..	..	..	..	..
Bulgaria	0.2	35	14	..	13	..	21	..	94	..	37	..	..
Burkina Faso	1.5	92	92	35	34	12	22	23	45	12	..	14	22
Burundi	0.6	94	92	71	56	5	11	22	43	14	..	14	20
Cambodia	..	79	74	..	51	13	19	14	36	..	..	..	8
Cameroon	1.5	85	70	31	39	16	15	51	46	16	14	21	16
Canada	1.7	8	3	5	..	22	19	43	71	19	21	45	59
Cape Verde	5.7	46	31	..	13	..	45	..	75	..	..	53	76
Cayman Islands	..	..	..	..	..	..	..	..	..	..	..	..	..
Central African Republic	−1.6	89	80	35	44	19	15	71	46	16	..	19	21
Chad	−0.1	92	81	47	44	18	9	54	46	..	..	20	14
Channel Islands	..	..	..	..	..	..	..	..	..	..	..	..	..
Chile	1.8	24	19	7	..	19	27	29	54	32	21	21	34
China	6.9	78	74	34	21	28	40	5	40	..	6	33	92
Colombia	1.9	41	25	25	14	20	20	30	35	12	17	17	19
Comoros	−0.6	82	97	..	39	..	17	..	64	14	..	..	20
Congo	1.7	66	48	18	10	24	27	93	128	35	..	15	15
Costa Rica	0.7	43	26	23	17	21	25	63	81	18	26	39	32
Côte d'Ivoire	−1.9	76	60	40	31	22	13	65	76	23	..	27	26
Croatia	..	51	15	..	12	..	14	..	93	..	45	..	22
Cuba	..	30	18	..	..	..	..	..	..	..	..	..	..
Cyprus	5.5	39	14	..	5	..	22	..	99	21	32	61	90
Czech Republic	..	17	11	..	6	..	25	..	108	..	41	..	81
Denmark	1.7	11	6	7	4	26	16	59	64	36	41	43	58
Djibouti	..	..	..	..	3	..	12	..	101	..	..	..	71
Dominica	2.5	..	..	..	21	..	26	..	109	..	..	50	61
Dominican Republic	1.4	48	25	23	15	19	20	42	55	14	17	18	24
Ecuador	1.5	51	33	24	12	18	19	33	56	13	16	21	27

	GNP per capita	Labor force in agriculture		Agriculture		Investment		Trade		Central government revenue		Money and quasi money (M2)	
	average annual % growth 1970–95	% 1970	1990	% of GDP 1970	1995	% of GDP 1970	1995	% of GDP 1970	1995	% of GDP 1980	1995	% of GDP 1980	1995
Egypt, Arab Rep.	3.7	52	43	29	20	14	17	33	54	46	41	52	97
El Salvador	–1.0	57	36	40	14	13	19	49	55	11	12	28	36
Equatorial Guinea	..	81	74	..	50	20	23	81	112	..	..	..	11
Eritrea	..	85	79	..	11	..	20	..	104	..	..	..	..
Estonia	–1.8	18	14	..	8	..	27	..	160	..	35	..	23
Ethiopia	..	91	80	..	57	..	17	..	39	16ª	14	22ª	42
Faeroe Islands	..	..	..	..	..	..	..	..	..	..	..	..	..
Fiji	0.9	52	45	29	..	22	14	100	104	..	..	32	50
Finland	1.9	20	8	17	6	30	16	53	68	27	33	40	57
France	1.8	14	5	..	2	27	18	31	43	40	41	72	64
French Guiana	..	..	..	..	..	..	..	..	..	..	..	..	..
French Polynesia	..	..	..	..	..	..	..	..	..	..	..	..	..
Gabon	–2.8	80	61	19	..	32	26	88	101	36	..	15	15
Gambia, The	0.2	86	82	33	28	5	21	66	103	23	23	21	23
Georgia	–1.9	37	26	..	67	..	3	..	46	..	..	..	..
Germany	..	9	4	..	..	..	21	..	46	..	32	..	62
Ghana	–1.2	60	60	47	46	14	19	44	59	7	17	16	15
Greece	1.5	42	23	29	21	28	19	28	57	31	28	50	53
Greenland	..	..	..	..	..	..	..	..	..	..	..	..	..
Grenada	..	..	..	..	11	..	32	..	47	..	..	63	77
Guadeloupe	..	28	7	..	..	..	..	..	..	..	..	..	..
Guam	..	..	..	..	..	..	..	..	..	..	..	..	..
Guatemala	–0.3	62	52	..	25	13	17	36	47	9	8	20	24
Guinea	..	92	87	..	24	..	15	..	46	..	..	..	9
Guinea-Bissau	0.1	89	85	47	46	30	16	34	48	..	..	..	14
Guyana	–2.6	32	22	19	36	23	19	113	159	35	..	49	56
Haiti	–1.3	74	68	..	44	11	2	31	17	11	..	24	43
Honduras	0.2	65	40	32	21	21	23	62	80	15	..	21	25
Hong Kong	5.7	4	1	..	0	20	35	181	297	..	..	61	..
Hungary	1.1	25	15	..	8	34	23	63	67	53	..	..	43
Iceland	3.3	17	11	..	..	24	15	87	70	25	30	20	38
India	2.4	71	64	45	29	17	25	8	27	12	13	35	46
Indonesia	4.7	66	57	45	17	16	38	28	53	21	18	13	..
Iran, Islamic Rep.	–2.4	44	41	..	25	..	29	..	39	22	25	54	35
Iraq	..	47	16	..	..	..	..	..	..	..	..	..	..
Ireland	2.6	26	14	..	..	..	13	79	136	35	37	44	50
Isle of Man	..	..	..	..	..	..	..	..	..	..	..	..	..
Israel	2.0	10	4	..	..	25	24	70	69	50	39	15	67
Italy	2.4	19	9	8	3	27	18	33	49	31	40	71	62
Jamaica	–0.8	33	24	7	9	32	17	71	145	29	..	33	44
Japan	3.2	20	7	6	2	39	29	20	17	12	21	83	113
Jordan	..	28	21	..	8	..	26	..	121	..	27	..	104
Kazakstan	..	27	22	..	12	..	22	..	69	..	..	..	..
Kenya	1.0	86	80	33	29	24	19	60	72	22	22	30	38
Kiribati	..	..	..	..	..	11	..	83	..	..	..	..	..
Korea, Dem. Rep.	..	55	38	..	..	..	..	..	..	..	..	..	..
Korea, Rep.	10.0	49	18	25	7	24	37	37	67	17	20	29	41
Kuwait	–3.5	2	1	0	0	12	12	84	104	89	..	33	78
Kyrgyz Republic	..	36	32	..	44	..	16	..	58	..	..	..	..
Lao PDR	..	81	78	..	52	..	..	..	..	..	..	..	13
Latvia	0.1	19	16	..	9	..	21	..	91	..	27	..	25
Lebanon	..	..	5	..	7	..	29	..	70	..	15	..	118
Lesotho	2.3	43	41	35	10	12	87	65	138	34	51	40	29
Liberia	–3.0	81	76	24	..	22	..	98	..	18	..	..	..
Libya	–4.8	24	11	2	..	17	..	89	..	..	..	35	..

	GNP per capita	Labor force in agriculture		Agriculture		Investment		Trade		Central government revenue		Money and quasi money (M2)	
	average annual % growth 1970–95	% 1970	% 1990	% of GDP 1970	% of GDP 1995	% of GDP 1970	% of GDP 1995	% of GDP 1970	% of GDP 1995	% of GDP 1980	% of GDP 1995	% of GDP 1980	% of GDP 1995
Liechtenstein	..	..	..	..	..	..	..	..	..	..	..	..	..
Lithuania	..	31	18	..	11	..	19	..	108	..	25	..	23
Luxembourg	3.0	8	4	3	..	23	..	162	184	45	47	..	..
Macao	..	..	..	..	..	..	31	..	111	..	..	..	..
Macedonia, FYR	..	55	22	..	..	..	15	..	86	..	..	..	..
Madagascar	–2.4	84	84	24	34	10	11	41	54	13	8	18	18
Malawi	–0.2	91	95	44	42	26	15	63	69	19	..	18	15
Malaysia	4.0	54	27	29	13	22	41	80	194	26	25	46	85
Maldives	..	67	33	..	..	..	..	..	..	14	35	36	43
Mali	0.2	93	93	66	46	16	26	33	60	11	..	18	20
Malta	6.1	7	3	7	3	33	29	129	198	35	35	114	139
Marshall Islands	..	..	..	..	..	..	..	..	..	..	..	..	..
Martinique	..	25	7	..	..	..	..	..	..	..	..	..	..
Mauritania	–0.7	85	55	29	27	22	15	74	104	..	..	21	19
Mauritius	0.5	34	17	16	9	10	25	85	120	21	21	40	73
Mayotte	..	..	..	..	..	..	..	..	..	..	..	..	..
Mexico	0.9	44	28	12	8	21	15	15	48	15	17	25	31
Micronesia, Fed. Sts.	..	43	..	..	..	..	..	..	..	..	..	..	..
Moldova	..	54	33	..	50	..	7	..	78	..	..	..	12
Monaco	..	..	..	..	..	..	..	..	..	..	..	..	..
Mongolia	..	48	32	..	..	..	..	..	..	..	27	..	26
Morocco	1.8	58	45	20	14	18	21	39	62	23	..	38	65
Mozambique	–0.2	86	83	..	33	..	60	..	102	..	..	..	..
Myanmar	1.2	78	73	38	63	14	12	14	4	16	7	24	..
Namibia	..	63	49	..	14	..	20	..	110	..	35	..	39
Nepal	1.3	94	95	67	42	6	23	13	60	8	11	22	34
Netherlands	1.5	7	5	..	3	..	22	89	99	49	46	67	82
Netherlands Antilles	..	..	..	..	..	..	..	..	..	14	..	52	..
New Caledonia	..	..	..	..	..	..	..	..	..	..	..	..	..
New Zealand	0.8	12	10	12	..	25	24	48	62	34	35	26	78
Nicaragua	–5.3	50	28	25	33	18	18	55	76	23	25	24	30
Niger	–2.6	93	91	65	39	10	6	29	30	14	..	13	14
Nigeria	–0.9	71	43	41	28	15	..	20	..	..	..	24	25
Northern Mariana Islands	..	..	..	..	..	..	..	..	..	..	..	..	..
Norway	2.9	12	6	5	..	28	23 [b]	77	71	37	40	47	56
Oman	3.3	57	48	16	..	14	17	93	89	38	32	14	31
Pakistan	2.9	59	56	37	26	16	19	22	36	16	19	39	41
Panama	0.7	42	26	..	11	..	24	..	79	27	28	33	68
Papua New Guinea	0.2	86	79	37	26	42	24	72	106	23	22	33	30
Paraguay	2.1	53	39	32	24	15	23	31	82	11	14	20	26
Peru	–1.1	48	36	19	7	16	17	34	30	17	16	17	17
Philippines	0.6	58	45	30	22	21	23	43	80	14	18	22	45
Poland	1.2	39	27	..	6	..	17	..	53	..	41	57	32
Portugal	2.5	32	18	..	..	..	28 [b]	49	66	26	34	70	78
Puerto Rico	0.6	14	4	3	1	29	17	107	..	..	..	..	..
Qatar	–5.9	10	3	..	..	..	..	..	..	..	..	17	67
Réunion	..	37	7	..	..	..	..	..	..	..	..	..	..
Romania	0.0	49	24	..	21	..	26	..	60	45	30	33	20
Russian Federation	1.3	19	14	..	7	..	25	..	44	..	17	..	12
Rwanda	–0.2	94	92	..	37	9	13	27	32	13	..	14	16
São Tomé and Principe	–1.0	..	..	..	23	18	50	76	108	..	..	..	..
Saudi Arabia	–2.9	64	20	4	..	12	20	89	70	..	..	14	50
Senegal	–0.6	83	76	24	20	16	16	59	69	24	..	27	20
Seychelles	3.3	..	..	..	4	..	26	..	129	..	50	29	45
Sierra Leone	–1.1	76	67	29	42	16	6	62	40	16	13	19	10

	GNP per capita	Labor force in agriculture		Agriculture		Investment		Trade		Central government revenue		Money and quasi money (M2)	
	average annual % growth 1970–95	% 1970	1990	% of GDP 1970	1995	% of GDP 1970	1995	% of GDP 1970	1995	% of GDP 1980	1995	% of GDP 1980	1995
Singapore	5.7	3	0	2	0	39	33	225	..	25	26	58	83
Slovak Republic	..	19	12	..	6	..	28	..	124	..	..	..	63
Slovenia	..	50	5	..	5	..	22	..	113	..	..	..	32
Solomon Islands	2.8	80	77	..	..	..	..	..	..	..	..	41	27
Somalia	–0.3	81	84	59	..	12	..	28	..	..	..	18	..
South Africa	–0.6	31	14	8	5	30	18	48	44	23	27	50	52
Spain	2.0	26	12	..	3	..	21	27	47	24	32	75	79
Sri Lanka	3.2	55	49	28	23	19	25	54	83	20	21	28	32
St. Kitts and Nevis	5.2	..	..	..	6	..	39	..	..	..	32	69	73
St. Lucia	..	..	..	..	11	..	25	..	141	25	..	44	60
St. Vincent and the Grenadines	3.7	..	..	..	11	..	..	..	..	..	..	62	58
Sudan	–0.7	77	69	43	..	14	..	31	..	14	..	28	20
Suriname	4.3	26	21	7	26	21	23	115	11	..	..	40	23
Swaziland	1.2	64	37	33	9	19	17	127	186	..	..	28	31
Sweden	1.1	..	..	..	2	..	14	48	77	35	38	..	..
Switzerland	1.1	8	6	..	..	28	23	67	68	20	22	107	126
Syrian Arab Republic	1.4	50	34	20	..	14	..	39	..	27	23	41	63
Tajikistan	..	46	41	..	..	..	17	..	228	..	..	..	..
Tanzania	..	90	84	..	58	..	31	..	96	18	..	41	31
Thailand	5.2	80	64	26	11	26	43	34	90	14	19	35	74
Togo	–1.1	74	66	34	38	15	14	88	65	30	..	29	29
Tonga	..	..	..	..	36	..	..	..	..	23	..	23	32
Trinidad and Tobago	–0.1	19	11	5	3	26	14	84	68	43	..	27	40
Tunisia	2.3	42	28	17	12	21	24	47	93	31	..	38	44
Turkey	1.7	71	53	40	16	14	25	10	45	18	18	14	25
Turkmenistan	..	38	37	..	..	..	..	..	..	..	..	..	..
Uganda	..	90	93	54	50	13	16	41	33	3	..	13	10
Ukraine	..	31	20	..	18	..	..	..	..	..	..	..	0
United Arab Emirates	–4.0	9	7	..	2	..	27	..	139	..	..	19	54
United Kingdom	1.8	3	2	3	2	20	16 [b]	45	57	35	36	..	..
United States	1.7	4	3	..	2	18	16	11	24	20	21	60	59
Uruguay	0.2	19	14	18	9	..	14	30	41	22	30	31	33
Uzbekistan	..	43	34	..	33	..	23	..	125	..	..	..	..
Vanuatu	..	..	..	..	..	..	..	..	..	16	..	73	118
Venezuela	–1.1	26	12	6	5	33	16	38	49	22	19	29	23
Vietnam	..	77	72	..	28	..	27	..	83	..	..	..	..
Virgin Islands (U.S.)	..	..	..	..	..	..	..	..	..	..	..	..	..
West Bank and Gaza	..	..	..	..	..	..	..	..	..	..	..	..	..
Western Samoa	..	..	..	..	..	..	..	..	..	..	..	17	..
Yemen, Rep.	..	70	58	..	22	..	12	..	88	..	21	..	47
Yugoslavia, Fed. Rep.	..	50	29	..	..	..	..	..	..	..	..	..	..
Zaire	–4.0	75	68	15	..	15	..	34	..	..	..	..	..
Zambia	–2.6	79	75	11	22	28	12	90	71	25	14	28	13
Zimbabwe	–0.3	77	69	15	15	20	22	..	74	24	..	29	26

a. Includes Eritrea. b. Includes statistical discrepancy.

Table 1.1

The indicators in this table provide an overview of the quality of life in the 209 economies with populations greater than 30,000 that are included in the *World Development Indicators*. Except for population density, GNP per capita, and the illiteracy rate, all these indicators appear elsewhere in the book.

Population density is computed from 1995 mid-year population estimates divided by the surface area of the country or economy. Different results may be obtained depending on whether land area or arable land area is used.

Gross national product (GNP) is the broadest measure of national income (see *Definitions*). GNP per capita in U.S. dollars is used by the World Bank to classify countries for analytical purposes and to determine borrowing eligibility. For definitions of the income groups used in this book, see the *Users guide*. In calculating GNP in U.S. dollars from GNP reported in national currencies, the World Bank follows its Atlas conversion method. This involves using a three-year average of exchange rates to smooth the effects of transitory exchange rate fluctuations. For further discussion of the Atlas method see *Statistical methods*.

Relative prices of goods and services not traded on the international market tend to vary substantially from one country to another, leading to big differences in the relative purchasing power of currencies and thus in welfare as measured by GNP per capita. To capture these differences in the relative purchasing power of currencies over equivalent goods and services, table 1.1 also shows GNP per capita estimates that are converted into international dollars using purchasing power parities (PPPs). For an explanation of PPPs see the notes to table 4.14.

Illiteracy rates are problematic statistics. Literacy and illiteracy are difficult both to define and to measure. The definition here is based on the concept of "functional" literacy. To measure literacy using such a definition requires census or sample survey measurements under controlled conditions. In practice, many countries estimate the number of illiterate adults from self-reported data or from estimates of school completion. Because of these problems comparisons across countries—and even over time for one country—should be made with caution.

For additional information on the other indicators see the notes to the tables indicated: population (table 2.1), people living on less than $1 a day (table 2.5), infant mortality rate (table 2.14), total fertility rate (table 2.2), and access to sanitation (table 2.12).

Table 1.2

Differences in the opportunities and resources available to men and women exist throughout the world, but are most prevalent in poor developing countries. This pattern begins at an early age: for example, boys receive a higher share of education and health spending than girls do. Such inequalities in the allocation of resources matter—because education, health, and nutrition are strongly associated with well-being, economic efficiency, and growth.

Girls in many developing countries are allowed less education by their families than boys are, as reflected in lower female primary school enrollment and higher female illiteracy rates (see table 1.1). They therefore have fewer employment opportunities, especially in the formal sector. Women who work outside the home do so in addition to taking on grueling household chores and childbearing and child-rearing responsibilities, often falling prey to the debilitating effects of undernourishment and ill health.

Female morbidity and mortality rates often exceed male rates, particularly during early childhood and the reproductive years. Life expectancy has increased for both men and women in all regions. But while in high-income countries women tend to outlive men by six to eight years on average, in low-income countries the difference is much narrower—about two to three years.

This female disadvantage is also reflected in the overall sex ratio of the population. Although the natural sex ratio at birth of 105 females per 100 males indicates female biological advantage, sex ratios in many countries are below 100. In developing countries this generally implies higher female mortality, although migration cannot be ruled out as a factor. Ratios exceeding 105 can be attributed to male migration in search of jobs or, increasingly in some parts of the world, to war losses. Data on sex ratios should be interpreted with caution, because it is not possible to isolate mortality and migration effects. For more information on these indicators see the tables indicated: sex ratio (table 2.1), gross primary enrollment (table 2.8), females as a percentage of the labor force (table 2.3), and life expectancy at birth (table 2.14).

For information on other aspects of gender differences see tables 2.1 (population), 2.2 (population dynamics), 2.3 (labor force structure), 2.4 (employment), 2.9 (educational attainment), 2.10 (gender and education), and 2.14 (mortality). See table 2.12 for data on the share of births attended by health staff.

Table 1.3

No single set of indicators can fully describe all the relevant characteristics of an economy. Those included here were chosen because they cover a broad range of issues and afford reasonably complete coverage.

For the indicators in this table, as for others in this book, differences in definition, collection methods, timeliness, and the capabilities of reporting agencies may affect accuracy, consistency, and comparability. For more information on the indicators see the tables indicated: GNP per capita (table 1.1), share of labor force in agriculture (table 4.5), value added in agriculture (table 4.3), gross domestic investment (tables 4.12 and 4.15), exports and imports of goods and services (tables 4.8–4.12), government revenues (table 4.18), and money supply (table 4.21). For additional information on national accounts indicators see the introduction to section 4 and the notes to tables 4.1 and 4.2.

Definitions

Table 1.1

● **Population density** is the midyear resident population divided by the surface area in square kilometers. ● **GNP** is the sum of gross value added by all resident producers plus any taxes (less subsidies) that are not included in the valuation of output plus net receipts of primary income (employee compensation and property income) from nonresident sources. ● **GNP per capita** is the gross national product, converted to U.S. dollars using the World Bank Atlas method, divided by the midyear population. ● **GNP per capita in PPP terms** is the gross national product converted to international dollars by adjusting for purchasing power parity, divided by the midyear population. ● **Poverty** is measured as the proportion of the population living on less than $1 a day measured at 1985 prices, adjusted for purchasing power parity. ● **Infant mortality rate** is the number of deaths of infants under one year of age per 1,000 live births in a given year. ● **Total fertility rate** is the number of children that would be born to a woman if she were to live to the end of her childbearing years and bear children at each age in accordance with prevailing age-specific fertility rates. ● **Adult illiteracy rate** is the proportion of adults aged 15 and above who cannot, with understanding, read and write a short, simple statement on their everyday life. ● **Access to sanitation** refers to the share of the population with at least adequate excreta disposal facilities that can effectively prevent human, animal, and insect contact with excreta. Suitable facilities range from simple but protected pit latrines to flush toilets with sewerage.

Table 1.2

● **Population sex ratio** is the number of women per 100 men in the population. Differences in this ratio across countries reflect differences in sex ratios at birth and in patterns of migration and mortality. ● **Gross primary enrollment** is the ratio of total enrollment, regardless of age, to the population of the age group that officially corresponds to the primary level of education. ● **Female labor force as a percentage of the total** is the proportion of economically active females in the labor force as defined by national authorities. ● **Life expectancy at birth** indicates the number of years a newborn infant would live if prevailing patterns of mortality at the time of its birth were to stay the same throughout its life.

Table 1.3

● **GNP per capita** is the gross national product converted to U.S. dollars using the World Bank Atlas method, divided by the midyear population. The growth rate is computed using the least-squares method and constant 1987 prices. ● **Labor force in agriculture** is the proportion of the total labor force recorded as working in agriculture, hunting, forestry, and fishing (ISIC major division 1). ● **Agriculture** is the value added of the agricultural sector (ISIC major division 1). ● **Investment** is gross domestic investment, which comprises gross additions to the fixed capital stock plus net changes in inventories. ● **Trade** is the sum of exports and imports of goods and services. ● **Central government revenue** includes all revenue to the central government from taxes and nonrepayable receipts (other than grants). ● **Money and quasi money (M2)** is the sum of currency outside banks and demand deposits other than those of the central government, plus the time, savings, and foreign currency deposits of resident sectors other than the central government. This measure of the money supply is commonly called M2.

Data sources

The indicators here and throughout the rest of the book have been compiled by World Bank staff from primary and secondary sources. For most of the indicators shown in the tables in this section, the sources are cited in the notes to the tables referred to in *About the data*. Data on surface area are from the Food and Agriculture Organization (see *Data sources* for table 3.1). GNP per capita is estimated by World Bank staff based on national accounts data collected by World Bank staff during economic missions or reported by national statistical offices to other international organizations such as the OECD. For high-income OECD economies the data come from the OECD. Data on illiteracy rates are supplied by UNESCO and published in its *Statistical Yearbook* (see *Data sources* for table 2.9).

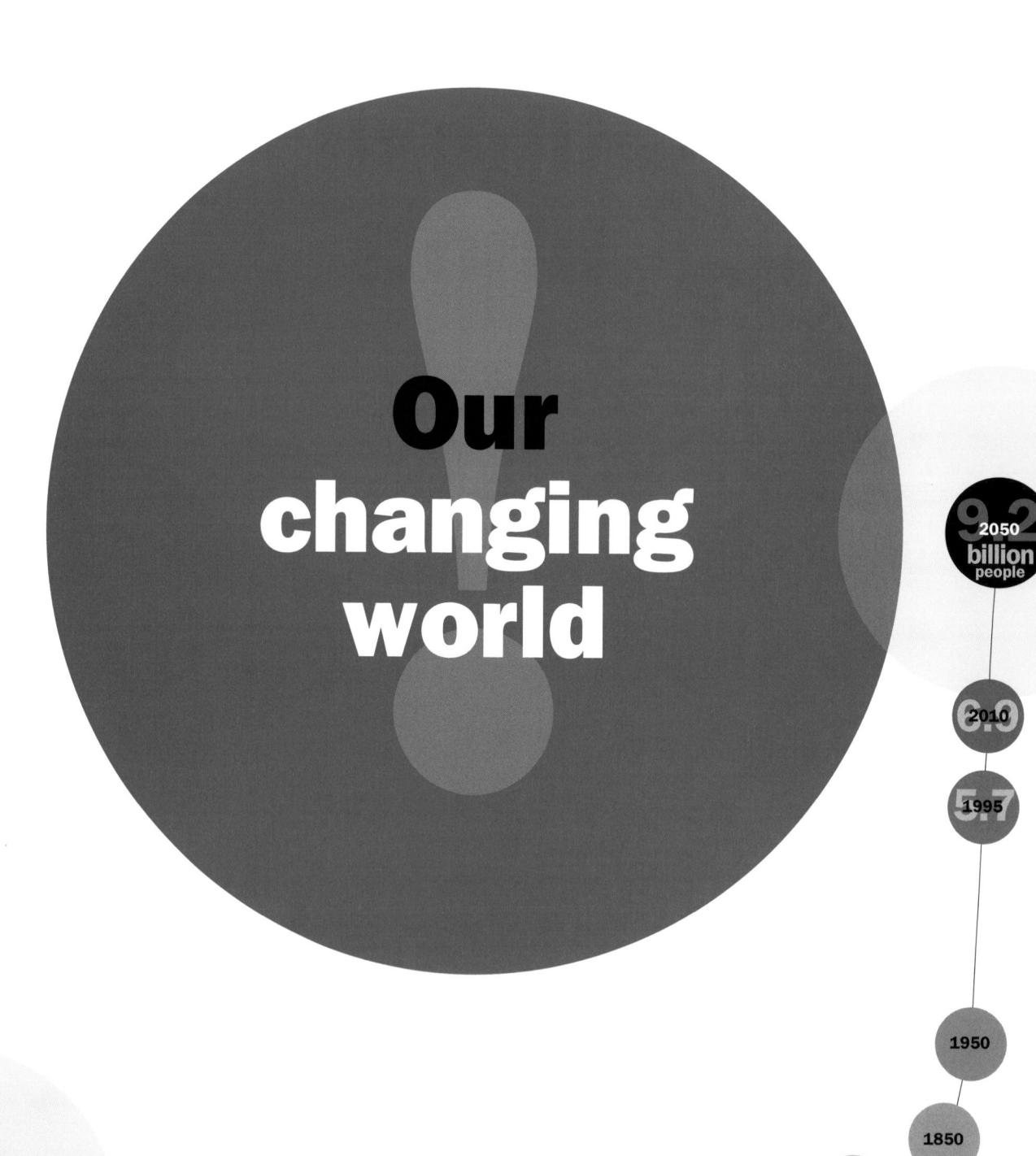

Our changing world

2000
B.C.

1000
B.C.

1
A.D.

1000

1500

1850

1950

5.7
1995

6.8
2010

9.2
2050
billion
people

The world's people are healthier, better educated, and better fed than they were 25 years ago. Life expectancy has increased by **9** years—from **55** years to **64**. And infant mortality rates have declined—from **107** per **1,000** live births in 1970 to **60** in 1995.

There are also twice as many people as there were in 1970—nearly **6** billion. And the next **35** years will add another **2.5** billion—**90** percent of them in the developing regions.

Infant mortality rate, 1970 and 1995
per 1,000 live births

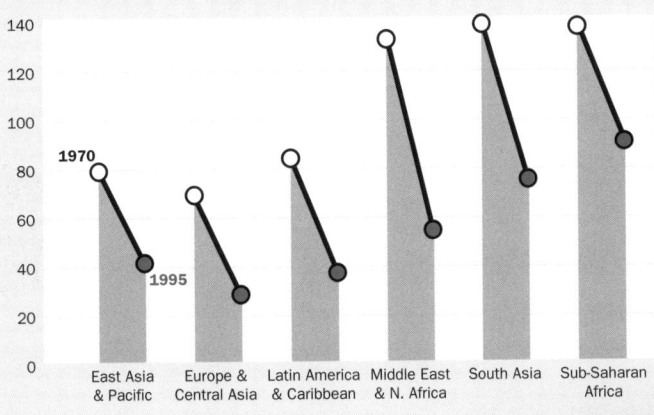

Urban population as a share of the total, 1980 and 1995
millions

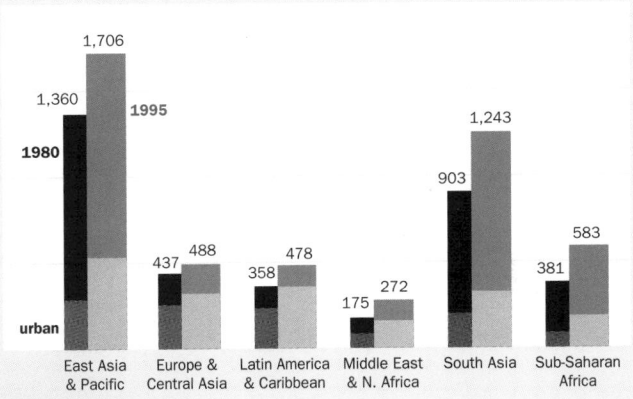

In the developing world nearly **2** billion people live in cities. Between **1980** and **1995** the urban population in low-income economies rose from **21** percent to **29** percent—that in middle-income economies from **52** percent to **61** percent. In high-income economies the urban population is now **78** percent.

More than **1.3** billion people live on less than a dollar a day, and **2** billion more are only marginally better off. About **60** percent of the poor live in South Asia and Sub-Saharan Africa, which together account for **39** percent of the developing world's people but only **14** percent of its aggregate GDP.

World's poor by region, 1993

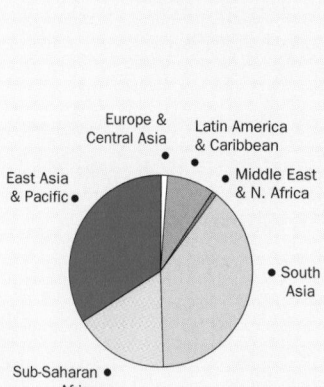

Europe & Central Asia

Latin America & Caribbean

East Asia & Pacific

Middle East & N. Africa

South Asia

Sub-Saharan Africa

Illiteracy, 1990 and 1995
percentage of people aged 15 and above

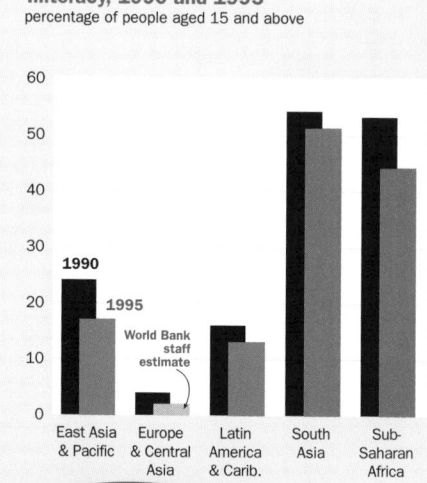

1990

1995

World Bank staff estimate

East Asia & Pacific

Europe & Central Asia

Latin America & Carib.

South Asia

Sub-Saharan Africa

Poverty is partly about failing to invest in people. In developing countries nearly **one** in **three** adults is still illiterate. In South Asia **256** million of the estimated **380** million women are illiterate—in Sub-Saharan Africa **87** million of the **164** million women are.

Better-educated people tend to be healthier, and the neglect of education takes its toll on human life. Of every **1,000** newborn babies in developing countries, **88** will not reach their **fifth** birthday. Of those who survive to their **15th** birthday, **21** percent will die before reaching their **60th**.

Energy consumption per capita in low- and middle-income economies is now **740** kilograms of oil equivalent, up from **690** kilograms in **1980**. Rising with income, per capita use in the high-income economies is now **5,100** kilograms, up from **4,600** kilograms in **1980**.

Fortunately, energy efficiency also rises with income. For every kilogram of oil equivalent, low-income economies generate **$1.10** in GDP—middle-income economies **$1.20**, and high-income economies **$3.40**.

Per capita energy use, by region, 1980 and 1994
kg of oil equivalent, thousands

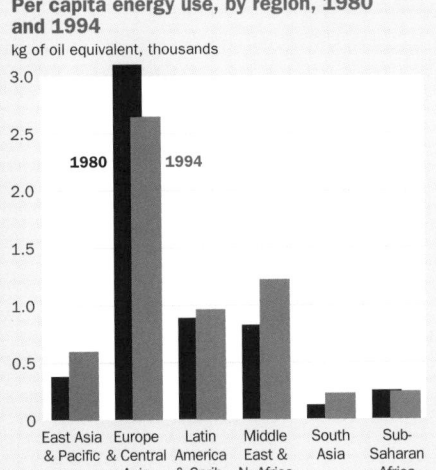

Per capita energy use, by income group, 1980 and 1994
kg of oil equivalent, thousands

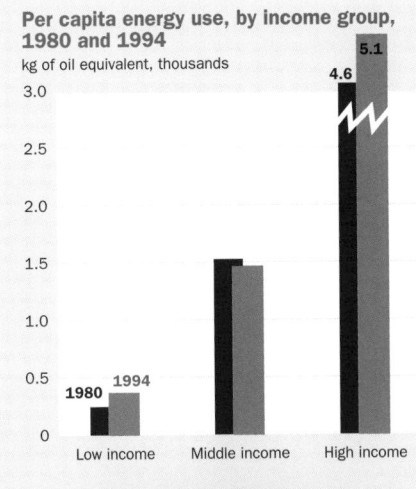

Arable land, 1994
as % of total land area

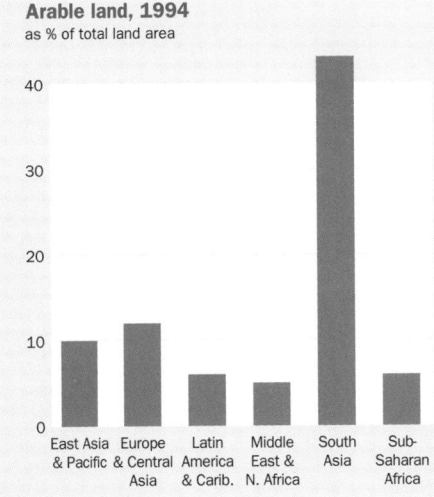

Of the world's **130** million square kilometers of land, a mere **10** percent is used for crops, pastures, and gardens. South Asia, with **45** percent of its land devoted to such uses, is rich in arable land. Sub-Saharan Africa, with only **6** percent, is poor in arable land by contrast.

Developing countries
(excluding the economies
of the former Soviet Union) recorded
a relatively modest **1.5** percent
GNP per capita growth rate between
1970 and **1995**, with population
gains eating into economic growth.
And growth has been uneven,
with periods of rapid growth
alternating with periods
of slow growth.

Growth has also been uneven
across regions. East Asia's economies
grew steadily over the period, recording
per capita income growth of **5.7** percent
between **1970** and **1995**,
while growth was negative
in the Middle East and North Africa
and Sub-Saharan Africa—at
–1.2 and **–0.8** percent.

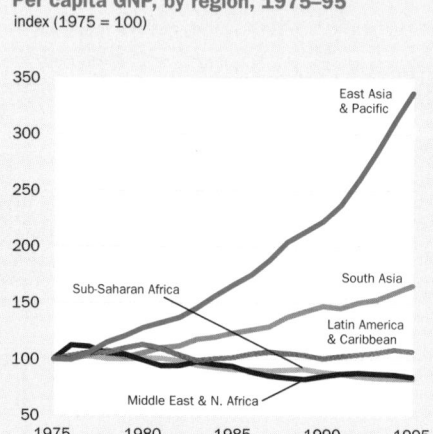

Per capita GNP, by region, 1975–95
index (1975 = 100)

East Asia & Pacific

South Asia

Sub-Saharan Africa

Latin America & Caribbean

Middle East & N. Africa

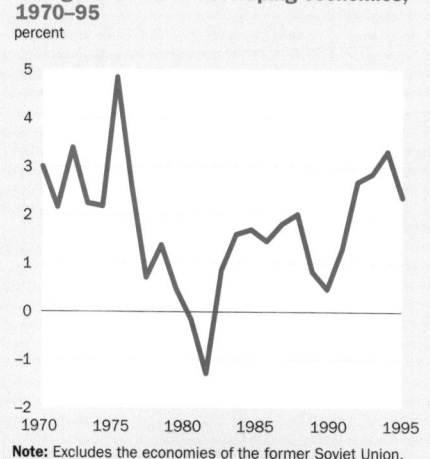

GNP growth rate in developing economies, 1970–95
percent

Note: Excludes the economies of the former Soviet Union.

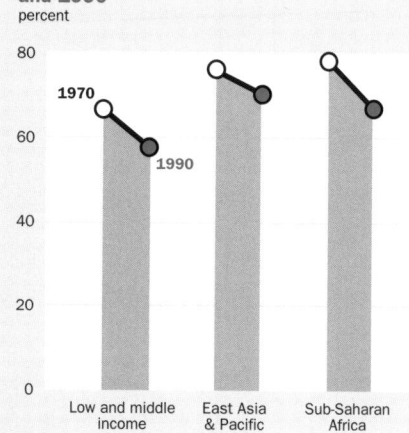

Share of labor force in agriculture, 1970 and 1990
percent

1970

1990

Low and middle income

East Asia & Pacific

Sub-Saharan Africa

Disparities in growth are
reflected in disparities in structural
change. Most low-income countries
remain predominantly agricultural.
But East Asia's rapidly growing economies
have seen their share of labor force
in agriculture fall dramatically—
Malaysia from **54** to **27** percent,
the Republic of Korea from **49**
to **18** percent.

The world economy is rapidly
integrating, and many developing
countries are leading the way.
World trade has consistently
outstripped world GDP growth
in the past four decades,
with the pace accelerating
in the 1990s.

**Foreign direct investment as a share of GDP,
1981–83 and 1991–93**

percent

Region	1981–83	1991–93
East Asia & Pacific	0.20	0.60
Europe & Central Asia	0.00	0.43
Latin America & Carib.	0.32	0.49
Middle East & N. Africa	0.16	0.00
South Asia	0.00	0.02
Sub-Saharan Africa	0.11	0.07
High income	0.29	0.61

Trade to GDP ratio, by region, 1980–95

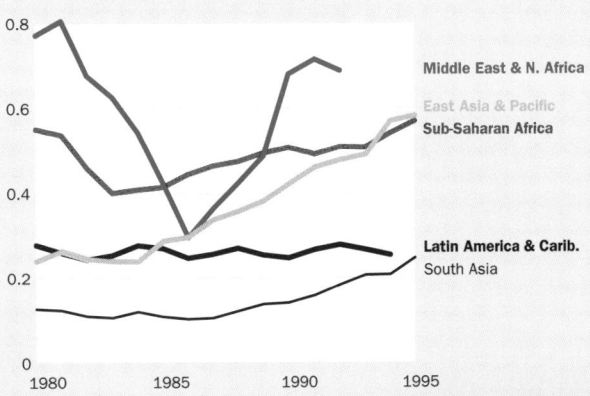

But there are wide disparities
in the speed of integration, with many
developing countries becoming
even less integrated. The ratio of
trade to GDP fell in **44** countries
over the past decade, and the ratio
of foreign direct investment to
GDP in more than a **third**.

Nevertheless, developing economies
are now important markets
for the industrial countries. Developing
economies account for
$1 in every **$4** of export earnings for
industrial countries—and
nearly **$2** of every **$5**
for Japan and the United States.

Net private capital flows to developing countries have soared—from **$44** billion in 1990 to **$184** billion in 1995—outstripping official flows. But so far, about **78** percent of this private money has been going to only a dozen or so countries.

Net foreign direct investment, by region, 1990 and 1995
billions of U.S. dollars

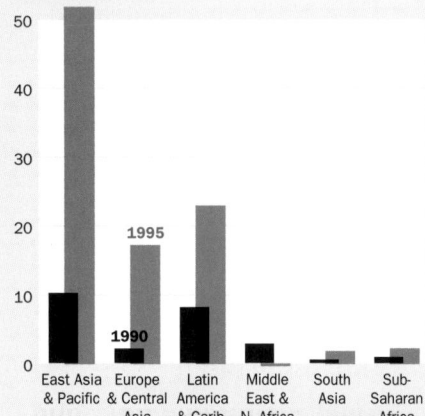

East Asia & Pacific | Europe & Central Asia | Latin America & Carib. | Middle East & N. Africa | South Asia | Sub-Saharan Africa

Net private capital flows, by region, 1990 and 1995
billions of U.S. dollars

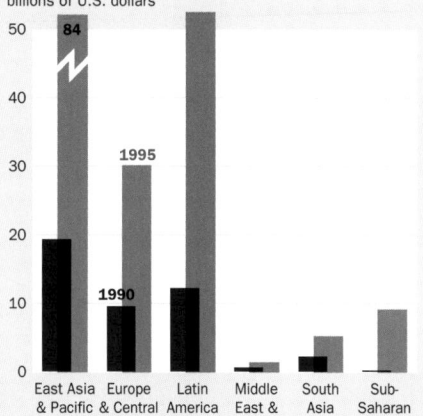

East Asia & Pacific | Europe & Central Asia | Latin America & Carib. | Middle East & N. Africa | South Asia | Sub-Saharan Africa

Top 12 recipients of net private capital, 1995

Economy	$ billions	Share of total (%)
China	44.3	24.1
Brazil	19.1	10.4
Mexico	13.1	7.1
Malaysia	11.9	6.5
Indonesia	11.6	6.3
Thailand	9.1	4.9
Hungary	7.8	4.2
Argentina	7.2	3.9
Czech Republic	5.6	3.0
Poland	5.1	2.8
Philippines	4.6	2.5
Chile	4.2	2.3
Total	**143.6**	**78.0**

Of these private flows to developing economies, foreign direct investment is up from **$25** billion to **$95** billion, bank and trade-related lending from **$14** billion to **$28** billion, bonds from **$2** billion to **$29** billion, and equity from **$3** billion to **$32** billion.

In part as a result of such flows, the market capitalization of the developing world's stock exchanges has also soared—from **$391** billion in **1990** to **$1,500** billion in **1995**.

Official flows of finance to developing countries, important until recently, have declined to some 27 cents of every $100 of OECD GNP.

Africa continues to receive the most aid per person—$32 dollars on average in 1994—while the Middle East and North Africa received $24.

Net aid received per person, 1994
U.S. dollars

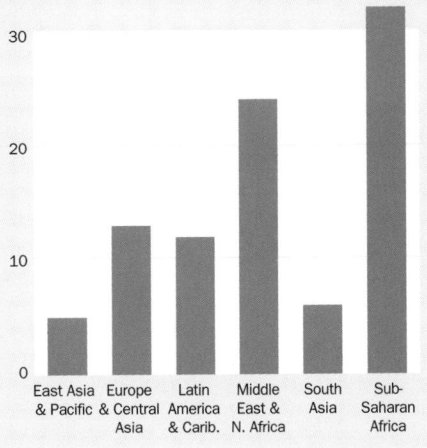

East Asia & Pacific | Europe & Central Asia | Latin America & Carib. | Middle East & N. Africa | South Asia | Sub-Saharan Africa

Net ODA flows, 1980–95
billions of 1994 U.S. dollars

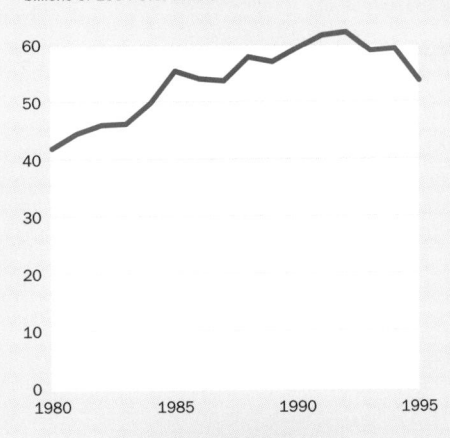

1980   1985   1990   1995

As countries develop, their dependence on aid naturally declines. For low-income economies (excluding China and India) aid accounted for 12.6 percent of GNP in 1994—and for middle-income economies 1.0 percent.

People

2

The ultimate aim of development is to improve human well-being in a substantial and sustainable way. Human capital development—the product of education and improvements in health and nutrition—is both a part of and a means of achieving this goal.

The importance of investing in human capital has become clearer in recent years, with increasing evidence on how and to what extent such investments interact with other factors in development as forces for change. This section allows readers to evaluate how well different economies are doing in building human capital and extending human welfare.

Living standards have been improving all over the world. Globally, real GNP per capita has increased by more than 3 percent a year on average since the mid-1960s. But while only the East Asian miracle economies have been able to sustain this (or even higher) income growth for long periods, improvements in social indicators have been sustained in all regions for much of the past 25 years. Many developing countries have succeeded in reducing poverty, a few by as much as 50 percent (World Bank 1990). Average infant mortality rates for low- and middle-income countries have declined from 107 per 1,000 live births in 1970 to 60 in 1995; life expectancy at birth increased from an average 55 years to 64 years. The world today is healthier, better educated, and better fed than it was 25 years ago.

These achievements nevertheless mask vast disparities across regions and countries. Infant mortality remains above 90 per 1,000 live births in Sub-Saharan Africa and 70 in South Asia, compared with 40 for East Asia. Average life expectancy at birth is only 52 years in Africa, compared with more than 60 for other regions. Primary school enrollment in some African countries has declined, and secondary school enrollment is only 24 percent, compared with over 50 percent for some other developing regions. And as the world approaches the turn of the century, more than 1.3 billion people are living on less than $1 a day, and another 2 billion are only slightly better off. Most of the poor—about 60 percent—live in South Asia and Sub-Saharan Africa, which together account for 14 percent of the aggregate GDP of developing countries and 3 percent of the world's.

Poverty reduction requires action simultaneously to stimulate growth through sound economic policies that promote sustainable, equitable development and to invest heavily in human capital through improvements in education, health, nutrition, and other social services (World Bank 1990). While this section focuses on human capital, sections 4 and 5 look at economic growth and its preconditions.

Why does human capital matter?

Because the poor's most significant asset is their labor, the most effective way to improve their welfare is to increase their employment opportunities and the productivity of their labor through investments in human capital. Often, the poor are unable to finance such investments. So the challenge is to create an enabling environment and to mobilize resources for human capital investments.

Human capital is critical in raising the living standards of the poor. Health care and good nutrition reduce sickness and mortality and improve labor productivity. Literacy and numeracy widen horizons, making it easier for people to learn new skills throughout their working lives, and thus ensure full participation in social and economic life. By raising productivity, investments in education stimulate growth, and by opening economic opportunities to more people, they help reduce income inequality. In turn, faster growth and greater equality increase the supply of, and demand for, education.

Better education and health enable couples to make more informed decisions about the number and spacing of their children and about their schooling, and to protect maternal and child health. The improved health of educated people motivates them to make still more investments in their education and health. The relationship between investments and outcomes is thus mutually reinforcing, justifying investments in human capital on both economic and equity grounds.

Developing countries have already made big investments in human capital development, assisted by private and official development agencies. More recently, governments have taken new initiatives to address social issues and identified specific goals, based on agreed targets, to measure progress (see box 1a in section 1).

The poverty of data

Many indicators have been proposed to measure progress in building human capital. Yet there are continuing problems with the quality of data that cast doubts on the reliability of the indicators and raise concerns about their use in decisionmaking (Srinivasan 1994). Data often suffer from conceptual problems, measurement biases and errors, and lack of comparability over time and across countries. The specialized United Nations agencies that standardize concepts and methods of data collection are underfinanced, and government commitment to data collection, including allocation of sufficient human and financial resources, often falls prey to budget cuts.

Not surprisingly, population censuses often become the main source of information on most aspects of human capital, supplemented by official estimates based on the censuses and surveys or broad generalizations. The problem is that censuses are infrequent (usually decennial), have long processing times, and fail to reflect such aspects of human capital development as access to and quality of social services. Important supplements to population censuses are specialized household surveys that gather information on the level and extent of poverty and on the impact of government policies on poor and vulnerable populations. Household surveys have other advantages. They can be conducted frequently and more cheaply than censuses and are increasingly used to measure living standards.

The indicators reported here share many of these shortcomings (detailed notes on their quality are presented with each table). With these caveats, the data nevertheless help quantify the consequences of poverty, allow intertemporal and cross-country comparisons, and highlight social problems that need to be resolved.

Population and the labor force

Worldwide, policymakers have tended to focus on the high population growth in many developing countries. Although the fertility rate has declined by one birth per woman in the past 15 years, average population growth rates have fallen less (tables 2.1 and 2.2). Between 1980 and 2030 the population of developing countries will more than double—to 7.2 billion, compared with

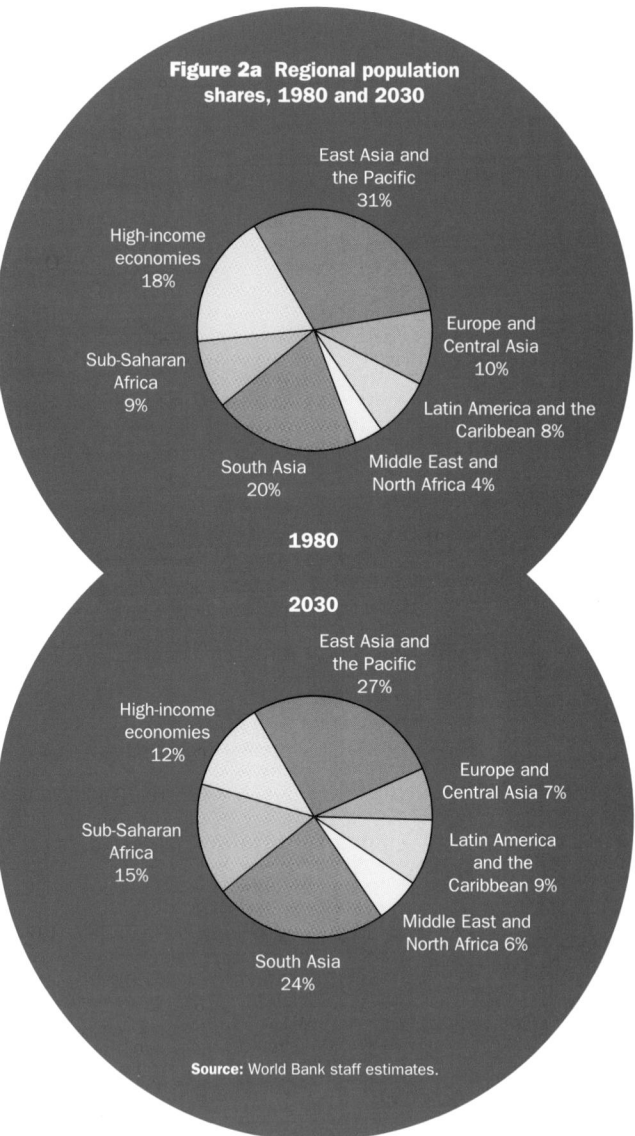

Figure 2a Regional population shares, 1980 and 2030

East Asia and the Pacific 31%

High-income economies 18%

Europe and Central Asia 10%

Sub-Saharan Africa 9%

Latin America and the Caribbean 8%

South Asia 20%

Middle East and North Africa 4%

1980

2030

East Asia and the Pacific 27%

High-income economies 12%

Europe and Central Asia 7%

Sub-Saharan Africa 15%

Latin America and the Caribbean 9%

South Asia 24%

Middle East and North Africa 6%

Source: World Bank staff estimates.

1 billion for high-income countries—further increasing the developing country share of world population (figure 2a).

Will this population boom depress economic growth and living standards? In the short run an increase in population means lower per capita income growth. High birth rates and young populations increase dependency ratios, making it more difficult to invest in human resources—the key to boosting labor productivity. But in the long run the larger number of workers may accelerate growth. According to the World Bank's *World Development Report 1995: Workers in an Integrating World,* poor labor outcomes may have little to do with the growth of labor supply. In the past 30 years growth in the working-age population (15–64) was remarkably similar across regions—ranging between 2.5 percent and 3.2 percent a year—but there were wide differences in GDP growth. In East Asia output growth exceeded expansion of the working-age population by about 5 percentage points a year; in Sub-Saharan Africa growth of the working-age population (roughly 3 percent a year) exceeded GDP growth. The dilemma remains, however, of what to do with future labor supply when economic growth is stagnant, populations continue to grow quickly, and most countries restrict immigration. It usually takes about a generation for a decline in fertility to appreciably slow growth in the labor supply.

At current and projected fertility rates, developing countries are expected to add about 640 million people to the world's labor force in the next 15 years (table 2.3). The fastest increases are expected in Sub-Saharan Africa and the Middle East and North Africa. In many countries almost all men between the ages of 25 and 54 are in the labor force (World Bank 1995g). The participation of women, however, often changes significantly as development proceeds. Female participation tends to be higher when an economy is organized around family-based production in agriculture, as in many Sub-Saharan African countries, and at higher levels of per capita income, when labor market options for women increase. Child labor, a sign of poverty, is pervasive in many parts of the world. While child labor may reduce household poverty, it is always at the expense of children's education and well-being. Income uncertainty, household size, and lack of schooling opportunities are strongly correlated with child labor.

How is the labor force deployed? In developing countries most workers are self-employed or work in family enterprises (table 2.4). As economies grow, however, more work for wages. In middle-income countries better educational opportunities and lower fertility have led more women to enter the labor market, and they now account for a growing share of wage employment. In low-income countries unpaid work and family responsibilities, as well as lack of investment in women's education, are strongly associated with their limited participation in the labor force.

How much poverty is there?

Without material assets or human capital, the poor hire out their labor, mostly in unskilled work. Poverty is the result when people cannot earn enough from their labor to maintain a minimal standard of living. An estimate of the number of poor depends, of course, on the choice of a poverty threshold. And while there

is little disagreement on one aspect of the threshold—the income needed to buy a minimum standard of living and nutrition—what constitutes minimum basic needs is more subjective. So the perception of poverty varies by culture, and criteria for distinguishing the poor from the nonpoor reflect national priorities. In general, as countries become richer, their perception of what constitutes an acceptable level of consumption changes, and so does the poverty line.

To allow comparisons across countries the World Bank has established an international poverty line based on $1 a day per person in 1985 purchasing power parity prices (table 2.5). According to this measure, inroads have been made in reducing poverty, although overall gains have been modest. While the proportion of poor in the world's population declined slightly, from 30 percent to 29 percent, between 1987 and 1993, the number of people living on less than $1 a day increased, from 1.2 billion to 1.3 billion (table 2a).

Where are the world's poor? South Asia is home to a quarter of the world's population but contains 39 percent of its poor and has the highest aggregate poverty level (43 percent). East Asia accounts for roughly a third of the world's poor, most in China and Indochina, with the incidence of poverty showing a modest decline between the late 1980s and the early 1990s. And while Sub-Saharan Africa has only 17 percent of the world's poor, the incidence of poverty has remained unchanged at around 39 percent. Its people remain among the poorest in the world, with poor access to productive resources and services, few employment opportunities, limited access to assets (particularly for women), and inadequate education, health, and water and sanitation services.

Does economic growth reduce poverty? Analysis of a new World Bank development database finds a strong positive relationship between growth and poverty reduction (Ravallion and Chen 1996; and Deininger and Squire 1996). This finding is confirmed by a World Bank research project on India, which estimated that a 10 percentage point increase in mean consumption resulted in a 12–13 percent decline in the proportion of the population living below the poverty line (Ravallion 1996).

While the relationship between growth and poverty is unambiguous, that between growth and inequality is less clear. Income inequality, with its political and economic overtones, stubbornly

Table 2a Population living on less than $1 a day in developing economies, 1987 and 1993

Region	Millions		Share of population %	
	1987	1993	1987	1993
East Asia and the Pacific	464.0	445.8	28.8	26.0
Europe and Central Asia	2.2	14.5	0.6	3.5
Latin America and the Caribbean	91.2	109.6	22.0	23.5
Middle East and North Africa	10.3	10.7	4.7	4.1
South Asia	479.9	514.7	45.4	43.1
Sub-Saharan Africa	179.6	218.6	38.5	39.1
Total	1,227.1	1,313.9	30.1	29.4

Source: World Bank 1996f.

persists in many countries (table 2.6). The question of whether, and under what conditions, economic growth is associated with changes in inequality has led to much empirical work—and to Kuznets's famous hypothesis that inequality increases with income at the early stages of development and decreases at higher levels of income. Lack of time-series data over a long period prevents the testing of this hypothesis. However, recent work at the World Bank suggests that there is no strong relationship between growth and changes in aggregate income inequality as measured by the Gini coefficient—that is, the Gini coefficient appears to change little with changes in income (Deininger and Squire 1996).

Big payoffs from investing in education

Investments in education create economic opportunities. The poor benefit most from basic education—rates of return are higher for primary education than for secondary. And developing countries are spending more on education, particularly primary education (table 2.7). Between 1980 and 1992 spending on primary education as a share of GDP increased in roughly four of every 10 countries. The impact of education spending depends on how and on what it is spent. Governments spend little on instructional materials, however, even though they have been shown to have a consistently positive effect on student achievement in developing countries (Lockheed, Verspoor, and associates 1991). Of the countries for which information is available, 90 percent direct less than 5 percent of primary and secondary education spending to teaching materials.

Because most students in postprimary education come from better-off families, skewing education spending toward primary education can increase the access of the poor to education. But despite increased expenditures on education in recent years, particularly primary education, many countries still suffer from low enrollment rates (table 2.8). In primary schools low enrollment typically reflects underenrollment of the poor, but it also has gender dimensions, reflecting mainly cultural norms and the value of female contributions to the household (Schultz 1993; and Hill and King 1993). One consequence of this long-standing

imbalance is that almost two-thirds of the world's illiterate adults—565 million—are women (table 2b).

Why does girls' education matter? Social returns to investments in female education are significantly greater than for similar investments in males, while private returns are the same or slightly higher (Heyneman 1996; Hill and King 1993; and Psacharopoulos 1994). Gender differences in persistence to grade 4 and in progression to secondary school are marginal in most countries, with rates for girls increasingly exceeding those for boys (table 2.9). Girls who enter school are more likely than boys to do so because of a strong motivation to obtain schooling or their parents' desire that they be educated—and so are more likely to complete their schooling. Women are not easily able to translate their educational achievements into social and economic gains, however. They are increasingly concentrated at the lower end of the professional ladder, often filling vacancies left by men as they move to better jobs (table 2.10).

Changing needs in health and nutrition

Along with education, improvements in health status and nutrition directly address the worst aspects of poverty. Access of the poor to health services is important both for increasing their income (illness reduces people's capacity to work) and for raising living standards even if income remains at poverty levels.

The public sector has been dominant in health improvements—training medical personnel, investing in clinics and hospitals, running subsidy and insurance schemes, and directly providing medical care. Government efforts have helped increase the number of doctors, nurses, and hospital beds throughout the developing world (table 2.11). But in many low-income countries private spending on health exceeds public spending, reflecting the inefficiency of the public system (with the distribution of political power explaining much of the allocation of resources) and ineffective social insurance systems (World Bank 1993c). The weakness of the health network means that patients seek care in hospitals or from private practitioners. Because the poor have worse access to health care, they generally use fewer health services.

Table 2b Estimated illiterate population aged 15 and above, 1980 and 1995

millions

Region or group	Total 1980	Female 1980	Female % 1980	Total 1995	Female 1995	Female % 1995
East Asia, including Oceania	276.1	186.3	67.5	209.9	149.5	71.2
Latin America and the Caribbean	44.1	24.7	56.1	42.9	23.4	54.7
Middle East and North Africa	55.8	34.5	61.8	65.5	41.2	41.2
South Asia	345.9	207.2	59.9	415.5	256.1	61.6
Sub-Saharan Africa	125.9	76.2	60.5	140.5	87.1	62.0
Least developed countries	135.4	81.2	59.9	166.0	101.0	60.8
Developing countries	848.4	530.6	62.5	871.8	556.7	63.9
Developed countries	29.0	20.9	72.0	12.9	7.9	61.6

Note: Some of the increase in the estimated illiterate population from 1980 to 1995 may reflect better reporting. The regional groupings are based on the United Nations country classification. Bulgaria, the former Czechoslovakia, Romania, and the former Soviet Union are included with developed countries.
Source: UNESCO 1995b.

Under the Health for All by the Year 2000 initiative adopted by the World Health Assembly in 1981, many developing countries are taking an important step in reducing inequities by emphasizing primary health care, including immunization, sanitation, access to safe water, family planning services, and safe motherhood initiatives (table 2.12). Even so, much remains to be done. Malnutrition, especially in women and children, remains a burden. And although the rate of measles immunization worldwide is 80 percent, ranging between 60 percent in Sub-Saharan Africa and 89 percent in the Middle East and North Africa, more than one million children are killed by the disease every year. Another 43 million cases occur annually, leaving many of the survivors prey to malnutrition and other debilitating conditions.

While most public health efforts have emphasized infant and child health, adult health is becoming a new issue for public health policy in developing countries. More than a third of the population in developing countries is between the ages of 15 and 60. The loss of an adult income earner not only may affect the family—by pushing the whole household into poverty—it also affects the economy. Adult mortality rates are highest in Sub-Saharan Africa and South Asia, where poverty is also the worst. Communicable diseases are still common. AIDS has emerged as a serious threat in developing countries, especially among people between the ages of 15 and 54. The rising consumption of tobacco in developing countries also adds to ill health. And as populations age, health care systems have to cope more with noncommunicable diseases, such as heart attacks and strokes, which are expensive to treat and can absorb considerable public health care resources for relatively small gains in overall health status (tables 2.13 and 2.14).

The answer requires more than money

Much has already been done to increase investments in human capital worldwide. Where necessary and possible, governments will also have to effectively mobilize private resources, while continuing to play a major role themselves if progress is to be sustained. But results do not depend on more resources alone; they also depend on how well resources are used and how successfully intersectoral linkages are exploited.

2.1 | Population

	Total			Average annual growth rate		Age dependency ratio		Population aged 60 and above		Women per 100 men aged 60 and above	
						dependents as % of working-age population					
		millions			%			% of total			
	1980	1995	2010	1980–95	1995–2010	1980	1995	1995	2010	1995	2010
Albania	3	3	4	1.3	1.0	0.7	0.6	9	12	119	117
Algeria	19	28	36	2.7	1.7	1.0	0.7	6	7	112	113
Angola	7	11	16	2.9	2.8	0.9	1.0	5	4	121	120
Argentina	28	35	40	1.4	1.0	0.6	0.6	13	14	133	135
Armenia	3	4	4	1.3	0.8	0.6	0.6	11	12	133	145
Australia	15	18	20	1.4	0.8	0.5	0.5	15	18	121	116
Austria	8	8	8	0.4	0.1	0.6	0.5	20	24	156	129
Azerbaijan	6	8	9	1.3	1.0	0.7	0.6	9	11	145	161
Bangladesh	87	120	150	2.2	1.5	1.0	0.9	5	6	81	96
Belarus	10	10	10	0.5	0.1	0.5	0.5	17	19	182	181
Belgium	10	10	10	0.2	0.1	0.5	0.5	21	24	136	131
Benin	3	5	8	3.1	2.6	0.9	1.0	4	4	122	121
Bolivia	5	7	10	2.2	2.1	0.9	0.8	6	6	119	122
Bosnia and Herzegovina	..	..	..	..	..	..	..	..	..	..	..
Botswana	1	1	2	3.2	1.7	1.0	0.8	4	4	174	167
Brazil	121	159	190	1.8	1.2	0.7	0.6	7	9	115	128
Bulgaria	9	8	8	–0.3	–0.3	0.5	0.5	21	23	125	135
Burkina Faso	7	10	15	2.7	2.6	0.9	1.0	5	4	109	140
Burundi	4	6	9	2.8	2.5	0.9	1.0	4	3	150	143
Cambodia	6	10	14	2.9	2.0	0.9	0.9	4	5	161	162
Cameroon	9	13	20	2.8	2.9	0.9	0.9	5	5	118	119
Canada	25	30	32	1.2	0.6	0.5	0.5	16	20	127	119
Central African Republic	2	3	4	2.3	2.0	0.9	0.9	6	5	132	137
Chad	4	6	9	2.4	2.4	0.8	0.9	6	6	119	119
Chile	11	14	17	1.6	1.1	0.6	0.6	9	13	138	134
China	981	1,200	1,347	1.3	0.8	0.7	0.5	10	12	102	100
Colombia	28	37	45	1.8	1.3	0.8	0.6	8	9	108	127
Congo	2	3	4	3.0	2.6	0.9	1.0	6	4	146	150
Costa Rica	2	3	4	2.7	1.5	0.7	0.7	7	10	113	114
Côte d'Ivoire	8	14	19	3.6	2.2	1.0	1.0	5	5	94	92
Croatia	5	5	5	0.3	0.0	0.5	0.5	20	24	149	138
Cuba	10	11	12	0.8	0.6	0.7	0.5	12	17	105	113
Czech Republic	10	10	10	0.1	0.0	0.6	0.5	18	22	149	141
Denmark	5	5	5	0.1	0.1	0.5	0.5	19	23	131	124
Dominican Republic	6	8	9	2.1	1.3	0.8	0.6	6	9	104	119
Ecuador	8	11	15	2.4	1.7	0.9	0.7	6	8	114	120
Egypt, Arab Rep.	41	58	73	2.3	1.6	0.8	0.7	6	7	118	111
El Salvador	5	6	8	1.4	2.0	1.0	0.8	6	6	132	146
Eritrea	..	..	..	..	..	..	..	..	..	..	..
Estonia	1	1	1	0.0	–0.5	0.5	0.5	19	23	175	174
Ethiopia	38	56	86	2.7	2.8	1.0	1.0	4	4	126	113
Finland	5	5	5	0.4	0.2	0.5	0.5	19	24	154	132
France	54	58	60	0.5	0.3	0.6	0.5	20	23	141	131
Gabon	1	1	2	3.0	2.3	0.6	0.8	9	8	121	118
Gambia, The	1	1	2	3.7	2.1	0.8	0.8	5	5	108	115
Georgia	5	5	6	0.4	0.1	0.5	0.5	17	20	157	165
Germany	78	82	82	0.3	0.0	0.5	0.5	20	25	153	125
Ghana	11	17	25	3.1	2.4	0.9	0.9	5	5	117	119
Greece	10	10	11	0.5	0.2	0.6	0.5	22	25	121	124
Guatemala	7	11	15	2.9	2.5	1.0	0.9	5	5	110	118
Guinea	4	7	10	2.6	2.8	0.9	1.0	4	4	110	98
Guinea-Bissau	1	1	1	1.9	2.1	0.8	0.9	5	4	126	135
Haiti	5	7	9	1.9	1.3	0.8	0.8	6	6	123	129
Honduras	4	6	9	3.2	2.5	1.0	0.9	5	5	111	117
Hong Kong	5	6	6	1.4	0.2	0.5	0.4	14	19	104	98

	Total			Average annual growth rate		Age dependency ratio		Population aged 60 and above		Women per 100 men aged 60 and above	
		millions			%	dependents as % of working-age population		% of total			
	1980	1995	2010	1980–95	1995–2010	1980	1995	1995	2010	1995	2010
Hungary	11	10	10	–0.3	–0.2	0.5	0.5	19	21	150	150
India	687	929	1,127	2.0	1.3	0.7	0.7	8	9	101	104
Indonesia	148	193	235	1.8	1.3	0.8	0.6	7	8	113	117
Iran, Islamic Rep.	39	64	91	3.3	2.4	0.9	0.9	6	6	92	100
Iraq	13	20	31	2.9	3.0	0.9	0.9	4	5	106	107
Ireland	3	4	4	0.4	0.7	0.7	0.5	15	18	123	119
Israel	4	6	7	2.4	1.4	0.7	0.6	11	13	122	116
Italy	56	57	56	0.1	–0.1	0.5	0.5	22	27	134	130
Jamaica	2	3	3	1.1	1.0	0.9	0.6	9	10	120	125
Japan	117	125	128	0.5	0.1	0.5	0.4	20	29	129	123
Jordan	2	4	6	4.4	2.4	1.1	0.8	4	6	77	97
Kazakstan	15	17	18	0.7	0.7	0.6	0.6	11	13	160	165
Kenya	17	27	37	3.2	2.2	1.1	1.0	4	4	113	116
Korea, Dem. Rep.	18	24	29	1.8	1.3	0.8	0.5	7	10	178	138
Korea, Rep.	38	45	50	1.1	0.8	0.6	0.4	9	14	146	138
Kuwait	1	2	2	1.3	2.6	0.7	0.6	4	8	69	97
Kyrgyz Republic	4	5	5	1.5	1.1	0.8	0.8	9	9	152	156
Lao PDR	3	5	7	2.8	2.8	0.8	0.9	5	5	120	115
Latvia	3	3	2	–0.1	–0.7	0.5	0.5	20	24	180	184
Lebanon	3	4	5	2.3	1.3	0.8	0.7	8	8	120	136
Lesotho	1	2	3	2.5	2.1	0.8	0.8	6	7	129	120
Libya	3	5	9	3.8	3.2	1.0	0.9	4	5	81	83
Lithuania	3	4	4	0.6	–0.1	0.5	0.5	17	20	171	173
Macedonia, FYR	2	2	2	0.8	0.8	0.6	0.5	13	17	120	119
Madagascar	9	14	21	3.0	2.8	0.9	0.9	5	5	117	116
Malawi	6	10	14	3.1	2.4	1.0	1.0	4	4	119	107
Malaysia	14	20	26	2.5	1.8	0.8	0.7	6	8	116	115
Mali	7	10	15	2.6	3.0	1.0	1.0	4	4	130	132
Mauritania	2	2	3	2.6	2.3	0.9	0.9	5	5	125	118
Mauritius	1	1	1	1.0	1.0	0.6	0.5	8	11	124	129
Mexico	67	92	114	2.1	1.5	0.9	0.7	6	8	124	130
Moldova	4	4	5	0.5	0.3	0.5	0.6	14	16	156	162
Mongolia	2	2	3	2.6	1.8	0.9	0.7	6	7	119	114
Morocco	19	27	34	2.1	1.6	0.9	0.7	6	7	112	126
Mozambique	12	16	23	1.9	2.4	0.9	0.9	5	5	123	121
Myanmar	34	45	57	1.9	1.6	0.8	0.7	7	7	116	120
Namibia	1	2	2	2.7	2.3	0.9	0.9	6	6	121	122
Nepal	15	21	30	2.5	2.2	0.9	0.8	5	6	92	102
Netherlands	14	15	16	0.6	0.3	0.5	0.5	18	23	131	118
New Zealand	3	4	4	1.0	0.8	0.6	0.5	15	17	122	120
Nicaragua	3	4	6	3.0	2.4	1.0	1.0	5	5	113	111
Niger	6	9	15	3.3	3.2	1.0	1.0	4	4	121	130
Nigeria	71	111	164	3.0	2.6	0.9	0.9	4	5	131	122
Norway	4	4	5	0.4	0.3	0.6	0.5	20	22	130	119
Oman	1	2	4	4.6	3.8	0.9	1.0	4	5	107	85
Pakistan	83	130	190	3.0	2.5	0.9	0.9	5	5	96	101
Panama	2	3	3	2.0	1.3	0.8	0.6	7	10	103	107
Papua New Guinea	3	4	6	2.2	2.0	0.8	0.7	5	6	97	102
Paraguay	3	5	7	2.9	2.1	0.8	0.8	5	7	123	114
Peru	17	24	30	2.1	1.6	0.8	0.6	6	8	118	115
Philippines	48	69	90	2.3	1.8	0.8	0.7	5	7	116	117
Poland	36	39	40	0.5	0.3	0.9	0.5	16	18	149	151
Portugal	10	10	10	0.1	0.1	0.6	0.5	19	21	139	156
Puerto Rico	3	4	4	1.0	0.8	0.7	0.6	15	17	139	135
Romania	22	23	22	0.1	–0.1	0.6	0.5	17	20	131	135
Russian Federation	139	148	145	0.4	–0.1	0.5	0.5	16	17	194	177

	Total			Average annual growth rate		Age dependency ratio		Population aged 60 and above		Women per 100 men aged 60 and above	
						dependents as % of working- age population					
	millions			%				% of total			
	1980	1995	2010	1980–95	1995–2010	1980	1995	1995	2010	1995	2010
Rwanda	5	6	11	1.4	3.5	1.0	1.1	4	3	122	131
Saudi Arabia	9	19	31	4.7	3.3	0.9	0.9	4	5	89	..
Senegal	6	8	12	2.8	2.5	0.9	1.0	4	4	116	112
Sierra Leone	3	4	6	1.7	2.7	0.9	0.9	4	3	130	140
Singapore	2	3	3	1.8	1.0	0.5	0.4	9	15	113	112
Slovak Republic	5	5	6	0.5	0.2	0.6	0.5	15	17	144	148
Slovenia	2	2	2	0.3	0.0	0.5	0.4	17	22	161	138
South Africa	29	41	55	2.3	1.9	0.8	0.7	7	8	119	132
Spain	37	39	39	0.3	0.0	0.6	0.5	20	23	133	136
Sri Lanka	15	18	21	1.4	1.1	0.7	0.6	8	12	103	116
Sudan	19	27	37	2.4	2.2	0.9	0.9	5	5	118	116
Sweden	8	9	9	0.4	0.2	0.6	0.6	22	25	126	119
Switzerland	6	7	7	0.7	0.2	0.5	0.5	20	26	135	126
Syrian Arab Republic	9	14	21	3.2	2.7	1.1	1.0	4	5	107	120
Tajikistan	4	6	8	2.6	1.9	0.9	0.9	7	6	134	127
Tanzania	19	30	44	3.1	2.6	1.0	0.9	4	4	120	114
Thailand	47	58	65	1.5	0.7	0.8	0.5	7	10	123	122
Togo	3	4	6	3.0	2.7	0.9	1.0	5	5	122	125
Trinidad and Tobago	1	1	1	1.2	1.0	0.7	0.6	8	11	121	125
Tunisia	6	9	11	2.3	1.5	0.8	0.6	7	8	101	116
Turkey	44	61	75	2.1	1.4	0.8	0.6	8	10	103	110
Turkmenistan	3	5	6	3.0	2.3	0.8	0.7	6	6	145	138
Uganda	13	19	28	2.7	2.6	1.0	1.1	4	2	108	110
Ukraine	50	52	50	0.2	−0.2	0.5	0.5	20	22	175	169
United Arab Emirates	1	2	3	5.7	2.2	0.4	0.5	3	10	48	..
United Kingdom	56	59	60	0.3	0.2	0.6	0.5	21	23	132	124
United States	228	263	297	1.0	0.8	0.5	0.5	16	19	138	128
Uruguay	3	3	3	0.6	0.6	0.6	0.6	17	18	131	146
Uzbekistan	16	23	31	2.4	2.0	0.9	0.8	7	7	138	139
Venezuela	15	22	28	2.5	1.7	0.8	0.7	6	9	117	120
Vietnam	54	73	93	2.1	1.6	0.9	0.7	7	7	133	140
West Bank and Gaza	1	2	4	3.9	4.1	0.9	0.9	4	4	102	116
Yemen, Rep.	9	15	25	3.9	3.3	1.1	1.0	4	4	117	139
Yugoslavia, Fed. Rep.	10	11	11	0.7	0.2	0.5	0.5	16	19	127	125
Zaire	27	44	..	3.2	..	1.0	..	..	..	..	..
Zambia	6	9	12	3.0	2.1	1.1	1.0	4	3	100	106
Zimbabwe	7	11	14	3.0	1.6	1.0	0.8	4	5	111	105
World	**4,429 t**	**5,673 t**	**6,850 t**	**1.6 w**	**1.3 w**	**0.7 w**	**0.6 w**	**10 w**	**11 w**	**122 w**	**118 w**
Low income	2,378 t	3,180 t	3,971 t	1.9 w	1.5 w	0.8 w	0.7 w	8 w	9 w	104 w	105 w
Excl. China & India	709 t	1,050 t	1,479 t	2.6 w	2.3 w	0.9 w	0.9 w	5 w	5 w	115 w	117 w
Middle income	1,236 t	1,591 t	1,916 t	1.7 w	1.2 w	0.7 w	0.6 w	10 w	12 w	137 w	131 w
Lower middle income	905 t	1,153 t	1,378 t	1.6 w	1.2 w	0.7 w	0.6 w	9 w	10 w	135 w	133 w
Upper middle income	331 t	438 t	539 t	1.9 w	1.4 w	0.7 w	0.6 w	13 w	15 w	140 w	127 w
Low & middle income	3,614 t	4,771 t	5,887 t	1.9 w	1.4 w	0.8 w	0.6 w	8 w	9 w	116 w	115 w
East Asia & Pacific	1,360 t	1,706 t	1,974 t	1.5 w	1.0 w	0.7 w	0.5 w	9 w	11 w	106 w	106 w
Europe & Central Asia	437 t	488 t	511 t	0.7 w	0.3 w	0.6 w	0.5 w	15 w	17 w	159 w	142 w
Latin America & Carib.	358 t	478 t	587 t	1.9 w	1.4 w	0.8 w	0.6 w	8 w	9 w	119 w	125 w
Middle East & N. Africa	175 t	272 t	383 t	3.0 w	2.3 w	0.9 w	0.8 w	5 w	6 w	99 w	102 w
South Asia	903 t	1,243 t	1,572 t	2.1 w	1.6 w	0.8 w	0.7 w	7 w	8 w	99 w	104 w
Sub-Saharan Africa	381 t	583 t	860 t	2.8 w	2.6 w	0.9 w	0.9 w	5 w	5 w	122 w	120 w
High income	816 t	902 t	963 t	0.7 w	0.4 w	0.5 w	0.5 w	18 w	22 w	133 w	125 w

Population and development

Population growth rates have started to decline in many countries, but the absolute numbers continue to increase, and more people will be added to the world's population in the 1990s than in any previous decade. The world's population was estimated to be 5.7 billion in mid-1995—and growing by 230,000 people a day.

Sub-Saharan Africa is projected to grow at 2.6 percent a year, Europe at a barely noticeable 0.1 percent a year. Such regional disparities will gradually change the relative distribution of people, with fast-growing continents dramatically increasing their share of the global population.

In low-income economies more than a third of the population is under age 15, compared with less than a fifth in high-income economies. In high-income economies there are roughly two people of working age to support each person who is either too young or too old to work. In low-income economies this ratio is

Nine of every 10 people added to the world's population over the next 15 years will be in developing economies ●

around 1.5 to 1 because of the large population under 15. But the transition to lower population growth also poses social and economic problems. As growth slows, the average age of the population rises, and the proportion of elderly people eventually increases. Many low-growth economies already face crises in their pension and social security systems.

About the data

Population estimates are based on national censuses. Precensus and postcensus estimates are interpolations or projections. The international comparability of population indicators is limited by differences in the concepts, definitions, data collection procedures, and estimation methods used by national statistical agencies and other organizations that collect the data. In addition, the frequency and quality of coverage of population censuses vary by country and region.

Of the 148 economies here, 117 conducted a census between 1987 and 1995. The proportion is 80 percent for high-income countries and 86 percent for low- and middle-income countries. The recentness of a census, along with the availability of complementary data from surveys or registration systems, is one of the many objective means for judging the quality of demographic data (see *Primary data documentation* for the most recent census or survey year and for registration completion status).

For developing countries that lack recent census-based population data, population figures are estimates provided by national statistical offices or the United Nations Population Division. Population projections require fertility, mortality, and net migration estimates based on demographic data collected from sample surveys, some of which may be small in size or have limited coverage. These estimates are the product of demographic modeling and are susceptible to biases and errors due to shortcomings of the model and the data.

The governmental and political climate also affects the quality of official demographic data. The trust and cooperation of the public, the government's commitment to full and accurate enumeration, the confidentiality and protection against misuse accorded to census data, and the independence of census agencies from unreasonable political influence all affect the quality and reliability of the data.

The population projections here are based on World Bank staff estimates using the cohort component method. Mortality, fertility, and net migration are projected separately by age-sex group and applied to the 1990 base year age-sex structure. For countries in which fertility has begun to decline to replacement level (countries making the "fertility transition"), this trend is assumed to continue. For countries in which this event has not yet occurred, the current fertility rate is assumed to decline at the average rate of countries making the fertility transition. Countries with below-replacement fertility are assumed to have constant fertility rates in 1995–2000 and to regain replacement fertility by 2030.

Definitions

● **Total population** is based on the de facto definition of population, which counts all residents regardless of legal status or citizenship. Refugees not permanently settled in the country of asylum are generally considered to be part of the population of their country of origin. The indicators shown are midyear estimates for 1980 and 1995 and projections for 2010. ● **Average annual growth rate** is calculated as the exponential change for the period indicated. See *Statistical methods* for more information. ● **Age dependency ratio** is calculated as the ratio of dependents—the population under age 15 and above age 65—to the working-age population—those aged 15–64. ● **Population aged 60 and above** represents the proportion of the population that is aged 60 and above. ● **Women per 100 men aged 60 and above** is the ratio of women to men in that age group.

Data sources

Population estimates are produced by the World Bank's Human Development and International Economics Departments in consultation with World Bank country departments. Important inputs to the World Bank's demographic work come from the following sources:

● Population censuses.

● United Nations Department of Economic and Social Information and Policy Analysis, *World Population Prospects: The 1996 Edition* and *Population and Vital Statistics Report*.

● Eurostat, *Demographic Statistics*.

● Council of Europe, *Recent Demographic Developments in Europe and North America* (1995).

● U.S. Bureau of the Census, *World Population Profile 1996*.

● Projections are based on the method discussed in Bos and others, *World Population Projections 1994–95*.

2.2 | Population dynamics

	Crude death rate		Crude birth rate		Total fertility rate		Contraceptive prevalence rate	Population momentum
	per 1,000 people		per 1,000 people		births per woman		% of women 15–49	
	1980	1995	1980	1995	1980	1995	1989–95	1995
Albania	6	6	29	21	3.6	2.6	..	1.5
Algeria	12	5	42	26	6.7	3.5	51	1.6
Angola	23	19	50	49	6.9	6.9	..	1.5
Argentina	9	8	24	20	3.3	2.7	..	1.4
Armenia	6	7	23	14	2.3	1.8	..	1.3
Australia	7	7	15	15	1.9	1.9	..	1.2
Austria	12	10	12	11	1.6	1.5	..	1.0
Azerbaijan	7	7	25	21	3.2	2.3	..	1.4
Bangladesh	18	10	44	28	6.1	3.5	45	1.6
Belarus	10	12	16	11	2.0	1.4	..	1.1
Belgium	12	11	13	12	1.7	1.6	..	1.0
Benin	19	15	49	43	6.5	6.0	..	1.6
Bolivia	15	10	39	35	5.5	4.5	45	1.6
Bosnia and Herzegovina	..	..	..	..	..	..	..	..
Botswana	14	12	48	34	6.7	4.4	..	1.7
Brazil	9	7	31	21	3.9	2.4	..	1.5
Bulgaria	11	13	15	10	2.1	1.2	..	1.0
Burkina Faso	20	18	47	46	7.5	6.7	8	1.5
Burundi	18	17	46	44	6.8	6.5	..	1.5
Cambodia	27	13	39	40	4.7	4.7	..	1.5
Cameroon	15	11	47	41	6.5	5.7	16	1.5
Canada	7	7	15	13	1.7	1.7	..	1.1
Central African Republic	19	17	43	38	5.8	5.1	15	1.4
Chad	22	18	44	43	5.9	5.9	..	1.4
Chile	7	6	24	20	2.8	2.3	..	1.4
China	6	7	18	17	2.5	1.9	83	1.3
Colombia	7	7	30	23	3.8	2.8	72	1.5
Congo	16	16	46	47	6.2	6.0	..	1.5
Costa Rica	4	4	30	25	3.7	2.8	75	1.7
Côte d'Ivoire	16	12	51	37	7.4	5.3	11	1.6
Croatia	..	11	..	11	..	1.5	..	1.0
Cuba	6	7	14	14	2.0	1.7	..	1.3
Czech Republic	13	11	15	10	2.1	1.3	69	1.0
Denmark	11	12	11	13	1.5	1.8	..	1.0
Dominican Republic	7	5	33	24	4.2	2.9	56	1.6
Ecuador	9	6	36	27	5.0	3.2	57	1.6
Egypt, Arab Rep.	13	8	39	26	5.1	3.4	47	1.5
El Salvador	11	6	39	30	5.3	3.7	53	1.7
Eritrea	..	..	..	..	..	..	..	..
Estonia	12	14	15	10	2.0	1.3	..	1.0
Ethiopia	20	17	47	47	6.6	7.0	4	1.5
Finland	9	10	13	13	1.6	1.8	..	1.0
France	10	9	15	12	1.9	1.7	..	1.1
Gabon	18	15	33	39	4.5	5.2	..	1.4
Gambia, The	24	18	48	41	6.5	5.3	12	1.4
Georgia	9	9	18	11	2.3	1.9	..	1.1
Germany	12	11	11	9	1.6	1.2	..	0.9
Ghana	15	10	45	37	6.5	5.1	20	1.6
Greece	9	9	15	10	2.2	1.4	..	1.1
Guatemala	11	7	43	35	6.2	4.7	31	1.7
Guinea	24	20	46	48	6.1	6.5	..	1.4
Guinea-Bissau	25	25	43	45	6.0	6.0	..	1.3
Haiti	15	12	37	35	5.9	4.4	18	1.5
Honduras	10	6	43	35	6.5	4.6	47	1.7
Hong Kong	5	5	17	11	2.0	1.2	..	1.1

Population momentum

Over the next several decades the populations of low- and middle-income countries will continue to grow. The rates of growth will decline, but the absolute increases will be large—and accompanied by substantial shifts in the age structure. Even when fertility reaches the replacement level of about two children per couple, the number of births will remain high—and population growth will not stop for several decades. This phenomenon, called "population momentum," is a facet of the youthful age structures typical of populations of developing countries. It occurs because large cohorts born in previous years move through the reproductive ages, generating more births than are offset by deaths in the smaller, older cohorts. Here population momentum is measured as the ratio of the population when zero growth has been achieved to the population in 1995, assuming that fertility is at replacement level in 1995 and remains at that level.

Because of population momentum, the full effect of lower fertility on the growth and age structure of a population takes several decades to be felt. As the population pyramids for low-income countries show, before the smaller birth cohorts born recently make their way through the age structures, the larger birth cohorts from the past will mean large increases in the number of women of reproductive age (figure 2.2a). In high-income countries, where fertility rates are well below replacement level and age structures are older, population will increase much less.

A longer-term effect of momentum is the large increase in absolute population size projected for developing regions during the next century. In China, where replacement fertility was reached around 1990, the population is expected to grow by another 400 million people before stabilizing. In India the combination of above-replacement fertility and momentum is projected to double its current population, which will surpass China's in 50 years.

In low- and middle-income economies slightly more than 85 percent of the projected increase between 1995 and 2035 is from population momentum and mortality decline—and the rest, from fertility above

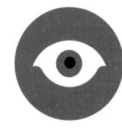

	Crude death rate		Crude birth rate		Total fertility rate		Contraceptive prevalence rate	Population momentum
	per 1,000 people		per 1,000 people		births per woman		% of women 15–49	
	1980	1995	1980	1995	1980	1995	1989–95	1995
Hungary	14	14	14	11	1.9	1.6	..	1.0
India	13	9	35	26	5.0	3.2	43	1.4
Indonesia	12	8	34	23	4.3	2.7	55	1.4
Iran, Islamic Rep.	11	6	44	32	6.1	4.5	..	1.7
Iraq	9	8	41	38	6.4	5.4	..	1.7
Ireland	10	9	22	14	3.2	1.9	60	1.3
Israel	7	6	24	20	3.2	2.4	..	1.5
Italy	10	10	11	9	1.6	1.2	..	1.0
Jamaica	7	6	28	22	3.7	2.4	67	1.6
Japan	6	7	14	10	1.8	1.5	..	1.0
Jordan	..	5	..	31	6.8	4.8	35	1.8
Kazakstan	8	9	24	18	2.9	2.3	59	1.3
Kenya	13	9	51	35	7.8	4.7	33	1.7
Korea, Dem. Rep.	6	6	22	22	3.0	2.2	..	1.4
Korea, Rep.	6	6	22	16	2.6	1.8	79	1.2
Kuwait	4	3	37	22	5.3	3.0	..	1.5
Kyrgyz Republic	9	8	30	25	4.1	3.3	..	1.5
Lao PDR	20	14	45	44	6.7	6.5	..	1.5
Latvia	13	16	15	9	2.0	1.3	..	0.9
Lebanon	9	8	30	26	4.0	2.8	..	1.5
Lesotho	15	11	41	33	5.6	4.6	23	1.5
Libya	12	7	46	41	7.3	6.1	..	1.7
Lithuania	10	12	16	11	2.0	1.5	..	1.0
Macedonia, FYR	7	7	21	16	2.5	2.2	..	1.2
Madagascar	16	11	46	41	6.5	5.8	17	1.5
Malawi	23	20	57	47	7.6	6.6	13	1.5
Malaysia	6	5	31	26	4.2	3.4	..	1.6
Mali	22	17	49	49	7.1	6.8	..	1.6
Mauritania	19	14	43	38	6.3	5.2	4	1.5
Mauritius	6	7	24	19	2.7	2.2	75	1.3
Mexico	7	5	33	26	4.5	3.0	..	1.7
Moldova	10	11	20	14	2.4	2.0	..	1.2
Mongolia	11	7	38	27	5.4	3.4	..	1.6
Morocco	12	7	38	27	5.4	3.4	50	1.6
Mozambique	20	18	46	44	6.5	6.2	..	1.5
Myanmar	14	10	36	28	5.1	3.4	..	1.5
Namibia	14	12	41	37	5.9	5.0	29	1.5
Nepal	18	12	44	36	6.4	5.3	23	1.4
Netherlands	8	9	13	12	1.6	1.6	..	1.0
New Zealand	9	8	16	16	2.1	2.1	..	1.2
Nicaragua	11	6	45	33	6.2	4.1	44	1.8
Niger	23	19	51	52	7.4	7.4	4	1.5
Nigeria	18	13	50	42	6.9	5.5	6	1.6
Norway	10	10	12	14	1.7	1.9	..	1.1
Oman	10	4	45	44	9.9	7.0	0	1.7
Pakistan	15	8	47	38	7.0	5.2	12	1.6
Panama	6	5	29	23	3.7	2.7	..	1.6
Papua New Guinea	14	10	37	33	5.7	4.8	..	1.4
Paraguay	7	5	36	31	4.8	4.0	48	1.6
Peru	11	6	35	26	4.5	3.1	59	1.5
Philippines	9	7	35	29	4.8	3.7	40	1.5
Poland	10	10	19	13	2.3	1.6	..	1.1
Portugal	10	10	16	11	2.2	1.4	..	1.1
Puerto Rico	6	8	23	17	2.6	2.1	..	1.3
Romania	10	12	18	11	2.4	1.4	57	1.1
Russian Federation	11	15	16	9	1.9	1.4	..	1.0

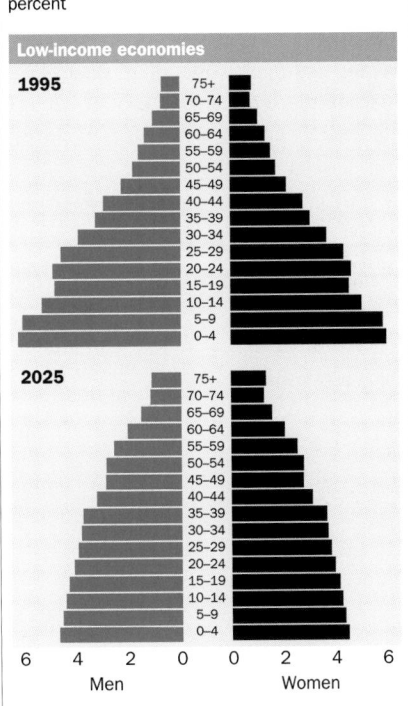

Figure 2.2a Composition of population by age and sex in low- and high-income economies, 1995 and 2025

percent

Low-income economies

1995

2025

| 6 | 4 | 2 | 0 | 0 | 2 | 4 | 6 |

Men | Women

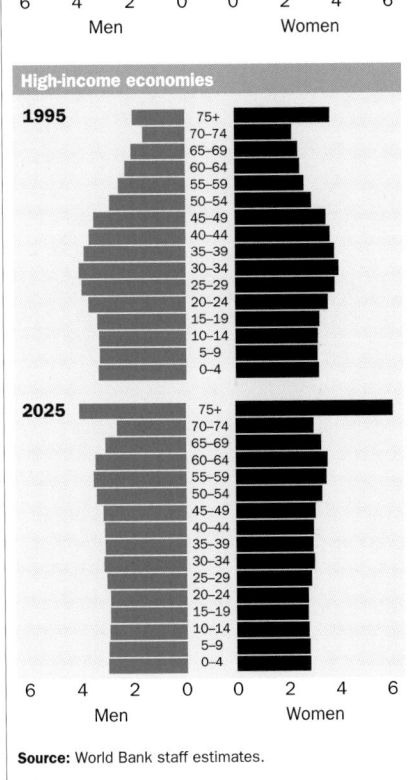

High-income economies

1995

2025

| 6 | 4 | 2 | 0 | 0 | 2 | 4 | 6 |

Men | Women

Source: World Bank staff estimates.

	Crude death rate		Crude birth rate		Total fertility rate		Contraceptive prevalence rate	Population momentum
	per 1,000 people		per 1,000 people		births per woman		% of women 15–49	
	1980	1995	1980	1995	1980	1995	1989–95	1995
Rwanda	19	22	51	41	8.3	6.2	21	1.5
Saudi Arabia	9	5	43	36	7.3	6.2	..	1.6
Senegal	20	14	46	40	6.7	5.7	7	1.4
Sierra Leone	29	29	49	48	6.5	6.5	..	1.4
Singapore	5	5	17	16	1.7	1.7	..	1.2
Slovak Republic	10	10	19	12	2.3	1.5	..	1.1
Slovenia	10	10	15	10	2.1	1.3	..	1.0
South Africa	12	8	36	30	4.9	3.9	..	1.5
Spain	8	9	15	10	2.2	1.2	..	1.1
Sri Lanka	6	6	28	19	3.5	2.3	..	1.4
Sudan	17	12	45	35	6.5	4.8	9	1.5
Sweden	11	10	12	13	1.7	1.7	..	1.1
Switzerland	9	9	12	12	1.6	1.5	..	1.0
Syrian Arab Republic	9	5	46	39	7.4	4.8	..	1.8
Tajikistan	8	7	37	28	5.6	4.2	..	1.7
Tanzania	15	14	47	42	6.7	5.8	20	1.5
Thailand	8	6	28	17	3.5	1.8	..	1.4
Togo	16	15	45	44	6.6	6.4	..	1.6
Trinidad and Tobago	7	6	29	19	3.3	2.1	..	1.4
Tunisia	9	6	35	24	5.2	2.9	..	1.5
Turkey	10	7	32	23	4.3	2.7	63	1.5
Turkmenistan	8	7	34	31	4.9	3.8	..	1.6
Uganda	18	19	49	49	7.2	6.7	..	1.5
Ukraine	11	14	15	10	2.0	1.5	..	1.0
United Arab Emirates	5	3	30	20	5.4	3.6	..	1.2
United Kingdom	12	11	13	13	1.9	1.7	..	1.0
United States	9	8	16	15	1.8	2.1	..	1.2
Uruguay	10	10	19	16	2.7	2.2	..	1.2
Uzbekistan	8	6	34	29	4.8	3.7	..	1.7
Venezuela	6	5	33	25	4.1	3.1	..	1.6
Vietnam	8	7	36	26	5.0	3.1	49	1.6
West Bank and Gaza	..	6	..	45	..	6.2	..	..
Yemen, Rep.	19	13	53	48	7.9	7.4	10	1.6
Yugoslavia, Fed. Rep.	10	10	18	14	2.3	1.9	..	1.1
Zaire	17	..	48	..	6.6	..	..	1.6
Zambia	15	18	50	45	7.0	5.7	15	1.5
Zimbabwe	13	10	49	31	6.8	3.8	48	1.6

World	12 w	9 w	27 w	23 w	3.7 w	2.9 w		1.4 w
Low income	13 w	10 w	31 w	26 w	4.3 w	3.2 w		1.4 w
Excl. China & India	17 w	13 w	45 w	37 w	6.3 w	5.0 w		1.5 w
Middle income	10 w	8 w	29 w	22 w	3.8 w	3.0 w		1.4 w
Lower middle income	10 w	8 w	28 w	22 w	3.7 w	3.0 w		1.4 w
Upper middle income	9 w	7 w	30 w	23 w	3.9 w	2.9 w		1.5 w
Low & middle income	12 w	9 w	30 w	25 w	4.1 w	3.1 w		1.4 w
East Asia & Pacific	8 w	7 w	22 w	19 w	3.1 w	2.2 w		1.3 w
Europe & Central Asia	10 w	11 w	20 w	14 w	2.5 w	2.0 w		1.1 w
Latin America & Carib.	8 w	7 w	31 w	24 w	4.1 w	2.8 w		1.5 w
Middle East & N. Africa	12 w	7 w	41 w	32 w	6.1 w	4.2 w		1.6 w
South Asia	14 w	9 w	37 w	28 w	5.3 w	3.5 w		1.4 w
Sub-Saharan Africa	18 w	15 w	47 w	41 w	6.7 w	5.7 w		1.5 w
High income	9 w	8 w	15 w	13 w	1.9 w	1.7 w		1.1 w

replacement level (figure 2.2b). Regional disparities among developing countries remain. Slightly less than half the increase in population growth in Sub-Saharan Africa is from high fertility (figure 2.2c), compared with only 7 percent in Asia (figure 2.2d).

In Europe and Central Asia fertility is below replacement level. In that region the increase

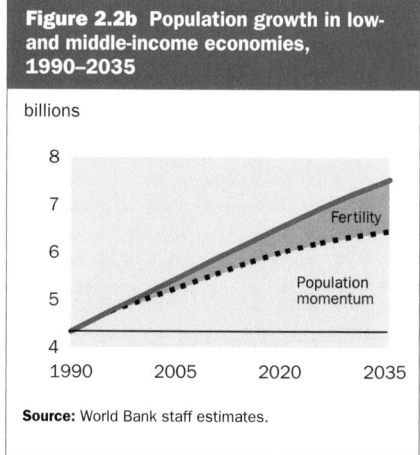

Figure 2.2b Population growth in low- and middle-income economies, 1990–2035

Source: World Bank staff estimates.

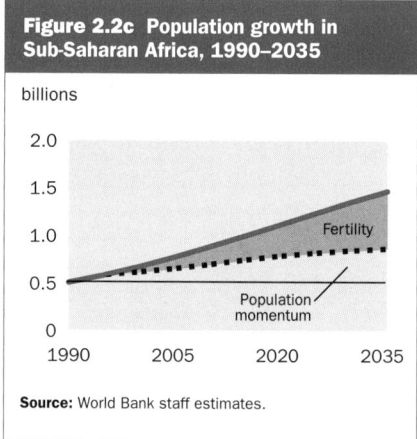

Figure 2.2c Population growth in Sub-Saharan Africa, 1990–2035

Source: World Bank staff estimates.

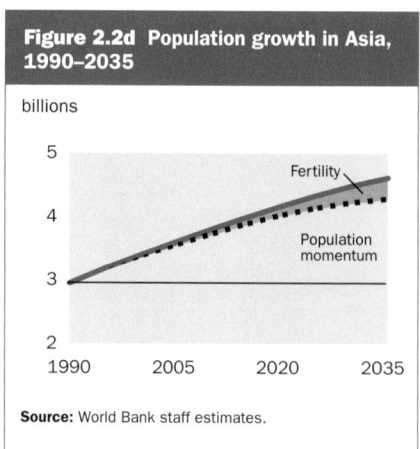

Figure 2.2d Population growth in Asia, 1990–2035

Source: World Bank staff estimates.

in population results from the dynamics of the current age structure, which produces more births than deaths (figure 2.2g).

Population dynamics indicators, or vital rates, are based on data derived from registration systems, censuses, and sample surveys conducted by national statistical offices. As with the basic demographic data in table 2.1, international comparisons are limited by differences in definitions, data collection, and estimation methods.

Registration systems in many developing countries in Africa, Asia, and Latin America are incomplete because of deficiencies in geographic coverage, in coverage of population groups, or both. For these countries vital rates are estimated by applying various estimation techniques to incomplete vital registration data or to data from demographic surveys.

The crude death, crude birth, and total fertility rates for 1995 are often based on projections from censuses or surveys from earlier years (see *Primary data documentation* for the most recent census or survey year and registration completion status). Contraceptive prevalence rates are obtained mainly from demographic and health surveys and contraceptive prevalence surveys (see *Primary data documentation* for the most recent survey year).

● **Crude death rate** and **crude birth rate** indicate the number of deaths and the number of live births occurring during the year, per 1,000 midyear population. The difference between the crude death and birth rates is the rate of natural increase. ● **Total fertility rate** represents the number of children that would be born to a woman if she were to live to the end of her childbearing years and bear children in accordance with prevailing age-specific fertility rates. ● **Contraceptive prevalence rate** is the percentage of women who are practicing, or whose sexual partners are practicing, any form of contraception and is usually measured for women aged 15–49. ● **Population momentum** is measured as the ratio of the population when zero growth has been achieved to the population in year t, given the assumption that fertility remains at replacement level from year t onward.

Vital rates estimates are produced by the World Bank's Human Development and International Economics Departments in consultation with World Bank country departments. Important inputs come from the following sources:

- Population censuses.
- Eurostat, *Demographic Statistics*.
- United Nations Department of Economic and Social Information and Policy Analysis, *World Population Prospects: The 1996 Edition* and *Population and Vital Statistics Report*.
- Demographic and health surveys from national sources.

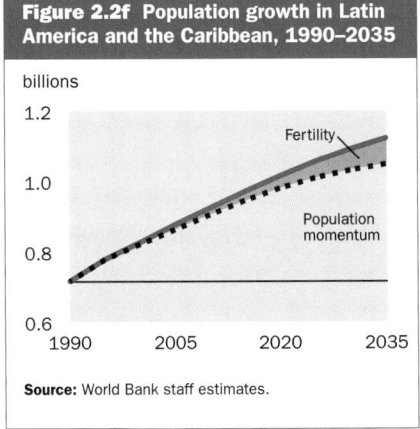

Figure 2.2e Population growth in the Middle East and North Africa, 1990–2035

billions

Source: World Bank staff estimates.

Figure 2.2f Population growth in Latin America and the Caribbean, 1990–2035

billions

Source: World Bank staff estimates.

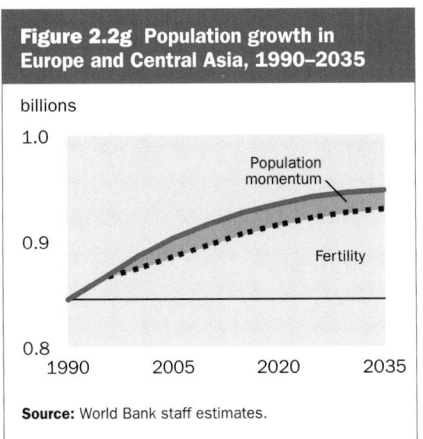

Figure 2.2g Population growth in Europe and Central Asia, 1990–2035

billions

Source: World Bank staff estimates.

2.3 | Labor force structure

	Population aged 15–64		Labor force								
	millions		Total millions			Average annual growth rate %		Female % of labor force		Children 10–14 % of age group	
	1980	1995	1980	1995	2010	1980–95	1995–2010	1980	1995	1980	1995
Albania	2	2	1	2	2	2.0	1.3	39	41	4	1
Algeria	9	16	5	9	15	3.8	3.7	21	24	7	2
Angola	4	5	3	5	8	2.4	2.9	47	46	30	27
Argentina	17	21	11	14	18	1.6	2.0	28	31	8	5
Armenia	2	2	1	2	2	1.4	1.3	48	48	0	0
Australia	10	12	7	9	10	2.0	0.9	37	43	0	0
Austria	5	5	3	4	4	0.5	0.0	40	41	0	0
Azerbaijan	4	5	3	3	4	1.2	1.9	47	44	0	0
Bangladesh	44	64	41	60	81	2.5	2.0	42	42	35	30
Belarus	6	7	5	5	6	0.4	0.3	50	49	0	0
Belgium	6	7	4	4	4	0.3	–0.1	34	40	0	0
Benin	2	3	2	2	4	2.7	2.6	47	48	30	28
Bolivia	3	4	2	3	4	2.6	2.6	33	37	19	14
Bosnia and Herzegovina	..	..	2	2	2	1.6	0.5	33	38	1	0
Botswana	0	1	0	1	1	3.1	2.1	50	46	26	17
Brazil	71	101	48	71	87	2.6	1.3	28	35	19	16
Bulgaria	6	6	5	4	4	–0.4	–0.5	45	48	0	0
Burkina Faso	4	5	4	5	8	2.0	2.2	48	47	71	51
Burundi	2	3	2	3	5	2.6	2.9	50	49	50	49
Cambodia	3	5	3	5	7	2.7	2.5	56	53	27	25
Cameroon	5	7	4	5	9	2.6	3.1	37	38	34	25
Canada	17	20	12	15	17	1.6	0.5	40	45	0	0
Central African Republic	..	2	1	2	2	1.7	1.9	48	47	39	31
Chad	2	3	2	3	5	2.3	2.5	43	44	42	38
Chile	7	9	4	6	8	2.5	2.0	26	32	0	0
China	586	811	539	709	802	1.8	0.8	43	45	30	12
Colombia	16	22	9	16	22	3.5	2.2	26	37	12	7
Congo	1	1	1	1	2	2.9	2.8	43	43	27	26
Costa Rica	1	2	1	1	2	3.4	2.1	21	30	10	5
Côte d'Ivoire	4	7	3	5	7	2.8	2.2	32	33	28	20
Croatia	3	3	2	2	2	0.2	0.0	40	43	0	0
Cuba	6	8	4	5	6	2.2	1.0	31	38	0	0
Czech Republic	6	7	5	6	5	0.3	–0.1	47	47	0	0
Denmark	3	4	3	3	3	0.5	–0.3	44	46	0	0
Dominican Republic	3	5	2	3	5	2.9	2.2	25	29	25	16
Ecuador	4	7	3	4	6	3.4	2.8	20	26	9	5
Egypt, Arab Rep.	23	34	14	21	31	2.5	2.6	26	29	18	11
El Salvador	2	3	2	2	3	2.3	3.1	26	34	17	15
Eritrea	..	..	1	2	3	2.6	3.0	47	47	44	40
Estonia	1	1	1	1	1	0.0	–0.5	51	49	0	0
Ethiopia	19	28	17	25	38	2.7	2.7	42	41	46	42
Finland	3	3	2	3	2	0.5	–0.3	46	48	0	0
France	34	38	24	26	27	0.5	0.4	40	44	0	0
Gabon	0	1	0	1	1	2.0	1.8	45	44	29	18
Gambia, The	0	1	0	1	1	3.4	2.4	45	45	44	37
Georgia	3	4	3	3	3	0.3	0.3	49	46	0	0
Germany	52	56	37	40	41	0.5	0.1	40	42	0	0
Ghana	6	9	5	8	12	3.0	2.7	51	51	16	13
Greece	6	7	4	4	5	1.1	0.5	29	36	5	0
Guatemala	4	6	2	4	6	3.1	3.4	22	26	19	16
Guinea	2	3	2	3	5	2.2	2.7	47	47	41	34
Guinea-Bissau	0	1	0	1	1	1.5	2.1	40	40	43	39
Haiti	3	4	3	3	4	1.4	1.4	45	43	33	25
Honduras	2	3	1	2	4	3.6	3.6	25	30	14	9
Hong Kong	3	4	2	3	3	1.5	0.6	34	37	6	0

	Population aged 15–64			Labor force								
	millions			Total millions			Average annual growth rate %		Female % of labor force		Children 10–14 % of age group	
	1980	1995		1980	1995	2010	1980–95	1995–2010	1980	1995	1980	1995
Hungary	7	7		5	5	5	–0.5	–0.3	43	44	0	0
India	394	562		300	398	518	1.9	1.7	34	32	21	14
Indonesia	83	120		59	89	123	2.8	2.2	35	40	13	10
Iran, Islamic Rep.	20	34		12	19	35	3.3	3.9	20	24	14	5
Iraq	7	11		4	5	9	2.8	3.6	17	18	11	3
Ireland	2	2		1	1	2	0.8	1.3	28	33	1	0
Israel	2	3		1	2	3	2.7	2.5	34	40	0	0
Italy	36	39		23	25	25	0.7	–0.1	33	38	2	0
Jamaica	1	2		1	1	2	2.0	1.6	46	46	0	0
Japan	79	87		57	66	67	1.0	0.1	38	41	0	0
Jordan	1	2		1	1	2	5.0	3.9	15	21	4	1
Kazakstan	9	10		7	8	9	0.9	1.0	48	47	0	0
Kenya	8	14		8	13	19	3.3	2.5	46	46	45	41
Korea, Dem. Rep.	10	16		8	12	15	2.8	1.5	45	45	3	0
Korea, Rep.	24	32		16	22	26	2.2	1.3	39	40	0	0
Kuwait	1	1		0	1	1	3.3	2.1	13	28	0	0
Kyrgyz Republic	2	3		2	2	3	1.5	1.8	48	47	0	0
Lao PDR	2	3		2	2	4	2.5	3.0	45	47	31	27
Latvia	2	2		1	1	1	–0.2	–0.6	51	50	0	0
Lebanon	2	2		1	1	2	3.3	2.7	23	28	5	0
Lesotho	1	1		1	1	1	2.3	2.4	38	37	28	22
Libya	2	3		1	2	3	3.3	3.5	18	21	9	0
Lithuania	2	2		2	2	2	0.4	–0.1	50	48	0	0
Macedonia, FYR	1	1		1	1	1	1.2	1.0	36	41	1	0
Madagascar	5	7		4	6	10	2.7	3.0	45	45	40	36
Malawi	3	5		3	5	7	2.8	2.4	51	49	45	35
Malaysia	8	12		5	8	12	2.8	2.7	34	37	8	3
Mali	3	5		3	5	8	2.4	2.9	47	46	61	55
Mauritania	1	1		1	1	2	2.2	2.5	45	44	30	24
Mauritius	1	1		0	0	1	2.1	1.3	26	32	5	3
Mexico	35	55		22	36	52	3.2	2.5	27	31	9	7
Moldova	3	3		2	2	2	0.2	0.5	38	42	3	0
Mongolia	1	1		1	1	2	3.0	2.5	46	46	4	2
Morocco	10	16		7	10	15	2.6	2.5	34	35	21	6
Mozambique	6	8		7	8	12	1.6	2.4	49	48	39	34
Myanmar	19	27		17	23	30	2.0	1.8	44	43	28	25
Namibia	1	1		0	1	1	2.4	2.5	40	41	34	22
Nepal	8	12		7	10	14	2.4	2.4	38	40	56	45
Netherlands	9	11		6	7	7	1.5	0.1	31	40	0	0
New Zealand	2	2		1	2	2	1.9	1.1	34	44	0	0
Nicaragua	1	2		1	2	3	3.3	3.6	29	36	19	14
Niger	3	4		3	4	7	3.0	3.2	45	44	48	45
Nigeria	38	58		30	44	67	2.7	2.8	36	36	29	26
Norway	3	3		2	2	2	0.9	0.3	40	46	0	0
Oman	1	1		0	1	1	4.0	4.6	7	15	6	1
Pakistan	44	70		29	46	77	3.1	3.4	23	26	23	18
Panama	1	2		1	1	1	2.9	2.1	30	34	6	4
Papua New Guinea	2	2		2	2	3	2.2	2.1	42	42	28	19
Paraguay	2	3		1	2	3	2.9	2.8	27	29	15	8
Peru	9	14		5	9	13	3.1	2.7	24	29	4	2
Philippines	27	40		19	28	41	2.7	2.5	35	37	14	8
Poland	19	26		19	19	21	0.3	0.4	45	46	0	0
Portugal	6	7		5	5	5	0.4	0.2	39	43	8	2
Puerto Rico	2	2		1	1	2	1.8	1.5	32	36	0	0
Romania	14	15		11	11	11	–0.1	0.1	46	44	0	0
Russian Federation	95	99		76	77	79	0.1	0.1	49	49	0	0

	Population aged 15–64 millions		Labor force									
			Total millions			Average annual growth rate %		Female % of labor force		Children 10–14 % of age group	
	1980	1995	1980	1995	2010	1980–95	1995–2010	1980	1995	1980	1995
Rwanda	3	3	3	4	6	2.8	2.7	49	49	43	42
Saudi Arabia	5	10	3	6	10	5.4	3.4	8	13	5	0
Senegal	3	4	3	4	6	2.7	2.6	42	42	43	31
Sierra Leone	2	2	1	2	2	1.9	2.5	36	36	19	15
Singapore	2	2	1	1	2	2.1	1.0	35	38	2	0
Slovak Republic	3	4	2	3	3	0.8	0.3	45	48	0	0
Slovenia	1	1	1	1	1	0.3	−0.2	46	46	0	0
South Africa	16	24	11	16	23	2.6	2.3	35	37	1	0
Spain	23	27	14	17	18	1.2	0.4	28	36	0	0
Sri Lanka	9	12	5	8	10	2.2	1.8	27	35	4	2
Sudan	10	14	7	10	15	2.5	2.6	27	28	33	29
Sweden	5	6	4	5	5	0.8	0.0	44	48	0	0
Switzerland	4	5	3	4	4	1.3	0.2	37	40	0	0
Syrian Arab Republic	4	7	2	4	7	3.2	3.6	23	26	14	6
Tajikistan	2	3	2	2	3	2.2	2.9	47	44	0	0
Tanzania	9	15	10	15	23	3.1	2.7	50	49	43	39
Thailand	26	39	24	34	38	2.2	0.8	47	46	25	16
Togo	1	2	1	2	3	2.6	2.9	39	40	36	29
Trinidad and Tobago	1	1	0	1	1	1.4	2.0	32	36	1	0
Tunisia	3	5	2	3	5	2.8	2.7	29	30	6	0
Turkey	25	38	19	28	37	2.6	2.0	35	35	21	24
Turkmenistan	2	3	1	2	3	2.9	3.4	47	45	0	0
Uganda	6	9	7	9	14	2.4	2.7	48	48	49	45
Ukraine	33	34	26	26	26	−0.2	−0.1	50	49	0	0
United Arab Emirates	1	2	1	1	2	4.7	2.1	5	13	0	0
United Kingdom	36	38	27	29	30	0.5	0.2	39	43	0	0
United States	151	172	110	133	152	1.3	0.9	42	46	0	0
Uruguay	2	2	1	1	2	1.4	1.0	31	40	4	2
Uzbekistan	9	12	6	9	14	2.4	2.9	48	46	0	0
Venezuela	8	13	5	8	13	3.3	2.7	27	33	4	1
Vietnam	28	43	26	37	48	2.4	1.7	48	49	22	9
West Bank and Gaza	..	1	..	..	..	..	..	..	..	..	..
Yemen, Rep.	4	8	2	5	9	4.1	4.2	33	29	26	20
Yugoslavia, Fed. Rep.	6	7	4	5	5	0.9	0.3	38	42	0	0
Zaire	14	22	12	18	30	2.9	3.3	45	44	33	30
Zambia	3	5	2	4	6	3.0	2.6	45	45	19	16
Zimbabwe	3	6	3	5	7	3.1	2.1	44	44	37	29
World	**2,590 t**	**3,521 t**	**2,037 t**	**2,695 t**	**3,365 t**	**1.9 w**	**1.5 w**	**38 w**	**40 w**	**21 w**	**14 w**
Low income	1,352 t	1,934 t	1,156 t	1,575 t	2,005 t	2.1 w	1.6 w	40 w	41 w	28 w	19 w
Excl. China & India	371 t	563 t	317 t	467 t	685 t	2.6 w	2.5 w	40 w	41 w	33 w	28 w
Middle income	717 t	981 t	513 t	688 t	895 t	2.0 w	1.7 w	36 w	38 w	13 w	8 w
Lower middle income	527 t	712 t	387 t	507 t	657 t	1.8 w	1.7 w	38 w	40 w	13 w	8 w
Upper middle income	191 t	269 t	126 t	182 t	238 t	2.4 w	1.8 w	29 w	34 w	11 w	8 w
Low & middle income	2,069 t	2,916 t	1,669 t	2,263 t	2,899 t	2.0 w	1.7 w	38 w	40 w	24 w	16 w
East Asia & Pacific	796 t	1,119 t	704 t	951 t	1,126 t	2.0 w	1.1 w	43 w	45 w	25 w	11 w
Europe & Central Asia	277 t	317 t	219 t	238 t	262 t	0.6 w	0.6 w	46 w	46 w	10 w	11 w
Latin America & Carib.	201 t	293 t	130 t	197 t	266 t	2.8 w	2.0 w	27 w	33 w	13 w	10 w
Middle East & N. Africa	91 t	151 t	54 t	88 t	144 t	3.2 w	3.3 w	24 w	26 w	13 w	5 w
South Asia	508 t	732 t	389 t	532 t	716 t	2.1 w	2.0 w	34 w	33 w	24 w	17 w
Sub-Saharan Africa	196 t	305 t	173 t	257 t	385 t	2.7 w	2.7 w	42 w	42 w	35 w	30 w
High income	522 t	605 t	368 t	432 t	465 t	1.1 w	0.5 w	39 w	42 w	0 w	0 w

Who is in the labor force?

The labor force includes both people who are currently employed and those who are unemployed. In practice, it is difficult to count the unemployed accurately, especially in developing countries. And it may be just as difficult to know who is fully employed.

According to the International Labour Organisation (ILO) definition, the unemployed are those "without work but available for and seeking work." Countries with unemployment insurance systems often base estimates of unemployment on those who file claims and thus certify that they are seeking work. But these systems do not count discouraged workers who have given up their job search because they believe that no employment opportunities exist or do not register as unemployed after their benefits have been exhausted. In developing economies rural women may not be counted as part of the labor force during seasons of low agricultural activity.

Some unemployment—often called "frictional unemployment"—occurs in all economies as a result of the normal operation of labor markets. At any time, some workers are temporarily unemployed—between jobs as employers look for the right workers and workers search for better jobs. In countries without unemployment insurance or other forms of social assistance, it may not be feasible to remain without work for a prolonged period. Instead, people find some form of work, often in informal or unrecorded activities.

Taking into account the underemployed—those engaged for only a few hours a week or employed in jobs requiring lower qualifications than they have—would yield a higher estimate of labor underutilization. Household surveys that examine unemployment and underemployment confirm that unemployment figures alone may seriously underestimate the underutilization of labor (table 2.3a).

Table 2.3a Unemployment and underemployment in three countries

percentage of the labor force

Country	Year	Un-employed	Dis-couraged workers	Under-employed
Ghana	1988–89	1.6	1.5	24.1
Ukraine	1994	0.4	..	14.5
Vietnam	1992–93	1.3	3.5	10.0

Source: World Bank 1995g.

About the data

Data on the labor force, or economically active population, are collected by the ILO from the latest census or survey of countries.

Despite the efforts of the ILO to encourage the use of international standards, labor force and employment and unemployment data are not fully comparable because of differences among economies, and sometimes within economies, in definitions (for example, daily or weekly rates) and coverage. Data comparability is also hampered by differences in methods of collection, classification, and tabulation. The reference period is another important source of differences: in some countries census data refer to the status of each person on the day of the census or survey or during a specific period before the inquiry date, while in others the data are recorded without reference to any period. And in some countries the statistics on labor force relate to people above a specific age, while in others there is no specific age provision. For a review of the problems relating to definitions, methods of collection, and classification of data on the labor force, see ILO (1990a) and the chapter notes in the ILO *Yearbook of Labour Statistics*.

The estimated population aged 15–64 typically provides a rough estimate of the economically active population. But in many developing economies children under 15 work full or part time. And in some high-income countries many workers postpone retirement past age 65.

Estimates of women in the labor force are not comparable internationally, because in many countries large numbers of women assist on farms or in other family enterprises without pay, and countries differ in the criteria used to determine the extent to which such workers are to be counted as part of the labor force.

Reliable estimates of child labor are hard to obtain. According to UNICEF's *The State of the World's Children 1997*, in many countries child labor is officially presumed not to exist, and so is not included in surveys or covered in official data. Data are also subject to underreporting because they do not include children engaged in agricultural or household activities with their families. Available statistics suggest that more boys than girls work, but the number of working girls is often underestimated because surveys do not include girls working as unregistered domestic help or those doing full-time household work in order to enable their parents to work outside the home.

Definitions

● **Population aged 15–64** is the number of people who could potentially be economically active, excluding children. ● **Total labor force** comprises people who meet the ILO definition of the economically active population: all people who supply labor for the production of goods and services during a specified period. It includes both the employed and the unemployed. While national practices vary in the treatment of such groups as the armed forces and seasonal or part-time workers, in general the labor force includes the armed forces, the unemployed, and first-time job-seekers, but excludes homemakers and other unpaid caregivers and workers in the informal sector. ● **Average annual growth rate** of the labor force is computed using the exponential end-point method. See *Statistical methods* for more information. ● **Females as a percentage of the labor force** shows the extent to which women are active in the labor force. ● **Children 10–14 in the labor force** is the share of that age group that is active in the labor force.

Data sources

Labor force estimates are calculated by the World Bank's International Economics Department by applying sex-specific activity rates from the ILO database, *Estimates and Projections of the Economically Active Population, 1950–2010*, to the World Bank's population estimates to create a labor force series consistent with its population estimates. This procedure sometimes results in estimates of the absolute size of the labor force that differ slightly from those published by the ILO in its *Yearbook of Labour Statistics*.

2.4 | Employment

	Employers and own-account workers				Employees				Unpaid family workers			
	Male % of economically active population		Female % of economically active population		Male % of economically active population		Female % of economically active population		Male % of economically active population		Female % of economically active population	
	1980	1993	1980	1993	1980	1993	1980	1993	1980	1993	1980	1993
Albania	..	..	..	..	..	..	..	..	..	..	..	..
Algeria	..	..	..	..	..	..	..	..	..	..	..	..
Angola	..	..	..	..	..	..	..	..	..	..	..	..
Argentina	..	..	..	..	..	..	..	..	..	..	..	..
Armenia	..	..	..	..	..	..	..	..	..	..	..	..
Australia	10.0	9.7	4.2	4.6	49.2	41.3	29.3	32.9	0.2	0.3	0.2	0.5
Austria	7.9	6.3	3.2	3.4	52.6	50.9	31.8	36.5	0.9	0.8	3.5	2.1
Azerbaijan	..	..	..	..	..	..	..	..	..	..	..	..
Bangladesh	36.9	23.8	2.0	2.5	43.0	9.5	2.3	2.0	15.0	13.5	0.8	32.7
Belarus	..	..	..	..	..	..	..	..	..	..	..	..
Belgium	8.8	9.3	3.0	3.5	49.9	50.8	26.1	25.6	0.5	0.5	2.6	2.6
Benin	..	31.2	..	27.2	..	4.2	..	1.1	..	18.3	..	12.2
Bolivia	..	18.4	..	17.2	..	35.1	..	17.8	..	2.3	..	3.4
Bosnia and Herzegovina	..	..	..	..	..	..	..	..	..	..	..	..
Botswana	1.9	3.3	1.2	3.2	28.3	39.8	12.7	22.7	24.6	11.1	20.9	6.0
Brazil	..	..	..	..	..	..	..	..	..	..	..	..
Bulgaria	..	..	..	..	..	..	..	..	..	..	..	..
Burkina Faso	..	..	..	..	..	..	..	..	..	..	..	..
Burundi	..	25.8	..	9.8	..	5.1	..	0.5	..	15.9	..	42.5
Cambodia	..	..	..	..	..	..	..	..	..	..	..	..
Cameroon	38.2	..	22.0	..	13.3	..	1.3	..	5.7	..	12.3	..
Canada	6.1	6.1	2.6	3.5	53.4	48.2	36.4	40.8	0.2	0.1	0.8	0.4
Central African Republic	..	..	..	..	..	..	..	..	..	..	..	..
Chad	..	..	..	..	..	..	..	..	..	..	..	..
Chile	17.1	19.3	5.0	6.6	32.3	43.9	16.1	22.7	6.5	1.5	3.4	1.6
China	..	..	..	..	..	..	..	..	..	..	..	..
Colombia	..	18.1	..	9.8	..	34.2	..	22.7	..	0.4	..	0.9
Congo	..	..	..	..	..	..	..	..	..	..	..	..
Costa Rica	..	18.1	..	5.6	..	49.5	..	22.8	..	2.2	..	1.2
Côte d'Ivoire	..	..	..	..	..	..	..	..	..	..	..	..
Croatia	..	..	..	..	..	..	..	..	..	..	..	..
Cuba	4.5	..	0.3	..	63.3	..	30.8	..	0.2	..	0.0	..
Czech Republic	..	1.7	..	0.5	..	49.9	..	46.4	..	0.0	..	0.0
Denmark	9.5	6.8	1.3	1.5	45.1	46.3	39.6	43.5	0.0	0.1	2.5	1.6
Dominican Republic	29.3	..	7.2	..	33.1	..	18.2	..	1.9	..	1.4	..
Ecuador	31.8	..	5.4	..	35.8	..	11.8	..	4.7	..	1.1	..
Egypt, Arab Rep.	27.3	29.2	1.0	2.0	48.4	45.4	5.5	5.1	12.5	14.2	0.2	0.5
El Salvador	16.0	15.6	12.3	11.5	40.5	42.2	18.6	19.0	8.2	8.6	2.7	2.7
Eritrea	..	..	..	..	..	..	..	..	..	..	..	..
Estonia	..	..	..	..	..	..	..	..	..	..	..	..
Ethiopia	..	..	..	..	..	..	..	..	..	..	..	..
Finland	6.0	8.6	4.1	3.9	45.7	42.6	40.2	41.1	0.9	0.4	1.1	0.3
France	..	..	..	..	..	..	..	..	..	..	..	..
Gabon	..	..	..	..	..	..	..	..	..	..	..	..
Gambia, The	..	43.6	..	34.4	..	0.4	..	0.1	..	5.2	..	9.1
Georgia	..	..	..	..	..	..	..	..	..	..	..	..
Germany	..	..	..	..	..	..	..	..	..	..	..	..
Ghana	..	..	..	..	..	..	..	..	..	..	..	..
Greece	30.4	26.1	6.0	6.4	33.0	32.6	13.2	19.0	2.5	2.8	10.9	8.3
Guatemala	27.4	35.3	10.3	3.8	41.3	39.4	8.3	9.0	9.1	11.8	1.6	0.8
Guinea	..	..	..	..	..	..	..	..	..	..	..	..
Guinea-Bissau	50.7	..	0.6	..	13.2	..	1.5	..	23.0	..	0.9	..
Haiti	36.1	..	23.3	..	9.1	..	7.5	..	6.5	..	4.0	..
Honduras	..	..	..	..	..	..	..	..	..	..	..	..
Hong Kong	8.3	9.1	1.5	1.2	53.7	52.6	30.9	34.3	0.4	0.1	1.0	0.7

	Employers and own-account workers				Employees				Unpaid family workers			
	Male % of economically active population		Female % of economically active population		Male % of economically active population		Female % of economically active population		Male % of economically active population		Female % of economically active population	
	1980	1993	1980	1993	1980	1993	1980	1993	1980	1993	1980	1993
Hungary	1.6	7.2	0.6	3.8	44.5	45.8	35.3	40.9	0.2	0.6	2.6	1.7
India	..	..	..	..	..	..	..	..	..	..	..	..
Indonesia	37.5	28.4	15.0	11.0	20.2	24.5	7.5	12.8	8.0	9.1	9.6	11.7
Iran, Islamic Rep.	..	..	..	..	..	..	..	..	..	..	..	..
Iraq	..	..	..	..	..	..	..	..	..	..	..	..
Ireland	16.5	18.7	1.7	2.0	45.3	46.3	23.7	23.0	1.8	2.0	0.4	1.2
Israel	15.0	11.0	4.2	3.7	45.3	41.9	28.5	32.7	0.6	0.2	1.6	0.6
Italy	16.3	16.4	4.6	5.2	45.7	40.4	21.1	23.5	1.6	1.4	3.2	2.3
Jamaica	16.5	..	5.4	..	26.1	..	18.3	..	0.7	..	0.5	..
Japan	11.6	8.5	5.2	3.8	46.3	48.3	24.0	30.4	2.0	1.1	8.7	5.2
Jordan	22.5	..	0.3	..	61.0	..	6.3	..	0.7	..	0.0	..
Kazakstan	..	..	..	..	..	..	..	..	..	..	..	..
Kenya	..	..	..	..	..	..	..	..	..	..	..	..
Korea, Dem. Rep.	..	..	..	..	..	..	..	..	..	..	..	..
Korea, Rep.	23.7	20.2	8.4	7.4	30.6	36.7	14.3	22.5	4.3	1.2	13.6	9.2
Kuwait	..	9.9	..	0.0	..	75.8	..	12.6	..	0.1	..	0.0
Kyrgyz Republic	..	..	..	..	..	..	..	..	..	..	..	..
Lao PDR	..	..	..	..	..	..	..	..	..	..	..	..
Latvia	..	..	..	..	..	..	..	..	..	..	..	..
Lebanon	..	..	..	..	..	..	..	..	..	..	..	..
Lesotho	..	..	..	..	..	..	..	..	..	..	..	..
Libya	..	..	..	..	..	..	..	..	..	..	..	..
Lithuania	..	..	..	..	..	..	..	..	..	..	..	..
Macedonia, FYR	..	44.6	..	27.2	..	6.4	..	2.6	..	1.0	..	2.1
Madagascar	..	..	..	..	..	..	..	..	..	..	..	..
Malawi	..	..	..	..	..	..	..	..	..	..	..	..
Malaysia	20.4	16.4	8.3	4.7	37.7	46.9	16.7	24.5	4.7	2.4	5.6	5.1
Mali	..	..	..	..	..	..	..	..	..	..	..	..
Mauritania	..	..	..	..	..	..	..	..	..	..	..	..
Mauritius	..	..	..	..	..	..	..	..	..	..	..	..
Mexico	20.3	22.9	6.7	7.2	32.3	36.3	12.0	17.5	3.5	8.3	1.9	5.3
Moldova	..	..	..	..	..	..	..	..	..	..	..	..
Mongolia	..	..	..	..	..	..	..	..	..	..	..	..
Morocco	24.2	27.6	2.9	3.1	33.4	38.3	7.1	10.2	12.2	14.8	5.4	6.0
Mozambique	..	..	..	..	..	..	..	..	..	..	..	..
Myanmar	..	..	..	..	..	..	..	..	..	..	..	..
Namibia	..	..	..	..	..	..	..	..	..	..	..	..
Nepal	..	..	..	..	..	..	..	..	..	..	..	..
Netherlands	8.1	6.0	1.5	2.8	55.6	51.0	25.0	31.7	0.3	0.2	1.7	1.3
New Zealand	..	37.4	..	33.9	..	13.0	..	5.2	..	0.4	..	0.6
Nicaragua	..	..	..	..	..	..	..	..	..	..	..	..
Niger	..	..	..	..	..	..	..	..	..	..	..	..
Nigeria	..	..	..	..	..	..	..	..	..	..	..	..
Norway	8.0	6.3	1.6	2.0	49.4	44.3	35.8	40.2	0.8	0.3	2.3	0.8
Oman	..	..	..	..	..	..	..	..	..	..	..	..
Pakistan	..	..	..	..	..	..	..	..	..	..	..	..
Panama	..	..	..	..	..	..	..	..	..	..	..	..
Papua New Guinea	..	..	..	..	..	..	..	..	..	..	..	..
Paraguay	36.6	16.1	6.6	11.8	30.4	37.4	7.4	27.6	8.2	0.8	1.0	1.2
Peru	..	21.5	..	14.4	..	37.1	..	17.7	..	1.2	..	2.2
Philippines	25.7	25.6	9.1	11.0	25.6	25.8	14.4	14.8	9.7	6.3	10.4	7.7
Poland	8.9	13.3	4.3	8.7	42.2	36.6	31.8	32.1	2.9	2.5	9.2	3.5
Portugal	12.5	13.6	3.5	9.5	42.6	40.5	23.7	33.7	2.8	0.8	10.2	1.0
Puerto Rico	11.8	11.7	1.5	2.3	52.7	48.6	31.2	35.4	0.4	0.1	0.8	0.6
Romania	..	5.8	..	8.1	..	46.4	..	33.3	..	0.6	..	1.3
Russian Federation	..	..	..	..	..	..	..	..	..	..	..	..

	Employers and own-account workers				Employees				Unpaid family workers			
	Male % of economically active population		Female % of economically active population		Male % of economically active population		Female % of economically active population		Male % of economically active population		Female % of economically active population	
	1980	1993	1980	1993	1980	1993	1980	1993	1980	1993	1980	1993
Rwanda	..	..	..	..	..	..	..	..	..	..	..	..
Saudi Arabia	..	..	..	..	..	..	..	..	..	..	..	..
Senegal	..	..	..	..	..	..	..	..	..	..	..	..
Sierra Leone	..	..	..	..	..	..	..	..	..	..	..	..
Singapore	10.3	10.3	1.8	2.0	51.6	47.8	30.7	36.3	1.1	0.1	1.4	0.7
Slovak Republic	..	7.8	..	5.5	..	40.5	..	37.2	..	0.7	..	1.2
Slovenia	..	..	..	..	..	..	..	..	..	..	..	..
South Africa	..	..	..	..	..	..	..	..	..	..	..	..
Spain	15.4	12.7	4.1	4.4	51.0	46.1	17.6	24.9	2.3	1.4	5.1	2.2
Sri Lanka	20.5	22.1	3.2	4.9	39.7	34.3	14.7	18.1	4.7	2.9	3.7	3.7
Sudan	..	..	..	..	..	..	..	..	..	..	..	..
Sweden	5.5	7.1	1.8	2.4	48.2	39.6	42.0	42.2	0.1	0.2	0.4	0.3
Switzerland	8.4	..	1.3	..	55.5	..	34.9	..	0.8	..	2.1	..
Syrian Arab Republic	..	..	..	..	..	..	..	..	..	..	..	..
Tajikistan	..	..	..	..	..	..	..	..	..	..	..	..
Tanzania	..	..	..	..	..	..	..	..	..	..	..	..
Thailand	22.9	23.8	8.2	7.3	13.7	12.4	7.9	7.3	15.6	16.3	30.1	32.1
Togo	..	..	..	..	..	..	..	..	..	..	..	..
Trinidad and Tobago	..	..	..	..	..	..	..	..	..	..	..	..
Tunisia	..	..	..	..	..	..	..	..	..	..	..	..
Turkey	..	24.9	..	2.6	..	34.1	..	7.4	..	8.3	..	19.4
Turkmenistan	..	..	..	..	..	..	..	..	..	..	..	..
Uganda	..	..	..	..	..	..	..	..	..	..	..	..
Ukraine	..	..	..	..	..	..	..	..	..	..	..	..
United Arab Emirates	6.8	..	0.0	..	87.8	..	4.9	..	0.0	..	0.0	..
United Kingdom	..	8.4	..	2.9	..	39.9	..	36.8	..	0.2	..	0.4
United States	5.9	5.6	2.1	2.6	51.7	48.8	38.8	42.1	0.1	0.1	0.5	0.2
Uruguay	..	14.9	..	8.0	..	41.0	..	31.3	..	0.7	..	1.6
Uzbekistan	..	..	..	..	..	..	..	..	..	..	..	..
Venezuela	..	..	..	..	..	..	..	..	..	..	..	..
Vietnam	..	..	..	..	..	..	..	..	..	..	..	..
West Bank and Gaza	..	..	..	..	..	..	..	..	..	..	..	..
Yemen, Rep.	..	33.8	..	3.1	..	37.1	..	2.5	..	8.9	..	14.6
Yugoslavia, Fed. Rep.	12.1	..	5.1	..	42.5	..	23.2	..	2.9	..	7.5	..
Zaire	..	..	..	..	..	..	..	..	..	..	..	..
Zambia	..	..	..	..	..	..	..	..	..	..	..	..
Zimbabwe	..	..	..	..	..	..	..	..	..	..	..	..

Women in the workplace

Labor force participation rates show how many women are in the labor force but do not show what work they do. Differences between women and men in where they work and what they do are as important as differences in their participation rates.

According to a recent International Labour Organisation (ILO) report, women's activities in developing countries remain highly concentrated in low-wage, low-productivity, and precarious forms of employment that tend to be outside the purview of labor regulations and therefore more prone to exploitation (Lim 1996). A high percentage of women work in the informal sector or in agriculture, where wages are generally among the lowest.

Women remain concentrated in certain occupations in all regions, whatever the level of development. In the industrial sector women tend to be concentrated in a limited number of manufacturing jobs—such as in the garment industry, where more than two-thirds of the

Fewer than 6 percent of senior management positions worldwide are held by women ●

global workforce is female and which accounts for more than one-fifth of the female labor force in manufacturing.

Most women in manufacturing are categorized as laborers, operators, and clerical workers. According to the ILO report, most women outside the agricultural sector earn on average about three-fourths of the male wage for the same work in both industrial and developing countries, and the gap is not narrowing.

In all regions, according to the ILO report, women work longer hours for lower wages than their male counterparts. In industrial countries women work at least two hours more a week than men, and differences of 5–10 hours are not unusual. The same pattern prevails in the home. In developing countries women spend 31–42 hours a week in unpaid work in the home, while men spend 5–15 hours in unpaid work.

About the data

Data on employment are drawn from the same sources as the labor force data in table 2.3 and are subject to the same caveats for quality and international comparability.

The ILO defines employment categories using the International Classification of Status in Employment (ICSE). Until 1993 the main ICSE groups were employers, own-account workers, employees, members of producers cooperatives, and unpaid family workers. In 1993 the group *own-account workers* was expanded to include people working in a family enterprise with the same degree of commitment as the head of the enterprise. These people, usually women, were formerly considered unpaid family workers.

According to the ILO, "experience has shown that because of the way countries measure 'status in employment,' the content of the groups is not easily comparable across countries" (*Yearbook of Labour Statistics 1995*, p. 4). Managers and directors of incorporated enterprises are classified as employees in most countries, but in some they are classified as employers. Similarly, family members who regularly receive remuneration in the form of wages, salaries, commissions, piece rates, or pay in kind are classified as employees in most countries, but some countries classify them as unpaid family workers.

In many instances the type of information needed to classify workers is not collected in labor force surveys. Some countries are unable to measure the employment status of unpaid family workers. And many cannot distinguish between own-account workers and employers in their basic observations, so only the sum of those two groups can be presented.

Differences between countries in the treatment of unemployed people are particularly pronounced. In general, unemployed people with previous job experience are included with employees and classified according to their last job. In some countries, however, they and unemployed people seeking their first job form much of the group *persons not classifiable by status*, and are not included in the table. The concept of unemployment is also poorly defined for the self-employed, the largest category of employment in many developing countries.

Definitions

The ICSE classifies workers with respect to the type of explicit or implicit contract of employment they have with other people or organizations. The basic criteria for defining classification groups are type of economic risk and type of authority over establishments and other workers that the job incumbent has or will have.
● **Employers** operate, alone or with one or more partners, their own economic enterprise, or engage independently in a profession or trade, and hire one or more employees on a continuous basis. The definition of "on a continuous basis" is determined by national circumstances. Partners may or may not be members of the same family or household. ● **Own-account workers** operate, alone or with one or more partners, their own economic enterprise, or engage independently in a profession or trade, and hire no employees on a continuous basis. As with employers, partners may or may not be members of the same family or household. ● **Employees** are people who work for a public or private employer and receive remuneration in wages, salary, commission, tips, piece rates, or pay in kind. ● **Unpaid family workers** (also referred to as *contributing family workers*) work without pay in an economic enterprise operated by a related person living in the same household and cannot be regarded as a partner because their commitment in terms of working time or other factors is not at a level comparable to that of the head of the establishment. In countries where it is customary for young people to work without pay in an enterprise operated by a related person, the requirement of living in the same household is often eliminated.

The above categories should add up to 100 percent. Where they do not, the difference was not classifiable by status (see *About the data* for composition and treatment).

Data sources

Employment data are compiled by the World Bank's International Economics Department using an ILO database corresponding to table 2a in the ILO's *Yearbook of Labour Statistics*.

2.5 | Poverty

	National poverty line				International poverty line		
			Population below the poverty line				Population below	Poverty
	Survey year	Rural %	Urban %	National %	Survey year	$1 a day %	gap %
Albania	1996	..	..	19.6	..	..	..
Algeria	..	..	..	..	1988	1.6	0.4
Angola	..	..	..	..	..	..	..
Argentina	1991	..	..	25.5	..	..	..
Armenia	..	..	..	..	..	..	..
Australia	..	..	..	..	..	..	..
Austria	..	..	..	..	..	..	..
Azerbaijan	..	..	..	..	..	..	..
Bangladesh	1991–92	47.6	46.7	47.5	..	..	..
Belarus	..	..	..	..	..	..	..
Belgium	..	..	..	..	..	..	..
Benin	1995	..	..	33.0	..	..	..
Bolivia	..	..	..	..	1990–91	7.1	1.1
Bosnia and Herzegovina	..	..	..	..	..	..	..
Botswana	..	..	..	..	1985–86	34.7	13.3
Brazil	1990	32.6	13.1	17.4	1989	28.7	11.6
Bulgaria	..	..	..	..	1992	2.6	0.8
Burkina Faso	..	..	..	..	..	..	..
Burundi	1990	..	..	36.2	..	..	..
Cambodia	..	..	..	..	..	..	..
Cameroon	1984	32.4	44.4	40.0	..	..	..
Canada	..	..	..	..	..	..	..
Central African Republic	..	..	..	..	..	..	..
Chad	..	..	..	..	..	..	..
Chile	..	..	..	..	1992	15.0	4.9
China	1990	11.5	0.4	8.6	1993	29.4	9.2
Colombia	1992	31.2	9.9	18.8	1991	7.4	2.3
Congo	..	..	..	..	..	..	..
Costa Rica	..	..	..	..	1989	18.9	7.2
Côte d'Ivoire	..	..	..	..	1988	17.7	4.3
Croatia	..	..	..	..	..	..	..
Cuba	..	..	..	..	..	..	..
Czech Republic	..	..	..	..	1993	3.1	0.4
Denmark	..	..	..	..	..	..	..
Dominican Republic	1992	..	..	20.6	1989	19.9	6.0
Ecuador	1994	47.0	25.0	35.0	1994	30.4	9.1
Egypt, Arab Rep.	..	..	..	..	1990–91	7.6	1.1
El Salvador	1992	55.7	43.1	48.3	..	..	..
Eritrea	..	..	..	..	..	..	..
Estonia	1994	14.7	6.8	8.9	1993	6.0	1.6
Ethiopia	..	..	..	..	1981–82	33.8	8.0
Finland	..	..	..	..	..	..	..
France	..	..	..	..	..	..	..
Gabon	..	..	..	..	..	..	..
Gambia, The	1992	..	..	64.0	..	..	..
Georgia	..	..	..	..	..	..	..
Germany	..	..	..	..	..	..	..
Ghana	1992	34.3	26.7	31.4	..	..	..
Greece	..	..	..	..	..	..	..
Guatemala	..	..	..	..	1989	53.3	28.5
Guinea	..	..	..	..	1991	26.3	12.4
Guinea-Bissau	1991	60.9	24.1	48.8	1991	87.0	57.8
Haiti	1987	..	..	65.0	..	..	..
Honduras	1992	46.0	56.0	50.0	1992	46.5	20.1
Hong Kong	..	..	..	..	..	..	..

Poverty lines—difficult to compare

International comparisons of poverty data entail both conceptual and practical problems. Different countries have different definitions of poverty, and consistent comparisons between countries can be difficult. Local poverty lines tend to have higher purchasing power in rich countries, where more generous standards are used than in poor countries.

Is it reasonable to treat two people with the same standard of living differently—in terms of their command over commodities—because one happens to live in a better-off country? It can be argued that to make consistent international comparisons, we should try to hold the real value of the poverty line constant, just as is typical when making comparisons over time.

The poverty measures given under the international poverty line attempt to do this. Here the poverty line is set for all countries at $1 a person per day, in 1985 international prices, and adjusted to local currency using exchange rates aimed at assuring purchasing power parity for consumption. The figure of $1 a day was chosen for the World Bank's *World Development Report 1990: Poverty* because it is typical of the poverty lines in low-income countries. Of course, by the same token, it is lower—often much lower—than the poverty lines found in middle- or high-income countries.

Currency conversions can be problematic, however. Using standard purchasing power parity (PPP) exchange rates, such as those from the Penn World Table, is clearly preferable to using official exchange rates, because many commodities are not traded internationally. But PPP rates were designed not for making international poverty comparisons, but for comparing aggregates from national accounts. It would be better to design special-purpose PPP rates for the poor. But with no such rates now available, the standard PPP rates for consumption appear to be the best option.

Just as there are problems in comparing a poverty measure for one country with that for another, there can also be problems in comparing poverty measures within countries. For example, the cost of living is typically higher in

	National poverty line				International poverty line		
			Population below the poverty line			Population below $1 a day %	Poverty gap %
	Survey year	Rural %	Urban %	National %	Survey year		
Hungary	1993	..	..	25.3	1993	0.7	0.3
India	..	..	..	..	1992	52.5	15.6
Indonesia	1990	14.3	16.8	15.1	1993	14.5	2.0
Iran, Islamic Rep.	..	..	..	..	..	..	..
Iraq	..	..	..	..	..	..	..
Ireland	..	..	..	..	..	..	..
Israel	..	..	..	..	..	..	..
Italy	..	..	..	..	..	..	..
Jamaica	1992	..	..	34.2	1993	4.7	0.9
Japan	..	..	..	..	..	..	..
Jordan	1991	..	..	15.0	1992	2.5	0.5
Kazakstan	..	..	..	..	..	..	..
Kenya	1992	46.4	29.3	42.0	1992	50.2	22.2
Korea, Dem. Rep.	..	..	..	..	..	..	..
Korea, Rep.	..	..	..	..	..	..	..
Kuwait	..	..	..	..	..	..	..
Kyrgyz Republic	1993	52.2	32.0	45.4	1993	18.9	5.0
Lao PDR	1993	53.0	24.0	46.1	..	..	..
Latvia	..	..	..	..	..	..	..
Lebanon	..	..	..	..	..	..	..
Lesotho	1993	53.9	27.8	49.2	1986–87	50.4	24.8
Libya	..	..	..	..	..	..	..
Lithuania	..	..	..	..	1993	2.1	0.5
Macedonia, FYR	1990	28.0	24.0	..	..	..	..
Madagascar	..	..	..	..	1993	72.3	33.2
Malawi	..	..	..	..	..	..	..
Malaysia	1989			15.5	1989	5.6	0.9
Mali	..	..	..	..	..	..	..
Mauritania	1990	..	..	57.0	1988	31.4	15.2
Mauritius	1992	..	..	10.6	..	..	..
Mexico	1988	..	..	10.1	1992	14.9	3.8
Moldova	..	..	..	..	1992	6.8	1.2
Mongolia	1995	33.1	38.5	36.3	..	..	..
Morocco	1990–91	18.0	7.6	13.1	1990–91	1.1	0.1
Mozambique	..	..	..	..	..	..	..
Myanmar	..	..	..	..	..	..	..
Namibia	..	..	..	..	..	..	..
Nepal	1995–96	44.0	23.0	42.0	1995–96	53.1	16.9
Netherlands	..	..	..	..	..	..	..
New Zealand	..	..	..	..	..	..	..
Nicaragua	1993	76.1	31.9	50.3	1993	43.8	18.0
Niger	..	..	..	..	1992	61.5	22.2
Nigeria	1992–93	36.4	30.4	34.1	1992–93	28.9	11.7
Norway	..	..	..	..	..	..	..
Oman	..	..	..	..	..	..	..
Pakistan	1991	36.9	28.0	34.0	1991	11.6	2.6
Panama	..	..	..	..	1989	25.6	12.6
Papua New Guinea	..	..	..	..	..	..	..
Paraguay	1991	28.5	19.7	21.8	..	..	..
Peru	1991	68.0	50.3	54.0	1994	49.4	20.5
Philippines	1991	71.0	39.0	54.0	1988	27.5	6.9
Poland	1993	..	..	23.8	1993	6.8	4.4
Portugal	..	..	..	..	..	..	..
Puerto Rico	..	..	..	..	..	..	..
Romania	1994	28.0	15.6	21.5	1992	17.7	4.2
Russian Federation	1994	..	..	30.9	1993	1.1	0.1

urban than in rural areas. (Food staples, for example, tend to be more expensive in urban areas.) So the urban poverty line should be higher than the rural poverty line. But it is not always clear that the difference between urban and rural poverty lines properly reflects the difference in the cost of living.

For some countries the urban poverty line in common use has a higher real value—meaning that it allows poor people to buy more commodities for consumption—than does the rural poverty line. Sometimes the difference has been so large as to imply that the incidence of poverty is greater in urban than in rural areas, even though the reverse is found when adjustments are made for differences in the cost of living. As with international comparisons, when the real

About 1.3 billion people live on less than $1 a day ●

value of the poverty line varies, it is not clear how meaningful such urban-rural comparisons are.

The problems of making poverty comparisons do not end there. Further issues arise in measuring household living standards. The choice between income and consumption as a welfare indicator is one issue. Incomes are generally more difficult to measure accurately, and it can also be argued that consumption accords better with the idea of the standard of living than does income, which can vary over time even if the standard of living does not. But consumption data are not always available, and when they are not there is little choice but to use income.

There are still other problems. In some countries an allowance is made for differences in household size and composition when determining who is poor, while in others no allowance is made. Household survey questionnaires can also differ widely, for example, in the number of distinct categories of consumer goods they identify and in the order in which questions are asked. Survey quality varies, and even similar surveys may not be strictly comparable.

Comparisons across countries at different

	National poverty line				International poverty line		
		Population below the poverty line				Population below $1 a day %	Poverty gap %
	Survey year	Rural %	Urban %	National %	Survey year		
Rwanda	1993	..	..	51.2	1983–85	45.7	11.3
Saudi Arabia	..	..	..	..	..	..	..
Senegal	..	..	..	..	1991–92	54.0	25.5
Sierra Leone	..	..	..	..	..	..	..
Singapore	..	..	..	..	..	..	..
Slovak Republic	..	..	..	..	1992	12.8	2.2
Slovenia	..	..	..	..	..	..	..
South Africa	..	..	..	..	1993	23.7	6.6
Spain	..	..	..	..	..	..	..
Sri Lanka	1991	24.4	18.3	22.4	1990	4.0	1.0
Sudan	..	..	..	..	..	..	..
Sweden	..	..	..	..	..	..	..
Switzerland	..	..	..	..	..	..	..
Syrian Arab Republic	..	..	..	..	..	..	..
Tajikistan	..	..	..	..	..	..	..
Tanzania	1991	..	..	51.1	1993	16.4	3.7
Thailand	1992	15.5	10.2	13.1	1992	0.1	0.0
Togo	1987–89	..	..	32.3	..	..	..
Trinidad and Tobago	1992	..	..	21.0	..	..	..
Tunisia	1990	..	..	14.1	1990	3.9	0.9
Turkey	..	..	..	..	..	..	..
Turkmenistan	..	..	..	..	1993	4.9	0.5
Uganda	1992–93	..	..	55.0	1989–90	50.0	14.7
Ukraine	1995	..	..	31.7	..	..	..
United Arab Emirates	..	..	..	..	..	..	..
United Kingdom	..	..	..	..	..	..	..
United States	..	..	..	..	..	..	..
Uruguay	..	..	..	..	..	..	..
Uzbekistan	..	..	..	..	..	..	..
Venezuela	1989	..	..	31.3	1991	11.8	3.1
Vietnam	1993	57.2	25.9	50.9	..	..	..
West Bank and Gaza	..	..	..	..	..	..	..
Yemen, Rep.	1992	19.2	18.6	19.1	..	..	..
Yugoslavia, Fed. Rep.	..	..	..	..	..	..	..
Zaire	..	..	..	..	..	..	..
Zambia	1993	..	..	86.0	1993	84.6	53.8
Zimbabwe	1990–91	..	..	25.5	1990–91	41.0	14.3

levels of development also pose a potential problem, because of differences in the relative importance of consumption of nonmarket goods. The local market value of all consumption in kind (including consumption from own production, particularly important in underdeveloped rural economies) should be included in the measure of total consumption expenditure. Similarly, the imputed profit from production of nonmarket goods should be included in income. This is not always done, though such omissions were a far bigger problem in surveys before the 1980s. Survey data now routinely include valuations for consumption or income from own production. Nonetheless, the methods of valuation vary—for example, some surveys use the price at the nearest market, while others use the average farm-gate selling price.

Table 2.5a Poverty gap in various regions, 1987 and 1993

percent

Region	1987	1993
East Asia and the Pacific	8.3	7.8
Europe and Central Asia	0.2	1.1
Latin America and the Caribbean	8.2	9.1
Middle East and North Africa	0.9	0.6
South Asia	14.1	12.6
Sub-Saharan Africa	14.4	15.3
Total	9.5	9.2

Note: The aggregates were derived by adjusting estimates from national surveys closest to 1987 and 1993 by the growth rate of real private per capita consumption from national accounts. The sample of countries covered by the surveys was assumed to be representative of the region. This assumption is less robust for the Middle East and North Africa and Sub-Saharan Africa. For further details on data and methodology see Ravallion and Chen 1996.
Source: World Bank 1996f.

About the data

It is impossible to create a data set on poverty and distribution that is strictly comparable across countries. But the poverty measures given under the international poverty line are designed to reduce the comparability problems in several ways. Nationally representative surveys have been used, surveys conducted either by national statistical offices or by private agencies under government or international agency supervision.

The poverty measures are based on the most recent purchasing power parity (PPP) estimates, from the latest version of the Penn World Table (PWT 5.6). These estimates include revisions to PPP exchange rates in the previous version of the table (PWT 5.0) to incorporate better data. The revisions resulted in significant changes, the most striking relating to China. Using the updated PPP exchange rates for consumption from PWT 5.6 produces an estimate of the percentage of China's population living on less than $1 a day (in international prices) in 1992 nearly triple that estimated using the PPP rates from PWT 5.0, with the same distribution data. For India, however, the revised PPP rates result in a lower estimate for this indicator. Such changes in the estimated incidence of poverty occur because a large change in the PPP for a country can produce dramatically different poverty lines in local currency.

Whenever possible, consumption has been used as the welfare indicator for deciding who is poor. A person is said to be poor if he or she lives in a household whose total consumption per person is less than the poverty line. The measure of consumption is generally comprehensive, including that from own production as well as all food and nonfood goods purchased. When only household incomes are available, the average level of income has been adjusted to accord with either a survey-based estimate of mean consumption (when available) or an estimate based on consumption data from national accounts. This procedure adjusts only the mean, however; nothing can be done to correct for the difference in Lorenz (income distribution) curves between consumption and income.

Empirical Lorenz curves were weighted by household size, so they are based on percentiles of population, not households. In all cases the measures of poverty have been calculated from primary data sources (tabulations or household data) rather than existing estimates. Estimation from tabulations requires an interpolation method; the method chosen was Lorenz curves with flexible functional forms, which have proved reliable in past work.

Definitions

● **Survey year** is the year in which the underlying data were collected. ● **Rural poverty rate** is the percentage of the rural population deemed poor. ● **Urban poverty rate** is the percentage of the urban population deemed poor. ● **National poverty rate** is the percentage of the population living below the poverty line deemed appropriate for the country by its authorities. National estimates are based on population-weighted subgroup estimates from household surveys. ● **Population below $1 a day** is the percentage of the population living on less than $1 a day at 1985 international prices, adjusted for purchasing power parity. ● **Poverty gap** is the mean shortfall below the poverty line (counting the nonpoor as having zero shortfall) expressed as a percentage of the poverty line. This measure reflects the depth of poverty as well as its incidence.

Data sources

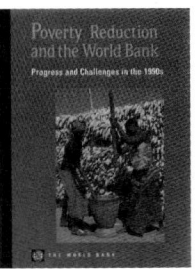

Poverty measures are prepared by the Poverty and Human Resources Division of the World Bank's Policy Research Department. National poverty lines are based on the World Bank's country poverty assessments. International poverty lines are based on primary household survey data obtained from government statistical agencies and World Bank country departments.

The World Bank has prepared an annual review of poverty trends since 1993. The most recent is *Poverty Reduction and the World Bank* (1996f).

2.6 | Distribution of income or consumption

	Survey year	Gini index	Percentage share of income or consumption						
			Lowest 10%	Lowest 20%	Second 20%	Third 20%	Fourth 20%	Highest 20%	Highest 10%
Albania		..	..	..	..	..	..	..	..
Algeria	1988 [a,b]	38.7	2.8	6.9	11.0	15.1	20.9	46.1	31.5
Angola		..	..	..	..	..	..	..	..
Argentina		..	..	..	..	..	..	..	..
Armenia		..	..	..	..	..	..	..	..
Australia	1985 [e,f]	..	..	4.4	11.1	17.5	24.8	42.2	25.8
Austria		..	..	..	..	..	..	..	..
Azerbaijan		..	..	..	..	..	..	..	..
Bangladesh	1992 [a,b]	28.3	4.1	9.4	13.5	17.2	22.0	37.9	23.7
Belarus	1993 [c,d]	21.6	4.9	11.1	15.3	18.5	22.2	32.9	19.4
Belgium	1978–79 [e,f]	..		7.9	13.7	18.6	23.8	36.0	21.5
Benin		..	..	..	..	..	..	..	..
Bolivia	1990 [c,d]	42.0	2.3	5.6	9.7	14.5	22.0	48.2	31.7
Bosnia and Herzegovina		..	..	..	..	..	..	..	..
Botswana		..	..	..	..	..	..	..	..
Brazil	1989 [c,d]	63.4	0.7	2.1	4.9	8.9	16.8	67.5	51.3
Bulgaria	1992 [c,d]	30.8	3.3	8.3	13.0	17.0	22.3	39.3	24.7
Burkina Faso		..	..	..	..	..	..	..	..
Burundi		..	..	..	..	..	..	..	..
Cambodia		..	..	..	..	..	..	..	..
Cameroon		..	..	..	..	..	..	..	..
Canada	1987 [e,f]	..		5.7	11.8	17.7	24.6	40.2	24.1
Central African Republic		..	..	..	..	..	..	..	..
Chad		..	..	..	..	..	..	..	..
Chile	1994 [c,d]	56.5	1.4	3.5	6.6	10.9	18.1	61.0	46.1
China	1995 [c,d]	41.5	2.2	5.5	9.8	14.9	22.3	47.5	30.9
Colombia	1991 [c,d]	51.3	1.3	3.6	7.6	12.6	20.4	55.8	39.5
Congo		..	..	..	..	..	..	..	..
Costa Rica	1989 [c,d]	46.1	1.2	4.0	9.1	14.3	21.9	50.7	34.1
Côte d'Ivoire	1988 [a,b]	36.9	2.8	6.8	11.2	15.8	22.2	44.1	28.5
Croatia		..	..	..	..	..	..	..	..
Cuba		..	..	..	..	..	..	..	..
Czech Republic	1993 [c,d]	26.6	4.6	10.5	13.9	16.9	21.3	37.4	23.5
Denmark	1981 [e,f]	..		5.4	12.0	18.4	25.6	38.6	22.3
Dominican Republic	1989 [c,d]	50.5	1.6	4.2	7.9	12.5	19.7	55.7	39.6
Ecuador	1994 [a,b]	46.6	2.3	5.4	8.9	13.2	19.9	52.6	37.6
Egypt, Arab Rep.	1991 [a,b]	32.0	3.9	8.7	12.5	16.3	21.4	41.1	26.7
El Salvador		..	..	..	..	..	..	..	..
Eritrea		..	..	..	..	..	..	..	..
Estonia	1993 [c,d]	39.5	2.4	6.6	10.7	15.1	21.4	46.3	31.3
Ethiopia		..	..	..	..	..	..	..	..
Finland	1981 [e,f]	..		6.3	12.1	18.4	25.5	37.6	21.7
France	1989 [e,f]	..		5.6	11.8	17.2	23.5	41.9	26.1
Gabon		..	..	..	..	..	..	..	..
Gambia, The		..	..	..	..	..	..	..	..
Georgia		..	..	..	..	..	..	..	..
Germany	1988 [e,f]	..		7.0	11.8	17.1	23.9	40.3	24.4
Ghana	1992 [a,b]	33.9	3.4	7.9	12.0	16.1	21.8	42.2	27.3
Greece		..	..	..	..	..	..	..	..
Guatemala	1989 [c,d]	59.6	0.6	2.1	5.8	10.5	18.6	63.0	46.6
Guinea	1991 [a,b]	46.8	0.9	3.0	8.3	14.6	23.9	50.2	31.7
Guinea-Bissau	1991 [a,b]	56.2	0.5	2.1	6.5	12.0	20.6	58.9	42.4
Haiti		..	..	..	..	..	..	..	..
Honduras	1992 [c,d]	52.7	1.5	3.8	7.4	12.0	19.4	57.4	41.9
Hong Kong	1980 [e,f]	..		5.4	10.8	15.2	21.6	47.0	31.3

	Survey year	Gini index	Percentage share of income or consumption						
			Lowest 10%	Lowest 20%	Second 20%	Third 20%	Fourth 20%	Highest 20%	Highest 10%
Hungary	1993 [a,b]	27.0	4.0	9.5	14.0	17.6	22.3	36.6	22.6
India	1992 [a,b]	33.8	3.7	8.5	12.1	15.8	21.1	42.6	28.4
Indonesia	1993 [a,b]	31.7	3.9	8.7	12.3	16.3	22.1	40.7	25.6
Iran, Islamic Rep.		..	..	..	..	..	..	..	..
Iraq		..	..	..	..	..	..	..	..
Ireland		..	..	..	..	..	..	..	..
Israel	1979 [e,f]	..		6.0	12.1	17.8	24.5	39.6	23.5
Italy	1986 [e,f]	..		6.8	12.0	16.7	23.5	41.0	25.3
Jamaica	1991 [a,b]	41.1	2.4	5.8	10.2	14.9	21.6	47.5	31.9
Japan	1979 [e,f]	..		8.7	13.2	17.5	23.1	37.5	22.4
Jordan	1991 [a,b]	43.4	2.4	5.9	9.8	13.9	20.3	50.1	34.7
Kazakstan	1993 [c,d]	32.7	3.1	7.5	12.3	16.9	22.9	40.4	24.9
Kenya	1992 [a,b]	57.5	1.2	3.4	6.7	10.7	17.0	62.1	47.7
Korea, Dem. Rep.		..	..	..	..	..	..	..	..
Korea, Rep.		..	..	..	..	..	..	..	..
Kuwait		..	..	..	..	..	..	..	..
Kyrgyz Republic		..	..	..	..	..	..	..	..
Lao PDR	1992 [a,b]	30.4	4.2	9.6	12.9	16.3	21.0	40.2	26.4
Latvia	1993 [c,d]	27.0	4.3	9.6	13.6	17.5	22.6	36.7	22.1
Lebanon		..	..	..	..	..	..	..	..
Lesotho	1986–87 [a,b]	56.0	0.9	2.8	6.5	11.2	19.4	60.1	43.4
Libya		..	..	..	..	..	..	..	..
Lithuania	1993 [c,d]	33.6	3.4	8.1	12.3	16.2	21.3	42.1	28.0
Macedonia, FYR		..	..	..	..	..	..	..	..
Madagascar	1993 [a,b]	43.4	2.3	5.8	9.9	14.0	20.3	50.0	34.9
Malawi		..	..	..	..	..	..	..	..
Malaysia	1989 [c,d]	48.4	1.9	4.6	8.3	13.0	20.4	53.7	37.9
Mali		..	..	..	..	..	..	..	..
Mauritania	1988 [a,b]	42.4	0.7	3.6	10.6	16.2	23.0	46.5	30.4
Mauritius		..	..	..	..	..	..	..	..
Mexico	1992 [a,b]	50.3	1.6	4.1	7.8	12.5	20.2	55.3	39.2
Moldova	1992 [c,d]	34.4	2.7	6.9	11.9	16.7	23.1	41.5	25.8
Mongolia		..	..	..	..	..	..	..	..
Morocco	1990–91 [a,b]	39.2	2.8	6.6	10.5	15.0	21.7	46.3	30.5
Mozambique		..	..	..	..	..	..	..	..
Myanmar		..	..	..	..	..	..	..	..
Namibia		..	..	..	..	..	..	..	..
Nepal	1995–96 [a,b]	36.7	3.2	7.6	11.5	15.1	21.0	44.8	29.8
Netherlands	1988 [e,f]	..		8.2	13.1	18.1	23.7	36.9	21.9
New Zealand	1981–82 [e,f]	..		5.1	10.8	16.2	23.2	44.7	28.7
Nicaragua	1993 [a,b]	50.3	1.6	4.2	8.0	12.6	20.0	55.2	39.8
Niger	1992 [a,b]	36.1	3.0	7.5	11.8	15.5	21.1	44.1	29.3
Nigeria	1992–93 [a,b]	37.5	1.3	4.0	8.9	14.4	23.4	49.3	31.3
Norway	1979 [e,f]	..		6.2	12.8	18.9	25.3	36.7	21.2
Oman		..	..	..	..	..	..	..	..
Pakistan	1991 [a,b]	31.2	3.4	8.4	12.9	16.9	22.2	39.7	25.2
Panama	1989 [c,d]	56.6	0.5	2.0	6.3	11.6	20.3	59.8	42.2
Papua New Guinea		..	..	..	..	..	..	..	..
Paraguay		..	..	..	..	..	..	..	..
Peru	1994 [a,b]	44.9	1.9	4.9	9.2	14.1	21.4	50.4	34.3
Philippines	1988 [a,b]	40.7	2.8	6.5	10.1	14.4	21.2	47.8	32.1
Poland	1992 [a,b]	27.2	4.0	9.3	13.8	17.7	22.6	36.6	22.1
Portugal		..	..	..	..	..	..	..	..
Puerto Rico		..	..	..	..	..	..	..	..
Romania	1992 [c,d]	25.5	3.8	9.2	14.4	18.4	23.2	34.8	20.2
Russian Federation	1993 [a,b]	49.6	1.2	3.7	8.5	13.5	20.4	53.8	38.7

	Survey year	Gini index	Percentage share of income or consumption						
			Lowest 10%	Lowest 20%	Second 20%	Third 20%	Fourth 20%	Highest 20%	Highest 10%
Rwanda	1983–85 [a,b]	28.9	4.2	9.7	13.2	16.5	21.6	39.1	24.2
Saudi Arabia		..	..	..	..	..	..	..	..
Senegal	1991 [a,b]	54.1	1.4	3.5	7.0	11.6	19.3	58.6	42.8
Sierra Leone		..	..	..	..	..	..	..	..
Singapore	1982–83 [e,f]	..	..	5.1	9.9	14.6	21.4	48.9	33.5
Slovak Republic	1992 [c,d]	19.5	5.1	11.9	15.8	18.8	22.2	31.4	18.2
Slovenia	1993 [c,d]	28.2	4.1	9.5	13.5	17.1	21.9	37.9	23.8
South Africa	1993 [a,b]	58.4	1.4	3.3	5.8	9.8	17.7	63.3	47.3
Spain	1988 [e,f]	8.3	13.7	18.1	23.4	36.6	21.8		
Sri Lanka	1990 [a,b]	30.1	3.8	8.9	13.1	16.9	21.7	39.3	25.2
Sudan		..	..	..	..	..	..	..	..
Sweden	1981 [e,f]	..	..	8.0	13.2	17.4	24.5	36.9	20.8
Switzerland	1982 [e,f]	..	..	5.2	11.7	16.4	22.1	44.6	29.8
Syrian Arab Republic		..	..	..	..	..	..	..	..
Tajikistan		..	..	..	..	..	..	..	..
Tanzania	1993 [a,b]	38.1	2.9	6.9	10.9	15.3	21.5	45.4	30.2
Thailand	1992 [a,b]	46.2	2.5	5.6	8.7	13.0	20.0	52.7	37.1
Togo		..	..	..	..	..	..	..	..
Trinidad and Tobago		..	..	..	..	..	..	..	..
Tunisia	1990 [a,b]	40.2	2.3	5.9	10.4	15.3	22.1	46.3	30.7
Turkey		..	..	..	..	..	..	..	..
Turkmenistan	1993 [c,d]	35.8	2.7	6.7	11.4	16.3	22.8	42.8	26.9
Uganda	1992–93 [a,b]	40.8	3.0	6.8	10.3	14.4	20.4	48.1	33.4
Ukraine	1992 [c,d]	25.7	4.1	9.5	14.1	18.1	22.9	35.4	20.8
United Arab Emirates		..	..	..	..	..	..	..	..
United Kingdom	1988 [e,f]	..	..	4.6	10.0	16.8	24.3	44.3	27.8
United States	1985 [e,f]	..	..	4.7	11.0	17.4	25.0	41.9	25.0
Uruguay		..	..	..	..	..	..	..	..
Uzbekistan		..	..	..	..	..	..	..	..
Venezuela	1990 [c,d]	53.8	1.4	3.6	7.1	11.7	19.3	58.4	42.7
Vietnam	1993 [a,b]	35.7	3.5	7.8	11.4	15.4	21.4	44.0	29.0
West Bank and Gaza		..	..	..	..	..	..	..	..
Yemen, Rep.		..	..	..	..	..	..	..	..
Yugoslavia, Fed. Rep.		..	..	..	..	..	..	..	..
Zaire		..	..	..	..	..	..	..	..
Zambia	1993 [a,b]	46.2	1.5	3.9	8.0	13.8	23.8	50.4	31.3
Zimbabwe	1990 [a,b]	56.8	1.8	4.0	6.3	10.0	17.4	62.3	46.9

a. Refers to expenditure shares by percentiles of population. b. Ranked by per capita expenditure. c. Refers to income shares by percentiles of population. d. Ranked by per capita income. e. Refers to income shares by percentiles of households. f. Ranked by household income.

Inequality in the distribution of income is reflected in the percentage share of income or consumption accruing to segments of the population ranked by income or consumption levels. The segments ranked lowest by personal or family income typically receive the smallest share of total income. The Gini index provides a convenient summary measure of the degree of inequality.

Data on personal or household income or consumption come from nationally representative household surveys. The data sets refer to different years between 1985 and 1994. Footnotes to the survey year indicate whether the rankings are based on per capita income or consumption, or, in the case of high-income economies, household income. Where the original data from the household survey were available, they have been used to directly calculate the income (or consumption) shares by quintile. Otherwise, shares have been estimated from the best available grouped data.

The distribution indicators for low- and middle-income economies have been adjusted for household size, providing a more consistent measure of per capita income or consumption. No adjustment has been made for spatial differences in cost of living within countries, because the data needed for such calculations are generally unavailable. For further details on the estimation method for low- and middle-income economies, see Ravallion and Chen (1996).

Because the underlying household surveys differ in method and in the type of data collected, the distribution indicators are not strictly comparable across countries. These problems are diminishing as survey methods improve and become more standardized, but achieving strict comparability is still impossible (see the notes to table 2.5).

The following sources of noncomparability should be noted. First, the surveys differ in whether they use income or consumption expenditure as the living standard indicator. For 37 of the 66 low- and middle-income economies the data refer to consumption expenditure. Income is typically more unequally distributed than consumption. In addition, the definitions of income used in surveys are usually very different from the economic definition of income (the maximum level of consumption consistent with keeping productive capacity unchanged). For these reasons, consumption is usually a much better measure. Second, the surveys differ in whether they use the household or the individual as their unit of observation. Further, household units differ in size (number of members) and in extent of income sharing among members. Individuals differ in age and consumption needs. Where households are used as the observation unit, the deciles or quintiles refer to the percentage of households rather than of population. Third, the surveys differ according to whether they rank the units of observation by household or per capita income (or consumption).

World Bank staff have made an effort to assure that the data for low- and middle-income economies are as comparable as possible. Whenever possible, consumption has been used rather than income. Households have been ranked by consumption or income per capita in forming the percentiles, and the percentiles are of population, not households. The comparability of the data for high-income economies is more limited, because the observation unit is usually a household unadjusted for size and households are ranked according to total household income rather than income per household member. These data are presented pending the publication of improved data from the Luxembourg Income Study, which ranks households by the average disposable income per adult equivalent. The estimates in the table should therefore be treated with considerable caution.

● **Survey year** is the year in which the underlying data were collected. ● **Gini index** measures the extent to which the distribution of income (or, in some cases, consumption expenditures) among individuals or households within an economy deviates from a perfectly equal distribution. A Lorenz curve plots the cumulative percentages of total income received against the cumulative number of recipients, starting with the poorest individual or household. The Gini index measures the area between the Lorenz curve and a hypothetical line of absolute equality, expressed as a percentage of the maximum area under the line. Thus a Gini index of zero represents perfect equality while an index of 100 percent implies perfect inequality. ● **Percentage share of income or consumption** is the share that accrues to subgroups of population indicated by deciles or quintiles. Percentage shares by quintiles may not add up to 100 because of rounding.

Data on distribution for low- and middle-income economies are compiled by the Poverty and Human Resources Division of the World Bank's Policy Research Department, using primary household survey data obtained from government statistical agencies and World Bank country departments. Data for high-income economies are from national sources, supplemented by:

• Luxembourg Income Study database, 1990.

• Eurostat, *Statistical Yearbook*.

• United Nations, *National Accounts Statistics: Compendium of Income Distribution Statistics* (1985).

Table 2.6a Income shares of lowest and highest quintiles, 1960s–1990s

percent

Region or group	1960s	1970s	1980s	1990s
Lowest quintile				
East Asia and the Pacific	6.4	6.0	6.3	6.9
Europe and Central Asia	9.7	9.8	9.8	8.8
Latin America and the Caribbean		3.4	3.7	3.7	4.5
Middle East and North Africa	5.7	..	6.6	6.9
South Asia	7.4	7.8	7.9	8.8
Sub-Saharan Africa	2.8	5.1	5.7	5.2
Industrial and high-income developing economies	6.4	6.3	6.7	6.3
Highest quintile				
East Asia and the Pacific	45.9	46.5	45.5	44.3
Europe and Central Asia	36.3	34.5	34.6	37.8
Latin America and the Caribbean	61.6	54.2	54.9	52.9
Middle East and North Africa	49.0	..	46.7	45.4
South Asia	44.1	42.2	42.6	39.9
Sub-Saharan Africa	62.0	55.8	48.9	52.4
Industrial and high-income developing economies	31.2	41.1	39.9	39.8

Source: Deininger and Squire 1996.

	Primary school starting age	Duration of primary education	Public spending on education						Spending on teaching materials		Primary school pupil-teacher ratio	
			Primary % of GDP		Secondary % of GDP		Tertiary % of GDP		Primary % of total for level	Secondary % of total for level	pupils per teacher	
	years	years	1980	1992	1980	1992	1980	1992	1992	1992	1980	1993
Albania	6	8	..	..	..	..	..	..	..	..	21	17
Algeria	6	6	1.4	1.7 [a]	1.3	3.2 [a]	0.9	..	..	..	35	27
Angola	6	4	..	3.4 [b]	..	..	..	0.1 [b]	0.7 [b]	..	..	32
Argentina	6	7	0.9	1.6	0.6	0.8	0.5	0.5	..	..	20	16
Armenia	7	3	..	..	..	..	..	..	..	..	..	..
Australia	6	6	..	..	3.3	3.0	1.1	1.4	..	..	19	17
Austria	6	4	0.8	0.9	2.5	2.4	0.7	0.9	..	..	15	12
Azerbaijan	7	4	..	..	..	..	..	..	..	..	..	4
Bangladesh	6	5	0.5 [b]	0.8 [b]	0.4 [b]	0.8 [b]	0.1 [b]	0.1 [b]	..	..	54	63
Belarus	6	4	..	3.0	..	1.0	..	0.7	..	..	..	5
Belgium	6	6	1.5 [b]	1.2 [b]	2.8	2.1 [b]	1.0 [b]	0.8 [b]	..	..	18	10
Benin	6	6	..	..	..	..	..	..	..	..	48	49
Bolivia	6	8	2.4	..	0.5	..	0.7	..	..	..	20	..
Bosnia and Herzegovina	..	..									..	..
Botswana	7	7	2.5	1.9 [b]	1.4	3.0 [b]	0.6	0.7 [b]	2.4 [b]	1.5 [b]	32	27
Brazil	7	8	1.6 [a]	..	0.3 [a]	..	0.7 [a]	..	..	..	26	23
Bulgaria	7	8	1.9	3.0	..	0.6	0.8	..	..	..	19	14
Burkina Faso	7	6	0.7	..	0.4	..	0.7	..	..	..	54	58
Burundi	7	6	1.2 [b]	1.6 [b]	1.1 [b]	1.0 [b]	0.7 [b]	0.9 [b]	..	..	37	63
Cambodia	6	6	..	..	..	..	..	..	..	..	..	..
Cameroon	6	6	1.6 [b]	2.1 [b]	..	..	0.5 [b]	0.3 [b]	..	..	52	48
Canada	6	6	..	..	4.3 [c]	4.6 [c]	1.8 [c]	2.1 [c]	..	..	..	16
Central African Republic	6	6	2.4 [b]	1.3 [b]	0.5 [b]	0.4 [b]	0.7 [b]	0.5 [b]	1.7 [b]	6.0 [b]	60	..
Chad	6	6	..	1.0	..	0.5	..	0.2	1.3	2.7	..	61
Chile	6	8	1.8	1.2	0.8	0.4	1.4	0.5	..	..	34	26
China	7	5	0.6	0.6	0.7 [d]	0.6 [d]	0.4	0.3	..	..	27	22
Colombia	6	5	0.8 [b]	1.3 [a,b]	0.5 [b]	1.1 [a,b]	0.4 [b]	0.6 [a,b]	..	..	31	28
Congo	6	6	2.1	..	1.7	..	1.5	..	..	..	..	..
Costa Rica	6	6	1.9	1.5	1.5	0.9	1.8	1.5	..	..	28	32
Côte d'Ivoire	6	6	2.7	..	2.1	..	0.9	..	..	..	39	39
Croatia	7	8	..	..	..	..	..	..	..	..	19	18
Cuba	6	6	..	..	..	..	..	..	2.5	1.2	17	13
Czech Republic	6	4	..	1.7	..	1.2	..	0.6	20.9	29.3	..	21
Denmark	7	6	3.2	1.4	1.1	2.9	1.0	1.2	..	..	..	10
Dominican Republic	7	8	0.6 [b]	0.4 [b]	0.4 [b]	0.1 [b]	0.4 [b]	0.1 [b]	..	..	64	34
Ecuador	6	6	1.0	0.7	0.9	0.7	0.8	0.5	..	..	36	31
Egypt, Arab Rep.	7	5	..	..	2.1	2.5	0.9	1.4	..	..	34	27
El Salvador	7	9	2.2	..	0.2	..	0.5	..	..	..	48	40
Eritrea	7	5	..	..	..	..	..	..	..	..	..	39
Estonia	7	6	..	..	..	3.1	..	0.9	..	..	..	18
Ethiopia	7	6	1.1	1.5	0.7	0.7	0.4	0.3	0.8	1.4	64	30
Finland	7	6	1.6 [c]	1.8 [c]	2.0 [c]	2.6 [c]	0.9 [c]	2.0 [c]	4.6 [c]	3.1 [c]	14	..
France	6	5	1.0	0.9	1.9	2.1	0.6	0.7	1.4	0.6	24	19
Gabon	6	6	..	1.0 [e]	..	1.3 [e]	..	..	0.4 [e]	0.3 [e]	..	..
Gambia, The	7	6	1.4	1.1	0.6	0.5	0.3	0.2	7.6	15.2	24	30
Georgia	..	..									..	..
Germany	6	4	..	..	..	..	..	..	..	..	..	16
Ghana	6	6	0.5	0.8	0.7	0.9	0.0 [f]	0.3	..	..	29	28
Greece	6	6	0.8	0.8	0.9	1.3	0.5	0.5	..	..	24	..
Guatemala	7	6	0.6 [b]	0.4 [b]	0.2 [b]	0.2 [b]	0.3 [b]	0.3 [b]	..	..	34	32
Guinea	7	6	..	0.8 [a]	..	0.7 [a]	..	0.4 [a]	..	..	36	49
Guinea-Bissau	7	6	3.0	..	0.6	..	0.1	..	..	..	23	..
Haiti	6	6	0.7	0.8	0.2	0.3	0.1	0.1	0.0	0.0	44	..
Honduras	7	6	1.7	1.8	0.5	0.6	0.5	0.7	..	..	37	37
Hong Kong	6	6	0.7	0.7	0.8	1.0	0.5	0.8	..	..	30	27

	Primary school starting age	Duration of primary education	Public spending on education						Spending on teaching materials		Primary school pupil-teacher ratio	
			Primary % of GDP		Secondary % of GDP		Tertiary % of GDP		Primary % of total for level	Secondary % of total for level	pupils per teacher	
	years	years	1980	1992	1980	1992	1980	1992	1992	1992	1980	1993
Hungary	6	8	1.5	2.5 ᵍ	0.8	1.5	0.8	1.0	..	..	15	11
India	6	5	1.0	1.4	0.7	1.0	0.4	0.5	..	..	55	64
Indonesia	7	6	..	..	..	..	..	..	..	..	32	23
Iran, Islamic Rep.	6	5	2.8	1.3	2.5	1.7	0.5	0.6	..	..	27	32
Iraq	6	6	1.4	..	0.5	..	0.7	..	..	..	28	*22*
Ireland	6	6	1.4	1.5	2.1	2.1	0.9	1.1	0.3	0.2	29	24
Israel	6	8	2.4 ᵍ	*1.7* ᵍ	2.1	*1.6*	1.8	*0.9*	16.3ᵍ	16.8	15	16
Italy	6	5	*1.1*	1.0	*1.6*	1.8	*0.3*	1.2 ʰ	0.4	0.2	16	11
Jamaica	6	6	2.1 ᵇ	1.0ᵇ	2.3ᵇ	1.0ᵇ	1.2ᵇ	0.8ᵇ	..	..	41	*40*
Japan	6	6	1.5 ⁱ	..	1.4ⁱ	..	0.4ⁱ	..	..	..	25	19
Jordan	6	10	..	..	..	2.9	..	..	..	..	32	22
Kazakstan	7	4	..	..	..	..	..	..	..	..	..	18
Kenya	6	8	3.6	2.8	0.9	0.8	0.7	0.8	..	..	38	31
Korea, Dem. Rep.	6	4	..	..	..	..	..	..	..	..	..	..
Korea, Rep.	6	6	1.5	1.4	1.0	1.3	0.3	0.2	1.5	1.6	*48*	31
Kuwait	6	4	0.8	3.8ᵃ	1.1	*1.7*ᵃ	0.4	5.5ᵃ	..	..	19	..
Kyrgyz Republic	..	..	..	..	..	..	..	..	..	..	..	..
Lao PDR	6	5	..	0.7	..	0.8	..	0.1	..	..	30	30
Latvia	7	4	..	..	1.8	2.9	0.4	0.6	..	..	..	14
Lebanon	6	5	..	..	..	..	..	..	..	..	18	6
Lesotho	6	7	2.7	3.8	2.3	2.3	1.5	1.2	..	..	48	49
Libya	6	9	..	..	..	..	..	0.4	..	..	18	*12*
Lithuania	7	4	..	..	..	2.6	..	1.1	..	..	25	17
Macedonia, FYR	7	8	..	2.9	..	1.2	..	0.9	..	..	23	20
Madagascar	6	5	1.5	*0.7*ᵉ	0.9	*0.5*ᵉ	1.0	..	..	..	44	40
Malawi	6	8	0.9	1.9	0.4	0.4	0.7	0.7	1.8	9.2	65	68
Malaysia	6	6	1.7	1.7 ᵇ	1.6	1.7ᵇ	0.6	0.7ᵇ	..	..	27	20
Mali	8	6	1.4	..	0.9	..	0.9	..	..	..	*42*	60
Mauritania	6	6	1.7	..	2.4	..	0.6	..	..	..	41	53
Mauritius	5	6	2.1	*1.2*	1.7	*1.2*	0.4	*0.5*	..	..	20	21
Mexico	6	6	0.9 ᵇ	0.9ᵇ	0.7ᵇ	0.8ᵇ	0.4ᵇ	0.5ᵇ	0.0ᵇ	0.0ᵇ	*39*	29
Moldova	6	4	..	..	..	..	..	..	..	..	..	23
Mongolia	8	3	..	4.9ᵃ	..	..	..	1.8ᵃ	..	..	32	..
Morocco	7	6	1.7 ᵇ	1.6ᵇ	2.2ᵇ	2.5ᵇ	0.9ᵇ	0.8ᵇ	..	..	*38*	28
Mozambique	7	5	..	*1.7*ʲ	..	0.5ʲ	..	0.3ʲ	..	..	81	55
Myanmar	5	5	..	..	..	..	..	..	..	..	52	..
Namibia	7	7	..	..	..	..	..	..	..	..	..	*32*
Nepal	6	5	1.1	1.3	..	0.5	0.6	0.8	..	..	38	39
Netherlands	6	6	1.3 ᶜ,ᵏ	*0.9*ᶜ,ᵏ	2.3ᶜ,ᵏ	*2.1*ᶜ,ᵏ	1.9ᶜ	*1.8*ᶜ	1.6ᶜ,ᵏ	0.7ᶜ,ᵏ	23	16
New Zealand	5	6	1.8	1.5	1.5	1.4	1.4	2.5	..	..	17	*16*
Nicaragua	7	6	1.2	1.7ᵃ,ᵉ	0.7	0.5ᵃ,ᵉ	0.3	..	0.3ᵃ,ᵉ	0.9ᵃ,ᵉ	*35*	37
Niger	7	6	*1.0*	1.4ᵇ	1.3	0.9ᵇ	0.5	..	..	..	41	34
Nigeria	6	6	*0.9*	..	2.0	..	1.2	..	..	..	37	37
Norway	7	6	2.8 ᶜ,ᵏ	*2.7*ᶜ,ᵏ	1.4ᶜ,ᵏ	1.9ᶜ,ᵏ	0.8ᶜ	1.2ᶜ	2.0ᶜ,ᵏ	2.8ᶜ,ᵏ	8	*6*
Oman	6	6	..	1.6	..	1.3	..	0.2	2.3	2.7	23	27
Pakistan	5	5	0.6	..	0.4	..	0.3	..	..	..	36	*45*
Panama	6	6	2.0	1.6	1.0	1.0	0.6	1.3	..	..	27	*23*
Papua New Guinea	7	6	..	..	..	..	..	..	..	..	31	33
Paraguay	7	6	..	1.2	..	0.5	..	0.6	..	..	27	24
Peru	6	6	1.3	..	0.6	..	0.1	..	..	..	37	29
Philippines	7	6	1.0	..	0.3	..	0.4	..	..	..	30	33
Poland	7	8	0.9	1.9	0.7	1.0	0.8	0.9	..	..	21	17
Portugal	6	6	1.7 ᵇ	1.8ᵇ	0.8ᵇ	1.8ᵇ	0.3ᵇ	0.7ᵇ	..	..	*18*	12
Puerto Rico	5	8	..	..	..	..	..	..	..	..	..	..
Romania	6	4	..	1.3ᵃ	..	0.9ᵃ	..	0.5ᵃ	..	..	21	21
Russian Federation	7	3	..	..	..	..	..	..	..	..	28	20

2.7 | Education policy and infrastructure

	Primary school starting age	Duration of primary education	Public spending on education						Spending on teaching materials		Primary school pupil-teacher ratio	
			Primary % of GDP		Secondary % of GDP		Tertiary % of GDP		Primary % of total for level	Secondary % of total for level	pupils per teacher	
	years	years	1980	1992	1980	1992	1980	1992	1992	1992	1980	1993
Rwanda	7	7	1.5	..	0.5	..	0.2	..	..	..	59	58
Saudi Arabia	6	6	..	5.1	..	..	0.7	1.3	..	..	18	14
Senegal	7	6	1.8	1.7	1.2	1.0	1.1	0.9	..	..	46	54
Sierra Leone	5	7	..	..	..	..	..	..	..	..	33	34
Singapore	6	6	0.8	..	1.0	..	0.4	..	..	..	31	26
Slovak Republic	6	4	..	1.5	..	1.0	..	0.8	..	..	..	22
Slovenia	7	4	..	1.2	..	2.3	..	1.0	0.9	0.4	..	16
South Africa	6	7	..	5.3	..	..	..	0.8	3.2	..	27	27
Spain	6	5	1.3	0.9	0.4	1.9	0.3	0.7	..	..	..	20
Sri Lanka	5	5	..	..	2.1 [b]	1.7 [b]	0.2 [b]	0.3 [b]	..	..	16	29
Sudan	7	6	2.1	..	1.3	..	0.9	..	..	..	34	34
Sweden	7	6	3.4 [k]	3.0 [i,k]	1.0 [k]	1.3 [i,k]	0.7	1.2 [i]	3.5 [i,k]	7.9 [i,k]	..	10
Switzerland	7	6	..	2.2 [k]	3.4	1.2 [k]	0.9	0.9	3.4 [k]	6.0 [k]	..	..
Syrian Arab Republic	6	6	1.4	1.6 [a]	1.0	0.9 [a]	1.2 [a]	0.8 [a]	1.0 [a]	1.7 [a]	28	24
Tajikistan	7	4	..	..	..	..	..	..	..	..	..	22
Tanzania	7	7	2.1	..	0.8	..	0.4	..	..	..	41	37
Thailand	6	6	1.4	1.6	0.4	0.6	0.5	0.5	3.3	8.3	25	19
Togo	6	6	1.5	1.9	1.6	1.7	1.6	0.7	1.0	1.1	55	53
Trinidad and Tobago	5	7	1.4	1.4	1.0	1.2	0.3	0.4	..	..	24	27
Tunisia	6	6	1.9	2.2	1.7	1.9	0.9	1.0	..	..	39	26
Turkey	6	5	0.8	1.5	0.4	0.7	0.5	..	0.0	0.1	27	27
Turkmenistan	..	..	..	..	..	..	..	..	..	..	..	..
Uganda	6	7	0.3 [b]	..	1.1 [b]	..	0.3 [b]	..	..	..	34	31
Ukraine	7	4	1.5	2.1	0.8	0.9	0.7	0.7	..	..	45	20
United Arab Emirates	6	6	..	..	..	..	..	..	..	..	16	17
United Kingdom	5	6	1.4	1.3	2.1	2.1 [g]	1.2	1.0	5.2	3.2 [g]	19	20
United States	6	6	2.5 [a,c]	1.9	1.7 [a,c]	1.8	2.6 [a,c]	1.2	..	..	..	14
Uruguay	6	6	1.0 [l]	0.9	0.7	0.7	0.3	0.6	..	..	22	21
Uzbekistan	7	4	..	..	..	..	..	..	..	..	..	20
Venezuela	6	9	0.6 [m]	0.5	0.6 [m]	0.1	1.5 [m]	1.0	..	..	34	23
Vietnam	6	5	..	..	..	..	..	..	..	..	39	35
West Bank and Gaza	..	..	..	..	..	..	..	..	..	..	..	..
Yemen, Rep.	..	..	..	..	..	..	..	..	..	..	..	..
Yugoslavia, Fed. Rep.	7	4	..	..	..	..	..	..	8.7	15.1	..	22
Zaire	6	6	1.0	..	1.7	..	0.8	..	..	..	..	44
Zambia	7	7	1.8	..	1.0	..	0.7	..	..	..	49	44
Zimbabwe	7	7	4.2	5.0	1.4	2.6	0.5	1.6	1.2	2.3	..	..
World			..	..	..	..	**1.4 w**	..	..	..	**31 w**	..
Low income			0.9 w	1.0 w	0.8 w	0.8 w	0.4 w	0.5 w	..	..	34 w	33 w
Excl. China & India			..	..	..	..	..	..	..	..	41 w	39 w
Middle income			..	..	..	..	0.7 w	..	..	..	28 w	23 w
Lower middle income			1.4 w	..	1.0 w	..	0.7 w	..	..	..	29 w	23 w
Upper middle income			..	2.2 w	..	..	0.6 w	..	..	..	..	22 w
Low & middle income			1.2 w	..	..	..	0.6 w	..	..	..	32 w	28 w
East Asia & Pacific			0.8 w	..	0.7 w	..	0.4 w	..	..	..	28 w	23 w
Europe & Central Asia			1.1 w	..	..	..	0.7 w	..	..	..	..	17 w
Latin America & Carib.			1.2 w	..	0.5 w	..	0.7 w	..	..	..	30 w	24 w
Middle East & N. Africa			..	2.8 w	..	2.1 w	0.7 w	1.0 w	..	..	29 w	24 w
South Asia			0.9 w	1.4 w	0.6 w	1.0 w	0.3 w	0.5 w	..	..	..	..
Sub-Saharan Africa			..	..	..	..	..	..	..	..	39 w	36 w
High income			1.9 w	..	1.9 w	..	1.6 w	..	..	..	..	..

a. Includes capital expenditure. b. Ministry of education expenditure only. c. Includes both public and private expenditure. d. Excludes expenditure on specialized secondary and technical and vocational schools. e. Ministry of primary and secondary education expenditure only. f. Excludes expenditure on universities. g. Includes special education. h. Includes capital expenditure on universities. i. Excludes public subsidies to private education. j. Includes foreign aid for education. k. Expenditure on primary education covers six grades of primary and the first three grades of secondary education. Expenditure on secondary education covers only the last three grades of secondary education (upper secondary). l. Includes expenditure on special and adult education. m. Central government expenditure only.

Statistics on education are compiled by the United Nations Educational, Scientific, and Cultural Organization (UNESCO) from official replies to surveys and from reports provided by education authorities in each country. Because coverage, definitions, and data collection methods differ across countries and may change over time within a country, caution should be exercised when using education statistics. Although exceptions are noted in the table, it is advisable to consult the country- and indicator-specific notes in the source cited below. See Behrman and Rosenzweig (1994) for a general discussion of the reliability of data on education.

For many countries the primary school starting age and duration of primary education changed between 1980 and 1993 (see the notes to table 2.8 for definitions of primary, secondary, and tertiary levels). As a result the relative size of public spending on education by level and primary pupil-teacher ratios also may have changed. These changes also may affect the comparability of school enrollment ratios over time and across countries (see table 2.8).

The data on public spending on education exclude foreign aid received for education. They may also exclude expenditures by religious schools, which play a significant role in many developing countries. Data for some countries and for some years refer to expenditures of the ministry of education only (excluding education expenditures by other ministries and departments, local authorities, and so on). Data for a few countries include private expenditures (all such cases are noted), although national practices vary with respect to whether parents or schools pay for books, uniforms, and other supplies.

The comparability of pupil-teacher ratios is affected by differences in whether both full- and part-time teachers are included and in whether teachers are assigned nonteaching duties and by differences in class size by grade and in number of hours taught. Moreover, the underlying enrollment levels are subject to a variety of reporting errors (see *About the data* for table 2.8 for further discussion of enrollment data). While the pupil-teacher ratio is often used to compare the quality of schooling across countries, it is not strongly related to the value added of schooling systems (Behrman and Rosenzweig 1994).

● **Primary school starting age** is the age at which children are officially accepted for primary school education. ● **Duration of primary education** is the minimum number of grades (years) a child is expected to cover in primary schooling. ● **Public spending on education** is the ratio of public expenditures on public education plus subsidies to private education at primary, secondary, and tertiary levels to current GDP. ● **Spending on teaching materials** is the ratio of public expenditure on teaching materials to total public expenditure on primary or secondary education. Expenditure on teaching materials includes purchases of textbooks, books, and other scholastic supplies. ● **Primary school pupil-teacher ratio** is the number of pupils enrolled in primary school divided by the number of primary school teachers (regardless of their teaching assignment).

International statistics on education are compiled by UNESCO's Division of Statistics, in cooperation with the National Commissions for UNESCO and national statistical services. Data reported in this table were compiled using a UNESCO electronic database corresponding to various tables in UNESCO's *Statistical Yearbook 1995*.

Table 2.7a Public education spending per pupil, by level of schooling, 1985 and 1992
percentage of per capita GNP

Region or group	All levels 1985	Pre-primary and primary 1985	Secondary 1985	Tertiary 1985	All levels 1992	Pre-primary and primary 1992	Secondary 1992	Tertiary 1992
East Asia, including Oceania	14.3	7.6	18.1	129.2	14.4	8.2	18.9	90.1
Latin America and the Caribbean	12.2	6.3	12.7	43.5	14.2	8.2	12.9	48.6
Middle East and North Africa	23.6	17.2[a]		115.1	18.8	15.0[a]		75.7
South Asia	18.3	10.9	18.2	79.8	19.6	10.7	22.9	76.3
Sub-Saharan Africa	23.5	14.0	42.0	423.7	27.9	15.1	53.7	507.8
Least developed countries	18.3	10.6	27.9	155.3	18.1	10.1	32.3	142.8
Developing countries	16.4	11.3[a]		98.1	18.0	13.0[a]		84.9
Developed countries	20.7	16.8[a]		34.1	21.4	17.7[a]		29.4

Note: The regional groupings are based on the United Nations country classification. Bulgaria, the former Czechoslovakia, Romania, and the former Soviet Union are included with developed countries. a. Data are for preprimary, primary, and secondary levels.
Source: UNESCO 1995b.

2.8 | Access to education

| | Gross enrollment ratio | | | | | | | Age efficiency ratio | | | |
| | Preprimary % of relevant age group | Primary % of relevant age group | | Secondary % of relevant age group | | Tertiary % of relevant age group | | Primary net enrollment as % of gross enrollment | | Secondary net enrollment as % of gross enrollment | |
	1993	1980	1993	1980	1993	1980	1993	1980	1993	1980	1993
Albania	..	113	96	67	..	8	10	..	..	..	..
Algeria	3	94 [b]	103 [a]	33	61 [c]	6	11	86 [b]	91 [a]	57	54 [c]
Angola	53	..	88	20	14	0	1	39	..	74	..
Argentina	47	106	107	56	72	22	41	..	88	..	81
Armenia	..	..	90	..	85	30	49	..	..	..	..
Australia	71	111	108	71	84	25	42	91	92	98	96
Austria	75	99	103	93	107	22	43	88	87	70	67
Azerbaijan	23	..	89	..	88	25	26	..	..	..	..
Bangladesh	..	62	111	18	19	3	..	69	..	88	..
Belarus	79	..	96	98	92	39	44	..	..	..	..
Belgium	111	104 [c]	99	91	103	26	..	94	96	90	85
Benin	3	64 [d]	64 [d]	16 [a]	12	2	..	..	80 [d]	..	..
Bolivia	..	87	..	37 [b]	..	16	23	91	..	44 [b]	..
Bosnia and Herzegovina	..	..	..	..	..	..	..	..	..	..	..
Botswana	..	91	116	19	19	1	3	84	83	80	80
Brazil	36	99 [d]	111 [c]	34 [a]	43 [b]	11	12	82 [d]	80 [c]	44 [a]	45 [b]
Bulgaria	56	98	92	84	72	16	23	99	96	90	91
Burkina Faso	..	18 [c]	38 [c]	3 [b]	8 [e]	0	..	83 [c]	81 [c]	..	79 [e]
Burundi	..	26 [e]	72 [d]	3 [b]	7	1	1	74	74	80	72
Cambodia	..	..	..	..	..	..	..	..	..	..	..
Cameroon	17	98 [e]	87	18 [c]	32	2	2	72 [e]	..	78 [c]	..
Canada	58	99	105	88	88	52	103	91	94	69	64
Central African Republic	..	71 [e]	..	14 [e]	..	1	2	80 [e]	..	..	..
Chad	..	..	59	..	9	..	1	..	..	..	..
Chile	86	109	98	52	70 [c]	12	27	..	89	..	79 [c]
China	27	112	109	46	52	1	6	..	81	..	..
Colombia	22	124	119 [a]	41	62 [a]	9	10	..	71 [a]	..	66 [a]
Congo	..	..	..	..	..	..	..	..	..	..	..
Costa Rica	66	105 [a]	105 [a]	48 [b]	47 [b]	21	30	85 [a]	86 [a]	83 [b]	..
Côte d'Ivoire	1	79 [d]	69 [e]	19 [b]	25 [c]	3	..	..	71 [e]	..	..
Croatia	26	91	85	..	83	..	27	..	..	..	..
Cuba	94	106 [a]	104	81	77	17	18	90 [a]	96	..	76
Czech Republic	88	..	103	..	86	18	16	..	..	..	..
Denmark	98	96	98	105	114	28	41	100	100	84	77
Dominican Republic	20	118 [c]	97	42	37	..	..	60 [c]	63	..	81
Ecuador	23	117 [b]	123	53 [b]	55	35	..	77 [b]	..	..	..
Egypt, Arab Rep.	7	73 [a]	97 [a]	50	76 [b]	16	17	..	76 [a]	..	81 [b]
El Salvador	25	75	79 [a]	24	29	4	15	92	90 [a]	..	..
Eritrea	4	..	47 [d]	..	14 [d]	..	..	..	55 [d]	..	74 [d]
Estonia	69	..	83	..	92	43	38	..	95	..	80
Ethiopia	1	34	23 [a]	8	11 [c]	0	1	..	75 [a]	..	..
Finland	37	96	100	100	119	32	63	..	..	..	..
France	84	111	106	85	106 [b]	25	50	90	94	93	85 [b]
Gabon	..	..	..	..	..	..	3	..	..	..	..
Gambia, The	24	51 [b]	73 [b]	11	19	..	..	95	82 [b]	..	96
Georgia	..	..	..	..	..	30	..	..	..	..	..
Germany	101	..	97	..	101	..	36	..	84	..	71
Ghana	..	80	76	41	36	2	..	..	..	..	..
Greece	..	103	..	81	..	17	..	94	96	90	88
Guatemala	31	71 [c]	84 [c]	18	24	8	..	82 [c]	..	68	..
Guinea	..	36 [d]	46 [d]	17 [e]	12 [d]	5	..	..	42 [d]	..	..
Guinea-Bissau	..	68	..	6	6	..	..	69 [e]	..	45	..
Haiti	..	76	..	14 [a]	..	1	..	50	..	..	..
Honduras	20	98 [c]	112 [b]	30	32 [b]	8	9	79 [c]	81 [b]	..	62 [b]
Hong Kong	81	107	102	64 [a]	..	10	21	89	..	95 [a]	..

| | Gross enrollment ratio | | | | | | | Age efficiency ratio | | | |
| | Preprimary % of relevant age group | Primary % of relevant age group | | Secondary % of relevant age group | | Tertiary % of relevant age group | | Primary net enrollment as % of gross enrollment | | Secondary net enrollment as % of gross enrollment | |
	1993	1980	1993	1980	1993	1980	1993	1980	1993	1980	1993
Hungary	114	96	95	70	81	14	17	98	*96*	..	*93*
India	..	83	105	30	..	5	..	..	..	..	..
Indonesia	35	107 [a]	114 [a]	29	43	..	10	82 [a]	85 [a]	..	86
Iran, Islamic Rep.	7	87	105 [a]	42	66 [b]	..	15	..	87 [a]	..	..
Iraq	*8*	113	91	57	44 [e]	9	..	*87*	87	*82*	85 [e]
Ireland	*106*	100	103	90	105	*18*	34	90	87	..	75
Israel	*81*	95	95	73	87	29	35	..	..	..	..
Italy	95	100	98	72 [a]	81 [a]	27	37	..	..	..	..
Jamaica	*73*	103	109	67	66	*7*	6	*93*	94	*96*	98
Japan	49	101	102	93	96	*31*	30	..	..	*100*	100
Jordan	*25*	104	94	76	53	*27*	19	97	94	89	70
Kazakstan	..	..	86	..	90	34	42	..	..	..	..
Kenya	34	115 [b]	91	20	25	1	..	79 [b]	..	..	..
Korea, Dem. Rep.	..	..	..	..	..	..	..	..	..	..	..
Korea, Rep.	71	110	101	78	93	15	48	64	60	90	94
Kuwait	45	102 [a]	..	80 [b]	..	11	..	83 [a]	*84*	81 [b]	77
Kyrgyz Republic	..	..	..	..	..	28	21	..	..	..	..
Lao PDR	7	113	107 [e]	21	25 [a]	0	2	..	63 [e]	..	72 [a]
Latvia	38	..	83	..	87	45	39	..	95	..	74
Lebanon	73	111	115	59	76	*30*	29	..	..	..	..
Lesotho	..	102 [d]	98 [d]	18	26	2	2	64 [d]	67 [d]	*73*	63
Libya	..	125 [a]	110	76 [b]	97	8	16	99	96	..	..
Lithuania	34	..	92	..	78	49	39	..	..	..	..
Macedonia, FYR	21	100	87	61	54	28	16	..	..	..	..
Madagascar	..	136	73 [e]	..	14 [d]	3	4	..	..	..	..
Malawi	..	60 [c]	80 [c]	3	4	1	1	72 [c]	77 [c]	..	38
Malaysia	35	93	93	48	59	4	..	..	..	..	..
Mali	2	27 [e]	31 [e]	9 [e]	9 [e]	1	..	69 [e]	70 [e]	..	..
Mauritania	..	37 [b]	69 [c]	11 [a]	15 [b]	..	4	..	..	..	..
Mauritius	..	93	106 [a]	50	59 [c]	*1*	4	..	..	..	..
Mexico	65	122 [b]	112 [a]	48	58	14	14	..	88 [a]	..	..
Moldova	59	..	77	..	69	29	35	..	..	..	..
Mongolia	..	107	..	91	78	..	..	93	..	95	..
Morocco	*62*	83 [e]	73	26 [c]	35 [c]	6	10	*74*	76	*78*	84 [c]
Mozambique	..	99 [e]	60 [e]	5	7 [e]	0	0	49 [e]	68 [e]	..	..
Myanmar	..	91	..	22	..	..	..	..	..	..	..
Namibia	*13*	..	136 [d]	..	55	..	3	..	66 [d]	..	55
Nepal	..	84	107 [e]	21	21 [a]	*3*	6	..	..	..	..
Netherlands	98	100	97	93 [b]	93	*29*	45	92	96	*88*	70
New Zealand	77	111	102	83	104	27	58	*96*	97	*98*	93
Nicaragua	15	99 [c]	103 [c]	42	41 [a]	*13*	9	75 [c]	77 [c]	54	63 [a]
Niger	*2*	25 [b]	29 [c]	5 [a]	7	*0*	1	83 [b]	..	79 [a]	..
Nigeria	..	119	93	21 [a]	29	2	..	..	..	..	..
Norway	113	100	99	94	116	26	54	99	100	89	79
Oman	3	52	85 [a]	12	61 [b]	..	5	84	86 [a]	*86*	88 [b]
Pakistan	..	39	65	14	..	..	..	..	..	..	..
Panama	..	106 [b]	105	61	64	*21*	23	83 [b]	..	75	..
Papua New Guinea	*0*	59	74	12	12	2	..	..	..	..	..
Paraguay	41	104 [b]	112 [a]	26	37	8	10	84 [b]	*86*	82	85
Peru	34	114 [c]	119	59 [a]	65	*17*	40	76 [c]	74	78 [a]	81
Philippines	12	113	111	64	79	24	26	89	88	70	..
Poland	42	100	98	77	84	18	26	98	98	..	..
Portugal	*48*	123	120	37	81	*11*	23	80	85	..	..
Puerto Rico	..	..	..	..	..	48	..	..	..	..	..
Romania	*76*	102	95	71	82 [a]	*12*	12	..	100	..	87 [a]
Russian Federation	63	102	107	96	88	46	45	..	90	..	..

| | Gross enrollment ratio | | | | | | | | Age efficiency ratio | | | |
	Preprimary % of relevant age group	Primary % of relevant age group		Secondary % of relevant age group		Tertiary % of relevant age group		Primary net enrollment as % of gross enrollment		Secondary net enrollment as % of gross enrollment	
	1993	1980	1993	1980	1993	1980	1993	1980	1993	1980	1993
Rwanda	..	63 [a]	50	3	10	0	..	88	93	..	78
Saudi Arabia	8	61 [c]	75 [a]	29 [c]	29 [c]	7	14	79 [c]	81 [a]	72 [c]	71 [c]
Senegal	2	46 [c]	54 [c]	11 [b]	11 [c]	3	3	77 [c]	83 [c]	..	..
Sierra Leone	..	52	..	14	..	1	..	..	..	..	..
Singapore	..	108 [a]	107	58 [b]	78	8	..	92 [a]	..	99 [b]	..
Slovak Republic	77	..	101	..	89	..	17	..	..	..	..
Slovenia	61	..	97	..	89	..	28	..	..	..	..
South Africa	24	..	111	..	77 [c]	..	13	..	82	..	65 [c]
Spain	67	109 [a]	104	87 [b]	113	23	41	93	95	85	82
Sri Lanka	..	103 [b]	106 [a]	55 [a]	74 [b]	3	6	..	..	..	..
Sudan	23	50	50	16	20	2	2	..	..	..	..
Sweden	67	97	100	88	99	31	38	99	99	93	94
Switzerland	91	..	101	..	91	18	31	94	92	71	69
Syrian Arab Republic	6	100 [a]	105 [a]	46 [b]	47 [b]	17	18	90 [a]	91 [a]	..	..
Tajikistan	16	..	89	..	100	24	25	..	..	..	..
Tanzania	..	93	70	3	5	..	..	73	72	..	..
Thailand	50	99 [a]	98	29	37	13	19	..	..	..	..
Togo	3	118 [e]	102 [e]	33 [e]	27 [e]	2	3	67 [e]	68 [e]	..	..
Trinidad and Tobago	9	99	94	70	76	4	8	90	93	78	71
Tunisia	9	103 [d]	118 [c]	27 [b]	52 [c]	5	11	80 [d]	83 [c]	67	59
Turkey	5	96	103 [a]	35	61	5	16	..	92 [a]	..	..
Turkmenistan	..	..	..	..	..	23	..	..	..	..	..
Uganda	..	50	91	5	13	1	1	74	..	..	..
Ukraine	54	102	87	94	80	42	46	..	..	..	..
United Arab Emirates	64	89 [a]	110	52 [a]	89 [a]	3	11	83 [a]	91	83 [a]	90
United Kingdom	27	103	112	83	92	19	37	94	85	95	92
United States	62	100	107	91	97	56	81	..	..	..	80
Uruguay	33	107 [c]	109 [a]	62	81	17	30	..	87 [a]	..	..
Uzbekistan	..	..	80	..	94	30	33	..	..	..	..
Venezuela	43	93	96 [b]	21 [a]	35	21	29	96	96 [b]	..	..
Vietnam	30	109	111	42	35	2	2	87	..	..	..
West Bank and Gaza	..	..	..	..	..	..	..	..	..	..	..
Yemen, Rep.	..	..	..	..	..	..	..	..	..	..	..
Yugoslavia, Fed. Rep.	25	99	72	82	65	..	19	..	..	..	..
Zaire	1	92 [c]	68 [d]	24	24 [e]	1	..	..	79 [d]	..	67 [e]
Zambia	..	90	104	16	..	2	..	86	..	..	..
Zimbabwe	..	85	119	8	45	1	6	..	..	..	..
World	..	**95 w**	**104 w**	**47 w**	..	**13 w**	..	..	..	..	..
Low income	..	92 w	105 w	33 w	..	3 w	..	..	..	..	..
Excl. China & India	..	75 w	83 w	19 w	..	3 w	..	..	..	..	..
Middle income	28 w	101 w	104 w	52 w	62 w	20 w	20 w	..	..	..	..
Lower middle income	22 w	101 w	104 w	54 w	64 w	24 w	23 w	..	..	..	..
Upper middle income	41 w	104 w	107 w	44 w	55 w	13 w	17 w	..	..	..	..
Low & middle income	..	95 w	104 w	39 w	..	8 w	..	..	..	..	..
East Asia & Pacific	26 w	110 w	117 w	43 w	55 w	3 w	5 w	..	..	..	..
Europe & Central Asia	30 w	101 w	97 w	81 w	86 w	31 w	32 w	..	..	..	..
Latin America & Carib.	43 w	106 w	110 w	42 w	51 w	14 w	15 w	..	..	..	..
Middle East & N. Africa	13 w	87 w	97 w	42 w	59 w	11 w	14 w	..	..	..	..
South Asia	..	76 w	98 w	27 w	..	5 w	..	..	..	..	..
Sub-Saharan Africa	..	80 w	72 w	15 w	24 w	1 w	..	..	..	..	..
High income	70 w	93 w	103 w	86 w	97 w	35 w	55 w	..	..	..	..

Percentage of repeaters in total enrollment: a. 5–9. b. 10–14. c. 15–19. d. 20–25. e. More than 25.

About the data

School enrollment data are important indicators of the size and capacity of the education system and may be useful measures of outcomes, but they are notoriously rife with errors. The data here are reported to the United Nations Educational, Scientific, and Cultural Organization (UNESCO) by national education authorities on the basis of annual enrollment surveys, typically conducted at the beginning of the school year. They do not reflect actual rates of attendance or the nonattendance of dropouts during the school year. Furthermore, school administrators may have incentives to exaggerate enrollments. Behrman and Rosenzweig (1994), comparing official school enrollment data for Malaysia in 1988 with gross school attendance rates from a household survey, found that the official statistics systematically overstated enrollment.

Overage or underage enrollments may occur, particularly when parents prefer for cultural or economic reasons to have children start school at other than the official age. Children's age at enrollment may also be inaccurately estimated or misstated, especially in communities where registration of births is not strictly enforced. Parents who choose to enroll their underage children in primary school may do so by over-reporting the age of the child. And in education systems where the authorities are willing to alter school records, ages for children repeating a grade may be deliberately underreported.

Other problems affecting cross-country comparisons of enrollment data stem from measurement errors in estimates of school-age populations. Age-sex structures from censuses or vital registration systems, the primary sources for school-age population data, are commonly subject to underenumeration (especially of young children) in order to circumvent laws or regulations or from age heaping resulting from parents' rounding up children's ages. While adjustments for age bias are commonly made in census data, such adjustments are rarely made for data from inadequate vital registration systems. Compounding these problems, pre- and post-census year estimates of school-age children are either interpolations or projections (see the discussion of demographic data in the notes to table 2.1).

In using enrollment data, it is important to consider repetition rates, which are quite high in some developing countries, leading to a substantial number of overage children enrolled in each grade. The gross enrollment ratios here provide an indication of the capacity of each level of education relative to the age group that should be enrolled at that level. But a high ratio does not necessarily indicate a successful education system. The quality of schools varies widely within countries, between countries, and over time. Thus a lower enrollment ratio could be consistent with greater aggregate, quality-adjusted educational capital if quality more than compensates for quantity.

The gross enrollment ratios for primary and secondary levels have been calculated by taking into account different national systems of education with different durations of schooling at the primary and secondary levels. For the tertiary level the ratios are expressed as a percentage of the population in the five-year age group following the secondary school leaving age. The population estimates used to calculate gross enrollment ratios are from the United Nations and are midyear estimates, while enrollments refer to the beginning of the school year.

The age efficiency ratio, a useful complement to the gross enrollment ratio, reflects the extent to which planned (net) enrollments match actual (gross) enrollments. It does not measure the cost-efficiency of the system. Nor does it reflect the quality of the education provided. However, lower efficiency ratios are likely to be associated with higher direct costs of schooling because of the cost of providing teachers, materials, and classrooms for repeaters, and with higher opportunity costs of providing schooling to overage students. Windham (1988) provides a general discussion of efficiency indicators.

In general, the enrollment data in this table cover both public and private schools but may exclude certain specialized schools and training programs. Interested readers should consult the notes to the appropriate tables in UNESCO's *Statistical Yearbook 1995*.

Definitions

● **Gross enrollment ratio** is the ratio of total enrollment, regardless of age, to the population of the age group that officially corresponds to the level of education shown. Estimates are based on UNESCO's classification of education levels, as follows: **Preprimary** provides education for children not old enough to enter school at the first level. **Primary**, or first level, provides the basic elements of education at elementary or primary school (see table 2.7 for duration of primary school). **Secondary** provides general or specialized instruction at middle, secondary, or high schools, teacher training schools, and vocational or technical schools; this level of education is based on at least four years of instruction at the first level. **Tertiary** requires, as a minimum condition of admission, the successful completion of education at the second level or evidence of attainment of an equivalent level of knowledge and is provided at a university, teachers college, or higher-level professional school. ● **Age efficiency ratio** is the ratio of net enrollment to gross enrollment at the primary and secondary levels. **Net enrollment ratio** is the ratio of the number of children of official school age enrolled in school to the number of children of official school age in the population.

Data sources

Gross enrollment ratios are from UNESCO's *Statistical Yearbook 1995*. Age efficiency ratios were compiled by World Bank staff using the UNESCO database on enrollment by level, age, and gender.

2.9 | Educational attainment

	Percentage of cohort reaching grade 4				Progression to secondary school				Expected years of schooling			
	Male		Female		Male %		Female %		Male		Female	
	1980	1990	1980	1990	1980	1990	1980	1990	1980	1992	1980	1992
Albania	97	..	96	..	..	..	..	..	..	..	..	..
Algeria	92 [b]	96 [b]	91	95 [a]	55 [j]	77	62 [i]	83 [f]	9	11	6	9
Angola	..	49	..	37	..	..	..	..	8	..	7	..
Argentina	73	..	76	..	..	..	..	..	..	13	..	14
Armenia	..	..	..	..	..	..	..	..	..	..	..	..
Australia	94	..	97	..	..	..	..	..	12	13	12	14
Austria	92	97	97	99	..	..	..	..	11	15	11	14
Azerbaijan	..	..	..	..	..	..	..	..	..	..	..	..
Bangladesh	29	44	30	46	..	..	..	..	..	..	..	..
Belarus	..	..	..	..	..	..	..	..	..	..	..	..
Belgium	78 [d]	..	81 [c]	..	..	..	..	..	14	14	13	14
Benin	77 [e]	58	73 [e]	58	62 [j]	..	48 [j]	..	..	..	..	..
Bolivia	52	..	50	..	..	..	..	..	9	11	8	9
Bosnia and Herzegovina	..	..	..	..	..	..	..	..	..	..	..	..
Botswana	91 [b]	..	98 [b]	..	..	84 [f]	..	85 [f]	7	10	8	11
Brazil	..	..	..	..	98	..	98	..	9	..	9	..
Bulgaria	98	93 [a]	95	91	..	..	..	..	11	11	11	12
Burkina Faso	79 [b]	86 [b]	79 [b]	90 [b]	..	27 [j]	..	27 [j]	2	3	1	2
Burundi	83 [b]	79 [d]	83 [b]	79 [d]	8	..	7	..	3	5	2	4
Cambodia	..	..	..	..	..	..	..	..	..	..	..	..
Cameroon	81 [d]	..	81 [d]	..	24 [g]	..	19 [g]	..	8	..	6	..
Canada	94	95	97	98	..	..	..	..	15	17	15	18
Central African Republic	..	..	..	..	38 [j]	..	35 [j]	..	..	..	..	..
Chad	..	74 [d]	..	65 [d]	..	..	..	..	..	..	..	..
Chile	78 [a]	..	81 [a]	..	79	..	80	..	..	12	..	12
China	..	..	..	..	..	..	..	..	..	..	..	..
Colombia	42 [a]	72 [a]	46 [a]	74	..	..	..	..	..	..	..	..
Congo	91 [e]	..	91 [e]	..	86 [i]	..	80 [i]	..	..	..	..	..
Costa Rica	80 [c]	90 [a]	84	91 [a]	52	66	53	67	10	10	10	9
Côte d'Ivoire	94 [c]	85 [c]	91 [d]	82 [d]	31 [j]	..	27 [j]	..	..	..	..	..
Croatia	..	..	..	..	..	16	..	28	..	11	..	11
Cuba	91 [b]	..	96	..	..	..	..	..	..	12	..	13
Czech Republic	..	..	..	..	..	..	..	..	..	..	..	..
Denmark	..	..	..	..	..	..	..	..	14	15	14	15
Dominican Republic	..	..	..	..	..	..	..	..	..	10	..	10
Ecuador	78 [b]	..	76	..	..	..	..	..	..	..	..	..
Egypt, Arab Rep.	75	..	83	..	..	82 [h]	..	85 [g]	..	11	..	9
El Salvador	52 [a]	..	55 [a]	..	28	22	26	17	..	9	..	9
Eritrea	..	..	..	..	..	84	..	70	..	..	..	..
Estonia	..	..	..	..	..	91	..	96	..	12	..	13
Ethiopia	42	..	48	..	..	82	..	77	..	..	..	..
Finland	99	98	99	98	..	..	..	..	..	..	..	..
France	..	..	..	..	..	..	..	..	13	14	13	15
Gabon	82 [d]	..	79 [d]	..	..	..	..	..	..	..	..	..
Gambia, The	..	..	..	..	41 [j]	..	42 [j]	..	..	5	6	3
Georgia	..	..	..	..	..	..	..	..	..	..	..	..
Germany	96	..	98	..	..	99	..	99	..	15	..	14
Ghana	87	..	82	..	..	..	..	..	..	..	..	..
Greece	98	..	98	..	..	..	..	..	12	13	12	13
Guatemala	66 [b]	..	56	..	..	..	..	..	..	..	..	..
Guinea	..	81 [c]	..	78 [d]	..	51 [j]	..	47 [j]	..	4	..	2
Guinea-Bissau	63 [e]	..	47 [e]	..	71 [g]	..	46 [h]	..	6	..	3	..
Haiti	63	60	64	60	38	..	45	..	..	..	..	..
Honduras	..	..	..	..	..	..	..	..	..	..	..	..
Hong Kong	100	..	99	..	87	..	93	..	12	..	12	..

	Percentage of cohort reaching grade 4				Progression to secondary school				Expected years of schooling			
	Male		Female		Male %		Female %		Male		Female	
	1980	1990	1980	1990	1980	1990	1980	1990	1980	1992	1980	1992
Hungary	96	..	96	..	14	15	28	29	9	12	10	12
India	57	..	52	..	..	..	..	..	..	..	..	..
Indonesia	..	..	..	..	..	..	..	..	..	10	..	9
Iran, Islamic Rep.	..	94 a	..	93	..	85 g	..	83 f	..	10	..	8
Iraq	88	..	85	..	46	..	51	..	12	9	9	7
Ireland	97	98	100	99	..	..	..	..	11	13	11	13
Israel	97	98	98	97	..	..	..	..	..	..	..	..
Italy	..	..	..	..	98	99	98	100	..	..	..	..
Jamaica	..	98	..	100	..	..	..	..	10	11	11	11
Japan	100	100	100	100	100	100	100	100	13	..	12	..
Jordan	95 a	99	95 a	97	88 f	60	88 f	75	12	11	12	12
Kazakstan	..	..	..	..	..	..	..	..	..	..	..	..
Kenya	84	..	85	..	..	..	..	..	..	..	..	..
Korea, Dem. Rep.	..	..	..	..	..	..	..	..	..	..	..	..
Korea, Rep.	96	100	96	100	99	..	96	..	12	14	11	13
Kuwait	..	..	..	..	98	97	98	97	11	..	11	..
Kyrgyz Republic	..	..	..	..	..	..	..	..	..	..	..	..
Lao PDR	31	..	31	..	..	70 h	..	66 h	..	8	..	6
Latvia	..	..	..	..	..	..	..	..	..	..	..	..
Lebanon	..	..	..	..	..	..	..	..	..	..	..	..
Lesotho	61 d	75 d	77 c	85 c	..	..	..	..	7	8	10	10
Libya	99	..	93	..	77	..	76	..	..	..	..	..
Lithuania	..	..	..	..	..	..	..	..	..	..	..	..
Macedonia, FYR	..	..	..	..	..	..	..	..	..	..	..	..
Madagascar	..	68 e	..	72 e	..	35	..	35 j	..	..	..	..
Malawi	62 a	73 b	55 a	68 a	..	..	..	..	..	6	..	5
Malaysia	..	98	..	99	..	..	..	..	..	..	..	..
Mali	73 e	..	77 e	..	41 j	64 j	36 j	60 j	..	2	..	1
Mauritania	96 e	82 b	86	83 c	..	34 j	..	28 j	..	..	..	..
Mauritius	97	..	97	..	47	49 j	47	54 j	..	..	..	..
Mexico	91 b	..	65	..	..	86	..	81	..	..	..	..
Moldova	..	..	..	..	..	96	..	97	..	..	..	..
Mongolia	..	..	..	..	..	..	..	..	..	..	..	..
Morocco	90 e	83	89 e	81	..	79 f	..	84 f	8	8	5	6
Mozambique	..	60 d	..	54 d	25	39	23	39 i	5	4	4	3
Myanmar	..	..	..	..	..	..	..	..	..	..	..	..
Namibia	..	..	..	..	..	76 h	..	72 h	..	12	..	13
Nepal	..	..	..	..	..	..	..	..	..	..	..	..
Netherlands	97	..	100	..	65	..	75	..	14	16	13	15
New Zealand	..	98	..	99	..	..	..	..	14	15	13	16
Nicaragua	51 a	..	55 a	..	..	..	..	..	8	8	9	9
Niger	82 c	..	79 c	..	38 j	..	30 i	..	..	3	..	1
Nigeria	..	74	..	76	..	..	..	..	..	..	..	..
Norway	99	..	100	..	..	..	..	..	13	15	13	16
Oman	..	..	..	..	74	88	83	93	5	8	2	7
Pakistan	53	55	41	45	..	..	..	..	..	..	..	..
Panama	87 b	85	88 a	88	..	..	..	..	11	11	11	11
Papua New Guinea	77	72	85	70	..	..	..	..	..	..	..	..
Paraguay	..	79 a	..	78 a	..	..	..	..	..	9	..	8
Peru	85	..	83	..	81 f	..	78 f	..	11	..	10	..
Philippines	..	..	..	..	..	..	..	..	10	11	11	11
Poland	..	..	..	..	..	..	..	..	12	12	12	12
Portugal	..	..	..	..	..	..	..	..	..	..	..	..
Puerto Rico	..	..	..	..	..	..	..	..	..	..	..	..
Romania	..	93	..	94	..	..	..	..	..	11	..	11
Russian Federation	..	..	..	..	..	..	..	..	..	..	..	..

2.9 Educational attainment

	Percentage of cohort reaching grade 4				Progression to secondary school				Expected years of schooling			
	Male		Female		Male %		Female %		Male		Female	
	1980	1990	1980	1990	1980	1990	1980	1990	1980	1992	1980	1992
Rwanda	73[b]	73[b]	74[b]	76[b]	5	..	2	..	..	6	..	6
Saudi Arabia	91[c]	..	90[b]	..	85[g]	..	94	..	7	9	5	8
Senegal	93[b]	..	90[b]	..	..	..	..	..	..	6	..	4
Sierra Leone	..	..	..	..	..	..	..	..	..	..	..	..
Singapore	96	..	98	..	72[h]	..	78[h]	..	11	..	11	..
Slovak Republic	..	..	..	..	..	98	..	99	..	..	..	..
Slovenia	..	..	..	..	..	..	..	..	..	..	..	..
South Africa	..	..	..	..	..	..	..	..	..	12	..	12
Spain	92	..	94	..	..	..	..	..	13	14	12	15
Sri Lanka	..	..	..	..	..	..	..	..	..	..	..	..
Sudan	83	..	71	..	..	..	..	..	..	..	..	..
Sweden	99	..	100	..	..	..	..	..	12	14	13	14
Switzerland	92	..	94	..	42	45	42	46	14	15	13	14
Syrian Arab Republic	94[a]	..	91[a]	..	76[g]	69[f]	76	62	11	10	8	9
Tajikistan	..	..	..	..	..	..	..	..	..	..	..	..
Tanzania	90	89[b]	89	90[b]	..	..	..	..	..	..	..	..
Thailand	..	..	..	..	..	..	..	..	..	..	..	..
Togo	90[e]	87[e]	84[e]	82[e]	39[j]	..	34[j]	..	..	11	..	6
Trinidad and Tobago	83	96	89	97	..	..	..	..	11	11	11	11
Tunisia	94[d]	95[c]	90[c]	93[b]	31[j]	57[j]	31[j]	59[j]	10	11	7	10
Turkey	..	98	..	98	47	..	33	..	..	..	..	..
Turkmenistan	..	..	..	..	..	..	..	..	..	..	..	..
Uganda	83	..	74	..	..	..	..	..	..	..	..	..
Ukraine	..	..	..	..	..	..	..	..	..	..	..	..
United Arab Emirates	..	94[a]	..	93	..	97	..	99	8	11	7	12
United Kingdom	..	..	..	..	..	..	..	..	13	15	13	15
United States	..	..	..	..	..	..	..	..	14	16	15	16
Uruguay	93	98[a]	99	98[a]	..	..	..	..	..	..	..	..
Uzbekistan	..	..	..	..	..	..	..	..	..	..	..	..
Venezuela	84[c]	..	83	..	69	..	70	..	..	10	..	11
Vietnam	71	..	67	..	..	..	..	..	..	..	..	..
West Bank and Gaza	..	..	..	..	..	..	..	..	..	..	..	..
Yemen, Rep.	..	..	..	..	..	..	..	..	..	..	..	..
Yugoslavia, Fed. Rep.	..	..	..	..	..	..	..	..	..	..	..	..
Zaire	73[c]	..	70[c]	..	..	25[f]	..	30[g]	..	7	..	4
Zambia	..	..	..	..	..	..	..	..	..	..	..	..
Zimbabwe	67	..	64	..	..	..	..	..	..	..	..	..

Percentage of repeaters in grade 4: a. 5–9. b. 10–14. c. 15–19. d. 20–24. e. More than 24.
Percentage of repeaters in final primary grade: f. 5–9. g. 10–14. h. 15–19. i. 20–24. j. More than 24.

Indicators of persistence or grade progression provide a measure of how successful an education system is in maintaining a flow of students from one grade to the next and thus of imparting a particular level of education. Although school attendance is mandatory in most countries, at least through the primary level, students drop out of school for a variety of reasons; discouragement over poor performance, the cost of schooling, and the opportunity cost of additional time spent in school are frequently cited. In addition, the progress of students to higher grades may be limited by the availability of teachers, classrooms, and educational materials.

Persistence measures the proportion of a single-year cohort of students that eventually reaches a particular grade or level of schooling. Tracking data for individual students are not available, so calculations are based on the reconstructed cohort method. This method uses data on average promotion, repetition, and dropout rates to calculate the flow of students from one grade to the next. Other flows caused by new entrants, reentrants, grade skipping, migration, or school transfers during the school year are not considered. The reconstructed cohort method makes three simplifying assumptions: dropouts never return to school; promotion, repetition, and dropout rates remain constant over the entire period in which the cohort is enrolled in school; and the same rates apply to all pupils enrolled in a given grade, regardless of whether they previously repeated a grade.

Because UNESCO data do not include dropouts or dropout rates, the number of dropouts was estimated as the difference between enrollments in successive grades in successive years, after netting out repeaters. The remaining students are assumed to be promoted. Repeated application of the same calculations leads to an estimate of the number of students entering each successive grade (Fredricksen 1991).

The percentage of the cohort reaching grade 4, rather than some other grade, is shown for two reasons. First, because of differences among countries in the duration of primary schooling, which ranges from three to 10 grades (see table 2.7 for each country's duration of primary schooling), grade 4 estimates are more comparable across countries than are estimates for other grades. Second, using grade 4 minimizes the effect of repetition at or close to the final grade of primary education.

Progression to secondary school measures the proportion of students in the final grade of primary school who enter the first year of the general secondary system. The comparability of this indicator across time and between countries may be affected by changes in the definition of the primary and secondary levels, rules governing repetition and promotion, and the availability of special programs and other alternatives to the general secondary education system. Enrollment in the final grade of primary school may be systematically overestimated because enrollment as reported at the beginning of the school year includes dropouts who may leave school during the year.

Expected years of schooling estimates the total number of years of schooling that an average child will receive. It may also be interpreted as an indicator of the total education resources, measured in school years, that a child will require over his or her "lifetime" in school. Because the calculation of this indicator assumes that the probability of a child's being enrolled in school at any future age is equal to the current enrollment ratio for that age, changes and trends in future enrollment ratios are not accounted for.

● **Percentage of cohort reaching grade 4** is the proportion of children enrolled in primary school in 1980 and 1990 who reach grade 4 in 1983 and 1993, respectively. The estimate is based on the reconstructed cohort method (see *About the data*).

● **Progression to secondary school** is the number of new entrants in the first grade of secondary (general) school divided by the number of children enrolled in the final grade of primary school in the previous year (according to the country's duration of primary education, as shown in table 2.7).

● **Expected years of schooling** are the average number of years of formal schooling that a child is expected to receive, including university education and years spent in repetition. They are the sum of the age-specific gross enrollment ratios for primary, secondary, and tertiary education.

Estimates of the percentage of cohort reaching grade 4 and progression to secondary school were compiled using the UNESCO database on enrollment by level, grade or field, and gender. Data on expected years of schooling are from UNESCO's *Statistical Yearbook,* supplemented by information from UNESCO's *World Education Report.*

2.10 | Gender and education

	Primary education				Secondary general				Secondary vocational			
	Teachers % female		Pupils % female		Teachers % female		Pupils % female		Teachers % female		Pupils % female	
	1980	1993	1980	1993	1980	1993	1980	1993	1980	1993	1980	1993
Albania	50	60	47	49	46	58	59	56	32	..	41	36
Algeria	37	43	42	46	..	44	39	46	..	19	21	34
Angola	..	..	47	..	..	..	33	..	..	..	21	..
Argentina	92	..	49	49	75	..	64	..	..	..	47	..
Armenia	..	..	..	50	..	..	..	..	..	..	..	..
Australia	70	74	49	49	45	51	50	49	..	..	..	..
Austria	75	84	49	49	54	61	49	49	36	44	41	43
Azerbaijan	..	60	..	47	..	..	..	48	..	..	32	38
Bangladesh	8	..	37	..	7	..	24	..	5	..	2	..
Belarus	..	..	..	49	..	..	..	51	..	..	..	..
Belgium	59	78	49	49	..	..	..	..	..	..	..	..
Benin	23	..	32	34	..	..	26	28	..	..	26	..
Bolivia	48	..	47	..	..	..	..	..	..	..	..	..
Bosnia and Herzegovina	..	..	..	..	..	..	..	..	..	..	..	..
Botswana	72	77	55	51	35	43	56	53	45	32	25	30
Brazil	85	..	49	..	..	..	52	..	..	..	47	..
Bulgaria	72	79	49	48	64	75	68	67	49	58	40	38
Burkina Faso	20	23	37	39	..	18	33	34	..	21	40	49
Burundi	47	47	39	45	18	..	25	38	10	14	18	39
Cambodia	..	36	..	45	..	..	..	37	..	..	..	..
Cameroon	20	32	45	47	18	20	34	40	24	25	39	41
Canada	..	69	49	48	..	53	49	49	..	..	..	..
Central African Republic	25	..	37	..	12	..	25	..	25	..	49	..
Chad	..	7	..	32	..	4	..	17	..	..	..	..
Chile	74	72	49	49	..	..	55	54	..	..	47	47
China	37	46	45	47	25	33	40	44	25	38	34	48
Colombia	79	80	50	50	41	..	50	51	42	..	45	59
Congo	25	34	48	48	8	..	40	41	..	23	54	47
Costa Rica	79	80	49	49	57	..	54	51	50	..	50	49
Côte d'Ivoire	15	20	40	42	..	..	28	34	..	..	49	..
Croatia	73	75	49	49	..	69	..	65	..	57	..	46
Cuba	75	78	48	49	50	60	51	54	25	34	46	46
Czech Republic	..	93	..	49	..	66	..	52	..	40	..	40
Denmark	..	58	49	49	..	..	51	52	..	..	41	46
Dominican Republic	..	71	40	50	..	..	..	57	..	..	..	64
Ecuador	65	65	49	49	38	44	48	47	37	..	60	55
Egypt, Arab Rep.	47	54	40	45	35	42	36	44	21	35	38	45
El Salvador	65	71	49	49	24	..	43	48	32	..	48	53
Eritrea	..	35	..	44	..	12	..	43	..	..	..	10
Estonia	..	96	49	49	..	83	..	53	..	72	..	49
Ethiopia	22	27	35	38	10	10	36	46	..	..	..	18
Finland	..	..	49	49	..	..	53	53	42	42	47	54
France	68	78	48	48	58	58	49	51	42	..	68	45
Gabon	27	..	49	50	28	27	42	..	17	..	28	..
Gambia, The	34	31	35	41	27		30	..	20	..	19	..
Georgia	..	..	..	..	..	..	..	..	..	..	..	..
Germany	..	85	..	49	..	48	..	50	..	35	..	44
Ghana	42	35	44	46	21	..	38	39	21	..	25	31
Greece	48	55	48	48	55	56	50	50	24	44	20	34
Guatemala	62	..	45	46	..	..	43	..	..	..	39	..
Guinea	14	22	33	33	..	14	28	24	..	..	..	25
Guinea-Bissau	24	..	32	..	20	..	22	..	3	..	14	..
Haiti	49	..	46	..	..	11	47	..	..	..	..	..
Honduras	74	73	50	50	..	..	50	53	..	..	49	56
Hong Kong	73	..	48	..	..	..	51	..	..	..	32	..

	Primary education				Secondary general				Secondary vocational			
	Teachers % female		Pupils % female		Teachers % female		Pupils % female		Teachers % female		Pupils % female	
	1980	1993	1980	1993	1980	1993	1980	1993	1980	1993	1980	1993
Hungary	80	83	49	49	61	67	65	64	40	..	39	44
India	26	30	39	43	30	34	32	38	..	..	32	13
Indonesia	..	52	46	48	..	39	36	46	..	27	27	40
Iran, Islamic Rep.	57	55	40	47	..	45	39	44	10	16	16	24
Iraq	48	68	46	45	42	55	32	39	24	52	29	26
Ireland	74	77	49	49	..	..	51	50	..	..	72	49
Israel	77	84	49	49	..	..	57	53	..	..	46	45
Italy	87	92	49	49	64	71	48	50	45	51	41	43
Jamaica	87	93	50	49	67	..	52	..	56	..	65	..
Japan	57	60	49	49	..	34	50	50	..	28	47	45
Jordan	59	60	48	49	44	53	46	55	28	37	30	35
Kazakstan	..	97	..	49	..	74	..	52	..	..	..	..
Kenya	29	44	47	49	24	36	42	44	..	..	..	..
Korea, Dem. Rep.	..	..	..	..	..	..	..	..	..	..	..	..
Korea, Rep.	37	54	49	48	28	39	46	47	20	25	44	53
Kuwait	56	71	48	49	50	54	46	49	..	23	..	33
Kyrgyz Republic	88	80	49	50	58	67	49	51	..	33	50	50
Lao PDR	30	42	45	43	26	39	38	39	..	26	28	31
Latvia	..	92	49	49	..	80	..	52	..	..	..	45
Lebanon	..	..	48	49	..	..	51	53	..	8	40	40
Lesotho	75	80	59	54	48	50	60	59	47	..	56	46
Libya	47	67	47	49	24	40	39	53	12	..	25	..
Lithuania	97	98	49	48	85	82	..	52	..	..	..	41
Macedonia, FYR	..	52	..	48	..	..	..	61	..	..	..	44
Madagascar	..	56	49	49	..	..	..	50	..	..	11	34
Malawi	32	34	41	48	..	..	29	39	..	..	..	4
Malaysia	44	59	49	49	46	54	48	51	22	34	29	27
Mali	20	23	36	39	..	17	29	34	..	..	8	34
Mauritania	9	18	35	45	8	11	21	36	..	4	7	23
Mauritius	43	47	49	49	39	57	48	51	17	..	22	..
Mexico	..	..	49	48	..	..	43	48	..	..	66	59
Moldova	96	96	49	49	..	..	51	51	..	..	..	57
Mongolia	82	..	49	..	53	..	52	..	41	..	62	..
Morocco	30	38	37	41	..	..	38	41	..	..	23	38
Mozambique	22	23	43	42	27	20	29	40	15	24	17	25
Myanmar	54	66	48	48	61	..	45	..	..	..	..	..
Namibia	..	65	..	50	..	46	..	55	..	20	..	21
Nepal	10	16	28	39	..	..	..	..	..	..	..	..
Netherlands	46	56	49	50	26	30	52	52	..	31	41	41
New Zealand	66	80	49	49	41	54	49	49	..	..	82	48
Nicaragua	78	84	51	50	..	55	52	53	..	..	56	49
Niger	30	34	35	38	22	18	29	33	15	12	8	13
Nigeria	33	45	43	44	8	..	36	..	38	..	17	..
Norway	56	63	49	49	..	..	51	51	..	..	47	41
Oman	34	49	34	48	27	46	25	47	..	..	0	17
Pakistan	32	..	33	31	30	..	26	32	20	42	17	33
Panama	80	..	48	..	55	..	51	..	47	..	54	..
Papua New Guinea	27	35	41	45	34	35	32	40	31	31	..	32
Paraguay	..	55	48	48	..	..	..	51	..	..	..	44
Peru	60	..	48	..	46	..	46	..	..	..	40	..
Philippines	80	..	49	50	..	..	53	..	..	..	..	..
Poland	83	..	49	49	69	..	71	71	47	..	44	42
Portugal	..	..	48	48	59	..	48	..	..	..	31	..
Puerto Rico	..	..	..	..	..	..	..	..	..	..	..	..
Romania	70	84	49	49	53	65	65	52	41	52	45	42
Russian Federation	98	98	49	49	76	79	51	52	..	..	..	..

	Primary education				Secondary general				Secondary vocational			
	Teachers % female		Pupils % female		Teachers % female		Pupils % female		Teachers % female		Pupils % female	
	1980	1993	1980	1993	1980	1993	1980	1993	1980	1993	1980	1993
Rwanda	38	*47*	48	*50*	..	..	28	*38*	..	..	55	*44*
Saudi Arabia	39	49	39	47	33	43	37	44	..	15	..	12
Senegal	24	25	40	43	*16*	*14*	34	*35*	..	..	25	*35*
Sierra Leone	..	..	42	..	..	..	30	..	..	..	..	..
Singapore	66	..	48	..	56	..	51	..	24	..	23	..
Slovak Republic	..	91	..	49	..	75	..	51	..	61	..	47
Slovenia	..	93	..	49	..	76	..	52	..	56	..	44
South Africa	..	*58*	..	50	..	*64*	..	53	..	*28*	..	..
Spain	67	74	49	48	43	53	51	51	31	*43*	46	52
Sri Lanka	..	80	48	48	..	64	51	51	..	..	..	..
Sudan	31	*52*	40	*43*	26	*33*	37	*45*	10	*15*	21	*17*
Sweden	..	79	49	49	..	..	51	51	..	..	52	45
Switzerland	..	..	49	49	..	..	49	50	..	..	39	41
Syrian Arab Republic	54	64	43	47	22	43	37	44	15	32	..	..
Tajikistan	..	50	..	49	..	35	..	47	..	..	..	..
Tanzania	37	42	47	49	*28*	20	33	43	..	..	..	..
Thailand	49	..	48	*49*	57	..	46	*50*	..	..	..	..
Togo	21	16	38	40	13	11	24	26	..	..	..	..
Trinidad and Tobago	66	74	50	49	*52*	56	*50*	51	..	..	..	..
Tunisia	29	48	42	47	..	..	39	46	..	..	..	..
Turkey	41	43	45	47	36	40	35	39	34	39	..	..
Turkmenistan	..	..	..	..	..	..	..	..	..	..	..	..
Uganda	30	31	43	44	*20*	..	29	*38*	..	..	..	..
Ukraine	97	98	49	49	..	..	..	51	..	..	..	..
United Arab Emirates	54	69	48	48	48	..	45	51	..	..	..	..
United Kingdom	78	77	49	*49*	49	*54*	49	*49*	..	..	57	*52*
United States	..	84	49	49	..	54	49	49	..	..	..	..
Uruguay	..	..	49	49	..	..	58	..	..	..	..	..
Uzbekistan	78	80	49	49	48	48	46	49	..	..	..	..
Venezuela	*83*	75	*50*	50	..	..	..	*58*	..	..	..	..
Vietnam	65	..	47	..	58	..	47	..	..	..	..	..
West Bank and Gaza	..	..	..	..	..	..	..	..	..	..	..	..
Yemen, Rep.	..	..	..	..	..	..	..	..	..	..	..	..
Yugoslavia, Fed. Rep.	..	*75*	..	49	..	..	..	51	..	..	..	..
Zaire	..	24	42	43	..	..	..	30	..	..	..	..
Zambia	40	..	47	..	..	..	35	..	3	..	..	..
Zimbabwe	*38*	42	*48*	48	*36*	32	*42*	44	..	..	..	..
World	..	..	**44 w**	..	..	..	..	..	..	..	..	..
Low income	32 w	38 w	42 w	44 w	26 w	33 w	36 w	41 w	..	..	30 w	31 w
Excl. China & India	30 w	..	40 w	*42* w	..	..	33 w	..	..	..	..	..
Middle income	..	..	47 w	48 w	..	..	46 w	*49* w	..	..	..	..
Lower middle income	..	70 w	47 w	48 w	..	..	45 w	49 w	..	..	..	..
Upper middle income	..	..	48 w	..	..	..	..	..	..	..	..	..
Low & middle income	..	..	43 w	..	..	..	..	..	..	..	..	..
East Asia & Pacific	41 w	46 w	45 w	47 w	28 w	35 w	40 w	44 w	25 w	36 w	33 w	45 w
Europe & Central Asia	84 w	84 w	49 w	49 w	..	67 w	53 w	52 w	..	..	..	..
Latin America & Carib.	..	..	49 w	..	..	..	..	..	..	..	..	..
Middle East & N. Africa	..	53 w	41 w	46 w	..	44 w	37 w	45 w	..	26 w	24 w	30 w
South Asia	24 w	31 w	38 w	41 w	27 w	34 w	31 w	38 w	..	..	27 w	15 w
Sub-Saharan Africa	29 w	37 w	42 w	44 w	..	..	34 w	41 w	..	..	..	..
High income	..	77 w	49 w	49 w	..	50 w	49 w	49 w	..	..	..	..

Progress—and gaps

Despite progress in raising both male and female enrollment rates in all regions during the past three decades, school enrollment remains lower among girls than among boys. This gap is widest in South Asia, the Middle East, and Sub-Saharan Africa and reflects both cultural norms and the value of girls' contribution to household work. Moreover, female enrollment rates often mask high absenteeism and dropout rates. Low female enrollment is, in part, a "bootstrap" problem: literate parents, especially mothers, are more likely than illiterate ones to enroll their daughters in school, and once enrolled, these girls are as likely as boys to remain in school.

Most education systems do not prepare boys and girls equally for occupations. Studies of learning styles in industrial countries have found that women leave school with fewer opportunities for continuing their education and poor prospects of translating their higher-level education into social and

The widest enrollment gaps between boys and girls are in South Asia, the Middle East, and Sub-Saharan Africa

economic advancement. At the postsecondary and higher levels, where the gap in enrollment between women and men is wider, there is implicit "gender streaming," or sex segregation by field of study. This phenomenon, widespread in both developing and industrial countries, discourages women from acquiring training in a variety of fields, especially the "hard" sciences, mathematics, and engineering.

In the teaching profession, one of the largest occupational fields requiring advanced training, women are well represented in many countries, often constituting more than half of the total qualified employed. But a hierarchical pattern of occupational segregation leads to inequality between women and men at both the top and the bottom of the profession. In many countries men move up to better-paid and more prestigious positions in secondary and higher education as these levels expand, while women predominate at the primary level.

The data on female enrollment suffer from the same problems affecting general school enrollment data discussed in the notes to table 2.8. To the extent that boys or girls may be more likely to drop out of school or repeat grades, male and female enrollment rates may misrepresent the actual pattern of attendance in some countries.

Data on teachers may not reflect the functions they perform. That is, teachers may be employed by schools in many capacities outside the classroom, and the responsibilities assigned to male and female teachers may differ systematically.

Definitions

● **Female teachers as a percentage of total teachers** includes full-time and part-time teachers. ● **Female pupils as a percentage of total pupils** includes enrollments in public and private schools but may exclude certain specialized schools and training programs.

Data sources

The estimates in this table were compiled using UNESCO's electronic database on institutions, teachers, and pupils.

	Health expenditure			People per physician		People per nurse		People per hospital bed	
	Total % of GDP 1990–95[a,b]	Public % of GDP 1990–95[a]	Private % of GDP 1990–95[a]	1980	1993	1980	1993	1980	1993
Albania	..	2.7	..	..	735	..	..	..	248
Algeria	4.6	3.3	1.3	..	1,062	..	330	..	390
Angola	..	4.0	..	..	23,725	..	..	..	774
Argentina	10.6	4.3	6.3	..	330	..	1,783	..	218
Armenia	7.8	3.1	4.7	284	261	122	101	119	120
Australia	8.4	5.8	2.7	559	..	146	..	..	178
Austria	9.7	6.2	3.6	440	231	170	..	90	95
Azerbaijan	7.5	1.4	6.1	298	257	118	106	103	96
Bangladesh	2.4	1.2	1.3	8,424	12,884	14,750	11,549	4,702	5,479
Belarus	6.4	5.3	1.1	295	236	102	89	80	80
Belgium	8.2	7.2	1.0	401	274	130	..	107	121
Benin	..	1.7	..	16,980	14,216	2,157	4,182	684	4,182
Bolivia	5.0	2.7	2.4	1,911	2,348	..	7,048	..	709
Bosnia and Herzegovina	..	..	..	..	..	..	..	..	..
Botswana	..	1.9	..	8,122	5,151	700	480	421	635
Brazil	7.4	2.7	4.7	1,301	844	1,140	3,379	..	299
Bulgaria	..	4.0	..	407	306	190	162	90	101
Burkina Faso	5.5	2.3	3.2	54,819	34,804	3,073	9,649	..	3,300
Burundi	..	0.9	..	..	17,153	..	4,778	..	1,519
Cambodia	7.2	0.7	6.5	..	9,374	..	1,231	..	453
Cameroon	1.4	1.0	0.4	..	11,996	..	1,999	..	381
Canada	9.8	7.0	2.7	560	464	122	107	..	150
Central African Republic	..	1.7	..	23,364	25,920	1,826	11,309	642	1,140
Chad	..	1.8	..	..	30,030	..	64,403	..	1,373
Chile	6.5	2.5	4.0	..	942	..	3,800	293	320
China	3.8	1.8	1.9	1,100	1,063	2,100	1,490	500	612
Colombia	7.4	3.0	4.4	..	1,105	..	2,717	627	732
Congo	6.8	3.6	3.2	8,425	3,713	595	1,401	..	306
Costa Rica	8.5	6.3	2.2	..	1,133	..	2,213	302	..
Côte d'Ivoire	3.4	1.4	2.0	..	11,739	..	3,244	..	1,223
Croatia	10.1	8.5	1.6	..	..	..	..	..	..
Cuba	..	7.9	..	721	275	..	180	..	184
Czech Republic	9.9	7.8	2.1	..	273	..	..	..	122
Denmark	6.6	5.5	1.1	420	360	140	153	..	177
Dominican Republic	5.3	2.0	3.3	..	949	1,239	9,423	..	506
Ecuador	5.3	2.0	3.2	..	652	..	1,853	524	608
Egypt, Arab Rep.	4.9	..	..	939	1,316	762	489	493	517
El Salvador	5.0	1.2	3.8	3,046	1,515	..	3,233	..	680
Eritrea	..	1.1	..	..	..	..	..	..	..
Estonia	..	5.9	..	239	253	95	127	80	104
Ethiopia	..	1.1	..	88,124	32,499	4,998	13,628	3,384	4,141
Finland	8.3	6.2	2.1	530	406	100	101	64	93
France	9.7	7.6	2.1	462	334	110	..	..	109
Gabon	..	0.5	..	2,184	1,987	225	1,173	..	305
Gambia, The	..	1.8	..	..	..	..	..	..	1,642
Georgia	..	0.3	..	208	182	90	85	94	95
Germany	9.5	7.0	2.5	452	367	..	..	..	118
Ghana	..	1.0	..	..	22,970	621	3,608	..	685
Greece	6.4	..	..	411	312	370	403	161	197
Guatemala	2.7	0.9	1.7	..	3,999	1,360	7,087	..	1,191
Guinea	..	0.9	..	45,457	7,445	5,056	5,166	..	1,712
Guinea-Bissau	..	1.1	..	7,491	..	1,130	..	562	671
Haiti	3.6	1.3	2.3	9,079	10,855	..	8,945	1,350	1,251
Honduras	5.6	2.8	2.8	3,100	1,266	..	4,582	775	1,276
Hong Kong	4.3	1.9	2.5	1,211	..	795	..	249	234

	Health expenditure			People per physician		People per nurse		People per hospital bed	
	Total % of GDP 1990–95[a,b]	Public % of GDP 1990–95[a]	Private % of GDP 1990–95[a]	1980	1993	1980	1993	1980	1993
Hungary	7.3	6.8	0.5	400	306	157	321	110	97
India	3.5	0.7	2.8	2,694	2,459	4,674	3,323	1,299	1,371
Indonesia	1.5	0.7	0.8	12,458	7,028	..	2,732	..	1,423
Iran, Islamic Rep.	4.8	2.8	2.0	2,949	3,142	1,179	..	675	724
Iraq	..	..	..	1,776	1,659	2,195	1,398	514	584
Ireland	7.9	6.0	1.9	784	632	141	153	103	101
Israel	4.1	..	..	401	..	130	..	197	164
Italy	8.3	5.9	2.5	750	207	250	333	..	131
Jamaica	5.4	3.0	2.3	2,786	6,420	..	489	..	476
Japan	7.0	5.5	1.5	740	608	210	..	89	64
Jordan	7.9	3.7	4.2	1,272	554	875	548	795	533
Kazakstan	..	2.2	..	312	254	99	91	76	75
Kenya	..	1.9	..	10,071	21,970	983	8,675	..	602
Korea, Dem. Rep.	..	..	..	419	..	..	..	..	..
Korea, Rep.	5.4	1.8	3.6	1,690	951	..	454	586	300
Kuwait	7.0	..	..	589	..	182	..	241	335
Kyrgyz Republic	..	3.5	..	343	303	115	105	83	92
Lao PDR	2.6	0.8	1.4	..	4,446	..	493	..	405
Latvia	..	3.7	..	242	278	102	118	73	82
Lebanon	5.3	2.1	3.3	550	537	..	2,971	..	606
Lesotho	..	3.5	..	..	24,095	..	2,040	..	..
Libya	..	..	..	750	957	355	340	207	246
Lithuania	..	4.8	..	255	235	92	92	83	84
Macedonia, FYR	7.7	6.8	0.9	..	427	..	..	..	189
Madagascar	..	1.0	..	9,891	8,385	1,721	3,736	..	1,072
Malawi	..	2.3	..	53,605	44,205	3,024	28,951	..	1,184
Malaysia	..	1.4	..	3,917	2,441	570	480	439	437
Mali	..	1.3	..	25,444	18,376	2,322	5,297	..	..
Mauritania	..	1.5	..	..	15,772	..	2,261	..	1,486
Mauritius	..	2.2	..	1,920	1,165	627	392	320	347
Mexico	5.3	2.8	2.6	1,149	615	..	..	..	1,704
Moldova	..	5.1	..	320	250	105	90	83	80
Mongolia	4.7	4.4	0.4	101	371	211	219	89	87
Morocco	3.4	1.6	1.7	18,558	4,665	898	..	814	775
Mozambique	..	4.6	..	39,142	36,225	4,629	4,937	918	1,156
Myanmar	0.9	0.5	0.4	4,952	12,528	4,943	1,227	1,171	1,605
Namibia	7.6	3.9	3.7	..	4,328	..	317	..	207
Nepal	5.0	1.2	3.8	30,062	13,634	7,783	2,257	5,728	4,210
Netherlands	8.8	6.9	2.0	480	399	168	123	80	170
New Zealand	7.5	5.7	1.7	638	518	81	..	..	149
Nicaragua	7.8	4.3	3.5	2,308	2,039	598	..	..	549
Niger	..	2.2	..	..	53,986	..	3,765	..	..
Nigeria	..	..	..	8,853	5,208	1,089	1,450	1,154	157
Norway	7.3	6.9	0.4	524	308	70	73	67	210
Oman	..	2.5	..	2,142	1,131	907	..	617	398
Pakistan	..	0.8	..	3,500	1,923	5,870	3,330	1,742	1,769
Panama	7.5	5.4	2.0	1,010	562	..	1,069	..	..
Papua New Guinea	..	2.8	..	16,073	12,754	1,000	1,569	180	290
Paraguay	4.3	1.0	3.3	1,746	1,231	..	7,098	..	762
Peru	4.9	2.6	2.3	1,395	939	..	..	..	664
Philippines	2.4	1.3	1.0	7,848	8,273	2,591	..	589	780
Poland	..	4.6	..	560	451	227	189	178	180
Portugal	7.6	4.3	3.4	494	353	..	..	..	227
Puerto Rico	..	..	6.0	..	..	..	..	..	..
Romania	..	3.3	..	678	538	280	..	114	127
Russian Federation	4.8	4.1	0.6	248	222	88	90	77	77

	Health expenditure			People per physician		People per nurse		People per hospital bed	
	Total % of GDP 1990–95[a,b]	Public % of GDP 1990–95[a]	Private % of GDP 1990–95[a]	1980	1993	1980	1993	1980	1993
Rwanda	..	1.9	..	31,482	24,967	10,314	8,133	654	1,152
Saudi Arabia	2.2	..	..	1,819	749	738	329	686	401
Senegal	1.6	..	..	12,683	18,192	1,931	13,174	..	1,923
Sierra Leone	..	1.6	..	17,305	..	1,869	..	823	..
Singapore	3.5	1.1	2.4	1,111	714	321	..	239	275
Slovak Republic	..	6.3	..	..	287	..	105	..	11
Slovenia	..	7.9	..	..	..	..	..	143	167
South Africa	7.9	3.6	4.3	..	..	..	..	..	..
Spain	7.4	5.8	1.6	361	261	281	262	..	209
Sri Lanka	1.9	1.4	0.4	7,172	6,843	1,262	1,745	340	365
Sudan	0.3	..	..	8,803	..	1,408	..	1,086	919
Sweden	7.7	6.4	1.3	454	394	107	108	68	161
Switzerland	9.6	6.9	2.7	..	580	128	..	..	93
Syrian Arab Republic	..	..	..	2,243	1,159	1,372	1,047	905	920
Tajikistan	..	6.4	..	422	424	152	139	100	95
Tanzania	..	2.8	..	..	..	..	..	716	976
Thailand	5.3	1.4	3.9	6,803	4,416	2,280	1,067	651	765
Togo	..	1.7	..	18,813	11,385	1,225	3,060	..	664
Trinidad and Tobago	3.9	2.6	1.3	1,377	1,520	381	247	..	308
Tunisia	5.9	3.0	2.9	3,694	1,549	956	411	470	350
Turkey	4.2	2.7	1.5	1,642	976	1,239	1,098	445	403
Turkmenistan	..	2.8	..	349	306	125	100	94	93
Uganda	3.9	1.8	2.2	21,405	22,399	2,009	6,762	661	760
Ukraine	..	5.4	..	274	227	97	87	80	77
United Arab Emirates	2.2	1.9	0.3	936	1,208	410	718	351	..
United Kingdom	6.9	5.8	1.1	611	..	207	202	107	161
United States	14.3	6.3	7.9	549	421	196	121	171	194
Uruguay	8.5	2.0	6.5	501	..	..	..	..	221
Uzbekistan	..	3.5	..	347	282	118	86	87	106
Venezuela	7.1	2.3	4.8	1,188	633	..	329	2,969	385
Vietnam	5.2	1.1	4.1	4,151	2,279	1,241	1,149	286	261
West Bank and Gaza	6.2	3.4	2.7	..	..	..	..	..	..
Yemen, Rep.	2.6	1.1	1.5	6,912	4,498	2,014	1,833	..	1,196
Yugoslavia, Fed. Rep.	..	..	..	290	232	..	810	71	73
Zaire	..	..	..	..	15,150	..	1,355	..	702
Zambia	3.3	2.6	0.7	13,221	10,917	1,693	4,937	289	..
Zimbabwe	..	2.1	..	6,105	7,384	921	1,594	..	..
World	..	..	..	**3,770 w**	..	..	..	**807 w**	**811 w**
Low income	..	..	..	4,913 w	..	..	..	1,088 w	1,152 w
Excl. China & India	..	..	..	..	..	5,410 w	..	1,953 w	2,131 w
Middle income	..	..	..	3,599 w	..	..	..	..	472 w
Lower middle income	..	..	..	4,287 w	..	..	..	385 w	402 w
Upper middle income	..	..	..	1,341 w	826 w	..	..	..	635 w
Low & middle income	..	..	..	4,243 w	..	..	..	921 w	950 w
East Asia & Pacific	..	..	..	1,834 w	1,063 w	2,084 w	1,490 w	518 w	612 w
Europe & Central Asia	..	..	..	478 w	371 w	111 w	260 w	133 w	140 w
Latin America & Carib.	..	..	..	1,458 w	970 w	..	..	..	688 w
Middle East & N. Africa	..	..	..	4,235 w	..	1,117 w	..	624 w	661 w
South Asia	..	..	..	3,857 w	2,847 w	5,788 w	3,313 w	1,731 w	1,889 w
Sub-Saharan Africa	..	..	..	..	..	..	..	..	..
High income	..	..	..	612 w	522 w	216 w	..	..	159 w

a. Data are for most recent year available. b. Totals may not add up due to rounding.

About the data

Most industrial countries have developed systems for tracking and comparing public and private health care expenditures over the past two decades.

By contrast, in developing countries data are rarely tabulated in national health accounts, which is necessary to ensure consistency and completeness. Compiling complete information on public health care spending has proved difficult in some developing countries. And estimates of private health spending are often lacking or incomplete. Data are provided here only for countries with actual data.

Data on physicians and nurses are mainly from the World Health Organization's (WHO) second evaluation of progress in implementing national health-for-all strategies. The data for developing countries here have been supplemented by country statistical yearbooks and World Bank sector studies.

Two factors affect the comparability of the WHO's physician ratios. First, in many developing countries a significant share of the population, particularly in rural areas, receives treatment from practitioners of indigenous medicine not included in the WHO definition of physician. Second, the extent to which homeopaths, osteopaths, and the like are included varies across countries.

Thus these are essentially indicators of availability, not of quality or use. They do not show how well trained physicians are or how well equipped hospitals or medical centers are—nor do they reveal the use of their services. Similarly, data on hospital beds and hospital usage may be misleading in poor countries, where hospital crowding can result in people sleeping on floors in wards and corridors.

The WHO reviews the international health statistics it compiles for validity and consistency, querying data that:

• Vary by more than a reasonable amount from the value reported for the previous period.

• Are not consistent with data reported for other indicators.

• Are not consistent with data from other sources. Inconsistent or grossly inaccurate data are not retained.

Definitions

• **Health expenditure** includes outlays for the provision of health services (preventive and curative), population activities, nutrition activities, and emergency aid designated for health. It does not include water and sanitation. • **Public health expenditure** comprises recurrent and capital government expenditures on health care (including government and social security expenditures for medical care) and donor assistance for health services. • **Private health expenditure** covers direct out-of-pocket expenditures by households, direct payments by employers for health services, and expenditures by nongovernmental and charitable organizations. • **Physicians** are defined as graduates of any faculty or school of medicine who are working in the country in any medical field (practice, teaching, research). • **Nurses** are defined as persons who have completed a program of basic nursing education, are qualified and registered or authorized to provide service for the promotion of health, prevention of illness, care of the sick, and rehabilitation, and are working in the country. The data do not cover auxiliary and paraprofessional personnel. • **Hospital beds** comprise those available in public and private, general and specialized hospitals and rehabilitation centers. Hospitals are establishments permanently staffed by at least one physician.

Data sources

Country information on public health expenditures is from national sources, supplemented by World Bank sector studies, including:

• Goldstein and others, *Trends in Health Status, Services, and Finance,* vol. 1.

• Chellaraj and others, *Trends in Health Status, Services, and Finance,* vol. 2.

• Klugman and Schieber, *A Survey of Health Reform in Central Asia.*

Data were also drawn from World Bank public expenditure reviews, the Pan American Health Organization, the International Monetary Fund's *Government Finance Statistics,* and other studies. Data for private expenditure are largely from household surveys, World Bank poverty assessments and sector studies, and other studies. Data on public and private health expenditures for industrial countries and Turkey are from the OECD. Data for physicians, nurses, and hospital beds come from government statistical yearbooks, the World Bank, the OECD, and the WHO.

2.12 | Access to health services

	Health care		Safe water		Sanitation		Child immunization				Births attended by health staff	
	% of population with access		% of population with access		% of population with access		Measles % of children under 12 months		DPT % of children under 12 months		% of total	
	1980	1993	1980	1994–95	1980	1994–95	1980	1995	1980	1995	1985	1990
Albania	100	..	92	..	..	100	90	91	94	97	99	..
Algeria	..	..	77	..	..	..	17	69	33	75	..	..
Angola	70	24	..	32	..	16	..	32	..	21	15	16
Argentina	..	..	..	64	..	89	..	76	46	66	..	..
Armenia	..	..	..	..	..	..	..	95	..	83	..	..
Australia	99	100	99	95	99	90	..	86	..	95	99	..
Austria	..	100	100	..	85	100	90	60	90	90	..	..
Azerbaijan	..	..	..	..	..	..	..	91	..	90	..	..
Bangladesh	80	74	..	83	..	30	..	96	..	91	..	7
Belarus	..	100	..	..	50	100	..	96	..	90	100	..
Belgium	..	100	..	..	99	100	..	70	..	97	100	..
Benin	..	42	..	70	..	22	..	72	..	79	34	51
Bolivia	..	..	..	60	..	44	..	83	..	88	36	29
Bosnia and Herzegovina	..	..	..	..	..	..	..	57	..	67	..	..
Botswana	..	86	..	70	..	55	..	68	64	78	52	..
Brazil	..	..	..	92	..	73	..	78	..	69	73	..
Bulgaria	..	100	96	..	..	99	98	93	97	100	100	..
Burkina Faso	..	..	35	..	5	14	23	55	2	47	..	33
Burundi	..	80	..	58	..	48	30	44	38	57	..	26
Cambodia	..	..	..	13	..	..	..	75	..	79	..	..
Cameroon	20	15	..	41	..	40	47	31	20	48	..	25
Canada	..	99	97	100	60	85	..	98	80	93	99	100
Central African Republic	..	13	16	..	..	..	19	70	21	40	..	..
Chad	..	26	..	29	..	32	..	24	..	18	..	21
Chile	..	95	..	96	..	71	..	93	..	92	95	..
China	..	..	..	46	..	..	..	89	..	93	..	51
Colombia	88	87	..	96	..	70	..	77	..	91	51	..
Congo	..	..	..	60	..	9	49	39	42	50	..	..
Costa Rica	..	97	..	100	..	99	..	94	..	85	..	..
Côte d'Ivoire	..	60	20	82	17	54	28	57	42	40	..	..
Croatia	..	..	..	96	..	68	..	90	..	87	..	..
Cuba	..	100	61	94	31	66	..	100	67	100	99	100
Czech Republic	..	..	..	..	..	..	..	96	..	96	..	..
Denmark	..	100	100	100	100	100	20	88	85	89	..	..
Dominican Republic	..	..	..	79	..	85	..	100	..	100	98	44
Ecuador	..	80	..	70	..	64	..	100	26	80	27	..
Egypt, Arab Rep.	100	99	90	84	70	..	..	82	..	82	..	24
El Salvador	..	..	..	62	..	73	..	94	..	100	35	..
Eritrea	..	..	..	..	..	..	..	45	..	45	..	..
Estonia	..	..	..	..	..	..	..	81	..	84	..	..
Ethiopia	..	55	4	27	..	10	7	54	6	57	58	..
Finland	..	100	..	100	100	100	80	98	92	100	..	..
France	..	..	..	100	85	96	30	76	79	89	..	..
Gabon	..	87	..	67	..	76	35	50	48	48	92	..
Gambia, The	90	..	42	61	..	34	70	88	88	93	54	65
Georgia	..	..	..	..	..	..	..	63	..	58	..	..
Germany	..	..	..	..	..	100	28	75	56	80	..	..
Ghana	..	25	..	56	..	42	..	68	22	71	73	42
Greece	..	..	..	..	..	96	..	70	31	78	..	..
Guatemala	..	60	..	64	..	71	..	84	..	78	..	22
Guinea	..	45	..	49	12	6	44	69	4	73	..	76
Guinea-Bissau	30	80	24	57	..	20	30	68	24	74	16	..
Haiti	..	45	..	28	..	24	..	24	..	30	20	..
Honduras	..	62	..	70	..	68	..	90	38	96	50	63
Hong Kong	..	..	..	..	..	..	..	42	84	83	..	..

	Health care		Safe water		Sanitation		Child immunization				Births attended by health staff	
	% of population with access		% of population with access		% of population with access		Measles % of children under 12 months		DPT % of children under 12 months		% of total	
	1980	1993	1980	1994–95	1980	1994–95	1980	1995	1980	1995	1985	1990
Hungary	..	..	..	..	..	94	99	100	99	100	..	..
India	50	..	..	63	..	29	..	84	..	92	33	75
Indonesia	..	43	..	63	..	55	..	89	..	91	31	..
Iran, Islamic Rep.	50	73	50	89	60	82	..	95	29	97	..	70
Iraq	..	98	74	45	..	36	..	95	13	91	24	74
Ireland	..	..	..	..	..	100	60	78	36	65	..	..
Israel	..	100	..	99	..	70	..	94	84	92	99	..
Italy	..	..	99	..	99	100	..	50	..	50	100	..
Jamaica	..	..	..	70	..	74	..	82	39	93	89	88
Japan	..	100	..	95	..	85	..	68	..	85	100	100
Jordan	..	90	89	89	76	30	..	92	..	100	75	86
Kazakstan	..	..	..	..	..	..	..	72	..	80	..	..
Kenya	..	..	..	49	..	43	..	73	..	84	..	..
Korea, Dem. Rep.	..	100	..	100	..	100	..	98	52	96	100	..
Korea, Rep.	..	100	..	89	..	100	89	92	61	93	65	95
Kuwait	100	100	100	..	100	..	..	93	54	100	99	..
Kyrgyz Republic	..	..	..	75	..	53	..	89	..	83	..	..
Lao PDR	..	..	..	41	..	30	..	65	7	51	..	..
Latvia	..	..	..	..	..	..	..	85	..	65	..	..
Lebanon	..	..	92	..	59	..	..	88	..	92	45	..
Lesotho	..	80	18	57	12	35	..	82	56	56	28	..
Libya	100	100	90	30	70	18	..	89	..	91	76	..
Lithuania	..	..	..	..	..	..	..	94	..	96	..	..
Macedonia, FYR	..	..	..	..	..	..	..	85	..	87	..	..
Madagascar	..	65	..	32	..	17	..	59	..	67	62	71
Malawi	40	80	..	54	..	63	..	99	..	98	59	41
Malaysia	..	88	..	90	75	94	..	81	58	90	82	92
Mali	20	..	..	44	..	44	11	49	18	46	27	..
Mauritania	..	..	..	72	..	64	..	53	..	50	23	..
Mauritius	100	99	..	100	..	100	53	85	88	89	84	91
Mexico	51	91	..	87	..	70	..	90	..	92	..	45
Moldova	..	..	..	..	..	50	..	98	..	96	..	..
Mongolia	90	100	..	54	..	..	..	85	..	88	100	100
Morocco	..	62	32	59	50	63	..	92	44	93	26	..
Mozambique	..	30	9	28	10	23	51	71	38	57	28	29
Myanmar	30	..	20	39	20	42	..	66	5	69	25	94
Namibia	..	..	..	57	..	36	..	57	..	61	..	71
Nepal	10	..	11	48	0	22	..	78	..	77	10	..
Netherlands	..	100	100	100	100	100	93	95	97	97	..	..
New Zealand	..	100	87	..	..	..	71	87	72	84	99	100
Nicaragua	..	..	..	57	..	..	..	81	23	85	..	42
Niger	..	30	..	57	..	15	16	38	5	19	47	21
Nigeria	40	67	..	43	..	38	20	50	24	44	..	45
Norway	..	100	..	100	100	100	80	93	90	92	..	100
Oman	75	89	15	56	..	72	..	98	9	99	60	90
Pakistan	65	85	38	60	16	30	..	53	..	55	24	70
Panama	..	82	..	82	..	87	..	84	49	86	83	85
Papua New Guinea	..	96	..	31	..	26	..	35	28	50	34	20
Paraguay	..	..	..	8	..	30	..	76	28	77	22	..
Peru	..	..	..	60	..	47	..	97	18	94	44	..
Philippines	..	..	..	84	..	75	..	86	51	85	..	76
Poland	100	100	67	..	50	100	89	96	95	95	..	..
Portugal	..	..	57	..	41	100	70	94	90	93	..	..
Puerto Rico	..	..	..	..	..	..	..	..	..	..	..	..
Romania	..	..	77	..	50	49	..	93	..	98	99	..
Russian Federation	..	..	..	..	..	..	..	91	..	72	..	..

2.12 | Access to health services

	Health care % of population with access		Safe water % of population with access		Sanitation % of population with access		Child immunization Measles % of children under 12 months		DPT % of children under 12 months		Births attended by health staff % of total	
	1980	1993	1980	1994–95	1980	1994–95	1980	1995	1980	1995	1985	1990
Rwanda	..	..	..	..	..	..	48	..	32	..	..	28
Saudi Arabia	85	98	91	93	76	86	..	94	53	97	79	..
Senegal	..	40	..	..	..	..	..	80	..	80	..	..
Sierra Leone	26	..	..	..	13	..	..	44	..	41	25	..
Singapore	..	100	100	100	..	100	57	88	87	95	100	100
Slovak Republic	..	..	..	..	43	51	..	99	..	99	..	..
Slovenia	..	..	..	..	..	90	..	91	..	98	..	..
South Africa	..	..	..	..	..	46	..	76	..	73	..	..
Spain	..	..	98	99	95	97	..	90	..	88	96	..
Sri Lanka	90	90	..	57	..	66	..	88	45	91	87	85
Sudan	..	70	..	77	..	55	1	74	..	76	20	..
Sweden	..	100	..	..	85	100	47	96	94	99	100	..
Switzerland	..	100	..	100	85	100	..	83	..	89	..	100
Syrian Arab Republic	..	99	71	87	45	78	..	98	14	100	37	80
Tajikistan	..	..	..	..	..	62	..	90	..	95	..	..
Tanzania	72	93	..	49	..	86	37	75	58	79	74	..
Thailand	30	59	..	81	..	87	..	86	..	93	59	71
Togo	..	..	..	67	..	20	..	65	9	73	..	..
Trinidad and Tobago	..	99	..	82	..	56	..	87	52	81	90	..
Tunisia	95	90	72	86	46	72	..	89	36	90	60	..
Turkey	..	100	67	92	10	94	45	75	64	86	78	..
Turkmenistan	..	..	..	85	..	60	..	90	..	87	..	..
Uganda	..	71	..	42	..	60	10	79	2	79	..	..
Ukraine	..	100	..	97	50	49	..	96	..	94	100	..
United Arab Emirates	96	90	100	98	75	95	..	90	45	90	96	97
United Kingdom	..	..	..	100	..	96	60	92	44	92	98	..
United States	..	..	..	90	98	85	96	89	37	94	99	..
Uruguay	..	..	..	34	..	82	..	80	..	86	..	100
Uzbekistan	..	..	..	..	..	18	..	71	..	65	..	..
Venezuela	..	..	..	88	..	55	..	94	..	63	..	82
Vietnam	75	97	..	38	..	21	..	95	..	93	..	..
West Bank and Gaza	..	..	..	..	..	..	..	..	..	..	..	..
Yemen, Rep.	16	..	..	52	..	51	..	49	..	52	..	..
Yugoslavia, Fed. Rep.	..	..	..	..	58	100	89	75	90	79	..	..
Zaire	80	59	..	25	..	9	..	41	..	35	..	..
Zambia	..	75	..	47	..	42	55	78	47	76	..	43
Zimbabwe	55	..	10	74	5	58	51	78	32	80	67	..
World	..	..	..	76 w	..	..	..	80 w	..	82 w	..	..
Low income	..	..	..	53 w	..	..	..	77 w	..	80 w	..	..
Excl. China & India	..	..	..	50 w	..	31 w	..	65 w	..	63 w	..	..
Middle income	..	..	..	..	..	..	..	86 w	..	86 w	..	..
Lower middle income	..	..	..	..	..	..	..	87 w	..	89 w	..	..
Upper middle income	..	..	..	86 w	..	75 w	..	83 w	..	79 w	..	..
Low & middle income	..	..	..	56 w	..	..	..	80 w	..	82 w	..	..
East Asia & Pacific	..	..	..	49 w	..	..	..	88 w	..	91 w	..	..
Europe & Central Asia	..	..	..	..	..	..	..	83 w	..	90 w	..	..
Latin America & Carib.	..	..	..	80 w	..	67 w	..	84 w	..	80 w	68 w	..
Middle East & N. Africa	..	..	..	85 w	..	..	..	89 w	..	91 w	58 w	..
South Asia	..	..	..	63 w	..	29 w	..	80 w	..	84 w	29 w	..
Sub-Saharan Africa	..	..	..	47 w	..	48 w	..	60 w	..	58 w	..	..
High income	..	..	..	94 w	..	92 w	..	83 w	..	89 w	..	..

Implementing primary health care

The Global Strategy for Health for All by the Year 2000, adopted by the World Health Assembly in 1981, marked a radical change in the orientation of health development. The strategy was aimed at attaining a socially and economically productive life for all people by redirecting national health systems toward an approach based on primary care. Equity in the availability of health services is an underlying principle of primary care and thus a critical element in monitoring progress in implementing the strategy.

The strategy includes a list of indicators for global monitoring and evaluation (WHO 1995, annex 2). The health-for-all global indicator of primary health care is expressed as the percentage of the population with access to at least the following:
• Safe water in the home or within 15 minutes' walking distance.
• Adequate sanitary facilities in the home or immediate vicinity.

Each year 43 million cases of measles occur—and one million deaths from the disease ●

• Immunization against the major infectious diseases.
• Local health care, including the availability of at least 20 essential drugs within one hour's walk or travel, trained personnel for attending pregnancy and childbirth, and family planning services.

Access to primary health care has been examined through demographic and health surveys in a limited number of countries. These studies note a wide discrepancy between the proportion of the population considered to have access to services and the rate of utilization of these services. This discrepancy indicates problems of community knowledge, perceived need, or motivation to use the services. The widest discrepancy between accessibility and use is noted for family planning services. But many of the constraints on the use of family planning services—transportation costs, difficulty of access, quality of service—also affect the use of other health services.

Most countries have made significant progress in providing access to primary health care; in others there has been little improvement or even a deterioration.

About the data

Data reported here are provided to the World Health Organization (WHO) by member states in the context of monitoring and evaluating their progress in implementing national health-for-all strategies. Reliable, observation-based statistical data for the indicators do not exist in many developing countries, so in most cases the data are estimates. Such assessments often may be biased by a country's inflated or deflated estimates designed to show either progress or a need for international assistance. Thus the resulting data cannot be used for analytical purposes—and are of limited use for monitoring progress in development efforts, national or international.

Access indicators measure the supply of services but reveal little about benefits or rate of use. For example, access to health care provides no information on the quality of health care or on how the consumption of services differs among groups within a country, region, or community. Moreover, such indicators, unless based on survey statistics, are becoming increasingly less informative in many developing countries. For the poor and for many in rural areas, services by nongovernmental organizations play an increasingly important role, widening the gap between official statistics and the actual production and consumption of many essential services. It is not known, however, whether such services truly replace publicly provided services, and if so, how they differ in quantity and quality from public services. Health care facilities also tend to be concentrated in urban areas. Separate figures for rural areas show much lower levels of coverage and access.

Similarly, while information on access to safe water is widely used, it may have different meanings in different countries, despite the official WHO definition (see *Definitions*). In many countries child immunization is difficult to measure because of data recording practices. Data on births attended by health staff are from the WHO, supplemented by data from UNICEF. They are based on national sources, derived from official community and hospital records; some reflect only births in hospitals and other medical institutions. Sometimes smaller private and rural hospitals are excluded, and sometimes even relatively primitive local facilities are included. Thus the coverage is not always comprehensive, and the figures should be treated with extreme caution. No cross-country comparison should be attempted for any of the indicators.

Definitions

● **Percentage of population with access to health care** is the share of the population covered for treatment of common diseases and injuries, including availability of essential drugs on the national list, within one hour's walk or travel. ● **Percentage of population with access to safe water** is the share of the population with reasonable access to an adequate amount of safe water (including treated surface water and untreated but uncontaminated water, such as from springs, sanitary wells, and protected boreholes). In urban areas the source may be a public fountain or standpost located not more than 200 meters away. In rural areas the definition implies that members of the household do not have to spend a disproportionate part of the day fetching water. An adequate amount of water is that needed to satisfy metabolic, hygienic, and domestic requirements, usually about 20 liters of safe water a person per day. The definition of safe water has changed over time. ● **Percentage of population with access to sanitation** refers to the share of the population with at least adequate excreta disposal facilities that can effectively prevent human, animal, and insect contact with excreta. Suitable facilities range from simple but protected pit latrines to flush toilets with sewerage. To be effective, all facilities must be correctly constructed and properly maintained. ● **Child immunization** measures the rate of vaccination coverage of children under one year of age for four diseases—measles and DPT (diphtheria, pertussis or whooping cough, and tetanus). A child is considered adequately immunized against measles after receiving one dose of vaccine, and against DPT after receiving two or three doses of vaccine, depending on the immunization scheme. ● **Births attended by health staff** refer to the percentage of deliveries attended by personnel trained to give the necessary supervision, care, and advice to women during pregnancy, labor, and the postpartum period, to conduct deliveries on their own, and to care for the newborn and the infant.

Data sources

The table was produced using information provided to the WHO by countries as part of their responsibility for monitoring progress toward "health for all" and reported in the WHO's *World Health Report 1996*. Data for delivery care are from WHO, *Progress Towards Health for All: Statistics of Member States*.

2.13 | Risk factors in health

	Low-birthweight babies		Prevalence of child malnutrition	Adult HIV-1 sero-prevalence	Tobacco consumption	
	% of births		% of children under 5	per 100 adults	kilograms a year per adult	
	1980–82	1990	1989–95	1994	1984–86	1995
Albania	..	..	..	0.0	..	..
Algeria	..	..	9	0.1	1.7	1.9
Angola	..	15	20	1.0	..	..
Argentina	..	6	..	0.4	2.0	1.9
Armenia	..	..	..	0.0	..	..
Australia	..	..	..	0.1	2.1	1.8
Austria	..	6	..	0.2	2.1	1.9
Azerbaijan	..	..	..	0.0	..	..
Bangladesh	..	34	84	0.0	0.9	1.0
Belarus	..	5	..	0.0	..	..
Belgium	..	6	..	0.2	..	..
Benin	..	10	36	1.2	..	..
Bolivia	10	9	13	0.1	..	..
Bosnia and Herzegovina	..	..	..	0.0	..	..
Botswana	..	..	..	18.0	274.8	242.8
Brazil	..	15	18	0.7	..	..
Bulgaria	..	6	..	0.0	3.9	4.4
Burkina Faso	21	12	..	6.7	..	..
Burundi	..	..	..	2.7	..	..
Cambodia	..	..	..	2.0	..	..
Cameroon	..	13	14	3.0	..	..
Canada	6	6	..	0.2	2.8	2.3
Central African Republic	23	18	..	5.8	..	..
Chad	11	..	..	2.7	..	..
Chile	..	7	1	0.1	0.9	0.9
China	..	6	17	0.0	2.5	2.8
Colombia	3	17	10	0.2	1.8	2.0
Congo	15	..	..	7.2	..	..
Costa Rica	..	..	2	0.5	..	..
Côte d'Ivoire	14	15	..	6.8	1.1	1.0
Croatia	..	..	..	0.0	..	..
Cuba	..	7	..	0.0	4.3	4.7
Czech Republic	..	..	..	0.0	..	..
Denmark	..	5	..	0.2	2.7	2.4
Dominican Republic	..	14	10	1.0	..	..
Ecuador	..	..	45	0.3	..	..
Egypt, Arab Rep.	7	12	9	0.0	1.8	1.8
El Salvador	9	8	22	0.6	1.1	1.1
Eritrea	..	..	..	3.2	..	..
Estonia	..	..	..	0.0	..	..
Ethiopia	..	..	47	2.5	..	..
Finland	4	5	..	0.0	1.7	1.5
France	5	..	..	0.3	2.4	2.2
Gabon	..	10	..	2.3	..	..
Gambia, The	35	10	..	2.1	..	..
Georgia	..	..	..	0.0	..	..
Germany	..	..	..	0.1	2.4	2.1
Ghana	..	5	27	2.3	..	..
Greece	6	9	..	0.1	2.9	3.0
Guatemala	10	..	..	0.4	..	..
Guinea	18	11	18	0.6	..	..
Guinea-Bissau	13	12	..	3.1	..	..
Haiti	..	15	27	4.4	..	..
Honduras	9	..	19	1.6	..	..
Hong Kong	..	..	..	1.6	..	..

Strengthening public health programs

Public health programs typically serve needs that cannot be met by private or market-based activities. Their objective is to prevent disease or injury and to provide information on self-cure and the importance of seeking care. By contrast, clinical services respond to demand from individuals who are already sick, and they are often provided, partly or entirely, through private resources. Providing essential clinical services is often the responsibility of public health programs, however.

Governments face difficult choices in the use of public money devoted to health. The World Bank's *World Development Report 1993: Investing in Health* identified six particularly cost-effective public health activities: providing population-based services, such as immunization and mass screening for widespread diseases; improving diet and nutrition; providing family planning and maternal health care; reducing the abuse of tobacco, alcohol, and other drugs; improving household and external environments, including mitigating occupational hazards; and preventing AIDS (table 2.13a). The report recommended that public health programs in developing countries include components in most or all of these six areas, depending on local epidemiological conditions. The criterion for including a service should be its cost-effectiveness in dealing with major threats to health. The report identified care for sick children, prenatal and delivery care, treatment of sexually transmitted diseases, and short-course therapy for tuberculosis as the most cost-effective essential clinical services.

Government action in many areas of public health has already had important payoffs in developing countries. Immunization saves an estimated 3 million lives a year, and diarrheal disease control more than one million. Contraceptive use has increased in developing countries from about 10 percent of married couples in the mid-1960s to 53 percent in 1990 (WHO 1996b), enabling women to space or avoid pregnancies. But governments need to expand their efforts and move forward with public health initiatives, especially in the areas of child malnutrition, tobacco use, and AIDS. The last two are high-risk factors in developing

	Low-birthweight babies		Prevalence of child malnutrition	Adult HIV-1 sero-prevalence	Tobacco consumption	
	% of births		% of children under 5	per 100 adults	kilograms a year per adult	
	1980–82	1990	1989–95	1994	1984–86	1995
Hungary	..	10	..	0.1	3.2	3.5
India	..	30	53	0.4	0.8	0.8
Indonesia	..	8	39	0.0	1.4	1.5
Iran, Islamic Rep.	4	12	16	0.0	0.9	0.8
Iraq	6	15	..	0.0	3.1	3.1
Ireland	..	4	..	0.1	2.6	2.4
Israel	..	..	..	0.1	2.4	2.2
Italy	7	..	..	0.3	1.9	1.9
Jamaica	10	11	10	0.9	..	..
Japan	..	6	3	0.0	2.6	2.1
Jordan	..	10	17	0.0	..	..
Kazakstan	..	..	..	0.0	..	..
Kenya	18	15	23	8.3	..	..
Korea, Dem. Rep.	..	0	..	0.0	..	..
Korea, Rep.	9	4	..	0.0	2.7	3.2
Kuwait	7	..	..	0.1	..	..
Kyrgyz Republic	..	..	..	0.0	..	..
Lao PDR	..	13	40	0.0	..	..
Latvia	..	..	..	0.0	..	..
Lebanon	..	..	..	0.1	..	..
Lesotho	8	10	21	3.1	..	..
Libya	5	5	..	0.1	..	..
Lithuania	..	..	..	0.0	..	..
Macedonia, FYR	..	..	..	0.0	..	..
Madagascar	..	10	32	0.1	..	..
Malawi	22	10	27	13.6	0.4	0.4
Malaysia	10	8	23	0.3	1.7	1.9
Mali	13	10	..	1.3	..	..
Mauritania	..	..	..	0.7	..	..
Mauritius	..	8	..	0.1	..	..
Mexico	..	5	..	0.4	1.1	1.1
Moldova	..	..	..	0.0	..	..
Mongolia	..	5	10	0.0	..	..
Morocco	9	..	9	..	1.8	1.8
Mozambique	16	11	..	5.8	0.4	0.4
Myanmar	..	13	31	1.5	2.9	3.1
Namibia	..	14	..	6.5	..	..
Nepal	..	26	70	0.1	..	..
Netherlands	4	..	..	0.0	3.1	2.8
New Zealand	5	6	..	0.1	2.3	2.0
Nicaragua	..	8	12	0.1	..	..
Niger	..	..	..	1.0	..	..
Nigeria	18	17	43	2.2	0.5	0.4
Norway	4	5	..	0.1	2.0	1.9
Oman	..	8	..	0.1	..	..
Pakistan	..	30	40	0.1	1.6	1.8
Panama	8	..	7	0.6	..	..
Papua New Guinea	..	23	..	0.2	..	..
Paraguay	7	5	4	0.1	0.9	0.9
Peru	9	..	16	0.2	..	..
Philippines	..	..	30	0.1	1.5	1.6
Poland	8	8	..	0.1	4.4	3.7
Portugal	8	5	..	0.2	1.8	2.0
Puerto Rico	..	..	..	..	..	..
Romania	..	..	..	0.0	1.9	2.1
Russian Federation	..	..	..	0.0	..	..

Table 2.13a Cost-effectiveness of public health interventions and essential clinical services in low-income economies, 1990

Program	Total global disease burden averted %	Annual cost per capita $
Care for sick children	14	1.6
Immunization[a]	6	0.5
Prenatal and delivery care	4	3.8
Family planning	3	0.9
AIDS prevention	2	1.7
Treatment of sexually transmitted diseases	1	0.2
Short-course chemotherapy for tuberculosis	1	0.6
School health	0.1	0.3
Discouraging tobacco and alcohol use	0.1	0.3

a. Refers to the Expanded Programme of Immunization, which focuses on preventing selected childhood diseases and, through support to national immunization programs, aims to achieve 90 percent immunization coverage of children born each year.
Source: World Bank 1993c.

countries and are expected to be among the main causes of death and disability in the next few decades.

Child malnutrition

Either directly or in association with such infectious diseases as measles, diarrhea, or respiratory diseases, malnutrition accounts for about a quarter of deaths among children under age five. According to World Health Organization (WHO) estimates, about a third of the children in developing countries are malnourished (table 2.13b). Because chronic malnutrition is mostly a consequence of poverty, governments need to ensure food distribution, especially during periods of seasonal variability, and control infectious diseases. But equally important is the need to encourage more healthy eating by providing information on improving diets.

Tobacco

Tobacco causes more deaths than all other psychoactive substances combined (World Bank 1993c). About 3 million premature

	Low-birthweight babies		Prevalence of child malnutrition	Adult HIV-1 sero-prevalence	Tobacco consumption	
	% of births		% of children under 5	per 100 adults	kilograms a year per adult	
	1980–82	1990	1989–95	1994	1984–86	1995
Rwanda	..	..	28	7.2	..	..
Saudi Arabia	..	..	..	0.0	1.9	1.8
Senegal	..	10	20	1.4	..	..
Sierra Leone	..	13	23	3.0	..	..
Singapore	8	7	14	0.1	3.6	3.2
Slovak Republic	..	..	..	0.0	..	..
Slovenia	..	..	..	0.0	..	..
South Africa	..	..	..	3.2	1.5	1.2
Spain	1	..	..	0.6	2.3	2.5
Sri Lanka	25	22	38	0.1	..	..
Sudan	17	..	..	1.0	..	..
Sweden	..	5	..	0.1	1.6	1.4
Switzerland	..	5	..	0.3	3.1	2.4
Syrian Arab Republic	10	8	..	0.0	3.3	3.4
Tajikistan	..	..	..	0.0	..	..
Tanzania	..	16	28	6.4	0.6	0.6
Thailand	12	10	13	2.1	1.9	2.0
Togo	..	32	..	8.5	..	..
Trinidad and Tobago	..	13	..	0.9	..	..
Tunisia	7	4	..	0.0	..	..
Turkey	8	..	..	0.0	2.0	2.2
Turkmenistan	..	..	..	0.0	..	..
Uganda	..	..	23	14.5	..	..
Ukraine	6	5	..	0.0	..	..
United Arab Emirates	8	..	..	0.2	..	..
United Kingdom	..	..	..	0.1	2.0	1.7
United States	7	7	..	0.5	2.9	2.3
Uruguay	..	8	..	0.3	..	..
Uzbekistan	..	..	..	0.0	..	..
Venezuela	..	10	6	0.3	1.4	1.6
Vietnam	..	17	45	0.1	1.0	1.1
West Bank and Gaza	..	..	..	..	..	..
Yemen, Rep.	..	..	30	0.0	..	..
Yugoslavia, Fed. Rep.	..	..	..	0.1	..	..
Zaire	13	10	35	3.7	0.5	0.5
Zambia	..	..	27	17.1	..	..
Zimbabwe	15	6	16	17.4	0.6	0.6
World	..	..	..	**0.6 w**	..	**2.0 w**
Low income	..	..	..	0.8 w	..	1.8 w
Excl. China & India	..	..	..	2.3 w	..	..
Middle income	..	..	..	0.3 w	..	..
Lower middle income	..	..	..	0.2 w	..	..
Upper middle income	..	..	..	0.7 w	..	..
Low & middle income	..	..	..	0.6 w	..	1.9 w
East Asia & Pacific	..	..	..	0.1 w	..	2.5 w
Europe & Central Asia	..	..	..	0.0 w	..	..
Latin America & Carib.	..	..	..	0.5 w	..	..
Middle East & N. Africa	..	..	..	0.0 w	..	1.8 w
South Asia	..	..	..	0.3 w	..	1.0 w
Sub-Saharan Africa	..	..	..	4.3 w	..	..
High income	..	..	..	0.3 w	..	2.2 w

Table 2.13b Prevalence of child malnutrition, 1985, 1990, and 1995
percentage of children under 5

Region	1985	1990	1995
Asia	41.7	36.8	37.3
Latin America and the Caribbean	10.5	9.3	7.7
Middle East and North Africa	14.2	12.1	12.4
Sub-Saharan Africa	29.2	29.7	31.2

Note: Data refer to 93 countries and are based on World Bank regional groupings.
Source: WHO estimates.

deaths a year (6 percent of the world total in 1990) are attributable to smoking. If current trends continue, annual deaths related to tobacco smoking are projected to reach 10 million by 2020, with most of the increase in developing countries. Effectively discouraging tobacco use involves slow changes, and public education is central to this process. Information on the risks of smoking—and taxes on tobacco—are changing behavior in some countries, although so far mostly in richer ones.

AIDS

AIDS has killed about 6 million people and infected 28 million (WHO 1996b). More than 80 percent of those infected in 1990 lived in developing countries; by 2000 this share is expected to increase to 95 percent. AIDS is the largest cause of death in many African cities, and it is likely to become a major cause of death in Sub-Saharan Africa and in India and other Asian countries unless action is taken now (Bobadilla and others 1994). A combination of strategies is required to stem the spread of AIDS. Most crucial is providing information on how to avoid infection and promoting condom use, which has proved successful in Uganda and Zaire (World Bank 1993c).

About the data

The limited availability of data on health status is a major constraint to assessing the health situation in developing countries. Surveillance data are lacking for a number of major public health concerns. Estimates of prevalence and incidence are available for only a few diseases and a handful of countries, and are notoriously unreliable and variable. National health authorities differ widely in their capability and willingness to collect or report information. Even when intentions are good, reporting is based on definitions that may vary widely across countries or over time. To compensate for the paucity of data and ensure a reasonable degree of reliability and international comparability, the World Health Organization (WHO) prepares estimates in accordance with epidemiological and statistical procedures.

Low birthweight is associated with maternal malnutrition, raises the risk of infant mortality, and leads to poor growth in infancy and childhood, thus increasing the incidence of other forms of retarded development. Estimates of low-birthweight infants are drawn from hospital records and community surveys. But since many births in developing countries take place at home without assistance from formal medical practitioners and are seldom recorded, these data should be treated with caution.

Estimates of child malnutrition, here defined by weight for age, are from survey data. The minimum criterion for including a survey in the global analysis is that it be at least a national survey. Weight for age is a composite indicator of both weight for height (wasting) and height for age (stunting). The disadvantage of this indicator is that it cannot indicate whether the malnutrition is due to stunting or wasting. This indicator is nevertheless useful for comparisons with earlier surveys, as weight for age was the first anthropometric measure in general use. Methods of assessment vary, but the indicator used here is less than minus 2 standard deviations from the median weight for age of the U.S. National Center of Health Statistics reference population aged 0–59 months. The reference population, adopted by the WHO in 1983, is based on children from the United States who are assumed to be well nourished. Where this indicator could not be estimated (because a different age range or assessment method was used), priority was given to deriving identically defined prevalence comparable within the country across time. This approach has minor effects on the estimated rates, which are considered generally comparable across countries by the WHO.

Adult HIV-1 seroprevalence rates reflect the rate of HIV-1 infection estimated by WHO for each country's adult population. The global HIV pandemic currently involves two HIV viruses: HIV-1 and HIV-2. HIV-1 is the dominant type worldwide. HIV-2 is found principally in West Africa, but cases have been reported in East Africa, Europe, Asia, and Latin America. There are at least 10 different genetic subtypes of HIV-1, but their biological and epidemiological significance is unclear at present. While the routes of transmission for the two viruses are the same, HIV-2 appears to be less easily transmitted than HIV-1 and the progression from HIV-2 infection to AIDS appears to be slower than that for HIV-1. AIDS is late-stage infection characterized by a severely weakened immune system that can no longer ward off life-threatening opportunistic infections and cancers. Surveys of HIV seroprevalence are not based on national samples. Most HIV data originate from diagnostic centers or screening programs and are therefore subject to selection (usually high-risk groups) and participation bias. The extent of bias in the estimates is determined by how different the sampled population group or geographical area is from the general population.

Tobacco consumption, where raw-leaf equivalents are not available, is derived from Food and Agriculture Organization (FAO) data by converting data on consumption or sale of products. In some cases consumption is calculated from production of and net trade in leaf and products. Estimates for 1995 are based on assumptions on the growth of private consumption expenditure to derive per capita demand for tobacco. The demand function and elasticities were based on an analysis of recent national family budget surveys and previous time-series data on consumption. Antismoking campaigns and other preventive activities that have influenced tobacco consumption were also considered for some countries through a trend factor, independent of income and price.

Definitions

● **Low-birthweight babies** are children born weighing less than 2,500 grams, with the measurement taken within the first hours of life, before significant postnatal weight loss has occurred. ● **Prevalence of child malnutrition** is the percentage of children under 5 whose weight for age is less than minus 2 standard deviations from the median of the reference population. ● **Adult HIV-1 seroprevalence** reflects the estimated rate of infection in each country's adult population (age 15 and older). ● **Tobacco consumption** is kilograms of dry-weight tobacco consumed per adult (aged 15 and older) per year.

Data sources

Data presented here are drawn from a variety of sources. In order of their appearance in the table, these are:

- WHO, *World Health Statistics Annual.*
- United Nations, *Update on the Nutrition Situation.*
- WHO.
- FAO, *Tobacco: Supply, Demand and Trade Projections 1995 and 2000.*

2.14 | Mortality

	Life expectancy at birth				Infant mortality rate	Under-5 mortality rate	Adult mortality rate		Maternal mortality ratio	Mortality rate by broad cause per 100,000 population		
	Male years		Female years		per 1,000 live births	per 1,000	per 1,000		per 100,000 live births	Communi-cable	Non-communi-cable	Injuries and accidents
	1980	1995	1980	1995	1995	1995	Male 1995	Female 1995	1989–95	1985–90	1985–90	1985–90
Albania	68	70	72	76	30	37	143	77	23[a]	..	..	..
Algeria	58	68	60	71	34	42	177	133	140[a]	..	..	..
Angola	40	45	43	48	124	209	493	406	..	..	..	..
Argentina	66	69	73	76	22	27	176	84	140[a]	107	530	59
Armenia	70	68	76	74	16	24	209	108	35[a]	60	580	66
Australia	71	74	78	80	6	8	129	63	..	31	424	48
Austria	69	74	76	80	6	7	130	64	..	30	437	55
Azerbaijan	64	66	72	75	25	31	231	91	29[a]	110	595	46
Bangladesh	49	57	48	58	79	115	314	292	887[b]	..	..	..
Belarus	66	64	76	75	13	20	301	100	25[a]	28	625	90
Belgium	70	73	77	80	8	10	135	63	..	52	459	68
Benin	46	49	49	52	95	156	472	399	..	..	..	..
Bolivia	50	59	54	62	69	96	292	237	373[c]	..	..	..
Bosnia and Herzegovina	..	..	..	..	..	..	..	..	..	..	..	..
Botswana	56	50	60	53	56	74	212	153	220[b]	..	..	..
Brazil	60	63	66	71	44	57	181	123	200[a]	..	..	..
Bulgaria	69	68	74	75	15	19	213	106	20[a]	73	619	64
Burkina Faso	43	45	45	47	99	164	426	340	939[b]	..	..	..
Burundi	45	45	49	48	98	162	481	403	1,327[b]	..	..	..
Cambodia	39	52	42	54	108	158	370	298	..	..	..	..
Cameroon	49	55	52	58	56	86	413	341	..	..	..	..
Canada	71	76	78	82	6	8	113	55	..	39	395	48
Central African Republic	43	46	49	51	98	160	505	406	649[b]	..	..	..
Chad	41	47	44	50	117	197	470	385	1,594[b]	..	..	..
Chile	66	72	73	78	12	15	162	77	..	131	444	88
China	66	68	68	71	34	43	186	142	115[d]	117	696	88
Colombia	63	67	68	73	26	31	214	118	107[b]	..	..	..
Congo	47	49	53	54	90	144	405	313	822[b]	..	..	..
Costa Rica	71	74	75	79	13	16	115	68	..	..	..	..
Côte d'Ivoire	50	53	53	56	86	138	392	333	887[b]	..	..	..
Croatia	66	70	74	78	16	18	176	78	10[a]	..	..	..
Cuba	72	74	75	78	9	10	122	78	36[a]	73	472	82
Czech Republic	67	70	74	77	8	10	195	88	12[a]	..	..	..
Denmark	71	72	77	78	6	7	148	80	..	..	..	..
Dominican Republic	62	68	66	73	37	44	155	100	..	..	..	..
Ecuador	61	67	65	72	36	45	179	100	..	..	..	..
Egypt, Arab Rep.	54	64	57	66	56	76	278	238	..	..	..	..
El Salvador	51	66	63	72	36	42	229	154	..	..	..	..
Eritrea	..	..	..	..	..	..	..	..	..	..	..	..
Estonia	64	65	74	76	14	16	284	95	41[a]	..	..	..
Ethiopia	39	47	42	51	112	188	442	352	1,528[b]	..	..	..
Finland	69	73	77	80	5	5	146	64	..	43	450	76
France	70	74	78	82	6	9	130	51	..	40	362	70
Gabon	47	53	50	56	89	145	386	322	483[b]	..	..	..
Gambia, The	39	45	42	48	126	213	511	419	..	..	..	..
Georgia	67	69	75	78	18	21	189	77	55[a]	69	591	56
Germany	69	73	76	79	6	7	140	69	..	35	468	45
Ghana	51	57	54	61	73	116	320	253	742[b]	..	..	..
Greece	72	75	77	81	8	10	113	61	..	51	393	48
Guatemala	56	63	60	68	44	58	245	166	464[b]	..	..	..
Guinea	39	44	40	45	128	220	498	497	880[a]	..	..	..
Guinea-Bissau	37	42	40	45	136	233	584	572	..	..	..	..
Haiti	50	54	54	57	72	101	391	329	600[c]	..	..	..
Honduras	58	64	62	69	45	59	166	111	..	..	..	..
Hong Kong	71	76	77	81	5	6	109	57	..	71	354	28

	Life expectancy at birth				Infant mortality rate	Under-5 mortality rate	Adult mortality rate		Maternal mortality ratio	Mortality rate by broad cause per 100,000 population		
	Male years		Female years		per 1,000 live births	per 1,000	per 1,000		per 100,000 live births	Communi- cable	Non- communi- cable	Injuries and accidents
	1980	1995	1980	1995	1995	1995	Male 1995	Female 1995	1989–95	1985–90	1985–90	1985–90
Hungary	66	66	73	74	11	14	276	116	10 [a]	55	690	90
India	55	62	54	63	68	95	229	219	437 [a]	..	..	..
Indonesia	53	62	56	66	51	75	262	205	390 [a]	..	..	..
Iran, Islamic Rep.	59	68	61	69	45	59	158	149	..	..	..	..
Iraq	61	60	63	62	108	145	182	143	..	..	..	..
Ireland	70	74	75	79	6	7	134	72	..	57	526	39
Israel	70	75	76	79	8	9	114	72	..	64	444	53
Italy	71	75	77	81	7	8	123	57	..	38	425	39
Jamaica	69	72	73	77	13	15	144	90	..	..	..	..
Japan	73	77	79	83	4	6	101	47	..	51	306	41
Jordan	..	69	..	72	31	33	171	120	132 [b]	..	..	..
Kazakstan	62	64	72	74	27	35	271	99	53 [a]	86	700	103
Kenya	53	57	57	60	58	90	362	295	..	..	..	..
Korea, Dem. Rep.	64	67	70	74	26	32	215	102	48 [a]	..	..	..
Korea, Rep.	64	68	70	76	10	14	230	96	30 [a]	..	..	..
Kuwait	69	74	73	79	11	14	126	68	18 [a]	..	..	..
Kyrgyz Republic	61	63	70	72	30	42	276	120	80 [a]	124	651	95
Lao PDR	44	51	47	54	90	147	444	375	..	..	..	..
Latvia	64	63	74	75	16	20	328	102	..	..	..	..
Lebanon	63	68	67	71	32	40	191	135	..	..	..	..
Lesotho	51	57	55	60	76	121	347	258	598 [b]	..	..	..
Libya	56	63	59	67	61	75	215	166	..	..	..	..
Lithuania	66	63	76	75	14	19	304	97	16 [a]	25	598	107
Macedonia, FYR	..	71	..	75	23	31	144	92	12 [a]	..	..	..
Madagascar	49	56	52	59	89	127	445	384	..	..	..	..
Malawi	43	43	45	44	133	225	553	487	620 [c]	..	..	..
Malaysia	65	69	69	74	12	14	194	123	34 [e]	..	..	..
Mali	41	48	43	51	123	192	412	326	1,249 [b]	..	..	..
Mauritania	45	51	48	54	96	158	467	396	..	..	..	..
Mauritius	63	68	69	75	16	20	222	116	112 [a]	..	..	..
Mexico	64	69	70	75	33	41	162	89	..	168	490	102
Moldova	62	65	69	73	22	26	275	128	34 [a]	54	704	104
Mongolia	57	64	59	66	55	74	221	182	..	..	..	..
Morocco	56	64	60	68	55	75	213	163	372 [f]	..	..	..
Mozambique	42	45	46	48	113	190	431	339	1,512 [b]	..	..	..
Myanmar	51	58	54	61	83	119	308	252	518 [b]	..	..	..
Namibia	52	55	54	57	62	78	356	304	..	..	..	..
Nepal	49	57	47	56	91	131	327	354	515 [f]	..	..	..
Netherlands	72	75	79	81	6	8	121	59	..	40	416	36
New Zealand	70	73	76	79	7	9	137	70	..	50	487	58
Nicaragua	56	65	62	70	46	61	177	130	..	..	..	..
Niger	40	44	43	49	119	200	510	401	593 [c]	..	..	..
Nigeria	44	51	48	54	80	176	450	377	..	..	..	..
Norway	73	75	79	81	5	8	118	59	..	52	399	53
Oman	58	68	61	73	18	22	201	134	..	..	..	..
Pakistan	55	62	56	64	90	127	208	228	..	..	..	..
Panama	68	71	72	76	23	28	139	88	..	..	..	..
Papua New Guinea	51	56	52	58	64	95	371	339	..	..	..	..
Paraguay	65	67	69	72	41	52	158	108	180 [a]	..	..	..
Peru	57	65	61	68	47	62	211	157	..	..	..	..
Philippines	59	64	63	68	39	53	254	189	208 [c]	..	..	..
Poland	67	67	75	76	14	16	228	89	10 [a]	73	603	80
Portugal	68	72	75	79	7	11	163	76	..	70	429	78
Puerto Rico	70	72	77	80	11	15	147	61	21 [a]	78	447	59
Romania	67	66	72	74	23	29	224	111	48 [a]	93	685	65
Russian Federation	62	58	73	72	18	21	430	143	52 [a]	47	704	115

	Life expectancy at birth				Infant mortality rate	Under-5 mortality rate	Adult mortality rate		Maternal mortality ratio	Mortality rate by broad cause per 100,000 population		
	Male years		Female years		per 1,000 live births	per 1,000	per 1,000		per 100,000 live births	Communicable	Non-communicable	Injuries and accidents
	1980	1995	1980	1995	1995	1995	Male 1995	Female 1995	1989–95	1985–90	1985–90	1985–90
Rwanda	44	38	48	40	133	200	542	461	1,512 [b]	..	..	..
Saudi Arabia	60	69	62	71	21	31	181	149	18 [a]	..	..	..
Senegal	44	49	46	51	62	97	561	496	..	..	..	..
Sierra Leone	34	35	37	38	179	236	589	470	..	..	..	..
Singapore	69	74	74	79	4	6	143	82	..	114	498	39
Slovak Republic	67	68	74	76	11	15	221	93	8 [a]	..	..	..
Slovenia	66	70	75	78	7	8	188	81	5 [a]	..	..	..
South Africa	54	61	60	67	50	67	281	173	404 [b]	..	..	..
Spain	73	74	79	81	7	9	132	57	..	45	410	42
Sri Lanka	66	70	70	75	16	19	172	108	30 [a]	..	..	..
Sudan	47	52	50	55	77	109	445	378	..	..	..	..
Sweden	73	76	79	81	4	5	112	57	..	41	397	46
Switzerland	73	75	79	82	6	7	118	53	..	..	..	..
Syrian Arab Republic	60	66	63	71	32	40	217	154	179 [a]	..	..	..
Tajikistan	64	66	69	66	42	61	200	197	39 [a]	182	558	53
Tanzania	48	50	52	52	82	133	485	417	748 [b]	..	..	..
Thailand	61	67	66	72	35	42	199	119	..	..	..	..
Togo	48	49	51	52	88	128	377	311	626 [b]	..	..	..
Trinidad and Tobago	66	70	71	75	13	18	177	108	..	..	..	..
Tunisia	61	68	62	70	39	50	171	148	139 [b]	..	..	..
Turkey	59	66	64	71	48	63	158	111	183 [f]	..	..	..
Turkmenistan	61	62	68	69	46	65	250	122	43 [a]	216	737	68
Uganda	48	44	49	44	98	160	622	558	506 [f]	..	..	..
Ukraine	65	64	74	74	15	21	294	112	33 [a]	32	673	93
United Arab Emirates	66	74	70	76	16	19	122	92	20 [b]	..	..	..
United Kingdom	71	74	77	79	6	7	128	69	..	49	478	31
United States	70	74	78	80	8	10	131	63	..	54	447	58
Uruguay	67	70	74	77	18	21	174	83	..	98	519	67
Uzbekistan	64	66	71	72	30	48	209	101	43 [a]	137	601	65
Venezuela	65	70	71	75	23	25	173	94	200 [a]	..	..	..
Vietnam	61	65	65	70	41	49	206	136	105 [a]	..	..	..
West Bank and Gaza	..	..	..	..	28	..	149	102	..	..	..	..
Yemen, Rep.	47	53	50	54	100	145	384	311	1,471 [b]	..	..	..
Yugoslavia, Fed. Rep.	68	70	73	75	18	22	170	99	..	..	..	..
Zaire	47	..	51	..	..	..	..	..	..	..	..	..
Zambia	49	45	52	46	109	180	534	494	..	..	..	..
Zimbabwe	53	56	57	58	55	83	391	393	..	..	..	..
World	**59 w**	**65 w**	**64 w**	**69 w**	**55 w**	**81 w**	**222 w**	**164 w**				
Low income	57 w	62 w	59 w	64 w	69 w	104 w	244 w	211 w				
Excl. China & India	50 w	55 w	52 w	57 w	89 w	143 w	353 w	303 w				
Middle income	61 w	65 w	67 w	71 w	39 w	53 w	235 w	139 w				
Lower middle income	60 w	64 w	66 w	70 w	41 w	56 w	253 w	148 w				
Upper middle income	62 w	66 w	68 w	73 w	35 w	45 w	187 w	113 w				
Low & middle income	56 w	63 w	59 w	66 w	60 w	88 w	241 w	186 w				
East Asia & Pacific	63 w	66 w	66 w	70 w	40 w	53 w	203 w	154 w				
Europe & Central Asia	64 w	64 w	72 w	73 w	26 w	35 w	289 w	116 w				
Latin America & Carib.	62 w	66 w	68 w	72 w	37 w	47 w	183 w	114 w				
Middle East & N. Africa	57 w	65 w	60 w	68 w	54 w	72 w	212 w	176 w				
South Asia	54 w	61 w	54 w	62 w	75 w	106 w	239 w	230 w				
Sub-Saharan Africa	46 w	50 w	49 w	53 w	92 w	157 w	434 w	359 w				
High income	70 w	74 w	77 w	81 w	7 w	9 w	132 w	62 w				

a. Official estimate. b. UNICEF-WHO estimate based on statistical modeling. c. Indirect estimate based on sample survey. d. Based on a survey covering 30 provinces. e. Based on civil registration. f. Based on sample survey.

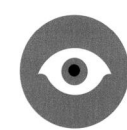

About the data

Mortality statistics and the indicators derived from them, such as life expectancy and infant mortality, are often cited as measures of a population's welfare or quality of life. They may be used to compare levels of socioeconomic development or to identify populations in need. Cause-specific mortality rates are useful both for placing the current health status of a population in an epidemiological context and for objective evaluation and planning in the health sector. As with all demographic indicators, mortality statistics should be used cautiously, with an awareness of the many difficulties involved in collecting and reporting them.

In developing countries mortality statistics from civil registers are notably defective. Estimates are derived by applying indirect estimation techniques to registration data, or from censuses or surveys, which also are subject to errors and biases. (See the notes to tables 2.1 and 2.2 for further discussion of demographic data.) Mothers may be reluctant to talk about children who have died, and may over- or underestimate the length of a year when answering survey questions about child deaths in the past 12 months (UNRISD 1977). And because many pregnant women die from lack of suitable health care, many maternal deaths go unrecorded, particularly in countries with remote rural populations. This may account for some of the low maternal mortality ratios in the table, especially for African countries. Differences in definitions may also affect the comparability of mortality data over time and across countries.

The available cause-specific mortality data are wholly inadequate; selected indicators are shown here to convey a sense of their potential utility. The main problem lies in determining the cause of death. In many developing countries, particularly in rural areas, trained medical personnel are not available to certify the cause of death. In such cases the cause of death is determined by a layperson, usually a (rural) health worker. The accuracy of such reporting is clearly lower than for cases that have been medically certified. Incomplete reporting introduces other potential biases, as does the use of hospital-based information to impute the health situation of a country as a whole.

Life expectancy and age-specific mortality rates for 1995 are generally estimates based on the most recent census or survey (see *Primary data documentation*). Maternal mortality ratios are drawn from diverse national sources. Where national administrative systems are weak, estimates are derived from demographic and health surveys using indirect estimation techniques or from other national sample surveys. For a number of countries maternal mortality ratios are derived by WHO and UNICEF (1996) using statistical modeling. Cause-specific mortality rates are standardized using the direct method: age-specific mortality rates are applied to the age distribution of a standard population—in this case the world—and the average is computed. This approach eliminates national differences in cause-specific rates due solely to the age distribution of the population. Cases in which the cause of death was ill defined are distributed among the three groups of causes of death in proportion to the number of deaths in each group.

Definitions

● **Life expectancy at birth** indicates the number of years a newborn infant would live if prevailing patterns of mortality at the time of its birth were to stay the same throughout its life. ● **Infant mortality rate** is the number of infants who die before reaching one year of age, per 1,000 live births in a given year. ● **Under-5 mortality rate** is the probability that a newborn baby will die before reaching age 5, if subject to current age-specific mortality rates. As with other demographic data (see notes to tables 2.1 and 2.2), 1995 estimates are often projected on the basis of the most recent census or survey (see *Primary data documentation*). ● **Adult mortality rate** is the probability of dying between the ages of 15 and 60, that is, the percentage of 15-year-olds who will die before their sixtieth birthday. ● **Maternal mortality ratio** is the number of female deaths that occur during pregnancy and childbirth per 100,000 live births. ● **Mortality rate by broad cause** is standardized for age using the world population as the reference population. ● **Deaths from communicable diseases** include deaths from infectious diseases listed in the WHO's *International Classification of Diseases, Ninth Revision* (1977), plus influenza and pneumonia, nutritional disorders and anemia, and maternal (including abortion) and perinatal (occurring at about the time of childbirth) causes of death. ● **Deaths from noncommunicable diseases** include all causes of death other than communicable diseases and injuries and accidents. ● **Deaths from injuries and accidents** include deaths from all violent causes, whether intentional, unintentional, or unknown.

Data sources

Mortality estimates are produced by the World Bank's Human Development and International Economics Departments in consultation with World Bank country departments. Important inputs came from the following sources:

• Bos and others, *World Population Projections 1994–95*.

• Eurostat, *Demographic Statistics*.

• United Nations Department of Economic and Social Information and Policy Analysis, *World Population Prospects: The 1996 Edition* and *Population and Vital Statistics Report*.

• Demographic and health surveys from national sources.

• UNICEF, *The State of the World's Children 1997*. Maternal mortality ratios are drawn from:

• WHO, *Maternal Mortality: A Global Factbook*.

• WHO and UNICEF, *Revised 1990 Estimates on Maternal Mortality: A New Approach*.

Mortality rates by cause are from WHO, *World Health Statistics Annual*.

Figure 2.14a Infant mortality, by region, 1970, 1980, and 1995

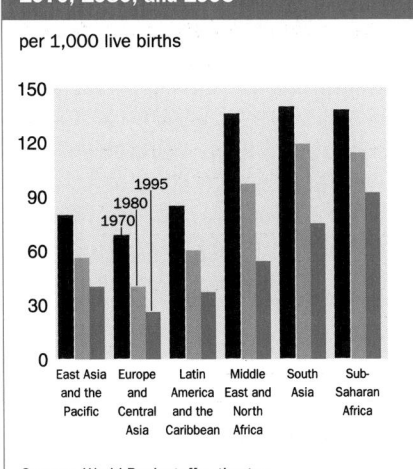

per 1,000 live births

Source: World Bank staff estimates.

Environment

3

Today some 1.5 billion people live exposed to dangerous levels of air pollution, 1 billion live without clean water, and 2 billion live without sanitation. Although food production doubled over the past quarter-century and outstripped population growth, the gains may have come at the cost of lost crop diversity and natural habitats—and more chemical contamination. Some estimates suggest that a seventh of the world's tropical forests have been lost in the past 25 years.

These problems are not just local or national—they are global, as evidenced by growing regional pollution, epidemics of disease, the loss of biodiversity, potential global climate effects, and the possibility of "environmental refugees" leaving severely degraded areas.

Poverty arising from lack of economic development is at the root of many environmental problems. Only with accelerated economic development in poor countries can environmental problems be tackled. True, economic growth can make some environmental problems worse, but without growth environmental problems will be harder to address. So it is not useful to think of development and the environment as involving a tradeoff. The only sensible approach is to ensure—through better environmental stewardship—that future economic development is socially and environmentally sustainable.

As we have come to better understand the links between economic development and the environment, it has become broadly accepted that inappropriate economic policies have a high cost for the environment, that poverty and environmental problems are closely linked, that environmental values have to be incorporated in the prices that guide economic growth, and that regional and global actions are essential to deal with environmental problems that cross national borders.

Broad acceptance of these propositions does not mean, however, that they have been translated into effective policies. Indeed, environmental problems continue to worsen in many countries. But growing national awareness of environmental issues and the way economic activities affect the environment is at last influencing the thinking of policymakers. For example, a few countries have reduced per capita carbon dioxide (CO_2) emissions over the past decade, and several others, mostly high-income countries, have exceeded the informal objective of designating 10 percent of total land area as protected areas.

We are learning more about how economic and environmental systems are interconnected—and how actions in one system can have important effects on the other. The environment can no longer be thought of as a source of "free" environmental goods and services—free forests, free fish, free freshwater. Nor can it be thought of as just a sink for disposing of waste products from homes, industries, and other sources.

Measuring the environment

The environment is a cross-cutting issue, and this must be reflected in environmental indicators. Some indicators deal with environmental "goods," such as protected areas or biodiversity. Others measure deforestation or soil loss, or pollution of the air or water. And still others monitor the effects of environmental degradation—such as waterborne disease, species loss, or number of threatened species. Such indicators are important because the links between the environmental and economic worlds are direct and immediate. Growth at the expense of the environment, or of the health of a nation's population, is likely to be unsustainable.

Many relevant indicators are not presented here, however, because of weaknesses in country coverage and concerns about the quality and comparability of data. Depletion issues in particular are inadequately captured. This lack of adequate and timely data of acceptable quality is a serious constraint on measuring the state of the environment and designing sound policies. While new techniques, such as geographic information systems (GIS), are now being used to analyze the environment, information on many aspects of the environment is sparse. The data available are usually of uneven quality, relate to different periods, and are sometimes out of date. As a result data are not only inadequate for policymaking, but may not always be comparable across countries. (Specific issues relating to each indicator are discussed in the *About the data* sections following each table.)

Another problem in measuring the state of the environment is that many environmental indicators are not meaningful at the national level. Although the world is organized into nation-states with sovereign governments, activities in one nation may sometimes have consequences for other nations. Air and water pollution do not observe national boundaries. On the other hand, some environmental issues are highly localized and location-specific. So in many cases global, regional, or city indicators are more meaningful than national aggregates. This is the direction environmental indicators are moving.

Land use and biodiversity

With growth and development, there is a tendency for forestland to be converted to agricultural land and urban land. But as development proceeds, some low-productivity agricultural land can revert to forests. This is less common, however, and for most developing countries the loss of forestland is a major issue. Of more direct importance for the environment is how land is used and whether agricultural and forestry practices are sustainable (table 3.1). Sustainability, however, is not captured well by current national indicators.

Closely linked to changes in land use are changes in protected areas and in biodiversity. The extent of protected areas and their management reveal how a country is protecting its biological resources. Many countries have an unofficial goal of protecting about 10 percent of their land area. But only some countries have achieved this goal (table 3.2). Protected areas in high-income countries approach 12 percent of their land area, while in low- and middle-income countries protected areas represent 3.0–6.5 percent of their land area. Protection has costs as well as benefits. Without appropriate analysis of both, it is hard to be certain whether protecting a specified percentage of land area is the right goal.

Water supply

The availability and quality of water are crucial to economic growth and development. For water the problem is often "too little, too much, or too dirty." Some countries have abundant untapped water to support growth far into the future. Others, such as Yemen, have already used up almost all sources, and major increases in supplies will be expensive (table 3.3).

Agriculture is typically responsible for 60–80 percent of annual withdrawals of freshwater, but industrial and domestic uses are much more important and produce more value per cubic meter.

In this century global water withdrawal has increased almost tenfold, with an increasing share going to industrial and domestic uses (figure 3a). Greater efficiency in the use of water within sectors and reallocation among sectors are needed to balance supply and demand.

Linked to the shortage of freshwater is the question of reliability of supply. In many developing countries water supply is handled largely by public utilities that are not operationally viable, resulting in a water supply of both poor quality and limited availability.

Total water available is an imperfect indication of the environmental and health consequences of the water supply, since water-short countries can, with proper management, do better than water-rich countries with inappropriate policies. This is especially true in agriculture, where water wastage is a costly and persistent problem. Raising water prices can usually help the environment without harming agricultural production.

Energy use and pricing

The link between economic growth and increased energy consumption is direct and positive—and only at the highest income levels are there signs of decreased per capita energy consumption despite economic growth. Per capita energy use in Germany has declined from 4,600 kilograms oil equivalent in 1980 to 4,100 in 1994, while energy use in the United States and Canada has been stable, around 7,850 kilograms oil equivalent in recent years (table 3.4). During this period low-income countries increased their per capita consumption from 250 to 370 kilograms oil equivalent (excluding China and India, the increase would be from 115 to 135 kilograms oil equivalent). But low-income countries use only 14 percent of total world energy (1.7 percent, excluding China and India), while high-income countries use 57 percent of the total (figure 3b). Fortunately, high-income countries now use energy more efficiently: their GDP per unit of energy use, measured in constant 1987 dollars per kilogram oil equivalent, increased from $2.90 in 1980 to $3.40 in 1994 (table 3.5). The energy efficiency of middle-income countries, however, declined slightly during the same period.

Energy use has important environmental consequences at all stages of production and consumption, not all of which are reflected in the prices paid by users of energy or in the costs borne by producers of energy. These consequences can be mitigated by pricing commercial energy (through taxes or subsidies) so as to encourage efficiency in energy use and by increasing reliance on renewable energy. A major byproduct of energy generation is emissions of CO_2, the principal greenhouse gas. In China 82 percent of greenhouse gas emissions were generated by energy use. The United States and China are the largest contributors to CO_2 emissions, accounting for some 35 percent of global emissions. On a per capita basis CO_2 emissions declined about 4 percent during 1980–92 in high-income countries, notably as a result of lower emissions in Germany. Total emissions in high-income countries increased only 4 percent during this period, with Germany reducing its emissions by 18 percent.

Urbanization and air pollution

In most countries urbanization is a natural consequence of economic growth. Rapid urbanization can yield important social benefits as people gain easier access to schools, medical care, and cultural facilities. But it can also lead to negative environmental consequences requiring a policy response.

Forty-five percent of the world's population lives in urban areas: two out of five people in low- and middle-income countries and four out of five in high-income countries (table 3.6). And the urban population grew faster (2.5 percent) than total population (1.7 percent) during 1980–95. It is easy to forget that many parts of the developing world are very urban. Most of Latin America is as urban as Europe, with 74 percent of the population living in urban areas. Asia is urbanizing rapidly, and even such traditionally rural countries as China and India now have hundreds of millions of people in towns and cities.

Increased urbanization usually means increases in air and water pollution—increases that can overwhelm the natural capacities of air and water to absorb pollution. The costs of controlling pollution and treating problems can be enormous. And pollution exposes people to severe health hazards.

Several major urban air pollutants—suspended particulate matter, lead, sulfur dioxide—are known to be harmful to health. Especially harmful is particulate matter, which contributes to respiratory diseases. Many of those pollutants come from vehicles, whose numbers are strongly linked to rising income (tables 3.7 and 3.8).

Government commitment

A crucial variable in all this, but one that is very difficult to measure, is a government's commitment to a cleaner environment and to better management of environmental resources (table 3.9). The strength of environmental policies in any country reflects the priority assigned by its government to problems of environmental degradation—and that priority reflects the benefits expected from using scarce financial resources that have competing uses. In addition to national environmental problems, governments are increasingly concerned about global environmental issues. To address these issues, agreements have been reached, and treaties signed, on areas related to the quality of life on earth. Many recent agreements resulted from the 1992 United Nations Conference on Environment and Development in Rio de Janeiro, which attracted representatives of almost every country. The conference produced Agenda 21, which proposes an array of actions to address environmental challenges. But perhaps more important, the conference caused countries to develop comprehensive environmental policy frameworks.

Government policies can make a difference, stimulating positive links between economic growth and the environment. And monitoring what is happening to the environment can guide policy toward a future that is more economically and environmentally sustainable.

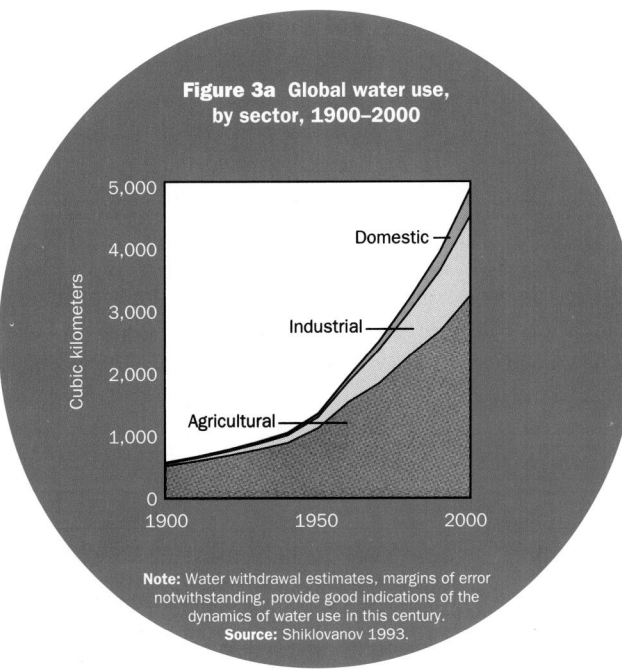

Figure 3a Global water use, by sector, 1900–2000

Cubic kilometers

Domestic
Industrial
Agricultural

Note: Water withdrawal estimates, margins of error notwithstanding, provide good indications of the dynamics of water use in this century.
Source: Shiklovanov 1993.

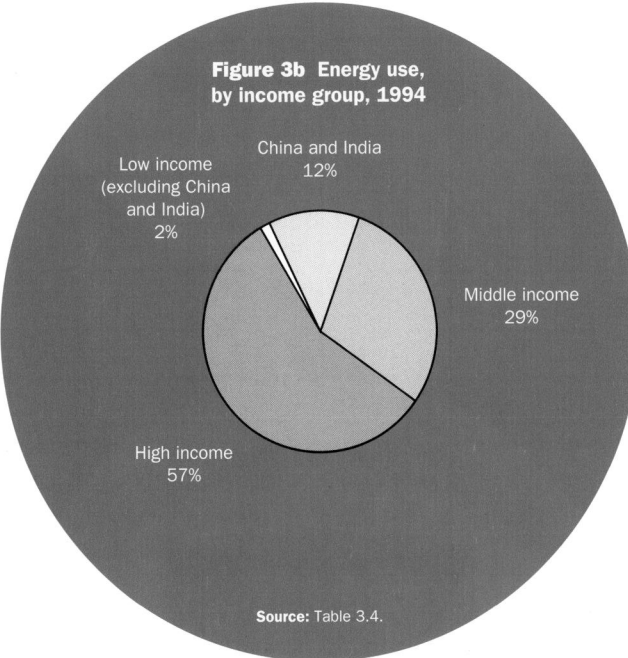

Figure 3b Energy use, by income group, 1994

China and India 12%
Low income (excluding China and India) 2%
Middle income 29%
High income 57%

Source: Table 3.4.

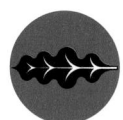

3.1 | Land use and deforestation

	Land area		Rural population density	Land use						Forest area	Annual deforestation	
	thousand sq. km 1994	share arable % 1994	people per sq. km 1994	Cropland % of land area 1980	1994	Permanent pasture % of land area 1980	1994	Other % of land area 1980	1994	thousand sq. km 1990	thousand sq. km 1980–90	% change 1980–90
Albania	27	21	349	26	26	15	15	59	59	14	–0.0	–0.0
Algeria	2,382	3	165	3	3	15	13	82	83	41	0.3	0.8
Angola	1,247	2	239	3	3	43	43	54	54	231	1.7	0.7
Argentina	2,737	9	17	10	10	52	52	38	38	592	0.9	0.1
Armenia	28	..	..	..	..	..	..	..	..	3	0.2	3.9
Australia	7,644	6	6	6	6	57	54	37	40	1,456	–0.0	–0.0
Austria	83	17	252	20	18	25	24	56	57	39	–0.1	–0.4
Azerbaijan	87	18	207	22	10	26	11	52	80	10	0.1	1.3
Bangladesh	130	73	1,026	70	74	5	5	25	21	8	0.4	4.1
Belarus	207	30	50	22	31	12	14	66	55	63	–0.3	–0.4
Belgium	33	23	39	..	24	..	21	..	55	6	–0.0	–0.3
Benin	111	13	219	16	17	4	4	80	79	49	0.7	1.3
Bolivia	1,084	2	145	2	2	25	24	73	73	493	6.3	1.2
Bosnia and Herzegovina	51	12	379	..	16	..	24	..	61	23	0.0	0.1
Botswana	567	1	238	1	1	45	45	54	54	143	0.8	0.5
Brazil	8,457	5	82	6	6	20	22	74	72	5,611	36.7	0.6
Bulgaria	111	36	63	38	38	18	16	44	46	37	–0.9	–0.2
Burkina Faso	274	13	212	10	13	22	22	68	65	44	0.3	0.7
Burundi	26	39	567	46	46	39	39	15	15	2	0.0	0.6
Cambodia	177	22	204	12	22	3	8	85	70	122	1.3	1.0
Cameroon	465	13	121	15	15	4	4	81	81	204	1.2	0.6
Canada	9,221	5	15	5	5	3	3	92	92	4,533	–47.1	–1.1
Central African Republic	623	3	101	3	3	5	5	92	92	306	1.3	0.4
Chad	1,259	3	152	3	3	36	36	62	62	114	0.9	0.7
Chile	749	5	50	6	6	17	18	77	76	88	–0.1	–0.1
China	9,326	10	910	11	10	36	43	53	47	1,247	8.8	0.7
Colombia	1,039	4	257	5	5	37	39	58	56	541	3.7	0.7
Congo	342	0	747	0	0	29	29	70	70	199	0.3	0.2
Costa Rica	51	6	589	10	10	39	46	51	44	14	0.5	3.0
Côte d'Ivoire	318	8	318	10	12	41	41	49	47	109	1.2	1.0
Croatia	56	20	158	29	22	28	20	42	59	20	0.0	0.2
Cuba	110	24	102	30	31	24	27	46	42	17	0.2	1.0
Czech Republic	77	41	114	41	44	13	12	45	45	26	–0.0	–0.0
Denmark	42	56	33	63	56	6	7	31	37	5	0.0	0.0
Dominican Republic	48	21	274	29	31	43	43	27	26	11	0.4	2.9
Ecuador	277	6	293	9	11	15	18	77	71	120	2.4	1.8
Egypt, Arab Rep.	995	3	1,012	2	4	0	0	98	96	0	0.0	0.0
El Salvador	21	27	536	35	35	29	29	36	35	1	0.0	2.3
Eritrea	101	4	661	..	5	..	69	..	26	..	..	..
Estonia	42	27	36	24	27	8	7	68	66	19	–0.2	–1.2
Ethiopia	1,000	10	455	..	11	..	20	..	69	142	0.4	0.3
Finland	305	9	73	8	9	1	0	91	91	234	–0.1	–0.0
France	550	33	86	34	35	23	19	42	45	135	–0.1	–0.1
Gabon	258	1	183	2	2	18	18	80	80	182	1.2	0.6
Gambia, The	10	17	471	16	17	19	19	65	64	1	0.0	0.8
Georgia	70	11	286	17	16	39	24	44	60	28	0.2	0.7
Germany	349	34	95	36	34	17	15	47	51	107	–0.5	–0.5
Ghana	228	12	381	15	19	37	37	48	44	96	1.4	1.4
Greece	129	19	152	30	27	41	41	29	32	60	0.0	0.0
Guatemala	108	12	450	16	18	12	24	72	58	42	0.8	1.8
Guinea	246	2	750	3	3	44	44	54	53	67	0.9	1.2
Guinea-Bissau	28	11	273	10	12	38	38	51	50	20	0.2	0.8
Haiti	28	20	864	32	33	18	18	49	49	0	0.0	5.2
Honduras	112	15	181	16	18	13	14	71	68	46	1.1	2.2
Hong Kong	1	6	5,239	7	7	1	1	92	92	0	–0.0	–0.5

	Land area		Rural population density	Land use						Forest area	Annual deforestation	
	thousand sq. km 1994	share arable % 1994	people per sq. km 1994	Cropland % of land area 1980	1994	Permanent pasture % of land area 1980	1994	Other % of land area 1980	1994	thousand sq. km 1990	thousand sq. km 1980–90	% change 1980–90
Hungary	92	51	77	58	54	14	12	28	34	17	–0.1	–0.5
India	2,973	56	404	57	57	4	4	39	39	517	3.4	0.6
Indonesia	1,812	9	738	14	17	7	7	79	77	1,095	12.1	1.1
Iran, Islamic Rep.	1,636	10	157	8	11	27	27	65	62	180	–0.0	–0.0
Iraq	437	13	84	12	13	9	9	78	78	19	0.0	0.1
Ireland	69	19	116	16	19	67	45	17	36	4	–0.1	–1.2
Israel	21	17	..	20	21	6	7	74	72	1	–0.0	–0.3
Italy	294	28	229	42	38	17	15	40	47	86	..	..
Jamaica	11	14	728	22	20	24	24	54	56	2	0.3	7.8
Japan	377	11	702	13	12	2	2	85	87	238	0.0	0.0
Jordan	89	4	374	4	5	9	9	87	87	1	–0.0	–1.1
Kazakstan	2,671	13	20	11	13	57	70	32	17	..	..	..
Kenya	569	7	476	8	8	37	37	55	55	12	0.1	0.6
Korea, Dem. Rep.	120	14	538	16	17	0	0	84	83	90	0.0	0.0
Korea, Rep.	99	19	478	22	21	1	1	77	78	65	0.1	0.1
Kuwait	18	0	1,043	0	0	8	8	92	92	0	0.0	0.0
Kyrgyz Republic	192	7	196	10	7	62	44	28	48	7	0.1	1.2
Lao PDR	231	4	428	3	4	3	3	94	93	132	1.3	0.9
Latvia	62	28	41	28	28	12	13	60	59	28	–0.1	–0.2
Lebanon	10	21	245	30	30	1	1	69	69	1	0.0	0.6
Lesotho	30	11	470	10	11	66	66	24	24	..	..	..
Libya	1,760	1	42	1	1	7	8	91	91	7	–0.1	–1.4
Lithuania	65	35	46	49	47	8	7	43	46	20	–0.0	–0.0
Macedonia, FYR	25	24	140	..	26	..	25	..	49	9	0.0	0.1
Madagascar	582	4	379	5	5	41	41	54	53	158	1.4	0.8
Malawi	94	18	493	14	18	20	20	66	62	35	0.5	1.4
Malaysia	329	6	508	15	23	1	1	85	76	176	4	2.1
Mali	1,220	2	280	2	2	25	25	74	73	121	1.1	0.8
Mauritania	1,025	0	515	0	0	38	38	62	62	6	0.0	0.0
Mauritius	2	49	661	53	52	3	3	44	44	1	0.0	0.2
Mexico	1,909	12	98	13	13	39	39	48	48	486	6.8	1.3
Moldova	33	53	122	67	66	11	13	23	21	4	–0.2	–6.7
Mongolia	1,567	1	75	1	1	79	75	20	24	139	1.3	0.9
Morocco	446	19	155	18	21	47	47	35	32	90	–1.2	–1.4
Mozambique	784	4	356	4	4	56	56	40	40	173	1.4	0.8
Myanmar	658	14	341	15	15	1	1	84	84	289	4.0	1.3
Namibia	823	1	145	1	1	46	46	53	53	126	0.4	0.3
Nepal	137	17	782	17	17	14	15	69	68	50	0.5	1.0
Netherlands	34	27	185	24	28	35	31	41	41	3	–0.0	–0.3
New Zealand	268	9	23	13	14	53	50	34	35	75	0.0	0.0
Nicaragua	121	9	151	10	10	40	45	50	44	60	1.2	1.9
Niger	1,267	3	188	3	3	8	8	90	89	24	0.1	0.4
Nigeria	911	33	220	33	36	44	44	23	20	156	1.2	0.7
Norway	307	3	130	3	3	0	0	97	97	96	–1.2	–1.4
Oman	212	0	11,439	0	0	5	5	95	95	41	0.0	0.0
Pakistan	771	27	400	26	28	6	6	67	66	19	0.8	3.4
Panama	74	7	232	7	9	17	20	75	71	31	0.7	1.9
Papua New Guinea	453	0	8,840	1	1	0	0	99	99	360	1.1	0.3
Paraguay	397	6	101	4	6	40	55	56	40	129	4.0	2.8
Peru	1,280	3	178	3	3	21	21	76	76	679	2.7	0.4
Philippines	298	19	569	29	31	3	4	67	65	78	3.2	3.5
Poland	304	47	96	49	48	13	13	38	39	87	–0.1	–0.1
Portugal	92	24	292	34	32	9	11	57	58	31	–0.1	–0.5
Puerto Rico	9	4	3,095	11	9	38	26	51	65	3	0.0	0.0
Romania	230	41	110	46	43	19	21	35	36	63	0.0	0.0
Russian Federation	16,889	8	31	8	8	..	5	..	87	7,681	15.5	0.2

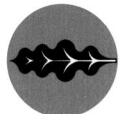

	Land area		Rural population density	Land use						Forest area	Annual deforestation	
	thousand sq. km 1994	share arable % 1994	people per sq. km 1994	Cropland % of land area 1980	1994	Permanent pasture % of land area 1980	1994	Other % of land area 1980	1994	thousand sq. km 1990	thousand sq. km 1980–90	% change 1980–90
Rwanda	25	35	674	41	47	28	28	30	24	2	0.0	0.2
Saudi Arabia	2,150	2	109	1	2	40	56	60	42	12	0.0	0.0
Senegal	193	12	206	12	12	30	30	58	58	75	0.5	0.7
Sierra Leone	72	7	540	7	8	31	31	62	62	19	0.1	0.6
Singapore	1	2	0	13	2	0	0	87	98	0	0.0	2.3
Slovak Republic	48	31	150	41	34	13	17	45	49	18	0.0	0.1
Slovenia	20	12	317	..	14	..	25	..	61	10	0.0	0.0
South Africa	1,221	10	162	11	11	67	67	22	23	45	–0.4	–0.8
Spain	499	31	59	41	40	22	21	37	38	256	–0.0	–0.0
Sri Lanka	65	14	1,531	29	29	7	7	64	64	17	0.3	1.4
Sudan	2,376	5	152	5	5	41	46	54	48	430	4.8	1.1
Sweden	412	7	53	7	7	2	1	91	92	280	–0.1	–0.0
Switzerland	40	10	673	10	11	40	29	49	60	12	–0.1	–0.6
Syrian Arab Republic	184	26	134	31	30	46	45	24	25	7	–0.3	–4.3
Tajikistan	141	6	476	13	6	50	25	37	69	5	0.0	0.6
Tanzania	884	3	732	3	4	40	40	57	56	336	4.4	1.2
Thailand	511	34	263	36	41	1	2	63	58	127	5.2	3.5
Togo	54	38	133	43	45	4	4	53	52	14	0.2	1.5
Trinidad and Tobago	5	15	557	23	24	2	2	75	74	2	–0.0	–2.1
Tunisia	155	19	128	30	32	22	20	48	48	7	–0.1	–1.9
Turkey	770	32	78	37	36	13	16	50	48	202	0.0	0.0
Turkmenistan	470	3	173	7	3	82	64	11	33	41	0.6	1.4
Uganda	200	25	323	28	34	9	9	63	57	63	0.7	1.0
Ukraine	579	57	47	61	59	12	13	27	28	92	–0.2	–0.3
United Arab Emirates	84	0	2,833	0	0	2	2	97	97	0	0.0	0.0
United Kingdom	242	25	104	29	25	47	46	24	29	24	–0.2	–1.1
United States	9,159	20	34	21	21	26	26	53	53	2,960	3.2	0.1
Uruguay	175	7	25	8	7	78	77	14	15	7	–0.0	–0.6
Uzbekistan	414	10	321	11	11	59	50	31	39	14	1	5.5
Venezuela	882	4	51	4	4	20	20	76	75	457	6	1.2
Vietnam	325	18	969	20	21	1	1	79	78	83	1.4	1.5
West Bank and Gaza	..	..	..	..	..	..	..	..	..	..	..	..
Yemen, Rep.	528	3	691	3	3	30	30	67	67	41	0.0	0.0
Yugoslavia, Fed. Rep.	102	37	125	..	40	..	21	..	39	29	0.1	0.2
Zaire	2,267	3	415	3	3	7	7	90	90	1,133	7.3	0.6
Zambia	743	7	91	7	7	40	40	53	53	323	3.6	1.1
Zimbabwe	387	7	269	7	7	44	44	49	48	89	0.6	0.7
World	**130,313 t**	**10 w**	**570 w**	**11 w**	**11 w**	**28 w**	**26 w**	**60 w**	**63 w**	**39,595 t**	**133.4 t**	**0.3 w**
Low income	39,442 t	12 w	636 w	12 w	12 w	31 w	32 w	57 w	55 w	7,916 t	65.5 t	0.8 w
Excl. China & India	27,143 t	7 w	536 w	8 w	8 w	32 w	32 w	60 w	60 w	6,152 t	53.3 t	0.8 w
Middle income	59,999 t	9 w	435 w	9 w	10 w	28 w	23 w	62 w	67 w	20,913 t	114.4 t	0.5 w
Lower middle income	39,649 t	10 w	454 w	10 w	11 w	..	18 w	..	71 w	13,525 t	65.6 t	0.5 w
Upper middle income	20,350 t	6 w	352 w	7 w	7 w	30 w	32 w	63 w	60 w	7,387 t	48.8 t	0.6 w
Low & middle income	99,441 t	10 w	593 w	10 w	11 w	29 w	27 w	60 w	63 w	28,828 t	179.8 t	0.6 w
East Asia & Pacific	15,869 t	10 w	854 w	11 w	12 w	30 w	34 w	59 w	54 w	3,986 t	43.5 t	1.0 w
Europe & Central Asia	24,114 t	12 w	115 w	13 w	13 w	..	16 w	..	71 w	8,630 t	16.7 t	0.2 w
Latin America & Carib.	20,064 t	6 w	224 w	7 w	7 w	28 w	29 w	65 w	63 w	9,786 t	74.8 t	0.7 w
Middle East & N. Africa	10,992 t	5 w	609 w	5 w	6 w	21 w	24 w	74 w	70 w	446 t	–1.4 t	–0.3 w
South Asia	4,775 t	43 w	493 w	44 w	45 w	11 w	10 w	45 w	45 w	658 t	5.5 t	0.8 w
Sub-Saharan Africa	23,628 t	6 w	358 w	6 w	7 w	34 w	34 w	60 w	59 w	5,322 t	40.7 t	0.7 w
High income	30,872 t	12 w	230 w	12 w	12 w	25 w	24 w	62 w	63 w	10,766 t	–46.4 t	–0.5 w

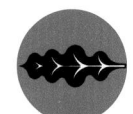

Figure 3.1a Land use in low-income economies, 1980 and 1994

percentage of land area

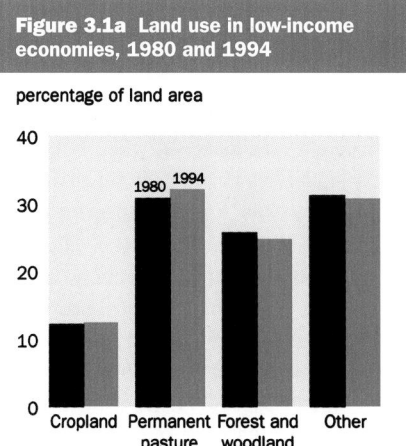

Source: Table 3.1.

Figure 3.1b Land use in middle-income economies, 1980 and 1994

percentage of land area

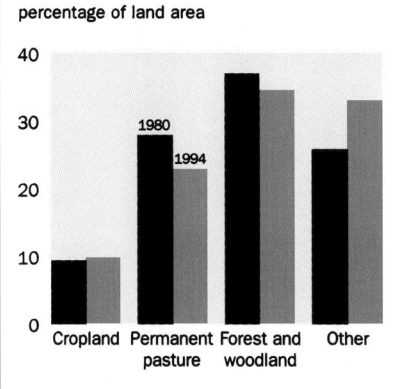

Source: Table 3.1.

Figure 3.1c Land use in high-income economies, 1980 and 1994

percentage of land area

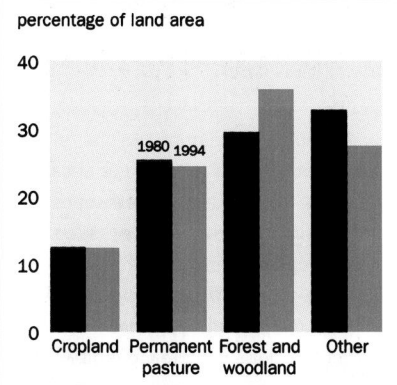

Source: Table 3.1.

About the data

The data indicate major differences in resource endowments and uses among countries, but true comparability is limited because of variations in definitions, statistical methods, and the quality of data collection. For example, countries sometimes use different definitions for land use. The Food and Agriculture Organization (FAO), the primary compiler of these data, often adjusts the definitions of land use categories—and sometimes substantially revises earlier data. Because the data thus reflect changes in data reporting procedures as well as actual changes in land use, apparent trends should be interpreted with caution. Increasingly sophisticated satellite images show land use different from that given by ground-based measures in terms of both total area under cultivation and type of land use. Furthermore, land use data in countries such as India are based on reporting systems that were geared to the collection of land revenue. With land revenue no longer a major source of government revenue, the quality and coverage of land use data (except for cropland) have declined. Data on forest area may be particularly unreliable.

Estimates of forest area are derived from country statistics assembled by the FAO and the United Nations Economic Commission for Europe (UNECE). In 1993 new assessments were published for tropical countries by the FAO and for temperate zones jointly by the UNECE and FAO—but with different definitions. The FAO defines natural forest in tropical countries either as closed forest, where trees cover a large portion of the ground with no continuous grass cover, or as open forest, a mix of forest and grasslands with at least 10 percent tree cover and a continuous grass layer on the forest floor. The UNECE-FAO assessment defines a forest as land where tree crowns cover more than 20 percent of the area. Also included are open forest formations, forest roads and firebreaks, small, temporarily cleared areas, young stands expected to achieve at least 20 percent crown cover on maturity, and windbreaks and shelter belts. The land use data here are based on the FAO definition of area under forests, and the forestry data on the UNECE-FAO definition.

Definitions

● **Land area** is the total area of the country, excluding area under inland water bodies. **Arable land** refers to land under temporary crops, temporary meadows for mowing or pasture, and land under market and kitchen gardens. ● **Rural population density** is the rural population divided by the arable land area. ● **Land use** is broken into three categories. **Cropland** includes land under temporary and permanent crops, temporary meadows, market and kitchen gardens, and land temporarily fallow. Permanent crops are those that do not need to be replanted after each harvest, excluding trees grown for wood or timber. **Permanent pasture** is land used for five or more years for forage, including natural and cultivated crops. **Other land uses** include forest and woodland, as well as logged-over areas to be forested in the near future. Also included are uncultivated land, grassland not used for pasture, wetlands, wastelands, and built-up areas—residential, recreational, and industrial lands and areas covered by roads and other fabricated infrastructure. ● **Forest area** refers to land under natural or planted stands of trees, whether productive or not (see *About the data*). ● **Annual deforestation** refers to the permanent conversion of natural forest area to other uses, including shifting cultivation, permanent agriculture, ranching, settlements, or infrastructure development. Deforested areas do not include areas logged but intended for regeneration or areas degraded by fuelwood gathering, acid precipitation, or forest fires. Negative numbers indicate an increase in forest area.

Data sources

Data on land area and land use are from the FAO's electronic files. They are also published in the FAO's *Production Yearbook*. The FAO gathers these data from national agencies through annual questionnaires and by analyzing the results of national agricultural censuses. Forestry data are from the World Resources Institute, which compiles data from the FAO and the UNECE.

3.2 | Biodiversity and protected areas

	Nationally protected areas		Mammals		Birds		Higher plants[a]	
	thousand sq. km 1994[b]	% of total land area 1994[b]	Species 1994[b]	Threatened species 1994[b]	Species 1994[b]	Threatened species 1994[b]	Species 1994[b]	Threatened species 1994[b]
Albania	0.3	1.2	68	3	306	5	2,965	50
Algeria	119.2	5.0	92	11	375	7	3,100	145
Angola	26.4	2.1	276	16	909	13	5,000	25
Argentina	43.7	1.6	320	20	976	40	9,000	170
Armenia	2.1	7.6	..	1	..	5	..	..
Australia	940.8	12.3	252	43	751	51	15,000	1,597
Austria	20.8	25.2	83	3	414	3	2,950	22
Azerbaijan	1.9	0.9	..	3	..	6	..	1
Bangladesh	1.0	0.7	109	16	684	28	5,000	24
Belarus	2.7	1.3	..	5	..	4	..	..
Belgium	0.8	2.3	58	2	429	3	1,400	3
Benin	7.8	7.0	188	7	423	1	2,000	3
Bolivia	92.3	8.5	316	21	1,274	27	16,500	49
Bosnia and Herzegovina	0.3	0.5	..	..	..	2	..	..
Botswana	106.6	18.8	164	8	550	5	..	4
Brazil	321.9	3.8	394	45	1,635	103	55,000	463
Bulgaria	3.7	3.3	81	1	374	11	3,505	94
Burkina Faso	26.6	9.7	147	6	453	1	1,100	0
Burundi	0.9	3.5	107	6	596	5	2,500	1
Cambodia	30.0	17.0	123	19	429	16	..	7
Cameroon	20.5	4.4	297	21	874	14	8,000	74
Canada	823.6	8.9	193	6	578	5	2,920	649
Central African Republic	61.1	9.8	209	9	662	2	3,600	0
Chad	114.9	9.1	134	13	532	3	1,600	12
Chile	137.3	18.3	91	11	448	15	5,125	292
China	580.8	6.2	499	94	1,186	183	30,000	1,009
Colombia	93.8	9.0	359	24	1,695	62	50,000	376
Congo	11.8	3.4	200	13	569	3	4,350	3
Costa Rica	6.5	12.7	205	8	850	10	11,000	456
Côte d'Ivoire	19.9	6.3	230	16	694	11	3,517	66
Croatia	3.9	7.0	..	..	..	4	..	..
Cuba	11.5	10.5	31	10	342	13	6,004	811
Czech Republic	10.7	13.8	..	3	..	5	..	..
Denmark	13.9	32.7	43	1	439	2	1,200	6
Dominican Republic	10.5	21.7	20	3	254	10	5,000	73
Ecuador	111.1	40.1	302	20	1,559	50	18,250	375
Egypt, Arab Rep.	7.9	0.8	98	7	439	10	2,066	84
El Salvador	0.1	0.2	135	2	420	0	2,500	35
Eritrea	..	..	112	3	537	3	..	..
Estonia	4.1	9.7	65	5	330	2	1,630	2
Ethiopia	60.2	6.0	255	21	813	17	6,500	153
Finland	27.4	9.0	60	3	425	4	1,040	11
France	56.0	10.2	93	5	506	5	4,500	117
Gabon	10.5	4.1	190	12	629	4	6,500	78
Gambia, The	0.2	2.3	108	3	504	1	966	0
Georgia	1.9	2.7	..	3	..	5	..	1
Germany	91.9	26.3	76	2	503	5	2,600	16
Ghana	11.0	4.9	222	12	725	7	3,600	32
Greece	2.2	1.7	95	5	398	9	4,900	539
Guatemala	13.3	12.3	250	5	669	4	8,000	315
Guinea	1.6	0.7	190	13	552	11	3,000	35
Guinea-Bissau	..	..	108	5	319	1	1,000	..
Haiti	0.1	0.4	3	3	220	10	4,685	28
Honduras	8.6	7.7	173	5	684	4	5,000	55
Hong Kong	..	..	..	..	..	..	..	..

Habitats for diversity

Losses of biodiversity are irreversible, and they compromise the choices of both current and future generations. Biologically diverse ecosystems often contain economically useful products that can be harvested or used as inputs in production—they provide economically valuable services, such as:

• Improving the quality of water available for agriculture, industry, or human consumption.

• Reducing sedimentation in reservoirs and irrigation works.

• Minimizing floods, landslides, coastal erosion, and droughts.

• Providing recreational opportunities.

• Filtering excess nutrients.

• Providing essential habitats for economically important species.

Ecosystems also are the reservoirs of genetic material from which new pharmaceuticals and improved crops are developed. And many people value ecosystems even if they do not use them.

The main cause of biodiversity loss has been habitat destruction, driven by such human activities as logging and by shifts in land use to agriculture, infrastructure development, or human settlement. Agriculture has played a major role in this process as the human activity that affects the largest portion of the earth's surface and the biggest user of

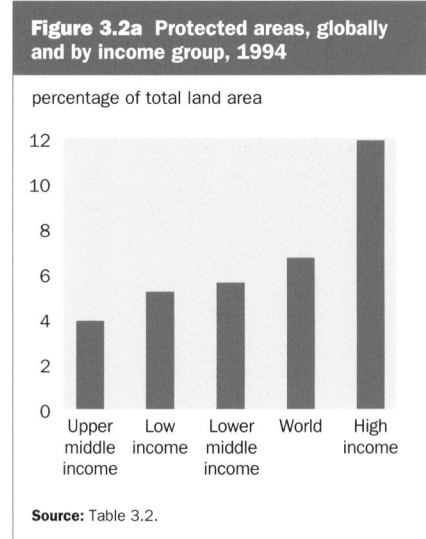

Figure 3.2a Protected areas, globally and by income group, 1994

percentage of total land area

Source: Table 3.2.

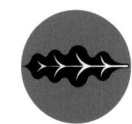

	Nationally protected areas		Mammals		Birds		Higher plants[a]	
	thousand sq. km 1994[b]	% of total land area 1994[b]	Species 1994[b]	Threatened species 1994[b]	Species 1994[b]	Threatened species 1994[b]	Species 1994[b]	Threatened species 1994[b]
Hungary	5.7	6.2	72	2	363	7	2,148	24
India	143.4	4.8	316	40	1,219	71	15,000	1,256
Indonesia	185.6	10.2	436	57	1,531	104	27,500	281
Iran, Islamic Rep.	83.0	5.1	140	9	502	12	..	1
Iraq	..	..	81	4	381	11	..	2
Ireland	0.5	0.7	25	0	417	1	892	9
Israel	3.1	14.9	92	7	500	8	..	38
Italy	22.8	7.7	90	4	490	6	5,463	273
Jamaica	0.0	0.2	24	2	262	7	2,746	371
Japan	27.6	7.3	132	17	583	31	4,700	704
Jordan	2.9	3.3	71	8	361	4	2,200	10
Kazakhstan	9.9	0.4	..	9	..	14	..	..
Kenya	35.0	6.2	359	16	1,068	22	6,000	158
Korea, Dem. Rep.	0.6	0.5	..	7	390	16	2,898	7
Korea, Rep.	6.9	7.0	49	6	372	19	2,898	69
Kuwait	0.3	1.5	21	2	321	3	234	0
Kyrgyz Republic	2.8	1.5	..	4	..	5	..	1
Lao PDR	..	..	172	25	651	23	..	5
Latvia	7.8	12.5	83	4	325	5	1,153	0
Lebanon	0.0	0.4	54	5	329	5	..	4
Lesotho	0.1	0.2	33	2	281	3	1,576	7
Libya	1.7	0.1	76	8	323	2	1,800	57
Lithuania	6.3	9.6	68	4	305	4	1,200	0
Macedonia, FYR	2.2	8.5	..	..	..	..	..	..
Madagascar	11.2	1.9	105	33	253	28	9,000	189
Malawi	10.6	11.3	195	6	645	9	3,600	61
Malaysia	14.8	4.5	286	20	736	31	15,000	510
Mali	40.1	3.3	137	12	622	5	1,741	14
Mauritania	17.5	1.7	61	10	541	3	1,100	3
Mauritius	0.0	2.0	4	3	81	9	700	222
Mexico	98.5	5.2	450	24	1,026	34	25,000	1,048
Moldova	0.1	0.4	68	1	270	6	..	1
Mongolia	61.7	3.9	134	8	390	11	2,272	1
Morocco	3.7	0.8	105	7	416	11	3,600	195
Mozambique	0.0	0.0	179	9	678	13	5,500	92
Myanmar	1.7	0.3	251	20	999	43	7,000	29
Namibia	102.2	12.4	154	12	609	6	3,128	23
Nepal	11.1	8.1	167	23	824	23	6,500	21
Netherlands	4.3	12.6	55	2	456	3	1,170	1
New Zealand	60.7	22.6	10	3	287	45	2,160	236
Nicaragua	9.0	7.4	200	6	750	3	7,000	78
Niger	84.2	6.6	131	10	482	2	1,170	0
Nigeria	29.7	3.3	274	22	862	8	4,614	9
Norway	55.4	18.0	54	3	453	3	1,650	20
Oman	9.9	4.6	56	5	430	5	1,018	4
Pakistan	37.2	4.8	151	10	671	22	4,929	12
Panama	13.3	17.8	218	11	929	9	9,000	561
Papua New Guinea	0.8	0.2	214	33	708	31	10,000	95
Paraguay	15.0	3.8	305	8	600	22	7,500	12
Peru	41.8	3.3	344	29	1,678	60	17,121	377
Philippines	6.1	2.0	153	22	556	86	8,000	371
Poland	30.7	10.1	79	4	421	5	2,300	27
Portugal	5.8	6.3	63	6	441	7	2,500	240
Puerto Rico	..	..	..	..	..	..	..	..
Romania	10.7	4.7	84	3	368	11	3,175	122
Russian Federation	705.4	4.2	..	17	..	35	..	127

freshwater worldwide. Agricultural expansion and intensification are both potentially important contributors to habitat and biodiversity losses worldwide. Conversion of land to agriculture is closely related to logging: many logged areas are later cultivated, and roads built for logging facilitate new settlement.

Conversion of habitat can lead directly to the extinction of species. Even if species survive the conversion of part of their habitat, their long-term survival may be threatened by fragmentation and disturbance of the rest. As habitats become smaller, the number of species they can support falls, and the populations of wide-ranging species often expand at the expense of species with more specialized habitat requirements. Species also are threatened by toxic chemicals and by changes in water regimes caused by human use.

Habitat conservation is vital for stemming the decline of biodiversity. Habitat conservation efforts traditionally have centered on protected areas, which have grown substantially in recent decades, particularly in low- and middle-income countries. Almost 7 percent of the world's land area is protected (figure 3.2a), with the proportion highest in North and Central America (table 3.2a). Although protected areas are important in conserving biodiversity, they have limits. Many are subject to encroachment and disturbance. Most were established to protect scenic or recreational resources, with

Table 3.2a Countries with largest shares of protected areas

Country	Share of total land area %
Ecuador	40.1
Denmark	32.7
Venezuela	29.8
Germany	26.3
Austria	25.2
New Zealand	22.6
Dominican Republic	21.7
United Kingdom	21.1
Slovak Republic	21.1
World	6.7

Source: Table 3.2.

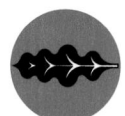

	Nationally protected areas		Mammals		Birds		Higher plants[a]	
	thousand sq. km 1994[b]	% of total land area 1994[b]	Species 1994[b]	Threatened species 1994[b]	Species 1994[b]	Threatened species 1994[b]	Species 1994[b]	Threatened species 1994[b]
Rwanda	3.3	13.3	151	14	666	6	2,288	0
Saudi Arabia	62.0	2.9	77	6	413	10	1,729	6
Senegal	21.8	11.3	155	9	610	5	2,062	32
Sierra Leone	0.8	1.1	147	12	622	12	2,090	12
Singapore	0.0	4.9	45	3	295	6	2,000	14
Slovak Republic	10.2	21.1	..	3	..	4	..	..
Slovenia	1.1	5.4	69	3	361	3	..	11
South Africa	69.7	5.7	247	25	790	16	23,000	953
Spain	42.5	8.5	82	7	506	10	..	896
Sri Lanka	8.0	12.3	88	4	428	11	3,000	436
Sudan	93.8	3.9	267	16	937	9	3,132	8
Sweden	29.8	7.2	60	3	463	4	4,916	19
Switzerland	7.3	18.5	75	2	400	3	1,650	9
Syrian Arab Republic	..	..	..	4	..	6	..	10
Tajikistan	0.9	0.6	..	6	..	9	..	0
Tanzania	139.4	15.8	322	16	1,005	30	10,000	406
Thailand	70.2	13.7	265	22	915	44	11,000	382
Togo	6.5	11.9	196	8	558	1	2,000	..
Trinidad and Tobago	0.2	3.1	100	1	433	2	1,982	16
Tunisia	0.4	0.3	78	5	356	6	2,150	24
Turkey	10.7	1.4	116	4	418	13	8,472	1,827
Turkmenistan	11.1	2.4	..	8	..	9	..	1
Uganda	19.1	9.6	338	15	992	10	5,000	6
Ukraine	4.9	0.8	..	4	..	10	2,927	16
United Arab Emirates	..	..	25	2	360	4	..	0
United Kingdom	51.1	21.1	50	1	219	2	1,550	28
United States	1,302.1	14.2	428	22	768	46	16,302	1,845
Uruguay	0.3	0.2	81	4	365	9	2,184	11
Uzbekistan	2.4	0.6	..	7	..	11	..	5
Venezuela	263.2	29.8	305	12	1,296	22	20,000	107
Vietnam	13.3	4.1	213	25	761	45	..	350
West Bank and Gaza	..	..	..	..	..	..	..	..
Yemen, Rep.	..	..	66	4	366	12	..	149
Yugoslavia, Fed. Rep.	3.5	3.4	..	..	..	..	..	..
Zaire	99.2	4.4	415	23	1,096	26	11,000	7
Zambia	63.6	8.6	229	7	736	10	4,600	9
Zimbabwe	30.7	7.9	270	9	648	7	4,200	94

World	**8,603.2 t**	**6.7 w**
Low income	2,001.1 t	5.2 w
Excl. China & India	1,276.9 t	4.9 w
Middle income	2,994.3 t	5.0 w
Lower middle income	2,199.7 t	5.6 w
Upper middle income	794.6 t	3.9 w
Low & middle income	4,995.4 t	5.1 w
East Asia & Pacific	966.3 t	6.2 w
Europe & Central Asia	860.0 t	3.6 w
Latin America & Carib.	1,303.4 t	6.5 w
Middle East & N. Africa	290.8 t	3.0 w
South Asia	212.4 t	4.4 w
Sub-Saharan Africa	1,362.5 t	5.8 w
High income	3,607.9 t	11.9 w

a. Flowering plants only. b. Data may refer to earlier years. They are the most recent reported by the World Conservation Monitoring Centre in 1994.

ecosystem protection only recently becoming an explicit objective.

Recognition of the limits of protected areas has spurred efforts to foster complementarities between biodiversity protection and economic activities. Such complementarities are particularly important for agriculture, which depends on many services provided by the environment, such as crop pollination and genes for developing improved crop varieties and livestock breeds. Moreover, exploiting biodiversity could substantially boost agricultural production. At the same time, damage to biodiversity often hurts agriculture. Reconciling biodiversity conservation with increased production to meet the needs of a growing human population will be a major challenge.

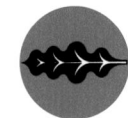

The data here are subject to variations in definition and in reporting to the World Conservation Monitoring Centre (WCMC)—a joint venture of the United Nations Environment Programme (UNEP), World Wide Fund for Nature (WWF), and World Conservation Union (IUCN)—which compiles and disseminates them. As a result cross-country comparability is limited. Compounding these problems, available data are of different vintages.

Nationally protected areas are areas of at least 1,000 hectares that fall into one of five management categories defined by the WCMC:

• Scientific reserves and strict nature reserves with limited public access.

• National parks of national or international significance (not materially affected by human activity).

• Natural monuments and natural landscapes with unique aspects.

• Managed nature reserves and wildlife sanctuaries.

• Protected landscapes and seascapes (which may include cultural landscapes).

The first three categories, referred to as "totally protected," are areas maintained in a natural state and closed to extractive uses. The last two categories, referred to as "partially protected," are areas that may be managed for specific uses, such as recreation or tourism, or that provide optimum conditions for certain species or communities of wildlife. Some extractive use is allowed within these areas. Designating land as a protected area does not necessarily mean, however, that protection is in force.

Threatened species are defined according to the IUCN's classification categories: endangered (in danger of extinction and survival unlikely if causal factors continue operating), vulnerable (likely to move into the endangered category in the near future if causal factors continue operating), rare (not endangered or vulnerable, but at risk), indeterminate (known to be endangered, vulnerable, or rare but not enough information is available to say which), out of danger (formerly included in one of the above categories, but now considered relatively secure because appropriate conservation measures are in effect), and insufficiently known (suspected but not definitely known to belong to any of the above categories). Figures on species are not necessarily comparable across countries because taxonomic concepts and coverage vary. And while the number of mammals and birds is fairly well known, it is difficult to make an accurate account of plants.

• **Nationally protected areas** are totally or partially protected areas of at least 1,000 hectares that are designed as scientific reserves with limited public access, national parks, natural monuments, nature reserves or wildlife sanctuaries, and protected landscapes and seascapes. The data do not include sites protected under local or provincial law. Total land area is used to calculate the percentage of total area protected (see table 3.1). • **Mammals** exclude whales and porpoises. • **Birds** are listed for countries included within their breeding or wintering ranges. • **Higher plants** refer to native vascular plant species. • **Threatened species** refer to species classified according to the IUCN categories endangered, vulnerable, rare, indeterminate, out of danger, and insufficiently known.

Data on protected areas are from the Protected Areas Data Unit of the WCMC, and those on species are from the WCMC's *Biodiversity Data Sourcebook*, the WCMC's *Global Biodiversity Status of the Earth's Living Resources*, and the IUCN's 1994 *Red List of Threatened Animals*, as reported by the World Resources Institute.

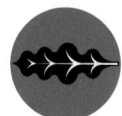

3.3 | Freshwater

	Freshwater resources	Annual freshwater withdrawals					Access to safe water			
	cubic meters per capita 1995	billion cu. m^a	% of total resources^a	% for agriculture^b	% for industry^b	% for domestic^b	Urban % of population 1985	1993	Rural % of population 1985	1993
Albania	6,534^c	0.2^d	0.9^c	76	18	6	100	..	95	..
Algeria	529^c	4.5	30.4^c	60^e	15^e	25^e	100	..	70	..
Angola	17,081	0.5	0.3	76^e	10^e	14^e	80	..	15	..
Argentina	28,674^c	27.6^d	2.8^c	73	18	9	63	73	17	17
Armenia	2,207^c	3.8	45.8^c	72	15	13	..	..	..	..
Australia	18,999	14.6^d	4.3	33	2	65	..	..	..	..
Austria	11,212^c	2.4	2.6^c	9	58	33	100	..	100	..
Azerbaijan	3,728^c	15.8	56.4^c	74	22	4	..	..	..	..
Bangladesh	19,680^c	22.5	1.0^c	96	1	3	29	47	43	85
Belarus	5,397^c	3.0	5.4^c	19	49	32	100	..	100	..
Belgium	1,232^c	9.0	72.2^c	4	85	11	..	..	..	..
Benin	4,712^c	0.1	0.4^c	67^e	10^e	23^e	45	82	9	63
Bolivia	40,464	1.2	0.4	85	5	10	81	82	27	21
Bosnia and Herzegovina	..	..	0.0	..	..	..	..	..	..	..
Botswana	10,138^c	0.1	0.6^c	48^e	20^e	32^e	98	100	72	53
Brazil	43,650^c	36.5	0.5^c	59	19	22	..	99	52	68
Bulgaria	24,379^c	13.9	6.8^c	22	76	3	..	..	..	..
Burkina Faso	2,698	0.4	1.4	81^e	0^e	19^e	50	..	26	..
Burundi	575	0.1	2.8	64^e	0^e	36^e	33	97	22	55
Cambodia	49,691	0.5	0.1	94	1	5	..	20	..	12
Cameroon	20,169	0.4	0.1	35^e	19^e	46^e	46	71	30	24
Canada	97,987	45.1	1.6	12	70	18	100	..	100	..
Central African Republic	43,053	0.1	0.0	74^e	5^e	21^e	24	..	5	..
Chad	6,669^c	0.2	0.4^c	82^e	2^e	16^e	27	..	30	..
Chile	32,900	16.8^d	3.6	89	5	6	97	100	22	31
China	2,333	460.0	16.4	87	7	6	..	..	..	..
Colombia	29,066	5.3	0.5	43	16	41	100	90	76	90
Congo	315,989^c	0.0	0.0^c	11^e	27^e	62^e	42	94	7	8
Costa Rica	27,949	1.4^d	1.4	89	7	4	100	..	82	..
Côte d'Ivoire	5,487	0.7	0.9	67^e	11^e	22^e	30	97	10	73
Croatia	12,851	..	0.0	..	..	..	..	98	..	74
Cuba	3,133	8.1^d	23.5	89	2	9	..	100	..	91
Czech Republic	5,633	2.7	4.7	2	57	41	100	..	100	..
Denmark	2,490^c	1.2	9.2^c	43	27	30	..	..	..	100
Dominican Republic	2,557	3	14.9	89	6	5	72	75	24	40
Ecuador	27,359	5.6	1.8	90	3	7	83	79	33	45
Egypt, Arab Rep.	1,005^c	56.4	97.1^c	85^e	9^e	6^e	93	95	61	74
El Salvador	3,379	1.0^d	5.3	89	4	7	76	95	47	16
Eritrea	2,462	..	0.0	..	..	..	..	..	..	..
Estonia	10,491^c	3.3	21.2^c	3	92	5	..	..	..	..
Ethiopia	1,950	2.2	2.0	86^e	3^e	11^e	93	90	42	20
Finland	22,114^c	2.2	1.9^c	3	85	12	99	100	90	100
France	3,410^c	37.7	19.1^c	15	69	16	100	100	100	100
Gabon	152,275	0.1	0.0	6^e	22^e	72^e	75	80	34	30
Gambia, The	7,188^c	0.0	0.3^c	91^e	2^e	7^e	100	87	33	86
Georgia	11,333^c	4.0	6.5^c	42	37	21	..	..	..	..
Germany	2,089^c	46.3	27.1^c	20	70	11	..	..	..	..
Ghana	3,116^c	0.3^d	0.6^c	52^e	13^e	35^e	57	76	40	46
Greece	5,608^c	5.0	8.6^c	63	29	8	100	..	95	..
Guatemala	10,922	0.7^d	0.6	74	17	9	89	84	39	51
Guinea	34,289	0.7	0.3	87^e	3^e	10^e	91	78	20	51
Guinea-Bissau	25,234^c	0.0	0.0^c	36^e	4^e	60^e	21	18	37	47
Haiti	1,535	0.0	0.4	68	8	24	59	55	32	34
Honduras	12,053^c	1.5	2.1^c	91	5	4	51	90	49	54
Hong Kong	..	..	0.0	..	..	..	..	..	..	..

	Freshwater resources	Annual freshwater withdrawals					Access to safe water			
	cubic meters per capita 1995	billion cu. m[a]	% of total resources[a]	% for agriculture[b]	% for industry[b]	% for domestic[b]	Urban % of population 1985	1993	Rural % of population 1985	1993
Hungary	11,731[c]	6.8	5.7[c]	36	55	9	100	..	95	..
India	2,243[c]	380[d]	18.2[c]	93	4	3	80	87	47	85
Indonesia	13,090	16.6	0.7	76	11	13	40	86	31	56
Iran, Islamic Rep.	1,833	45.4[d]	38.6	87	9	4	90	100	52	75
Iraq	4,976	42.8[d]	42.8	92	5	3	100	100	46	85
Ireland	13,943[c]	0.8[d]	1.6[c]	10	74	16	100	..	100	..
Israel	398[c]	1.9	84.1[c]	79[e]	5[e]	16[e]	..	..	..	..
Italy	2,919[c]	56.2	33.7[c]	59	27	14	100	..	100	..
Jamaica	3,291	0.3[d]	3.9	86	7	7	99	92	93	48
Japan	4,369	90.8	16.6	50	33	17	..	..	..	..
Jordan	332[c]	0.5[d]	32.1[c]	65	6	29	100	98	88	94
Kazakstan	7,551[c]	37.9	30.2[c]	79	17	4	..	..	..	..
Kenya	1,132[c]	2.1	7.0[c]	76[e]	4[e]	20[e]	61	74	21	43
Korea, Dem. Rep.	2,807	14.2	21.1	73	16	11	100	100	100	100
Korea, Rep.	1,474	27.6	41.8	46	35	19	..	..	..	..
Kuwait	0	0.5	0.0	4	32	64	100	..	100	..
Kyrgyz Republic	10,786	11.7	24.0	90	7	3	..	..	..	..
Lao PDR	55,305	1.0	0.4	82	10	8	..	34	..	36
Latvia	12,719[c]	0.7	2.2[c]	14	44	42	..	..	..	..
Lebanon	1,199	0.8[d]	15.6	85	4	11	98	..	98	..
Lesotho	2,626	0.1	1.0	56[e]	22[e]	22[e]	37	90	14	40
Libya	111	4.6	766.7	87[e]	2[e]	11[e]	92	..	75	..
Lithuania	6,245[c]	4.4	19.0[c]	3	90	7	..	..	..	..
Macedonia, FYR	..	..	0.0	..	..	..	..	..	..	..
Madagascar	24,687	16.3	4.8	99[e]	0[e]	1[e]	81	55	17	10
Malawi	1,917[c]	0.9	5.0[c]	86[e]	3[e]	10[e]	70	91	27	41
Malaysia	22,642	9.4[d]	2.1	47	30	23	..	100	..	80
Mali	10,217	1.4	1.4	97[e]	1[e]	2[e]	58	42	20	25
Mauritania	5,013[c]	1.6[d]	14.0[c]	92	2	6	80	49	16	86
Mauritius	1,950	0.4[d]	16.4	77[e]	7[e]	16[e]	100	..	98	..
Mexico	3,892	77.6[d]	21.7	86	8	6	95	90	50	66
Moldova	2,924[c]	3.7	29.1[c]	23	70	7	..	..	..	..
Mongolia	9,996	0.6	2.2	62	27	11	100	..	100	..
Morocco	1,129	10.9	36.2	92[e]	3[e]	5[e]	63	100	2	18
Mozambique	12,865[c]	0.8	0.3[c]	89[e]	2[e]	9[e]	82	44	2	17
Myanmar	23,988	4.0	0.4	90	3	7	36	38	21	36
Namibia	29,450[c]	0.1	0.4[c]	68[e]	3[e]	29[e]	..	97	..	37
Nepal	7,923	2.7	1.6	95	1	4	78	60	20	41
Netherlands	5,821[c]	7.8	8.7[c]	34	61	5	100	100	100	100
New Zealand	90,808	2.0	0.6	44	10	46	100	..	100	..
Nicaragua	40,000	0.9[d]	0.5	54	21	25	77	74	13	30
Niger	3,600[c]	0.3	1.5[c]	82[e]	2[e]	16[e]	48	58	34	54
Nigeria	2,516[c]	3.6	1.3[c]	54[e]	15[e]	31[e]	60	69	30	11
Norway	90,032[c]	2.0	0.5c	8	72	20	..	..	..	..
Oman	911	0.5[d]	24.0	94	3	3	90	98	55	56
Pakistan	3,603[c]	153.4[d]	32.8[c]	98	1	1	84	85	28	47
Panama	54,732	1.3[d]	0.9	77	11	12	100	..	64	..
Papua New Guinea	186,192	0.1	0.0	49	22	29	54	97	10	18
Paraguay	65,037[c]	0.4	0.1[c]	78	7	15	49	..	8	17
Peru	1,679	6.1	15.3	72	9	19	73	76	17	24
Philippines	4,709	29.5[d]	9.1	61	21	18	..	..	..	..
Poland	1,456[c]	12.3	21.9[c]	11	76	13	94	..	82	..
Portugal	7,011[c]	7.3	10.5[c]	48	37	15	97	..	90	..
Puerto Rico	..	..	0.0	..	..	..	..	..	..	..
Romania	9,166[c]	26.0	12.5[c]	59	33	8	100	..	90	..
Russian Federation	28,813[c]	117.0	2.7[c]	23	60	17	..	..	..	..

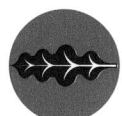

	Freshwater resources	Annual freshwater withdrawals					Access to safe water			
							Urban % of population		Rural % of population	
	cubic meters per capita 1995	billion cu. m[a]	% of total resources[a]	% for agriculture[b]	% for industry[b]	% for domestic[b]	1985	1993	1985	1993
Rwanda	984	0.8	12.2	94[e]	2[e]	5[e]	55	..	60	..
Saudi Arabia	116	3.6[d]	163.6	47	8	45	100	*98*	68	*54*
Senegal	4,653[c]	1.4	3.5[c]	92[e]	3[e]	5[e]	63	..	27	..
Sierra Leone	38,141	0.4	0.2	89[e]	4[e]	7[e]	58	85	8	..
Singapore	201	0.2[d]	31.7	4	51	45	*100*	100	..	..
Slovak Republic	5,737	1.8	5.8	..	..	..	..	..	..	..
Slovenia	..	..	0.0	..	..	..	..	..	..	..
South Africa	1,206[c]	13.3	26.6[c]	72[e]	11[e]	17[e]	..	..	..	..
Spain	2,839[c]	30.8	27.6[c]	62	26	12	100	..	100	..
Sri Lanka	2,385	6.3[d]	14.6	96	2	2	76	87	26	49
Sudan	5,766	17.8	11.6	94[e]	1[e]	4[e]	*49*	89	*45*	73
Sweden	20,385[c]	2.9	1.6[c]	9	55	36	..	..	..	..
Switzerland	7,103[c]	1.2	2.4[c]	4	73	23	..	*100*	..	..
Syrian Arab Republic	2,516	3.3	9.4	83	10	7	77	95	65	77
Tajikistan	16,330[c]	12.6	13.2[c]	88	7	5	..	..	..	..
Tanzania	3,002[c]	1.2	1.3[c]	89[e]	2[e]	9[e]	85	65	47	45
Thailand	3,073[c]	31.9	17.8[c]	90	6	4	..	89	..	72
Togo	2,938[c]	0.1	0.8[c]	25[e]	13[e]	62[e]	68	64	26	*54*
Trinidad and Tobago	3,963	0.2[d]	2.9	35	38	27	100	83	93	80
Tunisia	434[c]	3.1	79.5[c]	89[e]	3[e]	9[e]	98	100	79	67
Turkey	3,163[c]	33.5	17.3[c]	57[e]	19[e]	24[e]	100	100	70	*85*
Turkmenistan	15,528[c]	22.8	32.6[c]	91	8	1	..	..	..	..
Uganda	3,443[c]	0.2	0.3[c]	60[e]	8[e]	32[e]	45	..	12	..
Ukraine	1,684[c]	34.7	40.0[c]	30	54	16	100	..	100	..
United Arab Emirates	122	0.9	300	80	9	11	100	*98*	100	*98*
United Kingdom	1,213	11.8	16.6	3	77	20	100	100	100	100
United States	9,418[c]	467.3	18.9[c]	42[e]	45[e]	13[e]	100	..	100	..
Uruguay	38,945[c]	0.7[d]	0.5[c]	91	3	6	95	93	27	..
Uzbekistan	4,725[c]	82.2	76.4[c]	84	12	4	..	..	..	..
Venezuela	60,772[c]	4.1[d]	0.3[c]	46	11	43	88	68	65	67
Vietnam	5,117	28.9	7.7	78	9	13	90	*100*	30	*66*
West Bank and Gaza	..	..	..	..	..	..	..	..	..	..
Yemen, Rep.	164	3.4	136	93	2	5	..	88	..	17
Yugoslavia, Fed. Rep.	..	..	0.0	..	..	..	..	..	..	..
Zaire	23,239	0.7	0.0	23[e]	16[e]	61[e]	43	..	5	..
Zambia	12,920[c]	1.7	1.5[c]	77[e]	7[e]	16[e]	70	76	32	43
Zimbabwe	1,816[c]	1.2	6.1[c]	79[e]	7[e]	14[e]	100	99	10	65
World	**8,641 w**	..	..	**68 w**	**23 w**	**9 w**	..	..	..	..
Low income	5,069 w	..	..	90 w	5 w	5 w	..	..	..	..
Excl. China & India	10,722 w	..	..	92 w	4 w	4 w	64 w	71 w	30 w	45 w
Middle income	15,185 w	..	..	66 w	24 w	11 w	..	..	..	..
Lower middle income	12,248 w	..	..	64 w	26 w	10 w	..	..	..	..
Upper middle income	22,930 w	..	..	73 w	15 w	12 w	..	93 w	56 w	65 w
Low & middle income	8,411 w	..	..	80 w	13 w	7 w	..	..	..	..
East Asia & Pacific	5,558 w	..	..	84 w	8 w	7 w	..	..	..	..
Europe & Central Asia	12,927 w	..	..	53 w	37 w	11 w	..	..	..	..
Latin America & Carib.	28,340 w	..	..	77 w	11 w	12 w	..	89 w	47 w	57 w
Middle East & N. Africa	1,384 w	..	..	86 w	7 w	6 w	84 w	98 w	45 w	70 w
South Asia	4,239 w	..	..	95 w	3 w	2 w	77 w	84 w	43 w	80 w
Sub-Saharan Africa	9,106 w	..	..	85 w	4 w	10 w	63 w	..	28 w	..
High income	9,899 w	..	..	39 w	46 w	15 w	..	..	..	..

a. Refers to any year from 1980 to 1995, unless otherwise noted. b. Unless otherwise noted, sectoral withdrawal percentages are estimated for 1987. c. Total water resources include river flows from other countries. d. Data refer to estimates for years before 1980 (see *Primary data documentation*). e. Data refer to years other than the 1987 benchmark (see *Primary data documentation*).

Freshwater's scarcity

Freshwater may well be the oil of the late 20th century—an essential and increasingly scarce resource. For water, the concept of availability transcends physical quantities alone. Other important dimensions are quality, accessibility, and reliability of supply.

Although abundant globally, natural freshwater resources are unevenly distributed. Because of the central role of water in the functioning of economic, ecological, and social systems, its scarcity raises concerns for long-term development prospects in some regions.

Where water is not only scarce but also shared by more than one region or state, competition for limited supplies is a likely source of conflict, particularly in the Middle East. Uneven distribution makes it important to identify "hot spots" where pressures on water supply are likely to be greatest, as captured by annual freshwater withdrawals as a percentage of total water resources. In Saudi Arabia, the United Arab Emirates, and Yemen, for example, withdrawals exceed 100 percent, indicating a reliance on sources other than rivers and groundwater.

With expanding populations needing more water for human consumption and agricultural, industrial, and commercial uses, it is important to know which sector places the greatest strain on freshwater resources. As the indicators show, in most countries agriculture consumes the lion's share (60–80 percent in most countries and as much as 90 percent in some).

Access to reliable sources of freshwater depends to a large extent on the ability to treat water and transport it to consumers. In industrial countries water from natural sources is treated to render it pollutant-free and brought to consumers through piped networks. In developing countries such infrastructure may be lacking or poorly maintained. As a result, many people in the world still depend on water supplies that are unreliable in both quantity and quality.

About the data

The data on freshwater resources hide what can be significant variations in total renewable water resources from one year to the next. They also fail to distinguish between seasonal and geographic variations in water availability within a country. Data for small countries and countries in arid and semiarid zones are less reliable than those for larger countries and countries with higher rainfall. The data on freshwater resources are based on estimates of runoff into rivers and recharge of groundwater. These estimates are based on different sources and refer to different years, so the data on freshwater resources should be used with caution when comparing countries. Caution is also necessary in comparisons using the data on annual freshwater withdrawal, which are subject to variation in collection and estimation methods.

While information on access to safe water is widely used, it is extremely subjective, and such terms as "adequate amount" and "safe" may have very different meanings in different countries despite official World Health Organization (WHO) definitions (see the definitions for table 2.12). Even in industrial countries treated water may not always be safe to drink. While access to safe water is equated with connection to a public supply system, this does not take account of variation in the quality and cost (broadly defined) of the service once connected. Thus comparisons across countries must be made cautiously. Changes over time within countries may be a result of definitional or measurement changes.

Definitions

• **Freshwater resources** refer to both internal renewable resources and, where noted, river flows from other countries. Internal renewable water resources include flow of rivers and groundwater from rainfall in the country. • **Annual freshwater withdrawals** refer to total water withdrawal, not counting evaporation losses from storage basins. Withdrawals also include water from desalination plants in countries where that source is a significant part of all water withdrawal. Withdrawal data are for single years between 1980 and 1995. Withdrawals can exceed 100 percent of renewable supplies when extractions from nonrenewable aquifers or desalination plants are considerable or if there is significant water reuse. Withdrawals for agriculture and industry are the share of total withdrawal for agriculture (irrigation and livestock production) and the share for direct industrial use, including withdrawals for cooling thermoelectric plants. Withdrawals for domestic uses include drinking water, municipal use or supply, and use for public services, commercial establishments, and homes. For most countries sectoral withdrawal data are estimated for 1987–95. • **Access to safe water** refers to the percentage of people with reasonable access to an adequate amount of safe drinking water in a dwelling or located within a convenient distance from the user's dwelling (see *About the data*).

Data sources

Data are compiled by the World Resources Institute from various sources and published in *World Resources*. The Département Hydrogéologie in Orléans, France, compiles data on water resources and withdrawal from published documents, including national, United Nations, and professional literature. The Institute of Geography at the National Academy of Sciences in Moscow also compiles global water data on the basis of published work and, where necessary, estimates water resources and consumption from models that use other data, such as area under irrigation, livestock populations, and precipitation.

3.4 | Energy production and use

	Commercial energy production		Commercial energy use						Traditional fuel		Electricity production	
	thousand metric tons of oil equivalent		thousand metric tons of oil equivalent		average annual % growth		kg of oil equivalent per capita		% of total energy use		average annual % growth	kwh per capita
	1980	1994	1980	1994	1980–90	1990–94	1980	1994	1980	1993	1980–94	1994
Albania	3,053	1,064	3,058	1,093	–1.0	–15.6	1,145	341	11.1	21.8	–0.3	1,218
Algeria	66,730	103,833	12,078	24,834	6.2	2.1	647	906	2.7	1.7	7.4	725
Angola	7,700	24,914	937	931	1.2	–1.2	133	89	65.4	59.1	2.4	92
Argentina	36,683	60,625	39,669	51,405	1.1	5.0	1,411	1,504	5.7	5.0	3.2	1,930
Armenia	..	302	1,071	1,441	24.2	–35.9	346	384	..	..	–5.3	1,510
Australia	86,096	174,020	70,399	95,280	2.1	2.2	4,792	5,341	3.6	3.5	4.5	9,359
Austria	7,654	8,920	23,449	26,500	1.6	–0.3	3,105	3,301	1.4	3.0	1.9	6,487
Azerbaijan	14,821	16,065	15,001	16,274	5.2	–10.9	2,433	2,182	..	0.0	1.9	2,360
Bangladesh	1,113	5,460	2,809	7,566	9.0	5.4	32	64	73.5	53.2	11.5	84
Belarus	2,566	2,928	2,385	24,772	33.0	–13.2	247	2,392	..	0.4	0.7	3,032
Belgium	7,976	11,280	46,122	51,790	1.3	1.3	4,684	5,120	0.2	0.3	3.2	7,058
Benin	10	315	149	107	–1.4	–0.3	43	20	84.9	92.7	0.0	2
Bolivia	3,540	4,339	1,713	2,698	–0.6	8.6	320	373	19.2	17.5	3.4	390
Bosnia and Herzegovina	..	1,525	..	1,525	..	..	..	348	..	3.5	..	438
Botswana	260	248	384	549	3.1	0.7	426	387	..	..	..	..
Brazil	25,425	68,248	72,141	112,795	4.3	3.7	595	718	40.9	30.9	4.7	1,659
Bulgaria	7,541	8,969	28,476	20,568	0.3	–5.2	3,213	2,438	0.7	1.6	0.1	4,443
Burkina Faso	0	0	144	160	1.0	0.5	21	16	91.3	93.0	5.2	20
Burundi	1	5	58	143	7.3	5.2	14	23	92.9	14.4	50.5	20
Cambodia	13	22	393	512	2.5	0.5	60	52	..	72.9	..	..
Cameroon	2,855	5,782	774	1,335	4.1	3.2	89	103	70.6	67.7	3.9	212
Canada	207,360	337,730	193,170	229,730	1.6	2.3	7,854	7,854	0.6	0.7	2.7	18,944
Central African Republic	17	22	59	93	3.6	0.5	26	29	90.7	89.3	3.4	31
Chad	0	0	93	100	0.3	0.5	21	16	94.7	89.9	2.7	14
Chile	3,882	4,598	7,743	14,155	3.9	5.7	695	1,012	14.5	14.2	5.7	1,806
China	428,690	798,850	413,130	791,040	5.6	4.6	421	664	8.3	6.5	8.4	712
Colombia	13,057	44,825	13,972	22,470	3.7	1.5	501	622	21.4	21.8	5.3	1,199
Congo	3,387	9,428	262	847	0.6	28.6	157	331	56.1	53.6	9.2	172
Costa Rica	181	601	1,292	1,843	3.8	1.5	566	558	27.0	15.5	..	1,444
Côte d'Ivoire	192	425	1,435	1,406	1.6	1.1	175	103	..	65.4	1.3	170
Croatia	..	3,821	..	6,667	..	–1.7	..	1,395	..	3.5	..	1,733
Cuba	293	1,175	9,645	10,133	1.5	–0.9	992	923	27.6	24.4	1.5	1,000
Czech Republic	37,939	37,140	29,394	39,982	..	–4.7	2,873	3,868	..	0.9	1.1	5,680
Denmark	646	14,900	19,488	20,700	0.5	2.3	3,804	3,977	0.4	0.7	2.8	7,704
Dominican Republic	147	161	2,083	2,591	0.7	1.5	366	337	27.5	18.9	..	804
Ecuador	10,774	21,024	4,209	6,345	2.6	1.8	529	565	26.3	17.1	6.1	736
Egypt, Arab Rep.	33,374	60,931	15,176	34,071	7.2	2.7	371	600	4.9	3.2	7.7	915
El Salvador	366	608	1,000	2,032	1.9	11.5	220	370	51.8	48.0	..	585
Eritrea	..	..	..	..	..	..	..	..	..	..	..	..
Estonia	..	3,404	..	5,560	..	–15.6	..	3,709	..	3.3	–4.4	6,104
Ethiopia	55	156	624	1,193	6.4	1.6	17	22	90.8	90.4	3.6	24
Finland	6,888	12,740	24,998	30,520	2.3	1.4	5,230	5,997	3.8	3.3	3.4	12,880
France	46,999	12,480	190,660	234,160	1.9	1.2	3,539	4,042	1.3	1.0	4.9	8,156
Gabon	9,151	15,998	759	692	–3.6	6.1	1,098	652	27.4	50.7	3.6	876
Gambia, The	0	0	53	60	0.6	1.0	83	56	78.3	78.5	5.7	70
Georgia	4,706	502	..	3,325	..	..	..	614	..	1.1	–2.4	1,255
Germany	184,240	142,630	359,170	336,490	0.5	–1.4	4,587	4,128	..	1.2	1.3	6,431
Ghana	554	523	1,303	1,542	1.6	0.9	121	93	55.8	70.8	4.1	368
Greece	3,696	8,850	15,973	23,560	3.6	1.4	1,656	2,260	2.8	1.6	4.6	3,873
Guatemala	230	569	1,443	2,165	0.3	11.8	209	210	54.0	63.2	5.2	306
Guinea	38	57	356	418	1.5	0.4	80	65	66.8	69.2	0.6	86
Guinea-Bissau	0	0	31	39	2.0	1.6	38	37	75.5	71.5	11.3	41
Haiti	56	14	240	200	4.9	–13.0	45	29	83.3	84.7	..	51
Honduras	199	211	843	1,173	2.1	3.0	230	204	54.3	58.5	..	464
Hong Kong	0	0	5,628	13,243	7.0	6.8	1,117	2,185	0.8	0.4	8.8	4,412

	Commercial energy production		Commercial energy use						Traditional fuel		Electricity production	
	thousand metric tons of oil equivalent		thousand metric tons of oil equivalent		average annual % growth		kg of oil equivalent per capita		% of total energy use		average annual % growth	kwh per capita
	1980	1994	1980	1994	1980–90	1990–94	1980	1994	1980	1993	1980–94	1994
Hungary	14,340	13,025	28,322	24,450	0.8	–4.0	2,645	2,383	50.5	1.9	2.3	3,264
India	73,761	180,065	93,907	226,638	6.9	5.2	137	248	34.5	24.4	9.1	423
Indonesia	93,838	153,160	25,028	69,740	7.4	7.7	169	366	51.0	34.3	14.4	281
Iran, Islamic Rep.	83,430	222,019	38,347	94,159	7.5	8.1	980	1,505	0.3	0.8	9.2	1,265
Iraq	136,620	29,912	12,003	23,864	6.9	6.1	923	1,213	0.2	0.1	6.4	1,375
Ireland	1,894	3,530	8,485	11,200	2.1	1.5	2,495	3,137	48.9	0.0	3.6	4,713
Israel	151	531	8,616	14,624	4.5	5.9	2,222	2,717	0.0	0.0	7.4	6,090
Italy	20,027	29,830	139,190	154,600	1.4	–0.1	2,466	2,707	49.0	0.8	1.9	4,004
Jamaica	15	10	2,169	2,703	–0.3	1.7	1,017	1,083	6.2	7.4	3.3	938
Japan	43,247	89,260	347,120	481,850	2.4	2.5	2,972	3,856	0.1	0.1	4.0	7,650
Jordan	0	179	1,710	4,306	5.8	6.4	784	1,067	0.0	0.0	11.4	1,259
Kazakstan	76,799	70,851	76,799	56,664	3.6	–12.5	5,153	3,371	..	0.1	1.7	3,950
Kenya	91	488	1,991	2,872	4.2	3.9	120	110	75.1	76.9	6.5	136
Korea, Dem. Rep.	28,275	23,190	30,932	26,464	2.1	–7.7	1,694	1,129	3.9	3.3	3.5	1,621
Korea, Rep.	9,644	19,059	41,426	132,538	8.5	10.1	1,087	2,982	3.7	0.5	11.5	3,712
Kuwait	79,741	110,720	9,500	13,968	4.1	14.5	6,909	8,622	0.0	0.0	4.6	14,074
Kyrgyz Republic	2,190	1,450	..	2,755	..	–26.2	..	616	..	0.0	2.6	2,891
Lao PDR	236	215	107	182	1.8	2.5	33	38	88.4	84.8	..	..
Latvia	261	412	..	3,997	..	–17.5	..	1,569	..	11.2	–0.7	1,743
Lebanon	73	70	2,376	3,790	–0.8	14.0	840	964	2.0	3.4	0.1	1,318
Lesotho	0	0	..	..	..	..	..	..	..	..	..	..
Libya	96,537	74,658	7,122	13,039	4.4	3.2	2,340	2,499	..	..	11.1	3,411
Lithuania	186	2,254	..	7,555	0.9	–20.9	..	2,030	..	2.7	3.0	2,704
Macedonia, FYR	..	1,517	..	2,686	..	..	..	1,279	..	..	..	2,624
Madagascar	38	83	391	479	1.8	0.5	45	36	85.7	80.3	3.1	47
Malawi	99	152	334	370	1.0	1.2	54	39	83.1	86.4	5.5	86
Malaysia	15,049	57,011	9,522	33,410	9.4	11.0	692	1,699	..	6.5	9.8	1,987
Mali	21	42	164	205	2.1	0.4	25	22	85.0	87.0	10.7	36
Mauritania	0	0	214	229	0.2	0.5	138	103	0.0	0.0	3.3	68
Mauritius	21	34	339	431	3.5	0.5	351	387	47.8	47.2	7.1	901
Mexico	145,000	208,610	97,434	140,840	2.3	2.2	1,464	1,561	4.4	4.2	5.7	1,640
Moldova	..	24	..	4,763	2.1	–16.7	..	1,095	..	0.4	-3.1	1,892
Mongolia	1,195	2,167	1,943	2,550	3.1	–1.8	1,168	1,058	45.9	3.6	..	..
Morocco	618	463	4,927	8,509	3.6	5.3	254	327	5.1	4.0	5.0	426
Mozambique	1,293	161	1,123	619	–5.8	6.0	93	40	72.5	85.3	–21.5	31
Myanmar	1,940	2,164	1,858	2,181	–0.1	4.5	55	49	..	71.3	5.6	79
Namibia	0	0	..	..	..	..	..	..	..	..	..	..
Nepal	15	72	174	582	7.2	20.7	12	28	94.7	92.0	12.6	44
Netherlands	71,830	65,770	65,106	70,440	1.0	1.3	4,601	4,580	50.3	0.1	1.9	5,178
New Zealand	5,592	12,830	9,202	15,070	4.5	2.0	2,956	4,245	0.3	0.0	3.0	9,897
Nicaragua	130	476	756	1,273	2.9	7.2	270	300	49.5	43.6	..	398
Niger	14	55	210	327	2.3	1.2	38	37	77.9	78.7	0.3	21
Nigeria	105,510	102,138	9,879	17,503	2.9	4.6	139	162	62.7	59.9	5.6	144
Norway	55,743	170,150	18,865	23,060	1.9	1.5	4,611	5,318	65.3	1.1	2.3	26,061
Oman	15,133	44,508	1,346	5,018	12.4	6.2	1,223	2,392	..	..	15.8	2,950
Pakistan	7,217	19,429	11,698	32,133	8.0	6.3	142	254	27.1	19.7	9.6	463
Panama	38	206	1,376	1,597	–1.7	8.2	703	618	26.7	21.8	2.5	1,309
Papua New Guinea	80	2,472	705	990	2.4	2.3	228	236	64.2	59.4	..	..
Paraguay	64	3,130	550	1,402	6.8	12.1	175	299	65.6	52.6	45.4	7,759
Peru	11,094	8,515	8,139	8,555	–0.5	4.1	471	367	17.8	19.8	2.7	667
Philippines	2,839	6,081	13,406	21,199	2.6	4.2	277	316	36.0	31.3	3.4	404
Poland	120,720	94,437	124,500	92,537	–0.4	–1.1	3,499	2,401	50.1	0.8	1.1	3,512
Portugal	1,481	2,100	10,291	18,090	4.7	2.6	1,054	1,827	48.3	0.7	6.5	3,165
Puerto Rico	35	41	8,042	7,371	0.2	0.8	2,508	2,000	..	..	..	..
Romania	51,749	28,822	63,846	39,387	0.3	–9.0	2,876	1,733	53.5	2.8	–1.6	2,426
Russian Federation	749,290	910,609	750,240	595,440	4.2	–8.9	5,397	4,014	..	1.7	1.5	5,904

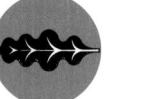

	Commercial energy production		Commercial energy use						Traditional fuel		Electricity production	
	thousand metric tons of oil equivalent		thousand metric tons of oil equivalent		average annual % growth		kg of oil equivalent per capita		% of total energy use		average annual % growth	kwh per capita
	1980	1994	1980	1994	1980–90	1990–94	1980	1994	1980	1993	1980–94	1994
Rwanda	29	46	190	209	3.1	–6.3	37	34	84.7	85.9	3.9	39
Saudi Arabia	518,700	471,344	35,496	83,772	5.8	5.7	3,787	4,566	0.0	..	9.9	4,961
Senegal	0	0	875	803	0.8	–2.7	158	97	48.1	57.3	3.7	121
Sierra Leone	0	0	310	323	–0.1	0.5	96	77	84.7	69.8	–1.5	56
Singapore	0	0	6,049	23,743	7.2	16.0	2,651	8,103	0.4	0.0	8.2	6,843
Slovak Republic	..	4,898	..	17,343	..	..	..	3,243	..	0.7	0.9	4,485
Slovenia	..	2,536	..	5,195	..	..	..	2,612	..	5.0	..	6,350
South Africa	69,065	117,691	60,511	86,995	3.6	–1.5	2,074	2,146	..	..	4.2	4,670
Spain	15,781	29,450	68,692	96,200	2.6	1.7	1,837	2,458	50.3	0.5	3.2	4,104
Sri Lanka	127	352	1,411	1,728	0.6	3.4	96	97	53.9	51.5	6.1	246
Sudan	68	81	1,150	1,731	4.8	–0.3	62	66	87.3	76.2	1.1	51
Sweden	16,133	31,340	40,992	50,250	2.1	0.6	4,933	5,723	9.0	5.9	3.5	16,236
Switzerland	7,030	11,030	20,840	25,380	2.1	0.3	3,298	3,629	1.1	..	1.3	9,271
Syrian Arab Republic	9,495	31,474	5,343	13,675	6.7	4.4	614	997	0.0	0.0	8.7	1,107
Tajikistan	1,986	1,654	..	3,542	..	–12.8	..	616	..	..	..	2,956
Tanzania	86	165	1,023	975	–0.7	2.9	55	34	89.0	89.3	5.3	66
Thailand	535	17,362	12,093	44,395	9.5	9.7	259	769	40.9	35.9	12.5	1,234
Togo	1	0	195	183	0.7	0.0	75	46	38.0	59.2	–4.2	24
Trinidad and Tobago	13,130	13,002	3,863	6,935	3.9	3.4	3,570	5,436	1.8	1.2	4.4	3,190
Tunisia	6,149	4,776	3,083	5,264	4.0	3.9	483	595	15.1	12.8	6.4	759
Turkey	17,190	26,790	31,314	57,580	5.8	2.5	705	957	16.8	3.7	9.8	1,302
Turkmenistan	8,035	30,279	..	10,401	..	–10.9	..	2,361	..	..	5.1	2,383
Uganda	153	179	320	425	4.6	–1.0	25	23	94.3	88.5	1.7	44
Ukraine	109,790	85,996	108,290	165,132	6.9	–10.5	2,164	3,180	..	0.4	0.2	3,910
United Arab Emirates	93,782	139,365	8,558	25,137	8.8	5.6	8,205	10,531	..	..	8.0	7,905
United Kingdom	197,770	241,300	201,200	220,270	1.0	0.7	3,572	3,772	0.0	0.0	1.4	5,547
United States	1,547,800	1,651,310	1,801,000	2,037,980	1.3	1.5	7,908	7,819	1.3	1.3	3.0	13,243
Uruguay	235	642	2,208	1,971	–0.9	2.7	758	622	13.2	25.0	4.0	2,406
Uzbekistan	..	41,894	..	41,825	2.5	–1.5	..	1,869	..	..	2.8	2,100
Venezuela	132,920	171,075	35,011	46,300	1.5	2.9	2,354	2,186	1.0	0.9	5.3	3,453
Vietnam	2,728	11,252	4,024	7,267	4.0	7.2	75	101	53.5	51.1	9.6	170
West Bank and Gaza	..	..	..	..	..	..	..	..	..	..	..	..
Yemen, Rep.	..	17,148	1,364	3,044	7.8	–0.1	160	206	..	2.6	11.4	146
Yugoslavia, Fed. Rep.	..	10,488	..	11,681	..	..	..	1,110	..	1.8	2.3	3,153
Zaire	1,478	1,877	1,487	1,902	2.0	1.1	55	45	80.7	83.5	3.0	131
Zambia	1,146	890	1,685	1,296	–3.0	2.3	294	149	54.9	71.0	–3.1	893
Zimbabwe	2,024	3,567	2,797	4,722	5.5	0.5	399	438	33.5	25.6	7.0	..
World	**6,231,383 t**	**8,044,554 t**	**6,249,745 t**	**8,011,531 t**	**5.0 t**	**0.6 t**	**1,419 w**	**1,433 w**	**10.7 w**	**4.3 w**	**4.9 t**	**2,365 w**
Low income	673,843 t	1,215,554 t	587,124 t	1,154,712 t	6.1 t	4.2 t	248 w	369 w	18.0 w	13.9 w	8.4 t	518 w
Excl. China & India	171,392 t	236,639 t	80,087 t	137,034 t	8.0 t	1.0 t	114 w	134 w	52.1 w	36.4 w	7.8 t	257 w
Middle income	2,788,780 t	3,447,268 t	1,873,142 t	2,313,337 t	12.5 t	–2.8 t	1,537 w	1,475 w	..	6.0 w	9.0 t	2,114 w
Lower middle income	1,779,584 t	2,237,535 t	1,448,776 t	1,647,009 t	16.3 t	–4.6 t	1,632 w	1,449 w	..	4.8 w	11.5 t	2,012 w
Upper middle income	1,009,196 t	1,209,733 t	424,366 t	666,328 t	4.4 t	2.6 t	1,282 w	1,544 w	18.7 w	10.7 w	4.9 t	2,382 w
Low & middle income	3,462,623 t	4,662,822 t	2,460,266 t	3,468,049 t	10.4 t	–0.8 t	686 w	739 w	..	8.6 w	8.7 t	1,066 w
East Asia & Pacific	575,418 t	1,074,050 t	514,066 t	1,000,586 t	5.6 t	4.7 t	378 w	593 w	14.2 w	10.9 w	8.3 t	704 w
Europe & Central Asia	1,226,858 t	1,412,506 t	1,279,071 t	1,288,624 t	21.6 t	–7.0 t	3,105 w	2,647 w	..	1.5 w	12.7 t	3,811 w
Latin America & Carib.	397,781 t	613,069 t	317,962 t	451,011 t	2.4 t	3.1 t	888 w	960 w	17.1 w	14.2 w	5.4 t	1,574 w
Middle East & N. Africa	971,980 t	1,068,548 t	143,540 t	323,064 t	6.4 t	5.4 t	825 w	1,220 w	1.9 w	1.6 w	8.5 t	1,299 w
South Asia	84,986 t	208,838 t	110,906 t	271,293 t	7.0 t	5.4 t	123 w	222 w	35.3 w	25.2 w	9.2 t	385 w
Sub-Saharan Africa	205,600 t	285,811 t	94,721 t	133,471 t	3.1 t	–0.3 t	249 w	237 w	64.9 w	64.2 w	3.5 t	571 w
High income	2,768,760 t	3,381,732 t	3,789,479 t	4,543,482 t	1.6 t	1.7 t	4,644 w	5,066 w	5.8 w	1.0 w	3.2 t	8,914 w

Energy use and the environment

Each stage in the production, transport, and use of energy has an impact on the environment. The quantity and mix of energy used in a country are an indicator both of potential environmental impact and, roughly, of the country's stage of development.

Commercial energy is widely traded, making it necessary to distinguish between its production and use. The production and transport of primary energy have a range of potential environmental consequences—from direct restructuring of the environment in the case of surface coal mines to the risk of leaks and catastrophic releases in the extraction and movement of crude oil and natural gas. Production of secondary energy (refined petroleum products and thermal electricity) and energy use in households, industry, and vehicles are by far the largest sources of air pollutants and CO_2 emissions (see table 3.5).

Growth in commercial energy use is closely related to the growth of the modern sectors—

People in high-income economies use nearly seven times as much commercial energy as do people in developing economies

industry, motorized transport, and urban areas—in developing countries, but more weakly correlated with growth in more developed countries. Commercial energy use per capita reflects the size of the modern sector as well as economic factors, such as the relative price of energy, and climatic and geographic factors.

Traditional fuels come from renewable sources, but the management of these resources—such as open-access forests—is often unsustainable. The burning of crop residues and manure reduces the nutrients available for maintaining soil quality. And traditional fuel use in the home, combined with inefficient combustion and poor ventilation, is a significant source of indoor air pollution and related health problems.

Electricity production has a large environmental impact, whatever the source of energy. Fossil fuel generation is the largest source of air pollution in most countries. Hydroelectric and nuclear power generation both have significant environmental consequences. And solar, wind, and wave generation, relatively benign environmentally, are still rare.

About the data

Energy data are compiled by the International Energy Agency (IEA) and the United Nations Statistical Division (UNSD). UNSD data are primarily from responses to questionnaires sent to national governments, supplemented by official national statistical publications and by data from intergovernmental organizations. When official data are not available, the UNSD prepares estimates based on the professional and commercial literature. The variety of sources affects the cross-country comparability of data.

Commercial energy use refers to domestic primary energy use before transformation to other end-use fuels (such as electricity and refined petroleum products). The use of firewood, dried animal manure, and other traditional fuels is not included. All forms of commercial energy—primary energy and primary electricity—are converted into oil equivalents. To convert nuclear electricity into oil equivalents, a notional thermal efficiency of 33 percent is assumed; for hydroelectric power, 100 percent efficiency is assumed. For traditional fuel, fuelwood and charcoal consumption data are estimated from population data and country-specific per capita consumption figures by the Food and Agriculture Organization (FAO) after an assessment of the available consumption data. Estimates of bagasse consumption, a traditional fuel, are based on sugar production data.

Electricity production includes both public and self-generating power plants. Self-generating power plants are operated by organizations or companies to produce electricity for internal operations. The energy source used in generating electricity is very important because of the effects different sources have on air quality, but this aspect of electricity production is not captured here.

Definitions

● **Commercial energy production** refers to commercial forms of primary energy—petroleum (crude oil, natural gas liquids, and oil from nonconventional sources), natural gas, solid fuels (coal, lignite, and other derived fuels), and primary electricity—all converted into oil equivalents (see *About the data*).
● **Commercial energy use** is indigenous production plus imports and stock changes, minus exports and international marine bunkers (see *About the data*).
● **Traditional fuel** includes estimates of the consumption of fuelwood, charcoal, bagasse, and animal and vegetable wastes. Total energy use comprises commercial energy use plus traditional fuel use.
● **Electricity production** includes that generated by nuclear, hydroelectric, geothermal, wind, tide, and wave power sources.

Data sources

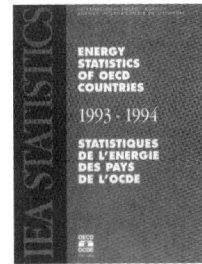

Data on commercial energy production and use are primarily from the IEA and the United Nations *Energy Statistics Yearbook*. Traditional fuel data are from the World Resources Institute's *World Resources* and the FAO.

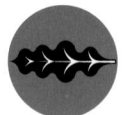

| | GDP per unit of energy use | | Net energy imports | | Carbon dioxide emissions from industrial processes | | | | | |
| | 1987 $ per kg oil equivalent | | % of commercial energy use | | Total million metric tons | | Per capita metric tons | | kg per 1987 $ of GDP | |
	1980	1994	1980	1994	1980	1992	1980	1992	1980	1992
Albania	0.6	2.4	0	3	7	4	2.8	1.2	4.0	1.8
Algeria	4.1	2.6	−452	−318	66	79	3.5	3.0	1.3	1.2
Angola	..	7.0	−722	−2,576	5	5	0.8	0.5	..	0.6
Argentina	2.9	2.7	8	−18	107	117	3.8	3.5	0.9	1.0
Armenia	4.3	1.4	100	79	..	4	..	1.1	..	1.8
Australia	2.4	2.6	−22	−83	203	268	13.8	15.3	1.2	1.2
Austria	4.6	5.4	67	66	52	57	6.9	7.2	0.5	0.4
Azerbaijan	..	0.2	1	1	..	64	..	8.7	..	13.6
Bangladesh	4.5	3.1	60	28	8	17	0.1	0.2	0.6	0.8
Belarus	..	0.8	−8	88	..	102	..	9.9	..	4.0
Belgium	2.8	3.2	83	78	128	102	13.0	10.1	1.0	0.6
Benin	8.3	18.0	93	−194	0	1	0.1	0.1	0.4	0.3
Bolivia	2.7	2.1	−107	−61	5	7	0.8	1.0	1.0	1.3
Bosnia and Herzegovina	..	..	..	0	..	15	..	3.4	..	..
Botswana	2.1	4.7	32	55	1	2	1.1	1.6	1.2	0.9
Brazil	3.4	2.8	65	39	184	217	1.5	1.4	0.7	0.8
Bulgaria	0.7	1.0	74	56	75	54	8.4	6.4	3.6	2.4
Burkina Faso	11.2	16.0	100	100	0	1	0.1	0.1	0.3	0.2
Burundi	13.9	8.3	98	97	0	0	0.0	0.0	0.1	0.1
Cambodia	..	2.4	97	96	0	0	0.0	0.1	..	0.4
Cameroon	10.0	6.9	−269	−333	4	2	0.4	0.2	0.5	0.2
Canada	1.7	2.0	−7	−47	430	410	17.5	14.4	1.3	0.9
Central African Republic	16.2	12.1	71	76	0	0	0.0	0.1	0.1	0.2
Chad	6.2	10.9	100	100	0	0	0.0	0.0	0.4	0.2
Chile	2.3	2.3	50	68	27	35	2.4	2.6	1.5	1.2
China	0.3	0.7	−4	−1	1,489	2,668	1.5	2.3	11.0	6.6
Colombia	2.1	2.1	7	−99	39	61	1.4	1.8	1.4	1.4
Congo	5.7	2.8	−1,193	−1,013	0	4	0.2	1.6	0.3	1.6
Costa Rica	3.1	3.4	86	67	2	4	1.1	1.2	0.6	0.7
Côte d'Ivoire	6.8	6.8	87	70	5	6	0.6	0.5	0.5	0.6
Croatia	..	..	..	43	..	16	..	3.4	..	..
Cuba	..	..	97	88	31	29	3.2	2.6	..	..
Czech Republic	..	0.8	−29	7	..	136	..	13.1	..	4.4
Denmark	4.4	5.5	97	28	63	54	12.3	10.4	0.7	0.5
Dominican Republic	2.0	2.5	93	94	6	10	1.1	1.4	1.5	1.7
Ecuador	2.3	2.2	−156	−231	13	19	1.7	1.8	1.4	1.4
Egypt, Arab Rep.	1.6	1.2	−120	−79	45	84	1.1	1.5	1.9	2.1
El Salvador	4.5	2.6	63	70	2	4	0.5	0.7	0.5	0.7
Eritrea	..	..	..	..	..	..	..	..	..	..
Estonia	..	0.7	..	39	0	21	0.3	13.5	0.1	4.9
Ethiopia	..	6.9	91	87	2	3	0.0	0.1	..	0.4
Finland	2.9	3.0	72	58	55	41	11.5	8.2	0.8	0.5
France	4.1	4.4	75	95	484	362	9.0	6.3	0.6	0.4
Gabon	5.0	5.5	−1,106	−2,212	5	6	6.9	5.5	1.3	1.3
Gambia, The	3.5	4.9	100	100	0	0	0.2	0.2	0.9	0.6
Georgia	..	0.7	..	85	..	14	..	2.5	..	3.0
Germany	..	..	49	58	1,068	878	13.6	10.9	..	..
Ghana	3.6	4.4	57	66	2	4	0.2	0.2	0.5	0.6
Greece	2.8	2.2	77	62	51	74	5.3	7.2	1.2	1.4
Guatemala	5.0	4.3	84	74	4	6	0.6	0.6	0.6	0.7
Guinea	..	6.1	89	86	1	1	0.2	0.2	..	0.4
Guinea-Bissau	3.8	5.8	100	100	0	0	0.2	0.2	1.2	1.0
Haiti	9.5	7.9	77	93	1	1	0.1	0.1	0.3	0.4
Honduras	4.2	4.4	76	82	2	3	0.6	0.6	0.6	0.6
Hong Kong	5.3	5.3	100	100	16	29	3.3	5.0	0.5	0.5

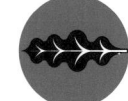

	GDP per unit of energy use		Net energy imports		Carbon dioxide emissions from industrial processes					
	1987 $ per kg oil equivalent		% of commercial energy use		Total million metric tons		Per capita metric tons		kg per 1987 $ of GDP	
	1980	1994	1980	1994	1980	1992	1980	1992	1980	1992
Hungary	0.8	1.0	49	47	82	60	7.7	5.8	3.7	2.6
India	1.9	1.6	21	21	350	769	0.5	0.9	1.9	2.3
Indonesia	2.1	1.8	−275	−120	95	185	0.6	1.0	1.8	1.7
Iran, Islamic Rep.	3.0	1.9	−118	−136	116	235	3.0	4.0	1.0	1.3
Iraq	7.2	..	−1,038	−25	44	65	3.4	3.4	0.5	..
Ireland	3.1	3.9	78	68	25	31	7.4	8.7	0.9	0.8
Israel	3.4	3.7	98	96	21	42	5.4	8.1	0.7	0.9
Italy	4.8	5.5	86	81	372	408	6.6	7.2	0.6	0.5
Jamaica	1.3	1.5	99	100	8	8	4.0	3.3	3.1	2.1
Japan	5.5	6.2	88	81	934	1,093	8.0	8.8	0.5	0.4
Jordan	..	1.5	100	96	5	11	2.2	3.0	..	1.9
Kazakstan	..	0.3	0	−25	..	298	..	17.6	..	12.6
Kenya	3.1	3.3	95	83	6	5	0.4	0.2	1.0	0.6
Korea, Dem. Rep.	..	..	9	12	126	254	6.9	11.2	..	..
Korea, Rep.	1.8	1.8	77	86	126	290	3.3	6.6	1.7	1.4
Kuwait	2.7	2.0	−739	−693	25	16	18.0	11.2	1.0	0.8
Kyrgyz Republic	..	0.9	..	47	..	15	..	3.4	..	4.3
Lao PDR	..	9.1	−121	−18	0	0	0.1	0.1	..	0.2
Latvia	..	1.2	..	90	..	15	..	5.6	..	2.6
Lebanon	..	..	97	98	6	11	2.2	2.9	..	..
Lesotho	..	..	..	..	..	..	..	..	..	..
Libya	5.6	..	−1,255	−473	27	40	8.8	8.1	0.7	..
Lithuania	..	0.8	..	70	..	22	..	5.9	..	3.1
Macedonia, FYR	..	..	..	44	..	4	..	2.0	..	..
Madagascar	6.7	5.6	90	83	2	1	0.2	0.1	0.6	0.4
Malawi	3.2	3.4	70	59	1	1	0.1	0.1	0.7	0.5
Malaysia	2.4	1.7	−58	−71	28	70	2.0	3.8	1.2	1.5
Mali	11.2	11.5	87	80	0	0	0.1	0.0	0.2	0.2
Mauritania	3.8	4.8	100	100	1	3	0.4	1.4	0.8	2.9
Mauritius	3.7	6.3	94	92	1	1	0.6	1.3	0.5	0.5
Mexico	1.3	1.2	−49	−48	260	333	3.9	3.8	2.0	2.0
Moldova	..	..	..	99	0	14	0.0	3.3	..	..
Mongolia	1.2	1.2	38	15	7	9	4.0	4.0	3.0	3.1
Morocco	3.1	2.9	87	95	16	27	0.8	1.1	1.1	1.2
Mozambique	1.4	3.3	−15	74	3	1	0.3	0.1	2.0	0.6
Myanmar	..	..	−4	1	5	4	0.1	0.1	..	..
Namibia	..	..	..	..	..	..	..	..	..	..
Nepal	12.5	7.3	91	88	1	1	0.0	0.1	0.3	0.3
Netherlands	3.0	3.7	−10	7	153	139	10.8	9.2	0.8	0.5
New Zealand	3.4	2.8	39	15	18	26	5.7	7.6	0.6	0.7
Nicaragua	5.1	2.7	83	63	2	2	0.7	0.6	0.5	0.7
Niger	12.1	7.3	93	83	1	1	0.1	0.1	0.2	0.5
Nigeria	3.1	2.2	−968	−484	68	97	1.0	0.9	2.2	2.6
Norway	3.9	4.6	−195	−638	40	60	9.8	14.1	0.5	0.6
Oman	2.9	2.4	−1,024	−787	6	10	5.3	5.3	1.5	0.9
Pakistan	1.8	1.5	38	40	32	72	0.4	0.6	1.5	1.6
Panama	3.2	3.9	97	87	4	4	1.9	1.7	0.8	0.8
Papua New Guinea	3.9	4.8	89	−150	2	2	0.6	0.6	0.7	0.6
Paraguay	6.0	3.5	88	−123	1	3	0.5	0.6	0.4	0.6
Peru	2.5	2.7	−36	0	24	22	1.4	1.0	1.2	1.2
Philippines	2.4	1.9	79	71	37	50	0.8	0.8	1.1	1.3
Poland	0.5	0.7	3	−2	460	342	12.9	8.9	7.7	6.0
Portugal	3.5	2.8	86	88	27	47	2.8	4.8	0.7	0.9
Puerto Rico	2.4	..	100	99	14	..	4.4	..	0.7	..
Romania	0.5	0.7	19	27	191	122	8.6	5.4	5.7	4.5
Russian Federation	0.6	0.5	..	−53	..	2,103	..	14.1	..	5.5

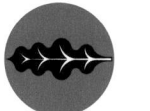

	GDP per unit of energy use		Net energy imports		Carbon dioxide emissions from industrial processes					
	1987 $ per kg oil equivalent		% of commercial energy use		Total million metric tons		Per capita metric tons		kg per 1987 $ of GDP	
	1980	1994	1980	1994	1980	1992	1980	1992	1980	1992
Rwanda	9.3	4.9	85	78	0	0	0.0	0.1	0.1	0.2
Saudi Arabia	2.7	1.1	−1,361	−463	131	221	14.0	13.1	1.4	2.3
Senegal	4.2	6.3	100	100	3	3	0.5	0.4	0.8	0.6
Sierra Leone	2.3	2.4	100	100	1	0	0.2	0.1	0.8	0.6
Singapore	2.2	1.6	100	100	30	50	13.2	17.7	2.2	1.6
Slovak Republic	..	0.9	..	72	..	37	..	7.0	..	2.5
Slovenia	..	..	..	51	..	6	..	2.8	..	..
South Africa	1.2	1.0	−14	−35	213	290	7.3	7.5	2.8	3.5
Spain	3.6	3.6	77	69	200	223	5.4	5.7	0.8	0.6
Sri Lanka	3.4	5.1	91	80	3	5	0.2	0.3	0.7	0.6
Sudan	12.7	12.1	94	95	3	3	0.2	0.1	0.2	0.2
Sweden	3.4	3.3	61	38	71	57	8.6	6.6	0.5	0.3
Switzerland	7.3	7.4	66	57	41	44	6.5	6.4	0.3	0.2
Syrian Arab Republic	1.9	1.2	−78	−130	19	42	2.2	3.3	1.9	2.8
Tajikistan	..	0.5	..	53	..	4	..	0.7	..	1.6
Tanzania	..	4.5	92	83	2	2	0.1	0.1	..	0.5
Thailand	2.8	2.2	96	61	40	112	0.9	2.0	1.2	1.3
Togo	6.3	6.9	99	100	1	1	0.2	0.2	0.5	0.6
Trinidad and Tobago	1.5	0.7	−240	−87	17	21	15.4	16.5	3.0	4.4
Tunisia	2.4	2.4	−99	9	9	14	1.5	1.6	1.3	1.1
Turkey	1.9	1.8	45	53	76	145	1.7	2.5	1.3	1.4
Turkmenistan	..	..	..	−191	..	42	..	10.5	..	..
Uganda	..	22.6	52	58	1	1	0.1	0.1	..	0.1
Ukraine	..	0.4	−1	48	..	611	..	11.7	..	6.9
United Arab Emirates	3.6	..	−996	−454	36	71	34.8	33.9	1.2	..
United Kingdom	2.8	3.5	2	−10	588	566	10.4	9.8	1.0	0.8
United States	2.1	2.6	14	19	4,623	4,881	20.3	19.1	1.2	1.0
Uruguay	3.4	4.6	89	67	6	5	2.0	1.6	0.8	0.6
Uzbekistan	..	0.3	..	0	..	123	..	5.7	..	8.5
Venezuela	1.3	1.2	−280	−269	90	116	6.0	5.7	2.0	2.0
Vietnam	..	7.5	32	−55	17	22	0.3	0.3	..	0.5
West Bank and Gaza	..	..	..	..	..	..	..	..	..	..
Yemen, Rep.	..	..	100	−463	3	10	0.4	0.7	..	..
Yugoslavia, Fed. Rep.	..	..	..	10	..	38	..	3.6	..	..
Zaire	4.4	..	1	1	3	4	0.1	0.1	0.5	0.7
Zambia	1.3	1.8	32	31	4	2	0.6	0.3	1.6	1.0
Zimbabwe	1.5	1.4	28	24	10	19	1.4	1.8	..	..
World	**2.2 w**	**2.4 w**			**14,770 t**	**21,347 t**	**3.6 w**	**4.0 w**	**1.1 w**	**1.2 w**
Low income	0.9 w	1.1 w			2,063 t	3,880 t	0.9 w	1.3 w	4.2 w	3.6 w
Excl. China & India	3.3 w	2.7 w			223 t	443 t	0.3 w	0.5 w	1.1 w	1.3 w
Middle income	1.3 w	1.2 w			2,831 t	7,221 t	2.9 w	4.8 w	1.7 w	..
Lower middle income	1.0 w	1.0 w			1,664 t	5,565 t	2.6 w	5.1 w	2.0 w	3.3 w
Upper middle income	2.2 w	1.6 w			1,167 t	1,656 t	3.7 w	4.0 w	1.4 w	..
Low & middle income	1.2 w	1.1 w			4,893 t	11,101 t	1.5 w	2.4 w	2.2 w	3.0 w
East Asia & Pacific	..	0.9 w			1,846 t	3,378 t	1.4 w	2.1 w	..	..
Europe & Central Asia	..	0.6 w			944 t	4,506 t	..	9.3 w	..	4.8 w
Latin America & Carib.	2.3 w	2.0 w			855 t	1,029 t	2.4 w	2.3 w	1.2 w	1.2 w
Middle East & N. Africa	3.3 w	1.6 w			500 t	849 t	2.9 w	3.4 w	1.1 w	..
South Asia	2.0 w	1.7 w			395 t	866 t	0.4 w	0.7 w	1.8 w	2.1 w
Sub-Saharan Africa	2.2 w	2.0 w			353 t	472 t	0.9 w	0.9 w	1.7 w	1.8 w
High income	2.9 w	3.4 w			9,877 t	10,246 t	12.4 w	11.9 w	0.9 w	0.7 w

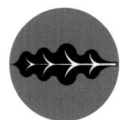

Moving toward energy efficiency

Energy is both a critical factor of production and, through its generation, a major source of pressure on the environment. The sustainability of energy supplies and the efficiency of energy use are therefore critical for countries aiming for environmentally sustainable development.

Carbon dioxide (CO_2) emissions, largely a byproduct of energy generation and use, are the largest source of greenhouse gases associated with global warming. Thus understanding the links between economic activity and CO_2 emissions has become increasingly important.

The ratio of real GDP to energy use provides a measure of energy efficiency. Differences in this ratio over time and across countries are influenced by:

- Structural changes in the economy.
- Changes in the energy efficiency of particular sectors of the economy.
- Differences in fuel mixes.

Technological changes in energy-intensive industries help increase overall energy effi-

Per dollar of GDP, developing economies produce four times the carbon dioxide that high-income economies do ⬤

ciency. Shifts to thermodynamically efficient fuels such as natural gas also can help. But the most important factor affecting energy efficiency is the rapid rise in energy use as countries approach middle-income status. The development of heavy industries and the large increase in private automobile ownership associated with income growth both increase demand for energy. Offsetting this tendency, especially for high-income economies, may be the growth of the less energy-intensive services sector. Growth in services also helps reduce oil-importing countries' dependence on external sources of energy. In the past two decades this dependency has put heavy pressure on these countries' foreign exchange earnings and has made their economies vulnerable to external shocks.

Anthropogenic CO_2 emissions result primarily from fossil fuel combustion and the manufacture of cement. Because fossil fuel consumption tends to rise with income, high-income countries are the largest emitters per capita.

The Carbon Dioxide Information Analysis Center (CDIAC), sponsored by the U.S. Department of Energy, calculates annual anthropogenic emissions of CO_2.

Estimates do not include bunker fuels used in international transport because of the difficulty of apportioning these fuels among the countries benefiting from that transport. Although the estimates of world emissions are probably within 10 percent of actual emissions (as calculated using global average fuel chemistry and use), individual country estimates may have larger error bounds.

For information on energy use and production see the notes to table 3.4.

Figure 3.5a Carbon dioxide emissions per capita, by income group, 1980 and 1992

metric tons

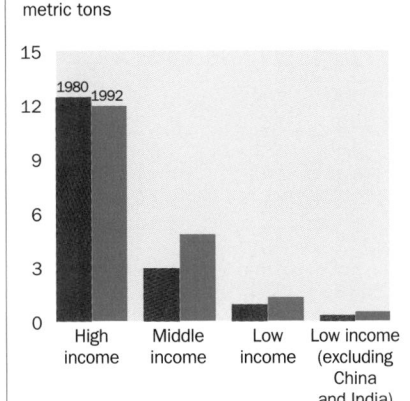

Note: Data refer to emissions from industrial processes.
Source: Table 3.5.

Figure 3.5b Carbon dioxide emissions, by income group, 1992

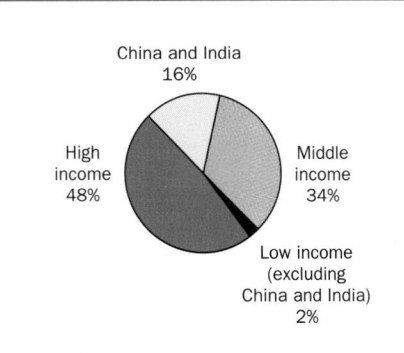

Source: Table 3.5.

Definitions

- **GDP per unit of energy use** is the U.S. dollar estimate of real GDP (at 1987 prices) per kilogram of oil equivalent of commercial energy use (see notes to table 3.4 on energy use). ● **Net energy imports** are calculated as energy use less production, both measured in oil equivalents. A minus sign indicates that the country is a net exporter. ● **Carbon dioxide emissions from industrial processes** are those stemming from the burning of fossil fuels and the manufacture of cement. They include contributions to the carbon dioxide flux from solid fuels, liquid fuels, gas fuels, and gas flaring.

Data sources

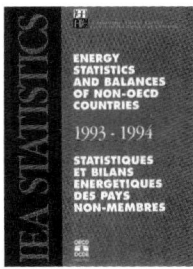

Underlying data on commercial energy use and production are primarily from International Energy Agency (IEA) and United Nations sources. Data on CO_2 emissions are based on several sources as reported by the World Resources Institute. The main source is the Carbon Dioxide Information Analysis Center, Environmental Sciences Division, Oak Ridge National Laboratory, in the state of Tennessee in the United States. CDIAC calculations of CO_2 emissions are based on data on the net apparent consumption of fossil fuels from the World Energy Data Set maintained by the United Nations Statistical Division and from data on world cement manufacture based on the Cement Manufacturing Data Set maintained by the U.S. Bureau of Mines.

	Urban population				Population in urban agglomerations of one million or more			Population in the largest city		Access to sanitation in urban areas	
	millions 1995	% of total population		average annual % growth		% of total population			% of urban population		% of urban population	
		1980	1995	1980–90	1990–95	1980	1995	2015	1980	1995	1985	1993
Albania	1.2	34	37	2.9	–0.9	0	0	0	..	20	100	100
Algeria	15.6	43	56	4.8	4.0	11	13	16	25	24	95	..
Angola	3.5	21	32	5.8	5.9	13	20	30	63	64	27	..
Argentina	30.5	83	88	1.9	1.7	35	39	37	42	44	76	100
Armenia	2.6	66	69	1.6	2.1	34	35	38	51	51	..	..
Australia	15.3	86	85	1.4	1.0	47	58	58	25	23	..	..
Austria	4.5	55	56	0.2	1.2	27	26	27	49	46	100	100
Azerbaijan	4.2	53	56	1.9	1.6	26	25	27	48	44	..	..
Bangladesh	21.9	11	18	5.9	5.0	5	9	15	33	36	21	42
Belarus	7.4	56	71	2.2	1.6	14	17	18	24	24	100	..
Belgium	9.8	95	97	0.2	0.5	12	11	11	13	11	100	100
Benin	2.3	32	42	5.2	4.9	0	0	0	..	9 [a]	45	49
Bolivia	4.3	46	58	4.2	3.2	14	17	19	30	26	51	64
Bosnia and Herzegovina	2.1	36	49	3.2	1.5	..	..	..	..	..	..	..
Botswana	0.4	15	31	8.9	7.4	0	0	0	..	34 [a]	79	91
Brazil	124.5	66	78	3.2	2.5	27	33	34	15	13	33	83
Bulgaria	5.9	61	71	1.0	–0.1	12	16	18	20	23	100	100
Burkina Faso	2.8	9	27	10.7	12.6	0	0	0	..	42 [a]	38	..
Burundi	0.5	4	8	6.9	6.5	0	0	0	..	68 [a]	90	71
Cambodia	2.1	12	21	6.8	6.5	..	..	..	..	63 [a]	..	..
Cameroon	6.0	31	45	5.4	5.3	6	10	13	19	22	25	73
Canada	22.7	76	77	1.4	1.4	29	36	36	16	20	..	..
Central African Republic	1.3	35	39	3.1	3.3	0	0	0	..	43 [a]	36	..
Chad	1.4	19	21	3.4	3.5	0	0	0	..	53 [a]	..	..
Chile	12.2	81	86	2.1	1.9	33	36	35	41	41	79	100
China	363.7	19	30	4.8	3.8	8	11	14	6	4	..	..
Colombia	26.8	64	73	2.8	2.6	22	28	30	20	21	96	70
Congo	1.5	41	59	5.9	5.1	0	0	0	67	65	17	11
Costa Rica	1.7	43	50	3.8	3.3	0	0	0	..	52	100	..
Côte d'Ivoire	6.1	35	44	5.4	4.9	15	20	29	44	46	13	60
Croatia	3.1	50	64	2.2	1.5	0	0	0	..	40	72	72
Cuba	8.4	68	76	1.7	1.5	20	20	21	29	27	..	100
Czech Republic	6.8	64	65	0.3	0.1	12	12	12	18	18	..	..
Denmark	4.4	84	85	0.2	0.4	27	25	25	32	30	100	100
Dominican Republic	5.1	51	65	4.1	3.4	25	33	37	49	51	72	75
Ecuador	6.7	47	58	4.2	3.6	14	26	30	29	26	79	69
Egypt, Arab Rep.	25.9	44	45	2.6	2.5	23	23	26	38	37	95	..
El Salvador	2.5	42	45	1.6	2.7	0	0	0	..	..	89	91
Eritrea	0.6	..	17	..	..	..	..	..	..	..	..	..
Estonia	1.1	70	73	1.0	–0.9	0	0	0	..	44 [a]	..	..
Ethiopia	7.6	11	13	4.7	3.4	3	4	6	30	29	..	..
Finland	3.2	60	63	0.7	1.1	0	0	0	22	33	100	100
France	42.3	73	73	0.4	0.6	21	21	20	23	22	100	100
Gabon	0.5	36	50	5.5	5.5	0	0	0	..	67 [a]	..	79
Gambia, The	0.3	18	26	6.0	6.8	0	0	0	..	100 [a]	99	99
Georgia	3.2	52	58	1.6	0.7	22	25	30	42	43	..	..
Germany	70.9	83	87	0.4	1.0	38	41	42	10	9	100	100
Ghana	6.2	31	36	4.3	4.3	9	10	14	30	27	47	61
Greece	6.8	58	65	1.3	1.5	31	35	36	54	54	100	100
Guatemala	4.4	37	42	3.4	4.0	0	0	0	29	21	73	82
Guinea	2.0	19	30	5.7	5.8	12	23	34	65	77	54	24
Guinea-Bissau	0.2	17	22	3.5	4.2	0	0	0	..	37 [a]	21	32
Haiti	2.3	24	32	3.9	3.9	13	18	28	55	56	42	43
Honduras	2.8	36	48	5.4	4.9	0	0	0	..	30 [a]	22	91
Hong Kong	5.9	92	95	1.6	1.4	91	90	91	100	95	..	..

	Urban population					Population in urban agglomerations of one million or more			Population in the largest city		Access to sanitation in urban areas	
	millions 1995	% of total population 1980	% of total population 1995	average annual % growth 1980–90	average annual % growth 1990–95	% of total population 1980	% of total population 1995	% of total population 2015	% of urban population 1980	% of urban population 1995	% of urban population 1985	% of urban population 1993
Hungary	6.6	57	65	0.5	0.6	19	20	21	34	30	100	*100*
India	249.1	23	27	3.2	2.9	6	10	12	6	6	30	46
Indonesia	66.3	22	34	5.3	3.9	7	13	17	18	17	30	81
Iran, Islamic Rep.	37.8	50	59	5.0	4.0	13	21	21	26	18	95	*100*
Iraq	15.7	66	78	4.3	3.5	26	22	21	39	29	100	95
Ireland	2.1	55	58	0.6	0.8	0	0	0	48	44	100	100
Israel	*4.3*	89	*92*	..	..	37	35	33	41	*42* [a]	*99*	100
Italy	38.0	67	66	0.1	0.2	26	20	21	14	11	100	100
Jamaica	1.4	47	55	2.3	2.1	0	0	0	..	*46* [a]	92	89
Japan	97.2	76	78	0.7	0.4	34	37	39	25	28	..	..
Jordan	3.0	60	72	5.1	7.9	29	28	36	49	39	91	91
Kazakstan	9.9	54	60	1.9	1.2	6	8	9	12	13	..	..
Kenya	7.4	16	28	7.5	6.2	5	8	13	32	28	75	69
Korea, Dem. Rep.	14.6	57	61	2.3	2.4	10	10	11	17	17	100	100
Korea, Rep.	36.5	57	81	3.8	2.9	37	52	54	38	32	100	..
Kuwait	1.6	90	97	5.1	–11.5	60	66	59	67	68	100	*100*
Kyrgyz Republic	1.7	38	39	1.9	1.1	0	0	0	..	*37* [a]	81	87
Lao PDR	1.1	13	22	6.2	6.5	0	0	0	..	*53* [a]	*30*	13
Latvia	1.8	68	73	1.0	–0.6	0	0	0	49	50	..	..
Lebanon	3.5	73	87	4.2	2.8	..	..	..	..	..	94	..
Lesotho	0.5	13	23	6.8	6.2	0	0	0	..	*50* [a]	*22*	*50*
Libya	4.7	70	86	5.9	4.4	38	61	59	54	70	100	..
Lithuania	2.7	61	72	2.1	1.0	0	0	0	..	*23* [a]	..	..
Macedonia, FYR	1.3	53	60	1.5	1.6	0	0	0	..	..	..	..
Madagascar	3.6	18	27	5.7	5.7	0	0	0	..	*25* [a]	8	*12*
Malawi	1.3	9	13	6.1	5.9	0	0	0	..	*31* [a]	88	82
Malaysia	10.8	42	54	4.4	4.0	7	6	7	16	11	*100*	100
Mali	2.7	19	27	5.1	5.7	0	0	0	..	*37* [a]	90	..
Mauritania	1.2	29	54	7.6	5.5	0	0	0	..	*75* [a]	7	..
Mauritius	0.5	42	41	0.4	1.3	0	0	0	..	*37* [a]	100	..
Mexico	69.1	66	75	3.2	2.7	27	28	26	31	23	77	81
Moldova	2.2	40	52	2.7	1.5	0	0	0	..	..	..	96
Mongolia	1.5	52	60	3.9	2.9	0	0	0	..	*45* [a]	100	..
Morocco	13.0	41	49	3.5	3.0	11	18	22	26	25	*85*	96
Mozambique	6.1	13	38	9.1	7.3	6	14	22	48	36	*51*	53
Myanmar	12.2	24	27	2.5	3.3	7	9	12	27	32	34	44
Namibia	0.6	23	38	6.2	6.2	0	0	0	..	*35* [a]	*36*	89
Nepal	2.9	7	14	8.0	7.5	0	0	0	..	*18* [a]	6	34
Netherlands	13.8	88	89	0.6	0.8	7	14	14	8	8	100	100
New Zealand	3.0	83	84	0.9	1.3	0	0	0	30	31	*100*	..
Nicaragua	2.7	53	62	3.9	4.1	23	27	33	42	44	35	..
Niger	2.1	13	23	7.5	6.9	0	0	0	..	*30* [a]	36	..
Nigeria	43.7	27	39	5.8	5.3	6	11	15	23	24	30	89
Norway	3.2	71	73	0.6	0.8	0	0	0	..	*22* [a]	100	100
Oman	0.3	8	13	8.7	8.6	0	0	0	..	*28* [a]	88	98
Pakistan	45.0	28	35	4.5	4.7	11	18	23	22	22	56	60
Panama	1.5	50	56	2.8	2.7	0	0	0	56	65	99	..
Papua New Guinea	0.7	13	16	3.6	3.7	0	0	0	..	*34* [a]	51	95
Paraguay	2.6	42	54	4.8	4.4	0	0	0	..	*30* [a]	66	..
Peru	17.1	65	72	3.0	2.7	26	31	32	40	44	67	60
Philippines	36.6	38	53	5.2	4.4	12	14	15	33	25	*76*	..
Poland	25.0	58	65	1.4	1.0	18	18	19	16	14	100	*100*
Portugal	3.5	29	36	1.4	1.2	13	19	24	46	53	100	*100*
Puerto Rico	2.6	67	71	1.6	1.4	34	30	30	51	42	..	..
Romania	12.6	49	55	1.3	0.0	9	9	10	18	17	100	85
Russian Federation	107.5	70	73	1.2	–0.2	16	19	19	8	9	..	..

	Urban population					Population in urban agglomerations of one million or more			Population in the largest city		Access to sanitation in urban areas	
	millions	% of total population		average annual % growth		% of total population			% of urban population		% of urban population	
	1995	1980	1995	1980–90	1990–95	1980	1995	2015	1980	1995	1985	1993
Rwanda	0.5	5	8	4.9	4.5	0	0	0	..	56 [a]	60	..
Saudi Arabia	14.9	67	79	6.9	4.0	19	21	22	16	17	100	100
Senegal	3.6	36	42	4.0	4.1	18	23	30	49	55	87	..
Sierra Leone	1.6	25	39	5.0	4.9	0	0	0	..	50 [a]	43	90
Singapore	3.0	100	100	1.7	2.0	100	100	100	100	100	85	100
Slovak Republic	3.2	52	59	1.5	1.1	0	0	0	..	15 [a]	..	..
Slovenia	1.3	48	64	2.6	1.0	0	0	0	..	22 [a]	..	95
South Africa	21.1	48	51	2.7	2.9	11	19	19	11	13	..	..
Spain	30.0	73	77	0.7	0.5	20	18	18	16	14	100	100
Sri Lanka	4.0	22	22	1.4	2.1	0	0	0	..	17 [a]	59	67
Sudan	6.9	20	26	4.0	4.6	6	9	14	31	35	20	85
Sweden	7.3	83	83	0.3	0.6	17	17	18	20	21	100	100
Switzerland	4.3	57	61	1.0	1.5	0	0	0	20	21	100	100
Syrian Arab Republic	7.5	47	53	4.1	4.3	28	28	33	34	27	70	100
Tajikistan	1.9	34	32	2.3	2.1	0	0	0	..	36 [a]	..	83
Tanzania	7.2	15	24	6.8	6.5	5	6	8	30	24	90	97
Thailand	20.9	17	36	2.8	2.3	10	18	23	59	50	50	..
Togo	1.3	23	31	5.3	4.8	0	0	0	..	51 [a]	34	56
Trinidad and Tobago	0.9	63	68	1.6	1.8	0	0	0	..	6 [a]	100	60
Tunisia	5.1	51	57	3.2	2.8	17	23	26	34	40	84	100
Turkey	42.6	44	70	5.8	4.7	17	24	25	23	18	95	99
Turkmenistan	2.0	47	45	2.0	5.7	0	0	0	..	25 [a]	..	70
Uganda	2.4	9	12	4.9	5.6	0	0	0	..	41 [a]	40	..
Ukraine	36.2	62	70	1.2	1.0	14	15	17	7	8	100	70
United Arab Emirates	2.1	72	84	6.1	3.8	0	0	0	..	45 [a]	93	..
United Kingdom	52.4	89	90	0.3	0.5	25	23	22	5	4	100	100
United States	200.5	74	76	1.2	1.3	36	39	38	9	8	..	..
Uruguay	2.9	85	90	1.0	0.9	42	42	40	49	46	59	92
Uzbekistan	9.5	41	42	2.5	2.6	11	10	11	28	24	..	46
Venezuela	20.1	83	93	3.5	2.9	16	27	28	20	15	57	55
Vietnam	15.3	19	21	2.5	3.1	5	7	9	27	23	..	..
West Bank and Gaza	..	..	..	..	..	..	..	..	..	..	..	..
Yemen, Rep.	5.1	20	34	7.0	9.4	0	0	0	..	15 [a]	..	70
Yugoslavia, Fed. Rep.	5.9	46	57	2.3	1.5	11	13	15	24	24	78	100
Zaire	12.8	29	29	3.1	4.0	..	..	..	28	33	8	..
Zambia	4.1	40	45	4.2	3.7	9	15	22	23	33	56	76
Zimbabwe	3.5	22	32	6.0	5.2	0	0	0	39	30	..	..
World	**2,554.4 t**	**40 w**	**45 w**	**2.7 t**	**2.2 t**	**14 w**	**16 w**	**18 w**	**18 w**	**17 w**	..	..
Low income	911.7 t	21 w	29 w	4.2 t	3.8 t	7 w	10 w	13 w	12 w	12 w	..	..
Excl. China & India	299.0 t	21 w	28 w	4.6 t	4.7 t	6 w	9 w	13 w	30 w	31 w	43 w	67 w
Middle income	962.3 t	52 w	61 w	3.0 t	2.4 t	16 w	20 w	21 w	22 w	21 w	..	..
Lower middle income	640.8 t	48 w	56 w	3.0 t	2.3 t	13 w	17 w	19 w	21 w	20 w	..	..
Upper middle income	321.5 t	64 w	73 w	3.0 t	2.5 t	24 w	28 w	28 w	25 w	22 w	60 w	86 w
Low & middle income	1,874.0 t	32 w	39 w	3.6 t	3.1 t	10 w	13 w	16 w	18 w	17 w	..	..
East Asia & Pacific	537.0 t	21 w	31 w	4.6 t	3.8 t	8 w	11 w	14 w	13 w	10 w	..	..
Europe & Central Asia	318.7 t	58 w	65 w	2.0 t	1.0 t	14 w	16 w	17 w	16 w	16 w	..	..
Latin America & Carib.	354.2 t	65 w	74 w	3.0 t	2.6 t	24 w	28 w	28 w	27 w	24 w	60 w	81 w
Middle East & N. Africa	153.5 t	48 w	57 w	4.4 t	3.8 t	17 w	20 w	22 w	31 w	27 w	81 w	..
South Asia	327.8 t	22 w	26 w	3.5 t	3.3 t	6 w	10 w	13 w	9 w	11 w	32 w	48 w
Sub-Saharan Africa	182.8 t	23 w	31 w	5.0 t	4.9 t	5 w	8 w	11 w	27 w	29 w	..	..
High income	680.4 t	75 w	78 w	0.9 t	0.1 t	31 w	33 w	34 w	17 w	17 w	..	..

a. Data are for 1990.

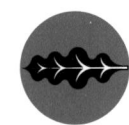

Exploding cities

Urbanization is a companion and stimulus of development, and in developing countries more than half of GDP originates in cities. As the process has accelerated, however, cities in Africa, Asia, the Middle East, and Latin America have also confronted congestion and pollution, with concentrated poverty and uncontrolled sprawl, and problems that at the least impede productive growth and at the worst stifle it.

The rapid growth of cities in developing countries is nearly universal. Whereas less than 22 percent of the developing world's population was urban in 1960, the proportion averaged 34 percent in 1990. By 2015 it is expected to exceed 50 percent, with the number of city residents due to reach 4 billion, more than twice today's total. By then there will be 225 urban agglomerations with populations of more than 2 million people, and 26 agglomerations with populations exceeding 10 million (table 3.6a).

About the data

Because the estimates here are based on different national definitions of what constitutes a city or metropolitan area and what is urban, cross-country comparisons should be made with caution. To arrive at estimates of urban population, the United Nations ratio of urban to total population is applied to the World Bank's estimates of total population (see table 2.1). The resulting series of urban population estimates are also used to compute the population in the largest city as a percentage of the urban population.

Definitions

● **Urban population** is the midyear population of areas defined as urban in each country. The definition varies slightly from country to country. ● **Population in urban agglomerations of one million or more** is the percentage of a country's population living in metropolitan areas that in 1990 had a population of one million or more people. ● **Population in the largest city** is the percentage of a country's urban population living in that country's largest metropolitan area. ● **Access to sanitation in urban areas** is the urban population served by connections to public sewers or household systems such as pit privies, pour-flush latrines, septic tanks, communal toilets, and other such facilities.

Data sources

Data on urban population, population in urban agglomerations, and population in the largest city come from the United Nations *World Urbanization Prospects: The 1994 Revision*. Total population figures are World Bank estimates. Data on access to sanitation in urban areas are from the World Health Organization.

Table 3.6a Urban agglomerations with populations of 10 million or more, 2015

City	Millions of people
Tokyo, Japan	28.7
Bombay, India	27.4
Lagos, Nigeria	24.4
Shanghai, China	23.4
Jakarta, Indonesia	21.2
São Paulo, Brazil	20.8
Karachi, Pakistan	20.6
Beijing, China	19.4
Dhaka, Bangladesh	19.0
Mexico City, Mexico	18.8
New York, U.S.A.	17.6
Calcutta, India	17.6
Delhi, India	17.6
Tianjin, China	17.0
Manila, Philippines	14.7
Cairo, Egypt	14.5
Los Angeles, U.S.A.	14.3
Seoul, Rep. of Korea	13.1
Istanbul, Turkey	12.3
Rio de Janeiro, Brazil	11.6
Lahore, Pakistan	10.8
Hyderabad, Pakistan	10.7
Osaka, Japan	10.6
Bangkok, Thailand	10.6
Lima, Peru	10.5
Teheran, Islamic Rep. of Iran	10.2

Source: United Nations 1995.

Figure 3.6a Urban population, by region, 1970–95

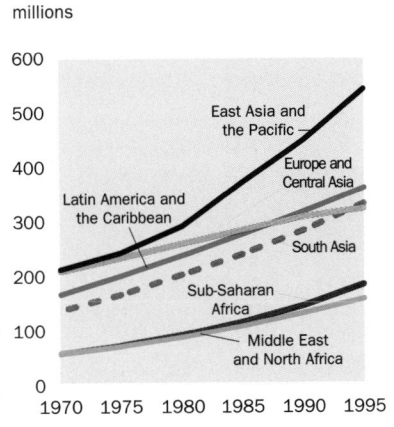

Source: United Nations Department of Economic and Social Information and Policy Analysis data and World Bank population estimates.

Figure 3.6b Urban population, by income group, 1980–95

Source: Table 3.6.

	Vehicles				Road traffic		Traffic accidents	
	per 1,000 people		per kilometer of road		million vehicle kilometers		people injured or killed per 1,000 vehicles	
	1980	1994	1980	1994	1980	1994	1980	1994
Albania	..	15	..	6	..	..	..	..
Algeria	..	33	..	10	..	124 [a]	..	44
Angola	..	..	..	..	..	..	..	..
Argentina	155	181	20	28	..	..	..	..
Armenia	..	4	..	2	..	..	..	150
Australia	502	574	..	13	204 [b]	138,501	5	2
Austria	330	471	23	29	35,430 [b]	..	27 [c]	15
Azerbaijan	..	49	..	15	..	2,207 [d]	..	12
Bangladesh	..	1	..	5	..	..	..	20
Belarus	..	..	..	..	..	..	..	..
Belgium	349	446	28	33	45,779 [e]	59,884	25	17
Benin	..	..	..	..	..	..	..	..
Bolivia	19	77	3	11	795	1,232	41	..
Bosnia and Herzegovina	..	..	..	..	..	..	..	..
Botswana	27	..	3	..	..	..	50	..
Brazil	85	..	7	..	..	..	..	..
Bulgaria	..	214	..	49	665 [b]	..	..	5
Burkina Faso	..	..	..	..	..	..	..	..
Burundi	..	..	..	..	..	..	..	..
Cambodia	..	5	..	1	..	1,145 [a]	..	6
Cameroon	8	..	4 [f]	..	..	..	112	..
Canada	548	630	..	19	205,515	..	..	14
Central African Republic	8	..	1	6	..	1,132	..	..
Chad	..	3	..	1	..	..	..	..
Chile	61	..	8	..	7,540	..	38	..
China	2	8	2	8	2,032 [d]	165,000	12	22
Colombia	..	..	..	..	2,480 [g]	..	..	..
Congo	..	18	..	4	..	103 [e]	..	10
Costa Rica	..	106	..	9	..	4,244 [e]	..	32
Côte d'Ivoire	24	..	..	..	..	..	..	..
Croatia	..	158	..	28	..	..	..	24
Cuba	..	..	..	..	..	..	..	..
Czech Republic	..	310	..	57	..	38,842 [h]	..	12
Denmark	322	364	24	24	26,300	39,895	10	5
Dominican Republic	36	..	11	..	..	..	18	..
Ecuador	..	38	..	10	..	11,851	..	16
Egypt, Arab Rep.	..	28	..	32	..	6,222 [h]	..	17
El Salvador	..	2	..	17	..	..	..	..
Eritrea	..	..	..	..	..	..	..	..
Estonia	..	267	..	27	..	..	..	5
Ethiopia	2	1	1	3	2	..	38	..
Finland	288	418	18	27	26,750	41,730	7	4
France	402	517	27	37	298,000	461,500	16 [i]	6
Gabon	..	..	..	..	..	..	..	..
Gambia, The	..	..	..	..	..	..	..	..
Georgia	..	..	..	..	..	..	..	..
Germany [j]	399	..	51	..	..	..	..	..
Ghana	..	..	..	..	..	..	..	..
Greece	134	282	35	23	..	510 [d]	23	11
Guatemala	..	..	..	..	..	..	..	..
Guinea	..	6	..	2	..	..	..	118
Guinea-Bissau	..	..	..	..	..	..	..	..
Haiti	..	..	..	..	..	..	..	..
Honduras	..	30	..	10	..	3,288	..	..
Hong Kong	54	78	234	289	4,407	10,341	77	44

More cars, more traffic

Traffic congestion in urban areas affects the health of people, their quality of life, and the productivity of the economy. Household income and the ownership of passenger cars have increased, and the expansion of economic activities has been associated with road transport of more goods and services over greater distances. These developments have increased demand for roads and vehicles, adding to congestion and air pollution in urban areas—and increasing health hazards and traffic accidents and injuries.

The number of vehicles registered worldwide in 1946 was close to 46 million, with 75 percent in the United States. By 1991 this number had grown to some 600 million, with only 32 percent in the United States (figure 3.7a). During this period the growth of private cars substantially exceeded that of commercial vehicles (figure 3.7b), leading to relatively less use of public and mass transportation and thus to more pollution. The number of vehicles (excluding motorized two- and three-wheel vehicles) is expected to reach 820 million by 2010. In Iran, Kenya, Mexico, the Republic of Korea, and Thailand about half the registered automobiles operate in the capital city.

Congestion, the most visible cost of expanding vehicle ownership, is usually associated

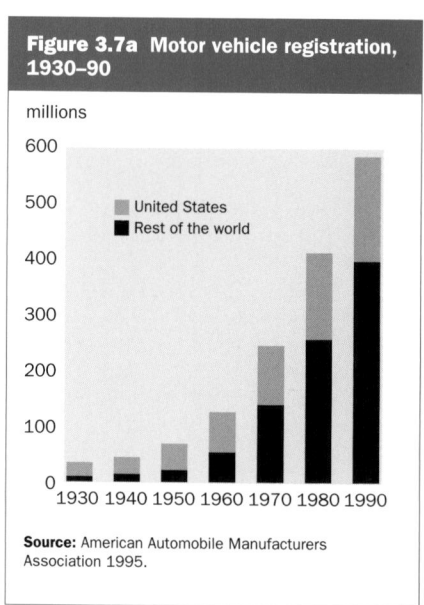

Figure 3.7a Motor vehicle registration, 1930–90

millions

United States
Rest of the world

Source: American Automobile Manufacturers Association 1995.

with the failure of urban transportation planning and, frequently, an inadequate road network. But expanding the road network is rarely the solution. The problem is that road users are heavily subsidized. Road users do not pay the full cost of building roads or of maintaining them. Until they do, urban traffic and congestion will continue to increase. In Asian cities, for example, rush hour traffic moves at an average of just 16 kilometers an hour—in Bangkok the average is closer to 9 kilometers an hour, and an average car is estimated to spend the equivalent of 44 days a year stuck in traffic (World Bank 1996d). Congested city streets exact a big toll on economic productivity.

How much does traffic congestion cost? In Bangkok the cost is about $400 million a year—the amount that could be saved just by making peak hour traffic move 10 percent faster. The hidden but all-too-real environmental tax on urban dwellers is high—the annual costs of dust and lead pollution in Bangkok, Jakarta, and Kuala Lumpur combined have been estimated at $5 billion, or about 10 percent of city income (World Bank 1996a). Another health threat associated with vehicles is particulate air pollution—the dust and soot from vehicle exhaust. This pollution is proving to be far more damaging to human health than once believed. Leaded

Figure 3.7b Motor vehicle production, 1950–90

millions

Source: American Automobile Manufacturers Association 1995.

	Vehicles				Road traffic		Traffic accidents	
	per 1,000 people		per kilometer of road		million vehicle kilometers		people injured or killed per 1,000 vehicles	
	1980	1994	1980	1994	1980	1994	1980	1994
Hungary	108	240	13	23	..	..	22	12
India	2	6[k]	1	3[k]	..	..	..	..
Indonesia	8	..	8	..	..	..	59	..
Iran, Islamic Rep.	..	..	..	..	..	..	..	..
Iraq	..	..	..	..	..	..	..	..
Ireland	236[l]	293	9[l]	11	14,917	25,530	11	10
Israel	123	240	114	93	10,442[d]	27,050	38	29
Italy	334	541	65	..	226,569	362,647	12[m]	8
Jamaica	..	..	..	..	..	..	..	..
Japan	323	520	34	57	389,052	683,754	16[n]	14
Jordan	56	60	25	37	623	31	63	54
Kazakstan	..	..	..	..	..	14,632	..	..
Kenya	8	14	3	5	..	4,620	74	6
Korea, Dem. Rep.	..	..	..	..	..	..	..	..
Korea, Rep.	14	167	11	100	8,728	48,376	212	49
Kuwait	390	..	..	..	12,189	..	7	..
Kyrgyz Republic	..	..	..	..	..	..	..	..
Lao PDR	..	8	..	2	..	..	..	85
Latvia	..	170	..	7	..	3,633	..	10
Lebanon	..	..	..	..	..	..	..	..
Lesotho	10	13	3	4	..	445	86	..
Libya	..	..	..	..	..	..	..	..
Lithuania	..	205	..	12	..	198[d]	..	6
Macedonia, FYR	..	151	..	35	..	4,119	..	11
Madagascar	..	..	3	..	1	..	..	..
Malawi	5	..	3	..	..	..	..	..
Malaysia	..	..	..	49	..	..	..	..
Mali	..	..	..	..	..	..	..	..
Mauritania	..	..	..	..	..	..	..	..
Mauritius	44	62	23	37	46[b]	..	..	59
Mexico	..	131	..	46	..	52,640	..	..
Moldova	..	67	..	20	..	805[d]	..	12[m]
Mongolia	..	..	..	..	..	..	..	..
Morocco	..	42	..	18	18[b]	..	..	60
Mozambique	..	2	..	1	..	..	..	84
Myanmar	..	..	..	..	..	..	..	..
Namibia	..	87	..	3	..	2,149	..	..
Nepal	..	..	..	..	..	..	..	..
Netherlands	343	235	..	65	70,825	98,400	12	4
New Zealand	492	554	17	21	16,545	..	11	9
Nicaragua	..	34	..	10	..	122	..	..
Niger	6	..	..	..	..	211	63[o]	..
Nigeria	4	..	3	..	..	..	123	..
Norway	342	464	17	22	..	22,646[e]	8	6
Oman	..	124	..	10	..	11,045[h]	..	27
Pakistan	2	6	5	4	..	27,547	71	29
Panama	..	..	..	..	..	..	..	..
Papua New Guinea	..	..	..	..	..	..	..	..
Paraguay	..	..	..	..	..	..	..	..
Peru	..	..	..	..	..	..	..	..
Philippines	..	10	..	4	..	193	..	12
Poland	86	223	10	22	44,597	113,000	..	8
Portugal	145	327	26	27	283[b]	73,780	31[p]	19
Puerto Rico	..	..	..	..	..	..	..	..
Romania	..	105	..	33	..	40[d]	..	5
Russian Federation	..	..	..	..	..	..	..	..

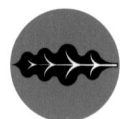

	Vehicles				Road traffic		Traffic accidents	
	per 1,000 people		per kilometer of road		million vehicle kilometers		people injured or killed per 1,000 vehicles	
	1980	1994	1980	1994	1980	1994	1980	1994
Rwanda	2	..	2	..	..	..	..	..
Saudi Arabia	163	166	26	43	..	94,141	..	12
Senegal	19	13	8	..	..	..	56	..
Sierra Leone	..	11	..	4	..	29	..	34
Singapore	..	154	..	152	..	..	..	18
Slovak Republic	..	215	..	65	..	651 d	..	10
Slovenia	..	349	..	47	..	6,924	..	9
South Africa	133	157	18	..	52,939	..	23	23
Spain	239	454	120	49	70,489	145,037	13	7
Sri Lanka	..	25	..	5	..	4,119	..	36
Sudan	..	..	..	..	..	..	..	..
Sweden	370	446	24	28	35,000	..	7	5
Switzerland	383	490	38	48	..	49,294	14	9
Syrian Arab Republic	..	..	..	..	..	..	..	..
Tajikistan	..	3	..	1	..	..	..	..
Tanzania	3	..	1	..	..	..	..	..
Thailand	13 q	70	13 q	73	16,824	81,444	29	9
Togo	..	1	1	1	..	386 e	..	..
Trinidad and Tobago	..	..	..	..	..	..	..	..
Tunisia	38	..	10	..	..	..	45	..
Turkey	23	62	4	9	14,785	31,251	26	..
Turkmenistan	..	..	..	..	..	..	..	..
Uganda	1	..	1	..	479	..	..	..
Ukraine	..	151	..	29	..	3,064 d	..	7
United Arab Emirates	..	..	..	..	..	..	..	..
United Kingdom	303 r	403 r	50	63	245,900	413,300	19	13
United States	..	748	25	31	2,418,619	3,504,934 a	..	18
Uruguay	..	..	..	..	..	..	..	..
Uzbekistan	..	..	..	..	..	..	..	..
Venezuela	112	..	27	..	56,900	..	32	..
Vietnam	..	..	..	..	..	..	..	..
West Bank and Gaza	..	..	..	..	..	..	..	..
Yemen, Rep.	..	32	..	8	1,251	10,866	..	15
Yugoslavia, Fed. Rep.	118	..	23	..	..	..	61	..
Zaire	..	29	..	8	..	..	..	..
Zambia	..	..	..	..	..	..	..	..
Zimbabwe	..	33	..	..	..	..	..	..

a. Passenger cars and goods vehicles only. b. Buses only. c. Deaths occurring within three days of accident. d. Buses and goods vehicles only. e. Passenger cars only. f. Does not include rural trailers. g. Goods vehicles only. h. Passenger cars and buses only. i. Deaths occurring within six days of accident. j. Data refer to the Federal Republic of Germany before unification. k. As of April 1. l. As of September 30. m. Deaths occurring within seven days of accident. n. Deaths occurring within 24 hours of accident. o. Only includes accidents after which driving licenses were revoked. p. Deaths on the spot or during transport to the hospital. q. Excludes data from Department of Land Transport. r. As of December 31; not comparable with earlier years.

gasoline causes about 90 percent of airborne lead pollution in cities. Yet in much of the world lead additives in gasoline are still used in alarmingly large quantities, especially in Africa. Lead poisoning does immense damage to children, affecting more than 90 percent of the population in African cities and 30 percent in Mexico City.

About the data

The data are compiled by the International Road Federation (IRF) through questionnaires sent to various national organizations. The IRF uses a hierarchy of sources to gather as much information as possible. The primary sources are national road associations. In the absence of such an association in a country, or in cases of nonresponse, other agencies are contacted, such as road directorates, ministries of transport or public works, or central statistical offices. As a result the compiled data are of uneven quality. In addition, the coverage of each indicator may differ across countries.

Definitions

• **Vehicles per 1,000 people** exclude buses.
• **Vehicles per kilometer of road** include cars, buses, and freight vehicles but do not include two-wheelers. Roads refer to motorways, highways, main or national roads, secondary or regional roads, and other roads. A motorway is a road specially designed and built for motor traffic. Except at special points, it provides carriageways separating the traffic flowing in opposite directions. • **Road traffic** is the number of vehicles multiplied by the distances they travel. • **Traffic accidents** refer to accident-related injuries and to deaths resulting from accidents that occur within 30 days of the accident.

Data sources

The data in the table are from the International Road Federation's annual *World Road Statistics*, except data for China, which are from Chinese statistical yearbooks.

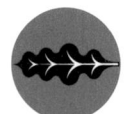

Country	City	Suspended particulate matter			Sulfur dioxide		
		metric tons per year 1990[a]	annual mean micrograms per cu. m 1987–90[b]	average annual % growth 1979–90	metric tons per year 1990[a]	annual mean micrograms per cu. m 1987–90[b]	average annual % growth 1979–90
Australia	Sydney	..	114[c]	2.2	..	28	–10.9
Belgium	Brussels	..	22	–3.3	..	42	–11.5
Brazil	São Paulo	77,000	98[c]	–9.1	122,000	41	–7.5
Canada	Montreal	..	61	–1.8	..	23	–11.0
China	Beijing	1,115,600	370[c]	–1.6	526,000	115[c]	–1.3
Denmark	Copenhagen	..	34	3.4	..	30	–0.5
Finland	Helsinki	..	81	2.0	..	20	–3.8
Germany	Frankfurt	..	42	0.5	..	36	–7.2
Ghana	Accra	..	137[c]	3.5	..	..	..
Greece	Athens	..	178[c]	–6.0	..	34	–4.8
Hong Kong	Hong Kong	..	132[c]	14.9	..	64[c]	47.3
India	Calcutta	200,000	393[c]	–1.0	25,500	54	4.6
Indonesia	Jakarta	96,733	271[c]	2.2	24,700	..	..
Iran, Islamic Rep.	Teheran	..	261[c]	–2.4	..	165[c]	6.9
Japan	Tokyo	..	50	–4.9	..	20	–8.9
Korea, Rep.	Seoul	139,000	..	..	518,000	..	..
Malaysia	Kuala Lumpur	..	119[c]	–3.9	..	24	–12.4
Mexico	Mexico City	451,000	..	..	206,000	..	..
Philippines	Manila	75,000	90[c]	0.8	148,000	34	–12.0
Russian Federation	Moscow	60,000	..	..	130,000	..	..
Portugal	Lisbon	..	99[c]	0.4	..	27	–3.0
Thailand	Bangkok	80,000	105[c]	–2.4	..	14	–1.7
United Kingdom	London	11,000	..	..	49,000	..	..
United States	New York	345,000	61	–2.2	404,000	60[c]	–5.8

a. Estimated emissions. b. Average concentration observed in the city's various monitoring sites. c. Exceeds World Health Organization guidelines.

Definitions

● **Suspended particulate matter** refers to smoke, soot, dust, and liquid droplets from combustion that are in the air. The amount indicates the quality of the air people are breathing and the state of a country's technology and pollution control. ● **Sulfur dioxide** is an air pollutant produced when fossil fuels are burned. It contributes to acid rain and can affect human health.

Data sources

The data in the table are drawn from the United Nations Environment Programme and World Health Organization's *Urban Air Pollution in Megacities of the World* and from the World Bank's *Environmental Data Book.*

The burden of air pollution

In many towns and cities exposure to air pollution is the main environmental threat to human health. Winter smogs—soot, dust, and sulfur dioxide—have long been associated with temporary spikes in the number of deaths. But long-term exposure to high levels of soot and small particles in the air provokes a wide range of chronic respiratory diseases and exacerbates heart disease and other conditions. The global burden of ill health caused by particulate pollution—on its own or in combination with sulfur dioxide—is very large. According to conservative estimates in the World Bank's *World Development Report 1992: Development and the Environment,* it includes at least 500,000 premature deaths a year and 4–5 million new cases of chronic bronchitis.

Summer smogs—from small particles and ground-level ozone produced by the action of the sun on nitrogen oxides and volatile organic compounds—are a major problem in southern California, Mexico City, Tokyo, and parts of Western Europe. Exposure to ozone makes it difficult for people to breathe, causing particu-

lar problems for asthmatics. And many plants and trees are susceptible to damage from ozone exposure, which reduces yields or kills them off.

Emissions of sulfur dioxide and nitrogen oxides lead to the deposition of acidic materials as acid rain or acidic compounds over long distances from their sources—often more than 1,000 kilometers. Lakes in Scandinavia, the northeastern United States, and eastern Canada have lost fish as a result. Such deposition changes the chemical balance of soils and can lead to the leaching of trace minerals and nutrients critical to trees and plants.

The links between forest damage and acid deposition are complex. Direct exposure to high levels of sulfur dioxide or acid deposition can cause defoliation and dieback. Extensive damage to forests in Central and Eastern Europe is usually thought to be the result of large emissions of sulfur dioxide from burning poor-quality brown coals and lignites. But the effects of soil acidification vary across species and seem to depend on many fac-

tors. The working hypothesis is that acidification increases the vulnerability of trees to such other stresses as drought and insect damage.

Where coal is the primary fuel for power plants, steel mills, industrial boilers, and domestic heating, the result is usually high levels of urban air pollution—especially particulates and sometimes sulfur dioxide—and widespread acid deposition if the sulfur content of the coal is high. Countries such as China, India, Poland, and Turkey fit this pattern today, as many high-income countries once did.

A second pattern is observed when coal is not an important primary fuel or is used by plants with effective dust controls, as in Brazil, Indonesia, Mexico, Thailand, and many high-income countries. Emissions of the worst air pollutants are caused by the combustion of petroleum products—diesel oil, heating oil, and heavy fuel oil. Industrial plants and vehicles—especially those with two-stroke engines—are typically the main offending sources.

3.9 | Government commitment

	National conservation strategy	Country environmental profile	Biological diversity profile	Frequency of reporting on trade in endangered species	Participation in treaties			
				% of years reported[a]	Climate change	Ozone layer	CFC control	Law of the Sea[b]
Albania	..	..	..	..[c]	CP	..	..	..
Algeria	..	..	..	50	CP	CP	CP	S
Angola	..	..	..	..[c]	S	..	..	CP
Argentina	..	..	..	82	CP	CP	CP	CP
Armenia	..	..	..	..	CP	..	..	..
Australia	1988	..	..	88	CP	CP	CP	CP
Austria	..	..	..	100	CP	CP	CP	CP
Azerbaijan	..	..	..	..	CP	..	..	..
Bangladesh	1991	1980	..	80	CP	CP	CP	S
Belarus	..	..	..	..	S	CP	CP	S
Belgium	..	..	..	100	S	CP	CP	S
Benin	..	..	..	0	CP	CP	CP	S
Bolivia	..	1986	..	62	CP	CP	CP	CP
Bosnia and Herzegovina	..	..	..	..	..	CP	CP	CP
Botswana	1990	..	1991	86	CP	CP	CP	CP
Brazil	..	..	1988	41	CP	CP	CP	CP
Bulgaria	..	..	..	0	CP	CP	CP	S
Burkina Faso	..	1982	..	0	CP	CP	CP	S
Burundi	..	1981	..	0	S	..	..	S
Cambodia	..	1994	..	..[c]	..	..	..	S
Cameroon	..	1981	..	92	CP	CP	CP	CP
Canada	1986	..	..	100	CP	CP	CP	S
Central African Republic	..	..	..	50	CP	CP	..	S
Chad	1990	..	..	0	CP	CP	CP	S
Chile	..	1990	..	65	CP	CP	CP	S
China	1990	1990	1994	100	CP	CP	CP	S
Colombia	IP	1990	1988	64	CP	CP	CP	S
Congo	..	..	..	100	S	CP	CP	S
Costa Rica	1990	1982	..	76	CP	CP	CP	CP
Côte d'Ivoire	..	..	1991	..[c]	CP	CP	CP	CP
Croatia	..	..	..	..	S	CP	CP	CP
Cuba	..	..	..	50	CP	CP	CP	CP
Czech Republic	..	..	..	100	CP	CP	CP	S
Denmark	..	..	..	100	CP	CP	CP	S
Dominican Republic	..	1981	..	80	S	CP	CP	S
Ecuador	IP	1987	1988	76	CP	CP	CP	..
Egypt, Arab Rep.	..	1980	..	0	CP	CP	CP	CP
El Salvador	..	1985	..	20	S	CP	CP	S
Eritrea	..	..	..	..	CP	..	..	..
Estonia	..	..	..	..	CP	..	..	..
Ethiopia	1990	..	1991	75	CP	CP	CP	S
Finland	..	..	..	75	CP	CP	CP	S
France	IP	..	..	100	CP	CP	CP	S
Gabon	..	..	..	67	S	CP	CP	S
Gambia, The	..	1981	..	20	CP	CP	CP	CP
Georgia	..	..	..	..	CP	..	..	..
Germany	..	..	..	100[d]	CP	CP	CP	CP
Ghana	1980	1980	1988	81	CP	CP	CP	CP
Greece	..	..	..	..[c]	S	CP	CP	CP
Guatemala	IP	1984	..	83	S	CP	CP	S
Guinea	..	1983	1988	45	CP	CP	CP	CP
Guinea-Bissau	IP	..	1991	0	CP	..	..	CP
Haiti	..	1985	..	..[c]	S	..	..	S
Honduras	..	1989	..	29	CP	CP	CP	CP
Hong Kong	..	..	..	..	..	..	..	..

National strategies—international treaties

Environmental degradation imposes high costs. Recognizing these costs, governments try to halt degradation by establishing or improving environmental laws and regulations, strengthening environmental management capacity, adjusting incentives for polluting agents, creating special funds, and working more closely with affected groups.

In many countries such efforts have not succeeded, often primarily because of the failure of government to assign priority to problems and interventions, a reflection of competing claims on scarce resources. To address this shortcoming, many countries have prepared national environmental management strategies—some focusing narrowly on environmental issues, others dealing with the integration of environmental, economic, and social concerns. Among such initiatives are national conservation strategies and national environmental action plans. Many countries have also prepared country environmental profiles and biological diversity profiles.

National conservation strategies—promoted by the World Conservation Union (IUCN)—provide a comprehensive, cross-sectoral analysis of conservation and resource management issues to help integrate environmental concerns with the development process. Such strategies discuss a country's current and future needs, institutional capabilities, prevailing technical conditions, and the status of natural resources.

National environmental action plans (NEAPs), supported by the World Bank and other development assistance agencies, describe a country's main environmental concerns, identify the principal causes of environmental problems, and formulate policies and actions to deal with them (table 3.9a). The NEAP is a continuing process in which governments develop comprehensive environmental policies, recommend specific actions, and outline the investment strategies, legislation, and institutional arrangements required to implement them.

Country environmental profiles identify how national economic and other activities can stay within the constraints imposed by the need to

	National conserva-tion strategy	Country environ-mental profile	Biological diversity profile	Frequency of reporting on trade in endangered species	Participation in treaties			
				% of years reported[a]	Climate change	Ozone layer	CFC control	Law of the Sea[b]
Hungary	..	..	..	57	S	CP	CP	S
India	IP	1980	1989	100	CP	CP	CP	CP
Indonesia	IP	1987	..	92	CP	CP	CP	CP
Iran, Islamic Rep.	..	..	..	31	S	CP	CP	S
Iraq	..	..	..	..[c]	..	..	..	CP
Ireland	..	..	..	..[c]	CP	CP	CP	S
Israel	..	..	..	25	S	CP	CP	..
Italy	..	..	..	86	CP	CP	CP	CP
Jamaica	..	1987	..	..[c]	CP	CP	CP	CP
Japan	..	..	..	92	CP	CP	CP	S
Jordan	IP	1979	..	31	CP	CP	CP	CP
Kazakstan	..	..	..	..	CP	..	..	..
Kenya	IP	..	1988	54	CP	CP	CP	CP
Korea, Dem. Rep.	..	..	..	..[c]	CP	CP	CP	S
Korea, Rep.	..	..	..	..[c]	CP	CP	CP	S
Kuwait	..	..	..	..[c]	CP	CP	CP	CP
Kyrgyz Republic	..	..	..	..	..	..	..	..
Lao PDR	1993	1996	..	..[c]	CP	..	..	S
Latvia	..	..	..	..	CP	CP	CP	..
Lebanon	..	..	..	..[c]	CP	CP	CP	CP
Lesotho	..	1982	..	..[c]	CP	CP	CP	S
Libya	..	..	..	..[c]	S	CP	CP	S
Lithuania	..	..	..	..	CP	CP	CP	..
Macedonia, FYR	..	..	..	..	..	CP	CP	CP
Madagascar	1984	..	1991	82	S	..	..	S
Malawi	IP	1982	..	70	CP	CP	CP	S
Malaysia	1991	1994	1988	86	CP	CP	CP	S
Mali	..	1989	..	..[c]	CP	CP	CP	CP
Mauritania	1987	1981	..	..[c]	CP	CP	CP	S
Mauritius	..	..	..	88	CP	CP	CP	CP
Mexico	..	..	..	100	CP	CP	CP	CP
Moldova	..	..	..	..	CP	..	..	..
Mongolia	..	..	..	..[c]	CP	..	..	S
Morocco	..	1980	..	44	S	S	S	S
Mozambique	..	..	..	73	CP	CP	CP	S
Myanmar	..	1994	1989	..[c]	CP	CP	CP	S
Namibia	..	..	..	0	CP	CP	CP	CP
Nepal	1987	1979	..	76	CP	CP	CP	S
Netherlands	..	..	..	100	S	CP	CP	S
New Zealand	1985	..	..	67	CP	CP	CP	S
Nicaragua	IP	1981	..	80	CP	CP	CP	S
Niger	..	1980	..	41	CP	CP	CP	S
Nigeria	1986	..	1988	18	CP	CP	CP	CP
Norway	IP	..	..	100	CP	CP	CP	S
Oman	IP	1981	..	..[c]	CP	..	..	CP
Pakistan	1991	1988	1991	94	CP	CP	CP	S
Panama	..	1980	..	86	CP	CP	CP	S
Papua New Guinea	..	..	..	75	CP	CP	CP	S
Paraguay	..	1985	..	60	CP	CP	CP	CP
Peru	IP	1986	1988	59	CP	CP	CP	..
Philippines	1990	1992	1988	82	CP	CP	CP	CP
Poland	..	..	..	0	CP	CP	CP	S
Portugal	..	..	..	55	CP	CP	CP	S
Puerto Rico	..	..	..	..	..	..	..	..
Romania	..	..	..	..[c]	CP	CP	CP	S
Russian Federation	..	..	..	..	CP	CP	CP	S

Table 3.9a Status of national environmental action plans

Completed	In preparation
Albania	Bangladesh
Benin	Congo
Bhutan	Dominican Republic
Bolivia	Ecuador
Burkina Faso	Gabon
China	Haiti
Costa Rica	Indonesia
Côte d'Ivoire	Korea, Rep.
El Salvador	Malaysia
Ethiopia	Nepal
Gambia, The	Paraguay
Grenada	St. Lucia
Guinea	St. Vincent
Guinea-Bissau	Tibet
Guyana	Togo
Honduras	Uganda
India	Vietnam
Kenya	
Lao PDR	
Lebanon	
Lesotho	
Madagascar	
Maldives	
Moldova	
Mongolia	
Mozambique	
Nicaragua	
Nigeria	
Pakistan	
Philippines	
Rwanda	
São Tomé and Principe	
Sierra Leone	
Sri Lanka	
St. Kitts and Nevis	

Source: World Resources Institute, International Institute for Environment and Development, and IUCN 1992.

conserve natural resources. Some profiles consider issues of equity, justice, and fairness. Biological diversity profiles—prepared by the World Conservation Monitoring Centre and the IUCN—provide basic background on species diversity, protected areas, major ecosystems and habitat types, and legislative and administrative support. They identify the status of sites of critical importance for biodiversity and ecosystem conservation, reporting concisely on the value and conservation needs of these sites and on the threats to them.

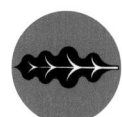

	National conservation strategy	Country environmental profile	Biological diversity profile	Frequency of reporting on trade in endangered species	Participation in treaties			
				% of years reported[a]	Climate change	Ozone layer	CFC control	Law of the Sea[b]
Rwanda	..	1987	..	27	S	..	..	S
Saudi Arabia	..	..	..	..[c]	CP	CP	CP	S
Senegal	..	1980	1991	80	CP	CP	CP	CP
Sierra Leone	1985	..	..	..[c]	CP	..	..	S
Singapore	1990	1988	..	100	S	CP	CP	CP
Slovak Republic	..	..	..	..	CP	CP	CP	S
Slovenia	..	..	..	..	CP	..	CP	CP
South Africa	1980	..	..	94	S	CP	CP	S
Spain	IP	..	..	100	CP	CP	CP	S
Sri Lanka	1988	1988	..	54	CP	CP	CP	CP
Sudan	..	1989	..	44	CP	CP	CP	CP
Sweden	..	..	..	94	CP	CP	CP	S
Switzerland	IP	..	..	100	CP	CP	CP	S
Syrian Arab Republic	..	1981	..	..[c]	..	CP	CP	..
Tajikistan	..	..	..	..	..	..	..	..
Tanzania	1986	..	1988	75	S	CP	CP	CP
Thailand	IP	1992	..	56	CP	CP	CP	S
Togo	1985	..	..	69	CP	CP	CP	CP
Trinidad and Tobago	IP	..	..	67	CP	CP	CP	CP
Tunisia	..	1980	..	100	CP	CP	CP	CP
Turkey	..	..	..	..[c]	..	CP	CP	..
Turkmenistan	..	..	..	..	CP	CP	CP	..
Uganda	1983	1982	1988	0	CP	CP	CP	CP
Ukraine	..	..	..	..	S	CP	CP	S
United Arab Emirates	..	..	..	0	..	CP	CP	S
United Kingdom	1990	..	..	100	CP	CP	CP	..
United States	..	..	..	88	CP	CP	CP	..
Uruguay	..	..	..	59	CP	CP	CP	CP
Uzbekistan	..	..	..	..	CP	CP	CP	..
Venezuela	..	..	..	79	CP	CP	CP	..
Vietnam	1985	..	1993	..[c]	CP	CP	..	CP
West Bank and Gaza	..	..	..	..	..	..	..	..
Yemen, Rep.	..	1982	..	..[c]	S	..	..	CP
Yugoslavia, Fed. Rep.[e]	IP	..	..	..[c]	S[f]	CP	CP[g]	CP
Zaire	1984	1981	..	69	CP	CP	..	CP
Zambia	1985	1982	..	45	CP	CP	CP	CP
Zimbabwe	1987	1982	..	83	CP	CP	CP	CP

CP = Contracting party (has ratified or taken equivalent action). S = Signatory (has signed but not ratified). IP = In preparation. a. Includes all trade reported by members of the Convention on International Trade in Endangered Species of Wild Flora and Fauna (CITES) as of May 1993. b. Convention became effective November 16, 1994. c. Not a member of CITES as of May 1993. d. Data refer to the Federal Republic of Germany before unification. e. Unless otherwise noted, data refer to the former Yugoslavia. f. The constituent republics of the former Yugoslavia inherited the status of signatories. g. Refers to Croatia, Slovenia, and the Federal Republic of Yugoslavia.

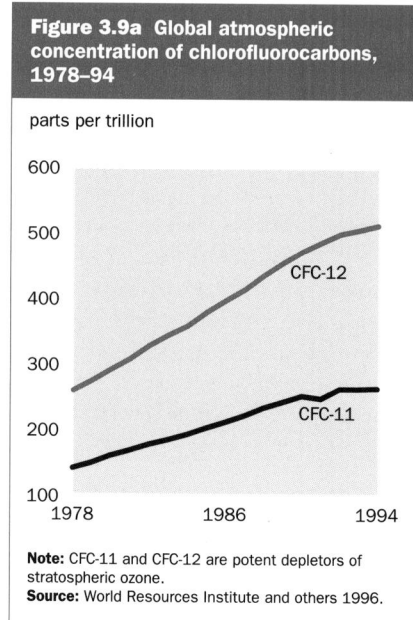

Figure 3.9a Global atmospheric concentration of chlorofluorocarbons, 1978–94

parts per trillion

CFC-12

CFC-11

Note: CFC-11 and CFC-12 are potent depletors of stratospheric ozone.
Source: World Resources Institute and others 1996.

To address global issues, many governments have also signed international treaties and agreements, launched in the wake of the 1972 United Nations Conference on Human Environment in Stockholm and the 1992 United Nations Conference on Environment and Development (UNCED) in Rio de Janeiro. The UNCED introduced and established principles covering a wide range of natural resources and issues of social and economic development and implementation. Among the major treaties and agreements are those on climate change, the ozone layer, chlorofluorocarbon control (the Montreal Protocol), the Law of the Sea, and the Convention on International Trade in Endangered Species.
• The Convention on Climate Change aims to stabilize atmospheric concentration of greenhouse gases at levels that will prevent human activities from interfering dangerously with the global climate system.
• The Vienna Convention for the Protection of the Ozone Layer protects human health and the environment by promoting research on the effects of changes in the ozone layer and on alternative substances (such as substitutes for chlorofluorocarbons) and technologies, monitoring the ozone layer, and taking measures to control the activities that produce adverse effects.
• The Montreal Protocol for CFC Control requires nations to help protect the earth from excessive levels of ultraviolet radiation by cutting chlorofluorocarbon consumption by 20 percent over their 1986 level by 1994 and

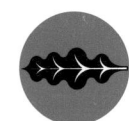

by 50 percent over their 1986 level by 1999, with allowances for increases in consumption by developing countries (figure 3.9a shows the global atmospheric concentration of chlorofluorocarbons in recent years).

• The United Nations Convention on the Law of the Sea, which became effective in November 1994, establishes a comprehensive legal regime for the sea and oceans, establishes rules for environmental standards and enforcement provisions, and develops international rules and national legislation to prevent and control marine pollution.

• Members of the Convention on International Trade in Endangered Species of Wild Flora and Fauna (CITES) agree to prohibit commercial trade in endangered species and to closely monitor trade in species that may become depleted by trade.

To help developing countries comply with their obligations under these international agreements, 32 countries created the Global Environment Facility (GEF) to focus on global improvement in biodiversity, climate change, international waters, and ozone layer depletion.

About the data

Unlike most other tables in this book, this table presents qualitative rather than quantitative indicators. Government commitment to sound national and international environmental programs is measured by the extent to which governments are proactive in preparing national environmental and conservation strategies and the extent to which they have of their own volition signed international treaties and accepted their obligations. But the signing of these treaties does not always imply ratification. Nor does it guarantee that governments will comply with treaty obligations.

Definitions

• **National conservation strategies** provide a comprehensive, cross-sectoral analysis of conservation and resource management issues to help integrate environmental concerns with the development process. The years shown refer to the year in which a strategy was completed. • **Country environmental profiles** identify how national economic and other activities can stay within the constraints imposed by the need to conserve natural resources. The years shown refer to the year in which a profile was completed. • **Biological diversity profiles** provide basic background on species diversity, major ecosystems and habitat types, protected area systems, and legislative and administrative support. • **Frequency of reporting on trade in endangered species** refers to the percentage of years for which a country has submitted an annual report to the CITES Secretariat since it became a party to the Convention on International Trade in Endangered Species. • **Participation in treaties** covers four international treaties (see facing page). Climate change refers to the Convention on Climate Change (signed in New York in 1993). Ozone layer refers to the Vienna Convention for the Protection of the Ozone Layer (1985). CFC control refers to the Montreal Protocol for CFC Control (formally, the Protocol on Substances that Deplete the Ozone Layer, signed in 1987). Law of the Sea refers to the United Nations Convention on the Law of the Sea (signed in Montego Bay, Jamaica, in 1982).

Data sources

Data are from the World Resources Institute's *World Resources 1994–95*; the World Resources Institute, International Institute for Environment and Development, and IUCN's *1993 Directory of Country Environmental Studies*; and the World Bank Environment Department's *National Environmental Strategies: Learning from Experience.*

Economy

4

In the past 25 years, in the expanding global economy, the developing economies have played an increasingly important role. This trend has four characteristics:

- *Steady growth and structural transformation,* led by low- and middle-income economies that have pursued successful adjustment policies.
- *Rapid integration of developing economies in the global economy,* marked by expanding trade and capital flows.
- *Improved policy environments in developing economies,* with better macroeconomic management and economic liberalization driving growth and integration.
- *Increasing disparities within the developing world,* with some regions pulling rapidly ahead (such as East Asia) and others in danger of being marginalized (Sub-Saharan Africa).

The indicators presented in this section attempt to measure changes in the global economy and the differential impact of these changes on developing economies. They are mainly indicators that traditionally appear in the *World Development Indicators,* measuring outcomes in the structure and rates of change of output, trade, and aggregate demand and in macroeconomic performance, including central government budgets, money supply, prices, balance of payments, and external debt. Like other data in this book, the data in this section are subject to conceptual and practical measurement problems that limit their comparability and usefulness (box 4a).

Developing economies outpace the world

The world economy grew at about 3 percent a year in the 1980s, slowing to 2 percent in the first half of the 1990s. Low- and middle-income economies, excluding Eastern Europe and the economies of the former Soviet Union, grew more rapidly, averaging 3.4 percent in the 1980s and 5 percent in the first half of the 1990s.

Growth among developing countries was dominated by the populous economies of East and South Asia. East Asia's economies grew at almost 8 percent a year in the 1980s and at 10 percent in the 1990s. In South Asia growth was almost 6 percent a year in the 1980s and roughly 5 percent in the 1990s. In the early 1980s Latin America's growth was hurt by the debt crisis and the halt in private capital flows. The debt crisis came to an end in the early 1990s, when these countries began to see much faster growth. In the same period Sub-Saharan Africa and the Middle East and North Africa had disappointing growth performance, reflecting poor policies, falling commodity prices, and, in Sub-Saharan Africa, growing official debt. Eastern Europe and the economies of the former Soviet Union—the transition economies—suffered from the collapse of the Soviet system and the end of state trading regimes; in the early 1990s their growth was negative.

Developing economies that have done well have some important similarities:

- *High rates of domestic savings have helped to sustain high rates of investment.* The fast-growing economies of East Asia are investing between 27 percent and 43 percent of GDP, while Chile is investing 27 percent and India 25 percent (tables 4.12 and 4.13).
- *Rapid growth in trade has increased the share of trade in GDP.* East Asia's export growth in the 1980s exceeded its GDP growth at around 9 percent a year—almost twice the rate for world exports. By the 1990s East Asian exports were growing at a remarkable 18 percent a year (almost three times the rate of growth of world exports). South Asian export growth has also been impressive—7 percent a year in the 1980s and 9 percent in the 1990s. As a result, the share of merchandise trade (exports plus imports) in GDP for developing economies as a group rose from 38 percent in 1980 to 44 percent in 1995.

Most of the increase, however, was in 10 economies, mostly in East Asia (tables 4.8 and 4.9).

● *Agriculture's importance is declining.* In China agriculture's share in GDP between 1980 and 1995 fell from 30 percent to 21 percent. In India it declined from 38 percent to 29 percent, in Indonesia from 24 percent to 17 percent, in Thailand from 23 percent to 11 percent, in Malaysia from 22 percent to 13 percent, and in the Republic of Korea, which moved from middle-income to high-income status during this period, from 15 percent to 7 percent (tables 4.1 and 4.2).

● *The share of manufactured exports is rising.* Further evidence of the structural transformation of these economies is seen in the increasing importance of manufactures in exports, a measure of access to learning, technology transfer, and the ability to produce at world standards. Between 1973–82 and 1983–92 the share of manufactures in merchandise exports rose in East Asia from 35 percent to 50 percent, and in South Asia from 45 percent to 65 percent (World Bank 1996c, p. 24).

The global economy integrates steadily

Since World War II international trade has consistently grown faster than output (table 4a). In the 1950s and 1960s this trend reflected recovery from the stagnation of the interwar years and a buoyant world economy. In the 1970s and 1980s world trade growth slowed but continued to outpace growth in the global economy. Led by rapid growth of East Asian exports, world trade in the 1990s is once again outstripping world output. In tandem with sharp growth in merchandise trade, there has been even sharper growth in services, whose share in world trade rose from 16 percent in 1980 to 18 percent in 1995.

Growth in trade has come from increasing trade liberalization, a result of successive international trade negotiations. Tariffs in industrial countries have fallen from 40 percent of imports in the 1950s to around 3–4 percent today. Developing countries, too, have reduced tariffs dramatically. In Latin America they have come down to around 15 percent, in Sub-Saharan Africa and the Middle East and North Africa to 25–30 percent, and in South Asia, which traditionally had high tariffs, to 45 percent (Finger, Ingco, and Reincke 1996). Under the Uruguay Round agreements countries are also progressively dismantling nontariff barriers.

In some developing countries trade integration goes hand in hand with financial integration, with private capital flows, particularly foreign direct investment (FDI), rising strongly (tables 4.22 and 5.2). Foreign direct investment to developing economies in 1995 accounted for 33 percent of all FDI, compared with 13 percent in 1990.

Policies make a difference . . .

Increased openness of economies and progressive dismantling of regulations and controls have been features of the economic policies of developing countries since 1980. Those that have seen the most rapid growth and integration have also had better macroeconomic management, as reflected in low inflation rates, stable real exchange rates, and small budget deficits (table

Box 4a The pitfalls of measuring national income

Accurate measurement of economic aggregates is crucial for understanding and managing the world economy. International statistics are a mix of quantifiable facts, guesses, conjectures, and missing data. Government financial statistics in many developing countries are poorly measured and erratically recorded. Reliable statistics on income, output, consumption, savings, and investment are crucial in assessing the health of an economy and its prospects for development, but these, too, are beset with theoretical and practical uncertainties.

The modern system of national accounts has its origins in the work of Richard Stone and a report prepared for the United Nations, *Measurement of National Income and the Construction of Social Accounts* (United Nations 1947). Since that time, standards for preparing national accounts have been updated. Most countries use the U.N. System of National Accounts, series F, no. 2, version 3 (universally referred to as the 1968 SNA), although version 4 of the SNA was completed in 1993.

National income may be compiled as the sum of incomes received by factors of production, or the sum of spending from income, or the sum of value added in each stage of production. Each approach uses different data from different sources, but each should arrive at the same total. Because these measures do not allow for the depreciation of physical capital, they are gross measures. When the sum is the total value of production by residents and domestic businesses, it is gross domestic product (GDP). When it also includes net income from abroad, it is gross national product (GNP) or, under version 4 of the SNA, gross national income (GNI).

It is easy to define national income, but compiling consistent, timely, and accurate national accounts is difficult and costly. There are three broad problems that face the analyst of national accounts: identifying and correctly accounting for all sources of income (or output) in the economy; adjusting data for price changes to allow comparisons of real values over time; and, when international comparisons are to be made, selecting the appropriate conversion factor to transform values in national currencies to a single, numeraire currency. Each has conceptual and practical difficulties.

Measuring income requires regular surveys of producers and households, supplemented by records of the tax system, customs service, and monetary authorities. In all economies, but particularly in developing economies with many small, unincorporated businesses, it may be difficult to identify the population to be surveyed and to distinguish business spending (investment or purchases of intermediate inputs) from household spending (consumption).

Measuring real output is especially vexing. As an economy grows, relative prices change, as does the underlying quality of goods. Over time, new products appear and others disappear. And the value of the output of the increasingly important service sector can often be measured only by the cost of inputs, mainly labor. The result of all these factors? Real growth and price change are difficult to measure.

Comparisons across countries are complicated by multiple exchange rates, some of which may be used only for official transactions, while others may not be officially reported. Moreover, relative prices of goods and services not traded on the international market may vary substantially from one economy to another, leading to big differences in the purchasing power of one currency compared with another and thus to differences in welfare as measured by GNP per capita.

Although the *World Development Indicators* points out the most obvious and serious deficiencies in international statistics, it can neither list nor correct for the many sources of error and noncomparability. The solution lies with the national statistical offices that collect and report the data and with the international agencies that assist their efforts and try to ensure comparability.

Table 4a Average annual growth of world trade and GDP, 1950–95

percent

	1950–60	1960–70	1970–80	1980–90	1990–95
World trade[a]	6.5	8.3	5.2	5.0	6.2
World output	4.2	5.3	3.6	3.1	2.0
Difference	2.3	3.0	1.6	1.9	4.2

a. Exports of goods and services on a national accounts basis.
Source: World Bank staff estimates.

4.15). Indeed, for the fastest growing economies inflation rates have been relatively low (around 13 percent), real exchange rates more stable, and budget deficits around 2–3 percent of GDP. By contrast, countries growing more slowly and weak and slow integrators have seen inflation rates approaching 20 percent, budget deficits of 4–6 percent or more, and volatile real exchange rates.

. . . but it is still an unequal world

While the economies of Asia fared remarkably well in 1980–95, per capita output fell in Sub-Saharan Africa and the Middle East and North Africa and stagnated in Latin America and the Caribbean. The poor outcomes reflected dependence on commodities and falling world prices (despite the commodity boom of the early 1990s), the debt crisis in Latin America, poor policies and weak institutions, and, in Sub-Saharan Africa, political instability and civil wars. In many countries population-weighted trade ratios fell. And while eight countries received two-thirds of all foreign direct investment flows, many have no access to private foreign capital and must depend heavily on official development assistance.

In this unequal world a handful of developing economies are emerging as potential giants in the global economy (table 4b). The 10 largest economies account for 83 percent of the developing world's population, 61 percent of its GNP (69 percent in purchasing power parity terms), and 66 percent of its exports. Although they have not all progressed at the same rate, their share of world output has grown from about 40 percent to 58 percent. Some smaller economies have higher output per capita, and others have grown faster, but the integration of these 10 into a growing world economy could transform the lives of billions of people in the next century.

Table 4b The emerging giants of the developing world, 1995

Country or group	Population millions	GNP $ billions	GNP in PPP terms $ billions	GNP per capita in PPP terms $	Exports of goods and services $ billions	Net foreign direct investment $ billions	Gross international reserves $ billions
China	1,201	745	3,522	2,940	147	38.0	80
India	929	325	1,357	1,460	40	1.3	23
Brazil	162	585	920	5,690	53	3.1	51
Indonesia	193	189	767	3,970	51	4.5	15
Russian Federation	147	328	683	4,640	94	1.5	18
Mexico	92	305	610	6,640	90	4.1	17
Thailand	59	160	456	7,760	70	2.3	37
Turkey	62	166	352	5,680	36	1.0	14
Pakistan	130	60	289	2,230	8	0.3	3
Argentina	36	269	288	8,640	24	3.9	16
Total	3,011	3,132	9,244	3,070[a]	613	60.0	274
Low- and middle-income economies	3,614	5,179	13,439	3,027[a]	1,395	91.0	515
World	5,673	27,687	31,165	5,929[a]	6,386	..	1,735

a. Weighted average; data refer only to countries for which PPP data are available.
Source: Tables 1.1, 2.1, 4.21, 4.22, and 5.2 and World Bank staff estimates.

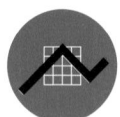

4.1 | Growth of output

	Gross domestic product		Agriculture		Industry		Manufacturing		Services	
	average annual % growth		average annual % growth		average annual % growth		average annual % growth		average annual % growth	
	1980–90	1990–95	1980–90	1990–95	1980–90	1990–95	1980–90	1990–95	1980–90	1990–95
Albania	3.0	1.4	2.4	7.6	3.2	−15.6	..	..	3.2	5.9
Algeria	2.8	0.1	4.6	1.3	2.3	−1.1	3.3	−9.0	3.8	1.3
Angola	3.7	−4.1	0.5	−1.8	6.4	0.9	−11.1	−11.1	2.2	−10.8
Argentina	−0.3	5.7	0.9	0.5	−0.9	5.9	−0.5	..	0.0	6.4
Armenia	3.3	−21.2	−3.9	−0.6	5.1	−28.7	..	..	4.6	−19.7
Australia	3.4	3.5	3.3	−2.4	2.8	3.3	1.9	4.4	3.7	3.7
Austria	2.1	1.9	1.1	−1.8	1.9	1.7	2.4	0.5	2.3	2.2
Azerbaijan	..	−20.2	..	..	..	..	..	..	..	..
Bangladesh	4.3	4.1	2.7	1.1	4.9	7.3	2.8	7.4	5.7	5.4
Belarus	..	−9.3	..	−11.2	..	−10.9	..	..	..	−6.9
Belgium	1.9	1.1	1.8	4.0	2.2	..	3.0	..	1.8	..
Benin	2.6	4.1	5.1	4.9	2.1	3.5	5.1	5.3	1.2	3.5
Bolivia	0.0	3.8	2.0	..	−2.9	..	−1.6	..	−0.1	..
Bosnia and Herzegovina	..	..	..	..	..	..	..	..	..	..
Botswana	10.3	4.2	2.2	0.7	11.4	1.4	8.8	2.2	11.0	7.7
Brazil	2.7	2.7	2.8	3.7	2.0	1.7	1.6	1.7	3.5	3.6
Bulgaria	4.0	−4.3	−2.1	−1.9	5.2	−7.5	..	..	7.2	−20.7
Burkina Faso	3.7	2.6	3.1	4.6	3.7	1.4	2.0	1.1	4.7	1.7
Burundi	4.4	−2.3	3.1	−4.1	4.5	−5.0	5.7	−7.2	5.4	−1.5
Cambodia	..	6.4	..	2.1	..	11.3	..	6.9	..	8.3
Cameroon	3.1	−1.8	2.2	2.2	5.9	−6.8	12.6	−2.2	2.1	−1.4
Canada	3.4	1.8	1.5	0.3	2.9	1.2	3.2	1.7	3.7	1.8
Central African Republic	1.7	1.0	2.7	1.5	3.1	−4.6	..	..	−0.1	−1.6
Chad	6.3	1.9	2.7	6.9	8.0	−9.9	4.4	−9.2	9.9	1.2
Chile	4.1	7.3	5.6	5.2	3.7	6.1	3.4	6.3	4.2	8.4
China	10.2	12.8	5.9	4.3	11.1	18.1	10.7	17.2	13.6	10.0
Colombia	3.7	4.6	2.9	1.4	5.0	3.0	3.5	3.3	3.1	6.4
Congo	3.6	−0.6	3.4	−0.9	5.2	1.2	6.9	−5.3	2.5	−2.1
Costa Rica	3.0	5.1	3.1	3.6	2.8	5.2	3.0	5.5	3.1	5.6
Côte d'Ivoire	0.1	0.7	−0.5	0.3	4.4	1.7	4.6	−2.2	−1.3	0.2
Croatia	..	..	..	..	..	..	..	..	..	..
Cuba	..	..	..	..	..	..	..	..	..	..
Czech Republic	1.7	−2.6	..	..	..	..	..	..	..	..
Denmark	2.4	2.0	3.1	0.3	2.9	1.6	1.4	0.9	2.3	1.3
Dominican Republic	2.7	3.9	0.4	2.5	2.2	3.3	0.9	3.6	3.7	4.5
Ecuador	2.0	3.4	4.4	2.5	1.2	4.9	0.0	3.2	1.8	2.7
Egypt, Arab Rep.	5.0	1.3	1.5	2.1	2.6	0.4	..	0.0	8.4	1.5
El Salvador	0.2	6.3	−1.1	1.2	0.1	2.9	−0.7	..	0.7	9.3
Eritrea	..	..	..	..	..	..	..	..	..	..
Estonia	2.1	−9.2	..	−8.9	..	−14.9	..	..	..	−3.8
Ethiopia[a]	2.3	..	1.4	..	1.8	..	1.2	..	3.1	..
Finland	3.3	−0.5	−0.2	0.0	3.3	−1.2	3.4	2.1	5.3	−2.7
France	2.4	1.0	2.0	−1.1	1.1	−1.0	0.8	−0.9	3.0	1.5
Gabon	0.5	−2.5	1.7	−0.2	1.0	2.7	9.8	−0.2	−0.3	−10.0
Gambia, The	3.4	1.6	0.4	2.6	6.0	0.4	7.2	1.2	3.9	2.5
Georgia	0.5	−26.9	0.7	−31.4	1.8	−34.1	0.3	−29.3	−1.4	−22.3
Germany[b]	2.2	..	1.7	..	1.2	..	..	..	2.9	..
Ghana	3.0	4.3	1.0	2.4	3.3	4.4	3.9	2.5	6.4	6.5
Greece	1.4	1.1	−0.1	3.1	1.3	−0.8	0.5	−1.7	4.9	0.6
Guatemala	0.8	4.0	2.3	2.5	2.1	4.2	..	..	2.1	4.9
Guinea-Bissau	4.5	3.5	6.7	4.8	0.4	1.9	..	0.5	3.3	2.2
Guinea	..	3.8	..	4.5	..	2.3	..	..	..	4.5
Haiti	−0.2	−6.5	..	..	..	..	..	..	..	..
Honduras	2.7	3.5	2.7	2.9	3.3	4.9	3.7	3.2	2.5	1.3
Hong Kong	6.9	5.6	..	..	..	..	..	..	..	..

Growth of output | 4.1

	Gross domestic product		Agriculture		Industry		Manufacturing		Services	
	average annual % growth		average annual % growth		average annual % growth		average annual % growth		average annual % growth	
	1980–90	1990–95	1980–90	1990–95	1980–90	1990–95	1980–90	1990–95	1980–90	1990–95
Hungary	1.6	–1.0	0.6	–7.0	–2.6	0.5	..	..	3.6	–4.6
India	5.8	4.6	3.1	3.1	7.1	5.1	7.4	5.4	6.7	6.1
Indonesia	6.1	7.6	3.4	2.9	6.9	10.1	12.6	11.2	7.0	7.4
Iran, Islamic Rep.	1.5	4.2	4.5	4.8	3.3	3.8	4.5	4.6	–0.4	6.0
Iraq	–6.8	..	..	..	..	..	..	..	..	..
Ireland	3.1	4.7								
Israel	3.5	6.4								
Italy	2.4	1.0	0.6	1.6	..	..	3.0	0.3		
Jamaica	2.0	2.9	0.6	8.3	2.4	–0.5	2.7	–1.9	1.9	6.0
Japan	4.0	1.0	1.3	–2.2	4.2	0.0	4.8	–0.9	3.9	2.3
Jordan	–1.5	8.2	13.2	10.2	–1.3	7.9	2.4	7.7	–8.2	6.2
Kazakstan	..	–11.9	..	–18.0	..	–19.2	..	–23.2	..	6.1
Kenya	4.2	1.4	3.3	–0.4	3.9	1.5	4.9	2.3	4.9	3.1
Korea, Dem. Rep.	..	..	..	..	..	..	..	..	..	..
Korea, Rep.	9.4	7.2	2.8	1.3	13.1	7.3	13.2	7.6	8.2	7.9
Kuwait	0.9	12.2	14.7	..	1.0	..	2.3	..	0.9	
Kyrgyz Republic	..	–14.7	..	–7.6	..	..	..	..	..	..
Lao PDR	..	6.5	..	..	..	..	..	..	..	..
Latvia	3.4	–13.7	2.3	–16.4	4.3	–25.1	4.4	–25.1	3.1	–2.1
Lebanon	..	..	..	..	..	..	..	..	..	..
Lesotho	4.3	7.5	2.6	–3.4	7.2	12.3	13.5	9.1	5.2	6.1
Libya	–5.7	..	..	..	..	..	..	..	..	..
Lithuania	..	–9.7	..	..	..	..	..	..	..	..
Macedonia, FYR	..	..	..	..	..	..	..	..	..	..
Madagascar	1.3	0.1	2.5	1.6	0.9	0.5	1.9	2.5	0.8	–0.6
Malawi	2.3	0.7	2.0	1.7	2.9	0.4	3.6	–0.2	3.4	–1.0
Malaysia	5.2	8.7	3.8	2.6	7.2	11.0	8.9	13.2	4.2	8.6
Mali	1.8	2.5	4.3	3.1	2.7	5.3	4.1	4.8	–1.7	1.2
Mauritania	1.7	4.0	1.7	4.9	4.9	3.9	–2.1	1.5	0.4	3.2
Mauritius	6.2	4.9	2.9	–1.4	10.3	5.6	11.1	5.2	5.4	6.4
Mexico	1.0	1.1	0.6	0.4	1.0	0.5	1.4	0.7	1.1	1.5
Moldova	..	..	..	..	..	..	..	..	..	..
Mongolia	5.5	–3.3	2.9	..	4.6	..	..	..	4.2	2.8
Morocco	4.2	1.2	6.7	–5.9	3.0	1.7	4.1	2.2	4.2	2.8
Mozambique	–0.2	7.1	1.6	2.4	–9.8	–2.4	..	..	–0.1	15.0
Myanmar	0.6	5.7	0.5	5.1	0.5	9.4	–0.2	7.0	0.7	5.5
Namibia	1.1	3.8	1.8	6.8	–1.1	2.9	5.3	8.4	2.7	4.6
Nepal	4.6	5.1	4.0	1.5	6.0	9.3	3.7	14.1	4.8	7.2
Netherlands	2.3	1.8	3.4	3.0	1.6	0.4	2.3	0.3	2.6	2.1
New Zealand	1.8	3.6	4.4	0.9	1.3	3.8	0.6	4.2	1.7	3.5
Nicaragua	–2.0	1.1	–2.2	0.3	–1.7	–4.4	–3.1	–0.7	–2.0	2.2
Niger	–1.1	0.5	1.8	..	–3.3	..	..	..	–5.2	..
Nigeria	1.6	1.6	3.3	2.3	–1.0	–1.2	4.6	–0.7	3.2	4.5
Norway	2.9	3.5	0.9	..	3.5	..	0.6	..	2.6	..
Oman	8.3	6.0	7.9	..	10.3	..	20.6	..	6.0	..
Pakistan	6.3	4.6	4.3	3.4	7.3	5.7	7.7	5.8	6.8	5.0
Panama	0.3	6.3	..	4.4	..	14.9	..	..	..	5.5
Papua New Guinea	1.9	9.3	1.8	4.7	1.9	17.8	0.1	5.9	2.0	4.8
Paraguay	2.5	3.1	3.6	1.4	–0.3	1.9	2.1	1.2	3.4	4.1
Peru	–0.2	5.3	..	..	..	..	..	..	..	..
Philippines	1.0	2.3	1.0	1.6	–0.9	2.2	0.2	1.8	2.8	2.7
Poland	1.9	2.4	–0.1	–2.0	–0.9	3.7	..	..	5.1	2.4
Portugal	2.9	0.8	..	..	..	..	..	..	..	..
Puerto Rico	4.1	3.0	1.8	..	3.6	..	1.5	..	4.6	..
Romania	0.5	–1.4	..	–0.4	..	–2.1	..	..	..	–2.8
Russian Federation	1.9	–9.8	..	..	..	..	..	..	..	..

World Development Indicators 1997 **131**

	Gross domestic product		Agriculture		Industry		Manufacturing		Services	
	average annual % growth		average annual % growth		average annual % growth		average annual % growth		average annual % growth	
	1980–90	1990–95	1980–90	1990–95	1980–90	1990–95	1980–90	1990–95	1980–90	1990–95
Rwanda	2.3	–12.8	0.7	–10.8	1.8	–17.0	2.6	–16.4	5.4	–12.3
Saudi Arabia	–1.2	1.7	13.4	..	–2.3	..	7.5	..	–1.2	..
Senegal	3.1	1.9	2.8	1.3	3.7	2.0	4.7	1.6	3.0	2.0
Sierra Leone	1.6	–4.2	4.4	–2.8	5.7	–2.8	3.4	4.4	–1.1	–5.9
Singapore	6.4	8.7	–6.2	0.5	5.4	9.2	6.6	8.3	7.2	8.4
Slovak Republic	2.0	–2.8	1.6	1.0	2.0	–10.4	..	..	0.8	6.2
Slovenia	..	..	..	..	..	..	..	..	..	..
South Africa	1.3	0.6	3.0	–0.3	–1.1	–0.1	–0.1	–0.2	3.1	0.9
Spain	3.2	1.1	..	–1.7	..	..	..	..	..	..
Sri Lanka	4.2	4.8	2.2	2.4	4.6	6.5	6.3	9.1	4.7	6.3
Sudan	0.6	6.8	0.0	..	2.8	..	3.7	..	1.5	..
Sweden	2.3	–0.1	1.5	–1.9	2.8	–0.7	2.6	0.8	2.5	–0.1
Switzerland	2.2	0.1	..	..	..	..	..	..	..	..
Syrian Arab Republic	1.5	7.4	–0.6	..	6.6	..	..	..	..	..
Tajikistan	..	–18.1	..	..	..	..	..	..	..	..
Tanzania[c]	3.8	3.2	4.9	4.1	3.4	8.4	1.1	3.6	1.6	1.7
Thailand	7.6	8.4	4.0	3.1	9.9	10.8	9.5	11.6	7.3	7.8
Togo	1.8	–3.4	5.6	3.3	1.1	–6.0	1.7	–7.7	–0.3	–8.6
Trinidad and Tobago	–2.5	1.0	–5.8	1.3	–5.5	0.2	–10.1	–0.6	–3.3	–0.1
Tunisia	3.3	3.9	2.8	–2.1	3.1	4.0	3.7	5.3	3.6	5.6
Turkey	5.3	3.2	1.3	0.9	7.8	4.2	7.9	4.7	4.4	3.3
Turkmenistan	..	–10.6	..	..	..	..	..	..	..	..
Uganda	3.1	6.6	2.3	3.8	6.0	11.0	4.0	12.2	3.0	8.2
Ukraine	..	–14.3	..	–9.7	..	–21.6	..	–20.2	..	..
United Arab Emirates	–2.0	..	9.6	9.3	–4.2	–1.8	3.1	1.3	3.4	4.9
United Kingdom	3.2	1.4	..	..	..	..	..	..	..	..
United States	3.0	2.6	4.0	3.6	2.8	1.2	3.1	1.6	3.1	2.1
Uruguay	0.4	4.0	0.0	4.5	–0.2	0.1	0.4	–1.6	0.9	6.2
Uzbekistan	..	–4.4	..	–0.9	..	–6.7	..	–5.3	..	–6.6
Venezuela	1.1	2.4	3.0	1.9	1.6	3.4	4.3	1.8	0.5	1.7
Vietnam	..	8.3	..	5.2	..	..	..	..	..	..
West Bank and Gaza	..	..	..	..	..	..	..	..	..	..
Yemen, Rep.	..	..	..	..	..	..	..	..	..	..
Yugoslavia, Fed. Rep.	..	..	..	..	..	..	..	..	..	..
Zaire	1.7	..	2.5	..	2.3	..	2.3	..	1.6	..
Zambia	0.8	–0.2	3.6	–0.5	1.0	–1.2	4.0	–1.0	0.1	0.7
Zimbabwe	3.5	1.0	2.4	1.6	3.6	–3.6	2.9	–5.6	2.9	1.7
World	**3.1 w**	**2.0 w**	**2.8 w**	**1.3 w**	**3.3 w**	**1.4 w**	**3.6 w**	**1.3 w**	**3.4 w**	**2.6 w**
Low income	6.0 w	6.8 w	3.6 w	3.1 w	7.7 w	11.6 w	8.5 w	12.7 w	6.9 w	6.4 w
Excl. China & India	2.7 w	1.8 w	2.6 w	1.9 w	2.9 w	..	..	..	2.8 w	..
Middle income	1.9 w	0.1 w	..	0.9 w	..	..	..	..	2.6 w	3.9 w
Lower middle income	2.3 w	–1.5 w	..	0.5 w	..	..	..	..	..	..
Upper middle income	1.3 w	2.6 w	2.4 w	1.8 w	0.7 w	2.6 w	1.2 w	2.7 w	2.0 w	3.4 w
Low & middle income	2.8 w	2.1 w	3.1 w	2.0 w	3.9 w	4.9 w	..	..	3.6 w	4.5 w
East Asia & Pacific	7.6 w	10.3 w	4.8 w	3.9 w	8.9 w	15.0 w	9.7 w	15.1 w	9.0 w	8.4 w
Europe & Central Asia	2.3 w	–6.5 w	..	..	..	..	..	..	..	..
Latin America & Carib.	1.7 w	3.2 w	2.0 w	2.3 w	1.4 w	2.5 w	1.1 w	2.2 w	1.9 w	3.8 w
Middle East & N. Africa	0.2 w	2.3 w	4.5 w	3.3 w	1.1 w	..	5.0 w	1.6 w	1.2 w	..
South Asia	5.7 w	4.6 w	3.2 w	3.0 w	6.9 w	5.3 w	7.2 w	5.6 w	6.6 w	6.0 w
Sub-Saharan Africa	1.7 w	1.4 w	1.9 w	1.5 w	0.6 w	0.2 w	1.7 w	0.0 w	2.5 w	1.5 w
High income	3.2 w	2.0 w	2.3 w	0.6 w	3.2 w	0.7 w	3.5 w	0.5 w	3.4 w	2.3 w

a. Data prior to 1992 include Eritrea. b. Data prior to 1990 refer to the Federal Republic of Germany before unification. c. In all tables GDP and GNP data cover mainland Tanzania.

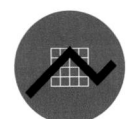

The growth of an economy is measured by the increase in value added produced by the individuals and enterprises operating in that economy. So, to measure real growth requires estimates of GDP and its components valued in constant prices from one period to the next. In principle, real value added can be estimated by measuring the quantity of goods produced in a period, valuing them at an agreed set of base year prices, and subtracting the cost of inputs, also in constant prices. This double deflation method, recommended by the U.N. System of National Accounts, depends on detailed information about prices of inputs and the quality of outputs. But in some sectors value added is extrapolated from the base year using volume indexes of output or inputs. In other sectors, particularly services, real output is imputed from labor inputs, such as the number of employees or real wages. The real output of governments and other unpriced services are calculated in the same way. Without well-defined measures of output, measuring the real growth of the service sector remains a vexing problem.

Technical progress can lead to improvements in both the production process and the quality of goods. Either effect, if not properly accounted for, can distort measures of value added and thus of growth. When inputs are used to estimate output, as in the service sector, unmeasured technical progress leads to underestimates of the quantity and value of output. Unmeasured changes in the quality of goods produced also lead to underestimates of value. The result can be underestimates of real growth and productivity and overestimates of inflation.

Nonmarket services pose a particular problem, especially in developing countries, where much economic activity may go unrecorded. Obtaining a complete picture of the economy requires estimating household production, barter exchanges, and illicit or deliberately unreported activity. How consistent and complete such estimates will be depends on the skill of the analysts and the resources available to them.

Rebasing national accounts

Countries occasionally "rebase" their national accounts by collecting a complete set of observations on the value and volume of production in a new base year. Using these data, they then update price indexes to reflect the relative importance of inputs and outputs in total output, and volume indexes to reflect relative price levels. The new base year should represent normal operation of the economy—a year not characterized by major shocks or distortions. But the choice of base year and the timing of economic surveys are also determined by administrative convenience and resource availability. Some developing countries have not rebased their national accounts for many years. Using an old base year can be misleading because implicit price and volume weights become progressively less useful and relevant.

The World Bank collects constant price national accounts series in national currencies and the country's original base year. To obtain comparable series of constant price data, the main sectoral components of GDP by industrial origin (agriculture, industry, and services) are rescaled to a common base year, currently 1987, and summed to provide a new estimate of constant price GDP. This process gives rise to a difference between the derived aggregate (based on the sum of its components) and directly rescaled GDP. It may also result in differences between the growth rates calculated from the original base year GDP series and those calculated from the rescaled aggregate. Such deviations are unavoidable when aggregating index numbers. To reconcile constant price GDP measured from the expenditure side with the rescaled GDP by industrial origin, a statistical discrepancy is calculated and added to the private consumption component of GDP expenditures.

Measuring growth rates

Country growth rates are calculated using constant price data in the local currency. Regional and income group growth rates are calculated after converting local currencies to U.S. dollars using the World Bank's International Economics Department (IEC) conversion factor. Growth rates are estimated by fitting a linear trend line to the logarithmic annual values of the given variable using the least-squares growth rate method. This produces an average growth rate that corresponds to a model of periodic compound growth. The least-squares growth rate method and the IEC conversion factor are described in *Statistical methods*.

Most countries use the definitions of the U.N. System of National Accounts (SNA), series F, no. 2, version 3, referred to as the 1968 SNA. Version 4 of the SNA was completed in 1993. Until new economic surveys can be implemented, most countries will continue to use the 1968 SNA. A few low-income countries still use concepts from older SNA guidelines, including valuations such as factor cost and market prices in describing major economic aggregates. • **Gross domestic product** at purchasers' prices is the sum of the gross value added by all resident and nonresident producers in the economy plus any taxes and minus any subsidies not included in the value of the products. It is calculated without making deductions for depreciation of fabricated assets or for depletion and degradation of natural resources. • **Agriculture** comprises value added from forestry, hunting, and fishing as well as cultivation of crops and livestock production. • **Industry** comprises value added in mining, manufacturing (also reported as a separate subgroup), construction, electricity, water, and gas. • **Manufacturing** refers to industries belonging to divisions 15–37 in the International Standard Industrial Classification, rev. 2. • **Services** include value added in all other branches of economic activity, such as wholesale and retail trade (including hotels and restaurants), transport, and government, financial, professional, and personal services such as education, health care, and real estate services. Also included are imputed bank service charges, import duties, and any statistical discrepancies noted by national compilers as well as discrepancies arising from rescaling.

National accounts data for developing countries are collected from national statistical organizations and central banks by visiting and resident World Bank missions. Data for industrial countries come from OECD data files. The World Bank rescales constant price data to a common base year. The complete national accounts time series is available on the *World Development Indicators* CD-ROM. For information on the OECD national accounts series see OECD, *National Accounts, 1960–1994*, volumes 1 and 2.

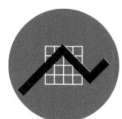

4.2 | Structure of output

	Gross domestic product		Agriculture value added		Industry value added		Manufacturing value added		Services value added	
	$ millions		% of GDP		% of GDP		% of GDP		% of GDP	
	1980	1995	1980	1995	1980	1995	1980	1995	1980	1995
Albania	..	2,192	..	56	..	21	..	..	..	23
Algeria	42,345	41,435	10	13	54	47	9	9	36	41
Angola	..	3,722	..	12	..	59	..	3	..	28
Argentina	76,962	281,060	6	6	41	31	29	20	52	63
Armenia	..	2,058	..	44	..	35	..	25	..	20
Australia	160,109	348,782	5	3	36	28	19	15	58	70
Austria	76,882	233,427	4	2	40	34	28	24	56	63
Azerbaijan	..	3,475	..	27	..	32	..	..	..	41
Bangladesh	12,950	29,110	50	31	16	18	11	10	34	52
Belarus	..	20,561	..	13	..	35	..	22	..	52
Belgium	118,022	269,081	2	2	34	..	24	..	64	..
Benin	1,405	1,522	35	34	12	12	8	7	52	53
Bolivia	3,074	6,131	18	..	35	..	15	..	47	..
Bosnia and Herzegovina	..	..	..	..	..	..	..	..	..	..
Botswana	971	4,318	13	5	44	46	4	4	43	48
Brazil	235,025	688,085	11	14	44	37	33	24	45	49
Bulgaria	20,040	12,366	14	13	54	34	..	..	32	53
Burkina Faso	1,709	2,325	33	34	22	27	16	21	45	39
Burundi	920	1,062	62	56	13	18	7	12	25	26
Cambodia	..	2,771	..	51	..	14	..	6	..	34
Cameroon	6,741	7,931	29	39	23	23	9	10	48	38
Canada	263,193	568,928	5	..	40	..	22	..	55	..
Central African Republic	797	1,128	40	44	20	13	7	..	40	43
Chad	727	1,138	54	44	12	22	..	16	34	35
Chile	27,572	67,297	7	..	37	..	21	..	55	..
China	201,688	697,647	30	21	49	48	41	38	21	31
Colombia	33,399	76,112	19	14	32	32	23	18	49	54
Congo	1,706	2,163	12	10	47	38	7	6	42	51
Costa Rica	4,831	9,233	18	17	27	24	19	19	55	58
Côte d'Ivoire	10,175	10,069	27	31	20	20	13	18	53	50
Croatia	..	18,081	..	12	..	25	..	20	..	62
Cuba	..	..	..	..	..	..	..	..	..	..
Czech Republic	29,123	44,772	7	6	63	39	..	..	30	55
Denmark	66,322	172,220	6	4	33	29	22	21	61	67
Dominican Republic	6,631	11,277	20	15	28	22	15	15	52	64
Ecuador	11,733	17,939	12	12	38	36	18	21	50	52
Egypt, Arab Rep.	22,913	47,349	18	20	37	21	12	15	45	59
El Salvador	3,574	9,471	38	14	22	22	16	..	40	65
Eritrea	..	579	..	11	..	20	..	11	..	69
Estonia	..	4,007	..	8	..	28	..	17	..	64
Ethiopia[a]	5,179	5,287	56	57	12	10	6	3	31	33
Finland	51,306	125,432	12	6	49	37	35	28	39	57
France	664,597	1,536,089	4	2	34	27	24	19	62	71
Gabon	4,285	4,691	7	..	60	..	5	..	33	..
Gambia, The	233	384	30	28	16	15	7	7	53	58
Georgia	..	2,325	..	67	..	22	..	18	..	11
Germany	..	2,415,764	..	..	..	..	..	..	..	..
Ghana	4,445	6,315	58	46	12	16	8	6	30	38
Greece	40,147	90,550	27	21	48	36	30	21	24	43
Guatemala	7,879	14,489	..	25	..	19	..	..	..	56
Guinea-Bissau	105	257	44	46	20	24	..	7	36	30
Guinea	..	3,686	..	24	..	31	..	5	..	45
Haiti	1,462	2,043	..	44	..	12	..	9	..	44
Honduras	2,566	3,937	24	21	24	33	15	18	52	46
Hong Kong	28,495	143,669	1	0	32	17	24	9	67	83

	Gross domestic product		Agriculture value added		Industry value added		Manufacturing value added		Services value added	
	$ millions		% of GDP		% of GDP		% of GDP		% of GDP	
	1980	1995	1980	1995	1980	1995	1980	1995	1980	1995
Hungary	22,163	43,712	..	8	..	33	..	24	..	59
India	172,321	324,082	38	29	26	29	18	19	36	41
Indonesia	78,013	198,079	24	17	42	42	13	24	34	41
Iran, Islamic Rep.	92,664	..	18	25	32	34	9	14	50	40
Iraq	47,562	..	..	..	..	..	..	..	..	..
Ireland	20,080	60,780	..	..	..	..	..	..	..	..
Israel	22,579	91,965	..	..	..	..	..	..	..	..
Italy	452,648	1,086,932	6	3	39	31	28	21	55	66
Jamaica	2,679	4,406	8	9	38	38	17	18	54	53
Japan	1,059,253	5,108,540	4	2	42	38	29	24	54	60
Jordan	..	6,105	..	8	..	27	..	14	..	65
Kazakstan	..	21,413	..	12	..	30	..	6	..	57
Kenya	7,265	9,095	33	29	21	17	13	11	47	54
Korea, Dem. Rep.	..	..	..	..	..	..	..	..	..	..
Korea, Rep.	63,661	455,476	15	7	40	43	29	27	45	50
Kuwait	28,639	26,650	0	0	75	53	6	11	25	46
Kyrgyz Republic	..	3,028	..	44	..	24	..	..	..	32
Lao PDR	..	1,760	..	52	..	18	..	14	..	30
Latvia	..	6,034	..	9	..	31	..	18	..	60
Lebanon	..	11,143	..	7	..	24	..	10	..	69
Lesotho	368	1,029	24	10	29	56	7	18	47	34
Libya	35,545	..	2	..	76	..	2	..	22	..
Lithuania	..	7,089	..	11	..	36	..	30	..	53
Macedonia, FYR	..	1,975	..	..	..	..	..	..	..	..
Madagascar	4,042	3,198	30	34	16	13	..	13	54	53
Malawi	1,238	1,465	37	42	19	27	12	18	44	31
Malaysia	24,488	85,311	22	13	38	43	21	33	40	44
Mali	1,629	2,431	61	46	10	17	4	6	29	37
Mauritania	709	1,068	30	27	26	30	..	13	44	43
Mauritius	1,132	3,919	12	9	26	33	15	23	62	58
Mexico	194,914	250,038	8	8	33	26	22	19	59	67
Moldova	..	3,518	..	50	..	28	..	26	..	22
Mongolia	..	861	..	..	..	..	..	..	..	..
Morocco	18,821	32,412	18	14	31	33	17	19	51	53
Mozambique	2,028	1,469	37	33	31	12	..	..	32	55
Myanmar	..	..	47	63	13	9	10	7	41	28
Namibia	2,190	3,033	12	14	53	29	5	9	35	56
Nepal	1,946	4,232	62	42	12	22	4	10	26	36
Netherlands	171,861	395,900	3	3	32	27	18	18	64	70
New Zealand	22,469	57,070	11	..	31	..	22	..	58	..
Nicaragua	2,144	1,911	23	33	31	20	26	16	45	46
Niger	2,538	1,860	43	39	23	18	4	..	35	44
Nigeria	93,082	40,477	27	43	40	27	8	9	32	31
Norway	63,283	145,954	4	..	36	..	15	..	60	..
Oman	5,982	12,102	3	..	69	..	1	..	28	..
Pakistan	23,690	60,649	30	26	25	24	16	17	46	50
Panama	3,592	7,413	..	11	..	15	..	..	..	74
Papua New Guinea	2,548	4,901	33	26	27	38	10	8	40	34
Paraguay	4,579	7,743	29	24	27	22	16	16	44	54
Peru	20,661	57,424	10	7	42	38	20	24	48	55
Philippines	32,500	74,180	25	22	39	32	26	23	36	46
Poland	57,068	117,663	..	6	..	39	..	26	..	54
Portugal	28,526	102,337	..	..	..	..	..	..	..	..
Puerto Rico	14,436	35,834	3	1	39	42	37	39	58	57
Romania	..	35,533	..	21	..	40	..	..	..	39
Russian Federation	..	344,711	..	7	..	38	..	31	..	55

	Gross domestic product		Agriculture value added		Industry value added		Manufacturing value added		Services value added	
	$ millions		% of GDP		% of GDP		% of GDP		% of GDP	
	1980	1995	1980	1995	1980	1995	1980	1995	1980	1995
Rwanda	1,163	1,128	50	37	23	17	16	3	27	46
Saudi Arabia	156,487	125,501	1	..	81	..	5	..	18	..
Senegal	3,016	4,867	19	20	25	18	15	12	57	62
Sierra Leone	1,166	824	33	42	21	27	5	6	47	31
Singapore	11,718	83,695	1	0	38	36	29	27	61	64
Slovak Republic	..	17,414	..	6	..	33	..	..	..	61
Slovenia	..	18,550	..	5	..	39	..	1	..	57
South Africa	78,744	136,035	7	5	50	31	23	24	43	64
Spain	211,543	558,617	..	3	..	..	..	..	..	..
Sri Lanka	4,024	12,915	28	23	30	25	18	16	43	52
Sudan	6,760	..	34	..	14	..	7	..	52	..
Sweden	125,557	228,679	4	2	37	32	25	23	59	66
Switzerland	101,646	300,508	..	..	..	..	..	..	..	..
Syrian Arab Republic	13,062	16,783	20	..	23	..	..	..	56	..
Tajikistan	..	1,999	..	..	..	..	..	..	..	..
Tanzania	5,702	3,602	46	58	18	17	11	8	37	24
Thailand	32,354	167,056	23	11	29	40	22	29	48	49
Togo	1,136	981	27	38	25	21	8	9	48	41
Trinidad and Tobago	6,236	5,327	2	3	60	42	9	9	38	54
Tunisia	8,743	18,035	14	12	31	29	12	19	55	59
Turkey	68,790	164,789	26	16	22	31	14	21	51	53
Turkmenistan	..	3,917	..	..	..	..	..	..	..	..
Uganda	1,267	5,655	72	50	4	14	4	6	23	36
Ukraine	..	80,127	..	18	..	42	..	37	..	41
United Arab Emirates	29,625	39,107	1	2	77	57	4	8	22	40
United Kingdom	537,382	1,105,822	2	2	43	32	27	21	54	66
United States	2,708,150	6,952,020	3	2	34	26	22	18	64	72
Uruguay	10,132	17,847	14	9	34	26	26	18	53	65
Uzbekistan	..	21,590	..	33	..	34	..	18	..	34
Venezuela	69,377	75,016	5	5	46	38	16	17	49	56
Vietnam	..	20,351	..	28	..	30	..	22	..	42
West Bank and Gaza	..	..	..	..	..	..	..	..	..	..
Yemen, Rep.	..	4,790	..	22	..	27	..	14	..	51
Yugoslavia, Fed. Rep.	..	..	..	..	..	..	..	..	..	..
Zaire	14,391	..	25	..	33	..	14	..	42	..
Zambia	3,884	4,073	14	22	41	40	18	30	44	37
Zimbabwe	5,355	6,522	14	15	34	36	25	30	52	48
World	10,768,090 t	27,846,241 t	7 w	5 w	38 w	33 w	23 w	21 w	53 w	63 w
Low income	739,236 t	1,352,256 t	34 w	25 w	32 w	38 w	21 w	27 w	32 w	35 w
Excl. China & India	390,472 t	316,889 t	25 w	33 w	..	25 w	..	13 w	..	41 w
Middle income	2,461,307 t	4,033,376 t	..	11 w	..	35 w	..	18 w	..	52 w
Lower middle income	..	2,025,853 t	..	13 w	..	36 w	..	..	..	49 w
Upper middle income	989,317 t	1,981,511 t	8 w	9 w	47 w	37 w	20 w	18 w	43 w	53 w
Low & middle income	3,192,729 t	5,393,142 t	..	14 w	..	36 w	..	20 w	..	48 w
East Asia & Pacific	464,719 t	1,341,265 t	27 w	18 w	39 w	44 w	27 w	32 w	32 w	38 w
Europe & Central Asia	..	1,103,330 t	..	..	..	..	..	..	..	..
Latin America & Carib.	758,570 t	1,688,195 t	10 w	10 w	37 w	33 w	25 w	21 w	51 w	55 w
Middle East & N. Africa	463,031 t	..	9 w	..	57 w	..	7 w	..	32 w	..
South Asia	219,283 t	439,203 t	39 w	30 w	24 w	27 w	15 w	17 w	35 w	41 w
Sub-Saharan Africa	292,557 t	296,748 t	24 w	20 w	36 w	30 w	12 w	15 w	38 w	48 w
High income	7,758,074 t	22,485,548 t	3 w	2 w	37 w	32 w	24 w	21 w	58 w	66 w

a. Data prior to 1992 include Eritrea.

Aggregate measures of output by industrial origin are obtained by summing the value of the gross output of producers and subtracting from that sum the value of intermediate goods consumed in production. No allowance is made in such gross measures for depreciation of fabricated assets or for depletion and degradation of natural resources. This concept is known as value added. The gross domestic product of a country represents the sum of value added by all producers in that country. Since 1968 the U.N. System of National Accounts (SNA) has called for estimates of GDP by industrial origin to be valued at either basic prices (excluding all indirect taxes on factors of production) or producer prices (including taxes on factors of production, but excluding indirect taxes on final output), but some countries report such data at purchasers' prices—the prices at which final sales are made. This may affect estimates of the distribution of output. Total GDP shown here and elsewhere in the report is measured at purchasers' prices. Components are measured at basic prices. When GDP components are valued at purchasers' prices, this is noted in *Primary data documentation*.

While GDP by industrial origin is generally considered more reliable than estimates compiled from income or expenditure accounts, there are still many differences in the definitions, methods, and reporting standards that countries have adopted (see also box 4a). World Bank staff review the quality of national accounts data and sometimes make adjustments to improve consistency with international guidelines. Nevertheless, significant discrepancies remain between international standards and actual practice. Many statistical offices, especially those in developing countries, face severe limits in the resources, time, training, and budgets required to produce reliable and comprehensive series of national accounts.

Data problems in measuring output

Among the difficulties faced by compilers of national accounts is the extent of unreported or informal economic activity. In developing countries a large share of agricultural output is either not exchanged (because it is consumed within the household) or not exchanged for money. Financial transactions may also go unrecorded.

Often agricultural production must be estimated indirectly, using a combination of methods. This sometimes leads to crude approximations that can differ over time and across crops for reasons other than climatic conditions or farming techniques. Similarly, the inputs to agriculture, which cannot easily be allocated to specific outputs, are frequently "netted out" using equally crude and ad hoc approximations. For further discussion of the measurement of agricultural production, see the notes to table 4.3.

The output of industry ideally should be measured through regular censuses and surveys of firms. But in most developing countries such surveys tend to be infrequent and quickly go out of date, so many results must be extrapolated. Moreover, much of industrial production is organized not in firms but in unincorporated or owner-operated ventures that are not captured by surveys aimed at the formal sector. Even in large industries, where surveys are more likely to be conducted regularly, evasion of excise and other taxes lowers the estimates of value added. As countries move through the transition from state control of industry to private enterprise, such problems become more acute as new firms enter business and growing numbers of established firms fail to report. Following the SNA, output should include all such missing values as well as the value of illegal activities and other unrecorded, informal, or small-scale operations. Data covering these areas need to be collected using techniques other than conventional surveys.

For sectors dominated by large organizations and enterprises, such as public utilities, information on output, employment, and wages is usually readily available and reasonably reliable. But in the service sector the many self-employed workers and one-person businesses are sometimes difficult to locate and have little incentive to respond to surveys, let alone report their full earnings. Compounding these problems are the many forms of economic activity that go unrecorded, including the work that women and children do for little or no pay. For further discussion of the problems of using national accounts data, see Srinivasan (1994) and Heston (1994).

Dollar conversion

To produce national accounts aggregates that are internationally comparable, the value of output must be converted to a common currency. The World Bank conventionally uses the U.S. dollar and applies the average official exchange rate reported by the International Monetary Fund (IMF) for the year shown. When the official exchange rate is judged to diverge by an exceptionally large margin from the rate effectively applied to domestic transactions in foreign currencies and traded products, an alternative conversion factor is applied. Note that the three-year averaging technique (the World Bank Atlas method) applied to GNP per capita in table 1.1 is not used here.

● **Gross domestic product** at purchasers' prices is the sum of the gross value added by all resident and nonresident producers in the economy plus any taxes and minus any subsidies not included in the value of the products. It is calculated without making deductions for depreciation of fabricated assets or for depletion and degradation of natural resources.
● **Value added** is the net output of a sector after adding up all outputs and subtracting intermediate inputs. It is calculated without making deductions for depreciation of fabricated assets or for depletion and degradation of natural resources. The industrial origin of value added is determined by the International Standard Industrial Classification (ISIC), rev. 2. **Agriculture** corresponds to ISIC divisions 1–5 and includes forestry and fishing. **Industry** corresponds to ISIC divisions 10–45 and includes **manufacturing** (ISIC divisions 15–37). **Services** correspond to ISIC divisions 50–99.

National accounts data for developing countries are collected from national statistical organizations and central banks by visiting and resident World Bank missions. Data for industrial countries come from OECD data files (see OECD, *National Accounts, 1960–1994*, volumes 1 and 2). The complete national accounts time series is available on the *World Development Indicators* CD-ROM.

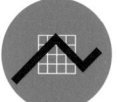

4.3 | Agricultural production

	Value added in agriculture		Agricultural production index		Food production index		Livestock production index	
	$ millions		1989–91 = 100		1989–91 = 100		1989–91 = 100	
	1980	1995	1980	1995	1980	1995	1980	1995
Albania	..	1,224	..	..	88	126	74	164
Algeria	3,466	4,267	70	113	72	114	52	111
Angola	..	463	98	103	92	104	87	104
Argentina	4,890	16,837	89	110	89	111	104	104
Armenia	..	879	..	..	..	..	..	..
Australia	8,454	9,710	83	111	84	117	89	107
Austria	3,423	4,330	94	99	94	99	93	102
Azerbaijan	..	1,281	..	..	..	..	..	..
Bangladesh	6,429	8,989	80	99	79	99	71	123
Belarus	..	2,475	..	..	..	..	..	..
Belgium	2,500	3,612	86 [a]	113 [a]	87 [a]	113 [a]	89 [a]	110 [a]
Benin	498	521	54	120	61	112	66	105
Bolivia	564	..	75	92	74	91	80	59
Bosnia and Herzegovina	..	..	..	..	..	..	..	..
Botswana	126	220	73	110	73	110	71	115
Brazil	23,385	84,725	74	116	74	119	74	127
Bulgaria	2,889	1,592	103	62	101	64	95	50
Burkina Faso	548	584	56	116	58	119	59	111
Burundi	530	508	77	95	78	96	91	94
Cambodia	..	1,421	59	94	60	92	30	132
Cameroon	1,933	3,105	83	108	82	111	62	107
Canada	10,005	..	79	111	79	110	89	108
Central African Republic	300	365	81	108	80	110	50	115
Chad	388	494	82	115	86	122	94	123
Chile	1,992	..	71	124	69	124	74	132
China	60,688	143,612	63 [b]	132 [b]	64 [b]	135 [b]	46 [b]	176 [b]
Colombia	6,466	7,485	76	100	73	102	68	101
Congo	199	223	81	105	79	105	78	110
Costa Rica	860	1,605	72	112	72	114	75	109
Côte d'Ivoire	2,633	3,030	71	108	70	114	75	118
Croatia	..	1,772	..	..	..	..	..	..
Cuba	..	..	83	64	85	62	90	73
Czech Republic	2,104	2,000	..	..	..	..	..	..
Denmark	3,161	4,765	82	106	82	106	95	112
Dominican Republic	1,336	1,654	87	99	84	102	69	116
Ecuador	1,423	2,138	75	105	76	102	67	121
Egypt, Arab Rep.	3,993	8,611	74	120	68	121	67	119
El Salvador	1,357	1,283	113	113	92	116	92	117
Eritrea	..	58	87	95	87	93	79	105
Estonia	..	284	..	..	..	..	..	..
Ethiopia	2,695 [c]	2,490	..	..	..	..	..	..
Finland	4,523	4,628	95	93	95	93	107	93
France	28,168	31,915	95	99	94	99	98	101
Gabon	290	387	80	105	80	105	86	104
Gambia, The	64	86	70	100	71	95	76	100
Georgia	..	1,531	..	..	..	..	..	..
Germany	16,791 [d]	..	90	87	90	87	99	83
Ghana	2,575	2,922	74	151	74	148	79	119
Greece	6,337	9,840	91	103	94	98	100	99
Guatemala	..	3,184	89	103	72	106	75	106
Guinea	..	890	91	123	94	123	87	106
Guinea-Bissau	47	118	67	113	67	114	78	111
Haiti	..	710	103	92	102	92	104	112
Honduras	544	701	87	102	89	100	88	108
Hong Kong	221	207	22	61	7	44	207	32

Agriculture's importance

Agriculture accounts for about 30 percent of GDP in South Asia, about 20 percent in East Asia and the Pacific and Sub-Saharan Africa, and about 10 percent in Europe and Central Asia and Latin America and the Caribbean. Even more striking regional differences are those in the relative size of the rural population. Rural people make up 70 percent of the total population in East Asia and the Pacific, South Asia, and Sub-Saharan Africa, about 50 percent in the Middle East and North Africa, but only 30 percent in Europe and Central Asia and Latin America and the Caribbean.

Increasing agricultural productivity, particularly for smallholders, can be a powerful factor in achieving poverty reduction, food security,

Food production in the low-income economies almost doubled between 1980 and 1995 ●

gender equity, and sustainable natural resource management. Nearly three-quarters of the world's poor live in rural areas, where they work as farmers, farm laborers, or artisans. Boosting agricultural productivity growth is particularly important in improving gender equity in countries with large rural populations, where as much as 80–90 percent of the female labor force works in agriculture.

Stronger agricultural growth is also critical for meeting the food needs of developing countries. In the next 30 years the world's population will increase by 2.5 billion. Most of this increase will take place in developing countries, doubling the demand for food. With land and water becoming increasingly scarce, growth in food supplies will have to come primarily from growth in yields rather than in cultivated area or irrigation. The challenge to more than double yields is enormous, and it will require major changes in international and domestic agricultural policies, institutional frameworks, and public expenditure patterns to support the development of high-productivity, environmentally sustainable production systems.

	Value added in agriculture		Agricultural production index		Food production index		Livestock production index	
	$ millions		1989–91 = 100		1989–91 = 100		1989–91 = 100	
	1980	1995	1980	1995	1980	1995	1980	1995
Hungary	..	2,794	96	71	95	71	96	68
India	59,102	86,628	67	114	66	114	62	117
Indonesia	18,701	34,046	67	112	66	112	51	122
Iran, Islamic Rep.	16,268	..	59	134	58	135	67	128
Iraq	..	..	79	106	80	107	82	78
Ireland	..	3,234	88	105	89	106	89	106
Israel	976	..	89	114	84	115	78	115
Italy	26,044	29,346	103	99	104	99	93	101
Jamaica	220	385	86	113	86	113	74	102
Japan	39,019	99,298	94	95	92	95	85	98
Jordan	..	412	70	136	70	137	51	166
Kazakstan	..	2,628	..	..	..	..	..	..
Kenya	2,019	2,267	65	104	66	102	60	97
Korea, Dem. Rep.	..	..	..	..	..	..	..	..
Korea, Rep.	9,250	26,759	74	116	72	116	54	138
Kuwait	52	114	110	122	108	122	118	128
Kyrgyz Republic	..	1,224	..	..	..	..	..	..
Lao PDR	..	684	69	119	69	118	64	145
Latvia	..	489	..	..	..	..	..	..
Lebanon	..	627	64	123	62	122	95	134
Lesotho	75	73	88	89	88	80	87	110
Libya	557	..	..	..	..	..	..	..
Lithuania	..	672	..	..	..	..	..	..
Macedonia, FYR	..	..	..	..	..	..	..	..
Madagascar	1,078	1,006	83	105	83	105	87	104
Malawi	413	547	81	111	90	107	81	106
Malaysia	5,365	11,110	66	116	55	123	41	140
Mali	950	1,070	72	111	75	112	93	110
Mauritania	202	224	85	98	85	98	89	91
Mauritius	119	324	78	106	77	107	63	133
Mexico	16,037	19,328	87	112	84	112	84	117
Moldova	..	1,636	..	..	..	..	..	..
Mongolia	231	..	86	77	85	76	91	80
Morocco	3,468	4,648	58	78	59	77	57	96
Mozambique	722	421	106	109	101	109	82	96
Myanmar	..	..	91	141	90	142	83	118
Namibia	241	360	112	107	109	106	117	111
Nepal	1,127	1,647	66	105	65	105	75	108
Netherlands	5,957	11,372	86	104	87	104	88	101
New Zealand	2,470	..	94	111	91	116	95	110
Nicaragua	497	618	105	107	102	110	122	98
Niger	1,080	855	103	117	103	118	110	114
Nigeria	24,673	16,584	61	132	61	132	86	137
Norway	2,221	..	93	101	93	101	95	101
Oman	152	..	59	92	60	91	62	90
Pakistan	6,279	14,133	62	121	66	125	59	131
Panama	..	766	83	106	83	106	71	111
Papua New Guinea	844	1,294	87	106	87	107	84	105
Paraguay	1,311	1,857	57	104	59	113	62	110
Peru	2,113	4,306	77	121	74	124	76	122
Philippines	8,163	16,069	88	115	89	116	75	143
Poland	..	7,640	84	84	84	85	101	78
Portugal	..	..	71	89	71	89	71	103
Puerto Rico	380	410	97	88	97	87	87	92
Romania	..	7,257	106	98	105	99	104	89
Russian Federation	..	21,641	..	..	..	..	..	..

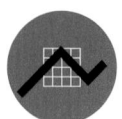

	Value added in agriculture		Agricultural production index		Food production index		Livestock production index	
	$ millions		1989–91 = 100		1989–91 = 100		1989–91 = 100	
	1980	1995	1980	1995	1980	1995	1980	1995
Rwanda	539	397	83	81	84	82	82	85
Saudi Arabia	1,675	..	30	90	30	89	34	110
Senegal	568	970	59	114	59	113	61	128
Sierra Leone	348	318	81	87	85	86	84	102
Singapore	150	146	156	43	156	43	176	42
Slovak Republic	..	982	..	..	..	..	..	..
Slovenia	..	789	..	..	..	..	..	..
South Africa	5,027	5,542	92	85	91	87	89	92
Spain	..	16,665	86	85	86	85	85	104
Sri Lanka	1,037	2,686	97	113	98	115	94	132
Sudan	2,097	..	102	124	103	124	91	111
Sweden	4,193	3,912	99	94	99	94	104	101
Switzerland	..	..	95	93	95	93	100	93
Syrian Arab Republic	2,642	..	98	127	103	129	72	94
Tajikistan	..	..	..	..	..	..	..	..
Tanzania	2,329	1,874	75	99	74	99	67	110
Thailand	7,519	18,290	81	110	83	108	69	118
Togo	312	372	68	102	76	101	49	116
Trinidad and Tobago	141	178	103	107	102	107	82	98
Tunisia	1,235	2,136	74	89	74	88	65	126
Turkey	17,215	23,530	76	106	75	106	79	104
Turkmenistan	..	..	..	..	..	..	..	..
Uganda	893	2,575	68	117	67	114	83	114
Ukraine	..	13,475	..	..	..	..	..	..
United Arab Emirates	223	773	49	147	48	148	42	134
United Kingdom	10,068	17,673	93	100	93	100	99	100
United States	68,300	109,100	90	109	90	109	89	112
Uruguay	1,371	1,584	85	108	86	111	86	109
Uzbekistan	..	5,627	..	..	..	..	..	..
Venezuela	3,363	3,998	77	119	78	120	82	125
Vietnam	..	5,606	62	124	62	122	52	125
West Bank and Gaza	..	..	102	141	102	141	50	136
Yemen, Rep.	..	952	77	113	76	113	71	119
Yugoslavia, Fed. Rep.	..	..	..	..	..	..	..	..
Zaire	3,646	..	73	100	72	101	76	108
Zambia	552	910	73	96	75	95	88	118
Zimbabwe	702	752	76	76	76	66	82	77

World	774,355 t	1,144,502 t	79 w	105 w	80 w	109 w	..	..
Low income	216,892 t	334,058 t	67 w	124 w	68 w	126 w	..	..
Excl. China & India	95,914 t	96,987 t	75 w	116 w	76 w	117 w	..	..
Middle income	..	401,957 t	82 w	88 w	81 w	98 w	..	..
Lower middle income	..	231,685 t	81 w	79 w	80 w	93 w	..	..
Upper middle income	74,283 t	174,944 t	82 w	108 w	81 w	109 w	..	..
Low & middle income	515,734 t	774,299 t	74 w	106 w	74 w	112 w	..	..
East Asia & Pacific	116,714 t	247,315 t	66 w	129 w	66 w	132 w	..	..
Europe & Central Asia	..	108,275 t	..	..	..	..	..	..
Latin America & Carib.	73,093 t	168,472 t	80 w	112 w	79 w	114 w	..	..
Middle East & N. Africa	37,790 t	..	68 w	115 w	67 w	116 w	..	..
South Asia	75,737 t	116,788 t	69 w	115 w	68 w	116 w	..	..
Sub-Saharan Africa	64,208 t	49,666 t	78 w	110 w	78 w	111 w	..	..
High income	265,206 t	414,416 t	91 w	103 w	91 w	103 w	..	..

a. Includes Luxembourg. b. Includes Taiwan, China. c. Includes Eritrea. d. Data refer to the Federal Republic of Germany before unification.

About the data

The agricultural production indexes here, prepared by the Food and Agriculture Organization (FAO), show the aggregate volume of agricultural production relative to the base period 1989–91. The FAO obtains data from official and semiofficial reports of crop yields, area under production, and livestock numbers. When data are not available, the FAO makes its own estimates. Market data on agricultural commodities are rarely sufficient to measure total production because significant amounts are not marketed. Estimates of crop yields and areas are subject to various sources of error that vary systematically over time across countries and by type of crop. Estimation practices vary from country to country but often involve rather coarse estimates based on outdated surveys applied to large crop districts. Allowances for feed, seed, and waste are generally based on fixed co-efficients and may not adequately reflect changes in seed varieties or harvesting practices (see Srinivasan 1994, pp. 6–9). Direct survey techniques, such as taking cutting samples at harvest time, generally yield better estimates. But such surveys are more difficult to administer, and if not carefully executed, the extrapolation of survey data into estimates of total production may be affected by excessive sampling error and nonrandom biases. Similarly, estimates of livestock products are often derived from baseline livestock censuses and then extrapolated using a sequence of assumptions about yields at each stage of processing. In a recent examination of food production data for South Asia, Evenson and Pray (1994) found that there has been some improvement in reliability but that further progress will require more resources and better measurement techniques.

The indexes are calculated using the Laspeyres formula: production quantities of each commodity are weighted by the average international commodity prices in the base period and summed for each year. Because the FAO indexes are based on the concept of agriculture as a single enterprise, estimates of the amounts retained for seed and feed are subtracted from the production data to avoid double counting. The resulting aggregate represents production available for any use except as seed and feed. The FAO indexes may differ from other sources because of differences in coverage, weights, concepts of production, time reference of data, the use of international prices, and methods of calculation.

To ease comparison among countries, the FAO uses international commodity prices to value production. These prices, expressed in international dollars (equivalent in purchasing power to the U.S. dollar), are derived using a Geary-Khamis formula for the agricultural sector (see Inter-Secretariat Working Group on National Accounts 1993, sections 16–93). This method assigns a single price to each commodity so that, for example, one metric ton of wheat has the same price regardless of the country in which it was produced. The FAO uses purchasing power parity (PPP) exchange rates for comparison of GNP or consumption expenditures across countries (see the notes to table 4.14). The use of international prices eliminates fluctuations in the value of output due to transitory movements of nominal exchange rates unrelated to the purchasing power of the domestic currency. Unlike the International Comparison Programme (ICP), the FAO calculates international prices only for agricultural products. Substantial differences may arise between the implicit exchange rate derived by the ICP and that of the FAO. For further discussion of the FAO's methods see FAO (1986).

Definitions

● **Value added in agriculture** measures the output of the agricultural sector (ISIC divisions 1–5) less the value of intermediate inputs. ● **Agricultural production index** shows the agricultural production for each year relative to the base period 1989–91. It includes all crops and livestock products except fodder crops. Regional and income group aggregates for the FAO production indexes are calculated from the underlying values in international dollars, normalized to the base period 1989–91. Missing observations have not been estimated or imputed. ● **Food production index** covers commodities that are considered edible and that contain nutrients. Coffee and tea are excluded because, although edible, they have no nutritive value. ● **Livestock production index** includes meat and milk from all sources, dairy products such as cheese, and eggs, honey, raw silk, wool, and hides and skins.

Data sources

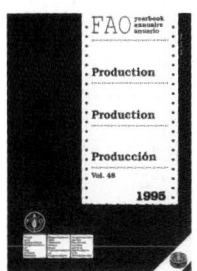 Data for value added in agriculture are from the World Bank's national accounts files. Agricultural production indexes are prepared by the FAO and published annually in its *Production Yearbook*. The FAO makes data available to the World Bank in electronic files that may contain more recent information than the published versions.

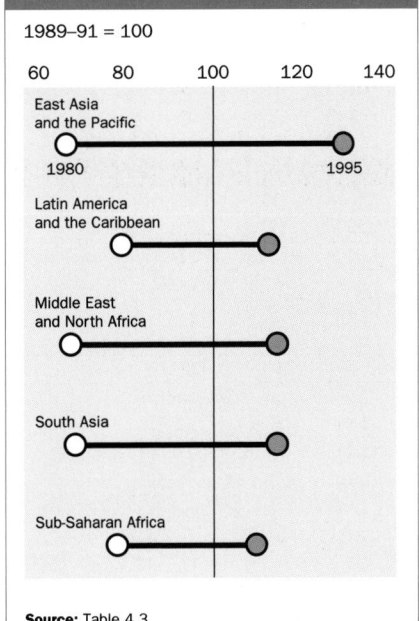

Figure 4.3a Food production, by region, 1980 and 1995

1989–91 = 100

Source: Table 4.3.

4.4 | Food crops

	Area under cereal production		Cereal yield		Cereal production		Roots and tubers production		Food aid in cereals		Cereal imports	
	thousand hectares		kilograms per hectare		thousand metric tons		thousand metric tons		thousand metric tons		thousand metric tons	
	1980	1995	1980	1995	1980	1995	1980	1995	1980–81	1994–95	1980	1994
Albania	373	258	2,362	2,547	881	657	99	70	..	34	44	270
Algeria	3,181	2,502	760	877	2,419	2,194	591	720	29	23	3,414	7,760
Angola	712	1,122	624	286	444	321	1,355	1,943	25	*217*	341	475
Argentina	9,924	8,150	1,866	2,878	18,521	23,456	2,092	2,410	..	..	8	28
Armenia	..	..	..	..	..	..	..	400	..	356	..	300
Australia	15,587	15,006	1,052	1,770	16,402	26,560	861	1,152	..	..	5	66
Austria	1,069	808	4,514	5,540	4,826	4,476	1,264	724	..	..	131	233
Azerbaijan	..	606	..	1,550	..	939	..	200	..	379	..	275
Bangladesh	10,818	10,699	2,006	2,424	21,698	25,931	1,708	1,864	737	888	2,194	952
Belarus	..	2,573	..	2,304	..	5,927	..	8,570	..	57	..	*1,250*
Belgium[a]	430	347	4,747	6,660	2,041	2,311	39	52	..	..	5,599	5,207
Benin	482	678	718	956	346	648	1,316	2,447	11	15	61	107
Bolivia	561	701	1,116	1,583	626	1,110	1,062	1,044	55	175	263	434
Bosnia and Herzegovina	..	252	..	2,845	..	717	..	377	..	..	..	..
Botswana	191	124	230	371	44	46	7	9	11	7	68	175
Brazil	21,081	19,832	1,576	2,504	33,217	49,653	26,310	29,009	3	33	6,740	8,971
Bulgaria	2,064	1,880	3,705	3,053	7,648	5,739	301	476	..	*156*	693	58
Burkina Faso	1,839	3,134	570	795	1,048	2,492	126	75	51	19	77	110
Burundi	204	209	1,064	1,287	217	269	1,030	1,326	12	48	18	105
Cambodia	1,447	1,359	1,256	1,374	1,818	1,867	202	60	133	64	195	58
Cameroon	1,032	936	864	1,346	892	1,260	1,634	2,080	10	2	140	226
Canada	19,319	18,373	2,141	2,705	41,365	49,693	2,478	3,774	..	..	1,383	1,022
Central African Republic	192	145	521	772	100	112	1,102	718	3	1	12	52
Chad	1,048	1,483	547	649	573	963	431	528	14	14	16	50
Chile	852	618	2,060	4,537	1,755	2,804	910	907	21	2	1,264	1,277
China[b]	95,054	89,361	2,948	4,664	280,262	416,796	149,508	152,813	..	..	17,061	16,331
Colombia	1,336	1,371	2,414	2,559	3,225	3,509	4,046	5,164	5	15	1,068	2,353
Congo	14	29	857	931	12	27	675	710	2	12	88	86
Costa Rica	119	66	2,924	2,424	348	160	45	181	1	2	180	453
Côte d'Ivoire	927	1,527	928	1,103	860	1,685	3,294	4,761	*1*	56	469	466
Croatia	..	655	..	4,220	..	2,764	..	500	..	*8*	..	82
Cuba	225	130	2,551	1,392	574	181	986	652	*2*	3	2,316	1,464
Czech Republic	..	1,577	..	4,184	..	6,598	..	1,330	..	..	..	287
Denmark	1,816	1,464	3,893	6,126	7,070	8,968	842	1,480	..	..	355	480
Dominican Republic	151	143	2,934	4,119	443	589	210	256	73	2	365	895
Ecuador	415	1,011	1,639	2,010	680	2,032	564	562	9	32	387	486
Egypt, Arab Rep.	1,978	2,841	4,095	6,048	8,100	17,182	1,394	1,734	1,865	179	6,028	9,200
El Salvador	428	440	1,706	2,030	730	893	26	107	50	7	144	448
Eritrea	..	296	..	517	..	153	..	109	..	140	..	281
Estonia	..	350	..	2,114	..	740	..	700	..	*231*	..	82
Ethiopia	..	5,478	..	1,505	..	8,245	..	2,018	..	720	..	928
Finland	1,171	978	2,823	3,408	3,306	3,333	736	798	..	..	367	130
France	9,894	8,301	4,854	6,458	48,025	53,606	6,618	5,754	..	..	1,570	1,228
Gabon	6	15	1,833	1,867	11	28	380	396	..	..	27	64
Gambia, The	62	89	1,274	1,213	79	108	6	6	16	2	47	97
Georgia	..	362	..	1,530	..	554	..	250	..	388	..	713
Germany[c]	7,738	6,589	4,228	6,051	32,713	39,870	17,146	10,382	..	..	9,500	3,321
Ghana	939	1,355	718	1,354	674	1,835	3,151	10,493	94	101	247	311
Greece	1,606	1,270	3,323	3,693	5,336	4,690	1,087	900	..	..	1,199	570
Guatemala	747	940	1,448	1,613	1,082	1,516	41	79	14	144	204	517
Guinea-Bissau	133	143	699	1,406	93	201	50	65	26	2	21	68
Guinea	759	722	955	1,071	725	773	636	801	34	29	171	384
Haiti	413	428	1,017	871	420	373	690	772	84	117	195	311
Honduras	421	500	1,131	1,542	476	771	18	30	36	73	139	278
Hong Kong	..	..	..	..	..	..	..	..	..	..	812	652

	Area under cereal production		Cereal yield		Cereal production		Roots and tubers production		Food aid in cereals		Cereal imports	
	thousand hectares		kilograms per hectare		thousand metric tons		thousand metric tons		thousand metric tons		thousand metric tons	
	1980	1995	1980	1995	1980	1995	1980	1995	1980–81	1994–95	1980	1994
Hungary	2,915	2,724	4,806	4,054	14,009	11,042	1,394	1,151	..	..	155	305
India	104,067	100,680	1,350	2,134	140,491	214,893	15,485	26,300	435	264	424	12
Indonesia	11,740	15,126	2,866	3,840	33,643	58,083	16,233	18,603	382	15	3,534	5,113
Iran, Islamic Rep.	8,045	9,796	1,067	1,767	8,583	17,312	1,339	3,200	..	54	2,779	5,450
Iraq	2,291	3,135	826	907	1,892	2,845	97	420	0	68	2,942	1,099
Ireland	444	272	4,651	6,658	2,065	1,811	880	620	..	..	553	444
Israel	131	115	2,313	2,200	303	253	173	288	10	..	1,601	2,311
Italy	5,111	4,225	3,521	4,666	17,995	19,713	2,945	2,076	..	..	7,629	6,014
Jamaica	4	3	1,750	1,333	7	4	214	337	37	46	469	335
Japan	2,724	2,342	4,843	5,737	13,192	13,437	5,416	5,157	..	..	24,473	29,937
Jordan	185	164	930	774	172	127	13	90	95	111	505	1,347
Kazakstan	..	18,763	..	564	..	10,583	..	1,950	..	60	..	100
Kenya	1,795	1,801	1,244	1,885	2,233	3,394	1,191	1,685	173	102	387	622
Korea, Dem. Rep.	1,611	1,548	3,130	3,386	5,042	5,241	1,920	2,050	..	..	510	310
Korea, Rep.	1,646	1,181	4,056	5,862	6,676	6,923	1,550	848	678	..	5,143	11,936
Kuwait	..	..	..	..	1	2	..	1	..	..	340	455
Kyrgyz Republic	..	546	..	1,432	..	782	..	431	..	19	..	120
Lao PDR	760	560	1,422	2,663	1,081	1,491	182	223	2	10	121	22
Latvia	..	382	..	1,835	..	701	..	927	..	390	..	65
Lebanon	26	40	1,731	1,925	45	77	136	222	43	7	678	577
Lesotho	203	61	956	672	194	41	18	62	44	15	107	99
Libya	..	..	..	..	..	..	..	..	..	..	908	1,790
Lithuania	..	1,141	..	2,191	..	2,500	..	1,594	..	77	..	19
Macedonia, FYR	..	242	..	3,000	..	726	..	154	..	..	..	133
Madagascar	1,331	1,401	1,681	1,984	2,238	2,780	2,302	3,375	27	26	110	140
Malawi	1,054	1,375	1,188	1,293	1,252	1,778	563	576	17	204	36	506
Malaysia	724	705	2,836	3,077	2,053	2,169	455	530	..	0	1,336	3,509
Mali	1,333	2,996	685	812	913	2,433	124	29	50	17	87	70
Mauritania	112	293	420	840	47	246	6	5	106	22	166	206
Mauritius	1	..	1,000	..	1	2	12	20	21	2	181	255
Mexico	9,542	10,289	2,189	2,463	20,887	25,344	1,156	1,252	..	44	7,226	8,100
Moldova	..	533	..	3,186	..	1,698	..	400	..	58	..	120
Mongolia	555	386	517	676	287	261	38	52	..	12	70	63
Morocco	4,429	4,021	1,019	453	4,515	1,823	544	783	120	13	1,821	1,678
Mozambique	1,113	1,727	596	653	663	1,127	3,715	4,310	155	320	368	496
Myanmar	5,261	6,985	2,599	2,962	13,673	20,690	190	244	7	5	16	49
Namibia	117	99	632	606	74	60	178	190	..	26	54	112
Nepal	2,248	3,031	1,687	1,795	3,792	5,440	348	984	45	21	56	62
Netherlands	224	196	5,692	8,112	1,275	1,590	6,267	7,363	..	..	5,246	6,676
New Zealand	192	149	3,938	5,738	756	855	229	282	..	..	63	316
Nicaragua	243	317	1,572	1,868	382	592	18	81	58	33	149	174
Niger	3,880	7,234	457	307	1,775	2,221	179	260	11	32	90	155
Nigeria	7,205	18,634	1,104	1,124	7,957	20,943	18,916	56,006	1	..	1,828	1,078
Norway	316	363	3,642	3,953	1,151	1,435	571	471	..	..	725	668
Oman	3	3	667	1,667	2	5	1	6	..	..	120	460
Pakistan	10,585	12,187	1,613	2,017	17,074	24,586	647	1,497	277	103	613	1,916
Panama	158	185	1,544	1,800	244	333	74	66	2	2	87	273
Papua New Guinea	2	2	2,000	1,500	4	3	1,122	1,267	..	0	152	275
Paraguay	306	523	1,510	2,166	462	1,133	2,147	2,708	11	1	75	31
Peru	640	813	1,816	2,635	1,162	2,142	2,319	3,369	116	348	1,309	2,289
Philippines	6,708	6,848	1,606	2,214	10,775	15,163	3,129	2,820	85	44	1,053	2,219
Poland	7,847	8,539	2,337	2,940	18,336	25,106	26,391	24,891	417	200	7,811	505
Portugal	1,104	701	1,275	1,863	1,408	1,306	1,268	1,477	255	..	3,372	2,351
Puerto Rico	1	..	6,000	..	6	1	40	10	..	..	..	..
Romania	6,469	6,194	2,994	3,210	19,367	19,885	3,942	3,020	..	75	2,369	529
Russian Federation	..	53,047	..	1,165	..	61,795	..	37,300	..	10	31,227	..

4.4 Food crops

	Area under cereal production		Cereal yield		Cereal production		Roots and tubers production		Food aid in cereals		Cereal imports	
	thousand hectares		kilograms per hectare		thousand metric tons		thousand metric tons		thousand metric tons		thousand metric tons	
	1980	1995	1980	1995	1980	1995	1980	1995	1980–81	1994–95	1980	1994
Rwanda	225	93	1,213	1,624	273	151	1,665	1,534	15	269	16	97
Saudi Arabia	453	815	587	4,196	266	3,420	4	170	..	..	3,061	6,182
Senegal	1,235	1,212	547	874	676	1,059	41	68	153	16	452	579
Sierra Leone	441	295	1,249	1,146	551	338	125	262	12	30	83	141
Singapore	..	..	..	..	..	..	2	..	..	..	1,324	776
Slovak Republic	..	859	..	4,107	..	3,528	..	442	..	..	..	201
Slovenia	..	113	..	5,044	..	570	..	430	..	3	..	512
South Africa	6,532	5,978	2,023	1,245	13,217	7,440	732	1,524	..	..	159	913
Spain	7,527	6,641	2,480	1,730	18,666	11,487	5,791	4,219	..	..	6,073	5,047
Sri Lanka	868	938	2,500	2,902	2,170	2,722	678	440	226	342	884	927
Sudan	4,261	8,071	670	473	2,857	3,821	293	156	195	132	236	1,022
Sweden	1,509	1,083	3,520	4,450	5,312	4,819	1,084	1,074	..	..	124	211
Switzerland	171	215	4,614	5,958	789	1,281	853	680	..	..	1,247	380
Syrian Arab Republic	2,702	3,686	1,437	1,665	3,884	6,136	292	553	44	59	726	952
Tajikistan	..	270	..	930	..	251	..	140	..	97	..	450
Tanzania	2,902	3,254	1,020	1,419	2,961	4,617	5,586	6,670	236	118	399	195
Thailand	10,786	10,630	1,911	2,386	20,612	25,358	16,940	18,382	26	3	213	740
Togo	465	674	637	691	296	466	914	865	4	8	41	69
Trinidad and Tobago	4	4	3,250	3,750	13	15	20	12	..	..	252	162
Tunisia	1,307	1,017	916	626	1,197	637	120	205	99	22	817	1,592
Turkey	13,163	14,242	1,855	1,977	24,419	28,163	3,002	4,750	9	2	6	878
Turkmenistan	..	565	..	2,211	..	1,249	..	11	..	50	..	940
Uganda	723	1,341	1,491	1,551	1,078	2,080	3,438	5,246	57	62	52	56
Ukraine	..	12,858	..	2,522	..	32,429	..	14,729	..	151	..	1,500
United Arab Emirates	1	1	5,000	7,000	2	7	1	4	..	..	426	759
United Kingdom	3,939	3,151	4,944	6,978	19,473	21,987	7,105	6,445	..	..	5,498	3,321
United States	71,629	59,614	3,771	4,647	270,122	276,999	14,285	20,764	..	..	199	7,363
Uruguay	552	564	1,618	2,645	893	1,492	159	208	..	..	45	277
Uzbekistan	..	1,658	..	1,691	..	2,803	..	500	..	..	..	4,100
Venezuela	808	793	1,915	2,576	1,547	2,043	603	655	..	..	2,484	2,015
Vietnam	5,992	7,154	2,016	3,523	12,080	25,205	6,613	5,077	150	64	1,160	387
West Bank and Gaza	..	..	..	..	..	..	..	..	..	..	..	..
Yemen, Rep.	851	756	1,016	1,091	865	825	136	200	34	91	..	..
Yugoslavia, Fed. Rep.	..	2,342	..	3,582	..	8,388	..	931	..	250	..	..
Zaire	1,113	2,123	799	799	889	1,697	13,748	18,358	77	83	350	253
Zambia	628	662	1,567	1,331	984	881	334	668	84	11	498	35
Zimbabwe	1,679	1,844	1,185	531	1,989	980	81	162	18	4	156	100
World	583,353 t	694,517 t	2,309 w	2,730 w	1,346,726 t	1,896,371 t	449,303 t	607,194 t	8,632 t	8,261 t	209,872 t	208,475 t
Low income	284,237 t	313,899 t	1,896 w	2,617 w	538,916 t	821,606 t	245,405 t	321,914 t	4,353 t	6,298 t	30,803 t	33,241 t
Excl. China & India	85,116 t	123,858 t	1,388 w	1,533 w	118,163 t	189,917 t	80,412 t	142,801 t	3,917 t	6,034 t	13,318 t	16,897 t
Middle income	145,369 t	248,426 t	2,014 w	2,100 w	292,764 t	521,848 t	125,190 t	209,044 t	3,331 t	1,963 t	100,198 t	87,905 t
Lower middle income	91,171 t	195,110 t	2,002 w	1,949 w	182,567 t	380,344 t	90,363 t	168,219 t	3,277 t	1,881 t	77,173 t	53,749 t
Upper middle income	54,198 t	53,316 t	2,033 w	2,654 w	110,197 t	141,504 t	34,827 t	40,825 t	53 t	82 t	23,025 t	34,156 t
Low & middle income	429,606 t	562,325 t	1,936 w	2,389 w	831,680 t	1,343,454 t	370,595 t	530,958 t	7,683 t	8,260 t	131,001 t	121,146 t
East Asia & Pacific	140,655 t	140,673 t	2,711 w	4,069 w	381,364 t	572,346 t	196,776 t	202,431 t	791 t	216 t	25,523 t	29,233 t
Europe & Central Asia	34,439 t	134,804 t	2,613 w	1,792 w	90,004 t	241,533 t	36,243 t	107,551 t	14 t	1,700 t	43,606 t	6,036 t
Latin America & Carib.	49,108 t	48,035 t	1,798 w	2,517 w	88,270 t	120,899 t	43,845 t	49,972 t	583 t	1,134 t	25,648 t	31,842 t
Middle East & N. Africa	25,492 t	28,776 t	1,254 w	1,827 w	31,979 t	52,628 t	4,674 t	8,320 t	2,328 t	481 t	23,881 t	38,211 t
South Asia	131,716 t	130,034 t	1,438 w	2,130 w	189,455 t	276,985 t	19,179 t	31,429 t	1,797 t	1,775 t	4,211 t	4,114 t
Sub-Saharan Africa	48,196 t	80,003 t	1,050 w	988 w	50,608 t	79,063 t	69,878 t	131,255 t	2,171 t	2,954 t	8,132 t	11,710 t
High income	153,747 t	132,192 t	3,350 w	4,183 w	515,046 t	552,917 t	78,708 t	76,236 t	949 t	..	78,871 t	87,329 t

a. Includes Luxembourg. b. Includes Taiwan, China. c. Data prior to 1990 refer to the Federal Republic of Germany before unification.

This table is concerned mainly with cereal production because cereals are widely produced and consumed as a primary source of nutrition. In countries where cereals are not extensively cultivated, roots and tubers are the principal alternatives. The indicators have been selected to show both the production of basic foodstuffs and the availability of grain through imports and, when countries cannot finance their import requirements, food aid.

The data on area under cereal production and on cereal yield and production relate to crops harvested for dry grain only. These data may be affected by a variety of reporting and timing differences. (See also the discussion in the notes to table 4.3.) The Food and Agriculture Organization (FAO) allocates production data to the calendar year in which the bulk of the harvest took place. But most of a crop harvested near the end of the year will be used in the following year. In general, cereal crops harvested for hay or harvested green for food, feed, or silage and those used for grazing are excluded. But millet and sorghum, which are grown as feed for livestock and poultry in Europe and North America, are used as food in Asia, Africa, and countries of the former Soviet Union.

Food aid in cereals is based on data for crop years (July through June) reported by donors and international organizations, including the International Wheat Council and the World Food Programme. Food aid information from donors may not correspond to actual receipts by beneficiaries during a given period because of delays in transport and recording or because aid sometimes is not reported to the FAO or other relevant international organizations. Aid receipts may also be omitted from customs reports of imports.

Cereal imports are generally based on calendar year customs data reported by the importing countries to the FAO. When official data are missing, the FAO uses estimates based on data from other sources. The FAO uses the Standard International Trade Classification (SITC), rev. 2, to categorize imports. Cereal imports include wheat flour. For further discussion of the classification of commodity imports see the notes to table 4.9.

- **Area under cereal production** relates to harvested area, although some countries report sown or cultivated area only. ● **Cereals** include wheat, rice, maize, barley, oats, rye, millet, sorghum, buckwheat, and mixed grains. Production data on cereals relate to crops harvested for dry grain only. Cereal crops harvested for hay or harvested green for food, feed, or silage and those used for grazing are excluded.
- **Roots and tubers** refer to potatoes, sweet potatoes, cassava, yams, taro, yautia, and arrowroot. Root crops grown principally for feed, such as turnips, mangels, and swedes, are not included. ● **Food aid in cereals** covers wheat and flour, bulgur, rice, coarse grains, and the cereal component of blended foods. The time reference for food aid is the crop year (July through June). ● **Cereal imports** are measured in grain equivalents and defined as comprising all cereals in Standard International Trade Classification (SITC), rev. 2, groups 041–046.

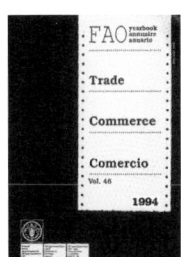

The data here come from the FAO. The most recent published source for commodity production data is the FAO's *Production Yearbook 1994*. Data on cereal imports come from the FAO's *Trade Yearbook 1994*. Data on food aid are published in the FAO's *Food Aid in Figures 1994*. The FAO makes data available to the World Bank in electronic files that may contain more recent information than the published sources.

4.5 | Key agricultural inputs

	Arable land		Irrigated land		Fertilizer consumption		Farm machinery		Share of labor force in agriculture	
	hectares per capita		% of arable land		hundreds of grams of plant nutrient per hectare of arable land		tractors		%	
	1980	1994	1980	1994	1980/81	1994/95	1980	1994	1980	1990
Albania	0.26	0.22	52.8	49.9	1,335	254	10,105	9,000	57	55
Algeria	0.40	0.29	3.4	6.9	314	153	47,000	98,799	36	26
Angola	0.49	0.34	2.2	2.1	49	29	10,250	10,300	76	75
Argentina	0.97	0.80	5.8	6.3	42	147	166,700	280,000	13	12
Armenia	..	..	..	..	..	..	13,000	16,000	21	17
Australia	3.01	2.65	3.4	4.5	263	352	327,000	315,000	6	5
Austria	0.22	0.19	0.2	0.3	2,491	1,685	320,100	343,000	10	8
Azerbaijan	0.32	0.27	61.4	50.0	..	195	35,300	32,000	35	31
Bangladesh	0.11	0.08	17.1	33.9	455	1,081	4,200	5,300	74	64
Belarus	0.66	0.61	2.6	1.6	..	995	117,200	123,000	26	20
Belgium	0.08 [a]	0.08 [a]	0.1 [a]	0.1 [a]	5,871 [a]	4,106 [a]	116,603 [a]	112,000 [a]	3	3
Benin	0.52	0.35	0.3	0.5	5	91	105	140	67	62
Bolivia	0.39	0.33	6.8	4.2	14	45	4,000	5,350	53	47
Bosnia and Herzegovina	..	0.18	..	0.3	..	55	..	29,000	28	11
Botswana	0.44	0.29	0.5	0.2	35	24	2,150	6,000	64	46
Brazil	0.41	0.32	3.3	5.9	855	933	545,205	735,000	37	23
Bulgaria	0.47	0.50	28.7	19.0	1,986	449	61,968	37,000	20	14
Burkina Faso	0.40	0.35	0.4	0.7	15	65	115	135	92	92
Burundi	0.29	0.19	0.8	1.2	9	26	90	170	93	92
Cambodia	0.32	0.39	4.8	4.5	39	33	1,350	1,365	76	74
Cameroon	0.80	0.54	0.2	0.3	46	43	572	500	73	70
Canada	1.86	1.56	1.3	1.6	424	490	657,400	740,000	7	3
Central African Republic	0.84	0.63	..	..	7	6	155	210	85	80
Chad	0.70	0.52	0.2	0.4	3	21	160	170	88	81
Chile	0.38	0.30	29.6	29.8	314	979	34,380	41,312	21	19
China[b]	0.10	0.08	45.4	51.5	1,530	3,088	747,893	709,654	76	74
Colombia	0.19	0.15	7.7	13.7	601	1,077	28,423	37,000	39	25
Congo	0.09	0.07	0.7	0.6	35	112	670	700	58	48
Costa Rica	0.22	0.16	12.1	23.8	1,453	2,585	5,950	7,000	35	26
Côte d'Ivoire	0.38	0.27	1.4	2.0	172	170	3,050	3,700	65	60
Croatia	0.36	0.26	..	0.2	..	1,482	5,438	4,006	24	15
Cuba	0.34	0.31	22.9	27.0	1,590	368	68,300	78,000	24	18
Czech Republic	..	0.33	..	0.7	..	887	..	60,000	13	11
Denmark	0.52	0.46	14.7	19.2	2,364	1,971	189,426	146,573	7	6
Dominican Republic	0.25	0.19	11.6	16.9	363	642	2,150	2,350	32	25
Ecuador	0.31	0.27	21.1	18.4	295	546	6,198	8,900	40	33
Egypt, Arab Rep.	0.06	0.06	100.0	100.0	2,714	2,433	36,000	78,099	61	43
El Salvador	0.16	0.13	15.2	16.4	832	1,325	3,300	3,430	43	36
Eritrea	..	0.15	..	5.4	..	..	..	850	..	79
Estonia	0.68	0.76	..	..	..	362	19,418	15,000	15	14
Ethiopia	..	0.20	..	1.7	..	42	..	3,000	86 [c]	80
Finland	0.54	0.51	2.3	2.5	1,908	1,484	212,000	230,000	12	8
France	0.35	0.34	4.6	7.6	2,972	2,418	1,473,600	1,440,000	8	5
Gabon	0.66	0.43	0.9	0.9	2	9	1,250	1,500	76	61
Gambia, The	0.25	0.16	0.6	1.2	127	47	45	45	84	82
Georgia	0.19	0.21	41.7	41.6	..	275	24,900	18,200	32	26
Germany[d]	0.16	0.15	3.7	4.0	4,126	2,419	1,613,502	1,300,000	7	4
Ghana	0.33	0.26	0.2	0.1	34	23	3,500	4,100	61	60
Greece	0.41	0.34	24.5	37.9	1,342	1,528	140,305	227,000	31	23
Guatemala	0.25	0.19	5.0	6.5	489	958	4,000	4,300	54	52
Guinea	0.16	0.11	12.8	12.7	4	15	150	290	91	87
Guinea-Bissau	0.35	0.33	6.0	5.0	7	18	16	19	86	85
Haiti	0.17	0.13	7.9	8.2	4	56	175	230	71	68
Honduras	0.48	0.35	4.1	3.6	162	281	3,250	4,900	56	40
Hong Kong	0.00	0.00	42.9	28.6	..	..	7	4	1	1

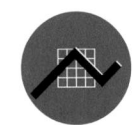

	Arable land		Irrigated land		Fertilizer consumption		Farm machinery		Share of labor force in agriculture	
					hundreds of grams of plant nutrient per hectare of arable land				%	
	hectares per capita		% of arable land				tractors			
	1980	1994	1980	1994	1980/81	1994/95	1980	1994	1980	1990
Hungary	0.50	0.49	2.5	4.2	2,624	631	55,452	36,200	18	15
India	0.25	0.19	22.9	28.3	329	797	382,869	1,257,630	70	64
Indonesia	0.18	0.16	16.5	15.2	451	848	9,240	55,608	59	57
Iran, Islamic Rep.	0.35	0.29	36.1	40.1	447	561	78,000	118,000	46	41
Iraq	0.42	0.28	32.2	44.3	170	654	23,350	32,000	28	16
Ireland	0.33	0.37	..	..	5,414	5,718	145,100	167,500	19	14
Israel	0.11	0.08	49.2	44.4	1,919	2,391	26,800	25,630	6	4
Italy	0.22	0.20	19.3	24.3	1,698	1,697	1,072,168	1,470,000	13	9
Jamaica	0.11	0.09	13.8	16.0	729	1,187	2,800	3,080	31	24
Japan	0.04	0.04	62.6	62.9	3,721	4,032	1,471,400	2,050,000	11	7
Jordan	0.16	0.10	11.0	15.8	427	346	4,561	7,634	24	21
Kazakstan	2.41	2.08	5.5	6.1	..	35	237,368	210,000	24	22
Kenya	0.26	0.17	0.9	1.5	144	305	6,546	14,000	83	80
Korea, Dem. Rep.	0.10	0.09	58.9	73.0	3,838	3,765	44,300	75,000	45	38
Korea, Rep.	0.06	0.05	59.5	65.0	3,657	4,672	2,664	80,000	37	18
Kuwait	0.00	0.00	100.0	100.0	4,400	2,000	25	100	2	1
Kyrgyz Republic	0.40	0.32	65.4	70.4	..	197	26,300	23,000	34	32
Lao PDR	0.22	0.19	16.7	17.2	58	23	464	890	80	78
Latvia	0.68	0.68	..	..	..	548	32,800	55,600	16	16
Lebanon	0.11	0.08	28.1	28.8	869	915	3,000	3,000	13	5
Lesotho	0.22	0.17	1.0	0.9	154	188	1,400	1,850	41	41
Libya	0.68	0.42	10.8	21.7	256	306	23,200	34,000	25	11
Lithuania	0.93	0.82	..	..	..	125	..	65,753	28	18
Macedonia, FYR	..	0.32	..	10.6	..	227	..	47,100	34	22
Madagascar	0.34	0.24	21.5	35.0	29	36	2,650	2,920	85	84
Malawi	0.22	0.18	1.4	1.6	250	214	1,200	1,420	88	95
Malaysia	0.35	0.39	6.7	4.5	944	1,586	7,430	38,926	41	27
Mali	0.31	0.26	2.9	3.2	69	84	830	840	93	93
Mauritania	0.13	0.09	25.1	23.6	67	192	270	330	72	55
Mauritius	0.11	0.10	15.0	17.0	2,492	2,754	325	370	27	17
Mexico	0.37	0.27	20.3	24.7	505	620	115,057	172,000	37	28
Moldova	0.55	0.50	9.9	14.3	..	528	50,300	53,300	43	33
Mongolia	0.71	0.56	3.0	6.1	69	42	9,700	11,700	40	32
Morocco	0.41	0.35	15.2	13.5	258	312	24,684	42,000	56	45
Mozambique	0.26	0.21	2.1	3.4	90	22	5,750	5,750	84	83
Myanmar	0.30	0.22	10.0	13.3	100	172	9,273	12,000	76	73
Namibia	0.64	0.44	0.6	0.9	..	..	2,550	3,150	56	49
Nepal	0.16	0.11	22.4	36.1	97	384	2,514	4,600	95	95
Netherlands	0.06	0.06	58.4	59.6	8,262	5,454	178,000	182,000	6	5
New Zealand	1.12	1.09	5.2	7.5	1,326	1,608	92,349	76,000	11	10
Nicaragua	0.45	0.31	6.4	6.9	435	244	2,200	2,700	39	28
Niger	0.64	0.41	0.6	1.8	8	3	96	180	93	91
Nigeria	0.43	0.30	0.7	0.7	57	120	8,600	11,900	55	43
Norway	0.20	0.21	9.1	10.8	3,174	2,297	130,700	148,100	8	6
Oman	0.04	0.03	92.7	92.1	259	1,587	95	150	50	48
Pakistan	0.25	0.17	72.3	80.3	532	1,023	97,373	283,300	62	56
Panama	0.28	0.26	5.0	4.8	551	481	5,458	5,000	29	26
Papua New Guinea	0.12	0.10	..	..	148	313	1,379	1,140	83	79
Paraguay	0.55	0.47	3.5	3.0	36	101	7,300	16,500	45	39
Peru	0.20	0.18	33.0	41.1	336	505	11,900	13,000	40	36
Philippines	0.18	0.14	14.0	17.2	383	655	10,533	11,500	52	45
Poland	0.42	0.38	0.7	0.7	2,339	976	619,353	1,310,690	30	27
Portugal	0.32	0.29	20.1	21.7	824	876	85,000	150,000	26	18
Puerto Rico	0.03	0.02	39.0	50.6	..	..	3,666	4,181	6	4
Romania	0.47	0.44	21.9	31.3	1,165	389	146,592	161,223	35	24
Russian Federation	0.98	0.89	3.7	4.1	..	116	1,324,000	1,147,500	16	14

	Arable land		Irrigated land		Fertilizer consumption		Farm machinery		Share of labor force in agriculture	
	hectares per capita		% of arable land		hundreds of grams of plant nutrient per hectare of arable land		tractors		%	
	1980	1994	1980	1994	1980/81	1994/95	1980	1994	1980	1990
Rwanda	0.20	0.19	0.4	0.3	1	9	84	90	93	92
Saudi Arabia	0.21	0.21	20.1	11.4	209	947	1,200	2,100	45	20
Senegal	0.42	0.28	2.6	3.0	83	85	460	550	81	76
Sierra Leone	0.15	0.12	4.0	5.4	36	56	317	550	70	67
Singapore	0.00	0.00	..	..	5,500	48,000	44	65	2	0
Slovak Republic	..	0.30	..	5.0	..	685	..	32,810	14	12
Slovenia	0.16	0.14	..	0.7	..	2,860	..	50,000	15	5
South Africa	0.45	0.33	8.5	9.6	803	631	172,725	125,885	17	14
Spain	0.55	0.51	14.8	18.2	811	916	523,907	789,747	19	12
Sri Lanka	0.13	0.11	28.0	29.2	882	1,131	24,263	33,000	52	49
Sudan	0.67	0.47	14.5	15.0	65	56	9,600	10,500	72	69
Sweden	0.36	0.32	2.3	4.1	1,624	1,148	181,000	165,000	..	..
Switzerland	0.07	0.06	6.1	5.8	4,409	3,364	94,717	114,000	6	6
Syrian Arab Republic	0.65	0.40	9.5	19.6	224	636	27,544	78,150	39	34
Tajikistan	0.22	0.15	69.3	83.5	..	814	31,700	30,000	44	41
Tanzania	0.15	0.12	4.2	4.3	125	114	10,000	6,600	86	84
Thailand	0.39	0.36	16.5	23.1	150	615	18,000	120,751	71	64
Togo	0.90	0.61	0.3	0.3	11	46	200	370	69	66
Trinidad and Tobago	0.11	0.09	18.1	18.0	688	492	2,350	2,650	11	11
Tunisia	0.74	0.56	5.2	7.8	132	180	25,800	27,500	39	28
Turkey	0.64	0.46	9.5	15.1	511	543	435,283	763,529	60	53
Turkmenistan	1.05	0.34	30.9	87.8	..	845	37,100	50,000	39	37
Uganda	0.44	0.37	0.1	0.1	1	4	2,600	4,700	89	93
Ukraine	0.71	0.66	5.7	7.5	..	349	408,837	436,713	25	20
United Arab Emirates	0.02	0.02	..	..	1,328	9,077	160	166	4	7
United Kingdom	0.12	0.10	2.0	1.8	2,936	3,837	512,494	500,000	3	2
United States	0.84	0.72	10.8	11.4	1,127	1,027	4,726,000	4,800,000	3	3
Uruguay	0.50	0.41	5.5	10.7	558	828	32,878	33,000	17	14
Uzbekistan	0.27	0.20	81.2	88.9	..	1,073	157,300	170,000	38	34
Venezuela	0.25	0.19	3.6	4.9	642	613	38,000	49,000	15	12
Vietnam	0.12	0.10	23.5	26.6	236	1,745	24,105	3,700	73	72
West Bank and Gaza	0.26	0.18	4.6	4.3	..	..	2,145	4,800	..	..
Yemen, Rep.	0.17	0.11	19.8	31.1	77	74	4,400	5,480	70	58
Yugoslavia, Fed. Rep.	..	0.39	..	1.8	..	230	..	414,889	39	29
Zaire	0.28	0.19	0.1	0.1	10	5	1,900	2,430	72	68
Zambia	0.89	0.57	0.4	0.9	154	112	4,640	6,000	76	75
Zimbabwe	0.37	0.27	3.1	4.1	676	593	16,717	19,500	74	69
World	**0.32 w**	**0.26 w**	**15.0 w**	**17.3 w**	**817 w**	**852 w**	**21,244,879 t**	**25,945,137 t**	**53 w**	**49 w**
Low income	0.21 w	0.16 w	24.8 w	27.8 w	522 w	1,022 w	1,553,073 t	2,613,438 t	73 w	69 w
Excluding China & India	0.30 w	0.22 w	15.8 w	17.1 w	161 w	296 w	422,311 t	646,154 t	72 w	67 w
Middle income	0.44 w	0.37 w	10.5 w	13.0 w	..	507 w	5,511,610 t	7,957,446 t	38 w	32 w
Lower middle income	0.45 w	0.38 w	10.9 w	13.6 w	..	424 w	4,206,993 t	6,106,698 t	41 w	36 w
Upper middle income	0.43 w	0.35 w	9.2 w	11.0 w	675 w	746 w	1,304,617 t	1,850,748 t	31 w	21 w
Low & middle income	0.29 w	0.23 w	17.0 w	19.7 w	591 w	740 w	7,064,683 t	10,570,884 t	63 w	58 w
East Asia & Pacific	0.14 w	0.11 w	32.2 w	34.8 w	1,027 w	1,976 w	888,118 t	1,049,457 t	73 w	70 w
Europe & Central Asia	0.75 w	0.63 w	8.3 w	9.8 w	..	319 w	3,984,991 t	5,628,963 t	27 w	23 w
Latin America & Carib.	0.38 w	0.30 w	9.8 w	12.3 w	541 w	647 w	1,101,134 t	1,517,156 t	34 w	25 w
Middle East & N. Africa	0.31 w	0.24 w	23.2 w	28.6 w	400 w	565 w	301,615 t	532,462 t	48 w	36 w
South Asia	0.23 w	0.18 w	27.8 w	34.1 w	346 w	803 w	511,989 t	1,584,670 t	70 w	64 w
Sub-Saharan Africa	0.40 w	0.28 w	3.7 w	4.1 w	145 w	135 w	276,836 t	258,176 t	72 w	68 w
High income	0.49 w	0.43 w	9.5 w	10.5 w	1,285 w	1,169 w	14,180,196 t	15,374,253 t	9 w	6 w

a. Includes Luxembourg. b. Includes Taiwan, China. c. Includes Eritrea. d. Data prior to 1990 refer to the Federal Republic of Germany before unification.

The Food and Agriculture Organization (FAO) collects data on agricultural inputs through annual questionnaires sent to participating governments. The FAO attempts to impose standard definitions and reporting methods, but exact consistency across countries and over time is not possible.

Comparative measures of the inputs to agriculture help in assessing differences in productivity and degree of modernization in the sector. However, levels of inputs and rates of application vary from country to country and over time depending on the type of crops, the climate and soils, and the production process used.

The FAO's definition of arable land includes land that is not under active cultivation. The calculation of arable land per capita is based on World Bank population estimates (see table 2.1). Available data on irrigated land do not distinguish the frequency, quantity, or method of irrigation. Fertilizer consumption measures the quantity of plant nutrients available for direct application and is calculated as production minus exports plus imports. Traditional nutrients—animal and plant manures—are not included. It should be noted that FAO measures of world exports and imports do not balance because of differences in reporting dates, time reference periods, and treatment of intermediate products.

Data on the labor force in agriculture should be used with caution. In many countries much of the agricultural employment is informal and unrecorded.

Definitions

● **Arable land** includes both land defined by the FAO as arable and land under permanent crops. The FAO defines arable land as land that is under temporary crops (double-cropped areas are counted once), temporary meadows for mowing or for pasture, land under market or kitchen gardens, and land temporarily fallow (less than five years). Land abandoned as a result of shifting cultivation is not included. ● **Irrigated land** is the area purposely provided with water, including land irrigated by controlled flooding. ● **Fertilizer consumption** measures the quantity of plant nutrients used per unit of arable land. Fertilizer products cover nitrogenous, potash, and phosphate fertilizers (including ground rock phosphate). The time reference for fertilizer consumption is the crop year (July through June). ● **Farm machinery** gives the number of wheel and crawler tractors (excluding garden tractors) in use in agriculture at the end of the calendar year specified or during the first quarter of the following year. ● **Share of labor force in agriculture** is the proportion of the total labor force recorded as working in International Standard Industrial Classification, rev. 2, major division 1 (agriculture, hunting, forestry, and fishing).

Data sources

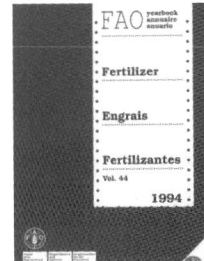

Data on arable land, irrigation, and farm machinery are published in the FAO's *Production Yearbook 1994*. Data on fertilizer consumption are published in the FAO's *Fertilizer Yearbook*. The FAO makes data available to the World Bank in electronic files that may contain more recent information than the published sources. Data on the share of the labor force in agriculture come from the International Labour Organisation's *Yearbook of Labour Statistics*.

4.6 Structure of manufacturing

	Value added in manufacturing		Food, beverages, and tobacco		Textiles and clothing		Machinery and transport equipment		Chemicals		Other manufacturing[a]	
	$ millions		% of total		% of total		% of total		% of total		% of total	
	1980	1994	1980	1994	1980	1994	1980	1994	1980	1994	1980	1994
Albania	..	..	..	..	..	..	..	..	..	..	..	..
Algeria	3,257	3,442	27	*13*	18	*14*	10	*15*	3	*5*	43	*54*
Angola	..	234	..	..	..	..	..	..	..	..	..	..
Argentina	22,685	56,500	19	..	13	..	19	..	9	..	41	..
Armenia	..	487	..	..	..	..	..	..	..	..	..	..
Australia	30,722	48,585	17	*18*	7	*6*	22	*20*	7	*8*	46	*48*
Austria	21,384	46,629	16	17	10	6	25	28	7	8	42	42
Azerbaijan	..	*2,559*	..	..	..	..	..	..	..	..	..	..
Bangladesh	1,422	2,536	24	..	43	..	4	..	16	..	14	..
Belarus	..	..	..	..	..	..	..	..	..	..	..	..
Belgium	28,515	..	17	17	8	8	24	24	11	14	40	37
Benin	112	114	59	..	14	..	..	..	6	..	21	..
Bolivia	449	..	28	*32*	11	*5*	4	*1*	3	*3*	54	*60*
Bosnia and Herzegovina	..	..	..	..	..	..	..	..	..	..	..	..
Botswana	36	160	..	..	..	..	..	..	..	..	..	..
Brazil	71,098	108,886	14	..	11	..	25	..	11	..	40	..
Bulgaria	..	..	..	*20*	..	*10*	..	*13*	..	*5*	..	*52*
Burkina Faso	261	357	59	..	19	..	3	..	1	..	17	..
Burundi	63	115	78	..	11	..	0	..	3	..	8	..
Cambodia	..	126	..	..	..	..	..	..	..	..	..	..
Cameroon	593	762	56	*26*	9	*12*	4	*1*	3	*8*	29	*54*
Canada	47,077	*81,478*	14	15	7	5	23	29	8	9	48	41
Central African Republic	54	..	49	..	22	..	8	..	11	..	10	..
Chad	..	*182*	..	..	..	..	..	..	..	..	..	..
Chile	5,911	..	27	30	9	6	6	6	8	11	51	47
China	81,836	203,589	10	*13*	18	*13*	22	*24*	11	*10*	38	*40*
Colombia	7,772	*9,893*	30	29	16	11	9	10	10	15	35	34
Congo	128	112	35	..	16	..	5	..	..	..	44	..
Costa Rica	899	1,547	46	*46*	10	*8*	8	*9*	7	*10*	28	*27*
Côte d'Ivoire	1,304	1,419	35	*35*	15	*11*	10	*7*	..	..	40	*47*
Croatia	..	2,491	..	*24*	..	*12*	..	*21*	..	*11*	..	*33*
Cuba	..	..	55	..	7	..	1	..	..	..	37	..
Czech Republic	..	..	..	..	..	..	..	..	..	..	..	..
Denmark	11,411	24,472	24	*23*	5	*4*	25	*23*	10	*12*	37	*38*
Dominican Republic	1,015	1,582	66	..	6	..	1	..	6	..	21	..
Ecuador	2,072	3,611	34	24	13	7	7	5	9	7	38	57
Egypt, Arab Rep.	2,678	5,782	19	*21*	30	*13*	11	*13*	9	*13*	31	*40*
El Salvador	589	..	37	*25*	22	*16*	4	*4*	11	*20*	27	*34*
Eritrea	..	38	..	..	..	..	..	..	..	..	..	..
Estonia	..	604	..	..	..	..	..	..	..	..	..	..
Ethiopia	275[b]	145	..	..	..	..	..	..	..	..	..	..
Finland	13,019	21,526	12	13	8	3	21	27	6	8	53	50
France	160,811	254,933	13	*15*	8	*6*	30	*29*	8	*9*	41	*41*
Gabon	195	435	24	..	4	..	9	..	4	..	58	..
Gambia, The	15	23	35	..	2	..	..	..	3	..	60	..
Georgia	..	459	..	..	..	..	..	..	..	..	..	..
Germany	..	..	..	..	..	..	..	..	..	..	..	..
Ghana	347	426	37	*36*	11	*5*	2	*2*	5	*10*	46	*47*
Greece	6,968	9,891	18	27	23	16	14	12	8	10	37	35
Guatemala	..	..	39	..	10	..	5	..	17	..	28	..
Guinea	..	157	..	..	..	..	..	..	..	..	..	..
Guinea-Bissau	..	18	..	..	..	..	..	..	..	..	..	..
Haiti	..	152	..	..	..	..	..	..	..	..	..	..
Honduras	344	501	51	*49*	9	*12*	2	*2*	5	*5*	34	*33*
Hong Kong	6,392	11,456	5	*10*	42	*35*	18	*22*	2	2	34	*31*

	Value added in manufacturing		Food, beverages, and tobacco		Textiles and clothing		Machinery and transport equipment		Chemicals		Other manufacturing[a]	
	$ millions		% of total		% of total		% of total		% of total		% of total	
	1980	1994	1980	1994	1980	1994	1980	1994	1980	1994	1980	1994
Hungary	..	8,066	11	21	11	8	28	19	11	10	38	42
India	27,422	47,288	9	11	21	13	25	25	14	19	30	32
Indonesia	10,133	41,186	32	26	14	15	13	12	11	10	30	36
Iran, Islamic Rep.	8,567	15,363	15	16	19	12	12	19	5	10	49	41
Iraq	..	..	..	13	..	9	..	8	..	11	..	60
Ireland	..	..	29	27	8	3	17	30	14	21	32	20
Israel	..	..	12	..	12	..	26	..	8	..	42	..
Italy	125,881	210,392	9	10	12	13	29	33	11	6	39	38
Jamaica	446	733	..	..	..	..	..	..	..	..	..	..
Japan	309,747	1,146,205	9	10	7	4	33	38	9	10	43	38
Jordan	..	651	23	27	7	6	1	4	7	16	62	48
Kazakstan	..	2,455	..	..	..	..	..	..	..	..	..	..
Kenya	796	645	34	42	12	9	15	10	9	9	30	30
Korea, Dem. Rep.	..	..	..	..	..	..	..	..	..	..	..	..
Korea, Rep.	18,260	102,049	17	10	19	12	17	34	10	9	36	36
Kuwait	1,581	2,616	7	8	5	7	4	7	7	2	76	76
Kyrgyz Republic	..	..	..	..	..	..	..	..	..	..	..	..
Lao PDR	..	179	..	..	..	..	..	..	..	..	..	..
Latvia	..	1,030	..	..	..	..	..	..	..	..	..	..
Lebanon	..	850	..	..	..	..	..	..	..	..	..	..
Lesotho	21	122	73	..	7	..	..	..	4	..	16	..
Libya	682	..	31	..	10	..	..	..	16	..	43	..
Lithuania	..	1,527	..	..	..	..	..	..	..	..	..	..
Macedonia, FYR	..	..	..	29	..	23	..	15	..	4	..	29
Madagascar	..	335	34	..	45	..	3	..	6	..	13	..
Malawi	129	215	58	..	12	..	4	..	5	..	20	..
Malaysia	5,054	22,387	24	9	7	6	20	36	5	10	43	39
Mali	70	119	29	..	51	..	8	..	..	..	11	..
Mauritania	..	106	..	..	..	..	..	..	..	..	..	..
Mauritius	147	694	36	32	30	45	6	2	6	4	23	16
Mexico	43,089	74,233	..	24	..	4	..	26	..	16	..	30
Moldova	..	913	..	..	..	..	..	..	..	..	..	..
Mongolia	..	..	..	37	..	48	..	1	..	1	..	13
Morocco	3,167	5,343	..	..	..	..	..	..	..	..	..	..
Mozambique	..	..	..	..	..	..	..	..	..	..	..	..
Myanmar	..	..	..	..	..	..	..	..	..	..	..	..
Namibia	90	234	..	..	..	..	..	..	..	..	..	..
Nepal	78	362	..	..	..	..	..	..	..	..	..	..
Netherlands	30,866	58,531	..	24	..	3	..	24	..	14	..	36
New Zealand	4,950	7,345	26	27	11	8	17	14	6	6	40	45
Nicaragua	549	304	53	..	8	..	1	..	10	..	28	..
Niger	94	..	30	..	25	..	2	..	16	..	28	..
Nigeria	7,229	3,607	21	..	13	..	13	..	13	..	39	..
Norway	9,239	..	15	23	4	2	27	26	7	8	48	40
Oman	39	495	..	..	..	..	..	..	..	..	..	..
Pakistan	3,389	8,214	32	..	22	..	9	..	12	..	25	..
Panama	..	..	49	47	10	7	2	2	6	8	34	35
Papua New Guinea	242	421	40	..	1	..	16	..	3	..	41	..
Paraguay	733	1,230	38	..	12	..	1	..	3	..	46	..
Peru	4,176	11,603	25	..	13	..	13	..	10	..	40	..
Philippines	8,354	14,917	30	31	13	11	12	14	14	16	31	28
Poland	..	..	12	31	17	8	32	19	8	7	31	35
Portugal	..	..	13	..	22	..	16	..	7	..	42	..
Puerto Rico	5,306	14,132	..	17	..	5	..	13	..	52	..	14
Romania	..	..	..	22	..	13	..	10	..	8	..	47
Russian Federation	..	97,357	..	20	..	9	..	15	..	10	..	46

	Value added in manufacturing		Food, beverages, and tobacco		Textiles and clothing		Machinery and transport equipment		Chemicals		Other manufacturing[a]	
	$ millions		% of total		% of total		% of total		% of total		% of total	
	1980	1994	1980	1994	1980	1994	1980	1994	1980	1994	1980	1994
Rwanda	172	18	..	..	..	..	..	..	..	..	..	..
Saudi Arabia	7,740	..	..	..	..	..	..	..	..	..	..	..
Senegal	456	479	50	58	19	2	4	3	8	14	20	23
Sierra Leone	54	48	51	69	5	1	..	..	..	..	44	30
Singapore	3,415	18,119	5	4	5	2	44	58	5	9	41	28
Slovak Republic	..	..	..	..	..	..	..	..	..	..	..	..
Slovenia	..	152	..	18	..	18	..	19	..	11	..	33
South Africa	16,607	25,298	12	15	9	8	21	19	9	10	48	48
Spain	..	120,931	16	19	12	7	23	25	9	11	41	38
Sri Lanka	668	1,629	32	48	14	23	6	2	6	8	42	19
Sudan	424	521	..	..	..	..	..	..	..	..	..	..
Sweden	26,293	38,821	10	10	3	2	33	37	7	11	47	41
Switzerland	..	..	..	10	..	3	..	32	..	..	..	55
Syrian Arab Republic	..	..	..	25	..	31	..	..	..	..	..	44
Tajikistan	..	..	..	..	..	..	..	..	..	..	..	..
Tanzania	555	242	23	..	33	..	8	..	6	..	30	..
Thailand	6,960	40,791	55	..	8	..	9	..	7	..	21	..
Togo	89	86	47	..	13	..	..	..	8	..	32	..
Trinidad and Tobago	557	444	22	35	4	2	9	4	4	20	61	38
Tunisia	1,030	2,863	18	19	19	22	7	6	15	5	42	46
Turkey	9,333	24,076	18	17	15	13	14	20	10	9	42	41
Turkmenistan	..	..	..	..	..	..	..	..	..	..	..	..
Uganda	53	242	..	..	..	..	..	..	..	..	..	..
Ukraine	..	34,232	..	..	..	..	..	..	..	..	..	..
United Arab Emirates	1,130	2,967	12	..	2	..	2	..	7	..	77	..
United Kingdom	125,830	185,594	13	14	6	5	33	31	10	13	38	37
United States	593,000	1,126,200	11	13	6	5	34	32	10	12	40	39
Uruguay	2,627	2,998	28	..	17	..	10	..	7	..	38	..
Uzbekistan	..	3,196	..	..	..	..	..	..	..	..	..	..
Venezuela	11,104	9,946	19	22	7	2	9	10	8	11	57	54
Vietnam	..	2,760	..	..	..	..	..	..	..	..	..	..
West Bank and Gaza	..	..	..	..	..	..	..	..	..	..	..	..
Yemen, Rep.	..	606	..	..	..	..	..	..	..	..	..	..
Yugoslavia, Fed. Rep.	..	..	..	..	..	..	..	..	..	..	..	..
Zaire	2,064	..	..	..	..	..	..	..	..	..	..	..
Zambia	718	1,026	44	..	13	..	9	..	9	..	25	..
Zimbabwe	1,248	1,477	23	31	17	15	8	7	9	5	42	42
World	**2,472,383 t**	**5,012,380 t**	..	..	..	..	..	..	..	..	..	..
Low income	151,808 t	294,045 t	..	..	..	..	..	..	..	..	..	..
Excl. China & India	..	38,690 t	..	..	..	..	..	..	..	..	..	..
Middle income	..	687,018 t	..	..	..	..	..	..	..	..	..	..
Lower middle income	..	..	..	..	..	..	..	..	..	..	..	..
Upper middle income	197,307 t	345,007 t	..	..	..	..	..	..	..	..	..	..
Low & middle income	..	963,642 t	..	..	..	..	..	..	..	..	..	..
East Asia & Pacific	124,518 t	341,881 t	..	..	..	..	..	..	..	..	..	..
Europe & Central Asia	..	..	..	..	..	..	..	..	..	..	..	..
Latin America & Carib.	186,165 t	312,017 t	..	..	..	..	..	..	..	..	..	..
Middle East & N. Africa	32,557 t	52,699 t	..	..	..	..	..	..	..	..	..	..
South Asia	33,695 t	61,355 t	..	..	..	..	..	..	..	..	..	..
Sub-Saharan Africa	36,114 t	40,925 t	..	..	..	..	..	..	..	..	..	..
High income	1,890,070 t	4,080,236 t	..	..	..	..	..	..	..	..	..	..

a. Includes unallocated data. b. Includes Eritrea.

Figure 4.6a Five largest developing manufacturing economies, 1994

share of value added in manufacturing for developing economies

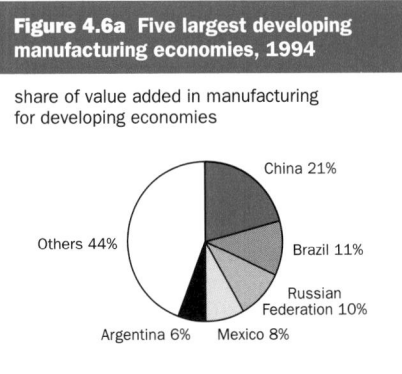

China 21%

Brazil 11%

Russian Federation 10%

Mexico 8%

Argentina 6%

Others 44%

Source: Table 4.6.

Figure 4.6b Shares of manufactured goods produced, by income group, 1994

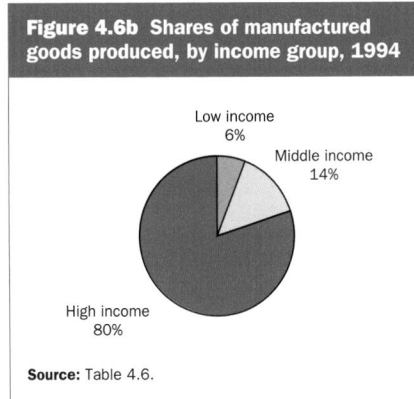

Low income 6%

Middle income 14%

High income 80%

Source: Table 4.6.

About the data

Data on the distribution of manufacturing value added by industry are provided by the United Nations Industrial Development Organization (UNIDO). The classification of manufacturing industries is in accordance with the United Nations International Standard Industrial Classification (ISIC), rev. 2. Manufacturing comprises all of ISIC major division 3.

UNIDO obtains data on manufacturing value added from a variety of national and international sources, including the Statistical Division of the United Nations Secretariat, the World Bank, the Organization for Economic Cooperation and Development, and the International Monetary Fund. To improve comparability of the data over time and across countries, UNIDO supplements originally reported data with information from industrial censuses, statistics supplied by national and international organizations, unpublished data that it collects in the field, and estimates by the UNIDO Secretariat. Nevertheless, coverage may be less than complete, particularly for the informal sector. To the extent that direct information on inputs and outputs is not available, estimates may be employed that may result in errors in industry totals. And there remain differences among countries in the reference period (calendar or fiscal year) and the valuation method (basic, producers', or purchaser prices) used in estimating value added. See also the notes to table 4.2.

Data on manufacturing value added in U.S. dollars are from the World Bank's national accounts files. These figures may differ from those used by UNIDO to calculate the shares of value added by industry. Thus estimates of value added in a particular industry group calculated by applying the shares to total value added will not match those found in UNIDO sources.

Definitions

● **Value added in manufacturing** is the sum of gross output, less the value of intermediate goods consumed in production, for industries classified in ISIC major division 3. ● **Food, beverages, and tobacco** comprise ISIC division 31. ● **Textiles and clothing** comprise division 32. ● **Machinery and transport equipment** comprise groups 382–84. ● **Chemicals** comprise groups 351 and 352. ● **Other manufacturing** includes wood and related products (division 33), paper and paper-related products (division 34), petroleum and related products (groups 353–56), basic metals and mineral products (divisions 36 and 37), fabricated metal products and professional goods (groups 381 and 385), and other industries (group 390). When data for textiles, machinery, or chemicals are shown as not available, they are included in other manufacturing.

Data sources

Data on value added in manufacturing in U.S. dollars are from the World Bank's national accounts files. The data used to calculate share of value added by industry are provided to the World Bank in electronic files by UNIDO. The most recent published source is UNIDO's *International Yearbook of Industrial Statistics 1996*.

4.7 | Growth of merchandise trade

	Export volume		Import volume		Export value		Import value		Net barter terms of trade		Income terms of trade	
	average annual % growth		average annual % growth		average annual % growth		average annual % growth		1987 = 100		1987 = 100	
	1980–90	1990–95	1980–90	1990–95	1980–90	1990–95	1980–90	1990–95	1980	1995	1980	1995
Albania	..	..	..	..	–1.7	0.5	1.0	13.3	..	..	..	..
Algeria	2.5	–0.8	–5.1	–5.7	–4.0	–9.7	–3.0	0.0	171	83	171	105
Angola	11.3	4.2	–3.4	–4.1	6.4	–3.6	–1.2	2.2	149	86	89	115
Argentina	3.1	–1.0	–8.6	45.8	2.1	10.5	–6.5	36.8	142	120	131	177
Armenia	..	..	..	..	..	..	..	..	..	..	..	..
Australia	5.8	8.1	4.9	5.1	6.6	5.2	6.4	7.9	123	101	84	161
Austria	6.4	3.9	5.8	1.9	10.2	1.6	8.7	2.0	93	93	68	149
Azerbaijan	..	..	..	..	..	..	..	..	..	..	..	..
Bangladesh	7.5	12.7	1.8	5.3	7.5	14.2	3.7	12.0	121	94	73	184
Belarus	..	..	..	..	..	..	..	..	..	..	..	..
Belgium[a]	4.4	4.2	4.0	0.3	7.8	2.5	..	..	96	101	76	139
Benin	7.7	–0.3	–6.3	29.4	9.9	31.4	–4.9	24.3	108	110	55	137
Bolivia	1.7	–5.4	–2.8	18.9	–1.9	4.3	–0.3	13.4	173	67	172	108
Bosnia and Herzegovina	..	..	..	..	..	..	..	..	..	..	..	..
Botswana	11.4	–0.8	7.7	–5.6	17.9	2.6	9.4	–1.9	99	152	32	96
Brazil	6.1	6.6	–1.5	8.5	5.1	9.0	–1.9	18.3	111	101	68	134
Bulgaria	..	..	..	..	4.4	–12.6	4.2	–10.4	..	..	..	..
Burkina Faso	5.4	1.3	2.1	8.3	7.2	–2.3	3.8	–2.3	102	103	69	84
Burundi	7.4	–4.8	1.4	–14.6	2.6	6.4	2.3	–0.9	133	52	75	62
Cambodia	..	..	..	..	..	50.1	..	41.0	..	..	..	..
Cameroon	4.5	–1.7	–1.4	–11.2	2.5	1.8	0.6	–5.2	145	79	176	202
Canada	5.7	8.4	6.2	6.3	6.8	8.7	7.9	6.8	113	100	77	167
Central African Republic	2.5	3.5	6.0	–3.3	3.3	8.6	7.6	4.9	116	91	92	86
Chad	5.4	–10.0	10.5	–12.1	9.4	–7.3	12.6	–8.4	87	103	66	104
Chile	5.7	10.5	1.4	14.5	8.0	12.0	2.7	14.9	120	94	88	153
China[†]	11.4	14.3	10.0	24.8	12.9	19.1	13.5	20.7	115	105	52	199
Colombia	9.7	4.8	–1.9	22.3	7.8	6.8	0.0	24.3	131	80	85	146
Congo	5.5	9.7	–2.0	2.5	0.4	–0.2	–0.5	3.2	142	93	92	96
Costa Rica	4.9	10.1	2.8	15.1	4.6	12.2	4.5	12.3	123	92	86	154
Côte d'Ivoire	3.3	–7.5	–4.0	5.4	1.7	3.5	–1.4	3.0	128	81	101	70
Croatia	..	..	..	..	..	3.8	..	12.2	..	..	..	..
Cuba	–1.1	–36.9	–0.4	–34.0	–0.9	–33.2	1.7	–29.0	136	109	102	20
Czech Republic	..	..	..	..	..	..	..	..	..	..	..	..
Denmark	4.4	5.4	3.6	3.4	8.5	5.9	6.3	4.5	91	100	68	151
Dominican Republic	–1.0	–10.2	2.6	8.9	–2.1	0.0	3.3	7.9	143	123	126	64
Ecuador	3.0	8.9	–3.9	10.0	–0.4	9.4	–1.4	16.6	147	71	137	129
Egypt, Arab Rep.	–0.2	–0.1	–0.7	–2.9	–3.7	2.7	1.4	5.8	142	95	147	94
El Salvador	–2.8	13.0	1.3	16.2	–4.6	12.1	2.4	18.7	158	89	155	108
Eritrea	..	..	..	..	..	..	..	..	..	..	..	..
Estonia	..	..	..	..	..	57.9	..	80.2	..	..	..	..
Ethiopia[b]	1.2	–9.4	3.3	–3.3	–0.8	11.9	4.3	4.3	145	74	116	49
Finland	2.3	8.7	4.4	–1.9	7.4	8.1	6.9	0.6	86	95	72	132
France	4.1	2.3	5.0	0.8	7.6	4.5	6.5	1.8	90	106	74	155
Gabon	0.6	5.7	–2.0	2.0	–3.3	2.0	1.1	–0.9	152	90	172	151
Gambia, The	2.3	26.9	1.0	9.0	1.2	–14.8	2.8	–5.1	123	111	75	113
Georgia	..	..	..	..	..	..	..	..	..	..	..	..
Germany[c]	4.6	2.2	4.9	2.9	9.2	3.8	7.1	3.7	86	96	65	138
Ghana	3.9	9.1	1.6	12.8	0.3	7.3	2.8	8.6	156	64	126	95
Greece	5.1	11.9	5.8	12.8	5.8	2.7	6.6	1.8	98	111	65	155
Guatemala	–1.3	8.2	–0.6	19.3	–2.2	11.6	0.6	13.7	142	93	151	120
Guinea	–3.6	–8.6	–2.9	–2.8	4.0	–4.1	9.9	–1.1	150	91	170	88
Guinea-Bissau	–5.1	–18.3	1.3	–5.4	3.8	9.5	3.6	–1.1	37	92	93	83
Haiti	–2.9	–11.2	–4.4	–6.8	–1.3	–10.6	–2.9	6.6	92	52	99	28
Honduras	1.3	10.7	–1.0	7.0	1.6	4.2	0.6	5.0	122	77	105	89
Hong Kong	15.4	15.3	11.0	15.8	16.8	15.9	15.0	18.1	116	87	47	211
†Data for Taiwan, China	11.6	5.9	12.8	14.1	14.8	9.5	12.3	12.7	78	112	32	144

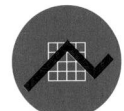

	Export volume		Import volume		Export value		Import value		Net barter terms of trade		Income terms of trade	
	average annual % growth		average annual % growth		average annual % growth		average annual % growth		1987 = 100		1987 = 100	
	1980–90	1990–95	1980–90	1990–95	1980–90	1990–95	1980–90	1990–95	1980	1995	1980	1995
Hungary	3.0	–1.8	0.7	7.9	1.7	3.6	0.1	10.9	112	97	87	96
India	6.3	7.0	4.5	2.7	7.2	11.5	4.2	8.0	96	150	68	314
Indonesia	5.3	21.3	1.2	9.1	–0.3	11.7	2.6	11.5	146	79	126	187
Iran, Islamic Rep.	7.4	10.2	–4.0	15.7	2.5	–0.6	0.1	–11.0	191	90	130	130
Iraq	0.2	–55.2	–13.2	–28.9	–5.9	–45.0	–11.1	–35.1	163	93	301	..
Ireland	9.3	11.4	4.7	5.6	12.7	12.7	7.0	8.4	93	90	52	211
Israel	5.9	10.0	4.6	12.3	8.3	11.0	5.9	11.5	95	109	59	178
Italy	4.3	6.0	5.3	–1.7	8.7	5.4	6.9	0.3	85	107	65	158
Jamaica	1.2	1.3	3.1	7.0	0.7	4.2	2.9	9.9	122	105	120	136
Japan	5.0	0.4	6.5	4.0	9.0	8.7	5.1	6.7	65	127	46	158
Jordan	7.4	7.1	–3.1	13.0	6.1	9.8	–1.9	8.1	133	128	59	159
Kazakstan	..	..	..	..	..	..	..	..	..	..	..	..
Kenya	2.6	16.6	1.1	–5.6	–1.1	12.5	1.5	6.5	136	98	122	161
Korea, Dem. Rep.	..	..	..	..	..	..	..	..	..	..	..	..
Korea, Rep.	13.7	7.4	11.2	7.7	15.0	12.8	11.9	12.1	94	102	34	216
Kuwait	–2.0	42.3	–6.3	23.0	–7.6	35.3	–4.1	13.3	156	88	246	105
Kyrgyz Republic	..	..	..	..	..	..	..	..	..	..	..	..
Lao PDR	..	..	..	..	10.3	38.5	20.3	29.3	..	..	..	..
Latvia	..	..	..	..	..	..	..	..	..	..	..	..
Lebanon	–1.2	–7.8	–7.4	23.5	–3.6	13.7	–5.4	19.4	125	95	147	93
Lesotho	..	..	..	..	3.4	27.5	1.8	4.9	..	..	..	..
Libya	0.2	–11.0	–6.4	7.7	–7.2	–16.5	–4.2	–0.1	189	93	257	74
Lithuania	..	..	..	..	..	..	..	65.0	..	..	..	..
Macedonia, FYR	..	..	..	..	..	4.0	..	4.2	..	..	..	..
Madagascar	–0.1	–6.8	–4.6	–5.6	–1.1	4.8	–2.8	–2.2	121	82	124	68
Malawi	0.1	–1.8	1.3	–1.6	2.0	–8.5	3.2	–5.7	96	87	109	100
Malaysia	11.5	17.8	6.0	15.7	8.6	20.0	7.7	20.3	139	92	72	229
Mali	2.6	–3.7	1.2	–3.4	6.0	–0.9	2.9	–0.9	91	103	113	167
Mauritania	7.8	3.5	1.1	4.4	8.2	–3.7	2.8	3.9	114	106	44	82
Mauritius	8.6	2.0	11.0	2.5	14.4	4.8	12.8	4.7	82	103	47	132
Mexico	12.2	14.7	5.7	18.7	8.2	13.7	8.6	12.8	146	92	58	160
Moldova	..	..	..	..	..	..	..	..	..	..	..	..
Mongolia	..	..	..	..	–0.4	–12.5	–3.8	–24.7	..	..	..	..
Morocco	4.2	0.8	2.9	1.7	6.1	1.1	3.6	3.5	96	90	81	105
Mozambique	–10.5	–0.3	–1.0	2.9	–9.6	3.4	0.1	–0.2	121	124	284	120
Myanmar	–7.0	27.2	–7.0	38.7	–7.9	21.1	–4.5	29.9	155	107	231	228
Namibia	..	..	..	..	..	3.8	..	0.9	..	..	..	..
Nepal	7.8	22.1	4.9	6.8	8.2	10.6	7.0	15.0	107	85	55	214
Netherlands	4.5	5.8	4.6	4.3	6.5	7.1	6.3	5.6	97	103	77	171
New Zealand	3.6	5.4	4.6	5.5	6.2	7.8	5.4	9.0	96	108	73	154
Nicaragua	–4.4	–8.7	–4.1	7.3	–5.8	9.6	–3.1	6.9	151	95	157	85
Niger	–6.4	–2.0	–4.5	2.5	–5.4	–8.1	–3.5	–8.0	113	101	174	64
Nigeria	–2.4	–1.9	–17.5	7.6	–8.4	–5.0	–15.6	2.9	178	86	363	115
Norway	6.8	6.5	4.2	0.7	5.3	2.8	6.2	3.0	123	95	83	169
Oman	13.1	9.8	–1.6	18.5	2.9	2.4	0.7	9.0	210	77	84	151
Pakistan	9.5	8.8	2.1	10.3	8.1	6.1	3.0	7.0	122	114	60	146
Panama	2.6	23.3	–4.1	14.3	–0.4	14.1	–3.6	10.7	129	86	94	137
Papua New Guinea	4.5	19.3	–0.2	2.1	4.8	20.6	1.3	2.0	120	90	87	181
Paraguay	9.9	–1.9	3.2	7.3	11.6	–3.3	4.2	13.6	113	101	84	179
Peru	–1.9	11.0	–1.0	12.1	–1.5	11.1	1.3	19.7	131	83	150	112
Philippines	2.9	10.2	2.4	15.2	3.9	16.2	2.9	18.0	115	114	94	174
Poland	4.8	3.9	1.5	26.4	1.4	9.2	–3.1	23.2	95	109	81	156
Portugal	12.2	0.5	9.8	2.4	15.1	5.0	10.3	3.3	99	92	44	152
Puerto Rico	..	..	..	..	..	..	..	..	..	..	..	..
Romania	–6.8	–4.7	–0.9	–5.3	–3.8	7.3	–3.8	2.4	64	111	99	43
Russian Federation	..	..	..	..	..	..	..	..	..	..	..	..

	Export volume		Import volume		Export value		Import value		Net barter terms of trade		Income terms of trade	
	average annual % growth		average annual % growth		average annual % growth		average annual % growth		1987 = 100		1987 = 100	
	1980–90	1990–95	1980–90	1990–95	1980–90	1990–95	1980–90	1990–95	1980	1995	1980	1995
Rwanda	5.6	–19.6	1.3	–1.9	2.9	–19.9	2.7	0.6	192	75	63	42
Saudi Arabia	–8.2	4.0	–8.4	5.9	–13.4	–0.8	–6.1	–0.5	155	92	489	156
Senegal	2.6	3.6	1.0	6.1	3.4	–18.0	1.6	–13.1	105	107	72	67
Sierra Leone	–2.1	–4.3	–9.9	–1.1	–2.4	–17.8	–8.7	–2.1	113	89	164	78
Singapore	12.2	16.2	8.6	12.1	9.9	17.6	8.0	15.5	109	89	60	308
Slovak Republic	..	..	..	..	..	..	..	..	..	..	..	..
Slovenia	..	..	..	..	..	16.7	..	20.1	..	..	..	..
South Africa	0.9	2.8	–0.8	5.3	0.8	3.2	–1.3	9.6	109	111	116	111
Spain	6.9	11.2	10.1	5.3	10.9	9.0	10.6	3.2	92	114	56	249
Sri Lanka	6.3	17.0	2.0	15.0	5.5	14.6	2.7	14.6	107	88	72	215
Sudan	–1.3	–7.4	–6.7	5.1	–0.8	–2.9	–5.3	5.3	132	105	103	65
Sweden	4.6	7.4	4.9	5.0	8.0	5.4	6.7	2.3	91	102	65	146
Switzerland	6.0	3.3	4.9	–6.7	9.5	3.4	8.8	0.9	79	60	66	110
Syrian Arab Republic	6.4	–3.2	–9.3	22.3	2.4	–1.1	–8.5	17.2	138	78	150	145
Tajikistan	..	..	..	..	..	..	..	..	..	..	..	..
Tanzania	–1.8	10.0	–3.3	12.7	–4.1	10.5	–2.0	6.5	142	83	173	137
Thailand	14.3	21.6	12.1	12.7	14.0	18.6	12.7	15.3	125	100	53	352
Togo	4.9	9.0	1.1	–11.2	1.2	–9.0	2.0	–13.1	159	90	130	49
Trinidad and Tobago	–4.3	4.9	–12.1	8.1	–9.9	4.2	–12.0	2.8	146	86	250	99
Tunisia	6.2	7.7	1.3	6.4	3.5	8.4	2.7	7.3	131	91	101	155
Turkey	12.0	8.8	11.3	11.2	14.0	10.3	9.3	8.7	88	109	22	132
Turkmenistan	..	..	..	..	..	..	..	..	..	..	..	..
Uganda	–1.4	3.9	–0.6	28.7	–4.3	26.4	1.4	43.5	157	58	116	47
Ukraine	..	..	..	..	..	..	..	..	..	..	..	..
United Arab Emirates	6.1	6.3	–1.3	21.0	–0.8	1.4	0.7	17.5	179	93	149	149
United Kingdom	4.4	1.8	6.3	0.9	5.8	4.7	8.4	2.9	105	102	83	143
United States	3.6	5.6	7.2	7.4	5.7	7.7	8.2	8.9	89	102	91	194
Uruguay	2.9	–3.1	–2.0	21.7	4.4	4.8	–1.3	17.1	108	112	85	122
Uzbekistan	..	..	..	..	..	..	..	..	..	..	..	..
Venezuela	1.6	–0.1	–6.1	19.3	–4.4	1.4	–3.2	5.1	168	82	189	118
Vietnam	..	..	..	..	18.8	16.9	8.8	24.2	..	..	..	..
West Bank and Gaza	..	..	..	..	..	..	..	..	..	..	..	..
Yemen, Rep.	1.5	7.2	–5.9	11.1	..	9.0	..	2.3	141	84	..	..
Yugoslavia, Fed. Rep.	..	..	..	..	..	–2.0	..	2.7	..	..	..	..
Zaire	1.8	–26.6	1.5	–26.8	3.3	–16.5	3.6	–15.7	118	85	166	32
Zambia	–3.5	26.9	–5.0	–6.2	1.4	–11.8	–3.5	0.5	118	85	147	85
Zimbabwe	2.2	–6.6	–2.2	–5.1	2.5	2.0	–0.4	2.7	120	84	105	92
World	**4.7 w**	**6.0 w**	**4.9 w**	**5.9 w**	**6.3 w**	**7.3 w**	**6.2 w**	**7.2 w**	..	..	..	..
Low income	5.3 w	8.3 w	1.6 w	13.0 w	5.1 w	12.7 w	3.9 w	13.4 w	121 m	91 m	105 m	89 m
Excl. China & India	1.4 w	2.7 w	–4.2 w	5.0 w	–0.7 w	3.0 w	–2.1 w	6.6 w	122 m	91 m	109 m	88 m
Middle income	2.6 w	6.9 w	–0.2 w	11.0 w	–0.3 w	7.6 w	0.8 w	10.8 w	131 m	94 m	..	..
Lower middle income	..	..	..	..	..	..	..	..	..	..	..	..
Upper middle income	1.7 w	7.3 w	–0.6 w	12.6 w	–1.5 w	8.5 w	0.6 w	12.9 w	134 m	95 m	87 m	132 m
Low & middle income	3.0 w	7.2 w	0.2 w	11.4 w	0.7 w	8.8 w	1.5 w	11.4 w	123 m	93 m	103 m	114 m
East Asia & Pacific	9.3 w	17.8 w	7.1 w	17.0 w	8.0 w	17.8 w	9.1 w	17.9 w	..	..	..	..
Europe & Central Asia	..	..	..	..	..	..	..	..	..	..	..	..
Latin America & Carib.	5.2 w	6.6 w	–0.5 w	15.1 w	3.0 w	9.1 w	1.1 w	14.3 w	134 m	94 m	123 m	120 m
Middle East & N. Africa	–2.0 w	1.1 w	–5.8 w	5.9 w	–7.6 w	–4.0 w	–3.7 w	0.6 w	142 m	92 m	147 m	119 m
South Asia	6.6 w	8.6 w	3.5 w	5.3 w	6.8 w	10.7 w	3.8 w	8.8 w	107 m	94 m	70 m	185 m
Sub-Saharan Africa	0.9 w	0.9 w	–3.8 w	1.9 w	–0.7 w	0.9 w	–2.8 w	5.0 w	120 m	91 m	105 m	88 m
High income	5.2 w	5.4 w	6.2 w	4.6 w	7.8 w	6.9 w	7.5 w	6.2 w	95 m	97 m	72 m	138 m

a. Includes Luxembourg. b. Data prior to 1992 include Eritrea. c. Data prior to 1990 refer to the Federal Republic of Germany before unification.

About the data

Statistics on international merchandise trade are based on transactions recorded by customs services. By international agreement these data are reported to the United Nations Statistical Office, which maintains a commodity trade database known as COMTRADE. The United Nations Conference on Trade and Development (UNCTAD) compiles a variety of international trade statistics, including price and volume indexes, based on the COMTRADE data. The World Bank supplements data from UNCTAD with data from the International Monetary Fund (IMF) and, to ensure that its information is the most recent available, with data taken directly from the COMTRADE database.

Merchandise trade includes all goods that add to or subtract from an economy's material resources. Currency in circulation, titles of ownership, and securities are excluded, but monetary gold is included.

Trade statistics are collected on the basis of the customs area of a country, which in most cases coincides with its geographic area. Goods under foreign aid programs are included, but goods destined for extraterritorial agencies (such as embassies) are not.

There are many difficulties in collecting and tabulating trade statistics. In principle, all transactions should be reported twice, once by the exporting country and once by the importing country. But timely and accurate reports are often lacking, particularly for developing countries. As a result, it is often necessary to estimate the trade of developing countries from the trade reported by their partners. This approach captures trade with high-income countries, but may miss trade between developing countries, particularly in Africa. In some cases national authorities may suppress or misrepresent data on certain trade flows (such as military equipment, oil, or the exports of a dominant producer) because of economic or political concerns. In other cases reported trade data may be distorted by deliberate under- or over-invoicing to effect capital transfers or avoid taxes. And in some regions smuggling and black market trading result in unreported trade flows. For these and other reasons trade values based on customs data differ from those calculated through the balance of payments accounts.

The growth rates here are calculated from 1987 base year volume indexes. They may differ from those derived from national sources because national price indexes may use base years and weighting procedures that differ from those used by UNCTAD or the IMF.

Terms of trade

The terms of trade measure the relative prices of a country's exports and imports. There are a number of ways to calculate terms of trade. The most common is the net barter, or commodity, terms of trade, con-

structed as the ratio of the export price index to the import price index. When the net barter terms of trade increase, a country's exports are becoming more valuable or its imports cheaper.

The income terms of trade provide another measure of the relative purchasing power of exports. When the prices of a country's exports rise relative to the prices of its imports, its residents can purchase more goods at a given level of domestic production. The U.N. System of National Accounts specifies that real GDP should be adjusted to reflect this trading gain or loss caused by changes in the terms of trade. (GDP adjusted for terms of trade effects is known as gross domestic income.) The World Bank measures trading gains or losses as the income terms of trade, or capacity to import. The capacity to import is calculated by deflating the export value index by the import price index. Because the terms of trade indexes are usually calculated using item- or category-level average unit values rather than actual prices (which may be difficult to collect), they are subject to significant variation and error, depending on the composition of trade from one reporting period to the next.

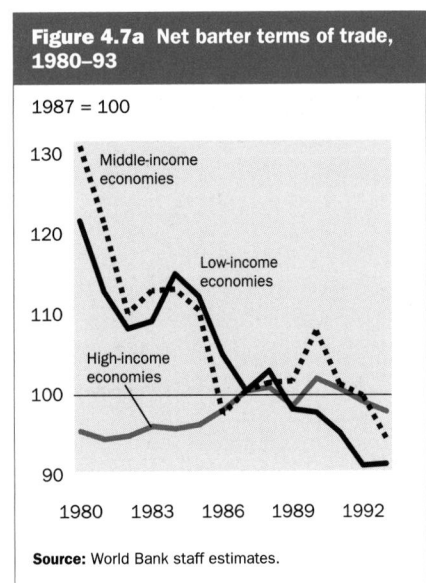

Figure 4.7a Net barter terms of trade, 1980–93

1987 = 100

Middle-income economies

Low-income economies

High-income economies

Source: World Bank staff estimates.

	Merchandise exports		Fuels, minerals, and metals		Other primary commodities		Machinery and transport equipment		Other manufactures		Textile fibers, textiles, and clothing[a]	
	$ millions		% of total		% of total		% of total		% of total		% of total	
	1980	1995	1980	1993	1980	1993	1980	1993	1980	1993	1980	1993
Albania	367	205	..	..	..	..	..	..	..	..	..	..
Algeria	13,900	8,594	99	96	1	1	..	1	0	2	..	0
Angola	1,880	3,508	78	100	9	0	..	..	13	..	0	..
Argentina	8,020	20,967	6	11	71	57	6	11	17	21	7	3
Armenia	..	271	..	..	..	..	..	..	..	..	..	..
Australia	21,900	52,692	34	36	46	29	5	8	15	28	10	9
Austria	17,500	45,200	5	4	12	7	28	38	56	52	11	8
Azerbaijan	..	612	..	..	..	..	..	..	..	..	..	..
Bangladesh	793	3,173	..	0	31	18	1	0	68	81	75	78
Belarus	..	4,621	..	..	..	..	..	..	..	..	..	..
Belgium[b]	64,500	136,864	..	..	..	..	..	..	..	..	..	..
Benin	63	163	5	..	87	..	1	..	7	..	25	..
Bolivia	942	1,101	86	56	11	25	1	2	2	17	0	3
Bosnia and Herzegovina	..	..	..	..	..	..	..	..	..	..	..	..
Botswana	502	2,130	..	..	..	..	..	..	..	..	..	..
Brazil	20,100	46,506	11	12	50	28	17	21	22	39	5	4
Bulgaria	10,400	5,100	..	..	..	..	..	..	..	..	..	..
Burkina Faso	161	274	..	..	..	..	..	..	..	..	..	..
Burundi	65	106	5	..	92	70	..	3	3	28	3	..
Cambodia	..	855	..	..	..	..	..	..	..	..	..	..
Cameroon	1,380	2,331	33	51	64	35	1	8	3	6	4	4
Canada	67,700	192,198	28	17	23	17	26	40	24	26	1	1
Central African Republic	116	187	0	..	71	..	0	..	29	..	8	..
Chad	71	156	1	..	92	..	4	..	4	..	..	..
Chile	4,710	16,039	65	43	25	38	2	3	8	16	1	2
China[†]	18,100	148,797	20	6	32	13	3	16	45	65	..	31
Colombia	3,920	9,764	3	26	77	34	2	6	18	34	9	10
Congo	911	952	90	..	4	..	0	..	7	..	0	..
Costa Rica	1,000	2,611	1	1	65	66	4	4	30	29	5	5
Côte d'Ivoire	3,130	3,939	..	15	..	68	..	2	..	15	..	..
Croatia	..	4,633	..	11	..	18	..	14	..	57	..	19
Cuba	5,580	1,100	5	..	90	..	..	..	6	..	..	..
Czech Republic	..	21,654	..	..	..	..	..	..	..	..	..	..
Denmark	16,700	49,036	5	4	38	29	24	27	32	40	5	5
Dominican Republic	962	765	3	6	73	41	1	2	23	50	1	2
Ecuador	2,480	4,307	63	42	34	50	1	2	2	5	1	2
Egypt, Arab Rep.	3,050	3,435	67	55	22	12	0	1	11	32	24	20
El Salvador	967	998	5	3	59	49	3	3	33	45	25	16
Eritrea	..	..	..	..	..	..	..	..	..	..	..	..
Estonia	..	1,847	..	..	..	..	..	..	..	..	..	..
Ethiopia[c]	425	423	8	1	92	95	0	0	0	4	3	3
Finland	14,200	39,573	8	6	22	11	18	32	52	51	7	2
France	116,000	286,738	8	5	18	17	33	38	41	40	6	5
Gabon	2,170	2,713	100	85	..	12	..	0	..	3	..	..
Gambia, The	31	16	0	..	90	63	1	..	9	37	3	..
Georgia	..	347	..	..	..	..	..	..	..	..	..	..
Germany[d]	193,000	523,743	7	4	7	6	44	48	42	42	5	5
Ghana	1,260	1,227	17	25	82	52	..	0	1	23	0	..
Greece	5,150	9,384	26	22	28	30	3	8	44	40	18	15
Guatemala	1,520	2,156	6	2	70	68	2	2	23	28	17	6
Guinea	401	583	..	..	..	..	..	..	..	..	..	..
Guinea-Bissau	11	23	..	..	..	..	..	..	..	..	..	..
Haiti	226	110	..	..	..	..	..	..	..	..	..	..
Honduras	830	1,061	7	3	81	84	..	0	13	13	4	3
Hong Kong	19,800	173,754	2	2	5	3	20	26	73	70	28	39
†Data for Taiwan, China	19,800	111,585	2	2	10	5	25	40	63	53	22	15

	Merchandise exports		Fuels, minerals, and metals		Other primary commodities		Machinery and transport equipment		Other manufactures		Textile fibers, textiles, and clothing[a]	
	$ millions		% of total		% of total		% of total		% of total		% of total	
	1980	1995	1980	1993	1980	1993	1980	1993	1980	1993	1980	1993
Hungary	8,670	12,540	9	8	25	24	32	24	34	44	8	12
India	8,590	30,764	8	7	33	18	8	7	51	68	26	30
Indonesia	21,900	45,417	76	32	22	15	1	5	2	48	1	17
Iran, Islamic Rep.	14,700	18,346	93	93	2	3	0	0	5	4	4	..
Iraq	26,300	380	99	..	1	..	0	..	0	..	..	..
Ireland	8,400	44,191	3	2	39	23	19	29	39	46	9	4
Israel	5,540	19,046	2	2	16	7	13	31	69	60	10	6
Italy	78,100	231,336	7	3	8	8	33	37	52	52	12	12
Jamaica	963	1,414	23	12	14	22	1	0	62	65	1	9
Japan	130,000	443,116	2	2	2	1	58	68	37	29	5	2
Jordan	574	1,769	41	27	26	22	2	4	32	47	5	5
Kazakhstan	..	5,197	..	..	..	..	..	..	..	..	..	..
Kenya	1,250	1,878	36	16	52	66	1	2	12	17	3	3
Korea, Dem. Rep.	..	..	..	..	..	..	..	..	..	..	..	..
Korea, Rep.	17,500	125,058	1	3	9	4	20	43	70	51	30	19
Kuwait	19,700	12,977	89	5	1	7	3	48	8	40	1	4
Kyrgyz Republic	..	409	..	..	..	..	..	..	..	..	..	..
Lao PDR	31	348	23	..	70	..	1	..	7	..	..	..
Latvia	..	1,305	..	..	..	..	..	..	..	..	..	..
Lebanon	868	982	8	..	27	..	17	..	48	..	8	..
Lesotho	58	143	..	..	..	..	..	..	..	..	..	..
Libya	21,900	7,540	100	95	..	1	..	0	..	4	..	0
Lithuania	..	2,707	..	11	..	25	..	24	..	40	..	18
Macedonia, FYR	..	1,244	..	..	..	..	..	..	..	..	..	..
Madagascar	401	364	10	8	84	72	2	2	4	18	4	13
Malawi	295	325	..	..	93	94	0	0	7	6	7	..
Malaysia	13,000	74,037	35	14	46	21	12	41	8	24	3	6
Mali	205	326	0	..	91	..	5	..	4	..	41	..
Mauritania	194	404	78	52	20	47	1	0	1	1	1	..
Mauritius	431	1,537	..	2	73	32	3	2	25	65	19	54
Mexico	15,600	79,543	73	17	15	9	4	49	8	26	3	4
Moldova	..	746	..	..	..	..	..	..	..	..	..	..
Mongolia	..	324	..	..	..	..	..	..	..	..	..	..
Morocco	2,490	4,802	45	14	31	29	1	6	23	51	10	25
Mozambique	281	169	11	14	87	66	1	3	2	18	..	..
Myanmar	472	846	..	..	..	..	..	..	..	..	..	..
Namibia	..	1,353	..	..	..	..	..	..	..	..	..	..
Nepal	80	348	0	..	69	16	..	..	31	84	39	..
Netherlands	74,000	195,912	26	11	23	25	17	24	34	40	5	4
New Zealand	5,420	13,738	6	7	74	66	4	6	17	22	20	7
Nicaragua	451	520	4	3	83	90	1	0	13	7	9	12
Niger	566	225	86	..	12	..	1	..	2	..	1	..
Nigeria	26,000	11,670	97	94	2	4	0	0	0	2	..	..
Norway	18,600	41,746	59	59	9	10	12	13	20	18	1	1
Oman	2,390	6,065	96	9	1	21	3	54	1	17	0	6
Pakistan	2,620	7,992	8	1	44	14	1	0	47	85	57	78
Panama	358	625	24	3	67	81	0	0	9	16	3	5
Papua New Guinea	1,030	2,644	49	52	48	37	..	10	3	2	..	0
Paraguay	310	817	..	0	88	83	..	1	12	16	42	23
Peru	3,900	5,575	63	50	19	33	2	1	16	16	9	11
Philippines	5,740	17,502	21	7	42	17	2	19	35	58	7	9
Poland	14,200	22,892	20	22	9	18	36	19	35	41	7	7
Portugal	4,640	22,621	7	9	21	13	13	17	59	61	27	25
Puerto Rico	..	..	..	..	..	..	..	..	..	..	..	..
Romania	11,200	7,548	..	13	..	10	..	17	..	60	..	17
Russian Federation	..	81,500	..	..	..	..	..	..	..	..	..	..

	Merchandise exports		Fuels, minerals, and metals		Other primary commodities		Machinery and transport equipment		Other manufactures		Textile fibers, textiles, and clothing[a]	
	$ millions		% of total		% of total		% of total		% of total		% of total	
	1980	1995	1980	1993	1980	1993	1980	1993	1980	1993	1980	1993
Rwanda	72	45	9	..	90	..	0	..	0	..	0	..
Saudi Arabia	109,000	46,624	99	90	0	1	0	2	0	7	..	..
Senegal	477	340	39	25	46	54	3	2	12	19	3	4
Sierra Leone	224	42	35	45	25	28	0	..	40	27	0	..
Singapore	19,400	118,268	31	14	18	6	27	55	24	25	4	4
Slovak Republic	..	8,585	..	..	..	..	..	..	..	..	..	..
Slovenia	..	8,286	..	8	..	6	..	27	..	58	..	15
South Africa	25,500	27,860	33	16	28	11	4	8	36	66	4	3
Spain	20,700	91,716	9	5	20	17	26	41	45	36	5	4
Sri Lanka	1,070	3,798	19	1	65	27	0	2	16	71	13	52
Sudan	543	493	2	..	98	98	..	1	1	1	41	..
Sweden	30,900	79,908	9	7	12	8	40	44	39	41	3	2
Switzerland	29,600	77,649	5	2	4	4	32	30	59	64	7	4
Syrian Arab Republic	2,110	3,970	78	71	16	20	1	0	5	9	13	13
Tajikistan	..	749	..	..	..	..	..	..	..	..	..	..
Tanzania	511	639	10	..	76	..	1	..	14	..	24	..
Thailand	6,510	56,459	14	2	58	26	6	28	22	45	10	15
Togo	338	209	66	52	23	42	2	1	9	5	4	25
Trinidad and Tobago	3,960	2,455	94	58	2	8	1	3	4	32	0	1
Tunisia	2,200	5,475	56	13	8	12	2	10	34	66	18	43
Turkey	2,910	21,600	8	4	65	25	3	8	24	64	28	40
Turkmenistan	..	2,008	..	..	..	..	..	..	..	..	..	..
Uganda	345	461	1	..	97	100	3	1	0	..	2	..
Ukraine	..	13,647	..	..	..	..	..	..	..	..	..	..
United Arab Emirates	20,700	25,650	96	..	1	..	1	..	2	..	..	..
United Kingdom	110,000	242,042	18	10	8	9	35	41	39	41	5	5
United States	226,000	584,743	9	4	23	14	39	49	29	33	4	3
Uruguay	1,060	2,106	1	0	61	57	4	8	34	35	36	28
Uzbekistan	..	3,805	..	..	..	..	..	..	..	..	..	..
Venezuela	19,221	18,457	98	84	0	3	0	3	1	11	..	1
Vietnam	339	5,026	..	..	..	..	..	..	..	..	..	..
West Bank and Gaza	..	..	..	..	..	..	..	..	..	..	..	..
Yemen, Rep.	..	1,937	0	..	49	..	25	..	26	..	6	..
Yugoslavia, Fed. Rep.	..	2,760	9	11	18	12	28	30	45	47	10	10
Zaire	1,630	438	56	69	14	13	1	1	30	17	0	..
Zambia	1,300	781	..	..	..	..	..	..	..	..	..	..
Zimbabwe	1,415	1,885	23	16	39	48	2	3	36	34	1	11
World	**2,003,797 t**	**5,144,770 t**	..	..	..	..	..	..	..	..	..	..
Low income	84,204 t	245,456 t	..	..	..	..	..	..	..	..	..	..
Excl. China & India	58,817 t	64,769 t	..	..	..	..	..	..	..	..	..	..
Middle income	586,567 t	893,331 t	..	..	..	..	..	..	..	..	..	..
Lower middle income	..	..	..	..	..	..	..	..	..	..	..	..
Upper middle income	246,329 t	372,898 t	..	..	..	..	..	..	..	..	..	..
Low & middle income	660,833 t	1,152,249 t	..	..	..	..	..	..	..	..	..	..
East Asia & Pacific	69,623 t	359,102 t	..	..	..	..	..	..	..	..	..	..
Europe & Central Asia	..	..	..	..	..	..	..	..	..	..	..	..
Latin America & Carib.	98,589 t	221,210 t	..	..	..	..	..	..	..	..	..	..
Middle East & N. Africa	203,379 t	106,441 t	..	..	..	..	..	..	..	..	..	..
South Asia	13,848 t	46,455 t	..	..	..	..	..	..	..	..	..	..
Sub-Saharan Africa	77,237 t	72,847 t	..	..	..	..	..	..	..	..	..	..
High income	1,393,926 t	3,997,288 t	..	..	..	..	..	..	..	..	..	..

a. Textile fibers are part of other primary commodities; textiles and clothing are part of other manufactures. b. Includes Luxembourg. c. Data prior to 1992 include Eritrea. d. Data prior to 1990 refer to the Federal Republic of Germany before unification.

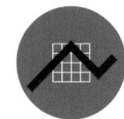
Figure 4.8a Merchandise exports from developing economies, 1980–94

percentage of world exports

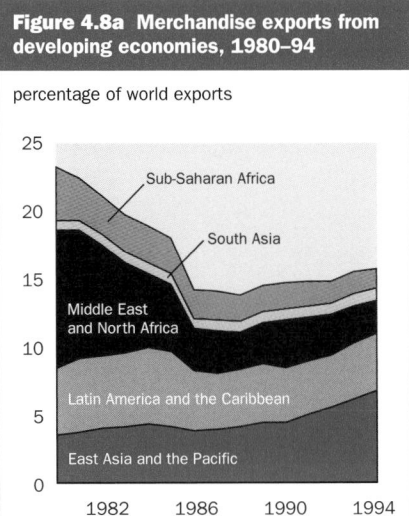

Source: World Bank staff estimates.

About the data

Data on trade in goods come from one of two sources: customs reports of goods entering an economy or reports of the financial transactions recorded in the balance of payments. Because of differences in timing and definitions, estimates of trade flows are likely to differ among sources. In addition, several international agencies process trade data, making estimates to correct for unreported or misreported data, which leads to other differences in the available data.

The most detailed source of data on international trade in goods is the COMTRADE database maintained by the United Nations Statistical Office (UNSO). The International Monetary Fund (IMF) collects data on total exports and imports as part of its balance of payments statistics. It also publishes customs-based statistics on international trade in its *Direction of Trade Statistics*.

The value of exports is recorded as the cost of the goods delivered to the frontier of the exporting country for shipment, the f.o.b. (free on board) value. Many countries collect and report trade data in U.S. dollars. When countries report in local currency, the UNSO applies the average official exchange rate for the period shown.

Countries may report trade according to the special or general system of trade (see *Primary data documentation*). Under the general system exports comprise outward-moving goods: (a) national goods wholly or partly produced in the country; (b) foreign goods, neither transformed nor declared for domestic consumption in the country, that move outward from customs storage; and (c) nationalized goods that have been declared from domestic consumption and move outward without having been transformed. Under the special system of trade, exports comprise categories (a) and (c). In some compilations categories (b) and (c) are classified as re-exports. Because of differences in reporting practices, data on exports may not be fully comparable across economies.

The data on total merchandise exports here have been taken principally from series reported in the IMF's *International Financial Statistics,* supplemented by data published in the United Nations *Monthly Bulletin of Statistics,* the IMF's *Direction of Trade Statistics,* UNCTAD's *Handbook of International Trade and Development Statistics,* and, in some cases, by World Bank staff estimates. Data on the structure of exports by major commodity groups are based on UNCTAD statistics. Because of delays in reporting and processing data, the most recent year for which shares of merchandise trade can be calculated is 1993.

Definitions

● **Merchandise exports** show the f.o.b. value of goods provided to the rest of the world valued in U.S. dollars. They are classified using the Standard International Trade Classification (SITC), series M, no. 34, revision 2. ● **Fuels, minerals, and metals** comprise the commodities in SITC section 3 (mineral fuels, lubricants, and related materials), divisions 27 and 28 (crude fertilizers and crude minerals, excluding coal, petroleum, precious stones, metalliferous ores, and metal scrap), and division 68 (nonferrous metals). ● **Other primary commodities** comprise SITC sections 0, 1, 2, and 4 (food and live animals, beverages and tobacco, inedible crude materials except fuels, and animal and vegetable oils and fats), excluding divisions 27 and 28. ● **Machinery and transport equipment** comprise the commodities in SITC section 7. ● **Other manufactures** comprise SITC sections 5–9, excluding section 7 and division 68. ● **Textile fibers, textiles, and clothing,** representing SITC divisions 26, 65, and 84 (textiles, textile fibers, yarn, fabrics, and clothing and accessories), are a subgroup of other primary commodities and of other manufactures.

Data sources

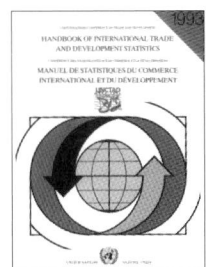

The principal sources of merchandise trade data are the UNSO's COMTRADE database; the United Nations *International Trade Statistics Yearbook;* UNCTAD's *Handbook of International Trade and Development Statistics;* and the IMF's *International Financial Statistics* and *Direction of Trade Statistics.*

	Merchandise imports		Food		Fuel		Other primary commodities		Machinery and transport equipment		Other manufactures	
	$ millions		% of total		% of total		% of total		% of total		% of total	
	1980	1995	1980	1993	1980	1993	1980	1993	1980	1993	1980	1993
Albania	354	679	..	..	..	..	..	..	..	..	..	..
Algeria	10,600	9,570	21	29	3	1	5	5	37	31	35	34
Angola	1,330	1,748	24	..	1	..	2	..	38	..	36	..
Argentina	10,500	20,122	6	5	10	2	7	4	40	50	37	39
Armenia	..	674	..	..	..	..	..	..	..	..	..	..
Australia	22,400	61,280	5	5	14	6	5	3	36	43	40	43
Austria	24,400	55,300	6	5	16	5	9	6	29	37	40	47
Azerbaijan	..	955	..	..	..	..	..	..	..	..	..	..
Bangladesh	2,600	6,496	24	15	10	14	9	30	25	14	33	28
Belarus	..	5,149	..	..	..	..	..	..	..	..	..	..
Belgium[a]	71,900	125,297	..	..	..	..	..	..	..	..	..	..
Benin	331	493	26	..	8	..	2	..	23	..	40	..
Bolivia	665	1,424	19	9	1	5	3	4	41	48	37	34
Bosnia and Herzegovina	..	..	..	..	..	..	..	..	..	..	..	..
Botswana	692	1,907	..	..	..	..	..	..	..	..	..	..
Brazil	25,000	53,783	10	10	43	16	6	7	20	33	21	33
Bulgaria	9,650	5,015	..	8	..	36	..	7	..	22	..	27
Burkina Faso	359	549	..	..	..	..	..	..	..	..	..	..
Burundi	168	234	..	..	..	..	..	..	..	..	..	..
Cambodia	..	1,213	..	..	..	..	..	..	..	..	..	..
Cameroon	1,600	1,241	9	16	12	3	2	2	34	27	44	51
Canada	62,500	168,426	8	6	12	4	7	4	46	50	27	35
Central African Republic	81	174	21	..	2	..	3	..	34	..	41	..
Chad	74	220	..	..	..	..	..	..	..	..	..	..
Chile	5,800	15,914	15	6	18	10	4	3	33	43	30	38
China[†]	19,900	129,113	..	3	..	6	..	7	..	42	..	43
Colombia	4,740	13,853	12	8	12	4	6	5	38	39	33	44
Congo	580	670	19	..	14	..	2	..	23	..	42	..
Costa Rica	1,540	3,253	9	8	15	9	4	3	24	26	48	55
Côte d'Ivoire	2,970	2,808	13	..	16	..	3	..	33	..	35	..
Croatia	..	7,582	..	9	..	10	..	5	..	24	..	52
Cuba	6,510	1,650	..	..	..	..	..	..	..	..	..	..
Czech Republic	..	26,523	..	..	..	..	..	..	..	..	..	..
Denmark	19,300	43,223	12	13	22	6	8	5	20	29	38	46
Dominican Republic	1,640	2,976	17	..	25	..	4	..	22	..	32	..
Ecuador	2,250	4,193	8	5	1	2	4	4	49	49	37	41
Egypt, Arab Rep.	4,860	11,739	32	24	1	2	8	10	27	31	32	34
El Salvador	966	2,853	18	15	18	14	4	5	13	26	47	41
Eritrea	..	..	..	..	..	..	..	..	..	..	..	..
Estonia	..	2,539	..	..	..	..	..	..	..	..	..	..
Ethiopia[b]	717	1,033	8	6	25	11	3	1	28	44	36	38
Finland	15,600	28,114	7	7	29	13	8	8	27	34	30	39
France	135,000	275,275	10	11	27	9	9	5	21	34	33	41
Gabon	674	882	19	..	1	..	2	..	37	..	41	..
Gambia, The	165	140	23	..	11	..	2	..	28	..	36	..
Georgia	..	687	..	..	..	..	..	..	..	..	..	..
Germany[c]	188,000	464,220	12	10	23	8	10	6	19	33	36	44
Ghana	1,130	1,580	10	..	27	..	3	..	30	..	31	..
Greece	10,500	21,466	9	6	23	25	8	6	36	38	24	25
Guatemala	1,600	3,293	8	11	24	14	4	3	22	32	42	41
Guinea	270	690	..	..	..	..	..	..	..	..	..	..
Guinea-Bissau	55	70	20	..	6	..	3	..	37	..	35	..
Haiti	375	653	24	..	13	..	3	..	20	..	40	..
Honduras	1,010	1,219	10	11	16	13	2	3	30	26	42	47
Hong Kong	22,400	192,774	12	6	6	2	6	3	22	33	54	56
†Data for Taiwan, China	19,700	103,698	8	6	25	8	15	10	28	40	24	36

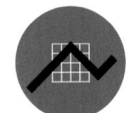

	Merchandise imports		Food		Fuel		Other primary commodities		Machinery and transport equipment		Other manufactures	
	$ millions		% of total		% of total		% of total		% of total		% of total	
	1980	1995	1980	1993	1980	1993	1980	1993	1980	1993	1980	1993
Hungary	9,220	15,073	8	6	16	13	13	5	29	37	33	39
India	14,900	34,522	9	4	45	30	8	10	13	14	25	42
Indonesia	10,800	40,918	13	7	16	8	6	9	34	42	32	34
Iran, Islamic Rep.	12,200	12,700	13	..	0	..	5	..	44	..	38	..
Iraq	13,900	490	13	..	0	..	3	..	54	..	31	..
Ireland	11,200	32,568	12	10	15	5	5	3	27	37	41	45
Israel	9,780	29,579	11	7	27	7	6	4	21	33	36	49
Italy	101,000	204,062	13	13	28	10	13	9	21	29	25	39
Jamaica	1,100	2,757	20	14	38	19	3	3	12	23	27	41
Japan	141,000	335,882	12	18	50	21	19	13	6	17	13	32
Jordan	2,400	3,698	18	20	17	13	3	3	28	27	34	37
Kazakstan	..	5,692	..	..	..	..	..	..	..	..	..	..
Kenya	2,120	2,949	8	8	34	33	3	5	28	25	28	29
Korea, Dem. Rep.	..	..	..	..	..	..	..	..	..	..	..	..
Korea, Rep.	22,300	135,119	10	6	30	18	17	13	22	34	21	29
Kuwait	6,530	7,784	15	13	1	1	3	3	36	42	46	41
Kyrgyz Republic	..	610	..	..	..	..	..	..	..	..	..	..
Lao PDR	29	587	..	..	..	..	..	..	..	..	..	..
Latvia	..	1,818	..	..	..	..	..	..	..	..	..	..
Lebanon	3,650	6,721	16	..	15	..	6	..	25	..	38	..
Lesotho	464	821	..	..	..	..	..	..	..	..	..	..
Libya	6,780	5,380	19	24	1	0	2	3	38	34	40	39
Lithuania	..	3,083	..	11	..	45	..	9	..	15	..	21
Macedonia, FYR	..	1,420	..	..	..	..	..	..	..	..	..	..
Madagascar	600	499	9	11	15	12	4	2	34	41	39	34
Malawi	439	491	8	..	15	..	2	..	34	..	41	..
Malaysia	10,800	77,751	12	7	15	4	6	4	39	54	28	30
Mali	439	529	19	..	35	..	1	..	23	..	23	..
Mauritania	286	700	30	..	14	..	1	..	27	..	28	..
Mauritius	609	1,959	26	13	14	9	5	3	16	25	39	50
Mexico	19,500	72,500	16	8	2	2	7	4	43	48	32	38
Moldova	..	841	..	..	..	..	..	..	..	..	..	..
Mongolia	..	223	..	..	..	..	..	..	..	..	..	..
Morocco	4,160	8,563	20	17	24	14	10	9	21	29	25	31
Mozambique	800	784	..	..	..	..	..	..	..	..	..	..
Myanmar	353	1,335	..	..	..	..	..	..	..	..	..	..
Namibia	..	1,196	..	..	..	..	..	..	..	..	..	..
Nepal	342	1,374	4	..	18	..	2	..	32	..	44	..
Netherlands	76,600	176,420	15	15	24	9	7	5	20	30	35	41
New Zealand	5,470	13,958	6	8	23	7	6	4	30	38	36	44
Nicaragua	887	962	15	23	20	15	2	1	14	26	49	34
Niger	594	309	14	..	26	..	4	..	27	..	29	..
Nigeria	16,700	7,900	17	..	2	..	3	..	39	..	39	..
Norway	16,900	32,702	8	7	17	3	8	7	29	39	39	45
Oman	1,730	4,248	15	19	11	3	2	2	39	44	33	32
Pakistan	5,350	11,461	13	14	27	17	6	7	25	35	29	27
Panama	1,450	2,511	10	10	31	13	1	2	21	31	37	45
Papua New Guinea	1,180	1,451	21	..	15	..	1	..	35	..	28	..
Paraguay	615	2,370	..	11	..	12	..	1	..	40	..	35
Peru	2,500	9,224	20	20	2	8	5	3	41	36	32	34
Philippines	8,300	28,337	8	8	28	12	5	5	24	32	35	43
Poland	16,700	29,050	14	12	18	17	11	6	27	29	30	36
Portugal	9,310	32,339	14	19	24	24	11	8	25	24	27	26
Puerto Rico	..	..	..	..	..	..	..	..	..	..	..	..
Romania	12,800	9,424	..	14	..	26	..	7	..	22	..	31
Russian Federation	..	58,900	..	..	..	..	..	..	..	..	..	..

	Merchandise imports		Food		Fuel		Other primary commodities		Machinery and transport equipment		Other manufactures	
	$ millions		% of total		% of total		% of total		% of total		% of total	
	1980	1995	1980	1993	1980	1993	1980	1993	1980	1993	1980	1993
Rwanda	243	235	12	..	13	..	11	..	25	..	39	..
Saudi Arabia	30,200	27,458	14	..	1	..	2	..	39	..	44	..
Senegal	1,050	704	25	29	25	11	1	3	23	23	25	34
Sierra Leone	427	135	24	..	2	..	2	..	40	..	32	..
Singapore	24,000	124,507	9	6	29	11	7	3	29	49	26	31
Slovak Republic	..	9,070	..	..	..	..	..	..	..	..	..	..
Slovenia	..	9,452	..	8	..	11	..	7	..	30	..	44
South Africa	19,600	30,555	3	6	0	1	5	4	38	44	54	46
Spain	34,100	115,019	13	14	39	11	11	6	18	35	20	35
Sri Lanka	2,040	5,185	20	16	24	9	3	3	25	21	28	51
Sudan	1,580	1,275	26	..	13	..	2	..	29	..	31	..
Sweden	33,400	64,438	7	8	24	9	7	5	27	36	35	42
Switzerland	36,300	76,985	8	7	11	4	10	5	24	29	47	55
Syrian Arab Republic	4,120	4,616	14	19	26	4	5	4	21	32	33	42
Tajikistan	..	799	..	..	..	..	..	..	..	..	..	..
Tanzania	1,250	1,619	13	..	21	..	3	..	35	..	28	..
Thailand	9,210	70,776	5	5	30	8	7	7	25	45	32	36
Togo	551	386	17	23	23	10	2	3	23	28	36	37
Trinidad and Tobago	3,160	1,714	11	15	38	16	3	3	25	33	24	32
Tunisia	3,540	7,903	14	8	21	8	8	6	23	32	34	46
Turkey	7,910	35,710	4	6	48	14	5	10	18	38	25	33
Turkmenistan	..	1,472	..	..	..	..	..	..	..	..	..	..
Uganda	293	1,058	8	..	30	..	2	..	27	..	34	..
Ukraine	..	15,945	..	..	..	..	..	..	..	..	..	..
United Arab Emirates	8,750	21,024	11	..	11	..	3	..	36	..	39	..
United Kingdom	116,000	263,719	13	11	14	5	11	6	26	39	36	39
United States	257,000	770,852	8	5	33	10	7	4	25	43	27	38
Uruguay	1,680	2,867	8	8	29	9	7	4	30	40	26	39
Uzbekistan	..	3,598	..	..	..	..	..	..	..	..	..	..
Venezuela	11,827	11,968	15	11	2	1	5	5	43	50	36	32
Vietnam	1,310	7,272	..	..	..	..	..	..	..	..	..	..
West Bank and Gaza	..	..	..	..	..	..	..	..	..	..	..	..
Yemen, Rep.	..	1,962	28	..	7	..	1	..	28	..	36	..
Yugoslavia, Fed. Rep.	..	4,300	8	9	24	19	12	6	28	23	29	43
Zaire	836	397	21	..	8	..	4	..	32	..	36	..
Zambia	1,340	1,258	5	..	22	..	2	..	35	..	36	..
Zimbabwe	1,448	2,241	3	18	1	12	4	4	64	36	28	31

World	**2,027,078 t**	**5,246,326 t**	..	..	..	..	..	..	..	..	..	..
Low income	97,748 t	251,806 t	..	..	..	..	..	..	..	..	..	..
Excl. China & India	65,465 t	86,058 t	..	..	..	..	..	..	..	..	..	..
Middle income	455,925 t	987,309 t	..	..	..	..	..	..	..	..	..	..
Lower middle income	..	..	..	..	..	..	..	..	..	..	..	..
Upper middle income	161,848 t	379,450 t	..	..	..	..	..	..	..	..	..	..
Low & middle income	547,417 t	1,233,749 t	..	..	..	..	..	..	..	..	..	..
East Asia & Pacific	65,139 t	368,683 t	..	..	..	..	..	..	..	..	..	..
Europe & Central Asia	..	..	..	..	..	..	..	..	..	..	..	..
Latin America & Carib.	107,971 t	237,576 t	..	..	..	..	..	..	..	..	..	..
Middle East & N. Africa	103,850 t	110,841 t	..	..	..	..	..	..	..	..	..	..
South Asia	25,863 t	60,512 t	..	..	..	..	..	..	..	..	..	..
Sub-Saharan Africa	66,593 t	77,574 t	..	..	..	..	..	..	..	..	..	..
High income	1,503,743 t	4,037,671 t	..	..	..	..	..	..	..	..	..	..

a. Includes Luxembourg. b. Data prior to 1992 include Eritrea. c. Data prior to 1990 refer to the Federal Republic of Germany before unification.

 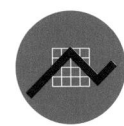

Structure of merchandise imports | 4.9

Figure 4.9a Merchandise imports of developing economies, 1980–95

percentage of world imports

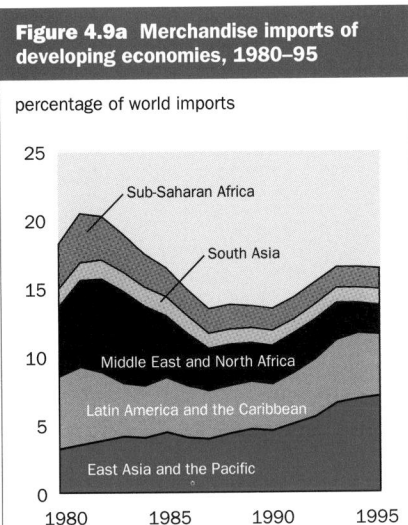

Source: World Bank staff estimates.

About the data

Imports are the mirror image of exports, and data on imports are derived from the same sources as data on exports. In principle, world exports and imports should be identical. Similarly, exports from an economy should equal the sum of imports by the rest of the world from that economy. But differences in timing and definitions result in discrepancies in reported values at all levels. For further discussion of indicators of merchandise trade see the notes to tables 4.7 and 4.8.

The value of imports is generally recorded as the cost of the goods when purchased by the importer plus the cost of transport and insurance to the frontier of the importing country—the c.i.f. (cost, insurance, and freight) value. A few countries, including Australia, Canada, and the United States, collect import data on an f.o.b. (free on board) basis and then adjust them for freight and insurance costs. Many countries collect and report trade data in U.S. dollars. When countries report in local currency, the United Nations Statistical Office applies the average official exchange rate for the period shown.

Countries may report trade according to the special or general system of trade (see *Primary data documentation*). In countries that report trade according to the general system, imports include both goods imported for domestic consumption and imports into bonded warehouses and free trade zones. Under the special system imports comprise goods imported for domestic consumption and withdrawals for domestic consumption from bonded warehouses and free trade zones. Goods shipped through a country for the purpose of transport are excluded.

Definitions

● **Merchandise imports** show the c.i.f. value of goods received from the rest of the world valued in U.S. dollars. Merchandise imports are classified using the Standard International Trade Classification (SITC), series M, no. 34, rev. 2. Group totals for merchandise imports are calculated by simple aggregation after estimating values for countries for which data are missing. Missing values are imputed for a group only when data are available for countries with at least 66 percent weight in 1987 for that group. Other indicators in the table are not aggregated because the coverage is generally poor. ● **Food** comprises the commodities in SITC sections 0, 1, and 4 and division 22 (food and live animals, beverages and tobacco, animal and vegetable oils and fats, oil seeds, oil nuts, and oil kernels). ● **Fuel** comprises the commodities in SITC section 3 (mineral fuels, lubricants, and related materials). ● **Other primary commodities** comprise SITC section 2 (inedible crude materials except fuels), excluding division 22 (oil seeds, oil nuts, and oil kernels) and division 68 (nonferrous metals). ● **Machinery and transport equipment** comprise the commodities in SITC section 7. ● **Other manufactures**, calculated residually from the total value of manufactured imports, represent SITC sections 5–9, excluding section 7 and division 68.

Data sources

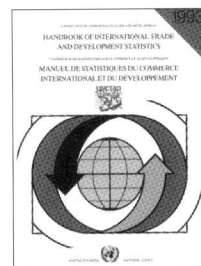

The principal sources of merchandise trade data are the UNSO's COMTRADE database; the United Nations *International Trade Statistics Yearbook;* UNCTAD's *Handbook of International Trade and Development Statistics;* and the IMF's *International Financial Statistics* and *Direction of Trade Statistics.*

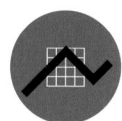

4.10 | Structure of service exports

	Service exports		Transport		Travel		Communications, computer, information, and other services		Insurance and financial services	
	$ millions		% of total		% of total		% of total		% of total	
	1980	1995	1980	1995	1980	1995	1980	1995	1980	1995
Albania	11	99	42.1	18.1	6.4	65.9	46.8	14.7	4.7	1.3
Algeria	476	628	41.0	..	24.1	..	29.5	0.0	5.4	..
Angola	..	112	..	34.2	..	0.0	..	57.5	..	8.3
Argentina	1,876	2,889	42.9	41.4	18.3	36.6	38.4	22.0	0.3	0.0
Armenia	..	29	..	49.9	..	4.9	..	45.2	..	..
Australia	3,860	15,556	49.3	31.9	29.5	47.2	19.9	16.6	1.3	4.3
Austria	9,423	23,506	7.3	11.1	68.9	55.7	21.3	22.6	2.6	10.6
Azerbaijan	..	172	..	..	..	..	..	..	..	..
Bangladesh	163	162	..	..	..	..	..	..	..	..
Belarus	..	123	..	..	..	..	..	..	..	..
Belgium[a]	12,925	38,655	32.7	25.1	14.1	14.8	48.5	41.0	4.7	18.4
Benin	62	104	56.8	56.8	14.1	22.5	26.8	20.6	2.3	0.0
Bolivia	88	231	33.5	26.3	41.0	31.3	16.6	34.5	8.9	7.9
Bosnia and Herzegovina	..	..	..	..	..	..	..	..	..	..
Botswana	101	260	41.7	14.7	22.2	62.2	32.0	16.0	4.1	7.1
Brazil	1,737	6,135	46.8	42.4	7.3	15.8	38.1	25.3	7.9	16.5
Bulgaria	1,211	1,420	36.3	34.0	28.7	33.3	31.0	32.7	4.0	..
Burkina Faso	49	56	17.3	11.8	10.2	32.6	72.5	55.6	0.0	0.0
Burundi	..	17	..	12.0	..	8.4	..	78.5	..	1.0
Cambodia	..	114	..	27.7	..	46.8	..	25.5	..	0.0
Cameroon	374	397	..	..	..	..	..	..	..	..
Canada	7,377	21,770	24.3	17.1	40.2	37.0	35.5	45.9	..	..
Central African Republic	54	33	6.5	0.0	5.1	0.0	86.1	100.0	2.4	0.0
Chad	0	55	0.0	1.9	100.0	21.3	0.0	76.1	0.0	0.7
Chile	1,263	3,153	32.2	42.9	13.9	26.6	51.9	27.1	2.1	3.3
China	2,512	19,130	52.3	17.5	28.0	45.6	11.7	27.2	8.0	9.7
Colombia	1,342	3,439	31.1	41.6	35.6	25.0	27.6	21.7	5.6	11.7
Congo	111	76	46.0	42.3	6.7	5.2	42.7	52.5	4.6	0.0
Costa Rica	194	1,310	24.9	13.7	43.7	51.2	30.7	35.1	0.7	0.0
Côte d'Ivoire	564	551	50.0	34.2	14.4	13.0	25.7	48.9	9.9	3.8
Croatia	..	2,569	..	25.5	..	61.6	..	12.9	..	..
Cuba	..	..	..	..	..	..	..	..	..	..
Czech Republic	..	6,725	..	21.8	..	42.8	..	34.4	..	1.0
Denmark	5,853	15,377	44.4	50.0	21.1	24.0	31.8	26.0	2.7	..
Dominican Republic	309	1,950	7.8	1.8	55.8	81.1	35.9	17.1	0.5	..
Ecuador	367	854	35.1	38.9	35.6	29.9	13.3	18.6	16.0	12.6
Egypt, Arab Rep.	2,393	6,767	..	..	..	..	..	..	..	..
El Salvador	139	388	18.3	24.9	9.6	22.0	50.5	46.3	21.6	6.9
Eritrea	..	91	..	..	..	..	..	..	..	..
Estonia	..	877	..	42.6	..	40.7	..	16.3	..	0.4
Ethiopia[b]	110	330	..	..	..	..	..	..	..	..
Finland	2,733	7,847	35.1	28.3	25.0	21.5	37.0	48.5	2.9	1.8
France	43,506	97,770	24.2	20.9	19.0	28.2	53.4	33.1	3.4	17.8
Gabon	325	253	21.5	32.0	5.2	2.4	67.7	60.0	5.6	5.4
Gambia, The	18	54	0.0	15.5	100.0	52.4	0.0	31.9	0.0	0.2
Georgia	..	..	..	..	..	..	..	..	..	..
Germany[c]	33,058	86,022	26.6	22.5	15.1	18.9	57.4	45.7	0.8	12.9
Ghana	107	142	33.6	57.5	0.4	7.7	64.9	32.0	1.2	2.7
Greece	3,947	9,605	23.6	3.9	43.9	43.1	32.4	52.8	0.1	0.2
Guatemala	211	666	18.9	8.1	29.2	31.9	46.5	56.2	5.4	3.8
Guinea	..	119	..	10.7	..	0.7	..	88.3	..	0.2
Guinea-Bissau	6	..	8.9	..	12.5	..	78.6	..	0.0	..
Haiti	90	100	5.9	5.0	85.0	82.1	7.8	12.3	1.2	0.6
Honduras	82	258	36.9	21.9	30.1	31.1	18.5	45.3	14.5	1.7
Hong Kong	3,686	..	..	..	..	..	..	..	..	..

	Service exports		Transport		Travel		Communications, computer, information, and other services		Insurance and financial services	
	$ millions		% of total		% of total		% of total		% of total	
	1980	1995	1980	1995	1980	1995	1980	1995	1980	1995
Hungary	*633*	4,271	*5.4*	10.4	*63.5*	40.4	*30.5*	45.4	*0.6*	3.8
India	2,949	6,893	..	..	..	..	..	..	..	..
Indonesia	*449*	5,681	*15.1*	*0.0*	*50.8*	95.9	*34.1*	4.1	*0.0*	*0.0*
Iran, Islamic Rep.	731	*438*	4.5	*20.8*	4.0	*2.5*	91.5	*65.5*	0.0	*11.2*
Iraq	..	..	..	..	..	..	..	..	..	..
Ireland	1,381	4,802	36.6	22.3	42.0	46.0	21.4	31.7	0.0	0.0
Israel	2,722	7,741	38.1	26.0	36.0	37.2	24.9	36.6	1.0	0.2
Italy	19,192	65,043	23.9	22.9	46.7	42.2	22.9	28.7	6.5	6.2
Jamaica	401	1,388	28.0	18.1	61.2	73.6	6.7	7.4	4.2	0.9
Japan	20,240	65,212	62.9	34.3	3.2	4.9	32.4	59.8	1.6	0.9
Jordan	997	1,719	..	..	..	..	..	..	..	..
Kazakstan	..	64	..	..	..	..	..	..	..	..
Kenya	577	1,034	38.0	30.1	41.4	47.0	19.8	21.8	0.8	1.1
Korea, Dem. Rep.	..	..	..	..	..	..	..	..	..	..
Korea, Rep.	4,710	26,243	33.5	40.3	7.8	19.6	53.1	37.6	5.6	2.5
Kuwait	1,225	1,491	57.7	76.6	30.8	7.2	11.5	16.2	0.0	0.0
Kyrgyz Republic	..	..	..	..	..	..	..	..	..	..
Lao PDR	..	97	..	15.6	..	52.8	..	31.2	..	0.4
Latvia	..	712	..	91.5	..	2.8	..	3.3	..	2.4
Lebanon	..	*55*	..	..	..	..	..	..	..	..
Lesotho	32	*38*	2.0	*8.2*	37.8	*46.0*	60.2	*45.8*	0.0	*0.0*
Libya	164	..	64.5	..	6.2	..	29.4	..	0.0	..
Lithuania	..	485	..	59.3	..	15.9	..	23.9	..	0.9
Macedonia, FYR	..	200	..	*20.5*	..	*15.3*	..	*64.2*	..	..
Madagascar	79	242	49.4	26.9	6.3	23.8	44.0	47.3	0.4	2.0
Malawi	32	16	49.8	*58.5*	29.5	*20.6*	19.8	*20.6*	0.9	*0.3*
Malaysia	1,135	7,308	41.6	*28.7*	28.0	*51.6*	29.8	*19.6*	0.6	*0.1*
Mali	58	77	30.9	*38.2*	25.8	*27.0*	42.2	*33.8*	1.0	*0.9*
Mauritania	56	31	26.3	*6.7*	11.9	*41.6*	61.8	*51.6*	0.0	*0.0*
Mauritius	140	778	38.4	25.7	30.2	55.3	31.2	19.0	0.2	0.0
Mexico	4,591	10,281	9.7	11.4	69.7	60.0	10.4	21.7	10.2	6.9
Moldova	..	103	..	1.0	..	55.1	..	27.7	..	16.1
Mongolia	*37*	57	*26.5*	26.2	*8.6*	36.0	*64.9*	33.5	..	4.4
Morocco	783	1,996	20.3	21.1	57.9	58.3	20.7	19.2	1.1	1.4
Mozambique	118	242	78.5	..	0.0	..	21.5	..	0.0	..
Myanmar	60	*309*	..	..	..	..	..	..	..	..
Namibia	..	297	..	0.0	..	88.3	..	9.8	..	1.9
Nepal	127	709	..	..	..	..	..	..	..	..
Netherlands	17,150	48,377	51.5	40.5	13.1	13.6	34.3	44.9	1.2	1.1
New Zealand	1,009	4,297	58.2	35.6	21.1	50.3	19.6	14.3	1.1	−0.3
Nicaragua	44	119	36.0	11.9	48.6	45.9	14.9	40.5	0.5	1.7
Niger	41	*30*	33.5	*1.2*	15.2	*15.3*	50.9	*83.5*	0.4	*0.0*
Nigeria	1,127	1,953	80.9	16.4	6.0	2.8	6.5	80.2	6.6	0.6
Norway	8,615	*13,105*	74.5	*56.9*	8.8	*16.7*	16.3	*19.0*	0.4	*7.4*
Oman	9	13	100.0	100.0	0.0	0.0	0.0	0.0	0.0	0.0
Pakistan	617	*1,622*	..	..	..	..	..	..	..	..
Panama	902	*1,319*	47.0	*51.1*	19.0	*17.7*	25.8	*26.9*	8.2	*4.2*
Papua New Guinea	43	309	33.8	12.5	28.3	8.1	36.9	79.4	1.0	0.0
Paraguay	118	1,229	..	..	..	..	..	..	..	..
Peru	715	1,234	30.9	27.4	40.9	41.8	24.9	24.7	3.2	6.0
Philippines	1,447	9,348	14.2	2.9	22.1	12.2	63.6	84.3	0.0	0.7
Poland	2,018	8,617	59.2	35.3	11.9	2.9	24.1	51.6	4.8	10.2
Portugal	2,006	8,173	23.5	17.9	57.3	59.2	18.1	18.5	1.2	4.4
Puerto Rico	..	..	..	..	..	..	..	..	..	..
Romania	1,063	1,494	37.6	31.5	30.5	39.5	27.8	23.6	4.2	5.4
Russian Federation	..	12,400	..	49.4	..	34.6	..	15.3	..	0.5

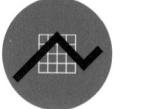

	Service exports $ millions		Transport % of total		Travel % of total		Communications, computer, information, and other services % of total		Insurance and financial services % of total	
	1980	1995	1980	1995	1980	1995	1980	1995	1980	1995
Rwanda	32	12	42.3	33.9	10.8	18.0	46.3	9.9	0.6	38.2
Saudi Arabia	5,191	3,480	15.3	..	25.9	..	58.8	..	0.0	..
Senegal	337	499	19.1	9.5	29.3	29.5	51.3	60.3	0.3	0.4
Sierra Leone	49	100	31.4	12.3	25.5	69.0	43.1	18.5	0.0	0.2
Singapore	4,856	29,375	26.9	16.8	29.5	28.2	42.5	53.6	1.1	1.3
Slovak Republic	..	2,378	..	25.9	..	26.2	..	43.0	..	4.9
Slovenia	..	2,018	..	25.0	..	53.5	..	21.1	..	0.4
South Africa	2,929	4,516	41.8	29.4	47.1	52.7	2.5	9.3	8.6	8.6
Spain	11,593	40,027	25.9	14.7	60.0	63.6	11.6	17.8	2.4	3.9
Sri Lanka	231	831	18.8	38.9	42.9	30.5	37.4	27.7	1.0	2.7
Sudan	216	106	..	..	..	..	..	..	..	..
Sweden	7,489	15,444	40.5	32.3	12.9	22.4	44.0	44.2	2.6	1.2
Switzerland	6,888	26,095	18.8	9.7	46.0	36.2	30.5	27.5	4.7	26.6
Syrian Arab Republic	365	1,966	17.2	12.1	42.9	67.4	39.9	20.5	0.0	0.0
Tajikistan	..	..	..	..	..	..	..	..	..	..
Tanzania	165	566	39.5	0.3	12.6	88.6	46.4	11.1	1.5	0.0
Thailand	1,490	14,845	20.1	16.5	58.2	54.1	21.2	28.7	0.5	0.7
Togo	74	73	38.3	14.2	35.2	32.6	25.0	52.7	1.4	0.5
Trinidad and Tobago	411	343	27.7	56.6	37.3	22.6	35.0	12.0	0.0	8.9
Tunisia	1,067	2,509	19.4	23.9	64.1	61.0	14.8	13.7	1.6	1.5
Turkey	711	14,606	37.4	11.7	45.9	33.9	16.3	52.8	0.4	1.5
Turkmenistan	..	..	..	..	..	..	..	..	..	..
Uganda	10	72	..	..	..	..	..	..	..	..
Ukraine	..	2,846	..	75.6	..	6.7	..	15.0	..	2.7
United Arab Emirates	1,090	..	..	..	..	..	..	..	..	..
United Kingdom	36,452	71,400	38.9	23.8	19.0	26.3	42.1	38.4	0.0	11.4
United States	47,550	208,550	29.9	22.3	22.3	33.5	44.6	40.6	3.2	3.6
Uruguay	468	1,171	18.6	23.1	63.7	52.2	14.8	24.7	2.9	1.2
Uzbekistan	..	..	..	..	..	..	..	..	..	..
Venezuela	693	1,487	41.1	38.6	35.1	45.7	9.5	15.5	14.4	0.2
Vietnam	..	2,074	..	..	..	..	..	..	..	..
West Bank and Gaza	..	..	..	..	..	..	..	..	..	..
Yemen, Rep.	..	173	..	..	..	..	..	..	..	..
Yugoslavia, Fed. Rep.	..	..	..	..	..	..	..	..	..	..
Zaire	57	..	40.4	..	15.8	..	42.1	..	1.8	..
Zambia	152	115	56.8	..	13.9	..	25.3	..	4.1	..
Zimbabwe	169	383	56.9	24.3	14.6	46.7	26.1	28.7	2.4	0.3

World	**357,753 t**	**1,126,092 t**	..	..	..	..	..	..	..	..
Low income	9,253 t	37,873 t	..	..	..	..	..	..	..	..
Excl. China & India	6,304 t	11,850 t	..	..	..	..	..	..	..	..
Middle income	46,384 t	175,214 t	..	..	..	..	..	..	..	..
Lower middle income	20,882 t	107,229 t	..	..	..	..	..	..	..	..
Upper middle income	25,502 t	67,986 t	..	..	..	..	..	..	..	..
Low & middle income	55,637 t	213,087 t	..	..	..	..	..	..	..	..
East Asia & Pacific	4,409 t	59,707 t	..	..	..	..	..	..	..	..
Europe & Central Asia	9,442 t	72,780 t	..	..	..	..	..	..	..	..
Latin America & Carib.	16,614 t	38,717 t	..	..	..	..	..	..	..	..
Middle East & N. Africa	12,509 t	19,910 t	..	..	..	..	..	..	..	..
South Asia	4,176 t	8,622 t	..	..	..	..	..	..	..	..
Sub-Saharan Africa	8,488 t	13,352 t	..	..	..	..	..	..	..	..
High income	302,116 t	913,005 t	..	..	..	..	..	..	..	..

a. Includes Luxembourg. b. Data prior to 1992 include Eritrea. c. Data prior to 1990 refer to the Federal Republic of Germany before unification.

Services go international

Services are the fastest-growing component of world trade. As the markets for services have expanded, so have foreign direct investment (FDI) flows to services, which now account for close to one-fifth of all trade and three-fifths of all FDI. Most of the FDI in services has flowed between OECD countries, but developing countries' share of this investment has been increasing.

Although services statistics have many deficiencies, it is clear that trade in services has grown faster than trade in merchandise in the past decade. During 1980–95 service trade grew an average 8 percent a year, compared with 6 percent for merchandise trade (in nominal terms). The rapid growth boosted commercial services' share in global trade from 16 percent in 1980 to 18 percent in 1995. The most dynamic trade is in such private services as financial, brokerage, and leasing services. Growing at an average annual rate of 9.5 percent, trade in these services rose from 37 percent of commercial services trade in 1980 to 45 percent in 1993.

International trade in services is not a new phenomenon: transport, travel, tourism, and insurance have long been important traded activities. What is new is the rapid expansion of international service transactions in the past decade or so. There are also new modes of supply, such as transmitting services over electronic networks. Many services considered nontradable only a few years ago are now actively traded. Seamless, around-the-clock, around-the-globe financial services, for example, have become standard.

Rapid advances in telecommunications and information technology have been a central force in the internationalization of services. Also important have been the deregulation of service industries and liberalization of foreign trade and investment regimes. For developing countries taking advantage of the more liberal trade and investment regimes, the internationalization of services offers opportunities for expanding into new exports and attracting more FDI. It should also broaden the range of producer services and technical capabilities that developing countries can provide by importing the new technologies.

By making more activities in industrial countries contestable and thus more subject to competition and by revealing new complementarities, technological progress has created important new opportunities for long-distance service exports from developing countries.

About the data

See the notes to table 4.11.

Definitions

● **Services** refer to economic output of intangible commodities that may be produced, transferred, and consumed at the same time. International transactions in services are defined by the IMF's *Balance of Payments Manual* (1993), but definitions may nevertheless vary among reporting economies.
● **Transport** covers all transport services (sea, air, land, internal waterway, space, and pipeline) performed by residents of one economy for those of another and involving the carriage of passengers, the movement of goods (freight), rental of carriers with crew, and related support and auxiliary services. Excluded are freight insurance, which is included in insurance services; goods procured in ports by nonresident carriers and repairs of transport equipment, which are included in goods; repairs of railway facilities, harbors, and airfield facilities, which are included in construction services; and rental of carriers without crew, which is included in other services. ● **Travel** covers goods and services acquired from an economy by travelers for their own use during visits of less than one year in that economy for either business or personal purposes. ● **Communications, computer, information, and other services** cover international telecommunications and postal and courier services; computer data; news-related service transactions between residents and nonresidents; construction services; royalties and license fees; miscellaneous business, professional, and technical services; personal, cultural, and recreational services; and government services not included elsewhere. ● **Insurance and financial services** cover various types of insurance provided to nonresidents by resident insurance enterprises and vice versa, and financial intermediary and auxiliary services (except those of insurance enterprises and pension funds) exchanged between residents and nonresidents.

Data sources

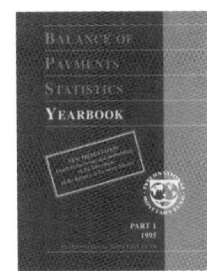 Data on exports and imports of services come from the balance of payments data files of the International Monetary Fund (IMF). The IMF publishes balance of payments data in the *International Financial Statistics* and in the *Balance of Payments Statistics Yearbook*. The feature text was adapted from the World Bank's *Global Economic Prospects and the Developing Countries 1995*.

Figure 4.10a World trade in goods and services, 1980–95

trillions of U.S. dollars

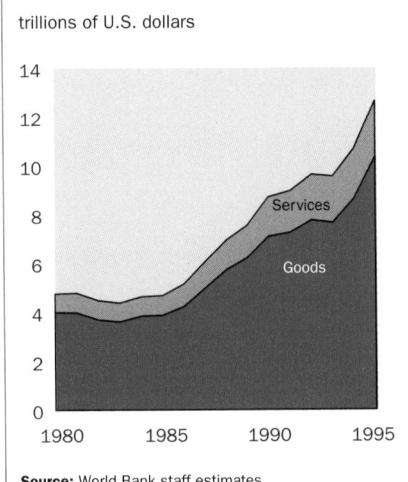

Source: World Bank staff estimates.

4.11 | Structure of service imports

	Service imports		Transport		Travel		Communications, computer, information, and other services		Insurance and financial services	
	$ millions		% of total		% of total		% of total		% of total	
	1980	1995	1980	1995	1980	1995	1980	1995	1980	1995
Albania	18	157	43.7	38.5	0.0	4.2	51.4	43.4	4.9	13.9
Algeria	2,697	*1,193*	39.9	..	12.4	..	40.9	..	6.8	..
Angola	..	*1,734*	..	*28.1*	..	*4.2*	..	*65.6*	..	*2.1*
Argentina	3,788	5,047	33.6	41.3	47.3	41.0	19.1	17.8	0.0	0.0
Armenia	..	52	..	82.6	..	6.2	..	0.9	..	10.3
Australia	6,532	17,611	47.4	36.9	28.1	28.3	23.2	29.4	1.3	5.4
Austria	6,204	21,034	12.7	9.2	50.6	50.2	32.4	25.7	4.2	14.9
Azerbaijan	..	312	..	..	..	..	..	..	..	..
Bangladesh	173	710	..	..	..	..	..	..	..	..
Belarus	..	174	..	..	..	..	..	..	..	..
Belgium[a]	12,827	35,520	29.7	21.1	25.7	25.9	39.5	38.6	5.2	14.4
Benin	109	*111*	56.9	*65.8*	7.1	*5.3*	25.9	*23.0*	10.1	*5.8*
Bolivia	259	*338*	53.3	*50.9*	21.3	*21.0*	16.2	*22.7*	9.1	*5.4*
Bosnia and Herzegovina	..	..	..	..	..	..	..	..	..	..
Botswana	216	444	42.4	42.2	26.0	32.7	27.8	17.1	3.7	8.0
Brazil	4,871	13,630	56.5	42.6	7.5	24.9	35.0	23.3	1.0	9.2
Bulgaria	549	1,191	51.3	37.3	8.6	16.4	34.4	46.4	5.7	0.0
Burkina Faso	209	*138*	58.0	*46.9*	15.3	*16.4*	21.6	*32.6*	4.8	*4.0*
Burundi	..	102	..	30.0	..	24.9	..	41.1	..	3.9
Cambodia	..	188	..	44.7	..	4.4	..	46.8	..	4.2
Cameroon	377	497	..	..	..	..	..	..	..	..
Canada	10,558	30,141	19.1	19.9	37.5	33.9	43.5	46.2	0.0	0.0
Central African Republic	142	*114*	47.3	*43.7*	24.5	*38.0*	23.5	*10.4*	4.7	*7.9*
Chad	24	*199*	6.4	*48.1*	57.5	*13.0*	35.4	*37.6*	0.7	*1.3*
Chile	1,583	3,306	52.4	49.2	12.6	21.5	32.3	26.7	2.7	2.6
China	*2,024*	25,223	*61.6*	37.8	*3.3*	14.6	*30.7*	30.7	*4.4*	16.9
Colombia	1,170	3,349	45.3	34.0	20.5	24.7	24.0	26.2	10.2	14.1
Congo	480	775	27.0	27.1	6.1	5.0	63.5	65.9	3.5	2.0
Costa Rica	286	947	58.2	40.1	21.1	34.6	13.9	*19.4*	6.7	6.6
Côte d'Ivoire	1,531	1,094	38.6	43.6	15.8	14.5	37.7	39.3	7.9	2.6
Croatia	..	2,708	..	49.7	..	28.5	..	21.8	..	..
Cuba	..	..	..	..	..	..	..	..	..	..
Czech Republic	..	4,882	..	16.4	..	33.5	..	43.8	..	5.2
Denmark	*4,663*	15,111	*47.7*	48.1	*27.4*	28.4	*22.9*	23.5	*2.0*	..
Dominican Republic	399	647	39.6	55.1	41.6	25.3	14.7	14.0	4.1	5.6
Ecuador	704	983	36.0	47.7	32.4	23.9	19.1	*15.5*	12.4	13.0
Egypt, Arab Rep.	2,343	3,761	..	..	..	..	..	..	..	..
El Salvador	273	237	29.3	..	38.8	..	20.7	..	11.2	..
Eritrea	..	44	..	..	..	..	..	..	..	..
Estonia	..	498	..	44.6	..	18.2	..	33.0	..	4.0
Ethiopia[b]	90	209	..	..	..	..	..	..	..	..
Finland	2,555	9,834	39.4	23.4	23.1	23.6	35.1	48.4	2.4	4.8
France	32,148	78,530	28.4	27.1	18.7	20.8	48.1	31.2	4.8	20.9
Gabon	789	894	22.0	*26.8*	12.2	*17.6*	60.1	*49.9*	5.7	*5.8*
Gambia, The	42	69	55.8	40.3	3.5	20.6	33.2	35.2	7.4	3.9
Georgia	..	..	..	..	..	..	..	..	..	..
Germany[c]	42,375	132,520	25.1	19.7	41.2	38.3	33.2	34.9	0.6	7.1
Ghana	270	408	39.7	*49.7*	12.1	*5.0*	45.8	*38.5*	2.3	*6.8*
Greece	1,428	4,368	41.5	27.4	21.6	30.3	31.1	38.1	5.8	4.2
Guatemala	487	695	37.0	40.1	33.6	20.3	26.0	31.2	3.3	8.4
Guinea	..	371	..	38.9	..	5.7	..	50.5	..	4.9
Guinea-Bissau	*14*	21	*47.9*	52.6	*11.0*	0.0	*36.0*	41.5	*5.0*	5.8
Haiti	162	233	49.3	56.5	25.1	14.9	23.0	26.9	2.7	1.7
Honduras	174	334	53.3	58.9	17.8	17.1	16.6	21.0	12.3	2.4
Hong Kong	2,643	..	..	..	..	..	..	..	..	..

	Service imports		Transport		Travel		Communications, computer, information, and other services		Insurance and financial services	
	$ millions		% of total		% of total		% of total		% of total	
	1980	1995	1980	1995	1980	1995	1980	1995	1980	1995
Hungary	*524*	3,629	*60.3*	10.2	*26.9*	29.5	*6.1*	53.9	*6.7*	5.1
India	1,516	6,954	..	..	..	..	..	..	..	..
Indonesia	*4,998*	13,475	*40.1*	35.2	*11.9*	16.1	*44.2*	45.4	*3.8*	3.2
Iran, Islamic Rep.	5,223	*3,405*	43.6	*29.1*	32.5	*4.4*	17.4	*59.1*	6.4	*7.4*
Iraq	..	..	..	..	..	..	..	..	..	..
Ireland	1,593	10,516	43.9	16.7	36.6	19.3	16.1	62.5	3.4	1.5
Israel	2,310	9,257	44.1	33.9	35.6	38.3	18.5	25.2	1.8	2.5
Italy	16,249	63,332	43.8	36.7	11.8	20.1	31.0	34.0	13.1	8.4
Jamaica	370	1,034	55.4	47.6	8.9	14.3	23.8	28.7	11.8	9.4
Japan	32,360	122,698	52.2	29.3	14.2	29.9	31.3	38.3	2.3	2.4
Jordan	828	1,209	..	..	..	..	..	..	..	..
Kazakstan	..	273	..	..	..	..	..	..	..	..
Kenya	502	871	66.2	55.4	4.6	16.6	18.0	22.5	11.2	5.5
Korea, Dem. Rep.	..	..	..	..	..	..	..	..	..	..
Korea, Rep.	4,089	27,885	55.8	38.2	8.6	22.7	30.0	36.0	5.6	3.1
Kuwait	3,067	4,936	38.8	32.5	43.7	47.0	16.9	19.1	0.6	1.3
Kyrgyz Republic	..	..	..	..	..	..	..	..	..	..
Lao PDR	..	125	..	32.5	..	23.6	..	43.1	..	0.7
Latvia	..	246	..	62.3	..	9.9	..	21.4	..	6.4
Lebanon	..	*403*	..	..	..	..	..	..	..	..
Lesotho	50	*64*	31.6	*50.8*	15.8	*10.6*	49.7	*33.6*	2.8	*5.0*
Libya	2,303	..	51.4	..	20.4	..	23.2	..	5.0	..
Lithuania	..	498	..	58.7	..	21.3	..	18.7	..	1.0
Macedonia, FYR	..	782	..	*49.4*	..	*7.5*	..	*43.1*	..	..
Madagascar	311	359	57.3	43.0	9.9	16.3	28.0	36.6	4.8	2.9
Malawi	179	217	81.7	*83.0*	5.6	*6.5*	5.3	2.0	7.4	*8.5*
Malaysia	2,957	10,101	44.3	49.0	24.5	*19.6*	31.2	*31.5*	0.0	*0.0*
Mali	212	394	65.8	*51.1*	9.6	*16.7*	18.3	*26.7*	6.2	*5.6*
Mauritania	128	249	59.1	*51.8*	13.6	*9.9*	24.2	*36.4*	3.1	*1.9*
Mauritius	174	641	64.7	39.2	12.9	24.8	15.2	31.5	7.2	4.5
Mexico	6,514	9,407	28.2	34.6	47.0	33.5	16.3	21.0	8.5	10.8
Moldova	..	185	..	51.8	..	30.5	..	7.9	..	9.7
Mongolia	*31*	95	*48.4*	63.7	*0.3*	20.4	*51.3*	*15.8*	0.0	0.0
Morocco	1,436	2,063	34.4	36.2	6.8	14.7	55.7	43.2	3.3	6.0
Mozambique	124	390	79.0	..	0.0	..	14.5	..	6.5	..
Myanmar	85	*122*	..	..	..	..	..	..	..	..
Namibia	..	467	..	26.0	..	17.5	..	47.7	..	8.2
Nepal	81	243	..	..	..	..	..	..	..	..
Netherlands	18,148	46,317	43.9	30.7	26.6	25.2	27.2	41.1	2.4	2.9
New Zealand	1,843	4,600	39.4	39.6	28.3	27.9	31.8	27.7	0.6	5.0
Nicaragua	104	218	50.7	37.5	29.9	18.4	14.2	40.9	5.2	3.2
Niger	279	*149*	43.0	*51.8*	6.6	*13.1*	43.7	*33.1*	6.7	*1.5*
Nigeria	5,285	..	33.7	..	18.7	..	43.8	..	2.8	..
Norway	6,996	*14,392*	52.2	*38.5*	21.1	*28.5*	23.3	*22.9*	3.4	*10.1*
Oman	518	964	34.1	42.7	6.2	4.9	55.9	47.7	3.8	4.7
Pakistan	853	*2,379*	..	..	..	..	..	..	..	..
Panama	588	*978*	65.4	*69.5*	9.5	*12.6*	14.9	*9.8*	10.2	*8.1*
Papua New Guinea	302	613	60.4	29.3	5.9	9.5	28.9	61.2	4.8	0.0
Paraguay	260	960	..	..	..	..	..	..	..	..
Peru	880	2,015	55.4	44.9	12.2	15.0	25.2	32.0	7.2	9.0
Philippines	1,439	6,926	52.1	29.6	7.4	6.1	39.8	62.1	0.8	1.6
Poland	2,023	7,158	59.9	24.7	12.9	6.0	25.3	55.3	2.0	13.3
Portugal	1,525	6,536	48.8	25.7	19.1	32.4	27.2	33.2	4.9	8.6
Puerto Rico	..	..	..	..	..	..	..	..	..	..
Romania	1,045	1,727	76.8	29.6	7.0	40.4	7.7	24.0	8.5	5.6
Russian Federation	..	20,500	..	..	..	..	..	..	..	..

	Service imports ($ millions)		Transport (% of total)		Travel (% of total)		Communications, computer, information, and other services (% of total)		Insurance and financial services (% of total)	
	1980	1995	1980	1995	1980	1995	1980	1995	1980	1995
Rwanda	123	115	63.5	50.3	9.3	13.1	27.3	36.6	0.0	0.0
Saudi Arabia	30,231	18,328	17.1	11.7	8.1	0.0	73.3	87.8	1.5	1.3
Senegal	340	552	46.9	36.7	17.6	9.7	28.9	48.8	6.5	4.7
Sierra Leone	85	108	54.8	14.5	9.8	57.5	23.4	24.8	11.9	3.2
Singapore	2,912	16,634	38.3	29.4	11.4	30.9	46.1	33.9	4.3	5.8
Slovak Republic	..	1,832	..	16.4	..	17.5	..	61.3	..	4.8
Slovenia	..	1,292	..	33.6	..	32.0	..	32.0	..	1.5
South Africa	3,805	5,970	48.4	47.7	20.3	29.5	20.0	14.6	11.3	8.2
Spain	5,732	22,161	38.6	28.8	21.5	20.1	34.6	43.4	5.4	7.6
Sri Lanka	351	1,245	60.4	55.5	9.5	16.1	23.5	22.7	6.5	5.7
Sudan	258	115	..	..	..	..	..	..	..	..
Sweden	7,018	17,206	35.9	28.2	31.6	31.6	28.1	38.8	4.4	1.4
Switzerland	4,885	15,402	30.4	24.6	48.8	50.1	19.3	24.2	1.6	1.1
Syrian Arab Republic	521	1,437	26.6	54.1	33.9	27.7	37.3	18.2	2.2	..
Tajikistan	..	25	..	..	..	..	..	..	..	..
Tanzania	295	754	62.1	28.8	6.7	47.8	25.6	20.8	5.5	2.7
Thailand	1,644	18,804	64.4	41.4	14.8	20.1	14.8	33.4	5.9	5.1
Togo	167	78	62.7	48.4	14.1	29.7	16.7	11.5	6.6	10.4
Trinidad and Tobago	645	242	45.7	38.9	21.6	28.7	23.5	24.9	9.2	7.3
Tunisia	600	1,352	51.1	41.7	17.7	18.5	25.5	33.7	5.7	5.9
Turkey	569	5,024	50.5	28.1	18.3	18.1	27.1	46.0	4.2	7.8
Turkmenistan	..	478	..	..	..	..	..	..	..	..
Uganda	123	281	..	..	..	..	..	..	..	..
Ukraine	..	1,334	..	34.0	..	15.7	..	42.9	..	7.3
United Arab Emirates	2,890	..	..	..	..	..	..	..	..	..
United Kingdom	27,933	61,717	47.5	27.9	22.9	39.9	29.6	30.9	0.0	1.3
United States	40,970	140,430	37.5	31.0	25.4	33.4	35.0	31.2	2.1	4.4
Uruguay	476	813	31.8	43.9	42.6	29.0	18.1	27.1	7.5	..
Uzbekistan	..	..	..	..	..	..	..	..	..	..
Venezuela	4,253	4,887	31.7	28.0	47.0	35.1	16.5	34.8	4.8	2.2
Vietnam	..	1,916	..	..	..	..	..	..	..	..
West Bank and Gaza	..	..	..	..	..	..	..	..	..	..
Yemen, Rep.	..	433	..	..	..	..	..	..	..	..
Yugoslavia, Fed. Rep.	..	..	..	..	..	..	..	..	..	..
Zaire	608	..	41.9	..	8.1	..	46.1	..	3.9	..
Zambia	651	375	53.5	..	8.5	..	33.9	..	4.0	..
Zimbabwe	395	712	43.3	50.7	40.3	16.9	12.9	29.8	3.5	2.6

	Service imports ($ millions)		Transport (% of total)		Travel (% of total)		Communications, computer, information, and other services (% of total)		Insurance and financial services (% of total)	
World	**397,366 t**	**1,145,244 t**	..	..	..	..	..	..	..	..
Low income	16,720 t	46,945 t	..	..	..	..	..	..	..	..
Excl. China & India	15,204 t	14,769 t	..	..	..	..	..	..	..	..
Middle income	92,963 t	196,587 t	..	..	..	..	..	..	..	..
Lower middle income	31,960 t	108,679 t	..	..	..	..	..	..	..	..
Upper middle income	61,002 t	87,908 t	..	..	..	..	..	..	..	..
Low & middle income	109,682 t	243,532 t	..	..	..	..	..	..	..	..
East Asia & Pacific	6,608 t	77,983 t	..	..	..	..	..	..	..	..
Europe & Central Asia	5,874 t	59,566 t	..	..	..	..	..	..	..	..
Latin America & Carib.	28,751 t	49,287 t	..	..	..	..	..	..	..	..
Middle East & N. Africa	47,174 t	30,427 t	..	..	..	..	..	..	..	..
South Asia	3,161 t	9,193 t	..	..	..	..	..	..	..	..
Sub-Saharan Africa	18,114 t	17,076 t	..	..	..	..	..	..	..	..
High income	287,683 t	901,712 t	..	..	..	..	..	..	..	..

a. Includes Luxembourg. b. Data prior to 1992 include Eritrea. c. Data prior to 1990 refer to the Federal Republic of Germany before unification.

Figure 4.11a Services as a share of total trade, 1980–95

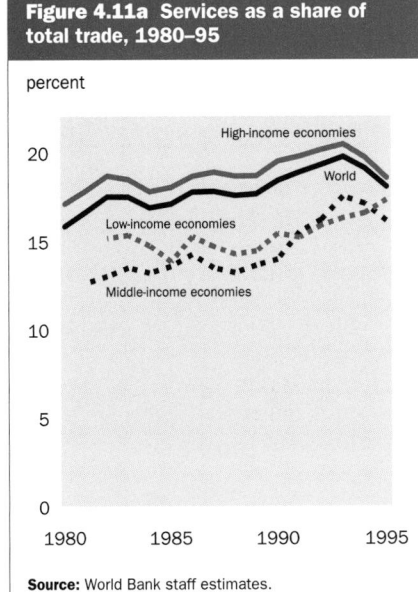

percent

High-income economies

World

Low-income economies

Middle-income economies

Source: World Bank staff estimates.

About the data

Balance of payments statistics, the main source of information for international trade in services, have many weaknesses. Until recently some large economies—such as the former Soviet Union—did not report data on trade in services. The level of disaggregation of important components may be limited and varies significantly across countries. There are inconsistencies in the methods used to report items, and the recording of major flows as net items is common practice (for example, insurance transactions are often recorded net as premiums less claims). These factors contribute to a downward bias in the value of the services trade reported in the balance of payments.

Efforts are being made to improve the coverage, quality, and consistency of the data. The Organization for Economic Cooperation and Development and Eurostat, for example, are working together to improve the collection of statistics on trade in services in member countries. And the International Monetary Fund is implementing the new classification of trade in services introduced in the fifth edition of its *Balance of Payments Manual* (1993).

But because of the difficulties in capturing all the dimensions of international trade in services, the record is likely to remain incomplete. Cross-border intrafirm service transactions, which are usually not captured in the balance of payments, are increasing rapidly as foreign direct investment expands and electronic networks become pervasive. One example of such transactions is transnational corporations' use of mainframe computers around the clock for data processing, exploiting time zone differences between their home country and the host countries of their affiliates. Another important dimension of services trade not captured by conventional balance of payments statistics is establishment trade—sales in the host country by foreign affiliates. By contrast, cross-border intrafirm transactions in merchandise may be reported as exports or imports in the balance of payments.

Definitions

• **Services** refer to economic output of intangible commodities that may be produced, transferred, and consumed at the same time. International transactions in services are defined by the IMF's *Balance of Payments Manual* (1993), but definitions may nevertheless vary among reporting economies.
• **Transport** covers all transport services (sea, air, land, internal waterway, space, and pipeline) performed by residents of one economy for those of another and involving the carriage of passengers, the movement of goods (freight), rental of carriers with crew, and related support and auxiliary services. Excluded are freight insurance, which is included in insurance services; goods procured in ports by nonresident carriers and repairs of transport equipment, which are included in goods; repairs of railway facilities, harbors, and airfield facilities, which are included in construction services; and rental of carriers without crew, which is included in other services. • **Travel** covers goods and services acquired from an economy by travelers for their own use during visits of less than one year in that economy for either business or personal purposes. • **Communications, computer, information, and other services** cover international telecommunications and postal and courier services; computer data; news-related service transactions between residents and nonresidents; construction services; royalties and license fees; miscellaneous business, professional, and technical services; personal, cultural, and recreational services; and government services not included elsewhere.
• **Insurance and financial services** cover various types of insurance provided to nonresidents by resident insurance enterprises and vice versa, and financial intermediary and auxiliary services (except those of insurance enterprises and pension funds) exchanged between residents and nonresidents.

Data sources

Data on exports and imports of services come from the balance of payments data files of the International Monetary Fund (IMF). The IMF publishes balance of payments data in the *International Financial Statistics* and in the *Balance of Payments Statistics Yearbook*.

4.12 | Structure of demand

	Private consumption		General government consumption		Gross domestic investment		Exports of goods and services		Imports of goods and services		Gross domestic savings	
	% of GDP		% of GDP		% of GDP		% of GDP		% of GDP		% of GDP	
	1980	1995	1980	1995	1980	1995	1980	1995	1980	1995	1980	1995
Albania	56	93	9	15	35	16	..	14	..	38	..	−8
Algeria	43	56	14	16	39	32	34	27	30	30	43	29
Angola	..	9	..	47	..	27	..	74	..	58	..	43
Argentina	76	82	..[a]	..[a]	25	18	5	9	6	8	24	18
Armenia	47	116	16	13	29	9	..	24	..	62	..	−29
Australia	59	60	18	17	25	23	16	20	18	20	24	22
Austria	56	55	18	19	28	27	37	38	39	39	26	26
Azerbaijan	..	96	..	..[a]	..	16	..	27	..	39	..	4
Bangladesh	92	78	6	14	15	17	6	14	18	22	2	8
Belarus	..	58	..	22	..	25	..	43	..	47	..	20
Belgium	63	62	18	15	22	18	63	74	65	69	19	24
Benin	96	82	9	9	15	20	23	27	43	37	−5	9
Bolivia	67	79	14	13	15	15	21	20	17	27	19	8
Bosnia and Herzegovina	..	..	..	..	..	..	..	..	..	..	..	..
Botswana	53	45	19	32	38	25	53	49	63	52	28	23
Brazil	70	62	9	17	23	22	9	7	11	8	21	21
Bulgaria	55	61	6	15	34	21	36	49	31	45	39	25
Burkina Faso	95	78	10	16	17	22	10	14	33	30	−6	6
Burundi	92	95	9	12	14	11	9	12	24	31	−1	−7
Cambodia	..	82	..	11	..	19	..	11	..	24	..	6
Cameroon	70	71	10	9	21	15	27	26	27	20	20	21
Canada	55	60	19	19	24	19	28	37	27	35	25	21
Central African Republic	94	80	15	13	7	15	26	18	43	27	−10	6
Chad	99	93	8	17	4	9	24	13	41	33	−6	−10
Chile	67	62	12	9	25	27	23	29	27	27	20	29
China	51	46	15	12	35	40	6	21	7	19	35	42
Colombia	70	75	10	9	19	20	16	15	16	20	20	16
Congo	47	64	18	12	36	27	60	62	60	66	36	23
Costa Rica	66	60	18	17	27	25	26	41	37	42	16	24
Côte d'Ivoire	63	67	17	12	27	13	35	41	41	34	20	20
Croatia	..	66	..	33	..	14	..	40	..	53	..	1
Cuba	..	..	..	..	..	..	..	..	..	..	..	..
Czech Republic	..	60	..	20	..	25	..	52	..	56	..	20
Denmark	56	54	27	25	19	16	33	35	34	29	17	21
Dominican Republic	77	80	8	4	25	20	19	26	29	29	15	16
Ecuador	60	67	15	13	26	19	25	29	25	27	26	21
Egypt, Arab Rep.	69	81	16	13	28	17	31	21	43	32	15	6
El Salvador	72	86	14	8	13	19	34	21	33	34	14	6
Eritrea	..	95	..	32	..	20	..	30	..	77	..	−27
Estonia	..	58	..	23	..	27	..	75	..	84	..	18
Ethiopia[b]	83	81	14	12	9	17	11	15	17	25	3	7
Finland	54	54	18	21	29	16	33	38	34	30	28	24
France	59	60	18	20	24	18	22	23	23	20	23	20
Gabon	26	42	13	10	28	26	65	61	32	39	61	48
Gambia, The	79	76	20	19	26	21	47	53	72	72	1	5
Georgia	56	103	13	7	29	3	..	17	..	29	..	−9
Germany	..	58	..	20	..	21	..	23	..	22	..	23
Ghana	84	77	11	12	6	19	8	25	9	34	5	10
Greece	60	74	16	19	29	19	21	22	26	34	23	7
Guatemala	79	86	8	6	16	17	22	19	25	28	13	8
Guinea	..	81	..	8	..	15	..	21	..	25	..	11
Guinea-Bissau	77	98	29	8	30	16	8	13	44	35	−6	−5
Haiti	82	101	10	6	17	2	22	4	31	13	8	−7
Honduras	70	73	13	14	25	23	36	36	44	45	17	14
Hong Kong	60	59	6	9	35	35	90	147	91	149	34	33

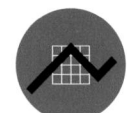

	Private consumption		General government consumption		Gross domestic investment		Exports of goods and services		Imports of goods and services		Gross domestic savings	
	% of GDP		% of GDP		% of GDP		% of GDP		% of GDP		% of GDP	
	1980	1995	1980	1995	1980	1995	1980	1995	1980	1995	1980	1995
Hungary	61	68	10	11	31	23	39	35	41	37	29	21
India	73	68	10	10	21	25	7	12	10	15	17	22
Indonesia	52	56	11	8	24	38	33	25	20	27	37	36
Iran, Islamic Rep.	53	53	21	13	30	29	13	21	16	16	26	34
Iraq	..	..	..	..	..	..	..	..	..	..	..	..
Ireland	67	57	19	15	27	13	48	75	61	61	14	27
Israel	50	58	39	29	22	24	40	29	51	40	11	13
Italy	61	62	15	16	27	18	22	26	25	23	24	22
Jamaica	64	80	20	9	16	17	51	69	51	76	16	10
Japan	59	60	10	10	32	29	14	9	15	8	31	31
Jordan	..	75	..	22	..	26	..	49	..	72	..	3
Kazakstan	..	65	..	15	..	22	..	34	..	37	..	19
Kenya	62	72	20	15	29	19	28	33	39	39	18	13
Korea, Dem. Rep.	..	..	..	..	..	..	..	..	..	..	..	..
Korea, Rep.	64	54	12	10	32	37	34	33	41	34	25	36
Kuwait	31	49	11	33	14	12	78	55	34	49	58	18
Kyrgyz Republic	..	67	..	23	..	16	..	26	..	32	..	10
Lao PDR	..	..	..	..	..	..	..	..	..	..	..	..
Latvia	60	65	8	20	26	21	..	43	..	48	..	16
Lebanon	..	110	..	12	..	29	..	10	..	60	..	−22
Lesotho	124	85	36	23	42	87	20	21	122	117	−60	−9
Libya	21	..	22	..	22	..	66	..	31	..	57	..
Lithuania	..	63	..	20	..	19	..	58	..	61	..	16
Macedonia, FYR	..	82	..	14	..	15	..	37	..	49	..	4
Madagascar	89	91	12	7	15	11	13	23	30	31	−1	3
Malawi	70	76	19	20	25	15	25	29	39	40	11	4
Malaysia	51	51	17	12	30	41	58	96	55	99	33	37
Mali	91	79	10	11	17	26	16	22	35	38	−2	10
Mauritania	68	80	25	9	36	15	37	50	67	54	7	11
Mauritius	75	65	14	12	21	25	51	58	61	61	10	22
Mexico	65	71	10	10	27	15	11	25	13	22	25	19
Moldova	..	81	..	20	..	7	..	35	..	43	..	−1
Mongolia	74	..	.. [a]	..	46	..	19	..	39	..	27	..
Morocco	68	71	18	15	24	21	17	27	28	35	14	13
Mozambique	78	75	21	20	22	60	20	23	42	79	1	5
Myanmar	82	89	.. [a]	.. [a]	21	12	9	2	13	2	18	11
Namibia	44	52	17	31	29	20	76	53	66	56	39	17
Nepal	82	79	7	8	18	23	12	24	19	35	11	12
Netherlands	61	57	17	14	22	22	51	53	52	46	22	29
New Zealand	62	60	18	15	21	24	30	32	32	30	20	26
Nicaragua	83	95	20	14	17	18	24	24	43	52	−2	−9
Niger	67	82	10	17	37	6	24	13	38	17	23	1
Nigeria	56	..	12	10	22	..	29	..	19	..	32	..
Norway	51	50	18	21	25	23[c]	43	38	37	32	31	29
Oman	28	42	25	31	22	17	63	49	38	40	47	27
Pakistan	83	73	10	12	18	19	12	16	24	19	7	16
Panama	..	64	..	15	..	24	..	39	..	40	..	22
Papua New Guinea	61	48	24	12	25	24	43	61	53	45	15	39
Paraguay	76	79	6	7	32	23	15	36	29	46	18	14
Peru	57	83	11	6	29	17	22	12	19	18	32	11
Philippines	67	74	9	11	29	23	24	36	28	44	24	15
Poland	67	63	9	18	26	17	28	28	31	26	23	19
Portugal	65	65	14	17	34	28[c]	24	28	37	38	21	18
Puerto Rico	75	..	16	14	17	17	65	..	73	..	10	..
Romania	60	66	5	12	40	26	35	28	40	32	35	21
Russian Federation	62	58	15	16	22	25	..	22	..	22	..	26

	Private consumption		General government consumption		Gross domestic investment		Exports of goods and services		Imports of goods and services		Gross domestic savings	
	% of GDP		% of GDP		% of GDP		% of GDP		% of GDP		% of GDP	
	1980	1995	1980	1995	1980	1995	1980	1995	1980	1995	1980	1995
Rwanda	83	93	12	14	16	13	15	6	26	26	5	−7
Saudi Arabia	22	43	16	27	22	20	71	40	30	30	62	30
Senegal	78	79	22	11	15	16	28	32	44	37	0	10
Sierra Leone	91	98	8	11	18	6	23	13	39	27	2	−9
Singapore	53	40	10	9	46	33	207	..	216	..	38	51
Slovak Republic	..	50	..	20	..	28	..	63	..	61	..	30
Slovenia	..	58	..	21	..	22	..	56	..	57	..	21
South Africa	50	61	13	21	28	18	36	22	28	22	36	18
Spain	66	62	13	16	23	21	16	24	18	23	21	22
Sri Lanka	80	74	9	12	34	25	32	36	55	47	11	14
Sudan	81	..	16	..	15	..	12	..	24	..	3	..
Sweden	51	55	29	26	21	14	29	41	31	36	19	19
Switzerland	67	59	13	14	24	23	37	36	40	32	20	27
Syrian Arab Republic	67	..	23	..	28	..	18	..	35	..	10	..
Tajikistan	..	71	..	11	..	17	..	114	..	114	..	18
Tanzania	69	97	12	10	29	31	14	30	24	68	19	−7
Thailand	65	54	12	10	29	43	24	42	30	48	23	36
Togo	53	80	22	11	30	14	51	31	56	35	25	9
Trinidad and Tobago	46	62	12	13	31	14	50	39	39	29	42	25
Tunisia	62	63	14	16	29	24	40	45	46	48	24	20
Turkey	78	70	10	10	18	25	5	20	12	25	11	20
Turkmenistan	..	..	..	..	..	..	..	..	..	..	..	..
Uganda	89	83	11	10	6	16	19	12	26	21	0	7
Ukraine	..	..	..	..	..	..	..	..	..	..	..	..
United Arab Emirates	17	54	11	18	28	27	78	70	34	69	72	27
United Kingdom	59	64	22	21	17	16c	27	28	25	29	19	15
United States	63	68	18	16	20	16	10	11	11	13	19	15
Uruguay	76	74	12	13	17	14	15	19	21	20	12	13
Uzbekistan	..	59	..	25	..	23	..	63	..	62	..	24
Venezuela	55	73	12	6	26	16	29	27	22	22	33	21
Vietnam	..	77	..	7	..	27	..	36	..	47	..	16
West Bank and Gaza	..	..	..	..	..	..	..	..	..	..	..	..
Yemen, Rep.	..	61	..	29	..	12	..	43	..	45	..	10
Yugoslavia, Fed. Rep.	..	..	..	..	..	..	..	..	..	..	..	..
Zaire	82	..	8	..	10	..	16	..	16	..	10	..
Zambia	55	88	26	9	23	12	41	31	45	40	19	3
Zimbabwe	64	64	20	19	19	22	30	34	33	40	16	17
World	**59 w**	**63 w**	**16 w**	**15 w**	**24 w**	**23 w**	**22 w**	**22 w**	**21 w**	**21 w**	**25 w**	**21 w**
Low income	66 w	59 w	12 w	12 w	24 w	32 w	13 w	19 w	15 w	21 w	22 w	30 w
Excl. China & India	..	80 w	..	13 w	..	20 w	..	24 w	..	30 w	..	10 w
Middle income	..	59 w	..	14 w	..	25 w	..	24 w	..	25 w	..	25 w
Lower middle income	..	..	..	..	..	..	..	..	..	..	..	..
Upper middle income	56 w	61 w	12 w	15 w	25 w	21 w	27 w	22 w	20 w	20 w	32 w	23 w
Low & middle income	57 w	63 w	14 w	14 w	26 w	27 w	23 w	22 w	20 w	24 w	30 w	22 w
East Asia & Pacific	58 w	51 w	12 w	11 w	28 w	39 w	16 w	29 w	15 w	31 w	28 w	38 w
Europe & Central Asia	..	..	..	..	..	..	..	..	..	..	..	..
Latin America & Carib.	67 w	67 w	11 w	12 w	25 w	20 w	16 w	17 w	18 w	18 w	23 w	19 w
Middle East & N. Africa	39 w	..	16 w	..	26 w	..	47 w	..	30 w	..	45 w	..
South Asia	75 w	69 w	9 w	11 w	20 w	23 w	8 w	14 w	13 w	18 w	15 w	20 w
Sub-Saharan Africa	60 w	67 w	14 w	17 w	23 w	19 w	31 w	28 w	27 w	31 w	27 w	16 w
High income	60 w	63 w	17 w	15 w	23 w	21 w	22 w	22 w	22 w	21 w	23 w	21 w

a. General government consumption figures are not available separately; they are included in private consumption. b. Data prior to 1992 include Eritrea. c. Includes statistical discrepancy.

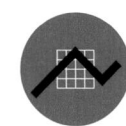

About the data

Government policymakers and statisticians—facing the tasks of mobilizing resources and strengthening different sectors—have tended to focus on the growth of output. Perhaps for this reason, and because production data are easier to collect than expenditure data, many countries continue to generate their primary estimate of GDP and underlying national accounts using the production approach. And many countries either do not estimate the separate components of national expenditure or, if they do, derive the main aggregates indirectly using GDP (output) as the control total.

Expenditures from GDP comprise private consumption, general government consumption, gross domestic fixed capital formation (private and public investment), changes in inventories, and exports (minus imports) of goods and services. Conventionally, such expenditures are recorded in purchasers' prices and therefore include net indirect taxes.

Private consumption is the market price or purchasers' price value of all goods and services purchased or received as income in kind by households and nonprofit institutions and, sometimes, unincorporated enterprises. It excludes purchases of dwellings but includes imputed rent for owner-occupied dwellings. Private consumption is often estimated as a residual, by subtracting from GDP all other known expenditures. The resulting aggregate may incorporate fairly large discrepancies. Even when private consumption is calculated separately, the household surveys on which the estimates are based tend to be one-year studies and limited in coverage. Consequently, they rapidly become outdated and must be supplemented by a variety of price- and quantity-based statistical procedures. Complicating the issue is that in many developing countries the distinction between cash outlays for personal business and those for household use may be blurred.

Gross domestic investment consists of outlays on additions to the fixed assets of the economy plus net changes in the level of inventories. In general, expenditures on national defense and security are regarded as part of general government consumption. Under the new 1993 U.N. System of National Accounts (SNA) guidelines, however, capital outlays on defense establishments used by the general public, such as schools and hospitals, and on certain types of private housing for family use are included in gross domestic investment.

Investment data may be estimated from direct surveys of enterprises and administrative records or based on the commodity flow method using data from trade and construction activities. While the quality of public fixed investment data depends on the quality of government accounting systems (which tend to be weak in developing countries), measures of private fixed investment, particularly capital outlays by small, unin-corporated enterprises, are usually very unreliable. Estimates of changes in stocks are rarely complete but usually include the most important activities or commodities. In some countries these estimates are derived as a composite residual along with aggregate private consumption. Adjustments should be made to the value of the stock change for holding gains due to price changes. In highly inflationary economies this element can be substantial.

Exports and imports are compiled from customs data and from balance of payments data obtained from central banks. While the data on exports and imports from the payments side provide reasonably reliable records of cross-border transactions, even these data may not adhere strictly to the appropriate valuation and timing definitions of the balance of payments or, more important, correspond with the change-of-ownership criterion. With increasing globalization of international business, this issue has assumed greater significance. Neither customs nor balance of payments data capture the illegal transactions that take place in many countries. Legal but unreported shuttle trade—goods carried by travelers across borders—may further distort trade statistics.

For further discussion of the problems of building and maintaining national accounts see Srinivasan (1994), Heston (1994), and Ruggles (1994). And for the classic analysis of the reliability of foreign trade and national income statistics see Morgenstern (1963).

Definitions

● **Private consumption** is the market value of all goods and services, including durable products (such as cars, washing machines, and home computers) purchased or received as income in kind by households and non-profit institutions. It excludes purchases of dwellings but includes imputed rent for owner-occupied dwellings. In practice, it may include any statistical discrepancy in the use of resources. ● **General government consumption** includes all current expenditures for purchases of goods and services by all levels of government, excluding most government enterprises. It also includes capital expenditure on national defense and security. ● **Gross domestic investment** consists of outlays on additions to the fixed assets of the economy plus net changes in the level of inventories. Fixed assets cover land improvements (fences, ditches, drains, and so on); plant, machinery, and equipment purchases; and the construction of roads, railways, and the like, including commercial and industrial buildings, offices, schools, hospitals, and private residential dwellings. ● **Exports and imports of goods and services** represent the value of all goods and other market services provided to the world. Included is the value of merchandise, freight, insurance, travel, and other nonfactor services. Factor and property income (formerly called factor services), such as investment income, interest, and labor income, is excluded. Transfer payments are excluded from the calculation of GDP. ● **Gross domestic savings** are calculated as the difference between GDP and total consumption.

Data sources

National accounts data for developing countries are collected from national statistical organizations and central banks by visiting and resident World Bank missions. Data for industrial countries come from OECD data files. For information on the OECD national accounts series see OECD, *National Accounts, 1960–1994*, volumes 1 and 2. The complete national accounts time series is available on the *World Development Indicators* CD-ROM.

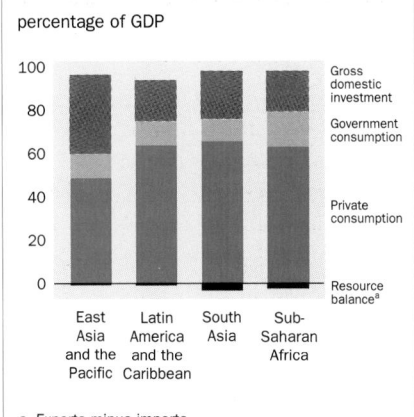

Figure 4.12a Structure of demand, 1995

percentage of GDP

a. Exports minus imports.
Source: World Bank staff estimates.

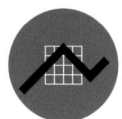

4.13 | Growth of consumption and investment

	Private consumption				Private consumption per capita		General government consumption		Gross domestic investment	
	$ millions		average annual % growth		average annual % growth		average annual % growth		average annual % growth	
	1980	1995	1980–90	1990–95	1980–90	1990–95	1980–90	1990–95	1980–90	1990–95
Albania	..	2,029	..	..	..	..	..	..	–0.3	38.4
Algeria	18,293	23,003	1.9	0.5	–1.1	–1.7	4.7	4.8	–2.3	–4.7
Angola	..	2,320	0.3	–14.0	–2.5	–16.6	2.7	–5.1	–6.8	0.1
Argentina	..	..	..	..	..	..	..	..	–4.7	16.0
Armenia	..	2,395	3.5	–17.6	2.2	–18.6	5.9	–8.9	6.2	–17.7
Australia	94,360	222,170	3.0	3.6	1.5	2.4	3.6	2.6	2.7	5.8
Austria	42,706	129,400	2.4	2.2	2.3	1.4	1.3	2.6	2.5	3.6
Azerbaijan	..	4,308	..	..	..	..	..	..	..	..
Bangladesh	11,857	22,683	4.0	0.9	1.5	–0.7	..[a]	3.4	1.4	8.2
Belarus	..	10,392	..	–10.1	..	–10.3	..	–8.4	..	–17.0
Belgium	74,274	165,441	1.7	1.4	1.6	1.0	0.5	1.1	3.2	–0.9
Benin	1,356	1,249	1.1	3.4	–2.1	0.4	1.3	–1.2	–6.2	12.1
Bolivia	2,064	4,353	0.6	3.1	–1.4	0.7	–3.1	5.8	–9.9	4.2
Bosnia and Herzegovina	..	..	..	..	..	..	..	..	..	..
Botswana	514	1,714	..	..	..	..	..	..	..	..
Brazil	163,832	425,391	1.6	4.4	–0.4	2.9	7.3	–1.3	0.2	3.5
Bulgaria	11,089	6,536	2.5	–6.5	2.6	–5.7	9.1	–6.7	2.4	–7.1
Burkina Faso	1,631	1,453	2.6	4.6	0	1.7	6.2	2.5	8.6	–5.8
Burundi	843	1,011	3.7	–0.7	0.8	–3.3	6.4	6.2	4.5	–5.0
Cambodia	..	1,976	..	..	..	..	..	..	..	..
Cameroon	4,710	5,611	3.9	–4.6	1.1	–7.3	5.3	–8.5	–2.7	–4.1
Canada	145,745	338,288	3.5	1.4	2.2	0.1	2.4	0.2	5.2	2.3
Central African Republic	753	907	3.1	–2.6	0.7	–4.7	–8.7	–6.2	4.8	–8.7
Chad	579	1,117	3.8	5.9	1.3	3.3	16.6	–9.1	19.0	–2.9
Chile	19,395	41,714	1.3	8.6	–0.4	7.0	0.4	3.5	9.6	11.9
China	103,442	333,360	9.7	10.9	8.1	9.7	7.8	12.3	11.0	15.5
Colombia	23,452	50,767	2.7	5.3	0.8	3.4	4.2	8.7	0.5	19.0
Congo	797	1,394	2.7	3.6	–0.5	0.7	4.0	–12.2	–11.9	–7.9
Costa Rica	3,167	5,509	2.9	4.6	0	2.2	1.1	2.7	5.3	6.6
Côte d'Ivoire	6,388	6,789	1.6	–0.2	–2.2	–3.3	–0.1	–0.2	–28.8	138.3
Croatia	..	11,883	..	..	..	..	..	..	..	..
Cuba	..	..	..	..	..	..	..	..	..	..
Czech Republic	..	26,646	..	..	..	..	..	..	2.3	0.9
Denmark	37,050	92,607	1.8	3.2	1.8	2.9	1.1	1.5	4.0	–1.1
Dominican Republic	5,109	8,618	1.7	4.9	–0.5	2.9	1.3	–3.9	3.7	4.9
Ecuador	6,995	11,972	1.9	2.5	–0.7	0.2	–1.4	–1.4	–3.8	5.3
Egypt, Arab Rep.	15,848	34,568	2.4	2.4	–0.1	0.3	4.5	1.2	2.7	–1.5
El Salvador	2,567	7,096	0.8	7.2	–0.2	4.9	0.1	2.3	2.2	14.7
Eritrea	..	541	..	..	..	..	..	..	..	..
Estonia	..	2,288	..	–5.9	..	–4.8	..	2.5	..	–13.4
Ethiopia[b]	4,282	4,314	..	..	..	..	..	..	3.5	21.9
Finland	27,761	69,032	3.8	–1.3	3.4	–1.8	3.4	–1.5	3.0	–8.3
France	391,263	919,222	2.6	1.2	2.1	0.7	2.2	2.6	2.8	–2.8
Gabon	1,120	1,966	0.4	–14.1	–2.4	–16.5	0.2	2.3	–4.6	–0.5
Gambia, The	185	277	3.6	7.3	–0.1	3.1	3.8	–10.9	0.8	3.0
Georgia	..	2,383	3.0	–22.4	2.2	–22.2	–0.4	–43.2	0.3	–21.2
Germany	..	1,375,151	..	..	..	..	..	..	..	..
Ghana	3,730	4,892	2.2	3.4	–1.2	0.6	4.2	9.2	4.5	0.9
Greece	25,919	67,172	2.3	1.6	1.8	1.0	2.6	0.6	–0.9	1.9
Guatemala	6,217	11,142	1.1	4.6	–1.7	1.6	2.7	5.2	–1.8	10.7
Guinea	..	2,981	..	4.3	..	1.5	..	1.0	..	0.6
Guinea-Bissau	81	251	4.6	2.0	2.8	–0.1	4.8	3.3	5.8	1.2
Haiti	1,197	1,635	0.9	–2.2	–1.0	–4.1	–4.4	–11.2	–0.6	–45.7
Honduras	1,806	2,864	2.7	2.0	–0.7	–1.0	3.3	4.6	2.9	10.0
Hong Kong	17,013	84,499	6.7	6.5	5.3	4.8	5.0	6.0	4.0	11.7

	Private consumption				Private consumption per capita		General government consumption		Gross domestic investment	
	$ millions		average annual % growth		average annual % growth		average annual % growth		average annual % growth	
	1980	1995	1980–90	1990–95	1980–90	1990–95	1980–90	1990–95	1980–90	1990–95
Hungary	13,562	29,714	0.8	1.4	1.2	1.7	2.5	−7.3	−0.4	6.6
India	125,809	219,943	5.3	4.5	3.1	2.6	7.7	3.5	6.5	5.3
Indonesia	40,821	110,900	5.5	4.7	3.6	3.0	4.6	3.1	7.0	16.3
Iran, Islamic Rep.	48,854	..	2.8	2.2	−0.8	−0.6	−5.0	8.6	−2.5	−0.8
Iraq	..	..	..	..	..	..	..	..	..	..
Ireland	13,585	32,917	2.2	3.0	1.9	2.5	−0.3	3.0	..	−3.8
Israel	11,397	53,387	5.3	7.7	3.5	4.2	0.5	2.5	2.2	11.5
Italy	276,261	660,193	3.0	0.2	2.9	0.0	2.7	−0.1	2.1	−3.2
Jamaica	1,710	3,528	4.5	*4.8*	3.3	*3.8*	6.2	*−0.9*	−0.1	*5.8*
Japan	623,284	3,083,912	3.7	1.7	3.2	1.5	2.4	2.0	5.3	−0.8
Jordan	..	*4,584*	−7.2	11.9	−10.5	5.7	−2.4	3.4	*7.3*	6.5
Kazakstan	..	13,943	..	−6.8	..	..	..	*−17.1*	..	*−16.7*
Kenya	4,506	6,572	4.7	4.5	1.1	1.8	2.6	11.3	0.8	0.0
Korea, Dem. Rep.	..	..	..	..	..	..	..	..	..	..
Korea, Rep.	40,534	241,030	8.1	7.1	6.9	6.1	5.5	5.1	11.9	7.2
Kuwait	8,836	13,045	−1.4	..	−5.5	..	2.2	..	−4.5	..
Kyrgyz Republic	..	2,039	..	..	..	..	..	..	..	..
Lao PDR	..	..	..	..	..	..	..	..	..	..
Latvia	..	3,914	..	..	..	..	5.0	1.2	3.4	−37.1
Lebanon	..	*10,045*	..	..	..	..	..	..	..	..
Lesotho	455	879	1.6	−1.2	−1.0	−3.3	2.8	8.4	6.9	12.1
Libya	7,171	..	..	..	..	..	..	..	..	..
Lithuania	..	4,476	..	..	..	..	..	..	..	..
Macedonia, FYR	..	1,625	..	..	..	..	..	..	..	..
Madagascar	3,611	2,898	−0.6	0.7	−3.5	−2.4	0.5	−2.6	4.9	−4.5
Malawi	866	1,111	1.7	0.3	−1.6	−2.4	6.3	0.3	−2.8	−11.2
Malaysia	12,378	43,222	3.7	7.2	1.0	4.7	2.7	8.6	2.6	16.0
Mali	1,490	1,917	1.1	0.4	−1.3	−2.5	6.5	−2.2	5.4	6.1
Mauritania	481	849	3.1	2.8	0.5	0.2	−6.8	1.6	−4.1	−1.3
Mauritius	854	2,565	6.7	4.8	5.8	3.4	3.3	4.4	10.2	1.7
Mexico	126,745	166,410	1.0	0.5	−1.3	−1.4	1.9	1.4	−3.1	−1.2
Moldova	..	2,852	..	..	..	..	..	..	..	..
Mongolia	..	..	..	..	..	..	..	..	1.7	..
Morocco	12,788	23,067	3.7	2.4	1.5	0.4	5.5	3.9	2.5	−2.5
Mozambique	1,591	*1,105*	0.9	2.8	−0.7	0.4	−2.0	9.8	−2.5	8.6
Myanmar	..	..	0.6	4.8	..	..	..	..	−4.1	*9.4*
Namibia	969	*1,510*	*2.4*	0.0	*−0.3*	−2.7	*2.6*	3.8	*11.9*	−2.8
Nepal	1,600	3,361	*6.6*	10.1	*4.0*	7.4	*4.6*	3.2	*1.8*	6.3
Netherlands	104,571	226,082	1.7	2.1	1.2	1.4	2.1	1.2	3.1	−0.3
New Zealand	13,801	34,913	2.0	2.3	1.3	0.9	1.2	−0.7	*1.7*	12.4
Nicaragua	1,770	*1,751*	−3.4	3.5	−6.2	0.3	3.0	−15.9	−4.7	4.1
Niger	1,704	*1,822*	−0.7	0.5	−3.9	−2.7	1.4	1.9	−5.9	0.3
Nigeria	51,920	..	−3.0	..	−5.9	..	−1.8	2.4	−8.6	..
Norway	28,955	72,450	2.3	2.9	1.9	2.3	3.1	2.6	0.6	..
Oman	1,657	*4,732*	..	..	..	..	..	..	..	..
Pakistan	19,688	43,977	4.7	5.3	1.6	2.3	10.3	0.6	5.9	4.0
Panama	..	*4,257*	..	6.3	..	4.6	..	0.5	..	15.3
Papua New Guinea	1,568	2,360	0.4	7.8	−1.7	5.4	−0.1	0.9	−0.9	0.4
Paraguay	3,467	*6,199*	2.4	4.5	−0.6	1.8	1.5	*8.6*	−0.8	2.6
Peru	12,006	48,826	1.2	3.3	−1.0	1.2	−1.4	3.2	−4.2	7.4
Philippines	20,910	54,938	2.6	3.2	0.2	1.0	0.6	2.9	−2.1	3.2
Poland	38,182	74,409	1.1	4.5	0.4	4.3	1.2	4.9	0.9	1.1
Portugal	19,035	66,159	2.6	1.8	2.5	1.8	4.8	1.2	..	..
Puerto Rico	10,756	*22,539*	3.5	*2.3*	2.5	*1.5*	5.1	*0.2*	6.9	*3.7*
Romania	..	23,626	..	−0.7	..	−0.2	..	2.4	..	−10.0
Russian Federation	..	*169,454*	..	..	..	..	..	..	..	..

	Private consumption				Private consumption per capita		General government consumption		Gross domestic investment	
	$ millions		average annual % growth		average annual % growth		average annual % growth		average annual % growth	
	1980	1995	1980–90	1990–95	1980–90	1990–95	1980–90	1990–95	1980–90	1990–95
Rwanda	969	1,045	1.5	–2.1	–1.5	..	4.9	–0.6	3.7	–6.3
Saudi Arabia	34,538	52,024	..	..	..	..	..	..	..	..
Senegal	2,365	3,821	2.5	1.3	–0.5	–1.4	2.8	–3.7	3.9	4.7
Sierra Leone	1,057	805	1.5	–2.0	–0.7	–2.9	0.2	2.5	–6.5	–20.0
Singapore	6,030	33,074	5.8	6.6	4.1	4.5	6.7	6.1	3.7	6.0
Slovak Republic	..	8,494	3.8	–6.0	3.5	–6.3	4.8	–3.5	1.1	–7.7
Slovenia	..	10,732	..	..	..	..	..	..	..	..
South Africa	39,543	82,709	2.3	1.0	–0.1	..	3.5	2.3	–4.8	4.7
Spain	139,348	350,559	2.7	0.9	2.4	0.7	5.3	1.9	5.7	–2.6
Sri Lanka	3,230	9,560	3.8	6.0	2.4	4.7	7.3	5.3	0.6	6.8
Sudan	5,447	..	0.2	..	–2.3	..	–0.3	..	–1.1	..
Sweden	64,624	120,153	1.8	–0.7	1.5	–1.3	1.5	–0.1	4.3	–7.2
Switzerland	64,650	178,266	1.7	0.4	1.2	–0.5	3.0	0.3	4.9	0.0
Syrian Arab Republic	8,690	..	3.4	..	0.1	..	–2.9	..	–7.0	..
Tajikistan	..	1,421	..	..	..	..	..	..	..	..
Tanzania	3,911	3,487	..	..	..	..	..	..	..	..
Thailand	21,175	90,267	5.9	8.1	3.9	7.1	4.2	5.0	9.4	10.2
Togo	600	1,011	4.6	1.4	1.6	–1.5	–2.2	–7.0	2.9	–16.4
Trinidad and Tobago	2,860	3,071	–1.3	–5.6	–2.6	–6.4	–1.7	1.2	–10.1	1.0
Tunisia	5,380	11,422	2.9	3.8	0.3	1.9	3.8	3.7	–1.8	1.4
Turkey	42,067	115,046	–4.7	3.5	–6.9	1.8	2.9	2.9	5.3	2.0
Turkmenistan	..	..	..	..	..	..	..	..	..	..
Uganda	1,935	4,696	2.9	6.4	0.2	3.0	1.8	6.8	9.6	7.9
Ukraine	..	..	..	..	..	..	..	..	..	..
United Arab Emirates	5,116	19,423	4.6	..	–0.5	..	–3.9	..	–8.7	..
United Kingdom	320,290	709,115	4.1	1.3	3.8	1.0	1.1	1.0	6.4	..
United States	1,708,280	4,692,418	3.4	2.7	2.4	1.7	3.0	–0.5	3.4	4.1
Uruguay	7,680	13,214	0.5	8.2	–0.1	7.5	1.8	2.6	–7.8	12.9
Uzbekistan	..	12,937	..	–7.2	..	–9.2	..	–4.0	..	–9.2
Venezuela	38,065	54,992	1.3	2.4	–1.3	0.0	2.0	–1.2	–5.3	3.8
Vietnam	..	15,622	..	..	..	..	..	..	..	..
West Bank and Gaza	..	..	..	..	..	..	..	..	..	..
Yemen, Rep.	..	2,750	..	..	..	..	..	..	..	..
Yugoslavia, Fed. Rep.	..	..	..	..	..	..	..	..	..	..
Zaire	11,736	..	2.9	..	–0.4	..	0.3	..	–0.4	..
Zambia	2,145	3,577	3.9	0.9	0.8	–2.0	–3.4	–3.3	–2.7	–10.2
Zimbabwe	3,453	3,608	0.8	6.5	–2.5	3.7	7.2	–3.7	1.3	1.5
World	**6,359,218 t**	**17,328,445 t**	**3.1 w**	**2.4 w**	**1.3 w**	**0.9 w**	**2.7 w**	**1.1 w**	**3.7 w**	**0.8 w**
Low income	433,839 t	809,268 t	5.1 w	5.9 w	3.0 w	4.0 w	5.9 w	5.9 w	6.2 w	10.4 w
Excl. China & India	216,008 t	245,968 t	1.8 w	1.1 w	–0.9 w	–1.4 w	3.1 w	..	–1.3 w	3.6 w
Middle income	..	2,298,093 t	..	..	..	..	..	..	..	..
Lower middle income	..	1,163,514 t	..	..	..	..	..	..	..	..
Upper middle income	554,295 t	1,159,357 t	1.7 w	2.8 w	–0.3 w	1.1 w	4.3 w	0.8 w	–1.4 w	5.6 w
Low & middle income	1,788,055 t	2,966,052 t	3.3 w	3.9 w	1.2 w	2.1 w	..	4.4 w	1.8 w	6.5 w
East Asia & Pacific	221,707 t	703,540 t	7.1 w	8.5 w	5.4 w	7.1 w	5.8 w	9.5 w	8.5 w	14.4 w
Europe & Central Asia	..	623,814 t	..	..	..	..	..	..	..	..
Latin America & Carib.	506,024 t	1,027,909 t	1.5 w	3.4 w	–0.6 w	1.6 w	4.2 w	0.4 w	–1.5 w	5.7 w
Middle East & N. Africa	178,543 t	..	..	..	..	..	..	..	..	..
South Asia	165,188 t	305,128 t	5.1 w	4.5 w	2.8 w	2.5 w	8.0 w	3.1 w	6.1 w	5.3 w
Sub-Saharan Africa	174,871 t	184,372 t	1.2 w	0.5 w	–1.7 w	–2.2 w	2.0 w	1.3 w	–4.0 w	3.4 w
High income	4,675,234 t	13,997,835 t	3.3 w	2.1 w	2.7 w	1.4 w	2.6 w	0.7 w	4.1 w	–0.2 w

a. General government consumption figures are not available separately; they are included in private consumption. b. Data prior to 1992 include Eritrea.

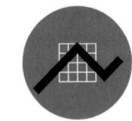

Figure 4.13a Private consumption per capita, 1980–95

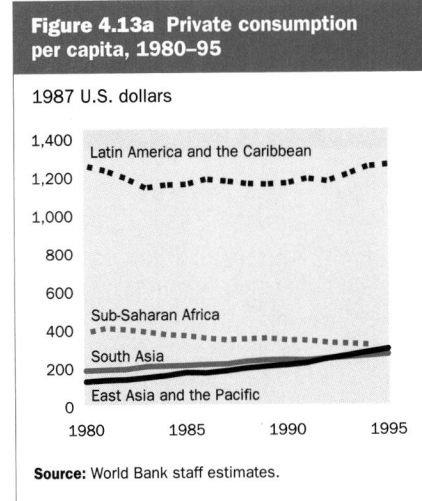

1987 U.S. dollars

Latin America and the Caribbean

Sub-Saharan Africa

South Asia

East Asia and the Pacific

Source: World Bank staff estimates.

About the data

The data here on private consumption in current U.S. dollars and growth rates of private and general government consumption and gross domestic investment are derived from the national accounts and converted using official exchange rates, except as noted in *Primary data documentation*. The estimate of consumption per capita here differs from that in table 4.14, where purchasing power parity conversion factors have been used to give a better estimate of domestic purchasing power. Consumption and investment as shares of current GDP are shown in table 4.12.

Measures of consumption and investment growth are subject to two kinds of inaccuracy. The first stems from the difficulty in measuring current price levels, as described in the notes to table 4.12. The second arises in deflating current price data to measure growth in real terms, where results are directly dependent on the relevance and reliability of the price indexes used. Measuring price changes is more difficult for investment goods than for consumption goods because of the one-time nature of many investments and because the rate of technological progress in capital goods makes capturing quality change difficult. Many countries estimate investment from the supply side, identifying capital goods entering an economy directly from detailed production and international trade statistics. This means that the price indexes used in deflating production and international trade will determine the deflator for investment expenditures on the demand side.

To obtain government consumption in constant prices, countries may adjust current values by applying deflators that use a weighted index of government wages and salaries, or simply take a government employment index as a measure of output. Neither technique captures improvements in productivity or changes in the quality of government services. Many countries estimate private consumption as a residual that includes statistical discrepancies accumulated from other domestic sources. Deflators for private consumption are usually calculated from consumer price series.

In rescaling constant price national accounts data to a common base year for the purpose of compiling international aggregates, the World Bank assigns discrepancies between the output and expenditure estimates of GDP to private consumption. This may lead to differences between the growth rate of private consumption measured on the basis of the country's original base year and the growth rates shown here.

Because the methods used to deflate consumption and investment can vary widely among countries, comparisons across countries, perhaps even more than those over time, should be treated with caution.

Definitions

● **Private consumption** is the market value of all goods and services, including durable products (such as cars, washing machines, and home computers) purchased or received as income in kind by households and nonprofit institutions. It excludes purchases of dwellings but includes imputed rent for owner-occupied dwellings. In practice, it may include any statistical discrepancy in the use of resources. ● **Private consumption per capita** is calculated using private consumption in constant prices and World Bank population estimates. ● **General government consumption** includes all current expenditures for purchases of goods and services by all levels of government, excluding most government enterprises, measured in constant prices. It also includes capital expenditure on national defense and security. ● **Gross domestic investment** consists of outlays on additions to the fixed assets of the economy plus net changes in the level of inventories, measured in constant prices. Fixed assets cover land improvements (fences, ditches, drains, and so on); plant, machinery, and equipment purchases; and the construction of roads, railways, and the like, including commercial and industrial buildings, offices, schools, hospitals, and private residential dwellings.

Data sources

National accounts data for developing countries are collected from national statistical organizations and central banks by visiting and resident World Bank missions. Data for industrial countries come from OECD data files. For information on the OECD national accounts series see OECD, *National Accounts, 1960–1994*, volumes 1 and 2. The complete national accounts time series is available on the *World Development Indicators* CD-ROM.

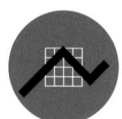

4.14 | Structure of consumption in PPP terms

	Private consumption per capita	Household consumption[a]									
	$ 1993	All food % 1985–93	Bread and cereals % 1985–93	Clothing and footwear % 1985–93	Gross rent, fuel, and power % 1985–93	Fuel and power % 1985–93	Health care % 1985–93	Education % 1985–93	Transport and communication % 1985–93	Other consumption % 1985–93	Consumer durables % 1985–93
Australia[b]	12,307	14.3	2.3	3.5	15.5	2.6	12.2	8.6	12.8	33.1	6.6
Austria[b]	12,960	13.0	2.6	7.0	17.5	3.5	12.6	10.6	12.7	26.6	6.7
Bangladesh	1,049	46.8	33.5	7.1	24.5	5.4	3.4	3.8	5.1	9.3	2.1
Belarus[b]	3,669	17.5	6.3	8.6	12.2	3.6	13.3	20.0	2.0	26.4	3.7
Belgium[b]	13,632	14.5	2.6	5.7	12.7	3.5	14.2	11.3	11.1	30.5	9.2
Benin	1,326	18.1	3.6	16.9	30.2	1.7	6.0	8.4	6.3	14.1	4.7
Botswana	2,888	11.6	5.1	11.6	15.3	1.2	8.7	27.5	3.3	21.9	6.8
Bulgaria[b]	3,452	16.0	2.8	5.8	18.3	4.8	10.0	16.9	7.1	26.0	2.7
Cameroon	1,427	11.4	1.2	9.4	25.5	1.2	13.4	16.0	7.2	17.1	2.0
Canada[b]	14,169	9.0	1.7	4.6	19.9	4.2	10.9	9.3	11.4	34.9	7.3
Congo	1,132	19.5	5.4	6.9	16.9	2.1	8.3	25.6	10.8	12.0	0.4
Côte d'Ivoire	894	25.1	3.9	9.2	9.0	0.8	15.5	10.5	5.2	25.6	6.7
Croatia[b]	3,825	18.9	5.4	3.3	21.6	3.1	10.9	10.7	13.9	20.7	3.2
Czech Republic[b]	5,802	16.2	4.2	4.9	20.8	5.5	10.3	12.4	5.7	29.7	4.7
Denmark[b]	14,002	10.1	1.3	3.9	19.8	3.1	8.9	12.6	9.2	35.6	6.1
Egypt, Arab Rep.	2,509	25.5	7.0	10.1	28.8	1.7	4.6	14.0	3.3	13.7	3.7
Ethiopia	372	27.6	5.5	13.8	23.6	3.6	4.0	8.0	8.0	14.9	4.7
Finland[b]	11,431	10.5	2.0	3.3	20.4	4.8	11.9	11.1	9.5	33.2	4.2
France[b]	13,811	12.4	2.0	4.1	16.8	2.7	21.2	8.1	11.8	25.6	5.8
Germany[b]	14,704	10.7	2.4	5.6	16.3	3.1	15.5	5.9	12.1	33.9	8.5
Greece[b]	8,544	28.1	3.0	5.0	13.1	1.7	7.3	5.6	15.5	25.5	3.1
Hong Kong	13,954	11.6	1.9	8.7	9.8	1.2	9.6	4.0	6.7	49.6	13.3
Hungary[b]	4,397	14.4	2.8	4.1	19.8	5.7	9.4	13.8	8.1	30.4	4.3
India	849	43.4	16.2	8.2	19.4	2.7	7.2	7.0	5.7	9.0	1.5
Iran, Islamic Rep.	3,624	28.5	8.5	7.7	28.2	4.9	11.8	4.4	6.8	12.6	3.5
Ireland[b]	8,500	13.8	3.4	5.8	16.0	3.3	11.4	13.2	7.7	32.0	4.7
Italy[b]	12,903	14.0	2.2	6.5	19.2	2.8	13.8	7.0	9.4	30.0	6.6
Japan[b]	13,322	10.9	3.5	5.3	16.6	1.8	17.5	8.3	9.5	31.9	4.4
Kenya	893	20.2	7.2	10.2	25.0	1.7	3.0	19.5	5.3	16.8	5.5
Korea, Rep.	5,878	26.9	13.9	6.7	12.0	3.0	8.5	9.9	7.6	28.4	6.4
Madagascar	568	32.0	9.7	10.1	23.8	5.2	3.5	15.0	3.7	12.0	1.9
Malawi	592	21.2	4.1	13.8	11.5	2.2	5.8	17.1	4.3	26.3	6.7
Mali	432	34.0	10.9	10.9	12.6	4.1	6.8	15.6	7.1	12.9	3.4
Mauritius	8,834	8.1	2.0	4.3	47.0	1.4	3.3	10.9	5.9	20.5	5.5
Moldova[b]	1,509	28.5	11.5	6.3	12.1	7.1	9.8	22.0	3.0	18.3	3.2
Morocco	2,454	23.6	6.9	16.0	18.5	0.9	5.0	15.7	5.8	15.5	4.8
Netherlands[b]	12,142	10.7	2.5	5.9	15.6	2.6	16.2	8.2	9.4	34.0	7.4
New Zealand[b]	10,571	11.8	2.7	4.1	19.9	3.4	10.5	9.3	13.4	30.9	6.8
Nigeria	984	28.2	4.3	6.5	14.0	1.5	4.3	7.6	3.6	35.8	7.6
Norway[b]	12,473	13.3	1.8	5.4	20.9	10.3	14.4	10.7	7.6	27.8	7.0
Pakistan	1,604	33.0	12.6	8.0	17.0	5.4	5.8	2.5	9.9	23.7	3.8
Philippines	1,970	47.0	24.4	3.9	16.6	4.4	3.9	9.4	1.5	17.7	2.7
Poland[b]	3,559	19.0	4.2	3.1	24.3	4.9	11.9	14.8	6.7	20.0	3.2
Portugal[b]	8,801	19.8	4.7	5.7	10.1	1.6	7.3	15.8	10.9	30.3	5.9
Romania[b]	2,547	27.6	8.7	8.9	16.4	4.9	5.7	11.9	5.2	24.3	4.2
Russian Federation[b]	2,648	18.2	6.6	7.7	20.1	9.6	12.9	18.2	6.5	16.4	3.4
Rwanda	760	18.8	1.5	13.2	21.0	4.3	5.9	13.7	4.6	22.8	12.4
Senegal	1,346	28.3	4.4	16.2	23.1	3.5	3.5	11.4	4.9	12.6	3.7
Sierra Leone	470	29.8	4.0	6.7	45.5	4.2	2.8	7.0	4.2	4.0	0.5
Slovak Republic[b]	4,309	16.6	4.9	4.9	24.5	6.6	14.3	16.5	3.5	19.7	2.9
Slovenia[b]	7,544	14.1	2.8	4.2	18.2	4.2	11.2	10.3	14.3	27.7	3.4
Spain[b]	9,326	16.8	2.5	7.0	14.4	2.3	11.0	7.7	12.2	30.9	4.7
Sri Lanka	2,373	37.1	18.2	8.5	6.2	2.4	9.0	8.9	12.5	18.0	4.2
Sweden[b]	12,502	10.4	2.2	5.1	23.2	4.6	11.2	8.6	10.6	31.0	5.9
Switzerland[b]	16,582	11.9	2.1	6.1	20.5	4.3	13.2	8.4	11.2	28.7	7.7
Tanzania	520	30.1	15.5	10.4	31.0	2.5	9.6	11.0	1.4	6.5	0.8

	Private consumption per capita	Household consumption[a]									
	$ 1993	All food % 1985–93	Bread and cereals % 1985–93	Clothing and footwear % 1985–93	Gross rent, fuel, and power % 1985–93	Fuel and power % 1985–93	Health care % 1985–93	Education % 1985–93	Transport and communication % 1985–93	Other consumption % 1985–93	Consumer durables % 1985–93
Thailand	4,102	29.1	11.9	9.4	9.7	2.6	12.2	10.0	10.2	19.4	4.8
Tunisia	2,494	24.3	2.8	9.6	19.5	2.0	8.5	16.9	4.7	16.5	7.5
Turkey[b]	3,878	23.3	6.2	7.4	23.2	3.7	4.9	9.5	7.3	24.4	6.6
Ukraine[b]	2,010	19.0	7.9	5.1	21.9	11.0	13.0	21.6	1.8	..	..
United Kingdom[b]	13,275	10.6	2.4	6.0	17.6	2.7	9.7	7.9	11.4	36.8	6.6
United States[b]	18,507	8.4	1.6	6.5	16.6	3.0	12.0	7.0	14.3	35.2	8.7
Zambia	659	13.9	1.7	12.2	23.1	3.3	11.0	27.6	4.4	7.8	0
Zimbabwe	1,275	21.4	5.3	12.0	29.8	3.6	2.6	10.0	3.4	20.8	6.3

Note: Except where otherwise indicated, data are based on results of the 1985 round of the International Comparison Programme (ICP). a. For the components constituting the shares see *Definitions* in the notes to this table. b. Data are based on results of the 1993 round of the ICP.

International comparisons of consumption

Cross-country comparisons of consumption expenditures are difficult to interpret. When the expenditures are denominated in national currencies or in a single currency using an exchange rate conversion, the comparisons do not account for the sometimes substantial differences in relative prices. As a result, they also do not reflect differences in the real relative quantities of different types of consumption embodied in each country's expenditure patterns.

This problem has led to the use of purchasing power parities (PPPs) to convert reported values to a common unit of account. PPPs measure the relative purchasing power of different currencies over equivalent goods and services. PPP-based expenditures therefore correct for differences in relative prices and so allow meaningful comparisons of consumption across countries. PPP-based figures also reveal the underlying relationships between the structure of consumption and income, because the quantities of different types of consumption are valued at average international prices. Thus PPPs provide a consistent and meaningful approach to analyzing how the structure of consumption changes with the level of development.

Table 4.14 presents the structure of private consumption for 65 countries with a popula-tion of more than 1 million using the most recent PPPs from the International Comparison Programme (ICP). The summary tables 4.14a and 4.14b divide the countries into five income groups based on their GDP per capita in PPP terms, and give the average shares for selected components of consumption based on both PPP and local currency values.

Comparison of the averages based on local currency and PPP values reveals some interesting differences. The most significant relates to the share of food in total consumption, used as a basic indicator in many poverty studies. While the share of food varies inversely with income in both summary tables, the size of the shares is quite different. For example, the average share of food for the lowest-income group is 48 percent of consumption in nominal terms, but only 29 percent in PPP terms. But the difference tends to disappear as income rises, because the relative price of food (measured by the ratio of the PPP for food to the PPP for GDP) is higher for lower-income economies. Because this tendency holds both for countries and for income groups within a country, one conclusion is that the incidence of poverty is likely to be higher if measured in PPP terms than if measured in nominal terms.

Another interesting difference relates to the relative shares of services in consumption.

For lower-income countries services generally account for a higher share of consumption in PPP terms than in nominal terms. The conventional view is that the share of income spent on services increases with per capita income. This is true only in nominal terms, however. In real terms the share of services remains more or less constant regardless of income level. But the relative prices of services are generally lower in poorer countries. So the implication is that people in higher-income countries do not buy proportionately more services—they just pay more for the services they buy.

Although PPPs are more useful than official exchange rates in comparing consumption patterns, caution should be used in interpreting PPP results. PPP estimates are based on price comparisons of comparable items, but not all items can be matched perfectly in quality across countries and over time. Services are particularly difficult to compare, in part because of differences in productivity. Many services are not sold on the open market in all countries—for example, government services—so they are compared using input prices (mostly wages). Because this approach ignores productivity differences, it may inflate estimates of real quantities in lower-income countries.

Table 4.14a Structure of consumption in PPP terms, by income group, 1993

percent

Income group (GDP per capita in PPP terms)	Food	Clothing and footwear	Rent	Health care	Education	Transport and communication	Other consumption
$1,000 or less	29	10	23	6	13	5	15
$1,001–4,000	25	10	18	8	14	6	19
$4,001–10,000	19	6	23	11	13	6	23
$10,001–20,000	15	5	16	11	9	11	33
$20,000+	11	5	18	14	9	11	31

Source: World Bank staff estimates.

Table 4.14b Structure of consumption in nominal local currency terms, by income group, 1993

percent

Income group (GDP per capita in PPP terms)	Food	Clothing and footwear	Rent	Health care	Education	Transport and communication	Other consumption
$1,000 or less	48	8	11	3	6	7	18
$1,001–4,000	38	9	10	6	7	9	21
$4,001–10,000	27	8	14	7	7	9	28
$10,001–20,000	15	7	15	9	7	13	34
$20,000+	11	5	18	12	8	12	33

Source: World Bank staff estimates.

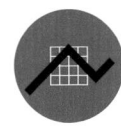

Figure 4.14a Expenditure on services in nominal and PPP terms as a share of total expenditure in selected economies

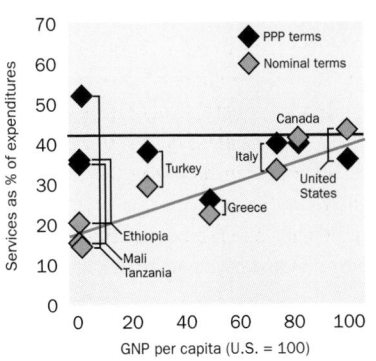

Note: The trend lines are based on data from 68 countries. The upper trend line is in PPP terms, the lower trend line in nominal terms. Data are for 1985 and 1993.
Source: World Bank staff estimates.

Figure 4.14b Expenditure on food in nominal and PPP terms as a share of total expenditure in selected economies

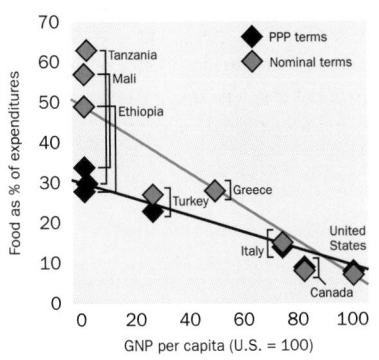

Note: The trend lines are based on data from 68 countries. The upper trend line is in nominal terms, the lower trend line in PPP terms. Data are for 1985 and 1993.
Source: World Bank staff estimates.

About the data

The data here are based on the most recent estimates from the International Comparison Programme (ICP). The ICP database is compiled in two steps. First, regional comparisons are carried out, and aggregate PPPs are computed for developing countries by region and for the OECD countries. Second, the results are linked across regions to establish global consistency. The figures for the OECD countries and for the countries of the former Soviet Union and Eastern Europe are from the 1993 round of the ICP. The rest are from the 1985 round.

Consumption refers to private (that is, household) and nonprofit (nongovernmental) consumption as defined in the U.N. System of National Accounts. Estimates of private consumption of education and health services include government as well as private outlays. The ICP concept of enhanced consumption, or total consumption of the population, focuses on who consumes goods and services rather than on who pays for them. That is, it emphasizes consumption rather than expenditure. This approach improves international comparability because aggregate measures based on consumption are less sensitive to differences in national practices in financing health and education services.

Because countries tend to concentrate on production numbers, however, estimating the detailed structure of consumption is one of the weaker aspects of national accounting in low- and middle-income economies. The composition of consumption is estimated through household expenditure surveys and related survey information and therefore shares any bias inherent in the original sample frames. For example, in some countries surveys are limited to urban areas or even more narrowly to capital cities and so are not representative of national expenditure patterns. Urban surveys show lower than average shares for food and higher than average shares for gross rent, fuel and power, transport and communication, and other consumption. Controlled food prices and incomplete national accounting for subsistence activities may also contribute to low shares for food. Adjustments based on other available indicators may have to be made to improve the cross-country comparability of consumption patterns. See Ahmad (1994) for an extensive discussion of the ICP and its methods.

Definitions

● **Private consumption** includes the consumption expenditures of individuals, households, and non-profit, nongovernmental organizations. It also includes government expenditures for education and health services. ● **Household consumption** shows the percentage shares of selected components of consumption computed from details of GDP converted using purchasing power parities. ● **Bread and cereals** comprise the main staple products—rice, flour, bread, all other cereals, and cereal preparations. ● **Gross rent** consists of both actual rent and imputed rent (the hypothetical cost of renting the same property in the open market) and repair and maintenance charges. ● **Fuel and power** exclude energy used for transport (rarely reported to be more than 1 percent of total consumption in low- and middle-income economies). ● **Health care** and **education** may include government as well as private expenditure. ● **Transport and communication** cover all personal costs of transport, telephones, and the like. ● **Other consumption** covers beverages and tobacco, nondurable household goods, household services, recreational services, and services (including meals) supplied by hotels and restaurants; the purchase of carryout food is also recorded here. This group also covers **consumer durables**, comprising household appliances, furniture, floor coverings, recreational equipment, and watches and jewelry.

Data sources

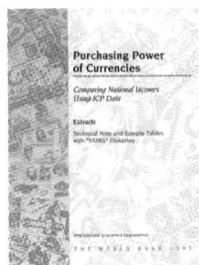

The source of purchasing power parity data is the International Comparison Programme (ICP), coordinated by the United Nations Statistical Division. The World Bank collects detailed ICP benchmark data from regional sources, establishes global consistency across the regional data sets, and computes regression-based estimates for non-benchmark countries. For detailed information on the regional sources and compilation of benchmark data see the World Bank's *Purchasing Power of Currencies: Comparing National Incomes Using ICP Data* (1993b). For information on how regression-based PPP estimates are derived see Ahmad (1992).

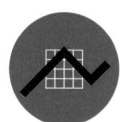

4.15 | Macroeconomic indicators

	Current account balance	Gross domestic savings	Gross domestic investment	Overall fiscal deficit	External debt (present value)	GDP deflator average annual	Seignor-age	Money and quasi money average annual	Real effective exchange rate	Real interest rate	Gross inter-national reserves months of import coverage
	% of GDP 1993–95	% of GDP 1993–95	% of GDP 1993–95	% of GDP 1993–95	% of GDP 1993–95	% growth 1993–95	% of GDP 1993–95	% growth 1993–95	1990 = 100 1993–95	% 1993–95	1993–95
Albania	−2.8	−21.0	14.3	..	41.3	22.4	..	23.8	..	−14.7	3.2
Algeria	−2.8	27.9	31.0	..	56.2	28.2	1.6	12.5	..	..	5.5
Angola	..	35.2	18.7	..	218.2	1,534.4	..	..	..	..	..
Argentina	−2.7	17.5	18.8	..	26.7	3.1	0.4	7.0	..	5.7	6.6
Armenia	−7.5	−20.8	9.8	..	10.2	943.8	14.9	..	..	..	..
Australia	−4.8	20.6	21.6	−2.0	..	1.0	0.3	9.2	85.2	..	2.2
Austria	−1.2	25.7	25.9	−3.6	..	2.8	0.3	5.1	94.9	−0.5	3.1
Azerbaijan	−5.8	1.3	16.1	..	3.8	935.1	14.9	288.1	..	..	..
Bangladesh	−2.6	8.3	15.4	..	32.5	6.6	1.2	15.7	..	2.5	6.1
Belarus	−1.6	19.2	30.8	..	4.5	1,142.1	..	158.4	..	−83.4	..
Belgium	..	23.0	17.7	−2.3	..	2.4	0.1	3.8	104.1	2.3	..
Benin	0.0	5.6	15.9	..	41.7	34.5	0.5	20.5	..	..	4.4
Bolivia	−7.8	6.8	15.2	−2.6	62.4	8.9	1.8	15.6	94.8	10.5	5.5
Bosnia and Herzegovina	..	..	..	..	..	..	..	..	..	..	..
Botswana	9.1	23.5	25.3	..	13.1	13.0	3.6	12.2	..	−0.2	24.0
Brazil	−0.9	21.9	21.0	..	27.1	542.4	7.0	316.0	..	55.0	8.2
Bulgaria	−2.6	18.8	20.3	−7.3	103.3	65.7	..	..	..	..	..
Burkina Faso	−0.8	7.6	22.2	..	26.4	17.5	1.5	25.9	..	..	6.1
Burundi	−1.8	−6.7	12.6	..	49.4	13.7	0.7	33.3	92.4	..	8.0
Cambodia	−6.0	6.7	14.5	..	69.2	8.6	..	39.5	..	..	0.7
Cameroon	−3.9	18.7	15.5	..	72.2	13.4	−0.2	9.0	71.2	−1.9	0.1
Canada	−3.0	19.7	18.8	..	..	1.8	0.0	7.1	82.8	4.3	0.9
Central African Republic	−3.4	5.0	12.5	..	45.1	20.1	4.1	36.4	69.9	−5.2	7.7
Chad	−6.8	..	..	..	37.7	23.6	1.3	39.8	..	−6.2	2.7
Chile	−1.8	28.0	27.6	1.9	39.4	13.1	4.8	18.4	114.6	2.6	9.2
China	−0.4	41.5	41.2	−2.0	16.4	16.0	8.7	32.2	..	−3.7	5.1
Colombia	−4.7	16.2	19.9	..	27.6	21.7	1.7	27.9	128.5	5.2	5.8
Congo	−30.9	21.8	35.3	..	222.8	22.1	0.9	13.2	..	−5.1	0.3
Costa Rica	−4.2	23.1	27.2	−2.9	42.0	20.3	3.0	13.1	100.7	2.1	3.0
Côte d'Ivoire	−3.5	16.8	11.2	..	177.5	27.8	2.0	31.7	76.7	..	0.8
Croatia	−2.6	8.9	14.0	0.0	16.5	..	3.3	56.0	..	..	2.0
Cuba	..	..	..	..	..	..	..	..	..	..	..
Czech Republic	−0.4	20.2	21.2	1.3	31.0	10.0	..	24.8	..	−4.5	4.6
Denmark	2.1	21.0	14.9	−2.2	..	1.6	1.2	−2.2	103.3	3.3	1.7
Dominican Republic	−2.1	16.8	20.8	..	38.4	8.2	1.4	13.5	109.9	..	0.9
Ecuador	−4.5	21.5	19.6	0.2	80.7	25.3	1.8	44.0	128.5	5.5	3.9
Egypt, Arab Rep.	−0.9	5.8	17.1	..	54.7	8.3	3.9	10.6	..	2.4	11.0
El Salvador	−0.9	4.7	18.9	−0.6	21.5	10.4	2.9	17.1	..	2.7	3.4
Eritrea	..	−28.8	15.1	..	..	..	..	..	..	..	..
Estonia	−2.9	19.4	27.3	0.2	5.2	37.2	4.1	30.6	..	..	2.8
Ethiopia	−1.4	5.0	15.5	−7.6	60.0	9.3	2.1	16.8	..	0.7	5.8
Finland	1.5	22.1	15.5	..	..	2.0	1.3	3.7	68.0	1.6	3.1
France	0.8	19.8	17.6	−4.9	..	1.6	0.1	8.8	99.9	2.6	1.6
Gabon	5.1	43.7	24.4	..	76.3	32.3	1.0	23.0	67.7	−9.2	0.6
Gambia, The	−0.5	4.3	21.0	..	59.4	6.5	0.9	4.8	99.4	6.3	..
Georgia	..	−20.2	3.3	..	37.4	1,477.9	..	..	..	..	..
Germany	−0.9	22.5	21.8	..	..	..	0.0	3.5	114.5	..	2.4
Ghana	−6.6	4.5	16.4	..	53.7	33.1	2.1	43.0	..	−4.0	3.6
Greece	−1.5	8.0	18.4	..	..	9.6	2.4	24.8	96.1	6.1	6.8
Guatemala	−5.0	8.9	17.5	−0.5	19.9	11.0	0.7	13.9	..	−1.7	3.1
Guinea	−4.8	10.2	14.9	..	57.8	5.2	0.3	3.6	..	11.6	1.2
Guinea-Bissau	−21.4	−1.2	20.6	..	220.5	32.7	2.6	45.8	..	−2.1	2.2
Haiti	−1.4	−8.4	3.1	..	24.4	30.4	5.2	29.3	..	..	..
Honduras	−8.0	15.4	26.3	−0.1	95.5	27.0	1.8	29.8	..	−8.5	1.1
Hong Kong	..	33.6	31.5	..	..	6.0	..	..	..	..	..

	Current account balance	Gross domestic savings	Gross domestic investment	Overall fiscal deficit	External debt (present value)	GDP deflator average annual % growth	Seignorage	Money and quasi money average annual % growth	Real effective exchange rate 1990 = 100	Real interest rate %	Gross international reserves months of import coverage
	% of GDP 1993–95	% of GDP 1993–95	% of GDP 1993–95	% of GDP 1993–95	% of GDP 1993–95	1993–95	% of GDP 1993–95	1993–95	1993–95	1993–95	1993–95
Hungary	–8.9	16.0	21.6	..	65.7	*21.8*	*3.4*	13.4	129.7	–0.8	5.6
India	–1.2	21.3	23.0	–6.5	24.9	9.5	2.5	15.6	..	..	5.7
Indonesia	–2.2	35.6	35.1	..	50.7	*7.9*	..	31.7	..	..	3.2
Iran, Islamic Rep.	..	30.3	27.6	–0.2	..	37.6	4.3	31.7	..	..	..
Iraq	..	..	..	..	..	..	..	..	..	..	..
Ireland	3.0	27.6	13.8	..	..	1.2	1.1	9.9	80.3	–1.1	1.9
Israel	–4.5	13.9	23.2	*–3.1*	..	*10.6*	–0.1	23.1	..	2.0	2.5
Italy	1.6	21.1	17.4	*–10.6*	..	*4.2*	..	..	77.5	2.5	2.6
Jamaica	–3.2	14.0	19.9	..	86.8	27.2	4.8	36.1	..	0.3	2.1
Japan	2.7	31.1	29.1	..	..	–0.1	0.6	2.9	145.6	1.4	3.6
Jordan	*–16.0*	*2.7*	*30.9*	2.7	*102.5*	*4.3*	5.9	4.5	..	–1.2	5.1
Kazakstan	–3.3	17.7	24.1	..	10.8	*575.8*	..	..	..	..	2.5
Kenya	–0.6	18.9	18.5	–2.3	74.7	14.3	3.8	23.7	..	..	1.9
Korea, Dem. Rep.	..	..	..	..	..	..	..	..	..	..	..
Korea, Rep.	–0.8	35.6	36.1	0.2	..	5.5	1.2	17.1	..	3.1	2.5
Kuwait	11.3	21.1	15.2	..	..	2.7	–0.3	6.8	..	9.2	4.5
Kyrgyz Republic	–7.6	9.3	15.8	..	11.3	*97.3*	..	23.9	..	2.0	1.6
Lao PDR	–13.7	..	..	..	42.7	13.4	1.5	23.9	..	2.0	1.6
Latvia	3.5	20.7	16.4	..	5.5	*31.3*	..	8.7	..	–10.9	4.3
Lebanon	–44.7	*–31.1*	*24.1*	..	21.3	..	6.7	20.8	..	..	15.2
Lesotho	7.0	–15.2	85.3	..	37.8	8.0	1.3	9.5	110.9	1.0	4.5
Libya	..	..	..	..	..	..	..	12.0	..	..	..
Lithuania	–3.8	14.3	20.4	..	6.6	*46.9*	..	29.8	..	–37.0	2.4
Macedonia, FYR	..	6.5	17.0	..	48.9	..	..	..	..	..	..
Madagascar	–8.5	2.7	11.1	..	93.8	*44.2*	1.8	33.0	..	..	..
Malawi	*–19.5*	0.3	14.3	..	60.6	59.2	4.0	46.1	75.2	–10.0	1.1
Malaysia	–4.7	36.7	38.1	2.1	34.5	5.1	3.9	16.3	103.3	..	4.6
Mali	*–8.6*	7.8	24.8	..	71.6	*22.4*	–0.1	22.7	..	..	4.1
Mauritania	–9.3	9.4	18.0	..	158.5	*5.5*	1.8	–2.9	..	..	1.2
Mauritius	–3.4	23.4	29.5	–0.5	33.9	*5.7*	–0.1	15.5	..	3.9	4.1
Mexico	–4.8	18.6	20.6	..	42.2	20.7	0.8	27.4	..	4.4	2.0
Moldova	..	–2.2	7.3	..	11.5	..	5.2	88.8	..	..	..
Mongolia	5.4	..	..	–3.3	40.4	47.1	4.3	53.7	..	0.3	2.6
Morocco	–3.0	14.9	21.1	..	64.8	3.5	1.2	8.6	109.1	..	4.5
Mozambique	..	*4.4*	*57.7*	..	280.5	*47.5*	..	..	..	..	3.4
Myanmar	..	*11.8*	*12.6*	–2.9	..	*16.4*	..	..	..	..	..
Namibia	4.1	*12.1*	*18.6*	..	..	10.1	0.6	25.9	..	0.7	1.2
Nepal	–7.7	13.5	23.0	..	27.8	*7.0*	2.3	18.1	..	..	6.5
Netherlands	4.2	26.2	20.3	–2.1	..	*2.2*	0.0	3.1	102.1	1.9	2.8
New Zealand	–4.6	24.6	22.4	0.3	..	0.0	0.1	4.1	94.5	6.8	2.5
Nicaragua	–37.4	*–10.9*	*17.9*	–2.1	496.4	10.8	2.7	52.1	88.3	–2.2	1.0
Niger	*–6.5*	..	..	..	52.2	*17.3*	–0.7	5.4	..	..	3.8
Nigeria	–3.7	..	..	..	105.5	76.9	*3.0*	36.5	114.0	–22.9	1.6
Norway	*2.4*	..	..	..	..	1.3	0.3	4.4	100.0	3.4	..
Oman	–9.2	*26.4*	*17.7*	–12.2	23.9	*0.7*	0.1	7.2	..	7.4	2.4
Pakistan	–4.5	15.7	19.6	–6.9	40.2	13.3	2.5	15.6	..	..	2.4
Panama	..	23.1	24.5	..	98.5	*2.1*	..	11.6	..	3.7	0.9
Papua New Guinea	12.2	33.8	19.4	–5.0	45.9	10.8	*0.5*	*–1.3*	98.3	2.4	0.9
Paraguay	–14.9	*12.8*	*23.1*	..	23.4	15.5	2.2	22.9	112.1	4.7	..
Peru	–5.9	14.6	19.0	0.5	45.9	15.5	2.0	32.9	..	1.7	8.2
Philippines	–4.3	16.0	23.5	..	56.1	8.7	1.4	24.3	116.0	1.3	3.0
Poland	–4.4	17.3	16.1	..	37.8	28.3	1.8	36.6	184.0	1.8	3.2
Portugal	–0.6	..	..	..	..	*4.5*	–3.6	9.7	113.0	3.6	7.4
Puerto Rico	..	..	..	..	..	..	..	..	..	..	..
Romania	–3.3	23.4	27.2	–1.0	16.5	79.8	4.1	101.2	..	..	3.6
Russian Federation	2.1	29.9	27.7	..	26.0	*249.6*	..	160.3	..	..	1.9

	Current account balance	Gross domestic savings	Gross domestic investment	Overall fiscal deficit	External debt (present value)	GDP deflator average annual	Seignor- age	Money and quasi money average annual	Real effective exchange rate	Real interest rate	Gross inter- national reserves months of import coverage
	% of GDP 1993–95	% of GDP 1993–95	% of GDP 1993–95	% of GDP 1993–95	% of GDP 1993–95	% growth 1993–95	% of GDP 1993–95	% growth 1993–95	1990 = 100 1993–95	% 1993–95	coverage 1993–95
Rwanda	..	–19.7	11.4	..	41.5	34.2	1.6	29.0	..	..	2.3
Saudi Arabia	–9.9	28.5	22.1	..	..	2.9	..	2.9	94.4	..	2.5
Senegal	–2.8	7.5	14.2	..	53.1	16.7	–0.1	22.0	..	..	1.2
Sierra Leone	–6.1	0.2	8.4	–4.6	115.8	22.5	0.7	14.1	108.4	–6.7	2.5
Singapore	13.9	..	34.9	5.3	..	3.1	1.1	11.4	..	–0.6	5.8
Slovak Republic	1.4	26.9	26.3	..	28.6	11.6	..	17.9	..	–3.4	2.9
Slovenia	1.7	21.5	21.0	..	14.8	..	1.2	36.4	..	..	1.9
South Africa	–0.5	19.0	17.1	–8.6	..	10.3	0.5	17.2	101.8	1.4	1.3
Spain	–0.8	20.4	20.5	..	..	4.3	0.6	6.9	90.2	3.6	4.3
Sri Lanka	–4.3	15.1	25.9	–5.0	41.9	9.1	2.0	19.3	..	6.6	4.3
Sudan	..	..	..	..	..	90.6	7.7	51.2	..	..	0.3
Sweden	0.1	17.9	13.9	–11.5	..	3.3	1.4	..	74.2	2.3	3.5
Switzerland	7.3	27.4	22.9	..	..	0.8	–0.1	4.4	107.9	1.5	..
Syrian Arab Republic	–2.4	..	..	–0.7	115.1	11.5	..	..	..	..	..
Tajikistan	–4.9	2.4	20.9	..	22.4	236.7	..	..	..	..	..
Tanzania	–19.4	–0.2	31.6	..	149.4	28.3	3.9	35.4	..	..	1.5
Thailand	–6.3	36.2	41.6	2.3	38.0	5.5	1.4	14.9	..	4.6	5.3
Togo	–9.0	4.3	9.7	..	66.7	34.9	–1.6	32.8	75.7	..	3.8
Trinidad and Tobago	4.1	23.4	13.6	..	44.4	8.2	1.2	10.1	87.2	–1.6	1.9
Tunisia	–5.5	21.2	25.8	..	50.8	5.1	0.6	7.3	..	..	1.9
Turkey	–1.0	21.3	24.4	–3.5	40.0	93.6	3.2	123.5	..	–4.8	3.2
Turkmenistan	11.3	..	..	..	7.5	1,230.5	..	..	..	..	..
Uganda	–9.1	4.2	15.5	..	45.7	7.5	1.1	23.9	87.2	–2.7	3.4
Ukraine	..	..	..	..	6.1	616.6	0.0	278.9	..	–76.2	..
United Arab Emirates	..	32.6	25.3	0.3	..	..	1.2	9.1	..	..	..
United Kingdom	–0.8	..	..	..	..	2.4	0.2	..	89.5	1.2	1.4
United States	–2.0	..	..	–3.1	..	2.3	0.4	2.9	96.1	..	2.1
Uruguay	–2.2	13.7	14.4	–0.9	30.8	41.2	3.7	41.6	151.9	–3.7	5.1
Uzbekistan	–1.2	24.7	31.3	..	5.5	639.1	..	..	..	..	..
Venezuela	1.3	20.2	16.0	–3.5	54.5	56.5	1.6	52.7	123.0	–5.0	7.9
Vietnam	–8.6	16.7	24.4	..	137.0	17.0	..	..	..	..	0.0
West Bank and Gaza	..	..	..	..	..	..	..	..	..	..	..
Yemen, Rep.	–6.8	–4.0	14.2	..	107.6	..	12.1	41.3	..	..	1.4
Yugoslavia, Fed. Rep.	..	..	..	..	..	..	..	..	..	..	..
Zaire	..	..	..	..	..	..	..	6,968.9	100.0	..	..
Zambia	..	5.0	9.7	..	137.5	51.3	..	62.0	110.8	..	..
Zimbabwe	–7.2	..	..	..	62.0	..	..	..	..	0.0	..

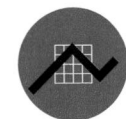

Increasing macroeconomic stability

For markets to function well, governments, businesses, and financial institutions need timely, accurate information on the macroeconomic and financial condition of a country. Improvements in the current account and in fiscal deficits are often viewed as signs of a strengthening economy. Lenders monitor a country's creditworthiness by watching trends in the level of reserves and in external debt ratios. Investors look at investment levels and money supply and exchange rate trends to assess the prospects for growth and financial stability. Portfolio managers, who frequently move large volumes of funds from one country to another in a search for high rates of return, look very closely at changes in key macroeconomic indicators in making decisions. And because the size and volatility of these movements in foreign capital can be destabilizing, governments have increasingly used macroeconomic indicators as a tool of economic management.

About 30 developing economies contained inflation to single digits during 1993–95 ●

In the short to medium term there are five key elements in macroeconomic stability: low and predictable inflation, appropriate real interest rates, stable and sustainable fiscal policy, an exchange rate that is not perceived to be over- or undervalued, and a viable balance of payments (see Fischer and Easterly 1990; and Fischer 1993). The two most susceptible to policy control are the inflation rate and the government's fiscal deficit. Uncertainty about either of these indicators tends to slow private investment and thus productivity growth. And inflation distorts price signals, leading to poor decisionmaking and costly efforts to hedge against the loss of monetary assets.

No single indicator by itself or in comparison to the value for another country is fully diagnostic. For example, a high level of debt may reflect the confidence of investors in the economy's future prospects. A large current account deficit may stem from high levels of private investment. And high inflation or a large fiscal deficit can occur despite good policies—the result of a supply-side shock caused by a poor harvest or deteriorating terms of trade.

About the data

The table shows three-year averages for key macroeconomic variables in the most recent period for which data are available. Most of the indicators appear elsewhere in this book. Readers may wish to consult the notes to tables 4.12, 4.16, 4.17, 4.20–4.22, 4.24, and 5.5 for further discussion of the sources and reliability of the data.

Seignorage, which does not appear elsewhere in this book, is the net revenue derived by the government or monetary authorities through the issuance of money. In the past seignorage was measured as the difference between the face value of money and the value of the metals it was made from. Now that money is printed, the cost of its production can be ignored. Seignorage is therefore measured by the change in holdings of reserve or base money, which in most countries is equal to the non-interest-bearing liabilities of the central bank.

Definitions

● **Current account balance** is the sum of net trade (exports minus imports) in goods, services, and income plus net current transfers. ● **Gross domestic savings** are the difference between GDP and total consumption. ● **Gross domestic investment** is the sum of all outlays on additions to capital assets, plus changes in inventories. ● **Overall fiscal deficit** is the overall budget deficit of the central government, calculated as current and capital revenue and official grants received, less total expenditure and lending minus repayments. ● **External debt (present value)** is the discounted present value of future debt service payments, including private, public, and publicly guaranteed short- and long-term debt. The discount rate reflects market lending rates for the currency in which the loan is denominated. ● **GDP deflator** is the price index that measures the change in the price level of GDP relative to real output. ● **Seignorage** is the annual change in holdings of reserve money (IFS line 14). ● **Money and quasi money** refer to the M2 definition of money supply (IFS lines 34 and 35). ● **Real effective exchange rate** is a trade-weighted index of a country's real exchange rates. An increase represents an appreciation of the currency. ● **Real interest rate** is the deposit interest rate (IFS line 60l) adjusted for the rate of inflation as measured by the GDP deflator. ● **Gross international reserves** comprise holdings of monetary gold, special drawing rights (SDRs), the reserve position of members in the International Monetary Fund (IMF), and holdings of foreign exchange under the control of monetary authorities, expressed in terms of the number of months of imports of goods and services they could pay for.

Data sources

The indicators in the table come from the World Bank's national accounts data files and the IMF's *International Financial Statistics* and *Government Finance Statistics*.

4.16 | Central government finances

	Current revenue[a]		Total expenditure		Overall budget deficit (including grants)		Financing from abroad		Domestic financing		Debt and interest payments	
	% of GDP		% of GDP		% of GDP		% of GDP		% of GDP		Total debt % of GDP	Interest % of current revenue
	1980	1994	1980	1994	1980	1994	1980	1994	1980	1994	1994	1994
Albania	..	..	..	..	..	..	..	..	..	..	..	..
Algeria	..	..	..	..	..	..	..	..	..	..	..	..
Angola	..	..	..	..	..	..	..	..	..	..	..	..
Argentina	15.6	12.3	18.2	12.0	−2.6	..	0.0	..	2.6	..	..	..
Armenia	..	..	..	..	..	..	..	..	..	..	..	..
Australia	21.7	23.3	22.7	27.2	−1.5	−2.8	0.2	0.7	1.3	2.1	20.7	6.2
Austria	34.6	36.0	37.4	40.5	−3.4	−5.6	0.9	2.1	2.5	3.5	54.6	10.7
Azerbaijan	..	..	..	..	..	..	..	..	..	..	..	..
Bangladesh	11.3	..	10.0	..	2.5	..	2.5	..	0.7	..	..	..
Belarus	..	31.4	..	37.8	..	−5.2	..	2.7	..	2.4	25.9	2.1
Belgium	43.7	45.3	51.0	50.4	−8.2	−0.3	2.4	−0.1	5.8	0.4	8.0	2.7
Benin	..	..	..	..	..	..	..	..	..	..	..	..
Bolivia	..	17.1	..	25.2	..	−3.6	..	4.9	..	−1.3	..	14.0
Bosnia and Herzegovina	..	..	..	..	..	..	..	..	..	..	..	..
Botswana	34.0	57.3	34.0	46.2	−0.2	11.5	1.4	1.0	−1.2	−12.5	14.0	..
Brazil	22.6	25.6	20.2	37.4	−2.2	−3.9	0.0	..	2.2	..	..	59.3
Bulgaria	..	37.4	..	43.1	..	−4.5	..	1.5	..	2.9	161.9	37.3
Burkina Faso	11.8	11.7	12.2	17.1	0.2	..	0.4	..	0.0	..	..	12.1
Burundi	13.9	..	21.5	..	−3.9	..	2.0	..	1.9	..	..	..
Cambodia	..	..	..	..	..	..	..	..	..	..	..	..
Cameroon	16.4	14.2	15.7	15.9	0.5	−1.7	0.7	1.9	−1.2	0.4	70.6	12.9
Canada	18.7	20.8	21.3	25.5	−3.5	−4.4	0.6	..	2.9	..	..	..
Central African Republic	16.5	..	22.0	..	−3.5	..	2.1	..	1.5	..	..	..
Chad	..	..	..	..	..	..	..	..	..	..	..	..
Chile	32.0	21.9	28.0	20.4	5.4	1.6	−0.8	..	−4.7	..	..	4.4
China	..	6.4	..	9.4	..	−1.9	..	0.2	..	1.7	..	..
Colombia	12.0	16.8	13.4	14.5	−1.8	−0.5	..	..	..	..	..	10.5
Congo	35.3	..	49.4	..	−5.2	..	3.8	..	1.4	..	..	..
Costa Rica	17.8	24.9	25.1	30.6	−7.4	−5.7	1.1	−0.1	6.3	5.8	..	16.2
Côte d'Ivoire	22.9	..	31.7	..	−10.8	..	6.5	..	4.4	..	..	..
Croatia	..	42.8	..	41.1	..	1.7	..	0.0	..	−1.6	..	3.1
Cuba	..	..	..	..	..	..	..	..	..	..	..	..
Czech Republic	..	41.0	..	42.5	..	0.9	..	−0.1	..	−0.8	18.7	3.5
Denmark	35.5	41.3	39.3	44.4	−2.7	−2.3	..	..	..	..	..	15.4
Dominican Republic	14.2	17.1	16.9	17.1	−2.6	0.0	1.4	−1.2	1.2	1.5	..	7.9
Ecuador	12.8	15.7	14.2	15.7	−1.4	0.0	0.5	..	0.9	..	..	..
Egypt, Arab Rep.	45.5	41.2	45.6	42.8	−6.3	2.0	2.1	−1.0	4.2	−1.0	..	24.8
El Salvador	11.4	12.0	17.1	14.5	−5.7	−0.8	0.3	1.0	5.5	−0.2	..	..
Eritrea	..	..	..	..	..	..	..	..	..	..	..	..
Estonia	..	35.0	..	31.9	..	1.4	..	0.1	..	−1.3	..	..
Ethiopia[b]	16.3	14.1	19.6	27.4	−3.1	−8.5	1.2	7.6	1.9	0.9	64.3	14.1
Finland	27.2	33.0	28.2	43.8	−2.2	−13.4	0.8	10.7	1.4	4.1	36.1	11.2
France	39.6	40.2	39.5	46.9	−0.1	−5.5	0.0	0.0	0.1	5.5	..	7.3
Gabon	35.5	..	36.5	..	6.1	..	0.0	..	−6.1	..	..	..
Gambia, The	23.4	23.2	32.2	20.4	−4.5	3.5	1.2	2.9	3.3	−6.4	..	..
Georgia	..	..	..	..	..	..	..	..	..	..	..	..
Germany	..	32.4	..	33.7	..	−2.5	..	0.1	..	1.2	30.2	6.3
Ghana	6.9	16.7	10.9	20.6	−4.2	−2.5	0.7	1.3	3.5	1.2	..	..
Greece	30.7	27.8	35.5	43.1	−5.0	−15.7	1.9	6.8	3.1	8.8	127.6	52.0
Guatemala	9.4	7.6	12.1	8.9	−3.4	−1.2	1.4	0.0	3.0	..	0.5	..
Guinea	..	13.3	..	20.9	..	−3.1	..	4.1	..	−1.0	..	9.8
Guinea-Bissau	..	..	..	..	..	..	..	..	..	..	..	..
Haiti	10.6	..	17.4	..	−4.7	..	..	..	..	..	..	..
Honduras	14.6	..	..	..	..	−0.1	..	..	..	0.1	..	0.0	1.5	..
Hong Kong	..	..	..	..	..	..	..	..	..	..	..	..

	Current revenue[a]		Total expenditure		Overall budget deficit (including grants)		Financing from abroad		Domestic financing		Debt and interest payments	
	% of GDP		% of GDP		% of GDP		% of GDP		% of GDP		Total debt % of GDP	Interest % of current revenue
	1980	1994	1980	1994	1980	1994	1980	1994	1980	1994	1994	1994
Hungary	53.4	..	56.2	..	–2.8	..	2.1	..	0.7	..	..	..
India	11.7	12.6	13.2	16.5	–6.5	–6.5	0.5	0.4	6.0	6.1	54.5	35.5
Indonesia	21.3	18.3	22.1	16.3	–2.3	0.6	2.1	–0.1	0.2	–0.5	37.5	11.3
Iran, Islamic Rep.	21.6	24.9	35.7	25.2	–13.8	–0.1	–0.6	0.0	14.4	0.1	..	0.1
Iraq	..	..	..	..	..	..	..	..	..	..	..	..
Ireland	34.7	37.5	45.0	42.6	–12.5	–2.2	..	..	..	..	..	18.6
Israel	50.4	37.5	70.2	43.2	–15.6	–2.9	7.9	2.6	7.8	0.3	127.8	16.5
Italy	31.2	39.6	41.0	49.9	–10.7	–10.5	0.2	..	10.5	..	83.8	28.0
Jamaica	29.0	..	41.5	..	–15.5	..	..	..	..	..	..	..
Japan	11.6	20.9	18.4	23.8	–7.0	–1.5	..	..	..	1.5	44.7	..
Jordan	..	27.2	..	30.7	..	1.1	..	–0.7	..	–0.4	120.0	..
Kazakstan	..	..	..	..	..	..	..	..	..	..	..	..
Kenya	21.9	21.7	25.2	27.5	–4.5	–3.2	2.4	..	2.1	..	..	..
Korea, Dem. Rep.	..	..	..	..	..	..	..	..	..	..	..	..
Korea, Rep.	17.4	19.5	17.0	17.6	–2.2	0.3	0.8	–0.1	1.4	–0.2	7.9	3.1
Kuwait	89.3	..	27.8	56.2	58.7	..	..	..	..	..	..	..
Kyrgyz Republic	..	..	..	..	..	..	..	..	..	..	..	..
Lao PDR	..	..	..	..	..	..	..	..	..	..	..	..
Latvia	..	25.5	..	27.6	..	–4.2	..	1.7	..	2.5	..	1.7
Lebanon	..	14.6	..	35.1	..	..	..	..	..	..	..	..
Lesotho	34.2	51.3	..	47.3	..	..	..	..	4.8	..	..	..
Libya	..	..	..	..	..	..	..	..	..	..	..	..
Lithuania	..	25.3	..	27.2	..	..	..	..	..	..	..	0.5
Macedonia, FYR	..	..	..	..	..	..	..	..	..	..	..	..
Madagascar	13.2	8.3	..	18.9	..	–4.8	..	2.9	..	1.9	51.2	41.1
Malawi	19.1	..	34.6	..	–15.9	..	8.3	..	7.7	..	..	..
Malaysia	26.3	28.8	28.5	24.7	–6.0	3.9	0.6	..	5.4	..	59.3	13.0
Mali	10.9	..	21.3	..	–4.6	..	4.3	..	0.4	..	..	..
Mauritania	..	..	..	..	..	..	..	..	..	..	..	..
Mauritius	20.8	22.4	27.3	22.8	–10.3	–0.3	2.5	–0.2	7.8	0.4	31.7	9.4
Mexico	15.1	16.7	16.8	16.8	–3.0	..	–0.1	..	3.1	..	..	..
Moldova	..	..	..	..	..	..	..	..	..	..	..	..
Mongolia	..	22.2	..	21.6	..	–1.9	..	1.5	..	0.4	5.3	2.7
Morocco	23.3	28.6	33.1	29.9	–9.7	–1.4	5.3	–0.2	4.4	1.6	83.7	18.4
Mozambique	..	..	..	..	..	..	..	..	..	..	..	..
Myanmar	16.0	7.2	15.9	11.0	1.2	–3.6	1.2	0.0	–2.4	3.6	..	..
Namibia	..	35.3	..	40.7	..	–4.8	..	0.1	..	4.7	..	2.4
Nepal	7.8	9.5	14.3	14.7	–3.0	..	1.9	..	1.2	..	..	..
Netherlands	49.4	48.1	53.0	52.4	–4.6	–0.5	0.0	–4.0	4.6	4.5	61.6	9.9
New Zealand	34.1	34.9	38.1	34.4	–6.7	0.8	3.6	..	3.1	..	59.3	..
Nicaragua	23.3	22.9	30.5	32.0	–7.2	–4.3	4.8	5.5	2.4	–1.2	..	20.3
Niger	14.4	..	18.4	..	–4.7	..	4.0	..	0.7	..	..	..
Nigeria	..	..	..	..	..	..	..	..	..	..	..	..
Norway	37.4	40.1	34.6	41.1	–1.7	–6.5	–0.7	3.0	2.4	3.5	23.2	5.7
Oman	38.2	31.7	38.5	43.9	0.4	–11.2	–3.6	7.9	3.1	3.3	33.6	..
Pakistan	16.2	18.7	17.5	24.4	–5.7	–6.9	2.3	2.2	3.4	4.7	..	34.2
Panama	26.9	28.2	32.3	28.2	–5.5	4.3	5.7	–0.9	–0.2	–3.4	..	6.4
Papua New Guinea	23.0	22.0	34.4	29.4	–1.9	–4.1	2.5	–0.2	–0.5	4.3	43.0	..
Paraguay	10.7	14.1	9.8	13.0	0.3	1.2	2.2	–0.8	–2.5	–0.4	12.8	5.6
Peru	17.1	15.0	19.4	17.0	–2.4	3.0	0.6	1.1	1.8	–4.2	..	14.0
Philippines	14.0	18.0	13.4	18.4	–1.4	–1.5	0.9	–0.7	0.5	0.6	56.4	..
Poland	..	41.7	..	44.1	..	–2.3	..	–0.6	..	2.9	69.5	10.0
Portugal	26.2	34.2	33.3	42.5	–8.5	–2.3	1.9	–0.1	6.6	2.3	..	22.1
Puerto Rico	..	..	..	..	..	..	..	..	..	..	..	..
Romania	45.3	29.9	44.7	31.9	0.5	–2.5	..	0.0	..	2.5	..	4.4
Russian Federation	..	20.2	..	27.0	..	–10.5	..	0.9	..	9.6	..	8.6

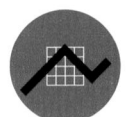

	Current revenue[a]		Total expenditure		Overall budget deficit (including grants)		Financing from abroad		Domestic financing		Debt and interest payments	
											Total debt % of GDP	Interest % of current revenue
	% of GDP		% of GDP		% of GDP		% of GDP		% of GDP			
	1980	1994	1980	1994	1980	1994	1980	1994	1980	1994	1994	1994
Rwanda	12.8	10.6	14.4	24.2	−1.7	−6.9	2.6	3.3	−0.9	2.3	48.4	16.7
Saudi Arabia	..	..	..	..	..	..	..	..	..	..	..	..
Senegal	24.1	..	23.1	..	0.9	0.1	−2.7	..	1.8	..	..	..
Sierra Leone	15.5	13.0	27.3	20.2	−12.1	−5.0	3.6	5.3	8.5	−0.2	89.4	..
Singapore	25.4	26.5	20.0	17.7	2.1	0.1	−0.2	0.0	−2.0	−15.8	76.9	4.9
Slovak Republic	..	..	..	..	..	..	..	..	..	..	..	..
Slovenia	..	..	..	..	..	..	..	..	..	..	..	..
South Africa	23.5	26.9	22.2	33.3	−2.3	−6.2	−0.2	1.2	2.5	5.1	55.8	21.0
Spain	24.2	32.0	26.7	39.4	−4.2	−7.0	0.0	8.0	4.2	−1.0	51.2	11.1
Sri Lanka	20.2	19.0	41.3	27.1	−18.3	−8.5	4.5	2.0	13.8	6.5	94.8	34.6
Sudan	13.8	..	19.6	..	−3.3	..	2.8	..	0.5	..	..	..
Sweden	35.0	36.8	39.4	48.7	−8.1	−12.8	3.2	13.4	4.9	−0.6	66.7	16.9
Switzerland	19.7	22.4	20.3	27.1	−0.2	−2.8	..	0.0	..	2.8	21.5	..
Syrian Arab Republic	26.8	22.5	48.2	26.6	−9.7	−3.8	−0.2	..	9.8	..	..	..
Tajikistan	..	..	..	..	..	..	..	..	..	..	..	..
Tanzania	17.9	..	27.9	..	−7.0	..	1.3	..	5.7	..	..	..
Thailand	14.3	18.5	18.9	16.4	−4.9	1.8	1.1	0.2	3.7	−2.0	6.1	3.3
Togo	30.3	..	30.8	..	−2.0	..	1.6	..	0.4	..	..	..
Trinidad and Tobago	42.5	..	30.3	..	7.2	..	..	..	..	..	..	..
Tunisia	31.3	28.8	31.6	32.0	−2.8	−2.5	2.3	..	0.5	..	51.8	11.4
Turkey	18.1	19.3	21.4	23.3	−3.1	−3.9	0.4	−1.8	2.6	5.7	44.0	23.8
Turkmenistan	..	..	..	..	..	..	..	..	..	..	..	..
Uganda	3.1	..	6.1	..	−3.1	..	0.0	..	3.1	..	..	..
Ukraine	..	..	..	..	..	..	..	..	..	..	..	..
United Arab Emirates	..	..	12.1	11.8	2.1	0.2	0.0	0.0	−2.1	−0.2	..	..
United Kingdom	35.2	35.3	38.3	41.7	−4.6	−6.6	0.3	−0.2	4.3	0.0	4.7	2.6
United States	20.2	20.0	22.0	23.0	−2.8	−3.0	0.0	0.4	2.8	2.6	51.9	16.0
Uruguay	22.3	32.2	21.8	35.1	0.0	−2.8	0.9	1.1	−0.9	1.7	26.4	6.1
Uzbekistan	..	..	..	..	..	..	..	..	..	..	..	..
Venezuela	22.3	18.9	18.7	18.8	0.0	−4.1	1.8	..	−1.9	..	..	20.6
Vietnam	..	..	..	..	..	..	..	..	..	..	..	..
West Bank and Gaza	..	..	..	..	..	..	..	..	..	..	..	..
Yemen, Rep.	..	21.4	..	38.4	..	−17.3	..	0.3	..	17.0	..	19.9
Yugoslavia, Fed. Rep.	..	..	..	..	..	..	..	..	..	..	..	..
Zaire	..	..	..	..	..	..	..	..	..	..	..	20.5
Zambia	25.0	12.0	37.2	18.2	−18.5	−6.5	8.8	..	9.7	..	..	19.5
Zimbabwe	24.1	..	34.9	..	−10.9	..	2.3	..	8.6	..	..	..

a. Excluding grants. b. Data prior to 1992 include Eritrea.

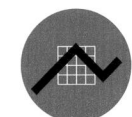

Fiscal deficits and economic growth

Many developing countries have implemented economic restructuring programs entailing sharp cuts in public spending and a reduced role for the government in the economy. The goal of these fiscal reforms is to increase domestic resources for investment, support market-oriented reforms, and promote a stable macroeconomic environment for growth. Several countries have made big strides in privatizing state-owned enterprises, liberalizing trade and financial policies, and strengthening tax administration. Other countries lag behind because of political or institutional constraints. But all developing countries face the challenge of improving fiscal management.

Fiscal discipline is critical to macroeconomic stability, although the consequences of a fiscal deficit depend on what it is financing and how it is financed. Large deficits may cause a resurgence of inflation, exchange and interest rate movements, and uncertainty about policy directions—and lead to weakening confidence and declining private sector investment. In general, the countries with the best growth records have been the most aggressive in pursuing conservative fiscal policies.

Since the 1980s the fiscal situation of many developing countries has markedly improved, as shown by declining deficit to GDP ratios and improving revenue to GDP ratios. But the overall reduction in fiscal deficits in developing countries conceals much variation among and within regions.

The difficulty for most governments arises from the need to strike a balance between making cuts in overall public spending and maintaining or increasing some types of spending. The reduction in fiscal deficits has come mostly from cuts in capital spending. But most developing countries need to increase government spending for infrastructure, health, and education and for improvements in public services. And they need to ensure that social safety nets protect the most vulnerable from the effects of spending cuts.

About the data

Tables 4.16–4.18 present an overview of the size and role of the central government in relation to the national economy. The IMF's *Manual on Government Finance Statistics* describes the government as the sector of the economy responsible for "implementation of public policy through the provision of primarily nonmarket services and the transfer of income, supported mainly by compulsory levies on other sectors" (1986, p. 3). In general, the definition of government excludes nonfinancial public enterprises and public financial institutions. Units of government meeting this definition exist at many levels, from local administrative units to the highest level of national government. But inadequate statistical coverage precludes the presentation of subnational data, making cross-country comparisons potentially misleading.

Central government can refer to one of two accounting concepts: consolidated or budgetary. For most countries central government finance data have been consolidated into one account, but for others only the budgetary central government accounts are available. Countries reporting budgetary data are noted in the *Primary data documentation*. Because budgetary accounts do not necessarily include all central government units, the picture of central government activities is usually incomplete. A key issue is the failure to include the quasi-fiscal operations of the central bank. Central bank losses arising from such operations can result in sizable quasi-fiscal deficits. Such deficits may also result from the operations of other financial intermediaries, such as public development finance institutions. Also missing from the data are governments' contingent liabilities for unfunded pension and insurance plans.

Government finance statistics are reported in local currency. Many countries report government finance data according to fiscal years. See *Primary data documentation* for the timing of fiscal years. For further discussion of government finance statistics see the notes to tables 4.17 and 4.18.

Definitions

● **Current revenue** includes all revenue from taxes and nonrepayable receipts (other than grants) from the sale of land, intangible assets, government stocks or fixed capital assets, or from capital transfers from nongovernmental sources. It also includes inheritance taxes and nonrecurrent levies on capital. ● **Total expenditure** includes nonrepayable current and capital expenditure. It does not include government lending or repayments to the government or government acquisition of equity for public policy purposes. ● **Overall budget deficit** is current and capital revenue and official grants received, less total expenditure and lending minus repayments. ● **Financing** refers to the means by which a government provides financial resources to cover a budget deficit or allocates financial resources arising from a budget surplus. It includes all government liabilities—other than those for currency issues or demand, time, or savings deposits with government—or claims on others held by government and changes in government holdings of cash and deposits. Government guarantees of the debt of others are excluded. Financing is broken down into **financing from abroad** (obtained from nonresidents) and **domestic financing** (obtained from residents). ● **Debt** is the entire stock of direct, government, fixed term contractual obligations to others outstanding at a particular date. It includes domestic debt (such as debt held by monetary authorities, deposit money banks, nonfinancial public enterprises, and households) and foreign debt (such as debt to international development institutions and foreign governments). It is the gross amount of government liabilities not reduced by the amount of government claims against others. Because debt is a stock rather than a flow, it is measured as of a given date, usually the last day of the fiscal year. ● **Interest** includes interest payments on government debt, including long-term bonds, long-term loans, and other debt instruments, to both domestic and foreign residents.

Data sources

Data on central government finances are from the IMF's *Government Finance Statistics Yearbook* (1995) and IMF data files. The accounts of each country are reported using the system of common definitions and classifications found in the IMF's *Manual on Government Finance Statistics* (1986). For complete and authoritative explanations of concepts, definitions, and data sources see these IMF sources.

4.17 | Central government revenues

	Income, profit, and capital gains		Social security		Goods and services		International trade		Other taxes		Nontax revenue	
	% of total current revenue		% of total current revenue		% of total current revenue		% of total current revenue		% of total current revenue		as % of total current revenue	
	1980	1994	1980	1994	1980	1994	1980	1994	1980	1994	1980	1994
Albania	..	..	..	..	..	..	..	..	..	..	..	..
Algeria	..	..	..	..	..	..	..	..	..	..	..	..
Angola	..	..	..	..	..	..	..	..	..	..	..	..
Argentina	..	..	..	..	..	..	..	..	..	..	..	..
Armenia	..	..	..	..	..	..	..	..	..	..	..	..
Australia	61	62	0	0	23	21	5	3	0	1	10	13
Austria	21	21	35	38	26	24	2	1	9	8	8	8
Azerbaijan	..	..	..	..	..	..	..	..	..	..	..	..
Bangladesh	..	..	..	..	..	..	..	..	..	..	..	..
Belarus	..	12	..	32	..	40	..	5	..	9	..	2
Belgium	39	35	31	34	24	25	0	0	2	3	4	4
Benin	..	..	..	..	..	..	..	..	..	..	..	..
Bolivia	..	3	..	6	..	42	..	7	..	9	..	32
Bosnia and Herzegovina	..	..	..	..	..	..	..	..	..	..	..	..
Botswana	..	..	..	..	..	..	..	..	..	..	..	..
Brazil	10	17	29	29	29	18	10	2	0	5	20	30
Bulgaria	..	14	..	22	..	28	..	8	..	4	..	23
Burkina Faso	18	21	8	0	16	..	44	..	4	4	11	25
Burundi	19	..	1	..	25	..	40	..	8	..	6	..
Cambodia	..	..	..	..	..	..	..	..	..	..	..	..
Cameroon	22	20	8	0	18	20	38	20	5	8	8	30
Canada	53	50	10	18	17	18	7	3	0	0	14	11
Central African Republic	..	..	..	..	..	..	..	..	..	..	..	..
Chad	..	..	..	..	..	..	..	..	..	..	..	..
Chile	18	19	17	7	36	46	4	9	6	4	20	16
China	..	..	..	..	..	..	..	..	..	..	..	..
Colombia	25	34	11	0	23	41	21	9	7	0	14	17
Congo	49	..	4	..	8	..	13	..	3	..	24	..
Costa Rica	14	11	29	30	30	32	19	14	2	1	6	12
Côte d'Ivoire	13	..	6	..	25	..	43	..	6	..	8	..
Croatia	..	10	..	32	..	44	..	10	..	1	..	4
Cuba	..	..	..	..	..	..	..	..	..	..	..	..
Czech Republic	..	16	..	39	..	32	..	4	..	1	..	7
Denmark	36	34	2	4	47	42	0	0	3	4	12	16
Dominican Republic	19	15	4	4	22	28	31	44	2	1	22	8
Ecuador	..	..	..	..	..	..	..	..	..	..	..	..
Egypt, Arab Rep.	..	21	..	10	..	14	..	10	..	10	..	36
El Salvador	..	..	..	..	..	..	..	..	..	..	..	..
Eritrea	..	..	..	..	..	..	..	..	..	..	..	..
Estonia	..	21	..	32	..	39	..	2	..	1	..	5
Ethiopia[a]	21	30	0	0	24	24	33	20	4	2	15	25
Finland	29	25	10	13	49	43	2	1	3	3	8	15
France	18	18	41	44	31	28	0	0	3	4	7	7
Gabon	40	..	0	..	5	..	20	..	2	..	34	..
Gambia, The	..	..	..	..	..	..	..	..	..	..	..	..
Georgia	..	..	..	..	..	..	..	..	..	..	..	..
Germany[b]	19	15	54	46	23	24	0	0	0	8	4	6
Ghana	..	..	..	..	..	..	..	..	..	..	..	..
Greece	17	29	26	2	32	64	5	0	10	0	11	7
Guatemala	..	..	..	..	..	..	..	..	..	..	..	..
Guinea	..	15	..	0	..	27	..	48	..	1	..	10
Guinea-Bissau	..	..	..	..	..	..	..	..	..	..	..	..
Haiti	14	..	0	..	15	..	48	..	9	..	13	..
Honduras	31	..	0	..	24	..	37	..	2	..	7	..
Hong Kong	..	..	..	..	..	..	..	..	..	..	..	..

	Income, profit, and capital gains		Social security		Goods and services		International trade		Other taxes		Nontax revenue	
	% of total current revenue		% of total current revenue		% of total current revenue		% of total current revenue		% of total current revenue		as % of total current revenue	
	1980	1994	1980	1994	1980	1994	1980	1994	1980	1994	1980	1994
Hungary	..	..	..	..	..	..	..	..	..	..	..	..
India	18	22	0	0	42	33	22	23	1	0	17	25
Indonesia	78	49	0	0	9	26	7	5	1	3	5	16
Iran, Islamic Rep.	4	9	7	5	4	7	12	10	5	3	68	67
Iraq	..	..	..	..	..	..	..	..	..	..	..	..
Ireland	34	38	13	15	30	31	9	7	2	3	11	7
Israel	41	41	10	7	25	35	4	1	8	4	14	12
Italy	30	37	35	30	25	28	0	0	4	3	8	3
Jamaica	34	..	4	..	49	..	3	..	6	..	4	..
Japan	71	36	0	27	21	15	2	1	3	6	5	16
Jordan	..	..	..	..	..	..	..	..	..	..	..	..
Kazakstan	..	..	..	..	..	..	..	..	..	..	..	..
Kenya	..	..	..	..	..	..	..	..	..	..	..	..
Korea, Dem. Rep.	..	..	..	..	..	..	..	..	..	..	..	..
Korea, Rep.	22	31	1	8	46	33	15	6	3	9	12	13
Kuwait	2	..	0	..	0	..	1	..	0	..	97	..
Kyrgyz Republic	..	..	..	..	..	..	..	..	..	..	..	..
Lao PDR	..	..	..	..	..	..	..	..	..	..	..	..
Latvia	..	16	..	35	..	39	..	4	..	0	..	6
Lebanon	..	..	..	..	..	..	..	..	..	..	..	..
Lesotho	..	..	..	..	..	..	..	..	..	..	..	..
Libya	..	..	..	..	..	..	..	..	..	..	..	..
Lithuania	..	23	..	34	..	32	..	7	..	0	..	4
Macedonia, FYR	..	..	..	..	..	..	..	..	..	..	..	..
Madagascar	17	16	11	0	39	23	28	43	3	2	2	16
Malawi	..	..	..	..	..	..	..	..	..	..	..	..
Malaysia	38	33	0	1	17	22	33	13	2	5	11	26
Mali	18	..	..	..	37	..	18	..	15	..	8	..
Mauritania	..	..	..	..	..	..	..	..	..	..	..	..
Mauritius	15	11	0	5	17	24	52	41	4	6	12	13
Mexico	37	..	14	..	29	8	28	2	–13	..	5	2
Moldova	..	..	..	..	..	..	..	..	..	..	..	..
Mongolia	..	34	..	12	..	23	..	12	..	1	..	19
Morocco	19	24	5	4	35	40	21	18	7	3	12	11
Mozambique	..	..	..	..	..	..	..	..	..	..	..	..
Myanmar	3	18	0	0	42	32	15	16	0	0	40	35
Namibia	..	29	..	0	..	29	..	31	..	1	..	11
Nepal	6	..	0	..	37	..	33	..	8	..	16	..
Netherlands	30	26	36	41	21	22	0	0	3	4	11	8
New Zealand	..	..	..	..	..	..	..	..	..	..	..	..
Nicaragua	8	8	9	13	37	47	25	22	10	6	10	5
Niger	24	..	4	..	18	..	36	..	3	..	15	..
Nigeria	..	..	..	..	..	..	..	..	..	..	..	..
Norway	27	15	22	25	40	37	1	1	1	2	9	20
Oman	..	..	..	..	..	..	..	..	..	..	..	..
Pakistan	14	16	0	0	34	32	34	23	0	0	18	29
Panama	21	17	21	22	17	12	10	14	4	3	27	32
Papua New Guinea	..	..	..	..	..	..	..	..	..	..	..	..
Paraguay	15	10	13	0	18	36	25	12	21	6	9	35
Peru	26	16	0	11	37	50	27	10	2	..	8	9
Philippines	..	..	..	..	..	..	..	..	..	..	..	..
Poland	..	28	..	24	..	28	..	9	..	1	..	10
Portugal	19	26	26	24	34	35	5	0	9	3	7	12
Puerto Rico	..	..	..	..	..	..	..	..	..	..	..	..
Romania	0	30	13	29	0	23	0	4	9	2	78	12
Russian Federation	..	14	..	36	..	29	..	15	..	0	..	7

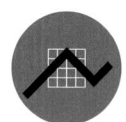

	Income, profit, and capital gains		Social security		Goods and services		International trade		Other taxes		Nontax revenue	
	% of total current revenue		% of total current revenue		% of total current revenue		% of total current revenue		% of total current revenue		as % of total current revenue	
	1980	1994	1980	1994	1980	1994	1980	1994	1980	1994	1980	1994
Rwanda	18	*16*	4	*2*	19	*35*	42	*31*	2	*4*	14	*12*
Saudi Arabia	..	..	..	..	..	..	..	..	..	..	..	..
Senegal	18	..	4	..	26	..	34	..	11	..	6	..
Sierra Leone	..	..	..	..	..	..	..	..	..	..	..	..
Singapore	32	*29*	0	*0*	16	*17*	7	*2*	14	*16*	31	*37*
Slovak Republic	..	..	..	..	..	..	..	..	..	..	..	..
Slovenia	..	..	..	..	..	..	..	..	..	..	..	..
South Africa	56	51	1	2	24	38	3	2	3	3	13	6
Spain	23	*31*	48	*38*	13	*22*	4	*1*	4	*0*	8	*8*
Sri Lanka	16	14	0	0	27	52	50	21	2	4	5	10
Sudan	..	..	..	..	..	..	..	..	..	..	..	..
Sweden	18	5	33	36	29	35	1	1	4	5	14	18
Switzerland	14	..	48	..	19	..	9	..	2	..	7	..
Syrian Arab Republic	10	*24*	0	*0*	5	*33*	14	*14*	10	*8*	61	*22*
Tajikistan	..	..	..	..	..	..	..	..	..	..	..	..
Tanzania	32	..	0	..	41	..	17	..	2	..	8	..
Thailand	18	30	0	1	46	39	26	17	2	3	8	9
Togo	34	..	6	..	15	..	32	..	–2	..	14	..
Trinidad and Tobago	..	..	..	..	..	..	..	..	..	..	..	..
Tunisia	15	*13*	9	*12*	24	*24*	25	*28*	4	*5*	22	*18*
Turkey	49	33	0	0	20	36	6	3	5	6	21	21
Turkmenistan	..	..	..	..	..	..	..	..	..	..	..	..
Uganda	..	..	..	..	..	..	..	..	..	..	..	..
Ukraine	..	..	..	..	..	..	..	..	..	..	..	..
United Arab Emirates	..	..	..	..	..	..	..	..	..	..	..	..
United Kingdom	38	*34*	16	*17*	28	*33*	0	*0*	6	*7*	13	*9*
United States	57	51	28	34	4	4	1	2	1	1	8	7
Uruguay	11	7	23	30	43	29	14	4	3	23	6	7
Uzbekistan	..	..	..	..	..	..	..	..	..	..	..	..
Venezuela	67	37	5	5	4	21	7	7	2	..	15	22
Vietnam	..	..	..	..	..	..	..	..	..	..	..	..
West Bank and Gaza	..	..	..	..	..	..	..	..	..	..	..	..
Yemen, Rep.	..	*23*	..	*0*	..	*12*	..	*21*	..	*5*	..	*39*
Yugoslavia, Fed. Rep.	..	..	..	..	..	..	..	..	..	..	..	..
Zaire	30	16	2	0	12	23	38	44	5	5	12	12
Zambia	38	34	0	0	43	46	8	16	3	0	7	4
Zimbabwe	46	..	0	..	28	..	4	..	1	..	20	..

a. Data prior to 1992 include Eritrea. b. Data prior to 1990 refer to the Federal Republic of Germany before unification.

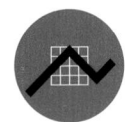

About the data

The International Monetary Fund (IMF) classifies government transactions as receipts or payments and according to whether they are repayable or nonrepayable. If nonrepayable, they are classified as capital (meant to be used in production for more than a year) or current, and as requited (involving payment in return for a benefit or service) or unrequited. Revenues include all nonrepayable receipts other than grants. Grants are unrequited, nonrepayable, noncompulsory receipts from other governments or international organizations. Transactions are generally recorded on a cash rather than an accrual basis. Measuring the accumulation of arrears on revenues or payments on an accrual basis would result in a higher deficit. Transactions within the same level of government are not included, but transactions between levels are included. In some instances the government budget may include transfers used to finance the deficits of autonomous, extrabudgetary agencies.

The IMF's *Manual on Government Finance Statistics* (1986) describes taxes as compulsory, unrequited payments made to governments by individuals, businesses, or institutions. They are unrequited because governments provide nothing specifically in return, although they may use the funds received to provide goods or services to individuals or to the community as a whole. The sources and relative size of revenues are determined by policy choices about where and how to impose taxes and by changes in the economy's structure. Tax policy may reflect concerns for distributional effects, economic efficiency, and the pragmatics of administering a tax system. There is no correct distribution of revenues among sources, nor is this distribution likely to remain constant.

Traditionally, taxes have been classified as either direct—those levied directly on the income or profits of individuals and corporations—or indirect—sales and excise taxes and duties. This distinction may be a useful simplification, but it has no particular analytical significance. The definitions used here are those followed by the IMF in its *Manual on Government Finance Statistics*. For further discussion of government revenues and expenditures see the notes to tables 4.16 and 4.18.

Definitions

● **Taxes on income, profit, and capital gains** are levied on the actual or presumptive net income of individuals, on the profits of enterprises, and on capital gains, whether realized on land, securities, or other assets. Intragovernmental payments are eliminated in consolidation. ● **Social security taxes** include employers' and employees' social security contributions and those of self-employed and unemployed people. ● **Taxes on goods and services** include general sales and turnover or value added taxes, selective excises on goods, selective taxes on services, taxes on the use of goods or property, and profits of fiscal monopolies. ● **Taxes on international trade** include import duties, export duties, profits of export or import monopolies, exchange profits, and exchange taxes. ● **Other taxes** include employers' payroll or labor taxes, taxes on property, and taxes not allocable to other categories. They may include negative values that are adjustments (for example, for taxes collected on behalf of state and local governments and not allocable to individual tax categories). ● **Nontax revenue** includes requited nonrepayable receipts for public purposes, such as fines, administrative fees, or entrepreneurial income from government ownership of property and voluntary, unrequited nonrepayable receipts other than from governmental sources. Proceeds of grants and borrowing, funds arising from the repayment of previous lending by governments, incurrence of liabilities, and proceeds from the sale of capital assets are not included.

Data sources

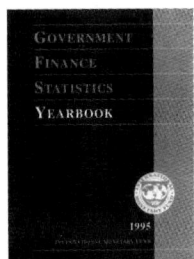

Data on central government revenues are from the IMF's *Government Finance Statistics Yearbook* (1995) and IMF data files. The accounts of each country are reported using the system of common definitions and classifications found in the IMF's *Manual on Government Finance Statistics* (1986). The IMF receives additional information on the tax revenues of some OECD members from the OECD. For complete and authoritative explanations of concepts, definitions, and data sources see these IMF sources.

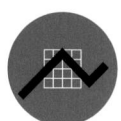

4.18 | Central government expenditures

	Goods and services		Wages and salaries[a]		Interest payments		Subsidies and other current transfers		Capital expenditure		Defense expenditure[b]	
	% of total expenditures		% of total expenditures		% of total expenditures		% of total expenditures		% of total expenditures		% of GDP	
	1980	1994	1980	1994	1980	1994	1980	1994	1980	1994	1980	1994
Albania	..	..	..	..	..	..	..	..	..	..	..	..
Algeria	..	..	..	..	..	..	..	..	..	..	..	..
Angola	..	..	..	..	..	..	..	..	..	..	..	..
Argentina	57	..	..	..	0	..	43	..	..	..	2.6	*0.8*
Armenia	..	..	..	..	..	..	..	..	..	..	..	..
Australia	22	24	..	..	7	5	65	67	7	4	2.1	2.1
Austria	26	25	11	10	5	9	60	58	9	7	1.1	0.9
Azerbaijan	..	..	..	..	..	..	..	..	..	..	..	..
Bangladesh	..	..	..	..	..	..	..	..	..	..	0.9	..
Belarus	..	*36*	..	*2*	..	*2*	..	*46*	..	*16*	..	*1.6*
Belgium	23	25	16	17	10	8	59	57	8	11	2.9	..
Benin	..	..	..	..	..	..	..	..	..	..	..	..
Bolivia	..	55	..	33	..	10	..	14	..	22	..	2.1
Bosnia and Herzegovina	..	..	..	..	..	..	..	..	..	..	..	..
Botswana	47	*52*	29	*28*	2	*2*	19	*27*	32	*18*	3.3	*5.6*
Brazil	22	*13*	11	*8*	11	*48*	67	*48*	11	*3*	0.8	*1.0*
Bulgaria	..	24	..	6	..	32	..	41	..	3	..	2.6
Burkina Faso	67	*46*	..	*38*	3	*8*	13	*12*	19	*34*	2.1	*2.1*
Burundi	*39*	..	*25*	..	*2*	..	*7*	..	*46*	..	..	..
Cambodia	..	..	..	..	..	..	..	..	..	..	..	..
Cameroon	55	*65*	32	*55*	1	*12*	11	*12*	33	*9*	1.4	*1.5*
Canada	22	..	10	..	12	..	65	..	1	..	1.6	*1.7*
Central African Republic	*67*	..	*54*	..	*1*	..	*16*	..	*6*	..	2.1	..
Chad	..	..	..	..	..	..	..	..	..	..	..	..
Chile	41	29	29	19	3	5	46	51	10	16	3.5	1.8
China	..	..	..	..	..	..	..	..	..	..	..	1.2
Colombia	36	*29*	23	*19*	4	*11*	38	*43*	31	*18*	1.1	*1.3*
Congo	..	71	..	51	..	3	..	16	*45*	9	..	..
Costa Rica	53	45	44	34	9	13	24	31	21	11	0.7	0.0
Côte d'Ivoire	..	..	..	..	..	..	..	..	28	..	..	..
Croatia	..	60	..	24	..	3	..	29	..	7	..	8.3
Cuba	..	..	..	..	..	..	..	..	..	..	..	..
Czech Republic	..	20	..	9	..	3	..	65	..	11	..	2.7
Denmark	22	19	13	11	7	13	65	64	7	3	2.6	1.8
Dominican Republic	50	35	39	23	6	6	12	8	31	51	1.3	0.8
Ecuador	28	47	26	42	9	22	34	9	16	21	1.8	..
Egypt, Arab Rep.	*38*	*32*	*19*	*18*	*6*	*24*	*36*	*25*	*20*	*19*	6.2	3.7
El Salvador	50	44	40	34	3	11	16	23	16	25	1.5	1.2
Eritrea	..	..	..	..	..	..	..	..	..	..	..	..
Estonia	..	..	..	..	..	..	..	..	..	..	..	1.0
Ethiopia[c]	85	*72*	37	*40*	3	*8*	4	*21*	15	*10*	6.8	3.7
Finland	22	*16*	11	*7*	2	*8*	66	*71*	11	*4*	1.6	1.8
France	30	24	20	16	2	6	62	64	5	5	2.9	*2.5*
Gabon	..	..	..	..	..	..	..	..	..	..	..	..
Gambia, The	46	..	23	..	1	..	4	..	48	23	..	..
Georgia	..	..	..	..	..	..	..	..	..	..	..	..
Germany[d]	34	*29*	9	*7*	3	*6*	55	*60*	7	*5*	..	..
Ghana	48	*45*	27	*28*	16	*17*	26	*23*	10	*15*	0.4	*1.0*
Greece	45	*32*	29	*22*	8	*29*	35	*29*	16	*10*	4.5	*3.8*
Guatemala	50	50	35	37	5	10	6	17	42	26	1.3	1.4
Guinea	..	39	..	23	..	6	..	5	..	50	..	..
Guinea-Bissau	..	..	..	..	..	..	..	..	..	..	..	..
Haiti	*82*	..	..	..	*2*	..	*5*	..	*20*	..	..	..
Honduras	..	..	..	..	..	..	..	..	..	..	..	..
Hong Kong	..	..	..	..	..	..	..	..	..	..	..	..

	Goods and services		Wages and salaries[a]		Interest payments		Subsidies and other current transfers		Capital expenditure		Defense expenditure[b]	
	% of total expenditures		% of total expenditures		% of total expenditures		% of total expenditures		% of total expenditures		% of GDP	
	1980	1994	1980	1994	1980	1994	1980	1994	1980	1994	1980	1994
Hungary	20	..	7	..	3	..	64	..	13	..	2.4	..
India	29	23	14	10	13	26	47	38	12	12	2.6	2.5
Indonesia	25	26	15	18	4	12	24	13	47	47	3.0	1.1
Iran, Islamic Rep.	57	52	45	39	1	0	19	13	22	35	5.7	1.6
Iraq	..	..	..	..	..	..	..	..	..	..	..	..
Ireland	19	18	13	13	14	15	57	59	10	8	1.7	1.3
Israel	50	35	12	14	11	14	35	41	4	10	27.9	8.4
Italy	18	15	13	11	11	22	63	59	5	4	1.4	..
Jamaica	..	..	..	..	..	..	..	..	..	..	..	..
Japan	13	..	..	..	13	..	54	..	19	..	..	1.0
Jordan	43	61	..	45	3	8	17	11	29	20	..	6.4
Kazakstan	..	..	..	..	..	..	..	..	..	..	..	..
Kenya	57	51	27	32	7	25	13	5	23	19	4.2	1.6
Korea, Dem. Rep.	..	..	..	..	..	..	..	..	..	..	..	..
Korea, Rep.	45	30	16	13	7	3	34	51	14	15	5.8	3.3
Kuwait	45	54	22	25	0	0	23	34	32	13	3.4	12.5
Kyrgyz Republic	..	..	..	..	..	..	..	..	..	..	..	..
Lao PDR	..	..	..	..	..	..	..	..	..	..	..	..
Latvia	..	35	..	18	..	2	..	59	..	4	..	0.9
Lebanon	..	..	..	..	..	..	..	..	..	..	..	..
Lesotho	..	..	..	..	..	..	..	..	..	..	..	2.8
Libya	..	..	..	..	..	..	..	..	..	..	..	..
Lithuania	..	39	..	14	..	0	..	52	..	8	..	0.5
Macedonia, FYR	..	..	..	..	..	..	..	..	..	..	..	..
Madagascar	..	29	..	19	..	20	..	8	..	38	..	0.9
Malawi	37	..	15	..	9	..	6	..	48	..	4.4	..
Malaysia	38	49	28	31	10	15	19	18	35	19	4.2	3.0
Mali	46	..	33	..	1	..	11	..	9	..	2.4	..
Mauritania	..	..	..	..	..	..	..	..	..	..	..	..
Mauritius	42	49	32	38	14	9	28	23	17	19	0.2	0.3
Mexico	32	..	25	..	10	..	25	..	33	..	0.4	0.8
Moldova	..	..	..	..	..	..	..	..	..	..	..	..
Mongolia	..	37	..	10	..	3	..	45	..	15	..	2.5
Morocco	47	50	33	37	7	18	15	9	31	23	5.9	4.2
Mozambique	..	..	..	..	..	..	..	..	..	..	..	..
Myanmar	..	..	..	..	..	..	..	..	24	42	3.5	4.1
Namibia	..	74	..	..	..	2	..	9	..	15	..	..
Nepal	..	..	..	..	..	..	..	..	..	..	1.0	0.9
Netherlands	16	15	11	9	4	9	72	72	9	4	3.0	2.1
New Zealand	29	49	21	10	10	12	55	37	6	3	2.0	1.2
Nicaragua	62	38	..	22	8	15	15	21	15	26	3.3	1.9
Niger	30	..	17	..	6	..	14	..	49	..	0.7	..
Nigeria	..	..	..	..	..	..	..	..	..	..	..	..
Norway	18	18	9	8	7	5	71	73	3	4	2.7	2.8
Oman	71	71	13	23	3	5	5	6	21	16	19.7	16.1
Pakistan	47	49	..	..	12	26	23	10	17	15	..	..
Panama	50	53	33	40	18	7	14	29	18	11	..	1.4
Papua New Guinea	58	48	37	28	5	9	23	32	15	11	1.5	1.0
Paraguay	61	56	34	46	3	6	12	23	24	15	1.2	1.4
Peru	45	33	..	17	18	13	14	35	23	18	4.1	..
Philippines	61	42	27	28	7	28	7	14	26	16	2.1	1.4
Poland	..	26	..	14	..	9	..	61	..	3	..	..
Portugal	34	38	24	29	8	18	45	31	13	13	2.5	..
Puerto Rico	..	..	..	..	..	..	..	..	..	..	..	..
Romania	11	34	2	16	0	4	55	49	33	13	1.7	2.4
Russian Federation	..	40	..	14	..	6	..	49	..	5	..	4.4

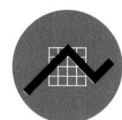

	Goods and services		Wages and salaries[a]		Interest payments		Subsidies and other current transfers		Capital expenditure		Defense expenditure[b]	
	% of total expenditures		% of total expenditures		% of total expenditures		% of total expenditures		% of total expenditures		% of GDP	
	1980	1994	1980	1994	1980	1994	1980	1994	1980	1994	1980	1994
Rwanda	58	65	30	27	2	9	5	8	35	26	..	..
Saudi Arabia	..	..	..	..	..	..	..	..	..	..	..	..
Senegal	72	..	45	..	6	..	18	..	8	..	3.9	..
Sierra Leone	..	34	..	19	..	15	..	23	20	32	..	..
Singapore	58	63	29	33	15	6	6	14	22	13	5.1	4.4
Slovak Republic	..	..	..	..	..	..	..	..	..	..	..	..
Slovenia	..	..	..	..	..	..	..	..	..	..	..	..
South Africa	47	37	20	26	8	16	31	40	14	7	..	..
Spain	40	20	32	14	1	11	48	62	11	7	1.2	1.3
Sri Lanka	31	35	13	19	8	24	20	22	40	19	0.7	3.3
Sudan	46	..	12	..	6	..	28	..	23	..	2.6	..
Sweden	17	15	8	6	7	13	71	71	5	1	3.0	2.7
Switzerland	27	33	6	8	3	3	63	63	7	5	2.1	1.7
Syrian Arab Republic	..	..	..	..	..	..	..	..	37	42	17.2	7.5
Tajikistan	..	..	..	..	..	..	..	..	..	..	..	..
Tanzania	52	..	19	..	7	..	4	..	40	..	3.4	..
Thailand	55	61	21	34	8	4	14	7	23	26	4.1	2.4
Togo	52	..	28	..	9	..	12	..	27	..	2.3	..
Trinidad and Tobago	34	..	28	..	3	..	24	..	40	..	..	..
Tunisia	42	..	29	..	5	..	24	..	30	..	3.8	1.7
Turkey	47	41	32	30	3	20	23	31	28	9	3.3	2.2
Turkmenistan	..	..	..	..	..	..	..	..	..	..	..	..
Uganda	..	..	..	..	..	..	..	..	13	..	1.5	..
Ukraine	..	..	..	..	..	..	..	..	..	..	..	..
United Arab Emirates	80	87	..	35	0	0	12	9	8	5	5.8	4.4
United Kingdom	32	29	14	11	11	7	53	58	5	7	5.3	3.6
United States	29	24	12	10	10	14	54	58	6	4	4.7	4.2
Uruguay	47	29	30	15	2	6	43	58	8	7	2.9	2.5
Uzbekistan	..	..	..	..	..	..	..	..	..	..	..	..
Venezuela	50	30	41	25	8	21	22	32	22	14	1.1	..
Vietnam	..	..	..	..	..	..	..	..	..	..	..	..
West Bank and Gaza	..	..	..	..	..	..	..	..	..	..	..	..
Yemen, Rep.	..	..	..	..	..	..	..	..	..	..	..	11.7
Yugoslavia, Fed. Rep.	..	..	..	..	..	..	..	..	..	..	..	..
Zaire	65	66	42	21	8	13	8	9	20	12	..	..
Zambia	55	36	27	22	9	10	25	20	11	34	0.0	..
Zimbabwe	56	..	31	..	7	..	32	..	5	..	8.7	..

Note: Includes expenditures financed by grants in kind and other cash adjustments. a. Part of goods and services. b. Classified by function; see *About the data*. c. Data prior to 1992 include Eritrea. d. Data prior to 1990 refer to the Federal Republic of Germany before unification.

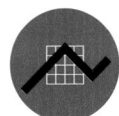

About the data

Government expenditures include all nonrepayable payments, whether current or capital, requited or unrequited. Total expenditure of the central government as presented in the International Monetary Fund's *Government Finance Statistics* (GFS) is a more limited measure of general government consumption than that shown in the national accounts (see table 4.12) because it excludes consumption expenditures by state and local governments. At the same time, the GFS concept of central government expenditure is broader than the national accounts definition because it includes government gross domestic investment and transfer payments.

Data on the revenues and expenditures of governments are collected by the IMF through questionnaires distributed to member governments and from the Organization for Economic Cooperation and Development (OECD). Despite the IMF's efforts to systematize and standardize the collection of public finance data, statistics on public finance are often incomplete, untimely, and noncomparable.

Expenditures can be measured either by function (education, health, and defense) or by economic type (wages and salaries, interest payments, and purchases of goods and services). Functional data are often incomplete, and coverage varies from country to country because functional responsibilities stretch across levels of government for which no data are available. Therefore, only defense expenditures, which are usually the responsibility of the central government, are shown here. For more information on education expenditure see table 2.7; for more information on health expenditure see table 2.11.

The classification of expenditures by economic type can also be problematic. For example, the distinction between current and capital expenditure may be arbitrary, and subsidies to state-owned enterprises or banks may be disguised as capital financing. For further discussion of government finance statistics see the notes to tables 4.16 and 4.17.

Definitions

● **Total expenditure** of the central government includes both current and capital (development) expenditures and excludes lending minus repayments. ● **Goods and services** include all government payments in exchange for goods and services, whether in the form of wages and salaries to employees or other purchases of goods and services. ● **Wages and salaries** consist of all payments in cash, but not in kind, to employees in return for services rendered, before deduction of withholding taxes and employees' contributions to social security and pension funds. ● **Interest payments** are payments for the use of borrowed money to domestic sectors and to nonresidents. (Repayment of principal is shown as a financing item, and commission charges are shown as purchases of services.) Interest payments do not include government payments as guarantor or surety of interest on the defaulted debts of others, which are classified as government lending. ● **Subsidies and other current transfers** include all unrequited, nonrepayable transfers on current account to private and public enterprises, and the cost of covering the cash operating deficits of departmental enterprise sales to the public. ● **Capital expenditure** is the expenditure to acquire fixed capital assets, land, intangible assets, government stocks, and nonmilitary, nonfinancial assets. Also included are capital grants. ● **Defense expenditure** comprises all expenditures, whether by defense or other departments, on the maintenance of military forces. Also in this category are such closely related items as military aid programs. Defense expenditure does not include that on public order and safety.

Data sources

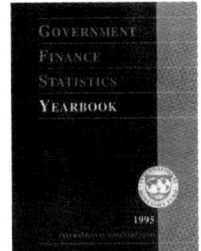

Data on central government expenditures are from the IMF's *Government Finance Statistics Yearbook* and IMF data files. The accounts of each country are reported using the system of common definitions and classifications found in the IMF's *Manual on Government Finance Statistics* (1986). For complete and authoritative explanations of concepts, definitions, and data sources see these IMF sources.

4.19 | Monetary indicators

	Money and quasi money		Net foreign assets		Domestic credit		Claims on private sector		Claims on governments and other public entities		Income velocity of money and quasi money	
	annual % growth of M2		annual growth as % of M2		annual growth as % of M2		annual growth as % of M2		annual growth as % of M2		GDP/M2	
	1990	1995	1990	1995	1990	1995	1990	1995	1990	1995	1990	1995
Albania	..	23.8	..	65.8	..	−10.4	..	1.3	..	−11.8	..	2.1
Algeria	11.4	9.0	0.0	−4.7	15.4	26.6	12.2	0.9	3.2	22.5	1.6	2.6
Angola	..	..	..	..	..	..	..	..	..	..	..	..
Argentina	1,113.3	−2.7	−21.9	−7.2	236.5	7.0	1,444.7	−1.1	1,573.2	8.1	16.1	5.3
Armenia	..	..	..	..	..	..	..	..	..	..	..	..
Australia	12.6	8.6	−3.7	−3.2	12.9	14.1	15.2	12.8	−2.2	0.5	1.8	1.6
Austria	9.7	5.0	−0.6	1.2	13.6	8.2	12.1	7.0	1.6	1.2	1.2	1.1
Azerbaijan	..	23.8	..	27.0	..	48.3	..	5.9	..	42.4	..	10.6
Bangladesh	10.2	12.2	5.8	−8.3	9.0	10.3	9.2	6.5	−0.2	3.3	3.3	2.8
Belarus	..	158.4	..	7.5	..	160.6	..	61.4	..	99.2	..	1.0
Belgium	4.1	4.9	−0.5	−2.1	7.8	6.3	3.5	0.5	4.8	4.8	2.1	1.2
Benin	28.6	−2.4	26.3	−5.5	11.1	7.6	−1.3	2.1	12.4	5.5	4.2	*4.0*
Bolivia	52.8	7.7	13.5	4.8	62.5	−3.0	40.7	13.4	17.5	−16.4	4.5	2.2
Bosnia and Herzegovina	..	..	..	..	..	..	..	..	..	..	..	..
Botswana	−14.0	9.4	61.8	52.8	−39.9	5.4	12.6	−1.4	−52.4	5.8	3.7	3.9
Brazil	1,289.2	38.9	314.8	10.2	4,280.6	36.0	1,566.4	27.9	2,704.2	8.0	7.6	3.8
Bulgaria	11.8	..	..	..	−23.3	..	4.9	..	−28.8	..	1.0	..
Burkina Faso	−0.4	22.4	−0.4	30.8	1.0	−4.4	3.6	2.9	−1.5	−7.2	4.9	4.5
Burundi	10.4	*33.3*	−3.5	*25.3*	11.1	*15.7*	16.3	*6.5*	−5.3	*11.1*	5.8	*5.0*
Cambodia	..	43.6	..	35.2	..	13.3	..	12.5	..	0.9	..	13.1
Cameroon	−1.7	−6.2	1.2	−3.8	−2.2	−0.9	0.9	0.3	−3.0	−1.9	4.4	6.2
Canada	7.7	6.3	−0.6	4.7	9.7	5.3	9.2	5.4	0.5	−0.1	2.1	1.7
Central African Republic	−3.7	4.3	−0.9	5.8	0.6	−2.4	−1.6	3.9	2.3	−6.3	5.6	4.8
Chad	−2.4	48.7	13.3	54.3	−18.7	−12.0	−1.3	6.4	−17.3	−18.4	4.7	7.3
Chile	23.5	25.8	32.8	12.9	37.9	34.6	21.4	37.3	16.4	−2.4	2.8	2.7
China	28.9	29.5	5.6	2.8	28.0	21.0	26.5	21.0	1.5	0.0	1.4	1.1
Colombia	32.7	21.5	*44.6*	8.4	*7.3*	36.3	*8.7*	28.6	−7.3	3.5	5.9	5.1
Congo	18.5	−0.1	25.1	6.2	−6.3	10.7	5.1	6.3	−12.6	4.2	4.9	6.8
Costa Rica	27.5	4.8	−6.9	9.2	15.4	5.1	7.3	0.0	8.2	5.6	2.6	3.1
Côte d'Ivoire	−2.6	18.1	−1.0	10.7	−7.7	13.8	−3.9	13.4	−3.0	0.2	3.4	3.8
Croatia	..	41.2	..	10.1	..	31.6	..	35.7	..	−4.3	..	4.5
Cuba	..	..	..	..	..	..	..	..	..	..	..	..
Czech Republic	..	29.3	..	13.3	..	25.1	..	14.1	..	11.0	..	1.2
Denmark	6.5	6.2	5.7	1.6	0.2	3.2	3.0	2.6	−3.1	−1.5	1.7	1.7
Dominican Republic	39.1	17.5	−3.8	7.6	23.2	16.6	20.8	16.4	0.8	0.8	5.5	4.1
Ecuador	101.6	36.8	31.1	0.7	17.7	−33.9	46.7	39.7	−22.4	−80.3	6.1	3.8
Egypt, Arab Rep.	28.7	9.9	0.2	−1.5	32.5	15.1	6.3	12.1	25.3	2.7	1.1	1.0
El Salvador	32.3	9.8	24.1	−2.9	9.6	18.4	8.8	17.4	9.6	−1.4	3.7	2.8
Eritrea	..	..	..	..	..	..	..	..	..	..	..	..
Estonia	*71.1*	27.1	*95.6*	6.3	*14.1*	24.9	*27.6*	22.7	*−13.5*	2.2	*3.9*	4.3
Ethiopia[a]	18.5	9.0	−1.6	4.5	24.0	10.9	−1.0	12.8	21.7	−2.7	2.7	2.4
Finland	5.0	6.0	−8.8	4.2	17.1	1.0	17.1	−3.7	−0.1	4.7	1.9	1.8
France	3.3	10.8	−4.0	3.2	16.1	8.6	15.8	3.5	0.3	5.1	1.6	1.6
Gabon	3.3	10.1	24.2	−13.7	−19.3	18.5	0.7	11.9	−20.6	5.6	5.2	6.8
Gambia, The	8.4	14.2	40.3	22.1	−27.5	10.2	7.8	−5.0	−35.4	15.2	5.3	*4.2*
Georgia	..	..	..	..	..	..	..	..	..	..	..	..
Germany[b]	18.6	4.6	2.1	−0.9	28.6	15.3	26.6	8.1	2.0	7.1	*1.7*	1.6
Ghana	13.3	40.4	12.2	15.5	4.1	66.1	4.9	12.4	−0.8	49.8	7.9	6.5
Greece	14.3	*24.8*	−4.2	*3.0*	22.3	*1.1*	4.6	*7.4*	16.3	−5.4	1.6	*1.9*
Guatemala	25.8	15.8	0.4	3.5	15.7	16.2	15.0	25.8	0.5	−9.4	5.2	4.2
Guinea	*23.3*	11.3	*15.1*	−3.9	*20.4*	20.9	*13.1*	12.1	*7.3*	8.6	*11.5*	11.3
Guinea-Bissau	65.3	43.1	26.2	17.6	167.4	−16.4	57.4	3.1	109.9	−19.5	7.3	7.2
Haiti	2.5	27.1	0.0	18.1	−1.4	16.2	−0.6	15.7	0.4	0.3	3.2	2.3
Honduras	21.4	29.2	−29.4	14.1	2.8	9.3	13.0	16.5	−10.9	−7.4	3.5	4.0
Hong Kong	..	..	..	..	..	..	..	..	..	..	..	..

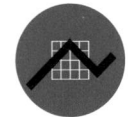

	Money and quasi money		Net foreign assets		Domestic credit		Claims on private sector		Claims on governments and other public entities		Income velocity of money and quasi money	
	annual % growth of M2		annual growth as % of M2		annual growth as % of M2		annual growth as % of M2		annual growth as % of M2		GDP/M2	
	1990	1995	1990	1995	1990	1995	1990	1995	1990	1995	1990	1995
Hungary	29.2	13.4	8.6	1.3	24.8	22.6	22.8	8.1	2.0	14.5	2.6	2.3
India	15.1	11.0	1.8	1.1	16.6	9.5	5.9	6.0	10.5	3.4	2.4	2.2
Indonesia	44.6	..	−3.3	..	60.4	..	66.9	..	−6.7	..	2.9	..
Iran, Islamic Rep.	18.0	30.1	−0.5	14.0	20.6	27.0	14.7	9.8	5.8	17.2	1.9	2.6
Iraq	..	..	..	..	..	..	..	..	..	..	..	..
Ireland	8.9	15.5	−0.3	10.2	7.8	5.8	0.6	7.3	1.9	−3.4	2.5	2.0
Israel	19.4	21.7	3.3	1.8	23.8	17.9	18.5	18.3	4.9	−0.5	1.6	1.5
Italy	8.8	7.4	1.4	−3.2	10.7	..	9.2	..	2.4	1.5	1.7	1.6
Jamaica	21.5	31.8	−2.2	17.1	−3.7	23.8	12.5	18.7	−16.0	4.9	2.6	2.3
Japan	8.2	2.8	−1.0	2.1	11.2	2.1	9.7	1.8	1.5	0.4	0.9	0.9
Jordan	8.3	5.7	8.0	2.6	4.8	8.1	4.7	9.5	1.0	−1.6	0.8	1.0
Kazakstan	..	..	..	..	..	..	..	..	..	..	..	..
Kenya	20.1	16.4	−6.4	−3.7	30.2	32.5	8.0	23.7	21.5	6.1	3.7	2.7
Korea, Dem. Rep.	..	..	..	..	..	..	..	..	..	..	..	..
Korea, Rep.	17.2	15.6	2.1	1.4	34.6	20.6	36.1	21.6	−1.5	−1.0	2.8	2.4
Kuwait	−0.5	8.4	−1.9	3.7	−15.6	7.1	−89.1	7.0	73.5	0.2	1.1	1.3
Kyrgyz Republic	..	..	..	..	..	..	..	..	..	..	..	..
Lao PDR	7.8	16.4	2.6	11.7	10.6	17.0	3.6	18.1	7.0	−1.1	14.4	7.9
Latvia	..	−21.4	..	−9.5	..	−17.2	..	−21.7	..	4.5	..	4.0
Lebanon	55.1	16.4	73.3	0.1	46.2	18.1	27.6	13.0	18.5	5.1	0.6	0.9
Lesotho	8.4	8.2	30.0	33.1	−11.2	−21.2	6.1	3.8	−17.4	−25.0	2.7	3.5
Libya	20.3	2.2	7.7	8.7	9.4	6.5	0.9	3.4	8.5	3.1	1.3	..
Lithuania	..	29.8	..	12.7	..	12.4	..	18.6	..	−6.2	..	4.4
Macedonia, FYR	..	..	..	..	..	..	..	..	..	..	..	..
Madagascar	4.5	15.9	−29.3	13.6	9.0	−3.4	23.8	9.6	−14.8	−13.1	6.3	5.6
Malawi	11.1	56.2	11.9	66.8	2.9	−2.7	15.8	2.1	−12.8	−4.8	5.6	6.6
Malaysia	10.6	20.0	4.9	−2.1	19.8	28.7	20.8	26.3	−1.2	−0.6	1.6	1.2
Mali	−4.9	6.8	9.3	5.3	−13.3	6.8	0.1	19.1	−13.4	−12.3	4.9	0.0
Mauritania	11.5	−5.1	−16.7	29.5	21.8	−71.5	20.2	−42.5	1.5	−28.9	3.7	5.2
Mauritius	21.2	18.7	17.7	6.4	12.0	12.1	10.8	9.1	0.8	3.0	1.8	1.4
Mexico	75.8	33.3	2.6	−0.5	74.6	6.7	64.0	−6.7	12.1	13.5	5.4	3.3
Moldova	358.0	65.3	−38.1	12.4	500.4	80.1	53.3	34.6	447.0	45.5	4.2	8.7
Mongolia	61.0	30.5	−31.9	28.1	76.0	−16.9	38.9	12.7	37.2	−29.5	3.5	3.9
Morocco	21.5	7.0	15.2	−3.7	−1.3	12.2	12.4	6.9	−4.9	5.1	2.0	1.5
Mozambique	..	..	..	..	..	..	..	..	..	..	..	..
Myanmar	37.7	..	2.4	..	39.0	..	12.8	..	23.4	..	4.2	..
Namibia	30.3	26.0	23.3	−3.5	8.4	34.8	15.4	31.8	−4.7	3.5	3.9	2.6
Nepal	18.5	18.1	13.9	7.2	12.8	15.5	5.7	18.5	7.3	−2.9	3.4	3.0
Netherlands	6.9	5.9	0.6	−1.5	6.8	13.1	6.7	13.3	0.1	−0.2	1.2	1.2
New Zealand	74.0	4.9	−9.1	−3.4	76.7	8.0	76.6	12.3	0.1	−4.3	1.9	1.3
Nicaragua	7,677.8	39.4	−192,285.8	38.3	22,002.3	10.5	4,932.9	31.0	12,679.3	−19.0	3.5	3.3
Niger	−4.1	3.6	1.9	−0.8	−3.7	−12.7	−5.0	−22.7	1.3	10.0	4.9	7.0
Nigeria	32.7	36.5	53.0	2.3	36.1	57.8	7.8	26.5	26.3	−97.7	5.2	4.0
Norway	5.6	3.8	1.9	0.2	2.9	6.3	5.0	9.5	−0.1	−2.6	1.7	1.8
Oman	10.0	7.7	19.8	3.1	−1.3	7.0	9.6	9.3	−10.9	−2.2	3.6	3.2
Pakistan	11.6	13.8	−0.4	−8.1	13.5	20.2	5.9	11.7	7.7	8.5	2.7	2.4
Panama	36.6	7.9	51.9	1.7	−24.8	10.9	0.8	15.5	−25.7	−4.6	2.6	1.5
Papua New Guinea	4.3	−1.3	−0.5	−1.5	8.6	7.8	1.3	9.4	7.2	−1.1	2.9	3.3
Paraguay	52.5	21.6	40.6	−0.2	23.8	6.8	33.1	14.1	−9.5	−9.0	6.1	3.8
Peru	6,384.9	26.6	1,626.7	9.8	4,784.1	21.9	2,123.7	31.2	2,127.1	−9.3	10.2	5.8
Philippines	22.5	24.2	−7.8	−1.0	19.7	32.0	15.7	28.8	3.4	2.6	3.2	2.2
Poland	160.1	35.0	87.5	29.4	96.3	21.4	20.8	14.9	75.6	6.5	4.2	3.1
Portugal	9.4	9.8	3.7	−5.9	13.2	12.9	7.4	11.5	3.2	−2.9	1.6	1.3
Puerto Rico	..	..	..	..	..	..	..	..	..	..	..	..
Romania	26.4	70.1	−12.0	−7.9	−30.8	73.7	..	..	133.3	73.7	1.8	5.0
Russian Federation	..	114.0	..	8.3	..	131.1	..	46.2	..	84.5	..	8.6

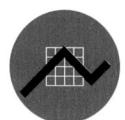

	Money and quasi money		Net foreign assets		Domestic credit		Claims on private sector		Claims on governments and other public entities		Income velocity of money and quasi money	
	annual % growth of M2		annual growth as % of M2		annual growth as % of M2		annual growth as % of M2		annual growth as % of M2		GDP/M2	
	1990	1995	1990	1995	1990	1995	1990	1995	1990	1995	1990	1995
Rwanda	5.6	72.8	–11.0	61.6	16.4	–9.0	–10.0	32.1	26.8	–41.0	6.9	6.4
Saudi Arabia	4.6	2.9	–3.0	–9.3	–0.2	8.6	–4.5	3.4	4.2	–1.1	2.1	2.0
Senegal	–4.8	6.5	6.9	12.7	–13.9	1.1	–8.4	1.1	–5.3	0.2	4.3	5.0
Sierra Leone	74.0	19.6	–406.7	–7.8	39.9	3.7	4.9	1.6	35.0	2.1	9.7	10.2
Singapore	20.0	8.5	13.3	4.6	8.8	11.6	13.7	19.7	–4.9	–8.1	1.2	1.2
Slovak Republic	..	18.4	..	16.1	..	–1.5	..	12.1	..	–16.0	..	1.6
Slovenia	123.6	29.3	93.1	7.1	86.1	35.1	96.3	29.4	–10.5	4.7	5.2	3.1
South Africa	11.4	16.0	0.4	1.1	15.5	14.9	13.7	18.9	1.8	–4.0	1.9	1.9
Spain	13.6	6.6	–1.0	3.6	15.2	10.2	8.4	7.1	5.3	3.3	1.4	1.3
Sri Lanka	21.1	19.4	6.5	–1.7	27.8	23.9	16.2	18.2	6.8	3.2	3.8	3.1
Sudan	48.8	51.2	–10.7	–238.0	42.1	38.4	12.6	16.3	29.4	22.2	4.1	5.0
Sweden	..	..	..	..	..	..	..	..	..	..	..	..
Switzerland	0.8	4.6	–3.2	1.4	12.7	4.1	11.7	4.0	1.0	0.2	0.9	0.8
Syrian Arab Republic	26.1	20.9	12.9	3.0	14.8	20.7	3.4	2.7	11.4	17.1	2.0	1.6
Tajikistan	..	..	..	..	..	..	..	..	..	..	..	..
Tanzania	41.9	35.4	–22.6	12.5	103.2	12.4	22.6	–3.9	80.6	16.3	4.8	3.3
Thailand	26.7	17.0	4.9	–5.1	26.8	27.0	30.0	27.8	–4.0	–2.9	1.6	1.4
Togo	9.5	22.4	1.3	–6.0	7.9	31.7	2.4	17.6	6.3	15.1	2.9	3.9
Trinidad and Tobago	6.2	4.0	2.9	–3.2	0.9	15.7	2.7	9.0	–1.9	6.7	2.3	2.5
Tunisia	7.6	6.6	–1.6	–0.6	7.7	9.2	5.9	10.4	1.8	–1.2	2.0	2.3
Turkey	53.2	103.6	1.4	17.3	53.3	87.0	42.9	63.6	9.7	22.4	5.1	4.0
Turkmenistan	..	..	..	..	..	..	..	..	..	..	..	..
Uganda	60.2	15.0	..	21.3	..	–37.1	..	8.2	..	–45.2	16.2	9.9
Ukraine	..	115.0	..	–15.1	..	172.6	..	7.7	..	164.8	..	..
United Arab Emirates	–8.2	10.2	–1.9	8.7	–2.2	6.3	1.3	10.7	–4.8	–4.3	2.0	1.9
United Kingdom	..	..	..	..	..	..	..	..	..	..	..	..
United States	4.9	5.7	–0.5	0.4	1.8	9.3	1.1	9.3	0.7	0.0	1.5	1.7
Uruguay	115.8	42.3	95.2	20.6	103.0	44.4	58.5	36.4	28.0	4.2	2.2	2.9
Uzbekistan	..	..	..	..	..	..	..	..	..	..	..	..
Venezuela	69.0	36.7	36.1	21.0	57.6	70.0	16.2	14.9	40.7	34.1	3.8	4.3
Vietnam	..	..	..	..	..	..	..	..	..	..	..	..
West Bank and Gaza	..	..	..	..	..	..	..	..	..	..	..	..
Yemen, Rep.	11.3	50.7	2.6	25.5	11.6	22.7	1.4	6.0	10.2	16.7	1.5	2.1
Yugoslavia, Fed. Rep.	..	..	..	..	..	..	..	..	..	..	..	..
Zaire	195.4	6,968.9	–218.4	..	449.0	2,832.1	18.0	885.3	429.7	1,934.2	..	..
Zambia	47.1	55.7	–151.5	–86.7	217.3	251.7	31.5	32.7	185.8	219.0	5.5	7.9
Zimbabwe	15.1	25.5	–4.7	–3.7	18.5	19.1	13.5	20.5	5.0	–1.4	3.6	3.9

a. Data prior to 1992 include Eritrea. b. Data prior to 1990 refer to the Federal Republic of Germany before unification.

About the data

Money and the financial accounts that record the supply of money lie at the heart of a country's financial system. There are several commonly used definitions of the money supply. The narrowest, often called M1, encompasses currency held by the public and demand deposits with banks. M2 includes M1 plus time and savings deposits with banks that require a notice for withdrawal. A broader definition is M3, which includes M2 plus assorted money market instruments, such as certificates of deposit issued by banks, bank deposits denominated in foreign currency, and deposits with financial institutions other than banks. However defined, money is a liability of the banking system, distinguished from other bank liabilities by the special role it plays as a medium of exchange, a unit of account, and a store of value.

A change in money occurs when any other liability or asset in banks' balance sheets changes, because the assets and liabilities must always balance. Net foreign assets comprise the international reserves of the central bank held in short-term foreign assets, such as claims on other central and commercial banks, treasury bills and other short-term bonds of foreign governments or international institutions, holdings of gold, and special drawing rights, adjusted for all short-term foreign exchange liabilities of the banking system. The change in money supply resulting from a change in net foreign assets depends on a country's trade position, capital inflows and outflows, and trade financing and is therefore not entirely within the control of the monetary authorities.

Net domestic credit consists of bank credit to the nonfinancial public sector—investments in short- and long-term government securities and loans to state enterprises—and credit to the private sector, netting out public and private sector deposits with the banking system. Net domestic credit is the main vehicle through which the authorities regulate changes in the money supply, with central bank lending to the government often playing the most important role. The central bank can regulate lending to the private sector in three ways: by adjusting the cost of its refinancing facilities provided to banks, by changing market interest rates through open market operations, or by controlling the availability of credit through changes in the reserve requirements imposed on banks and ceilings on the credit provided by banks to the private sector.

The income velocity of money is defined as the number of times a given quantity of money is used to mediate transactions. At the World Bank it is usually measured by the ratio of nominal GDP, a proxy for transactions, to the quantity of money. The velocity of money tends to decline secularly with the development of the economy, because money, particularly deposit money, tends to increase as monetization accelerates and banking facilities expand. But the velocity of money fluctuates widely in the short term, depending on the macroeconomic situation. In an inflationary environment there is often a flight from money into goods, which increases the velocity of money.

Monetary accounts are derived from the balance sheets of financial institutions—the central bank, commercial banks, and nonbank financial intermediaries. Although these balance sheets are usually reliable, they are subject to errors of classification and valuation and differences in accounting practices. For example, whether interest income is recorded on an accrual or a cash basis can make a substantial difference, as can the treatment of nonperforming assets. Errors of valuation typically arise with respect to foreign exchange transactions, particularly in countries with flexible exchange rates or in those that have undergone a currency devaluation during the reporting period. Banks may use different exchange rates to convert accounts denominated in foreign currency into local currency values. They are also likely to use the prevailing exchange rate on the day of the transaction in converting foreign exchange into local currency or vice versa. Such practices may result in differences between the value in foreign currency converted at an average exchange rate for the year or for each quarter and that based on reporting by commercial banks in local currency. Similar problems may arise in valuing gold or in renegotiating foreign exchange liabilities (as in a debt rescheduling agreement).

The quality of commercial bank reporting also may be adversely affected by delays in reports from bank branches, especially in countries where branch accounts have not been computerized. Thus the data in the balance sheets of commercial banks may be based on preliminary estimates subject to constant revision. This problem is likely to be even more acute for nonbank financial intermediaries.

Definitions

● **Money and quasi money** comprise the sum of currency outside banks, demand deposits other than those of the central government, and the time, savings, and foreign currency deposits of resident sectors other than the central government. This definition of the money supply is frequently called M2 (IFS lines 34 and 35). The change in money supply is measured as the difference in end-of-year totals relative to the level of M2 in the preceding year. ● **Net foreign assets** (IFS line 31n) are the sum of foreign assets held by monetary authorities and deposit money banks, less their foreign liabilities. ● **Domestic credit** (IFS line 32) is the sum of net credit to the nonfinancial public sector, credit to the private sector, and other accounts. ● **Claims on the private sector** (IFS line 32d) include gross credit from the financial system to individuals, enterprises, nonfinancial public entities not included under net domestic credit, and financial institutions not included elsewhere. ● **Claims on governments and other public entities** (IFS lines 32an + 32b + 32bx + 32c) usually comprise direct credit for specific purposes such as financing of the government budget deficit or loans to state enterprises, advances against future credit authorizations, and purchases of treasury bills and bonds. Public sector deposits with the banking system also include sinking funds for the service of debt and temporary deposits of government revenues. ● **Income velocity of money and quasi money** is the ratio of GDP at purchasers' prices to the money supply measured as M2.

Data sources

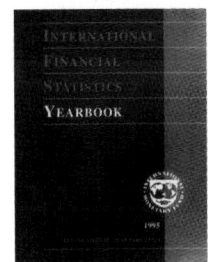

The International Monetary Fund (IMF) collects data on the financial systems of its member countries. The data in the table are published in the monthly *International Financial Statistics* and the annual *International Financial Statistics Yearbook*. The World Bank receives data from the IMF in electronic files that may contain more recent revisions than the published sources. GDP is from the World Bank's national accounts files. The discussion of monetary indicators draws heavily from the IMF publication by Marcello Caiola, *A Manual for Country Economists* (1995).

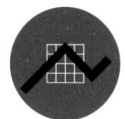

4.20 | Inflation

	GDP implicit deflator		Wholesale prices		Consumer prices		Food prices	
	average annual % growth		average annual % growth		average annual % growth		average annual % growth	
	1980–90	1990–95	1980–90	1990–95	1980–90	1990–95	1980–90	1990–95
Albania	–1.9	76.4	–0.8	..	..	64.2	..	82.7
Algeria	8.0	25.8	..	..	9.1	27.1	6.8	28.6
Angola	5.9	774.5	..	..	..	..	..	847.9
Argentina	389.0	20.5	454.7	14.5	486.6	26.3	206.9	25.8
Armenia	0.3	896.6	..	..	..	..	..	..
Australia	7.3	1.3	7.0	1.8	7.9	2.2	7.4	1.9
Austria	3.7	3.5	0.7	0.3	3.2	3.3	2.6	2.6
Azerbaijan	..	747.6	..	..	..	1,005.5	1.5	585.5
Bangladesh	9.5	4.6	..	..	10.5	3.7	10.4	3.8
Belarus	..	878.8	..	..	..	1,247.2	2.4	971.1
Belgium	4.4	3.1	2.0	–0.7	4.3	2.5	4.0	0.5
Benin	1.6	7.9	..	..	..	18.9	..	..
Bolivia	316.7	10.5	343.5	..	322.6	11.2	322.0	11.8
Bosnia and Herzegovina	..	..	..	..	..	..	..	..
Botswana	13.1	9.2	..	..	10.0	12.9	10.7	13.2
Brazil	284.5	965.3	317.0	956.1	314.9	1,044.8	238.2	1,235.4
Bulgaria	1.2	81.2	..	..	..	..	..	121.5
Burkina Faso	3.1	6.2	..	..	3.4	6.3	–0.5	3.3
Burundi	4.4	8.5	..	..	7.1	10.8	6.1	6.7
Cambodia	..	56.2	..	..	..	..	..	..
Cameroon	5.9	5.1	..	..	8.7	8.2	3.9	..
Canada	4.4	1.5	3.3	3.2	5.3	1.9	4.6	1.4
Central African Republic	5.6	8.5	5.4	–0.7	3.2	6.4	2.0	2.1
Chad	1.1	8.9	..	..	0.6	7.3	..	5.3
Chile	20.9	14.7	22.3	10.7	20.6	13.6	20.8	13.8
China	5.8	12.4	..	..	..	13.4	8.8	..
Colombia	24.6	23.3	24.1	18.6	22.7	24.8	24.5	22.3
Congo	0.3	7.8	6.9	0.5	6.1	4.2	4.1	9.4
Costa Rica	23.5	19.1	21.0	17.3	23.0	17.8	23.0	15.7
Côte d'Ivoire	3.4	10.4	..	..	5.4	9.3	6.0	..
Croatia	..	..	..	279.4	..	328.0	246.3	324.5
Cuba	..	..	..	..	..	..	..	..
Czech Republic	1.5	18.3	..	..	..	..	..	11.9
Denmark	5.5	1.8	3.3	0.3	5.5	1.9	4.8	1.4
Dominican Republic	21.5	11.7	..	..	23.6	12.7	22.5	..
Ecuador	36.4	37.2	32.3	40.7	35.8	40.0	43.0	38.1
Egypt, Arab Rep.	11.7	13.3	15.8	12.8	17.4	13.1	19.0	9.9
El Salvador	16.4	11.2	10.9	6.7	19.6	13.3	21.4	16.5
Eritrea	..	..	..	..	..	..	..	..
Estonia	2.4	151.4	..	..	..	52.8	..	154.9
Ethiopia[a]	3.4	..	..	..	4.0	..	3.7	..
Finland	6.8	1.8	3.4	1.6	6.2	2.0	5.8	–0.5
France	6.0	2.1	10.5	..	5.8	2.3	5.7	1.0
Gabon	1.9	13.0	7.0	..	5.1	5.8	2.8	0.3
Gambia, The	18.7	5.0	..	..	20.0	6.4	20.4	6.3
Georgia	1.9	2,280.2	..	..	..	..	..	..
Germany[b]	..	..	1.5	1.0	2.2	3.3	..	2.6
Ghana	42.4	23.8	55.7	..	39.1	24.6	33.1	23.8
Greece	18.3	13.1	16.3	11.0	18.7	14.0	18.0	13.5
Guatemala	14.6	14.2	9.5	..	14.0	13.5	14.6	16.6
Guinea	..	10.1	..	..	..	..	..	17.0
Guinea-Bissau	56.1	49.5	..	..	..	45.1	..	..
Haiti	7.5	22.4	..	..	5.2	25.5	4.1	19.2
Honduras	5.7	19.2	..	..	6.3	18.4	5.1	19.1
Hong Kong	7.7	8.1	..	..	7.2	9.3	6.8	8.0

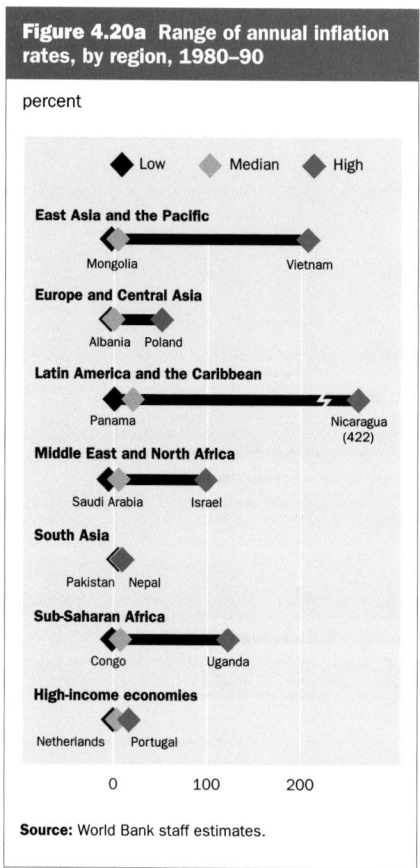

Figure 4.20a Range of annual inflation rates, by region, 1980–90

percent

◆ Low   ◆ Median   ◆ High

East Asia and the Pacific
Mongolia — Vietnam

Europe and Central Asia
Albania Poland

Latin America and the Caribbean
Panama — Nicaragua (422)

Middle East and North Africa
Saudi Arabia   Israel

South Asia
Pakistan Nepal

Sub-Saharan Africa
Congo — Uganda

High-income economies
Netherlands Portugal

0   100   200

Source: World Bank staff estimates.

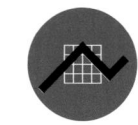

	GDP implicit deflator		Wholesale prices		Consumer prices		Food prices	
	average annual % growth		average annual % growth		average annual % growth		average annual % growth	
	1980–90	1990–95	1980–90	1990–95	1980–90	1990–95	1980–90	1990–95
Hungary	8.6	22.3	5.9	6.0	9.6	24.2	9.5	24.8
India	8.0	10.1	6.7	10.3	8.6	10.0	8.4	11.1
Indonesia	8.5	7.6	9.4	5.8	8.3	8.8	8.6	9.2
Iran, Islamic Rep.	14.6	32.3	16.8	34.6	18.1	27.7	16.3	31.8
Iraq	10.3	..	..	..	..	..	14.3	..
Ireland	6.6	2.2	4.2	2.1	6.8	2.4	10.5	1.6
Israel	101.5	12.2	99.8	10.0	101.7	12.5	102.4	9.8
Italy	9.9	4.7	6.8	..	9.1	4.9	8.2	4.1
Jamaica	18.6	38.5	..	..	15.1	39.9	16.2	40.9
Japan	1.7	0.9	–1.8	–1.9	1.7	1.3	1.6	1.1
Jordan	7.0	4.7	5.7	1.8	5.7	4.5	4.7	3.9
Kazakstan	..	805.5	..	..	..	..	..	..
Kenya	9.0	18.5	..	..	11.1	27.3	..	28.7
Korea, Dem. Rep.	..	..	..	..	..	..	..	..
Korea, Rep.	5.9	6.2	1.9	2.9	4.9	6.1	5.0	6.7
Kuwait	–2.4	–2.0	2.2	4.1	2.9	2.3	1.6	..
Kyrgyz Republic	..	337.3	..	..	..	..	..	262.3
Lao PDR	37.8	10.1	..	..	..	10.0	..	..
Latvia	..	149.1	..	..	..	83.1	..	86.1
Lebanon	..	..	..	..	75.5	36.8	..	..
Lesotho	13.6	11.0	..	..	13.6	13.0	13.2	14.9
Libya	..	..	..	..	..	..	..	..
Lithuania	..	241.4	..	102.0	..	124.1	..	219.3
Macedonia, FYR	..	..	..	..	..	397.9	242.1	277.5
Madagascar	16.9	23.5	..	..	16.7	22.0	15.7	22.6
Malawi	15.0	30.4	..	..	16.9	21.9	16.3	35.3
Malaysia	1.7	3.9	1.7	2.6	2.6	4.3	1.3	5.2
Mali	5.3	10.1	..	..	..	2.5	..	1.8
Mauritania	8.6	6.8	..	..	7.1	8.4	..	..
Mauritius	9.4	6.7	..	..	6.9	7.3	7.4	7.7
Mexico	70.4	15.5	73.2	14.9	73.8	15.5	73.1	13.4
Moldova	..	..	..	..	..	..	..	..
Mongolia	–1.2	126.7	..	..	..	..	..	..
Morocco	7.2	3.9	7.7	4.3	7.0	5.8	6.7	8.8
Mozambique	38.4	48.6	..	..	..	47.8	24.4	..
Myanmar	12.2	24.4	..	..	11.5	26.9	11.9	28.6
Namibia	13.6	9.3	..	..	12.6	11.7	14.9	11.3
Nepal	11.1	11.0	..	..	10.2	11.0	10.0	12.2
Netherlands	1.6	2.2	1.6	1.1	2.0	2.7	1.2	1.9
New Zealand	10.8	0.6	8.7	1.7	10.9	1.9	9.9	0.6
Nicaragua	422.6	98.3	..	..	..	85.2	..	..
Niger	2.9	6.5	..	..	0.7	6.1	–1.5	..
Nigeria	16.6	47.1	..	..	21.5	49.1	21.6	42.1
Norway	5.5	1.3	5.5	0.9	7.4	2.3	7.8	0.8
Oman	–3.6	–2.9	..	..	..	..	..	..
Pakistan	6.7	11.2	7.3	11.8	6.3	11.0	6.6	11.1
Panama	2.4	1.8	–1.8	1.3	1.4	1.2	1.9	1.6
Papua New Guinea	5.3	5.7	..	..	5.6	4.6	4.6	3.6
Paraguay	24.4	18.0	24.3	..	21.9	18.2	24.9	18.6
Peru	229.6	62.4	221.6	57.7	283.6	69.0	..	85.1
Philippines	14.9	9.2	16.7	4.9	14.4	9.8	14.1	8.5
Poland	53.7	34.9	50.1	32.2	51.0	41.5	52.4	35.2
Portugal	18.1	8.7	21.3	..	17.1	7.2	16.9	5.3
Puerto Rico	3.4	2.3	..	..	..	..	2.8	6.6
Romania	2.5	158.4	..	184.6	..	151.5	1.8	169.4
Russian Federation	3.2	517.0	..	424.4	..	381.6	..	787.4

Figure 4.20b Range of annual inflation rates, by region, 1990–95

percent

◆ Low   ◆ Median   ◆ High

East Asia and the Pacific

Singapore   Mongolia

Europe and Central Asia

Greece   Georgia (2,300)

Latin America and the Caribbean

Panama   Brazil (1,000)

Middle East and North Africa

Oman Iran, Islamic Rep.

South Asia

Bangladesh Pakistan

Sub-Saharan Africa

The Gambia   Angola (800)

High-income economies

New Zealand Portugal

0   100   200

Source: World Bank staff estimates.

	GDP implicit deflator		Wholesale prices		Consumer prices		Food prices	
	average annual % growth		average annual % growth		average annual % growth		average annual % growth	
	1980–90	1990–95	1980–90	1990–95	1980–90	1990–95	1980–90	1990–95
Rwanda	3.9	18.2	..	..	3.9	13.2	6.1	..
Saudi Arabia	–3.7	1.0	6.0	2.4	–0.8	1.7	–0.4	2.0
Senegal	6.5	7.6	..	..	6.2	7.3	5.3	5.3
Sierra Leone	62.2	39.6	35.5	..	72.4	41.9	71.0	..
Singapore	2.0	3.7	–2.2	–2.8	1.6	2.5	0.9	2.0
Slovak Republic	1.8	16.0	..	..	..	..	1.6	20.8
Slovenia	..	..	..	60.4	..	62.1	252.3	63.3
South Africa	14.8	11.5	13.9	8.6	14.7	11.1	15.1	14.5
Spain	9.3	5.2	6.8	3.0	9.0	5.2	9.3	3.6
Sri Lanka	10.8	10.4	9.2	7.7	10.9	10.4	10.9	10.3
Sudan	37.1	86.2	..	..	37.6	114.3	38.0	..
Sweden	7.4	3.2	5.8	3.8	7.0	4.0	8.2	0.1
Switzerland	3.7	2.3	1.1	..	2.9	3.1	3.1	1.0
Syrian Arab Republic	15.3	8.5	22.2	8.9	23.2	12.1	24.5	7.1
Tajikistan	..	399.1	..	..	..	..	..	..
Tanzania	35.7	22.4	..	..	31.0	27.2	30.2	25.9
Thailand	3.9	4.6	2.4	3.0	3.5	4.6	2.7	5.4
Togo	4.7	5.7	..	..	2.5	0.5	1.2	..
Trinidad and Tobago	4.1	7.2	7.3	1.9	10.7	7.4	14.6	10.8
Tunisia	7.4	5.4	9.3	2.1	7.4	5.5	8.3	5.2
Turkey	45.3	75.6	43.5	75.6	44.9	79.3	..	80.3
Turkmenistan	..	1,167.0	..	..	..	..	..	..
Uganda	125.6	23.7	..	..	102.4	19.7	..	17.2
Ukraine	..	1,040.5	..	1,381.9	..	1,180.4	2.0	..
United Arab Emirates	0.7	..	..	..	..	..	..	..
United Kingdom	5.7	3.6	5.2	3.7	5.8	3.1	4.6	2.5
United States	4.1	2.4	1.9	1.3	4.1	3.1	3.8	3.5
Uruguay	61.3	55.6	63.2	58.2	61.1	59.3	62.0	53.7
Uzbekistan	..	628.4	..	..	..	..	..	..
Venezuela	19.3	38.4	23.9	42.1	20.9	43.8	29.7	38.0
Vietnam	210.7	26.3	..	..	..	..	..	..
West Bank and Gaza	..	..	..	..	..	..	..	..
Yemen, Rep.	..	..	..	..	..	..	2.6	..
Yugoslavia, Fed. Rep.	..	..	..	..	..	..	..	..
Zaire	58.6	..	..	..	57.1	3558.3	..	..
Zambia	42.4	107.8	48.2	..	42.7	112.5	42.8	166.4
Zimbabwe	11.5	27.6	..	38.2	13.8	28.2	14.6	35.2

World	**15.0 w**	**56.6 w**
Low income	13.4 w	62.0 w
Excl. China & India	28.4 w	170.8 w
Middle income	64.8 w	298.8 w
Lower middle income	17.5 w	286.7 w
Upper middle income	138.0 w	320.5 w
Low & middle income	50.6 w	235.8 w
East Asia & Pacific	10.1 w	11.5 w
Europe & Central Asia	12.2 w	461.5 w
Latin America & Carib.	179.4 w	380.9 w
Middle East & N. Africa	8.2 w	19.4 w
South Asia	8.0 w	9.9 w
Sub-Saharan Africa	19.0 w	47.4 w
High income	4.8 w	2.4 w

a. Includes Eritrea. b. Data prior to 1990 refer to the Federal Republic of Germany before unification.

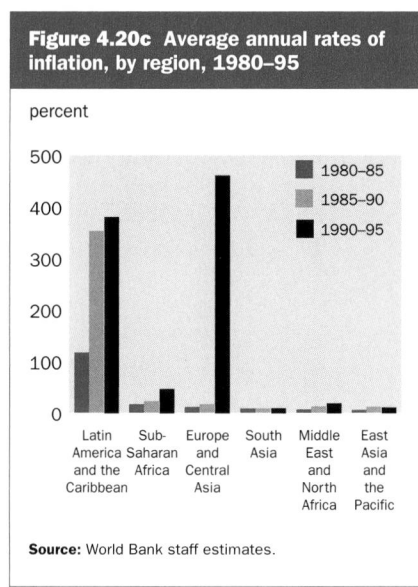

Figure 4.20c Average annual rates of inflation, by region, 1980–95

percent

Legend: 1980–85, 1985–90, 1990–95

Regions: Latin America and the Caribbean; Sub-Saharan Africa; Europe and Central Asia; South Asia; Middle East and North Africa; East Asia and the Pacific

Source: World Bank staff estimates.

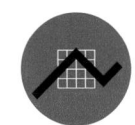

About the data

Inflation is measured by the rate of change in a price index. Which index to use depends on which set of prices in the economy is being examined. The most general measure of the overall price level is the GDP deflator. This measure takes into account changes in government costs, inventory appreciation, and investment expenditures. The GDP deflator is usually derived implicitly as the ratio of current to constant price GDP. It may also be calculated explicitly as a Laspeyres price index in which the weights are base period quantities of output.

Consumer price indexes are constructed explicitly, based on surveys of the cost of a defined consumer market basket. Index numbers of consumer prices should be interpreted with caution. The definition of a household and the geographic (urban or rural) and income group coverage of consumer price surveys can vary widely across countries. Furthermore, the weights are derived from household expenditure surveys, which for budgetary reasons tend to be conducted infrequently in developing countries, leading to poor comparability over time. Consumer price indexes should be distinguished from retail price indexes, which are used in a few countries. Retail price indexes are based on prices at retail outlets weighted by sales turnover, so the weights may differ from country to country and over time. In addition, the basket of goods chosen varies from country to country. Although a useful indicator for measuring consumer price inflation within a country, the consumer price index is of limited value for comparisons across countries. The wholesale and food price indexes should be interpreted with similar caution.

Traditionally, index numbers of wholesale prices have been based on the prices of commodities that have some significance in the output or consumption of the country. Many wholesale price indexes now refer to a mix of agricultural and industrial goods at various stages of production and distribution, including imports and import duties. In general, a Laspeyres index is used.

Recently, some countries have compiled more specialized price indexes. Core inflation, for example, is measured by price changes for goods that affect the whole structure of prices. Such commodities as gasoline, electricity, food staples, and transport fares form the core elements of the basket. And many countries maintain price indexes for baskets of goods typically consumed by specific groups, such as the old, or industrial workers. In some economies these indexes are used in making cost-of-living adjustments to social welfare benefits or in indexing wages.

Definitions

- **GDP implicit deflator** measures the average annual rate of price change in the economy as a whole for the periods shown. The least-squares method is used to calculate the growth rate of the GDP deflator. The regional and income group averages for the GDP implicit deflator are calculated by weighting the ratios by the 1987 GDP in U.S. dollars. • **Wholesale price** indexes refer to a mix of agricultural and industrial goods at various stages of production and distribution, including imports and import duties. The Laspeyres formula is generally used. • **Consumer price** indexes reflect changes in the cost to the average consumer of acquiring a fixed basket of goods and services. The Laspeyres formula is generally used. • **Food price** indexes are a subindex of the consumer price index.

Data sources

The primary sources of data on price levels are national statistical agencies and central banks. The GDP deflator is calculated from the World Bank's national accounts files. Consumer and wholesale price indexes are published in the International Monetary Fund's *International Financial Statistics*. Food price indexes are published by the United Nations in the *Statistical Yearbook* and *Monthly Bulletin of Statistics*.

4.21 | Balance of payments current account

	Goods and services				Net income		Net current transfers				Current account balance	
	Exports $ millions		Imports $ millions		$ millions		Total $ millions		Net workers' remittances $ millions		$ millions	
	1980	1995	1980	1995	1980	1995	1980	1995	1980	1995	1980	1995
Albania	378	304	371	836	4	44	6	477	0	385	16	−12
Algeria	14,128	10,822	12,311	10,900	−1,869	−2,400	301	168	241	..	249	−2,310
Angola	..	3,644	..	3,672	..	−936	..	166	..	−83	..	−769
Argentina	9,897	23,853	13,182	23,774	−1,512	−2,901	23	432	0	0	−4,774	−2,390
Armenia	..	300	..	726	..	−13	..	160	..	12	..	−279
Australia	25,752	68,688	27,053	74,757	−2,733	−13,049	−416	−67	..	..	−4,450	−19,184
Austria	26,650	95,615	29,921	98,590	−528	−636	−66	−1,503	−67	28	−3,865	−5,113
Azerbaijan	..	784	..	1,267	..	−6	..	110	..	..	..	−379
Bangladesh	885	4,130	2,545	6,544	14	−41	802	1,426	197[a]	1,198[a]	−844	−1,029
Belarus	..	2,773	..	3,163	..	−47	..	182	..	..	..	−254
Belgium[b]	70,498	196,592	74,259	184,644	61	6,253	−1,231	−3,241	−270	−393	−4,931	14,960
Benin	226	489	421	708	8	−41	151	149	75	65	−36	36
Bolivia	1,030	1,272	833	1,569	−263	−199	60	225	0	−1	−6	−218
Bosnia and Herzegovina	..	..	..	..	..	..	..	..	..	..	..	..
Botswana	645	2,425	818	2,023	−33	−32	55	−27	−17	−157	−151	342
Brazil	21,869	52,641	27,826	63,293	−7,018	−11,105	144	3,621	−80	2,773	−12,831	−18,136
Bulgaria	9,302	6,530	7,994	5,873	−412	−455	58	132	0	0	954	334
Burkina Faso	210	345	577	604	−3	−29	322	255	100	29	−49	15
Burundi	..	129	..	277	..	−9	..	151	..	0	..	−6
Cambodia	..	969	..	1,375	..	−57	..	277	..	10	..	−186
Cameroon	1,792	2,058	1,829	1,570	−628	−668	−17	9	11[a]	39[a]	−682	−171
Canada	74,869	211,625	70,044	197,654	−6,689	−22,294	173	−370	..	..	−1,691	−8,693
Central African Republic	201	234	327	292	3	−23	81	63	−19	−27	−43	−25
Chad	71	267	79	525	−4	−7	20	191	−4	−15	9	−38
Chile	5,968	19,191	7,052	17,961	−1,000	−1,430	113	357	0	0	−1,971	157
China[†]	23,637	147,240	18,900	135,282	451	−11,774	486	1,435	538	350	5,674	1,618
Colombia	5,328	13,813	5,454	16,270	−245	−2,337	165	679	68	172	−206	−4,116
Congo	1,021	1,249	1,025	1,425	−162	−396	−1	3	−38	−27	−167	−570
Costa Rica	1,195	3,790	1,661	3,901	−212	−186	15	154	0	0	−664	−143
Côte d'Ivoire	3,577	4,490	4,145	3,562	−553	−903	−706	−294	−716	−449	−1,826	−269
Croatia	..	7,202	..	9,466	..	−93	..	646	..	..	..	−1,712
Cuba	..	..	..	..	..	..	..	..	..	..	..	..
Czech Republic	..	28,202	..	30,044	..	−104	..	572	..	0	..	−1,374
Denmark	21,989	64,230	21,727	57,139	−1,977	−4,716	−161	−961	0	0	−1,875	1,413
Dominican Republic	1,271	2,915	1,919	3,222	−277	−347	205	529	183	795	−720	−125
Ecuador	2,887	5,216	2,946	5,078	−613	−1,191	30	231	0	0	−642	−822
Egypt, Arab Rep.	6,246	10,083	9,157	15,275	−318	−824	2,791	5,060	2,696	5,060[a]	−438	−956
El Salvador	1,214	2,049	1,170	3,421	−62	−87	52	1,389	11	1,061	34	−70
Eritrea	..	171	..	448	..	8	..	288	..	..	..	19
Estonia	..	2,738	..	3,051	..	2	..	126	..	−1	..	−184
Ethiopia[c]	569	804	782	1,316	7	−60	80	532	22[a]	312[a]	−126	−93
Finland	16,802	47,924	17,307	37,377	−783	−4,561	−114	−343	0	..	−1,403	5,642
France	153,197	368,171	155,915	337,755	2,680	−7,446	−4,169	−6,526	−2,591	−1,364	−4,208	16,443
Gabon	2,409	2,789	1,475	1,686	−426	−724	−124	0	−143	−152	384	378
Gambia, The	66	177	179	232	−2	−5	28	52	0	0	−87	−8
Georgia	..	452	..	..	..	..	..	..	..	..	..	..
Germany[d]	224,220	609,239	225,481	589,619	914	370	−12,858	−40,967	−4,437	−5,305	−13,205	−20,976
Ghana	1,210	1,563	1,178	2,098	−83	−143	81	264	−4	12	30	−414
Greece	8,122	15,523	11,145	24,711	−273	−1,684	1,087	8,008	1,066	2,982	−2,209	−2,864
Guatemala	1,731	2,821	1,960	3,728	−44	−159	110	493	0	350	−163	−572
Guinea	..	701	..	993	..	−85	..	179	..	−10	..	−197
Guinea-Bissau	17	24	75	80	−8	−15	−14	30	−14	−1	−80	−41
Haiti	306	205	481	754	−14	−24	89	505	52	0	−101	−67
Honduras	942	1,635	1,128	1,852	−152	−226	22	243	0	120	−317	−201
Hong Kong	23,417	..	25,096	..	421	..	0	..	..	..	−1,258	..
†Data for Taiwan, China	21,495	126,126	22,361	121,082	48	2,814	−95	−2,202	..	..	−913	5,656

	Goods and services				Net income		Net current transfers				Current account balance	
	Exports $ millions		Imports $ millions		$ millions		Total $ millions		Net workers' remittances $ millions		$ millions	
	1980	1995	1980	1995	1980	1995	1980	1995	1980	1995	1980	1995
Hungary	9,671	17,135	9,152	18,926	–1,113	–1,804	63	1,060	0	–14	–531	–2,535
India	11,265	39,682	17,378	48,536	331	–4,455	2,860	7,478	2,786 [a]	6,000 [a]	–2,922	–5,830
Indonesia	23,797	51,160	21,540	53,244	–3,073	–5,778	250	839	0	629	–566	–7,023
Iran, Islamic Rep.	13,069	20,613	16,111	17,263	606	–271	–2	1,198	0	0	–2,438	4,777
Iraq	..	..	..	..	..	..	..	..	..	..	..	..
Ireland	9,610	48,121	12,044	40,710	–902	–7,814	1,204	1,782	0	..	–2,132	1,379
Israel	8,668	26,735	11,511	35,998	–757	–1,827	2,729	5,600	0	0	–871	–5,491
Italy	97,298	296,379	110,265	250,586	1,278	–15,461	1,101	–4,626	1,609	98	–10,587	25,706
Jamaica	1,363	3,180	1,408	3,640	–212	–320	121	535	51	414	–136	–245
Japan	146,980	494,529	156,970	419,942	770	44,406	–1,530	–7,747	0	..	–10,750	111,246
Jordan	1,573	3,490	3,226	4,905	117	–179	594	1,118	715 [a]	1,244 [a]	–942	–476
Kazakstan	..	5,261	..	5,692	..	–147	..	59	..	..	..	–519
Kenya	2,007	2,949	2,846	3,524	–194	–325	156	499	0	–4	–878	–400
Korea, Dem. Rep.	..	..	..	..	..	..	..	..	..	..	..	..
Korea, Rep.	21,924	149,446	25,687	155,834	–2,102	–2,276	592	413	96	486	–5,273	–8,251
Kuwait	21,857	14,123	9,823	12,089	4,847	4,011	–1,580	–1,846	–692	–1,347	15,302	4,198
Kyrgyz Republic	..	409	..	672	..	–68	..	43	..	..	..	–288
Lao PDR	..	445	..	666	..	0	..	–3	..	0	..	–224
Latvia	..	2,080	..	2,193	..	19	..	68	..	..	..	–27
Lebanon	..	1,065	..	6,880	..	374	..	350	..	..	..	–5,092
Lesotho	90	218	475	977	266	330	175	471	0	0	56	108
Libya	22,084	..	12,671	..	–65	..	–1,134	..	–1,052	..	8,214	..
Lithuania	..	3,191	..	3,902	..	–13	..	109	..	1	..	–614
Macedonia, FYR	..	1,486	..	2,070	..	–93	..	..	..	..	..	..
Madagascar	516	749	1,075	987	–44	–167	47	129	–30	–2	–556	–276
Malawi	313	415	487	851	–149	–82	63	124	0	0	–260	–450
Malaysia	14,098	81,692	13,526	86,248	–836	–3,673	–2	163	0	0	–266	–4,147
Mali	263	528	520	913	–17	–49	144	231	40	69	–130	–164
Mauritania	253	531	449	588	–27	–46	90	76	–27	–20	–134	–27
Mauritius	574	2,349	690	2,454	–23	–19	22	101	0	0	–117	–22
Mexico	22,622	89,824	27,601	81,861	–6,277	–12,579	834	3,962	687	3,672	–10,422	–654
Moldova	..	844	..	958	..	–20	..	40	..	..	..	–95
Mongolia	475	508	1,272	521	–11	–25	0	77	0	0	–808	39
Morocco	3,233	8,867	5,207	11,331	–562	–1,318	1,130	2,261	989	1,890	–1,407	–1,521
Mozambique	399	411	844	1,121	22	..	56	..	0	..	–367	..
Myanmar	539	1,120	806	1,669	–48	–101	7	312	0	0	–307	–339
Namibia	..	1,666	..	1,934	..	84	..	233	..	4	..	50
Nepal	224	1,068	365	1,556	13	5	36	108	..	101 [a]	–93	–375
Netherlands	90,380	221,680	91,622	200,338	1,535	1,189	–1,148	–6,339	–320	–423	–855	16,191
New Zealand	6,403	17,782	6,934	17,184	–538	–4,454	96	78	143	174	–973	–3,778
Nicaragua	495	648	907	1,070	–124	–359	124	75	0	75	–411	–706
Niger	617	274	956	448	–33	–30	95	67	–47	–41	–277	–126
Nigeria	27,071	11,779	20,014	10,972	–1,304	–1,990	–576	673	–410	2,567	5,178	–510
Norway	27,264	48,027	23,749	40,993	–1,922	–1,769	–515	–1,620	–23	–236	1,079	3,645
Oman	3,757	6,078	2,298	5,014	–257	–332	–260	–1,711	–362	–1,740	942	–979
Pakistan	2,958	8,307	5,709	11,064	–281	–1,729	1,895	2,390	1,748 [a]	1,866 [a]	–1,137	–1,965
Panama	3,422	7,588	3,394	7,603	–399	–90	40	203	–36	–7	–331	–141
Papua New Guinea	1,029	2,980	1,322	1,876	–179	–505	184	75	0	0	–289	674
Paraguay	701	4,071	1,314	5,478	–4	–108	0	42	2	..	–618	–1,473
Peru	4,631	6,810	3,970	9,701	–909	–1,823	147	491	0	334	–101	–4,223
Philippines	7,235	26,795	9,166	33,317	–420	3,662	434	880	202	296	–1,917	–1,980
Poland	16,061	32,080	17,842	33,845	–2,357	–1,995	721	–485	0	35	–3,417	–4,245
Portugal	6,674	32,102	10,136	38,948	–608	–513	3,006	7,131	2,928	3,348	–1,064	–229
Puerto Rico	..	..	..	..	..	..	..	..	..	..	..	..
Romania	12,087	9,013	13,730	10,477	–777	–241	0	363	0	3	–2,420	–1,342
Russian Federation	..	93,900	..	79,500	..	–5,100	..	304	..	..	..	9,604

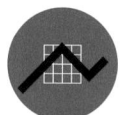

	Goods and services				Net income		Net current transfers				Current account balance	
	Exports $ millions		Imports $ millions		$ millions		Total $ millions		Net workers' remittances $ millions		$ millions	
	1980	1995	1980	1995	1980	1995	1980	1995	1980	1995	1980	1995
Rwanda	165	78	319	329	2	–6	104	188	–14	–7	–48	–129
Saudi Arabia	106,765	50,104	55,793	43,399	526	2,803	–9,995	–17,616	–4,094	–16,616	41,503	–8,108
Senegal	807	1,461	1,215	1,718	–98	–139	120	388	–15	13	–387	3
Sierra Leone	275	136	471	313	–22	–56	52	47	–2	0	–165	–89
Singapore	24,285	148,394	25,312	134,028	–429	1,615	–106	–888	0	0	–1,563	15,093
Slovak Republic	..	10,935	..	10,366	..	–14	..	93	..	0	..	648
Slovenia	..	10,362	..	10,591	..	147	..	45	..	53	..	–37
South Africa	28,627	32,395	22,073	33,103	–3,285	–2,814	239	23	0	0	3,508	–3,500
Spain	32,140	132,653	38,004	132,508	–1,362	–3,967	1,646	5,102	1,647	2,119	–5,580	1,280
Sri Lanka	1,293	4,630	2,197	5,691	–26	–137	272	790	152	715	–657	–546
Sudan	810	609	1,597	1,341	–70	–868	293	143	209[a]	54[a]	–564	–1,457
Sweden	38,151	94,626	39,878	80,416	–1,380	–6,586	–1,224	–2,992	0	106	–4,331	4,633
Switzerland	48,595	123,234	51,843	109,303	4,186	11,797	–1,140	–4,105	–603	–2,519	–201	21,622
Syrian Arab Republic	2,477	5,824	4,531	5,438	11	–863	2,293	917	774	385	251	440
Tajikistan	..	657	..	653	..	–28	..	25	..	..	..	1
Tanzania	748	1,249	1,384	2,095	–14	–137	128	354	0	0	–522	–629
Thailand	7,939	70,292	9,996	82,219	–229	–2,114	210	487	0	0	–2,076	–13,554
Togo	550	513	691	588	–40	–45	86	30	1	5	–95	–57
Trinidad and Tobago	3,139	2,799	2,434	2,110	–306	–390	–42	–4	1	30	357	294
Tunisia	3,262	7,979	3,766	8,811	–259	–716	410	811	304	659	–353	–737
Turkey	3,621	36,581	8,082	40,211	–1,118	–3,205	2,171	4,496	2,071	3,327	–3,408	–2,339
Turkmenistan	..	2,425	..	2,134	..	..	..	..	..	..	..	320
Uganda	329	627	441	1,367	–7	–58	36	370	..	0	–83	–428
Ukraine	..	17,090	..	18,280	..	–434	..	472	..	..	..	–1,152
United Arab Emirates	23,090	..	10,490	..	1,400	..	..	..	..	..	..	..
United Kingdom	146,072	311,783	134,200	320,486	–418	15,072	–4,592	–11,001	0	..	6,862	–4,632
United States	271,800	786,370	290,730	890,240	29,580	–9,170	–8,500	–35,190	–810	–12,230	2,150	–148,230
Uruguay	1,526	3,277	2,144	3,495	–100	–173	9	32	0	0	–709	–358
Uzbekistan	..	3,657	..	3,094	..	–70	..	0	..	..	..	–8
Venezuela	19,968	20,357	15,130	16,467	329	–1,746	–439	111	–418	–173	4,728	2,255
Vietnam	..	7,272	..	9,459	–72	–310	..	477	..	..	–792	–2,021
West Bank and Gaza	..	..	..	..	..	..	..	..	..	..	..	..
Yemen, Rep.	..	2,111	..	2,395	..	–637	..	1,067	..	1,080[a]	..	146
Yugoslavia, Fed. Rep.	..	..	..	..	..	..	..	..	..	..	..	..
Zaire	1,658	..	1,905	..	–496	..	150	..	..	..	–593	..
Zambia	1,609	1,392	1,765	1,409	–205	–175	–155	..	–61	..	–516	..
Zimbabwe	1,610	2,344	1,730	2,515	–61	–294	31	40	8	–2	–149	–425
World	**2,383,840 t**	**6,386,911 t**	**2,380,069 t**	**6,255,176 t**								
Low income	81,433 t	272,246 t	109,903 t	302,361 t								
Excl. China & India	69,239 t	83,941 t	83,934 t	115,725 t								
Middle income	647,208 t	1,120,266 t	638,866 t	1,179,850 t								
Lower middle income	..	..	..	..								
Upper middle income	268,801 t	431,483 t	216,488 t	448,255 t								
Low & middle income	640,062 t	1,394,962 t	679,494 t	1,467,965 t								
East Asia & Pacific	77,284 t	396,141 t	85,128 t	421,691 t								
Europe & Central Asia	..	..	..	..								
Latin America & Carib.	120,648 t	288,664 t	141,492 t	313,772 t								
Middle East & N. Africa	205,720 t	162,572 t	149,924 t	163,556 t								
South Asia	17,450 t	60,542 t	29,271 t	78,069 t								
Sub-Saharan Africa	90,056 t	89,635 t	84,166 t	98,586 t								
High income	1,706,503 t	4,975,163 t	1,740,074 t	4,801,178 t								

a. World Bank estimate referring to receipts only. b. Includes Luxembourg. c. Data prior to 1992 include Eritrea. d. Data prior to 1990 refer to the Federal Republic of Germany before unification.

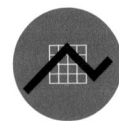

Changes in the current account

In September 1995 the International Monetary Fund (IMF) revised its presentation of balance of payments data in *International Financial Statistics* to conform to the fifth edition of its *Balance of Payments Manual* (1993). The new edition of the manual has been strengthened and, to the extent possible, harmonized with the revised U.N. System of National Accounts and the IMF's forthcoming manual on money and banking and government finance statistics.

The revision introduced several important changes in the current account:

• Some transactions previously included in the current account have been redefined as capital transfers. These include debt forgiveness, migrants' capital transfers, and foreign aid to acquire capital goods. Thus the current account balance now reflects more accurately net current transfer receipts in addition to transactions in goods, services (previously nonfactor services), and income (previously factor income).

• The category of merchandise has been

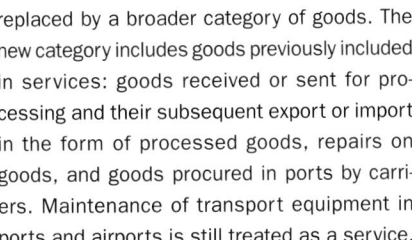

Between 1980 and 1995 East Asia doubled its share of world export trade to 6 percent

replaced by a broader category of goods. The new category includes goods previously included in services: goods received or sent for processing and their subsequent export or import in the form of processed goods, repairs on goods, and goods procured in ports by carriers. Maintenance of transport equipment in ports and airports is still treated as a service.

• Earnings from royalties, license fees, and similar nonfinancial intangible assets have been reclassified from income to services.

• A clear distinction is made between income and services with regard to the compensation of employees. For example, earnings of resident workers in foreign embassies and international agencies are now treated as income rather than services. And current expenditures by nonresident workers are now treated as services rather than income.

• Investment income is recorded on a full accrual basis. It also includes net payments from interest rate derivatives.

• Residence, valuation, time of recording, and reinvested earnings on direct investment are defined in the same manner as in the System of National Accounts.

About the data

The balance of payments is divided into two groups of accounts. The current account refers to goods and services, income, and current transfers. The capital and financial account refers to capital transfers, the acquisition or disposal of nonproduced, nonfinancial assets, and financial assets and liabilities. This table presents data from the current account, and table 4.22 data from the capital and financial account.

The balance of payments is a double-entry accounting system that shows all real flows of goods and services into and out of the country; all transfers that are the counterpart of real resources or financial claims provided to or by the rest of the world without a quid pro quo, such as donations and grants; and all changes in residents' claims on, and liabilities to, nonresidents that arise from economic transactions. All transactions are recorded twice, once as a credit and once as a debit. In principle the net balance should be zero, but in practice the accounts often do not balance. In these cases a balancing item, net errors and omissions, is included to balance the accounts.

Discrepancies may arise in the balance of payments because there is no single source for balance of payments data and therefore no way to ensure that the data are fully consistent. Sources include customs data, the monetary accounts of the banking system, external debt records, information provided by enterprises, surveys to estimate service transactions, and foreign exchange records. Differences in the methods of collecting these data—such as in timing, definitions of residence and ownership, and the exchange rate used to value transactions—all contribute to net errors and omissions. In addition, smuggling and other illegal or quasi-legal transactions may be unrecorded or misrecorded.

The concepts and definitions underlying the data here are based on the fifth edition of the IMF's *Balance of Payments Manual* (1993). However, many countries maintain their data collection systems according to the fourth edition. Where necessary, the IMF converts data reported in earlier systems to conform with the fifth edition. Values are in U.S. dollars converted at market exchange rates.

Definitions

• **Exports and imports of goods and services** comprise all transactions between residents of a country and the rest of the world involving a change of ownership of general merchandise, goods sent for processing and repairs, nonmonetary gold, and services. • **Net income** refers to employee compensation paid to nonresident workers and investment income (receipts and payments on direct investment, portfolio investment, other investments, and receipts on reserve assets). Income derived from the use of intangible assets is excluded from income and recorded under business services. • **Net current transfers** are recorded in the balance of payments whenever an economy provides or receives goods, services, income, or financial items without a quid pro quo. All transfers not considered to be capital are current. • **Net workers' remittances** are current transfers by migrants who are employed or intend to remain employed for more than a year in another economy in which they are considered residents. Some developing countries classify workers' remittances as a factor income receipt (and thus as a component of GNP). The World Bank adheres to international guidelines in defining GNP, and its classification of workers' remittances may therefore differ from national practices. • **Current account balance** is the sum of net exports of goods and services, income, and current transfers.

Data sources

More information about the design and compilation of the balance of payments can be found in the IMF's *Balance of Payments Manual*, fifth edition (1993), *Balance of Payments Textbook* (1996a), and *Balance of Payments Compilation Guide* (1995).

The data come from the IMF's balance of payments database, *Balance of Payments Statistics*, and *International Financial Statistics* (IFS). The World Bank exchanges data with the IMF through electronic files, which in most cases are more up to date and cover a longer period than the published sources. The IFS is also available on CD-ROM.

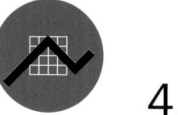

Balance of payments capital
4.22 and financial account

	Net capital account		Net direct and portfolio investment		Other net investment		Net errors and omissions[a]		Reserves and related items		Gross international reserves	
	$ millions		$ millions		$ millions		$ millions		$ millions		$ millions	
	1980	1995	1980	1995	1980	1995	1980	1995	1980	1995	1980	1995
Albania	..	389	..	70	−2	−481	−11	54	−3	−21	..	265
Algeria	..	..	315	..	640	..	136	..	−1,340	..	7,064	4,164
Angola	..	..	..	302	..	−576	..	−277	..	1,320	..	..
Argentina	..	..	942	5,865	1,260	−5,740	−308	55	2,880	2,210	9,297	15,979
Armenia	..	8	..	..	..	141	..	71	..	59	..	..
Australia	179	630	3,305	4,686	1,026	8,430	537	5,808	−598	−369	6,366	14,952
Austria	−22	10	1,713	9,735	71,410	−5,090	−67,896	2,189	−1,340	−1,730	17,725	23,369
Azerbaijan	..	..	..	..	..	..	..	..	..	..	..	84
Bangladesh	..	890	..	67	455	192	65	−632	324	512	331	2,376
Belarus	..	..	..	..	..	..	..	..	..	..	..	377
Belgium[b]	..	..	2,045	−16,975	2,455	6,523	981	−2,349	−550	−219	27,974	24,120
Benin	..	..	4	..	34	−34	−25	54	23	−56	15	202
Bolivia	..	..	43	22	−53	221	−412	−10	429	−15	553	1,005
Bosnia and Herzegovina	..	..	..	..	..	..	..	..	..	..	..	..
Botswana	8	3	109	−1	35	−33	89	−105	−90	−207	344	4,764
Brazil	25	352	1,898	12,710	7,545	16,620	−347	1,454	3,710	−13,000	6,875	51,477
Bulgaria	..	..	..	57	−870	−205	151	178	−235	−363	..	..
Burkina Faso	..	..	−1	..	64	−14	−8	−8	−7	7	75	352
Burundi	..	−1	..	1	..	26	..	16	..	−36	105	216
Cambodia	..	78	..	..	..	−28	..	163	..	−26	..	192
Cameroon	..	..	105	−2	393	−181	262	−131	−78	880	206	15
Canada	156	650	1,976	14,453	−600	−10,110	−1,120	3,232	1,280	467	15,462	16,369
Central African Republic	..	..	5	−4	49	56	−12	−15	1	−13	62	238
Chad	..	..	0	27	−11	50	−21	−33	24	−6	12	147
Chile	..	..	170	1,027	2,998	153	53	−257	−1,250	−1,080	4,128	14,860
China[†]	..	..	407	34,639	−69	4,033	288	−17,790	−6,300	−22,500	10,091	80,288
Colombia	..	..	49	2,217	907	2,803	169	−542	−919	−362	6,474	8,205
Congo	..	..	40	..	135	−80	38	76	−47	575	93	64
Costa Rica	..	..	170	366	74	−86	−70	94	490	−231	197	1,060
Côte d'Ivoire	..	..	98	19	1,140	21	−75	−14	664	242	46	546
Croatia	..	..	..	..	..	412	..	1,388	..	−88	..	2,036
Cuba	..	..	..	..	..	..	..	..	..	..	..	..
Czech Republic	..	7	..	3,901	..	4,330	..	586	..	−7,450	..	14,613
Denmark	..	..	24	7,672	1,420	−7,630	−281	914	713	−2,370	4,347	11,652
Dominican Republic	..	..	93	271	456	98	48	−116	123	−127	279	373
Ecuador	..	..	70	..	889	1,104	−71	−775	−246	493	1,257	1,788
Egypt, Arab Rep.	2	958	541	515	410	−2,366	95	19	−610	1,830	2,480	17,122
El Salvador	−3	..	5	107	20	326	−318	−214	262	−148	382	940
Eritrea	..	..	..	..	..	..	..	..	..	..	..	..
Estonia	..	−1	..	183	..	50	..	35	..	−84	..	583
Ethiopia[c]	..	..	..	1	158	113	−134	−57	102	36	262	815
Finland	−7	22	−76	−1,362	1,590	−2,681	175	−1,993	−280	372	2,451	10,657
France	..	−27	493	−8,200	7,500	−12,300	2,276	4,796	−6,060	−712	75,592	58,510
Gabon	..	..	24	−104	−289	−377	−22	−52	−96	154	115	153
Gambia, The	..	..	..	8	−2	17	53	−16	36	−1	6	106
Georgia	..	..	..	..	..	..	..	..	..	..	..	..
Germany[d]	−917	−654	−8,113	780	13,800	32,400	−1,204	−4,329	9,640	−7,220	104,702	121,816
Ghana	−1	..	16	233	54	278	−113	−154	14	−93	330	804
Greece	..	..	672	1,053	1,801	2,110	−400	−322	136	23	3,607	16,119
Guatemala	..	59	115	−16	−259	438	−18	−61	325	152	753	783
Guinea	..	35	..	..	..	120	..	−39	..	80	..	87
Guinea-Bissau	..	49	..	..	24	−26	32	−26	23	44	..	20
Haiti	..	..	13	..	63	83	−12	205	37	−221	27	106
Honduras	..	17	6	..	232	65	−33	86	113	33	159	270
Hong Kong	..	..	250	..	..	..	..	..	..	..	..	..

†Data for Taiwan, China

| | | | | | | | | | | | 4,055 | 95,559 |

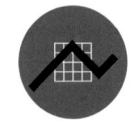

	Net capital account		Net direct and portfolio investment		Other net investment		Net errors and omissions[a]		Reserves and related items		Gross international reserves	
	$ millions		$ millions		$ millions		$ millions		$ millions		$ millions	
	1980	1995	1980	1995	1980	1995	1980	1995	1980	1995	1980	1995
Hungary	..	59	..	6,688	−474	−111	465	1,299	540	−5,400	..	12,095
India	643	..	8	..	483	..	128	..	1,660	..	12,010	22,865
Indonesia	..	..	180	3,745	1,681	2,540	−1,669	2,308	374	−1,570	6,803	14,908
Iran, Islamic Rep.	..	..	..	..	−8,239	−2,226	827	−1,321	9,850	−1,230	12,783	..
Iraq	..	..	..	..	..	..	..	..	..	..	..	..
Ireland	..	817	467	1,212	2,260	−1,900	117	831	−712	−2,340	3,071	8,770
Israel	296	1,404	29	2,317	1,060	772	27	2,247	−541	−1,250	4,055	8,123
Italy	298	1,693	−1,099	33,901	13,180	−37,210	−995	−21,289	−797	−2,800	62,428	60,690
Jamaica	−30	37	28	78	80	35	−28	125	87	−29	105	681
Japan	..	−2,265	7,250	−58,726	11,700	−6,000	−3,170	14,345	−5,030	−58,600	38,919	192,620
Jordan	..	..	27	26	297	163	1,062	−56	−445	265	1,745	2,279
Kazakstan	..	..	..	..	..	..	..	..	..	..	..	1,660
Kenya	−10	0	79	38	428	209	9	11	371	142	539	384
Korea, Dem. Rep.	..	..	..	..	..	..	..	..	..	..	..	..
Korea, Rep.	−47	−487	127	9,072	5,838	8,100	−334	−1,394	−311	−7,040	3,101	32,804
Kuwait	..	..	−736	−298	−10,570	−6,617	−2,945	2,630	−1,050	87	5,425	4,543
Kyrgyz Republic	..	..	..	..	..	..	..	..	..	..	..	..
Lao PDR	..	13	..	43	..	−36	..	−27	..	230	..	99
Latvia	..	..	..	245	..	484	..	−735	..	33	..	602
Lebanon	..	..	..	..	..	..	..	..	..	..	7,025	8,100
Lesotho	..	..	4	19	−8	14	−11	−20	−41	−121	50	457
Libya	..	..	−1,249	..	−459	..	−96	..	−6,410	..	14,905	..
Lithuania	..	−39	..	88	..	149	..	287	..	129	..	829
Macedonia, FYR	..	..	..	..	..	2	..	187	..	18	..	275
Madagascar	0	45	..	10	381	−207	−73	98	248	330	9	109
Malawi	..	..	10	..	142	122	86	293	22	35	76	115
Malaysia	−19	..	923	2,698	512	−1,188	−682	−523	−468	3,160	5,755	24,699
Mali	..	..	2	45	126	−51	−31	107	33	64	26	330
Mauritania	..	..	27	2	96	−13	−32	−23	43	105	146	90
Mauritius	−2	−1	1	191	65	−166	24	107	28	−109	113	887
Mexico	..	..	2,133	−3,840	9,370	−7,940	−272	−1,266	−809	13,700	4,175	17,046
Moldova	..	0	..	63	..	15	..	9	..	8	..	240
Mongolia	..	..	..	..	808	−27	−1	20	1	−32	..	158
Morocco	−12	−6	89	278	996	−150	46	635	288	763	814	3,874
Mozambique	..	..	..	..	364	..	−30	..	32	..	..	..
Myanmar	..	166	..	245	371	..	8	−411	−31	..	409	651
Namibia	..	44	..	146	..	−225	..	14	..	−29	..	225
Nepal	64	107	..	..	22	369	−6	−85	13	−15	272	646
Netherlands	−250	−1,209	−491	−12,480	2,950	5,000	−94	−9,412	−1,260	1,910	37,549	47,162
New Zealand	−38	1,239	71	1,882	−715	−1,356	234	2,347	1,420	−334	365	4,410
Nicaragua	..	..	..	70	43	−631	−75	66	443	1,200	75	142
Niger	..	..	53	−9	254	44	−35	20	5	71	132	99
Nigeria	..	..	−739	..	679	..	−737	..	−4,380	..	10,640	1,709
Norway	19	..	−336	−854	200	−470	918	−870	−1,880	−1,450	6,746	22,976
Oman	..	..	98	147	−183	−44	−62	445	−796	432	704	1,251
Pakistan	268	..	68	..	575	..	14	..	211	..	1,568	2,528
Panama	..	..	−719	−794	220	220	842	460	−11	255	117	782
Papua New Guinea	−23	..	60	147	36	−625	132	−53	84	−142	458	267
Paraguay	5	..	30	180	416	277	−23	686	−151	−394	783	1,040
Peru	..	10	27	..	−75	−112	414	3,186	−264	1,140	2,804	8,653
Philippines	..	..	−102	2,269	2,791	3,040	119	−2,089	−891	−1,240	3,978	7,757
Poland	..	..	−11	4,788	2,878	9,449	−87	−242	637	−9,750	574	14,957
Portugal	..	..	136	−1,617	67	4,890	1,218	−3,343	−357	299	13,863	22,063
Puerto Rico	..	..	..	..	..	..	..	..	..	..	..	..
Romania	..	32	..	396	2,173	596	1	−182	246	500	2,511	2,624
Russian Federation	..	−348	..	520	..	−13,090	..	−7,786	..	11,100	..	18,024

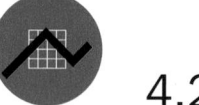
	Net capital account $ millions		Net direct and portfolio investment $ millions		Other net investment $ millions		Net errors and omissions[a] $ millions		Reserves and related items $ millions		Gross international reserves $ millions	
	1980	1995	1980	1995	1980	1995	1980	1995	1980	1995	1980	1995
Rwanda	0	..	17	0	56	83	-2	-5	-23	51	187	126
Saudi Arabia	..	..	-25,200	2,148	-12,395	7,182	32	-2	-3,940	-1,220	26,129	10,399
Senegal	..	..	16	48	349	-20	-37	-57	58	26	25	283
Sierra Leone	0	..	-20	-4	132	-23	-22	56	76	59	31	52
Singapore	..	..	1,151	-4,121	429	-2,754	646	382	-663	-8,600	6,567	68,695
Slovak Republic	..	46	..	383	..	775	..	-61	..	-1,790	..	3,863
Slovenia	..	-12	..	160	..	235	..	-122	..	-224	..	1,821
South Africa	..	15	-1,155	1,844	-107	3,405	-1,451	746	-795	-2,510	7,888	4,464
Spain	407	5,974	1,182	23,365	4,065	-30,920	-868	-6,189	795	6,490	20,474	40,531
Sri Lanka	..	..	43	158	282	727	16	-41	316	-298	283	2,088
Sudan	..	..	..	..	-264	474	302	89	526	-63	49	78
Sweden	-73	15	-640	2,794	1,097	-5,570	-1,452	-3,042	5,400	1,170	6,996	25,909
Switzerland	..	-132	-7,068	-13,616	-4,230	-4,740	11,836	-3,076	-337	-57	64,748	68,620
Syrian Arab Republic	..	20	..	..	196	1,640	-701	-1,320	254	-780	828	..
Tajikistan	..	..	..	..	..	..	..	..	..	..	..	..
Tanzania	..	237	..	150	219	4	-47	-54	350	292	20	270
Thailand	6	..	283	5,263	1,759	16,660	-178	-1,209	206	-7,160	3,026	36,939
Togo	..	..	45	..	18	-16	-1	-24	33	97	85	135
Trinidad and Tobago	-22	-12	165	9	61	-587	87	380	-648	-84	2,813	379
Tunisia	-7	-7	249	295	119	663	69	-117	-76	-97	700	1,689
Turkey	..	..	18	2,496	627	2,230	1,433	2,273	1,330	-4,660	3,298	13,891
Turkmenistan	..	..	..	..	..	..	..	..	..	..	..	..
Uganda	38	303	..	2	-67	-6	-103	64	214	65	3	459
Ukraine	..	6	..	261	..	-783	..	48	..	1,620	..	1,069
United Arab Emirates	..	..	..	..	..	..	..	..	..	..	2,355	7,778
United Kingdom	..	..	-8,015	-17,701	-1,400	18,100	1,864	3,269	689	964	31,755	49,144
United States	140	100	1,800	58,120	-38,900	-37,800	25,410	31,910	9,400	95,900	171,413	175,996
Uruguay	..	..	278	412	460	-22	90	196	-118	-228	2,401	1,813
Uzbekistan	..	..	..	..	..	..	..	..	..	..	..	..
Venezuela	..	..	1,365	944	-1,204	-3,640	-1,129	-579	-3,760	1,020	13,360	10,715
Vietnam	..	..	..	..	..	..	..	..	..	..	..	3
West Bank and Gaza	..	..	..	..	..	..	..	..	..	..	..	..
Yemen, Rep.	..	37	..	-218	..	-601	..	161	..	475	..	638
Yugoslavia, Fed. Rep.	..	..	..	..	..	..	..	..	..	..	..	..
Zaire	..	..	..	..	-75	..	-28	..	696	..	380	131
Zambia	-21	..	62	..	225	..	26	..	225	..	206	192
Zimbabwe	-94	..	-26	80	-4	-106	187	365	86	86	419	888

World											954,407 t	1,735,308 t
Low income											40,397 t	122,496 t
Excl. China & India											18,296 t	19,343 t
Middle income											173,531 t	392,309 t
Lower middle income											82,224 t	198,859 t
Upper middle income											91,307 t	193,450 t
Low & middle income											213,928 t	514,805 t
East Asia & Pacific											30,740 t	166,478 t
Europe & Central Asia											..	107,646 t
Latin America & Carib.											57,381 t	139,037 t
Middle East & N. Africa											76,217 t	50,854 t
South Asia											15,404 t	30,680 t
Sub-Saharan Africa											22,950 t	20,111 t
High income											740,478 t	1,220,503 t

a. Derived as a residual. b. Includes Luxembourg except for gross international reserves. c. Data prior to 1992 include Eritrea. d. Data prior to 1990 refer to the Federal Republic of Germany before unification.

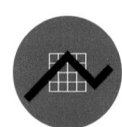

Changes in the capital and financial account

In the fifth edition of the *Balance of Payments Manual* the International Monetary Fund (IMF) introduces changes in the capital account, now designated the capital and financial account. The principal changes are these (see the notes to table 4.21 for the corresponding changes in the current account):

• Capital transfers are newly defined to include debt forgiveness, migrants' transfers, and foreign aid to acquire capital goods. These transactions are now separately recorded in the capital and financial account, not in the current account.

• The acquisition or disposal of nonproduced, nonfinancial assets (for example, patents, copyrights, goodwill, and leases) is newly recognized and included in the capital category of the capital and financial account.

• Portfolio investment now includes money market instruments (debt and short-term tradable instruments) and newly identified financial

East Asia's high-income economies hold nearly a quarter of the world's reserves ●

derivatives, in addition to long-term debt and equity securities.

• Other investment now includes use of IMF credit and loans from the IMF.

• Reserves are now restricted to assets, and exclude such nontransactions as the allocation or cancellation of special drawing rights and the monetization or demonetization of gold.

About the data

The concepts and definitions underlying the data here are based on the fifth edition of the IMF's *Balance of Payments Manual* (1993). The presentation of the capital and financial accounts follows that of the IMF's *International Financial Statistics*. Reserve transactions equal the sum of net transactions in the current account and the capital and financial accounts, with the residual category, net errors and omissions, acting as the balancing item. Because the World Bank makes adjustments to the current account balances of some economies, principally to correct for differences between fiscal and calendar year timing (see *Primary data documentation*), the value for errors and omissions shown here may differ from that reported in the *International Financial Statistics*.

The concept of direct investment used in the balance of payments is broader than the U.N. System of National Accounts concept of foreign-controlled (as opposed to domestically controlled) resident enterprises. In the balance of payments, direct investment includes all international investments by an entity resident in one economy to obtain a lasting interest in an enterprise resident in another. According to the *Balance of Payments Manual*, the primary distinction between direct investment and portfolio investment is that the direct investor seeks a significant voice in the management of an enterprise.

One of the frequently watched indicators of the balance of payments is the level of reserve assets available to and controlled by monetary authorities for directly financing payments imbalances and for indirectly regulating the size of imbalances through intervention in exchange markets. Gross international reserves, shown here, include monetary gold, special drawing rights, the reserve position in the IMF, and foreign exchange and other claims. Because of differences in the definition of international reserves, in the valuation of gold, and in reserve management practices, the levels of reserve holdings published in national sources may not be strictly comparable. The reserve levels for 1980 and 1995 refer to the end of the year and are in current U.S. dollars at prevailing exchange rates.

For additional discussion of the balance of payments see the notes to table 4.21.

Definitions

• **Net capital account** includes government debt forgiveness, investment grants in cash or in kind by a government entity, and taxes on capital transfers. Also included are migrants' transfers and debt forgiveness and investment grants by nongovernmental entities.
• **Net direct and portfolio investment** comprises direct investment in equity capital, reinvested earnings, and other capital associated with intercompany transactions and transactions with nonresidents in financial securities (such as corporate securities, bonds, notes, money market instruments, and financial derivatives.) Excluded are flows of direct investment capital for exceptional financing, such as debt-for-equity swaps, and reserve transactions. • **Other net investment** reflects all other transactions with nonresidents in financial assets and liabilities except for exceptional financing, liabilities constituting foreign authorities' reserves, and reserve assets. Examples include short- and long-term loans, trade credits, and transactions in currency. • **Net errors and omissions** constitute a residual category needed to ensure that all debit and credit entries in the balance of payments statement sum to zero. In the *International Financial Statistics* presentation, this is equal to the difference between reserves and related items and the sum of the balances of the current, capital, and financial accounts. • **Reserves and related items** are the sum of transactions in reserve assets, exceptional financing, liabilities constituting foreign authorities' reserves, and use of IMF credit and loans. A minus sign denotes an increase in reserves. • **Gross international reserves** comprise holdings of monetary gold, special drawing rights, the reserve position of members in the IMF, and holdings of foreign exchange under the control of monetary authorities. The gold component of these reserves is valued at year-end (December 31) London prices ($589.50 an ounce in 1980 and $386.75 an ounce in 1995).

Data sources

More information about the design and compilation of the balance of payments can be found in the IMF's *Balance of Payments Manual,* fifth edition (1993), *Balance of Payments Textbook* (1996a), and *Balance of Payments Compilation Guide* (1995). The data come from the IMF's balance of payments database, *Balance of Payments Statistics,* and *International Financial Statistics.*

	Total external debt $ millions		Long-term debt $ millions		Public and publicly guaranteed debt				Private nonguaranteed external debt $ millions		Use of IMF credit $ millions	
					Total $ millions		IBRD loans and IDA credits $ millions					
	1980	1995	1980	1995	1980	1995	1980	1995	1980	1995	1980	1995
Albania	..	709	..	557	..	557	0	109	0	0	0	65
Algeria	19,365	32,610	17,040	30,442	17,040	30,442	253	2,049	0	0	0	1,478
Angola	..	11,482	..	9,533	150	9,533	0	81	0	0	0	0
Argentina	27,157	89,747	16,774	73,446	10,181	62,181	404	4,913	6,593	11,265	0	6,131
Armenia	..	374	..	300	..	300	0	96	0	0	0	70
Australia	..	..	..	..	..	..	..	..	..	..	..	..
Austria	..	..	..	..	..	..	..	..	..	..	..	..
Azerbaijan	..	321	..	206	..	206	0	30	0	0	0	101
Bangladesh	4,230	16,370	3,594	15,543	3,594	15,543	981	5,692	0	0	424	622
Belarus	..	1,648	..	1,255	..	1,255	0	116	0	0	0	283
Belgium	..	..	..	..	..	..	..	..	..	..	..	..
Benin	424	1,646	334	1,514	334	1,514	52	498	0	0	16	84
Bolivia	2,702	5,266	2,273	4,692	2,181	4,452	239	865	92	239	126	268
Bosnia and Herzegovina	..	..	..	..	..	..	0	472	0	0	0	48
Botswana	147	699	143	682	143	682	66	108	0	0	0	0
Brazil	71,520	159,131	57,981	128,495	41,375	96,609	2,035	6,038	16,605	31,887	0	142
Bulgaria	..	10,887	392	9,574	392	9,574	0	444	0	0	0	717
Burkina Faso	330	1,267	281	1,136	281	1,136	77	608	0	0	15	75
Burundi	166	1,157	118	1,095	118	1,095	37	591	0	0	36	48
Cambodia	..	2,031	..	1,942	..	1,942	0	65	0	0	0	72
Cameroon	2,588	9,350	2,251	8,258	2,073	8,060	298	1,082	178	197	59	51
Canada	..	..	..	..	..	..	..	..	..	..	..	..
Central African Republic	195	944	147	852	147	852	29	414	0	0	24	35
Chad	285	908	260	840	260	840	36	379	0	0	14	49
Chile	12,081	25,562	9,399	18,607	4,705	7,178	184	1,383	4,693	11,429	123	0
China	4,504	118,090	4,504	95,764	4,504	94,675	0	14,248	0	1,090	0	0
Colombia	6,940	20,760	4,604	15,486	4,088	12,983	1,012	2,559	515	2,503	0	0
Congo	1,526	6,031	1,257	4,955	1,257	4,955	61	279	0	0	22	19
Costa Rica	2,744	3,800	2,112	3,346	1,700	3,132	183	303	412	214	57	24
Côte d'Ivoire	7,462	18,952	6,339	14,559	4,327	11,899	314	2,386	2,012	2,660	65	427
Croatia	..	3,662	..	2,950	..	1,693	0	117	0	1,257	0	221
Cuba	..	..	..	..	..	..	..	..	..	..	..	..
Czech Republic	..	16,576	..	11,504	..	9,610	0	434	0	1,894	0	0
Denmark	..	..	..	..	..	..	..	..	..	..	..	..
Dominican Republic	2,002	4,259	1,473	3,570	1,220	3,550	83	300	254	19	49	160
Ecuador	5,997	13,957	4,422	12,471	3,300	12,032	146	1,108	1,122	440	0	174
Egypt, Arab Rep.	19,131	34,116	14,693	31,638	14,428	31,325	728	2,356	265	313	411	103
El Salvador	911	2,583	659	2,060	499	2,055	114	327	161	5	32	0
Eritrea	..	..	..	..	..	..	..	..	..	..	..	..
Estonia	..	309	..	187	..	182	0	50	0	6	0	92
Ethiopia[a]	824	5,221	688	4,958	688	4,958	304	1,494	0	0	79	74
Finland	..	..	..	..	..	..	..	..	..	..	..	..
France	..	..	..	..	..	..	..	..	..	..	..	..
Gabon	1,514	4,492	1,272	4,099	1,272	4,099	19	110	0	0	15	97
Gambia, The	137	426	97	384	97	384	16	162	0	0	16	26
Georgia	..	1,189	..	988	..	988	0	84	0	0	0	116
Germany	..	..	..	..	..	..	..	..	..	..	..	..
Ghana	1,398	5,874	1,162	4,595	1,152	4,568	213	2,434	10	27	105	648
Greece	..	..	..	..	..	..	..	..	..	..	..	..
Guatemala	1,166	3,275	831	2,635	549	2,493	144	158	282	142	0	0
Guinea	1,133	3,242	1,019	2,975	1,019	2,975	87	847	0	0	35	94
Guinea-Bissau	145	894	138	849	138	849	5	210	0	0	1	6
Haiti	303	807	242	752	242	752	66	389	0	0	46	29
Honduras	1,472	4,567	1,168	4,093	976	3,979	216	828	191	114	33	99
Hong Kong	..	..	..	..	..	..	..	..	..	..	..	..

	Total external debt $ millions		Long-term debt $ millions		Public and publicly guaranteed debt				Private nonguaranteed external debt $ millions		Use of IMF credit $ millions	
					Total $ millions		IBRD loans and IDA credits $ millions					
	1980	1995	1980	1995	1980	1995	1980	1995	1980	1995	1980	1995
Hungary	9,764	31,248	6,416	27,660	6,416	23,572	0	2,218	0	4,088	0	385
India	20,581	93,766	18,333	86,343	17,997	79,725	5,969	27,348	336	6,618	977	2,374
Indonesia	20,938	107,831	18,163	85,481	15,021	65,347	1,605	13,259	3,142	20,134	0	0
Iran, Islamic Rep.	4,500	21,935	4,500	17,392	4,500	17,078	622	316	0	314	0	0
Iraq	..	..	..	..	..	..	..	..	..	..	..	..
Ireland	..	..	..	..	..	..	..	..	..	..	..	..
Israel	..	..	..	..	..	..	..	..	..	..	..	..
Italy	..	..	..	..	..	..	..	..	..	..	..	..
Jamaica	1,913	4,270	1,505	3,537	1,430	3,409	176	595	75	128	309	240
Japan	..	..	..	..	..	..	..	..	..	..	..	..
Jordan	1,971	7,944	1,486	6,904	1,486	6,904	102	805	0	0	0	252
Kazakstan	..	3,712	..	2,899	..	2,833	0	295	0	65	0	432
Kenya	3,383	7,381	2,489	6,372	2,052	5,927	528	2,412	437	445	254	374
Korea, Dem. Rep.	..	..	..	..	..	..	..	..	..	..	..	..
Korea, Rep.	..	..	..	..	..	..	..	..	..	..	..	..
Kuwait	..	..	..	..	..	..	..	..	..	..	..	..
Kyrgyz Republic	..	610	..	474	..	474	0	141	0	0	0	124
Lao PDR	350	2,165	333	2,091	333	2,091	6	285	0	0	16	64
Latvia	..	462	..	270	..	270	0	55	0	0	0	160
Lebanon	510	2,966	216	1,600	216	1,550	27	113	0	50	0	0
Lesotho	72	659	58	611	58	611	24	207	0	0	6	38
Libya	..	..	..	..	..	..	..	..	..	..	..	..
Lithuania	..	802	..	491	..	491	0	62	0	0	0	262
Macedonia, FYR	..	1,213	..	1,062	..	773	0	181	0	289	0	57
Madagascar	1,241	4,302	911	3,691	911	3,691	152	1,121	0	0	87	73
Malawi	821	2,140	625	1,978	625	1,978	156	1,306	0	0	80	116
Malaysia	6,611	34,351	5,256	27,077	4,008	15,857	504	1,059	1,248	11,220	0	0
Mali	732	3,066	669	2,840	669	2,840	121	863	0	0	39	147
Mauritania	843	2,467	717	2,184	717	2,184	38	347	0	0	62	100
Mauritius	467	1,801	318	1,449	294	1,182	55	157	24	267	102	0
Mexico	57,378	165,743	41,215	112,614	33,915	94,027	2,063	13,823	7,300	18,587	0	15,828
Moldova	..	691	..	455	..	455	0	152	0	0	0	230
Mongolia	..	512	..	452	..	452	0	59	0	0	0	47
Morocco	9,247	22,147	8,013	21,678	7,863	21,347	578	3,999	150	331	457	52
Mozambique	..	5,781	..	5,299	..	5,251	0	890	0	48	0	202
Myanmar	1,500	5,771	1,390	5,378	1,390	5,378	146	777	0	0	106	0
Namibia	..	..	..	..	..	..	..	..	..	..	..	..
Nepal	205	2,398	156	2,328	156	2,328	76	1,023	0	0	42	48
Netherlands	..	..	..	..	..	..	..	..	..	..	..	..
New Zealand	..	..	..	..	..	..	..	..	..	..	..	..
Nicaragua	2,192	9,287	1,671	7,937	1,671	7,937	135	341	0	0	49	39
Niger	863	1,634	687	1,509	383	1,376	66	598	305	133	16	52
Nigeria	8,921	35,005	5,368	29,002	4,271	28,701	554	3,489	1,097	301	0	0
Norway	..	..	..	..	..	..	..	..	..	..	..	..
Oman	599	3,107	436	2,566	436	2,563	14	25	0	3	0	0
Pakistan	9,930	30,152	8,519	25,305	8,501	23,711	1,151	6,403	18	1,593	674	1,613
Panama	2,975	7,180	2,271	3,905	2,271	3,905	133	175	0	0	23	111
Papua New Guinea	719	2,431	624	2,303	486	1,614	110	407	139	689	31	50
Paraguay	954	2,288	780	1,504	630	1,488	124	189	151	17	0	0
Peru	9,386	30,831	6,828	20,199	6,218	18,929	359	1,729	610	1,270	474	955
Philippines	17,417	39,445	8,817	33,438	6,363	29,908	960	5,185	2,454	3,531	1,044	728
Poland	..	42,291	..	42,085	..	41,073	0	2,067	0	1,012	0	0
Portugal	..	..	..	..	..	..	..	..	..	..	..	..
Puerto Rico	..	..	..	..	..	..	..	..	..	..	..	..
Romania	9,762	6,653	7,131	4,311	7,131	3,896	806	844	0	416	328	1,038
Russian Federation	..	120,461	..	100,279	..	100,279	0	1,524	0	0	0	9,617

	Total external debt $ millions		Long-term debt $ millions		Public and publicly guaranteed debt Total $ millions		IBRD loans and IDA credits $ millions		Private nonguaranteed external debt $ millions		Use of IMF credit $ millions	
	1980	1995	1980	1995	1980	1995	1980	1995	1980	1995	1980	1995
Rwanda	190	1,008	150	948	150	948	58	512	0	0	14	26
Saudi Arabia	..	..	..	..	..	..	..	..	..	..	..	..
Senegal	1,473	3,845	1,114	3,235	1,105	3,191	156	1,160	9	44	140	347
Sierra Leone	435	1,226	323	968	323	968	43	234	0	0	59	165
Singapore	..	..	..	..	..	..	..	..	..	..	..	..
Slovak Republic	670	5,827	..	3,656	..	3,570	0	263	0	85	0	457
Slovenia	..	3,489	..	2,966	..	1,491	0	187	0	1,475	0	4
South Africa	..	..	..	..	..	..	..	..	..	..	..	..
Spain	..	..	..	..	..	..	..	..	..	..	..	..
Sri Lanka	1,841	8,230	1,230	7,099	1,227	7,010	129	1,512	3	90	391	595
Sudan	5,177	17,623	4,147	10,275	3,822	9,779	236	1,279	325	496	431	960
Sweden	..	..	..	..	..	..	..	..	..	..	..	..
Switzerland	..	..	..	..	..	..	..	..	..	..	..	..
Syrian Arab Republic	3,552	21,318	2,921	16,757	2,921	16,757	257	472	0	0	0	0
Tajikistan	..	665	..	612	..	612	0	0	0	0	0	0
Tanzania	2,460	7,333	1,970	6,129	1,886	6,085	440	2,269	84	44	171	197
Thailand	8,297	56,789	5,646	38,476	3,943	17,231	703	1,906	1,702	21,245	348	0
Togo	1,052	1,486	899	1,297	899	1,297	47	541	0	0	33	105
Trinidad and Tobago	829	2,556	712	1,849	712	1,759	57	72	0	90	0	50
Tunisia	3,526	9,938	3,390	9,007	3,210	8,814	337	1,766	180	193	0	293
Turkey	19,131	73,592	15,575	57,207	15,040	50,128	1,347	5,069	535	7,079	1,054	684
Turkmenistan	..	393	..	375	..	375	0	1	0	0	0	0
Uganda	689	3,564	537	3,054	537	3,054	47	1,792	0	0	89	417
Ukraine	..	8,434	..	6,668	..	6,585	0	491	0	84	0	1,542
United Arab Emirates	..	..	..	..	..	..	..	..	..	..	..	..
United Kingdom	..	..	..	..	..	..	..	..	..	..	..	..
United States	..	..	..	..	..	..	..	..	..	..	..	..
Uruguay	1,660	5,307	1,338	3,950	1,127	3,823	72	513	211	127	0	21
Uzbekistan	..	1,630	..	1,260	..	1,260	0	157	0	0	0	158
Venezuela	29,344	35,842	13,795	30,508	10,614	28,494	133	1,639	3,181	2,013	0	2,239
Vietnam	..	26,495	..	22,962	..	22,962	2	231	0	0	0	377
West Bank and Gaza	..	..	..	..	..	..	..	..	..	..	..	..
Yemen, Rep.	1,684	6,212	1,453	5,528	1,453	5,528	137	828	0	0	48	0
Yugoslavia, Fed. Rep.[b]	..	..	..	..	..	..	..	..	..	..	..	..
Zaire	4,770	13,137	4,071	9,621	4,071	9,621	246	1,413	0	0	373	485
Zambia	3,261	6,853	2,227	5,091	2,141	5,077	348	1,434	87	14	447	1,239
Zimbabwe	786	4,885	696	3,741	696	3,360	3	896	0	381	..	..
World	..	..	..	..	..	..	..	..	..	..	..	..
Low income	106,209 t	534,794 t	87,521 t	452,108 t	82,430 t	437,814 t	14,004 t	96,113 t	5,091 t	14,294 t	5,797 t	14,299 t
Excl. China & India	..	..	..	..	..	..	..	..	..	..	..	..
Middle income	509,503 t	1,530,883 t	364,768 t	1,174,269 t	301,591 t	1,010,832 t	18,203 t	87,328 t	63,176 t	163,437 t	5,767 t	46,805 t
Lower middle income	..	..	..	..	..	..	..	..	..	..	..	..
Upper middle income	..	..	..	..	..	..	..	..	..	..	..	..
Low & middle income	..	..	..	..	..	..	..	..	..	..	..	..
East Asia & Pacific	64,600 t	404,457 t	48,438 t	322,568 t	39,687 t	264,542 t	4,077 t	37,604 t	8,751 t	58,026 t	1,551 t	1,337 t
Europe & Central Asia	87,919 t	425,319 t	63,299 t	330,224 t	51,759 t	309,715 t	3,512 t	16,913 t	11,540 t	20,509 t	2,143 t	16,946 t
Latin America & Carib.	257,266 t	636,594 t	187,256 t	490,344 t	144,798 t	409,830 t	8,133 t	38,576 t	42,458 t	80,514 t	1,413 t	26,719 t
Middle East & N. Africa	83,793 t	216,046 t	61,733 t	165,088 t	61,138 t	161,825 t	3,053 t	12,730 t	595 t	3,263 t	916 t	2,177 t
South Asia	38,014 t	156,778 t	33,052 t	142,435 t	32,695 t	134,134 t	8,307 t	42,036 t	357 t	8,301 t	2,507 t	5,252 t
Sub-Saharan Africa	84,119 t	226,483 t	58,509 t	175,717 t	53,942 t	168,600 t	5,126 t	35,582 t	4,567 t	7,117 t	3,033 t	8,673 t
High income	..	..	..	..	..	..	..	..	..	..	..	..

a. Includes Eritrea. b. Data refer to the former Yugoslavia.

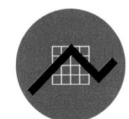

About the data

Data on the external debt of developing countries are gathered by the World Bank through its Debtor Reporting System. World Bank staff calculate the total external indebtedness of developing countries using loan-by-loan reports submitted by these countries on public and publicly guaranteed borrowing, along with information obtained from creditors through the debt data collection systems of such agencies as the Bank for International Settlements and the Organization for Economic Cooperation and Development. The data are also supplemented by information on loans and credits of major multilateral banks and loan statements of official lending agencies in major creditor countries and by estimates by country economists of the World Bank and desk officers of the International Monetary Fund (IMF).

Despite an ongoing effort to standardize the reporting of external debt (see, for example, International Working Group of External Debt Compilers 1987), the coverage, quality, and timeliness of debt data vary across countries. Coverage varies for both debt instruments and borrowers. With a widening spectrum of debt instruments and investors and the expansion of private nonguaranteed borrowing, comprehensive coverage of long-term external debt becomes more complex. Reporting countries differ in their ability to monitor debt, especially private nonguaranteed debt. Last year more than 30 countries reported their private nonguaranteed debt to the World Bank; estimates were made for approximately 30 additional countries known to have significant private debt. Even public and publicly guaranteed debt is affected by coverage and accuracy in reporting—again because of monitoring capacity and, sometimes, willingness to provide information. A key part that is often underreported is military debt.

Variations in reporting rescheduled debt also affect cross-country comparability. For example, when rescheduling under the auspices of the Paris Club, some countries calculate the effects of rescheduling according to the date of the general agreement with the Paris Club, while others use the completion dates for the individual bilateral (post–Paris Club) agreements. To ensure consistency, the World Bank estimates the effect of the Paris Club agreement for the second group until the authorities reflect it in the reported data. Other areas of inconsistency include country differences in treatment of arrears, reporting of debt owed to Russia, and treatment of nonresident national deposits denominated in foreign currency.

Definitions

- **Total external debt** is the sum of public, publicly guaranteed, and private nonguaranteed long-term debt, use of IMF credit, and short-term debt. ● **Long-term debt** is debt that has an original or extended maturity of more than one year and that is owed to nonresidents and repayable in foreign currency, goods, or services. It has three components: public, publicly guaranteed, and private nonguaranteed loans. ● **Public and publicly guaranteed debt** comprises long-term external obligations of public debtors, including the national government, political subdivisions (or an agency of either), and autonomous public bodies, and external obligations of private debtors that are guaranteed for repayment by a public entity. ● **IBRD loans and IDA credits** are the market-rate loans (from the International Bank for Reconstruction and Development) and the concessional loans (from the International Development Association) owed to the World Bank. ● **Private nonguaranteed external debt** comprises long-term external obligations of private debtors that are not guaranteed for repayment by a public entity. ● **Use of IMF credit** denotes repurchase obligations to the IMF for all uses of IMF resources (excluding those resulting from drawings on the reserve tranche). It is shown for the end of the year specified. It comprises purchases outstanding under the credit tranches, including enlarged access resources, and all special facilities (the buffer stock, compensatory financing, extended fund, and oil facilities), trust fund loans, and operations under the structural adjustment and enhanced structural adjustment facilities.

Data sources

The principal sources of external debt information are reports to the World Bank through its Debtor Reporting System from member countries that have received IBRD loans or IDA credits. Additional information has been drawn from the files of the World Bank and the IMF. Summary tables of the external debt of developing countries are published annually in the World Bank's *Global Development Finance* (formerly *World Debt Tables*).

4.24 External debt management

	Present value of debt				Total debt service				Public and publicly guaranteed debt service	
	% of GNP		% of exports of goods and services		% of GNP		% of exports of goods and services		% of central government current revenue	
	1993	1995	1993	1995	1980	1995	1980	1995	1980	1995
Albania	46.5	32.1	146.0	94.7	..	0.3	..	1.0	..	0.4
Algeria	51.7	63.9	217.9	221.9	9.9	11.2	27.4	38.7	..	..
Angola	314.6	260.0	312.3	310.5	..	11.0	..	12.5	..	..
Argentina	26.5	30.6	379.9	296.0	5.5	3.5	37.3	34.7	6.1	11.8
Armenia	6.9	13.7	..	92.8	..	0.3	..	2.9	..	..
Australia	..	..	..	..	..	..	..	..	..	..
Austria	..	..	..	..	..	..	..	..	..	..
Azerbaijan	0.7	8.0	..	..	..	0.3	..	..	..	..
Bangladesh	33.5	31.5	205.1	166.7	2.1	2.5	23.7	13.3	..	..
Belarus	2.7	6.4	..	..	..	0.9	..	..	..	..
Belgium	..	..	..	..	..	..	..	..	..	..
Benin	38.6	45.7	136.7	159.5	1.4	2.4	6.3	8.4	..	..
Bolivia	62.2	67.1	354.8	303.7	12.6	6.4	35.0	28.9	..	27.1
Bosnia and Herzegovina	..	..	..	..	..	..	..	..	..	..
Botswana	13.4	13.1	..	..	1.7	2.2	2.1	3.2	..	..
Brazil	35.2	22.9	324.1	257.4	6.5	3.3	63.3	37.9	15.3	4.7
Bulgaria	130.9	87.3	278.6	278.6	0.2	10.7	0.5	18.8	..	14.4
Burkina Faso	21.1	28.0	137.4	148.3	1.3	2.1	5.9	11.1	8.4	8.3
Burundi	50.4	49.8	471.4	375.0	1.0	3.7	..	27.7	4.8	..
Cambodia	77.5	52.0	485.3	145.2	..	0.2	..	0.6	..	..
Cameroon	54.8	96.6	272.3	354.8	4.6	5.8	15.3	20.1	17.0	19.3
Canada	..	..	..	..	..	..	..	..	..	..
Central African Republic	40.2	52.2	253.9	253.9	1.3	1.4	4.9	6.8	3.2	..
Chad	32.3	39.6	187.4	196.6	0.8	1.4	8.3	5.8	..	8.0
Chile	43.8	41.3	156.9	138.5	10.2	7.8	43.1	25.7	15.6	20.2
China	17.9	16.4	84.2	70.6	0.5	2.2	8.4	9.9	..	..
Colombia	30.5	27.0	150.2	132.8	2.9	5.1	16.0	25.2	13.2	29.4
Congo	201.8	324.9	374.1	374.1	7.1	10.1	10.6	14.4	11.7	..
Costa Rica	48.1	39.6	116.9	89.6	7.7	7.1	29.1	16.4	23.9	23.8
Côte d'Ivoire	188.1	184.9	510.5	366.6	14.5	11.6	38.7	23.1	37.4	..
Croatia	16.5	18.1	..	..	..	2.3	..	5.7	..	2.2
Cuba	..	..	..	..	..	..	..	..	..	..
Czech Republic	29.0	36.0	..	54.8	1.6	5.7	..	8.7	..	10.6
Denmark	..	..	..	..	..	..	..	..	..	..
Dominican Republic	47.5	33.1	94.1	70.0	5.9	3.7	25.3	7.8	16.3	16.9
Ecuador	97.1	75.8	356.3	237.3	9.0	8.5	33.9	26.7	..	..
Egypt, Arab Rep.	58.9	55.6	142.5	157.7	5.8	5.1	13.4	14.6	8.6	11.5
El Salvador	22.3	22.0	78.9	66.5	2.7	3.0	7.5	8.9	..	..
Eritrea	..	..	..	..	..	..	..	..	..	..
Estonia	3.8	6.5	..	10.2	..	0.5	..	0.8	..	2.4
Ethiopia[a]	50.4	65.7	397.3	301.5	1.1	3.0	7.3	13.6	..	..
Finland	..	..	..	..	..	..	..	..	..	..
France	..	..	..	..	..	..	..	..	..	..
Gabon	71.7	89.1	127.9	127.9	11.2	12.0	17.7	15.8	26.1	14.4
Gambia, The	64.9	59.3	94.9	96.2	1.9	6.7	6.3	14.0	..	..
Georgia	19.8	44.4	..	..	..	0.9	..	..	..	..
Germany	..	..	..	..	..	..	..	..	..	..
Ghana	51.4	61.1	249.3	236.1	3.6	6.0	13.1	23.1	..	..
Greece	..	..	..	..	..	..	..	..	..	..
Guatemala	21.6	19.0	106.1	86.7	1.8	2.3	7.9	10.6	..	..
Guinea	60.7	59.4	..	294.3	..	5.1	..	25.3	..	20.2
Guinea-Bissau	219.1	230.2	3,251.9	3,251.9	4.5	6.3	31.6	66.9	..	..
Haiti	29.3	19.5	384.4	627.1	1.8	4.7	6.2	45.2	13.2	..
Honduras	101.0	101.2	252.3	207.4	8.5	15.1	21.4	31.0	26.0	..
Hong Kong	..	..	..	..	..	..	..	..	..	..

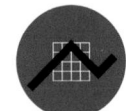

	Present value of debt				Total debt service				Public and publicly guaranteed debt service	
	% of GNP		% of exports of goods and services		% of GNP		% of exports of goods and services		% of central government current revenue	
	1993	1995	1993	1995	1980	1995	1980	1995	1980	1995
Hungary	64.7	72.4	211.3	173.1	8.8	16.7	24.9	39.1	15.2	..
India	27.9	22.6	229.2	159.6	0.8	4.1	9.3	27.9	5.6	21.8
Indonesia	54.0	54.5	195.7	194.2	4.1	8.7	14.0	30.9	10.6	29.0
Iran, Islamic Rep.	14.6	14.6	119.7	103.2	1.0	..	6.8	..	4.7	20.2
Iraq	..	..	..	..	..	..	..	..	..	..
Ireland	..	..	..	..	..	..	..	..	..	..
Israel	..	..	..	..	..	..	..	..	..	..
Italy	..	..	..	..	..	..	..	..	..	..
Jamaica	90.4	123.1	133.8	103.3	11.4	21.3	19.0	17.9	26.6	..
Japan	..	..	..	..	..	..	..	..	..	..
Jordan	116.0	108.4	152.0	140.7	..	9.7	8.4	12.6	..	..
Kazakstan	6.1	21.8	..	..	..	1.1	..	4.6	..	..
Kenya	106.3	72.3	232.8	183.8	6.2	8.7	21.0	25.7	..	..
Korea, Dem. Rep.	..	..	..	..	..	..	..	..	..	..
Korea, Rep.	..	..	..	..	..	..	..	..	25.1	5.7
Kuwait	..	..	..	..	..	..	..	..	..	..
Kyrgyz Republic	6.8	14.9	..	..	..	2.0	..	4.8	..	..
Lao PDR	46.4	42.9	183.1	154.5	..	1.5	..	5.8	..	..
Latvia	4.0	7.0	..	..	..	0.6	..	1.6	..	1.7
Lebanon	17.1	24.8	100.3	154.8	..	2.1	..	13.1	..	9.1
Lesotho	22.5	26.0	45.0	63.5	0.9	2.7	1.5	6.0	7.9	8.3
Libya	..	..	..	..	..	..	..	..	..	..
Lithuania	3.4	8.8	11.8	21.7	..	0.6	..	1.4	..	1.1
Macedonia, FYR	51.9	56.6	..	..	..	1.6	..	11.8	..	..
Madagascar	86.0	105.0	517.0	416.8	2.6	2.3	20.3	9.1	13.7	19.1
Malawi	42.1	79.3	236.0	237.4	7.7	7.6	27.7	25.9	..	..
Malaysia	37.7	38.6	42.1	33.6	4.0	8.1	6.3	7.8	5.9	12.2
Mali	58.2	74.7	266.9	282.4	1.0	3.3	5.1	12.6	5.3	..
Mauritania	177.3	166.2	362.9	311.6	7.1	11.4	17.3	21.4	..	..
Mauritius	..	..	43.3	43.3	4.7	5.5	9.1	9.0	14.7	15.1
Mexico	33.0	67.2	174.2	163.8	5.8	9.9	44.4	24.2	26.9	18.8
Moldova	5.2	16.1	..	..	..	1.8	..	8.0	..	..
Mongolia	44.3	39.5	70.0	70.0	..	5.6	..	9.1	..	14.8
Morocco	73.9	61.7	206.8	180.7	7.9	11.3	33.4	32.1	27.5	44.8
Mozambique	316.2	339.9	1,045.9	904.0	..	13.3	..	35.3	..	..
Myanmar	7.7	6.5	469.1	432.5	..	..	25.4	14.5	11.9	3.3
Namibia	..	..	..	..	..	..	..	..	..	..
Nepal	25.4	26.2	125.9	97.4	0.4	2.2	3.2	7.8	2.6	18.5
Netherlands	..	..	..	..	..	..	..	..	..	..
New Zealand	..	..	..	..	..	..	..	..	..	..
Nicaragua	687.8	520.3	2,423.5	1,122.9	5.7	17.9	22.3	38.6	26.3	53.7
Niger	46.3	56.7	273.7	312.0	5.7	3.1	21.7	19.8	10.6	..
Nigeria	109.9	132.3	240.6	88.8	1.3	6.3	4.1	12.3	..	..
Norway	..	..	..	..	..	..	..	..	..	..
Oman	26.5	28.0	43.4	45.8	4.7	4.6	6.4	7.5	..	..
Pakistan	39.3	38.4	205.9	223.8	3.7	5.1	18.3	35.3	15.4	25.2
Panama	110.1	98.2	84.6	80.3	13.4	5.3	6.2	3.9	48.3	15.4
Papua New Guinea	58.2	45.1	93.7	68.2	6.0	13.7	13.8	20.8	..	..
Paraguay	20.4	27.2	..	..	3.1	3.5	18.6	..	16.0	27.9
Peru	47.1	52.2	376.6	385.4	10.9	2.1	44.5	15.3	42.7	9.5
Philippines	61.7	49.4	178.1	113.5	6.7	7.0	26.6	16.0	..	..
Poland	47.8	30.5	220.1	107.6	5.3	3.5	17.9	12.2	..	4.4
Portugal	..	..	..	..	..	..	..	..	..	..
Puerto Rico	..	..	..	..	..	..	..	..	..	..
Romania	15.3	18.3	55.2	68.7	..	2.7	12.6	10.6	7.5	2.8
Russian Federation	20.4	34.9	..	..	..	2.0	..	6.6	..	9.1

	Present value of debt				Total debt service				Public and publicly guaranteed debt service	
	% of GNP		% of exports of goods and services		% of GNP		% of exports of goods and services		% of central government current revenue	
	1993	1995	1993	1995	1980	1995	1980	1995	1980	1995
Rwanda	21.9	42.4	397.6	397.6	0.7	1.8	4.2	..	2.9	8.5
Saudi Arabia	..	..	..	..	..	..	..	..	..	..
Senegal	47.2	53.7	189.1	158.6	8.9	6.3	28.7	18.7	30.1	..
Sierra Leone	156.4	100.0	595.3	471.4	5.6	10.8	23.2	60.3	..	..
Singapore	..	..	..	..	..	..	..	..	..	..
Slovak Republic	27.6	31.3	..	48.6	..	6.2	..	9.7	..	..
Slovenia	11.4	18.0	18.9	31.2	..	3.9	..	6.7	..	..
South Africa	..	..	..	..	..	..	..	..	..	..
Spain	..	..	..	..	..	..	..	..	..	..
Sri Lanka	42.4	43.6	104.1	99.2	4.5	3.2	12.0	7.3	10.3	19.1
Sudan	244.1	244.1	2,985.3	2,418.1	3.9	0.5	25.5	0.5	..	..
Sweden	..	..	..	..	..	..	..	..	..	..
Switzerland	..	..	..	..	..	..	..	..	..	..
Syrian Arab Republic	132.1	118.3	320.9	295.4	2.9	1.9	11.4	4.6	8.6	2.3
Tajikistan	12.3	33.0	..	..	..	0.0	..	0.0	..	..
Tanzania	..	..	660.6	430.0	3.1	6.3	21.1	17.4	8.1	..
Thailand	38.5	35.3	94.8	77.6	5.0	4.6	18.9	10.2	9.5	7.7
Togo	65.5	74.8	226.0	172.5	4.8	2.5	9.0	5.7	11.0	..
Trinidad and Tobago	47.6	52.2	108.1	85.7	3.9	9.1	6.8	14.8	..	..
Tunisia	54.4	51.8	120.9	101.7	6.4	8.7	14.8	17.0	15.6	27.2
Turkey	36.2	42.8	212.9	162.3	2.3	6.9	28.0	27.7	8.5	30.1
Turkmenistan	4.5	9.4	..	..	..	2.5	..	4.1	..	..
Uganda	57.1	33.4	748.8	291.0	4.5	2.4	17.3	21.3	..	..
Ukraine	2.8	10.0	..	..	..	1.2	..	5.3	..	..
United Arab Emirates	..	..	..	..	..	..	..	..	..	..
United Kingdom	..	..	..	..	..	..	..	..	..	..
United States	..	..	..	..	..	..	..	..	..	..
Uruguay	35.8	31.2	157.7	139.1	3.1	4.9	18.8	23.5	8.8	14.4
Uzbekistan	4.1	6.9	..	..	..	1.0	..	6.0	..	..
Venezuela	62.6	46.8	205.8	205.8	8.7	6.7	27.2	21.7	19.1	19.4
Vietnam	161.0	114.6	..	..	..	1.9	..	5.2	..	..
West Bank and Gaza	..	..	..	..	..	..	..	..	..	..
Yemen, Rep.	150.0	127.7	194.5	158.0	..	2.6	..	3.2	..	3.3
Yugoslavia, Fed. Rep.[b]	..	..	..	..	..	..	..	..	..	..
Zaire	173.9	226.0	..	..	3.9	0.5	13.2	..	29.2	..
Zambia	164.3	138.6	..	..	11.4	68.4	25.3	174.4	29.6	53.5
Zimbabwe	68.0	64.9	177.8	147.4	1.2	10.5	3.8	25.6	..	..
World	..	..	..	..	..	..	..	..	..	..
Low income	..	..	..	..	1.5 w	3.2 w	9.6 w	15.4 w	..	..
Excl. China & India	..	..	..	..	..	..	..	..	..	..
Middle income	..	..	..	..	3.6 w	4.9 w	13.6 w	17.4 w	..	..
Lower middle income	..	..	..	..	..	..	..	..	..	..
Upper middle income	..	..	..	..	..	..	..	..	..	..
Low & middle income	..	..	..	..	..	..	..	..	..	..
East Asia & Pacific	..	..	..	..	2.2 w	4.3 w	11.5 w	12.8 w	..	..
Europe & Central Asia	..	..	..	..	1.6 w	4.2 w	7.4 w	13.8 w	..	..
Latin America & Carib.	..	..	..	..	6.5 w	5.1 w	36.3 w	26.2 w	..	..
Middle East & N. Africa	..	..	..	..	2.5 w	4.2 w	5.7 w	14.9 w	..	..
South Asia	..	..	..	..	1.3 w	3.4 w	11.7 w	24.6 w	..	..
Sub-Saharan Africa	..	..	..	..	3.3 w	4.9 w	9.8 w	14.5 w	..	..
High income	..	..	..	..	..	..	..	..	..	..

a. Includes Eritrea. b. Data refer to the former Yugoslavia.

Debt sustainability

When is the burden of debt on a country so great that national solvency is threatened? Debt sustainability analysis looks at the future path of the economy and the expected evolution of the country's current obligations to determine when and if debt service problems are likely to arise.

The method typically used involves choosing a time horizon (often 10–20 years) and projecting the change in the main macroeconomic variables to that horizon. These projections, together with estimates of future inflows of private and official capital, are then used to construct the balance of payments accounts and the estimated financing requirement for the country. This requires much explicit or implicit economic modeling based on assumptions about the indebted country's future economic policy.

For external debt to be judged sustainable, the projected scenario must satisfy two conditions. First, during the projection period balance of payments equilibrium must be achieved without resorting to exceptional financing (such as debt restructuring or emergency borrowing from official sources). Second, indebtedness at the end of the period must be low enough to make future debt service problems unlikely. The second condition is typically evaluated by computing indebtedness indicators such as the ratio of debt to GDP or of debt service to exports (possibly on a present value basis) for the last years of the projection period.

There are no absolute rules on what values are too high for these ratios. But empirical analysis of the experience of developing countries and their debt service performance has shown that debt service difficulties become increasingly likely when the ratio of the present value of debt to exports reaches 200–250 percent and the debt service ratio exceeds 20–25 percent. What constitutes a sustainable debt burden nevertheless varies from one country to another. Countries with fast-growing economies and exports are likely to be able to sustain higher debt levels than countries with inefficient tax systems, distorted prices, and high current expenditure rates.

About the data

Data on debt are in U.S. dollars converted at official exchange rates. The data include private nonguaranteed debt reported by more than 30 developing countries and complete or partial estimates for an additional 30 that do not report this type of debt but for which it is known to be significant. Government debt denominated in local currency is not reported here because data availability is poor.

The present value of external debt provides a measure of current and future debt obligations that can be compared with the current value of such indicators as GNP and exports of goods and services. It is calculated by discounting the debt service (interest plus amortization) due on long-term external debt over the life of existing loans. Short-term debt (debt with a maturity of one year or less) is included at its face value. The discount rate applied to long-term debt is determined by the currency of repayment of the loan and is based on the OECD's commercial interest reference rates. IBRD loans and IDA credits are discounted using the latest IBRD lending rates, and obligations to the IMF are discounted at the SDR lending rate. When the discount rate is greater than the interest rate of the loan, the present value is less than the nominal sum of future debt service.

Data on the present value of debt and debt service are from the World Bank's Debtor Reporting System. The ratios shown here may differ from those published elsewhere, however, because estimates of exports of goods and services and gross national product have been revised to incorporate data available as of February 1, 1997.

Definitions

● **Present value of debt** is the sum of short-term external debt plus the discounted sum of total debt service payments due on public, publicly guaranteed, and private nonguaranteed long-term external debt over the life of existing loans. ● **Total debt service** is the sum of principal repayments and interest paid in foreign currency, goods, or services on long-term debt and interest payments only on short-term debt. ● **Public and publicly guaranteed debt service** is the sum of principal repayments and interest paid on long-term obligations of public debtors.

Data sources

The principal sources of information on external debt are reports to the World Bank through its Debtor Reporting System from member countries that have received IBRD loans or IDA credits. Additional information has been drawn from the files of the World Bank and the International Monetary Fund. Summary tables of the external debt of developing countries are published annually in the World Bank's *Global Development Finance* (formerly *World Debt Tables*).

States and markets

It is increasingly recognized that "governments need to do less in those areas where markets work or can be made to work reasonably well" (World Bank 1991b) and more in those areas—such as education, health, nutrition, and regulation—where markets alone cannot be relied upon. By unleashing competitive forces and enhancing international competitiveness, a healthy private sector can provide both growth and jobs.

Many developing country governments are shifting their priorities from preserving jobs in a stagnant public sector to creating jobs in a vibrant private sector. This shift implies a fundamental change in the role of government—from owner and operator to policymaker and regulator, working closely with the private sector to develop a competitive, outward-looking economy (World Bank 1995e). This section provides indicators that reflect these shifting roles.

The new strategy requires that developing countries:

- *Establish a more inviting business environment.* Sound macroeconomic management has to supplant stop-go policies that undermine the confidence of the private sector. But governments also have to promote competition and reduce risk—and especially to cut the high costs of doing business. This means pressing ahead on an array of policy, legal, regulatory, and institutional reforms in partnership with business and labor.
- *Accelerate financial reform.* Governments also have to restructure and, when appropriate, privatize banks, strengthen regulation and supervision, and develop the basic financial infrastructure to service a broad segment of the population, especially small businesses.
- *Go faster and farther with public enterprise reform.* Governments have to privatize utilities and large enterprises—and, where appropriate, liquidate major loss-makers. Employing only a small fraction of the labor force, these enterprises absorb a large part of government expenditures and account for a large part of the losses of the banking system. Failure to deal with these losses threatens reform programs and diverts resources from pressing social needs.

Two major objectives of the new strategy are to stop the hemorrhaging of the banking system and to improve infrastructure services essential for competing in a dynamic global economy.

Many countries have implemented parts of this new strategy for private sector development, and the response has been impressive. But even in countries with well-established institutions and legal systems—and the human resources to translate commitment into action—reform is a long process that may take more than a decade and is subject to reversal and fragility.

The poorest countries lack many of the prerequisites for such a sustained effort—and have little latitude for error. The challenges are particularly daunting in Africa, where the business environment for entrepreneurs is shaky, markets are small, skills are shallow and narrow, the supporting infrastructure is weak, and laws and regulations are very restrictive.

Tracking progress

How to track countries' progress in developing the private sector? By following three sets of indicators (World Bank 1991a). A changing *public-private balance* is reflected in an expanding private sector and a dwindling government role in the economy. Private sector growth shows up in higher private sector credit and investment, in flows of private capital, and in expanding capital markets. As the private sector grows, the government shifts out of providing services and into building human resources—and its intervention in the economy subsides. This shift shows up in the amount and composition of central government expenditure, in the amounts of public investment, publicly guaranteed debt, and domestic borrowing, and in the shares of government and state-owned enterprises in economic activity. To capture the potential of the economic environment to promote private sector development, *incentives* for investment are measured by integration with the global economy, trade policies, key prices in the economy, trade competitiveness, tax policies, and the legal and regulatory framework. And because *support systems* are essential for increasing the potential for private sector development, we look at the financial sector's depth and efficiency, the level of people's skills, the dependability of infrastructure, and scientific and technological capacity.

Going private

The private sector's share in economic activity has increased dramatically in many countries and in the developing world as a whole, but in far too many countries excessive fiscal deficits still crowd out private investment and raise the cost of domestic borrowing.

Even so, some countries have begun to attract sizable amounts of private capital flows in recent years (tables 5.1 and 5.2). For countries, this reflects their greater receptivity to foreign capital, and for investors, their search for higher returns and for better diversification of risk (box 5a).

Developing country stock markets are also beginning to attract significant inflows of foreign portfolio equity investment—as well as domestic funds. In 1990–95 the stock market capitalization in developing economies rose from $390 billion to $1.5 trillion, up from 4 percent to 8 percent of global stock market capitalization (table 5.3).

Stock market development is closely related to economic development. In the initial stages of economic development, commercial banks tend to dominate the financial system. As economies grow, specialized financial intermediaries and equity markets develop. The reason? Many profitable investments require a long-term commitment of capital, but investors are typically reluctant to relinquish control of their savings. By allowing savers to acquire liquid assets, equity markets make investments less risky and more attractive—and allow companies to tap capital for their longer-term investments. The development of stock markets also makes it easier for governments to sell off state-owned enterprises.

But despite more than a decade of divestiture efforts, state enterprises remain as ubiquitous in developing economies as they were 20 years ago. Indeed, their presence has shrunk significantly only in the former socialist economies and a few middle-income countries. In most developing countries, particularly the poorest, bureaucrats run as large a share of the economy as ever (table 5.4).

State enterprises often are less efficient than private firms, and their deficits are typically financed in ways that undermine macroeconomic stability. In addition, subsidies to state enter-

Box 5a Private capital flows prove resilient

Spurred by favorable world market conditions and strong growth in equity flows, private capital flows to developing economies increased fourfold between 1990 and 1995. Together, foreign direct investment and portfolio equity flows accounted for more than 70 percent of the increase in capital flows to developing countries during 1990–95.

The continuing growth of private capital flows to developing economies despite the cyclical recovery in industrial economies suggests that these flows have reached a new phase, driven by increased financial integration. Two forces are behind this: high expected rates of return and the opportunities for risk diversification.

Economic growth in developing economies has been on an upswing in the 1990s and, unlike in the 1980s, is expected to remain significantly stronger than that in industrial economies. The creditworthiness of major recipients of private capital also has been improving steadily, reflecting better economic performance and underlying policy improvements. And risk diversification is more possible because of the low correlation between returns in developing and industrial economies. The correlation between the Standard & Poor's 500 and the IFC composite return index for emerging markets is less than 0.4—and for many individual emerging markets, it is much lower.

Recent changes in the composition of flows have been associated with important shifts in the investor base. Commercial bank lending has recovered, but it no longer occupies center stage—and it is increasingly oriented toward project financing. The most important component of private flows: foreign direct investment (more than 50 percent), propelled by the globalization of production and growing trade integration.

An important new feature of international financial markets is the expanding role of institutional investors, especially mutual and pension funds. Since the mid-1980s these investors have allocated an increasing portion of their rapidly growing portfolios to international assets. Mutual funds have led the surge in investments in emerging market equities. In 1986 there were 17 emerging market country funds and nine regional or global emerging market funds. By 1995 there were nearly 500 country funds and more than 800 regional and global funds. The exposure of U.S. open-end mutual funds to emerging markets rose from just $1.5 billion in 1990 to $35 billion in 1995, or 14 percent of their international exposure.

Pension fund managers have followed suit, investing through mutual funds or directly on their own account. Even though they began to invest in emerging markets more recently, allocations of U.S. pension funds to emerging markets are now comparable to those of mutual funds, with some of the bigger pension funds investing considerably larger portions of their portfolios.

Despite these increases, the share of emerging markets in the portfolios of institutional investors remains small—well below their share in world market capitalization. Even in the United States, where institutional investors have been fastest to increase their exposure to emerging markets, mutual funds and pension funds are estimated to hold an average of only 2 percent of their portfolios in emerging markets. For most other industrial economies these shares are much smaller.

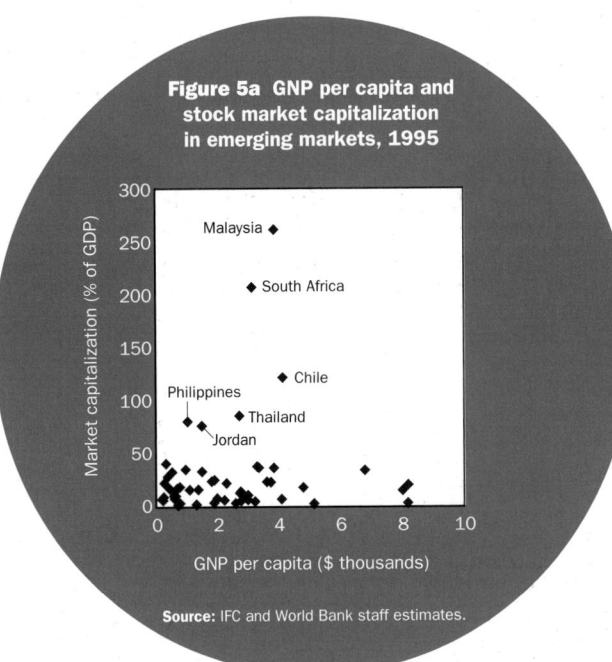

Figure 5a GNP per capita and stock market capitalization in emerging markets, 1995

Market capitalization (% of GDP)

Malaysia
South Africa
Chile
Philippines
Thailand
Jordan

GNP per capita ($ thousands)

Source: IFC and World Bank staff estimates.

prises often divert scarce funds from public spending on education and health. And because state enterprises tend to loom large in low-income countries, they are likely to be most costly in countries that can least afford them.

Privatizations of state enterprises in developing countries generally have so far had more qualitative effects than quantitative effects—increased efficiency, more new domestic firms, and a proven government commitment to private sector development. And even though sales have yet to generate much revenue, public enterprises are accruing fewer losses than they once did.

Getting the incentives right

If the private sector is to lead economic growth, incentives must be in place to increase private investment, boost the productivity of private firms, and spur competition. Perhaps even more important is removing constraints to private sector development. Distorted incentive policies call for reforms that address product and factor prices, special tax incentives, trade protection, state subsidies, and preferential access to foreign exchange and other scarce resources.

Real exchange rates, real wages, real interest rates, and relative commodity prices convey vital information about the interaction of the agents in an economy—and that economy's interaction with the rest of the world (table 5.5). Some relative price movements are immutable. For a small, open economy the real exchange rate in the long run is determined by the country's endowments, tastes, and technologies. But policymakers can influence relative prices only in the short run—and whether their policy initiatives stick depends on the behavior of real wages and the accompanying monetary and fiscal policies.

Relative prices also reflect an economy's openness by showing how far domestic prices of traded goods are from international prices. Trade restrictions account for most of the gap between domestic and international prices (table 5.6). They push investment to the wrong projects, and they force consumers to pay higher than world prices.

Openness to trade goes hand in hand with faster economic growth. Many developing economies have been lowering their tariffs and reducing the coverage of nontariff barriers, with further progress expected now that the Uruguay Round is coming into force. But tariffs are still high in many countries, in part because the countries need the revenues tariffs generate. For example, tariffs in South Asia averaged 30 percent after the Uruguay Round, substantially lower than in the 1980s, but still much higher than those in East Asia (around 12 percent). Industrial country tariffs now average around 3 percent (see table 6.4). As countries develop, they usually build up their capacity to tax residents directly, and indirect taxes become less important as a source of revenue. Thus the share of direct taxes in total revenues is one measure of the development of the tax system.

Openness to foreign competition, foreign knowledge, and foreign resources energizes the development process in many ways, and lowering trade taxes enhances openness. The fastest-

Figure 5b
Implementing the private sector development agenda

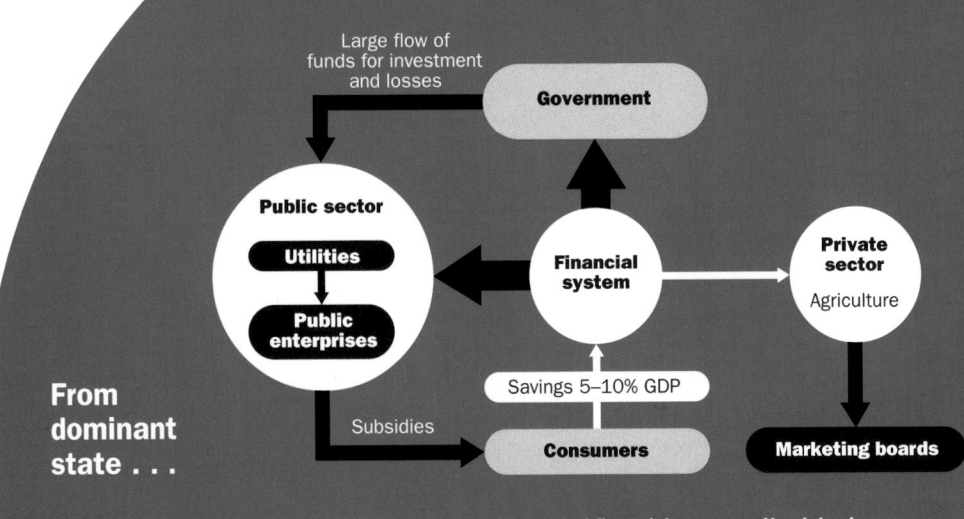

From dominant state . . .

Large flow of funds for investment and losses

Government

Public sector
- Utilities
- Public enterprises

Financial system

Private sector
Agriculture

Savings 5–10% GDP

Subsidies

Consumers

Marketing boards

Overbearing public sector
- Utilities and large public enterprises absorb a large share of government resources
- They crowd out investment in social sectors and infrastructure, particularly in rural areas
- Public enterprises and large urban consumers receive bulk of subsidies provided by utilities

Distressed financial system
- Fiscal deficits, public enterprises, and privileged private firms drain system
- Remaining private sector crowded out
- Public sector banks dominate, with large amounts of nonperforming loans
- Financial repression provides little incentive for saving
- Weak prudential regulation and supervision

Harsh business environment
- Weak legal system
- Private sector overregulated and overprotected
- Incentives and regulations unevenly applied
- Agriculture oppressed by price controls and marketing boards
- Goods and services provided by public sector increase the cost of private firms by 20–30%

. . . to competitive markets

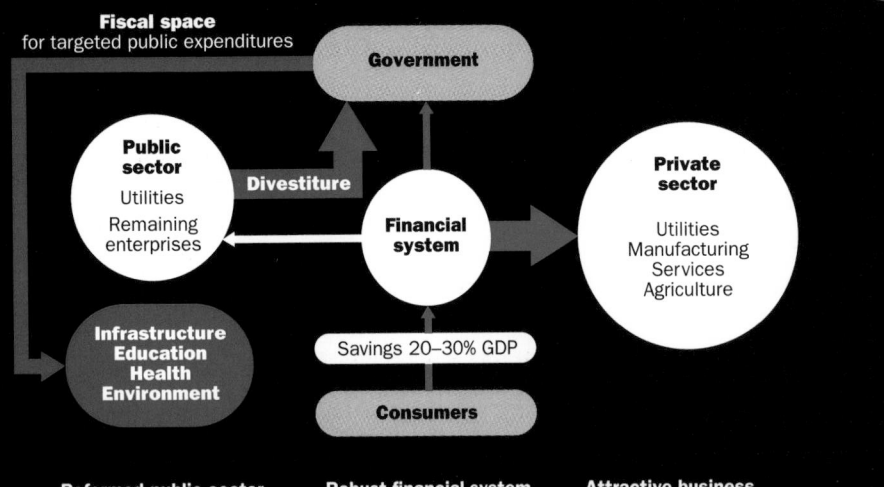

Fiscal space
for targeted public expenditures

Government

Public sector
Utilities
Remaining enterprises

Divestiture

Financial system

Private sector
Utilities
Manufacturing
Services
Agriculture

Infrastructure Education Health Environment

Savings 20–30% GDP

Consumers

Reformed public sector
- Rationalize subsidies; target them to poor
- Sell large public enterprises on a priority basis; use sales proceeds to retire debt
- Attract private sector utilities (requires pricing reform, competition, and regulation)
- Operate remaining public enterprises on commercial basis
- Prune public expenditures and focus them on public goods

Robust financial system
- Cut off nonperforming borrowers—public and private—from further credit; make a vigorous collection effort
- Privatize banks and allow new entry by reputable banks where appropriate
- Build payment systems
- Strengthen prudential regulation and supervision
- Serve small savers and borrowers

Attractive business environment
- Reform legal and regulatory system
- Reform tax and customs administration
- Deregulate economy to complement liberalization of internal and external trade
- Promote foreign investment and regional integration
- Conduct these activities in partnership with the private sector and labor

Source: World Bank 1995e.

growing economies over the past 15 years have not relied on tax revenues from exports, and, seeing this pattern, many other countries have pulled down their export taxes. High export taxes—typically levied on primary products, particularly agriculture—are inadvisable because they reduce the incentive to export and encourage a shift to other crops. Similarly, high marginal income taxes tend to penalize work and savings (table 5.8). The progressivity of a tax system—as measured roughly by the highest marginal tax rate on individual and corporate income—can show how the tax system builds or reduces the incentives for succeeding on the job or in business. International investors, for example, use such data as an indicator of the hospitality of governments to their interests. Of course, considerations of equity and incentives need to be balanced in a tax policy geared to socially sustainable development.

The overall incentive framework determines how private investors see risk, perceptions that usually are highly subjective. To get a handle on the reality a country faces in trying to attract private capital, country risk ratings take account of objective indicators as well as policies and prevailing prejudices (table 5.9).

Putting support systems in place

An efficient and vibrant financial system is an important precondition for private sector development. It mobilizes savings and allocates them to investments by private entrepreneurs (table 5.10). It links savers and borrowers, manages risk, and operates the payment and settlement systems. And it helps shift resources from declining to dynamic sectors.

Yet in many developing economies, particularly the poorest, inappropriate policies have hobbled fledgling financial systems. Large budget deficits were monetized, and inflation flowered. To keep nominal rates from rising, governments controlled interest rates. The resulting reduction in real rates reduced incentives for the formal banking system to intermediate savings, encouraging capital flight and overborrowing. This neutralized commercial banks, and credit was allocated by government decree. Banks lost their ability to screen and assess credit risks, and central banks allowed their oversight functions to wither.

The unhappy outcomes? Bad loans accumulated, and the losses were periodically covered by printing money. Weak financial sectors are proving a threat to middle-income countries trying to attract large private capital flows.

Financial reforms are now at the top of the agenda for economic reform in many countries. Measures include stopping the hemorrhaging of public enterprises, privatizing banks when appropriate, improving bank management, and strengthening bank supervision.

Infrastructure is a second key support system for private sector growth. The quality and adequacy of infrastructure services are important determinants of how successful firms are in delivering products and services of high quality at low prices in the shortest possible time (tables 5.11 and 5.12). Poor infrastructure increases private costs by increasing investment and transactions costs and restricting access to domestic and international markets.

Low-income countries have improved their infrastructure but are far behind middle-income countries. In Sub-Saharan Africa telecommunications coverage is among the lowest in the world, averaging 11 lines per 1,000 people compared with 34 in East Asia and the Pacific and 91 in Latin America. Indeed, there are more telephones in Tokyo than in the whole of Sub-Saharan Africa. National transport systems also fail to deliver the logistical support needed by private firms, and poorly maintained roads add to excessive freight costs.

Private sector growth is also enhanced by expediting access to technology (table 5.13). Technology is the knowledge that leads to improved machinery products and processes. It is embodied in imported inputs and capital goods, sold directly through licensing agreements, and transmitted through foreign direct investment. The ability to assimilate technology is a function of the pool of trained manpower and investments in research and development, but public spending on research and development has often been wasteful and misdirected. Information technology is now at the vanguard of technological change, with countries rapidly expanding their use of computers and tapping the World Wide Web (table 5.14).

The shift in emphasis from states to markets constitutes a tall agenda requiring simultaneous and difficult actions in many areas over long periods (figure 5b). Future editions of the *World Development Indicators* should enrich our capacity to monitor these trends further, as data coverage and quality improve, particularly in the area of institutional development.

	Private investment		Foreign direct investment				Credit to private sector		Private non-guaranteed debt		Central government expenditure	
	% of gross domestic fixed investment		% of gross domestic investment		% of GDP		% of GDP		% of external debt		% of GDP	
	1980	1995	1980	1995	1980	1995	1980	1995	1980	1995	1980	1995
Albania	..	..	..	19.4	..	3.2	..	4.1	..	0.0	..	34.1
Algeria	..	..	2.1	0.0	0.8	0.0	42.2	5.2	0.0	0.0	..	..
Angola	..	..	..	39.4	..	10.7	..	..	0.0	0.0	..	..
Argentina	..	..	3.5	1.1	0.9	0.5	25.4	18.3	24.3	12.6	18.2	..
Armenia	..	..	..	4.3	..	0.4	..	7.3	..	0.0	..	..
Australia	..	..	..	..	..	..	51.9	75.5	..	..	22.7	27.6
Austria	..	..	..	..	..	..	75.8	94.8	..	..	37.4	40.5
Azerbaijan	..	..	..	19.9	..	3.2	..	1.0	..	0.0	..	..
Bangladesh	58.9	55.0	0.0	0.0	0.0	0.0	8.1	21.0	0.0	0.0	10.0	..
Belarus	..	..	..	0.4	..	0.1	..	6.2	..	0.0	..	..
Belgium	..	..	..	..	..	..	29.3	65.5	..	..	51.0	50.4
Benin	..	33.6	1.9	1.7	0.3	0.3	28.6	8.9	0.0	0.0	..	..
Bolivia	51.3	40.2	10.3	2.5	1.5	2.4	15.5	52.8	3.4	4.5	..	23.1
Bosnia and Herzegovina	..	..	..	..	..	..	..	..	..	0.0	..	..
Botswana	..	..	30.6	6.5	11.5	1.6	12.1	13.2	0.0	0.0	34.0	46.2
Brazil	72.0	76.2	3.5	3.2	0.8	0.7	42.5	34.8	23.2	20.0	20.2	37.4
Bulgaria	..	..	0.0	5.2	0.0	1.1	..	..	0.0	0.0	..	43.1
Burkina Faso	..	..	0.0	0.2	0.0	0.0	16.7	6.9	0.0	0.0	12.2	..
Burundi	..	..	0.0	1.7	0.0	0.2	9.8	19.8	0.0	0.0	21.5	..
Cambodia	..	..	..	15.0	..	5.4	..	4.1	0.0	0.0	..	..
Cameroon	..	..	9.2	8.9	1.9	1.3	29.5	9.0	6.9	2.1	15.7	15.9
Canada	..	..	..	..	..	..	73.6	81.4	..	..	21.3	..
Central African Republic	..	..	9.0	3.3	0.6	0.3	13.9	4.1	0.0	0.0	22.0	..
Chad	..	..	0.0	13.3	0.0	0.6	24.4	4.9	0.0	0.0	..	..
Chile	67.6	80.4	3.1	10.4	0.8	2.5	46.8	52.7	38.8	44.7	28.0	19.2
China	..	..	0.0	12.7	0.0	5.1	53.4	88.6	0.0	0.9	..	9.4
Colombia	58.3	59.7	2.5	16.4	0.5	3.3	30.5	40.6	7.4	12.1	13.4	14.5
Congo	..	..	6.6	0.2	2.3	0.0	15.5	7.9	0.0	0.0	49.4	..
Costa Rica	61.3	79.4	4.1	16.8	1.1	4.3	27.9	13.4	15.0	5.6	25.1	28.4
Côte d'Ivoire	53.2	64.1	3.5	1.4	0.9	0.2	40.8	20.2	27.0	14.0	31.7	..
Croatia	..	..	..	3.2	..	0.4	..	33.8	..	34.3	..	46.5
Cuba	..	..	..	..	..	..	..	..	..	..	..	..
Czech Republic	..	..	0.0	23.2	0.0	5.7	..	67.5	0.0	11.4	..	42.0
Denmark	..	..	..	..	..	..	42.1	32.6	..	..	39.3	43.5
Dominican Republic	68.4	54.1	5.6	12.2	1.4	2.4	30.8	26.7	12.7	0.5	16.9	17.1
Ecuador	59.7	60.9	2.3	14.0	0.6	2.6	22.8	34.3	18.7	3.2	14.2	15.7
Egypt, Arab Rep.	30.1	58.7	8.7	7.5	2.4	1.3	15.2	47.1	1.4	0.9	45.6	42.8
El Salvador	47.5	79.9	1.3	2.1	0.2	0.4	33.6	35.5	17.6	0.2	17.1	14.5
Eritrea	..	..	..	..	..	..	..	..	..	..	..	..
Estonia	..	..	..	17.9	..	5.0	..	14.6	..	1.8	..	31.9
Ethiopia	..	..	0.0	0.8	0.0	0.1	20.1	16.0	0.0	0.0	19.6	27.4
Finland	..	..	..	..	..	..	48.5	64.5	..	..	28.2	43.8
France	..	..	..	..	..	..	104.8	85.8	..	..	39.5	46.4
Gabon	..	..	2.7	-4.1	0.7	-1.1	15.8	8.4	0.0	0.0	36.5	..
Gambia, The	..	..	0.0	13.1	0.0	2.6	24.2	9.8	0.0	0.0	32.2	20.4
Georgia	..	..	..	0.0	..	0.0	..	..	..	0.0	..	..
Germany	..	..	..	..	..	..	..	99.7	..	..	..	33.8
Ghana	..	27.4	6.4	19.6	0.4	3.6	2.2	5.2	0.7	0.5	10.9	20.6
Greece	..	..	5.9	6.2	1.7	1.2	53.2	43.7	..	..	35.5	43.1
Guatemala	63.8	84.1	8.9	3.0	1.4	0.5	16.2	19.5	24.2	4.3	12.1	8.9
Guinea	..	55.4	..	6.4	..	0.9	..	5.0	0.0	0.0	..	..
Guinea-Bissau	..	..	0.0	2.4	0.0	0.4	..	7.3	0.0	0.0	..	..
Haiti	..	..	5.3	7.3	0.9	0.1	19.6	16.5	0.0	0.0	17.4	..
Honduras	..	..	0.9	5.6	0.2	1.3	28.8	24.9	13.0	2.5	..	..
Hong Kong	..	..	..	..	..	..	22.4	..	..	..	..	..

	Private investment		Foreign direct investment				Credit to private sector		Private non-guaranteed debt		Central government expenditure	
	% of gross domestic fixed investment		% of gross domestic investment		% of GDP		% of GDP		% of external debt		% of GDP	
	1980	1995	1980	1995	1980	1995	1980	1995	1980	1995	1980	1995
Hungary	..	..	0.0	44.0	0.0	10.3	*48.3*	*26.2*	0.0	13.1	*56.2*	..
India	55.5	61.6	0.2	1.6	0.0	0.4	25.4	25.0	1.6	7.1	13.2	16.1
Indonesia	*56.5*	76.0	0.9	5.8	0.2	2.2	8.8	..	15.0	18.7	22.1	*16.3*
Iran, Islamic Rep.	52.3	61.0	0.0	..	0.0	..	43.8	23.2	0.0	1.4	35.7	*25.2*
Iraq	..	..	..	..	0.0	..	..	..	..	..	..	..
Ireland	..	..	..	..	..	..	44.0	54.8	..	..	45.0	*42.6*
Israel	..	..	..	..	..	..	68.3	66.8	..	..	70.2	44.8
Italy	..	..	..	..	..	..	36.4	..	..	..	41.0	*49.9*
Jamaica	..	..	6.6	21.8	1.0	3.8	21.9	31.6	3.9	3.0	41.5	..
Japan	..	..	..	..	..	..	132.7	210.1	..	..	18.4	23.8
Jordan	..	..	..	*0.2*	..	*0.0*	..	71.6	0.0	0.0	..	*30.7*
Kazakstan	..	..	..	8.1	..	1.3	..	7.1	..	1.8	..	..
Kenya	54.8	49.6	3.7	1.8	1.1	0.4	29.5	33.8	12.9	6.0	25.2	*27.5*
Korea, Dem. Rep.	..	..	..	..	..	..	..	..	..	..	..	..
Korea, Rep.	75.7	73.8	..	..	..	..	50.9	69.9	..	..	17.0	17.7
Kuwait	..	..	..	..	..	..	41.6	22.4	..	..	27.8	51.4
Kyrgyz Republic	..	..	..	3.2	..	0.5	..	..	..	0.0	..	..
Lao PDR	..	..	..	..	..	5.0	..	9.1	0.0	0.0	..	..
Latvia	..	..	..	14.3	..	3.0	..	7.4	..	0.0	..	30.3
Lebanon	..	..	..	*0.3*	..	0.3	..	57.7	0.0	1.7	..	*35.1*
Lesotho	..	..	3.2	2.6	1.4	2.2	9.8	19.8	0.0	0.0	..	47.3
Libya	..	..	−13.9	..	−3.1	..	11.2	..	..	..	..	..
Lithuania	..	..	..	4.8	..	1.0	..	17.2	..	0.0	..	27.4
Macedonia, FYR	..	..	..	0.0	..	0.0	..	..	..	23.8	..	..
Madagascar	..	53.3	−0.2	2.7	0.0	0.3	19.2	11.5	0.0	0.0	..	17.2
Malawi	21.4	14.1	3.3	0.5	0.8	0.1	20.7	7.8	0.0	0.0	34.6	..
Malaysia	62.6	65.1	12.5	16.8	3.8	6.8	49.9	129.5	18.9	32.7	28.5	23.0
Mali	..	51.7	0.7	0.2	0.1	0.0	23.8	10.7	0.0	0.0	21.3	..
Mauritania	..	..	10.5	1.9	3.8	0.3	31.0	22.7	0.0	0.0	..	..
Mauritius	*61.4*	62.0	0.4	1.5	0.1	0.4	21.6	48.3	5.1	14.8	27.3	23.3
Mexico	56.1	80.7	4.1	18.2	1.1	2.8	19.7	41.0	12.7	11.2	16.8	*16.8*
Moldova	..	..	..	27.1	..	1.8	..	5.0	..	0.0	..	..
Mongolia	..	..	0.0	..	0.0	1.2	..	13.3	..	0.0	..	23.6
Morocco	53.1	37.3	2.0	4.3	0.5	0.9	27.0	48.9	1.6	1.5	33.1	..
Mozambique	..	..	0.0	3.7	0.0	2.5	..	..	0.0	0.8	..	..
Myanmar	..	..	..	..	..	..	5.5	..	0.0	0.0	15.9	*11.0*
Namibia	40.7	61.0	0.0	*8.9*	0.0	1.5	..	56.9	..	..	..	*40.7*
Nepal	..	70.6	0.0	0.8	0.0	0.2	8.6	*18.6*	0.0	0.0	14.3	17.5
Netherlands	..	..	..	..	..	..	93.6	98.6	..	..	53.0	50.8
New Zealand	..	..	..	..	..	..	18.3	89.8	..	..	38.1	36.1
Nicaragua	..	..	0.0	*11.7*	0.0	3.7	48.3	36.0	0.0	0.0	30.5	32.8
Niger	..	..	5.3	*0.8*	1.9	0.1	16.9	4.5	35.3	8.2	18.4	..
Nigeria	30.8	..	−3.6	..	−0.8	2.4	12.1	7.8	12.3	0.9	..	..
Norway	..	..	..	..	..	..	51.5	72.1	..	..	34.6	*41.1*
Oman	..	..	7.3	*6.8*	1.6	1.2	13.7	29.2	0.0	0.1	38.5	42.3
Pakistan	*42.7*	52.8	1.4	3.5	0.3	0.7	24.0	27.1	0.2	5.3	17.5	23.2
Panama	59.3	84.0	..	12.6	−1.3	3.0	61.6	82.3	0.0	0.0	32.3	*28.2*
Papua New Guinea	58.6	79.6	11.8	38.3	3.0	9.2	17.6	19.6	19.3	28.4	34.4	*29.4*
Paraguay	82.1	76.9	2.2	9.8	0.7	2.6	18.4	21.8	15.8	0.7	9.8	*13.0*
Peru	*70.6*	81.3	0.5	19.6	0.1	3.3	12.9	15.3	6.5	4.1	19.4	19.0
Philippines	68.9	80.1	−1.1	8.9	−0.3	2.0	42.2	45.0	14.1	9.0	13.4	*18.4*
Poland	..	..	0.1	17.0	0.0	3.1	6.4	12.8	0.0	2.4	..	43.4
Portugal	..	..	..	..	..	..	54.4	58.3	..	..	33.3	*42.5*
Puerto Rico	..	..	..	..	..	..	..	..	..	..	..	..
Romania	..	..	..	4.6	..	1.2	..	..	0.0	6.3	44.7	*31.9*
Russian Federation	..	..	..	2.3	..	0.6	..	7.6	0.0	0.0	..	22.2

	Private investment		Foreign direct investment				Credit to private sector		Private non-guaranteed debt		Central government expenditure	
	% of gross domestic fixed investment		% of gross domestic investment		% of GDP		% of GDP		% of external debt		% of GDP	
	1980	1995	1980	1995	1980	1995	1980	1995	1980	1995	1980	1995
Rwanda	..	..	8.7	0.7	1.4	0.1	5.7	8.8	0.0	0.0	14.4	24.2
Saudi Arabia	..	..	-9.4	1.5	-2.0	-1.5	22.8	63.7	..	..	..	..
Senegal	..	..	3.3	0.1	0.5	0.0	42.3	14.7	0.6	1.1	23.1	..
Sierra Leone	..	..	-9.2	2.1	-1.6	0.1	7.4	2.8	0.0	0.0	27.3	20.2
Singapore	..	..	..	..	..	..	81.0	106.7	..	..	20.0	17.7
Slovak Republic	..	..	..	3.7	..	1.1	..	27.7	0.0	1.5	..	..
Slovenia	..	..	..	4.2	..	0.9	..	27.3	..	42.3	..	..
South Africa	50.8	72.8	-0.1	0.0	0.0	0.0	60.3	130.6	..	..	22.2	33.3
Spain	..	..	..	..	..	..	78.2	74.0	..	..	26.7	39.4
Sri Lanka	41.2	0.2	3.2	1.9	1.1	0.5	17.2	26.7	0.2	1.1	41.3	28.3
Sudan	..	..	0.0	..	0.0	..	14.9	5.3	6.3	2.8	19.6	..
Sweden	..	..	..	..	..	..	78.0	107.9	..	..	39.4	45.0
Switzerland	..	..	..	..	..	..	114.9	172.2	..	..	20.3	27.1
Syrian Arab Republic	..	..	0.0	..	0.0	0.4	5.7	10.9	0.0	0.0	48.2	26.6
Tajikistan	..	..	..	4.3	..	0.8	..	..	..	0.0	..	..
Tanzania	..	..	1.1	13.1	0.3	4.2	2.6	8.9	3.4	0.6	27.9	..
Thailand	68.1	77.1	2.0	2.9	0.6	1.2	41.7	139.9	20.5	37.4	18.9	15.8
Togo	..	..	12.3	0.0	3.7	0.0	27.5	20.8	0.0	0.0	30.8	..
Trinidad and Tobago	..	..	9.7	39.5	3.0	5.6	28.7	43.6	0.0	3.5	30.3	..
Tunisia	46.9	52.7	9.0	6.1	2.7	1.5	46.4	68.4	5.1	1.9	31.6	..
Turkey	45.6	80.0	0.1	2.2	0.0	0.5	13.6	19.0	2.8	9.6	21.4	22.8
Turkmenistan	..	..	..	..	..	0.0	..	..	..	0.0	..	..
Uganda	..	..	0.0	13.1	0.0	2.1	3.9	4.1	0.0	0.0	6.1	..
Ukraine	..	..	..	..	..	0.3	..	0.0	..	1.0	..	..
United Arab Emirates	..	..	..	..	..	..	22.9	50.0	..	..	12.1	11.8
United Kingdom	..	..	..	..	..	..	27.6	118.2	..	..	38.3	41.8
United States	..	..	..	..	..	..	80.0	109.0	..	..	22.0	22.9
Uruguay	68.2	70.1	16.5	7.6	2.9	0.7	37.2	28.6	12.7	2.4	21.8	31.2
Uzbekistan	..	..	..	1.1	..	0.5	..	..	..	0.0	..	..
Venezuela	..	40.3	0.3	7.6	0.1	1.2	48.2	12.2	10.8	5.6	18.7	18.8
Vietnam	..	..	..	16.4	..	6.9	..	..	0.0	0.0	..	..
West Bank and Gaza	..	..	..	..	..	..	..	..	..	..	..	..
Yemen, Rep.	..	..	..	3.1	..	0.0	..	5.5	0.0	0.0	..	38.4
Yugoslavia, Fed. Rep.[a]	..	..	..	..	..	..	..	..	..	..	..	..
Zaire	..	..	0.0	..	0.0	..	0.0	..	0.0	0.0	0.0	..
Zambia	..	..	6.9	13.8	1.6	1.6	19.9	7.2	2.7	0.2	37.2	16.8
Zimbabwe	..	..	0.2	2.2	0.0	0.6	18.6	35.3	0.0	7.8	34.9	..
World	..	..	..	..	..	..	..	..	..	..	..	..
Low income	..	..	..	..	..	..	..	..	4.8 w	2.7 w	..	..
Excl. China & India	..	..	..	..	..	..	..	..	..	..	..	..
Middle income	..	..	..	..	..	..	..	..	12.4 w	10.7 w	..	..
Lower middle income	..	..	..	..	..	..	..	..	..	..	..	..
Upper middle income	..	..	..	..	..	..	..	..	..	..	..	..
Low & middle income	..	..	..	..	..	..	..	..	..	..	..	..
East Asia & Pacific	..	..	..	..	..	..	..	..	13.5 w	14.3 w	..	..
Europe & Central Asia	..	..	..	..	..	..	..	..	13.1 w	4.8 w	..	..
Latin America & Carib.	..	..	..	..	..	..	..	..	16.5 w	12.6 w	..	..
Middle East & N. Africa	..	..	..	..	..	..	..	..	0.7 w	1.5 w	..	..
South Asia	..	..	..	..	..	..	..	..	0.9 w	5.3 w	..	..
Sub-Saharan Africa	..	..	..	..	..	..	..	..	5.4 w	3.1 w	..	..
High income	..	..	..	..	..	..	..	..	..	..	..	..

a. Data for 1980 refer to the former Yugoslavia.

How big should a government be?

And what should its role be in nurturing, regulating, or monitoring the functioning of markets? The model state for many classical economists and philosophers in the 19th century was a minimal one that left most activities to markets. In the 1870s governments were generally small: in what are today's major industrial countries government spending amounted to just over 8 percent of GDP. In 1994 government spending for the same countries averaged 47 percent of GDP, reflecting large increases in defense spending and the provision of goods and services, such as infrastructure, education, health care, and social safety nets (Tanzi and Schuknecht 1995). Developing countries generally have much smaller governments, largely reflecting a much smaller commitment to a welfare state.

Governments have two principal responsibilities: providing rules to make markets work efficiently and taking corrective actions when markets fail. These responsibilities encompass many of the traditional functions of the state: establishing law and order, ensuring property rights, and providing goods and services that the private sector cannot or will not provide, including universal education, public health services, and basic infrastructure.

The indicators in the table measure the relative size of the state and markets in the national economy. There is no ideal size for the state, and size alone does not capture its full effect on markets. Large states may support prosperous and effective markets; small states may be predatory toward markets. The resources of a large state may be used to correct genuine market failures in key areas—or merely to subsidize state enterprises making goods or providing services that the private sector might have produced more efficiently. A large share of private domestic investment in total investment may reflect a highly competitive and efficient private sector—or one that it is subsidized and protected. Thus, like other indicators in this volume, the indicators here provide an important but far from complete picture of what they measure—in this case the roles of states and markets.

About the data

Because data on subnational units of government—state, provincial, and municipal—are not readily available, the size of the public sector is measured here by the size of the central government. While the central government is usually the largest single economic agent in a country and typically accounts for most of the revenues, expenditures, and deficits of the public sector, in some countries state, provincial, and local governments are important participants in the economy. In addition, the activities covered under "central government" can vary depending on the accounting concept used (consolidated or budgetary). For most countries central government finance data have been consolidated into one overall account, but for others only budgetary central government accounts are available, which often omit the operations of state-owned enterprises (see *Primary data documentation*).

When direct estimates of private gross domestic fixed investment are not available, such investment is estimated residually as the difference between total gross domestic investment and consolidated public investment. Total investment may be estimated directly from surveys of enterprises and administrative records or indirectly using the commodity flow method. Consolidated measures of public investment may omit important subnational units of government. In addition, public investment data may include financial as well as physical capital investment. As the difference between two estimated quantities, private investment may be undervalued or overvalued and subject to large errors over time.

Statistics on foreign direct investment are based on balance of payments data reported by the International Monetary Fund (IMF), supplemented by data on net foreign direct investment reported by the OECD and official national sources. The data suffer from deficiencies relating to definitions, coverage, and cross-country comparability (see the notes to table 5.2 for a detailed discussion of data on foreign direct investment).

Data on domestic credit to the private sector are taken from the banking survey of the IMF's *International Financial Statistics* or, when the broader aggregate is not available, from its monetary survey. The monetary survey includes monetary authorities (the central bank) and deposit money banks. In addition to these, the banking survey includes other banking institutions such as savings and loan institutions, finance companies, and development banks. In some cases credit to the private sector may include credit to state-owned or partially state-owned enterprises.

Definitions

- **Private investment** covers outlays by the private sector (including private nonprofit agencies) on additions to its fixed assets. Gross domestic fixed investment includes similar outlays by the public sector.
- **Foreign direct investment** is net inflows of investment to acquire a lasting management interest (10 percent or more of voting stock) in an enterprise operating in an economy other than that of the investor. It is the sum of equity capital, reinvestment of earnings, other long-term capital, and short-term capital as shown in the balance of payments. Gross domestic investment is gross domestic fixed investment plus changes in stocks. ● **Credit to private sector** refers to financial resources provided to the private sector—such as through loans, purchases of nonequity securities, and trade credits and other accounts receivable—that establish a claim for repayment. For some countries these claims include credit to public enterprises. ● **Private nonguaranteed debt** consists of external obligations of private debtors that are not guaranteed for repayment by a public entity. Total external debt is the sum of public and publicly guaranteed long-term debt, private nonguaranteed long-term debt, IMF credit, and short-term debt. ● **Central government expenditure** comprises the expenditures of all government offices, departments, establishments, and other bodies that are agencies or instruments of the central authority of a country. It includes both current and capital (development) expenditures.

Data sources

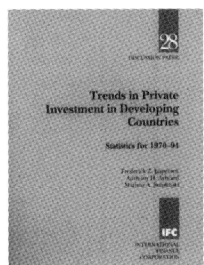

Private investment data are from the International Finance Corporation's *Trends in Private Investment in Developing Countries 1996*. Data on foreign direct investment are based on estimates compiled by the IMF in the *Balance of Payments Statistics Yearbook,* supplemented by World Bank staff estimates. Data on domestic credit are from the IMF's *International Financial Statistics,* and government expenditure data are from the IMF's *Government Finance Statistics Yearbook.* External debt figures are from the World Bank's Debtor Reporting System as reported in the World Bank's *Global Development Finance 1997* (formerly *World Debt Tables*).

	Net private capital flows		Foreign direct investment		Portfolio investment				Bank and trade-related lending	
					Bonds $ millions		Equity $ millions			
	$ millions		$ millions		$ millions		$ millions		$ millions	
	1990	1995	1990	1995	1990	1995	1990	1995	1990	1995
Albania	31	70	0	70	0	0	0	0	31	0
Algeria	-493	129	0	5	-15	-278	0	1	-477	401
Angola	195	523	-335	400	0	0	0	0	530	123
Argentina	-203	7,204	1,836	1,319	-857	4,906	13	211	-1,196	768
Armenia	0	8	0	8	0	0	0	0	0	0
Australia	..	..	..	..	..	..	..	..	..	..
Austria	..	..	..	..	..	..	..	..	..	..
Azerbaijan	0	110	0	110	0	0	0	0	0	0
Bangladesh	70	10	3	2	0	0	0	33	67	-25
Belarus	0	103	0	20	0	0	0	0	0	83
Belgium	..	..	..	..	..	..	..	..	..	..
Benin	1	1	1	1	0	0	0	0	0	0
Bolivia	-13	191	11	150	0	0	0	0	-24	41
Bosnia and Herzegovina	..	..	..	..	..	..	..	..	..	..
Botswana	77	64	95	70	0	0	0	0	-19	-6
Brazil	505	19,097	989	4,859	129	2,636	0	4,411	-613	7,190
Bulgaria	-42	489	4	135	65	-6	0	400	-111	-41
Burkina Faso	0	0	0	0	0	0	0	0	0	0
Burundi	-5	1	1	2	0	0	0	0	-6	-1
Cambodia	0	164	0	151	0	0	0	0	0	13
Cameroon	-124	49	-113	102	0	0	0	0	-12	-53
Canada	..	..	..	..	..	..	..	..	..	..
Central African Republic	0	3	1	3	0	0	0	0	-1	0
Chad	-1	7	0	7	0	0	0	0	-1	0
Chile	2,098	4,230	590	1,695	-7	489	320	274	1,194	1,772
China	8,107	44,339	3,487	35,849	-48	317	0	2,807	4,668	7,303
Colombia	363	3,741	500	2,501	-4	855	0	131	-133	254
Congo	-100	-49	0	1	0	0	0	0	-100	-50
Costa Rica	23	384	163	396	-42	-4	0	1	-99	-9
Côte d'Ivoire	57	36	48	19	-1	0	0	3	10	14
Croatia	0	346	0	81	0	0	0	0	0	265
Cuba	..	..	1	7	..	..	0	0	..	..
Czech Republic	843	5,596	207	2,568	0	38	0	82	636	2,907
Denmark	..	..	..	..	..	..	..	..	..	..
Dominican Republic	130	237	133	271	0	0	0	0	-3	-34
Ecuador	183	561	126	470	0	1	0	1	57	90
Egypt, Arab Rep.	698	294	734	598	-1	0	0	2	-35	-306
El Salvador	8	8	2	38	0	0	0	0	6	-30
Eritrea	..	..	..	..	..	..	..	..	..	..
Estonia	0	207	0	201	0	0	0	7	0	-1
Ethiopia[a]	-44	-42	12	7	0	0	0	0	-56	-49
Finland	..	..	..	..	..	..	..	..	..	..
France	..	..	..	..	..	..	..	..	..	..
Gabon	103	-125	74	-50	0	0	0	0	29	-75
Gambia, The	-7	10	0	10	0	0	0	0	-7	0
Georgia	0	0	0	0	0	0	0	0	0	0
Germany	..	..	..	..	..	..	..	..	..	..
Ghana	-5	525	15	230	0	0	0	267	-20	29
Greece	..	..	1,005	1,053	..	..	0	43	..	..
Guatemala	42	85	48	75	-11	46	0	0	5	-35
Guinea	-1	20	18	35	0	0	0	0	-19	-15
Guinea-Bissau	2	1	2	1	0	0	0	0	0	0
Haiti	8	2	8	2	0	0	0	0	0	0
Honduras	75	65	44	50	0	-13	0	0	31	28
Hong Kong	..	..	..	..	..	..	..	..	..	..

	Net private capital flows		Foreign direct investment		Portfolio investment				Bank and trade-related lending	
					Bonds $ millions		Equity $ millions			
	$ millions		$ millions						$ millions	
	1990	1995	1990	1995	1990	1995	1990	1995	1990	1995
Hungary	−308	7,841	0	4,519	921	2,094	150	483	−1,379	745
India	1,851	3,592	162	1,300	147	210	105	1,517	1,438	566
Indonesia	3,235	11,648	1,093	4,348	26	2,248	312	4,873	1,804	180
Iran, Islamic Rep.	−392	..	−362	17	0	0	0	0	−30	..
Iraq	..	..	0	0	..	..	0	0	..	..
Ireland	..	..	..	..	..	..	..	..	..	..
Israel	..	..	..	..	..	..	..	..	..	..
Italy	..	..	..	..	..	..	..	..	..	..
Jamaica	92	188	138	167	0	13	0	0	−46	8
Japan	..	..	..	..	..	..	..	..	..	..
Jordan	254	−143	38	43	0	0	0	11	216	−197
Kazakstan	0	500	0	284	0	0	0	0	0	216
Kenya	124	−42	57	32	0	0	0	0	67	−74
Korea, Dem. Rep.	..	..	0	1	..	..	0	0	..	..
Korea, Rep.	..	..	..	..	..	..	..	..	..	..
Kuwait	..	..	..	..	..	..	..	..	..	..
Kyrgyz Republic	0	15	0	15	0	0	0	0	0	0
Lao PDR	6	88	6	88	0	0	0	0	−1	0
Latvia	0	224	0	180	0	43	0	0	0	1
Lebanon	12	1,153	6	35	0	750	0	34	6	333
Lesotho	17	32	17	23	0	0	0	0	0	9
Libya	..	..	159	90	..	..	0	0	..	..
Lithuania	0	194	0	73	0	60	0	4	0	57
Macedonia, FYR	0	0	0	0	0	0	0	0	0	0
Madagascar	6	4	22	10	0	0	0	0	−16	−6
Malawi	−3	−14	0	1	0	0	0	0	−3	−15
Malaysia	1,799	11,924	2,333	5,800	−212	2,240	293	2,299	−614	1,585
Mali	−8	1	−7	1	0	0	0	0	−1	0
Mauritania	6	3	7	3	0	0	0	0	−1	0
Mauritius	85	304	41	15	0	150	0	4	44	135
Mexico	8,155	13,068	2,549	6,963	661	4,321	563	520	4,382	1,265
Moldova	0	79	0	64	0	0	0	0	0	15
Mongolia	16	−4	0	10	0	0	0	0	16	−14
Morocco	350	572	165	290	0	0	0	150	185	132
Mozambique	30	67	9	36	0	0	0	0	26	28
Myanmar	−3	61	5	10	0	0	0	16	−8	36
Namibia	..	..	29	47	..	..	0	0	..	..
Nepal	−9	−2	6	8	0	0	0	0	−15	−10
Netherlands	..	..	..	..	..	..	..	..	..	..
New Zealand	..	..	..	..	..	..	..	..	..	..
Nicaragua	21	−7	0	70	0	0	0	0	21	−77
Niger	9	−23	−1	1	0	0	0	0	10	−24
Nigeria	469	453	588	650	0	0	0	6	−119	−203
Norway	..	..	..	..	..	..	..	..	..	..
Oman	−259	126	141	150	0	0	0	5	−400	−28
Pakistan	182	1,443	244	409	0	0	0	729	−63	305
Panama	127	962	132	220	−2	0	0	20	−3	−12
Papua New Guinea	204	578	155	453	0	−32	0	450	49	−293
Paraguay	67	174	76	200	0	0	0	0	−9	−26
Peru	59	3,532	41	1,895	0	0	0	1,611	18	26
Philippines	639	4,605	530	1,478	395	1,060	0	1,961	−286	449
Poland	71	5,058	89	3,659	0	250	0	921	−18	228
Portugal	..	..	..	..	..	..	..	..	..	..
Puerto Rico	..	..	..	..	..	..	..	..	..	..
Romania	4	687	0	419	0	0	0	1	4	267
Russian Federation	5,604	1,116	0	2,017	310	−810	0	141	5,294	−232

	Net private capital flows		Foreign direct investment		Portfolio investment				Bank and trade-related lending	
					Bonds $ millions		Equity $ millions			
	$ millions		$ millions						$ millions	
	1990	1995	1990	1995	1990	1995	1990	1995	1990	1995
Rwanda	6	1	8	1	0	0	0	0	-2	0
Saudi Arabia	..	..	1,864	-1,877	..	..	0	0	..	..
Senegal	42	-24	57	1	0	0	0	0	-15	-25
Sierra Leone	36	-28	32	1	0	0	0	0	4	-29
Singapore	..	..	..	..	..	..	..	..	..	..
Slovak Republic	278	653	0	183	0	0	0	60	278	410
Slovenia	0	838	0	176	0	0	0	0	0	662
South Africa	..	..	-5	3	..	..	0	4,571	..	..
Spain	..	..	..	..	..	..	..	..	..	..
Sri Lanka	54	140	43	63	0	0	0	61	11	15
Sudan	0	0	0	0	0	0	0	0	0	0
Sweden	..	..	..	..	..	..	..	..	..	..
Switzerland	..	..	..	..	..	..	..	..	..	..
Syrian Arab Republic	18	43	71	65	0	0	0	0	-53	-22
Tajikistan	0	15	0	15	0	0	0	0	0	0
Tanzania	5	137	0	150	0	0	0	0	5	-13
Thailand	4,498	9,143	2,444	2,068	-87	2,023	449	2,154	1,692	2,898
Togo	0	0	0	0	0	0	0	0	0	0
Trinidad and Tobago	-69	271	109	299	-52	97	0	0	-126	-125
Tunisia	-122	751	76	264	-60	588	0	0	-138	-102
Turkey	1,736	2,000	684	885	597	616	35	630	420	-131
Turkmenistan	0	20	0	0	0	0	0	0	0	20
Uganda	16	112	0	121	0	0	0	0	16	-10
Ukraine	0	247	0	267	0	0	0	0	0	-20
United Arab Emirates	..	..	..	..	..	..	..	..	..	..
United Kingdom	..	..	..	..	..	..	..	..	..	..
United States	..	..	..	..	..	..	..	..	..	..
Uruguay	-192	217	0	124	-16	63	0	4	-176	26
Uzbekistan	0	235	0	115	0	0	0	0	0	120
Venezuela	-133	848	451	900	345	-328	0	7	-929	-110
Vietnam	18	1,487	16	1,400	0	0	0	155	2	-67
West Bank and Gaza	..	..	..	..	..	..	..	..	..	..
Yemen, Rep.	30	-2	-131	0	0	0	0	0	161	-2
Yugoslavia, Fed. Rep.[b]	..	..	..	..	..	..	0	0	..	..
Zaire	-24	1	-12	1	0	0	0	0	-12	0
Zambia	194	30	203	66	0	0	0	0	-9	-36
Zimbabwe	85	99	-12	40	-30	-30	0	18	128	71

World	..	..	..	..	..	..	..	..	..	..
Low income	11,415 t	53,446 t	4,509 t	41,570 t	67 t	483 t	105 t	5,611 t	6,734 t	5,782 t
Excl. China & India	..	..	..	..	..	..	..	..	..	..
Middle income	31,962 t	130,742 t	20,040 t	53,919 t	2,255 t	28,025 t	2,134 t	26,476 t	7,533 t	22,322 t
Lower middle income	..	..	..	..	..	..	..	..	..	..
Upper middle income	..	..	..	..	..	..	..	..	..	..
Low & middle income	43,377 t	184,188 t	24,549 t	95,489 t	2,322 t	28,508 t	2,239 t	32,087 t	14,267 t	28,104 t
East Asia & Pacific	19,323 t	84,137 t	10,179 t	51,776 t	75 t	7,856 t	1,750 t	14,714 t	7,319 t	9,791 t
Europe & Central Asia	9,514 t	30,059 t	2,102 t	17,215 t	3,089 t	5,290 t	235 t	2,772 t	4,088 t	4,782 t
Latin America & Carib.	12,483 t	54,261 t	8,121 t	22,897 t	101 t	13,114 t	1,099 t	7,190 t	3,162 t	11,060 t
Middle East & N. Africa	609 t	1,414 t	2,757 t	-347 t	-148 t	1,060 t	0 t	202 t	-2,000 t	499 t
South Asia	2,152 t	5,191 t	464 t	1,791 t	147 t	210 t	105 t	2,340 t	1,436 t	850 t
Sub-Saharan Africa	247 t	9,128 t	926 t	2,157 t	-941 t	978 t	0 t	4,868 t	262 t	1,125 t
High income	..	..	..	..	..	..	..	..	..	..

Note: Totals for low- and middle-income economies may not add up to regional totals due to unallocated amounts. a. Includes Eritrea. b. Data for 1990 refer to the former Yugoslavia.

The data on foreign direct investment (FDI) are based on balance of payments data reported by the International Monetary Fund (IMF), supplemented by data on net foreign direct investment reported by the OECD and official national sources. The data suffer from deficiencies relating to definitions, coverage, and cross-country comparability.

The internationally accepted definition of FDI is that provided in the fifth edition of the IMF's *Balance of Payments Manual* (1993). To ensure a common definition of FDI, the OECD has also published a definition, in consultation with the IMF, Eurostat, and the United Nations. Both definitions describe FDI as having three components: equity investments, reinvested earnings, and short- and long-term intercompany loans between parent firms and foreign affiliates. But many economies report data that exclude at least one of these components—often reinvested earnings—and that can lead to serious underestimation. In addition, the definition of "long-term" differs among economies. And the balance of payments data on FDI do not include capital raised in the host economies, which has become an important source of financing for FDI projects. Because of the widely differing definitions and collection methods used, relying on a variety of sources for FDI data can lead to very different results for a single economy. There is also increasing awareness that FDI data are limited because they capture only cross-border investment flows involving equity participation and omit nonequity cross-border transactions such as intrafirm flows of goods and services.

Despite the drawbacks, the data on FDI are invaluable for analytical purposes. For a detailed discussion of FDI data issues see the World Bank's *World Debt Tables 1993–94* (volume 1, chapter 3).

Portfolio flow data are compiled from several official and market sources, including Euromoney databases and publications, Micropal Inc., Lipper Analytical Services, published reports of private investment houses, central banks, national securities and exchange commissions, national stock exchanges, and the World Bank's Debtor Reporting System (DRS).

Gross statistics on international bond and equity issues are produced by aggregating individual transactions reported by market sources. The net values of public and publicly guaranteed bonds are reported through the DRS by member economies that have received either IBRD loans or IDA credits. Information on private nonguaranteed bonds is collected from market sources, since official national sources reporting to the DRS are not asked to report the breakdown between private nonguaranteed bonds and private nonguaranteed loans. Information on transactions by nonresidents in local equity markets is gathered from national authorities, investment positions of mutual funds, and market sources.

The volume of portfolio investment reported by the World Bank generally differs from that reported by other sources because of differences in the classification of economies, in the sources, and in the method used to adjust and disaggregate reported information (there are differences in particular with the balance of payments data reported by the IMF; see table 4.22). Differences in reporting arise particularly for foreign investments in local equity markets, where there is a lack of clarity, adequate disaggregation, and comprehensive and periodic reporting in many developing economies. By contrast, capital flows through international debt and equity instruments are well recorded, and the differences in reporting lie primarily in differences in the classification of economies, in the exchange rates used, in whether particular tranches of the transactions are included, or in the treatment of certain offshore issuances.

● **Net private capital flows** consist of private debt and nondebt flows. Private debt flows include commercial bank lending, bonds, and other private credits; nondebt private flows are foreign direct investment and portfolio equity investment. ● **Foreign direct investment** is net inflows of investment to acquire a lasting management interest (10 percent or more of voting stock) in an enterprise operating in an economy other than that of the investor. It is the sum of equity capital, reinvestment of earnings, other long-term capital, and short-term capital as shown in the balance of payments. ● **Portfolio investment flows** are net and include non-debt-creating portfolio equity flows (the sum of country funds, depository receipts, and direct purchases of shares by foreign investors) and portfolio debt flows (bond issues purchased by foreign investors). ● **Bank and trade-related lending** covers commercial bank lending and other private credits.

The principal source of information for the table is reports to the World Bank's DRS from member economies that have received IBRD loans or IDA credits. These data are compiled and published in the World Bank's annual *Global Development Finance* (formerly *World Debt Tables*). Additional information has been drawn from the data files of the World Bank and the IMF.

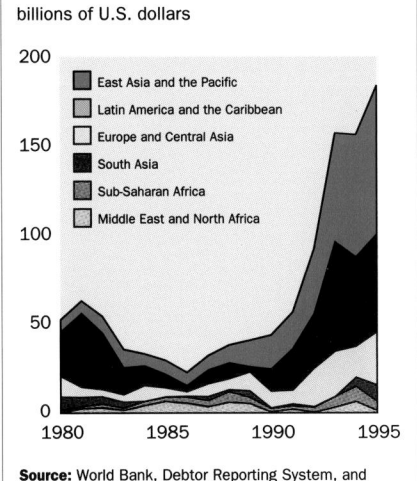

Figure 5.2a Net private capital flows to developing economies, by region, 1980—95

billions of U.S. dollars

- East Asia and the Pacific
- Latin America and the Caribbean
- Europe and Central Asia
- South Asia
- Sub-Saharan Africa
- Middle East and North Africa

Source: World Bank, Debtor Reporting System, and World Bank staff estimates.

5.3 | Stock markets

	Market capitalization				Value traded		Turnover ratio		Listed domestic companies		IFC Global Index price-earnings ratio	
	$ millions		% of GDP		% of GDP		value of shares traded as % of capitalization					
	1990	1995	1990	1995	1990	1995	1990	1995	1990	1995	1990	1995
Albania	..	..	..	..	..	..	..	..	..	..	..	..
Algeria	..	..	..	..	..	..	..	..	..	..	..	..
Angola	..	..	..	..	..	..	..	..	..	..	..	..
Argentina	3,268	37,783	2.3	13.5	0.6	1.6	22.7	12.3	179	149	–3.1	15.0
Armenia	..	3	..	0.1	..	0.0	..	66.7	..	1	..	..
Australia	107,611	245,218	36.4	70.3	13.3	28.1	31.6	42.2	1,089	1,178	..	..
Austria	11,476	32,513	7.2	13.9	11.7	11.0	110.3	82.1	97	109	..	..
Azerbaijan	..	..	..	..	..	..	..	..	..	..	..	..
Bangladesh	321	1,323	1.4	4.5	0.0	0.5	0.0	13.3	*138*	183	..	..
Belarus	..	..	..	..	..	..	..	..	..	..	..	..
Belgium	65,449	104,960	34.1	39.0	3.3	5.7	9.2	16.1	182	143	..	..
Benin	..	..	..	..	..	..	..	..	..	..	..	..
Bolivia	..	97	..	1.6	..	0.0	..	1.7	..	7	..	..
Bosnia and Herzegovina	..	..	..	..	..	..	..	..	..	..	..	..
Botswana	*261*	397	*7.1*	9.2	0.2	0.9	*6.1*	9.8	*9*	12	..	..
Brazil	16,354	147,636	3.4	21.8	1.2	11.7	18.4	47.0	581	543	4.7	36.3
Bulgaria	..	62	..	0.5	..	0.0	..	7.7	..	26	..	..
Burkina Faso	..	..	..	..	..	..	..	..	..	..	..	..
Burundi	..	..	..	..	..	..	..	..	..	..	..	..
Cambodia	..	..	..	..	..	..	..	..	..	..	..	..
Cameroon	..	..	..	..	..	..	..	..	..	..	..	..
Canada	241,920	366,344	42.6	64.4	12.5	32.3	26.7	53.9	1,144	1,196	..	..
Central African Republic	..	..	..	..	..	..	..	..	..	..	..	..
Chad	..	..	..	..	..	..	..	..	..	..	..	..
Chile	13,645	73,860	44.9	120.8	2.6	18.1	6.7	15.6	215	284	7.9	17.2
China	*2,028*	42,055	*0.5*	6.0	0.2	7.1	*80.9*	116.3	*14*	323	..	16.7
Colombia	1,416	17,893	3.5	23.5	0.2	1.6	5.6	7.9	80	190	8.4	11.3
Congo	..	..	..	..	..	..	..	..	..	..	..	..
Costa Rica	*311*	434	*5.5*	1.7	0.1	*0.0*	5.8	4.6	*82*	118	..	..
Côte d'Ivoire	549	867	5.1	8.6	0.2	0.1	3.3	2.2	23	31	..	..
Croatia	..	581	..	3.2	..	0.3	..	8.6	..	61	..	..
Cuba	..	..	..	..	..	..	..	..	..	..	..	..
Czech Republic	..	15,664	..	35.0	..	8.1	..	33.6	..	1,635	..	11.2
Denmark	39,063	56,223	30.3	32.6	8.6	15.1	28.0	46.9	258	213	..	..
Dominican Republic	..	..	..	..	0.0	0.4	..	..	..	..	..	..
Ecuador	*69*	2,627	*0.5*	14.6	0.0	0.4	*0.0*	2.1	*65*	65	..	..
Egypt, Arab Rep.	1,765	8,088	5.0	17.1	0.4	1.4	7.3	11.0	573	746	..	..
El Salvador	..	..	..	..	..	..	..	..	..	..	..	..
Eritrea	..	..	..	..	..	..	..	..	..	..	..	..
Estonia	..	..	..	..	..	..	..	..	..	..	..	..
Ethiopia	..	..	..	..	..	..	..	..	..	..	..	..
Finland	22,721	44,138	16.9	35.2	2.9	15.2	14.7	46.1	73	73	..	..
France	314,384	522,053	26.3	34.0	9.8	47.5	34.4	149.8	578	450	..	..
Gabon	..	..	..	..	..	..	..	..	..	..	..	..
Gambia, The	..	..	..	..	..	..	..	..	..	..	..	..
Georgia	..	..	..	..	..	..	..	..	..	..	..	..
Germany	355,073	577,365	*22.9*	23.9	22.1	47.5	139.3	218.9	413	678	..	..
Ghana	*76*	1,680	*1.1*	26.6	0.0	0.3	*0.0*	1.2	*13*	19	..	..
Greece	15,228	17,060	22.9	18.8	5.9	6.7	36.3	38.1	145	212	16.7	10.5
Guatemala	..	..	..	..	..	..	..	..	..	..	..	..
Guinea	..	..	..	..	..	..	..	..	..	..	..	..
Guinea-Bissau	..	..	..	..	..	..	..	..	..	..	..	..
Haiti	..	..	..	..	..	..	..	..	..	..	..	..
Honduras	*40*	338	*1.3*	8.6	..	3.3	*0.0*	67.2	*26*	99	..	..
Hong Kong	83,397	303,705	111.5	211.4	46.3	74.4	43.1	37.3	284	518	..	..

	Market capitalization				Value traded		Turnover ratio		Listed domestic companies		IFC Global Index price-earnings ratio	
	$ millions		% of GDP		% of GDP		value of shares traded as % of capitalization					
	1990	1995	1990	1995	1990	1995	1990	1995	1990	1995	1990	1995
Hungary	505	2,399	1.5	5.4	0.4	0.8	46.3	17.7	21	42	..	12.0
India	38,567	127,199	12.9	39.2	7.3	4.2	66.5	10.8	6,200	7,985	17.8	14.2
Indonesia	8,081	66,585	7.1	33.6	3.5	7.3	77.3	25.3	125	238	20.3	21.4
Iran, Islamic Rep.	34,282	6,561	28.0	..	4.3	..	30.4	15.9	97	169	..	..
Iraq	..	..	..	..	..	..	..	..	..	..	..	..
Ireland	..	25,817	..	42.5	..	21.8	..	77.4	..	80	..	..
Israel	3,324	36,399	6.0	39.6	10.1	10.0	95.8	26.5	216	654	..	..
Italy	148,766	209,522	13.6	19.3	3.9	8.0	26.8	44.6	220	250	..	..
Jamaica	911	1,391	21.4	31.6	0.8	7.7	3.4	21.7	44	51	..	..
Japan	2,917,679	3,667,292	98.2	71.8	54.0	24.1	43.8	33.3	2,071	2,263	..	..
Jordan	2,001	4,670	49.8	75.2	10.1	10.3	19.6	11.2	105	97	7.8	18.2
Kazakstan	..	..	..	..	..	..	..	..	..	..	..	..
Kenya	453	1,889	5.3	20.8	0.1	0.7	2.1	2.6	54	56	..	..
Korea, Dem. Rep.	..	..	..	..	..	..	..	..	..	..	..	..
Korea, Rep.	110,594	181,955	43.6	39.9	29.9	40.7	60.4	99.1	669	721	16.5	19.8
Kuwait	..	13,623	..	51.1	..	24.0	0.0	52.9	..	52	..	..
Kyrgyz Republic	..	..	..	..	..	..	..	..	..	..	..	..
Lao PDR	..	..	..	..	..	..	..	..	..	..	..	..
Latvia	..	..	..	..	..	..	..	..	..	..	..	..
Lebanon	..	..	..	..	..	..	..	..	..	..	..	..
Lesotho	..	..	..	..	..	..	..	..	..	..	..	..
Libya	..	..	..	..	..	..	..	..	..	..	..	..
Lithuania	..	158	..	2.0	..	0.5	..	37.2	..	351	..	..
Macedonia, FYR	..	..	..	..	..	..	..	..	..	..	..	..
Madagascar	..	..	..	..	..	..	..	..	..	..	..	..
Malawi	..	..	..	..	..	..	..	..	..	..	..	..
Malaysia	48,611	222,729	113.6	261.1	25.4	90.0	24.6	36.4	282	529	23.6	25.1
Mali	..	..	..	..	..	..	..	..	..	..	..	..
Mauritania	..	..	..	..	..	..	..	..	..	..	..	..
Mauritius	268	1,381	10.1	35.2	0.2	1.8	4.5	4.8	13	28	..	..
Mexico	32,725	90,694	13.2	36.3	4.9	13.7	44.2	31.1	199	185	10.3	28.4
Moldova	..	..	..	..	..	..	..	..	..	..	..	..
Mongolia	..	..	..	..	..	..	..	..	..	..	..	..
Morocco	966	4,376	3.7	14.4	0.2	2.6	0.0	0.0	71	51	..	..
Mozambique	..	..	..	..	..	..	..	..	..	..	..	..
Myanmar	..	..	..	..	..	..	..	..	..	..	..	..
Namibia	21	189	0.8	6.2	0.0	0.1	0.0	1.7	3	10	..	..
Nepal	..	244	..	5.5	..	0.4	..	6.7	..	83	..	..
Netherlands	119,825	356,481	42.2	90.0	14.2	62.8	29.0	77.7	260	387	..	..
New Zealand	8,835	31,950	20.3	56.0	4.4	14.7	17.3	28.4	171	205	..	..
Nicaragua	..	..	..	..	..	..	..	..	..	..	..	..
Niger	..	..	..	..	..	..	..	..	..	..	..	..
Nigeria	1,372	2,033	4.2	7.6	0.0	0.1	0.9	0.6	131	181	6.0	12.5
Norway	26,130	44,587	22.7	30.5	12.1	16.7	54.4	60.3	112	151	..	..
Oman	945	1,980	9.0	16.4	1.1	1.8	12.3	11.5	55	80	..	..
Pakistan	2,850	9,286	7.1	15.3	0.6	5.3	8.7	29.8	487	764	7.0	15.0
Panama	226	831	3.8	11.2	0.0	0.1	0.9	1.2	13	16	..	..
Papua New Guinea	..	..	..	..	..	..	..	..	..	..	..	..
Paraguay	..	..	..	..	..	..	..	..	..	..	..	..
Peru	812	11,795	2.5	20.5	0.3	6.9	11.4	39.4	294	246	25.9	14.5
Philippines	5,927	58,859	13.4	79.3	2.7	19.9	13.6	25.8	153	205	11.3	19.0
Poland	144	4,564	0.2	3.9	0.0	2.4	38.9	72.7	9	65	..	7.0
Portugal	9,201	18,362	13.7	17.9	2.5	4.1	17.0	24.5	181	169	11.9	14.8
Puerto Rico	..	..	..	..	..	..	..	..	..	..	..	..
Romania	..	..	..	..	..	..	..	..	..	..	..	..
Russian Federation	..	15,863	..	4.6	..	0.1	..	2.0	43	170	..	..

	Market capitalization				Value traded		Turnover ratio		Listed domestic companies		IFC Global Index price-earnings ratio	
	$ millions		% of GDP		% of GDP		value of shares traded as % of capitalization					
	1990	1995	1990	1995	1990	1995	1990	1995	1990	1995	1990	1995
Rwanda	..	..	..	..	..	..	..	..	..	..	..	..
Saudi Arabia	..	40,961	..	32.6	..	4.9	..	15.6	..	69	..	..
Senegal	..	..	..	..	..	..	..	..	..	..	..	..
Sierra Leone	..	..	..	..	..	..	..	..	..	..	..	..
Singapore	34,308	148,004	94.0	176.8	55.6	72.2	57.8	42.8	150	212	..	..
Slovak Republic	..	1,235	..	7.1	..	4.8	..	71.5	..	18	..	..
Slovenia	..	302	..	1.6	..	1.9	..	77.0	24	17	..	..
South Africa	137,540	280,526	128.9	206.2	7.6	12.5	6.1	6.7	732	640	13.2	18.8
Spain	111,404	197,788	22.6	35.4	8.3	10.7	35.0	33.9	427	362	..	..
Sri Lanka	917	1,998	11.4	15.5	0.5	1.7	5.8	9.1	175	226	..	8.2
Sudan	..	..	..	..	..	..	..	..	..	..	..	..
Sweden	92,102	178,049	40.1	77.9	6.8	40.8	14.9	60.3	122	223	..	..
Switzerland	160,044	433,621	70.8	144.3	29.8	103.5	0.0	86.6	182	233	..	..
Syrian Arab Republic	..	..	..	..	..	..	..	..	..	..	..	..
Tajikistan	..	..	..	..	..	..	..	..	..	..	..	..
Tanzania	..	..	..	..	..	..	..	..	..	..	..	..
Thailand	23,896	141,507	27.9	84.7	26.7	34.1	92.4	41.8	214	416	8.7	21.7
Togo	..	..	..	..	..	..	..	..	..	..	..	..
Trinidad and Tobago	696	1,138	13.7	21.4	1.1	2.6	9.9	15.2	30	27	..	..
Tunisia	533	4,006	4.3	22.3	0.2	3.7	3.2	20.2	13	26	..	..
Turkey	19,065	20,772	12.7	12.6	3.9	31.2	45.2	242.5	110	205	13.2	8.5
Turkmenistan	..	..	..	..	..	..	..	..	..	..	..	..
Uganda	..	..	..	..	..	..	..	..	..	..	..	..
Ukraine	..	..	..	..	..	..	..	..	..	..	..	..
United Arab Emirates	..	..	..	..	..	..	..	..	..	..	..	..
United Kingdom	848,866	1,407,737	87.0	127.3	28.6	92.3	33.3	77.9	1,701	2,078	..	..
United States	3,059,434	6,857,622	55.7	98.6	31.9	73.5	53.4	85.7	6,599	7,671	..	..
Uruguay	38	170	0.5	1.1	0.0	0.1	0.0	0.0	36	21	..	..
Uzbekistan	..	..	..	..	..	..	..	..	..	..	..	..
Venezuela	8,361	3,655	17.2	4.9	4.6	0.7	45.4	13.1	76	90	26.0	12.0
Vietnam	..	..	..	..	..	..	..	..	..	..	..	..
West Bank and Gaza	..	..	..	..	..	..	..	..	..	..	..	..
Yemen, Rep.	..	..	..	..	..	..	..	..	..	..	..	..
Yugoslavia, Fed. Rep.	..	..	..	..	..	..	..	..	..	..	..	..
Zaire	..	..	..	..	..	..	..	..	..	..	..	..
Zambia	..	..	..	..	..	..	..	..	..	..	..	..
Zimbabwe	2,395	2,038	35.3	31.2	0.8	2.3	2.9	7.8	57	64	8.4	7.3

World	**9,393,545 t**	**17,781,749 t**							**28,918 t**	**38,825 t**		
Low income	47,424 t	190,953 t							7,127 t	10,015 t		
Excl. China & India	8,857 t	21,699 t							927 t	1,707 t		
Middle income	343,349 t	1,308,574 t							4,339 t	8,065 t		
Lower middle income	73,751 t	372,144 t							1,858 t	3,541 t		
Upper middle income	269,598 t	936,430 t							2,481 t	4,524 t		
Low & middle income	390,773 t	1,499,527 t							11,466 t	18,080 t		
East Asia & Pacific	86,515 t	531,735 t							774 t	1,711 t		
Europe & Central Asia	34,293 t	79,902 t							255 t	2,808 t		
Latin America & Carib.	78,506 t	390,235 t							1,748 t	2,088 t		
Middle East & N. Africa	6,210 t	66,266 t							817 t	1,187 t		
South Asia	42,655 t	140,050 t							6,862 t	9,241 t		
Sub-Saharan Africa	142,594 t	291,339 t							1,010 t	1,045 t		
High income	9,002,772 t	16,282,222 t							17,452 t	20,745 t		

World stock markets are booming

During 1990–95 world stock market capitalization rose from $9.4 trillion to $17.8 trillion, and developing economies increased their share in this capitalization from less than 4 percent to almost 8 percent. Emerging markets also saw an increase in the value of shares traded—from 3 percent of world trading in 1985 to 9 percent in 1995.

Part of the impetus for this growth has come from market liberalization. As these relative newcomers on the global economic stage have become more integrated with established world capital markets, they have reformed laws and regulations and removed capital controls and other barriers to foreign portfolio flows. Investors in industrial countries have responded with a substantial increase in portfolio flows to these markets (see table 5.2).

Opinion is divided on the importance of stock markets to economic growth. Some analysts view stock markets in developing countries as "casinos" with potentially negative consequences for growth. Others argue that stock markets have a positive effect on economic activity through the creation of liquidity.

Many profitable investments require a long-term commitment of capital, but investors typically are reluctant to relinquish control of their savings for long periods. Liquid equity markets make investment less risky and more attractive because they allow savers to acquire an asset and to sell it quickly and cheaply if they need access to their savings or wish to alter their portfolios. At the same time, companies enjoy permanent access to capital raised through equity issues. By facilitating longer-term, more profitable investments, liquid markets improve the allocation of capital and enhance prospects for economic growth. Further, by making investments less risky and more profitable, stock market liquidity can also lead to more savings and investment. Investors will come if they can leave.

But an increased return on investment may reduce overall savings, and reduced uncertainty may reduce precautionary savings. And since investors can leave when they want to, they may not bother to stay and exercise their rights as shareholders to improve corporate governance. Nevertheless, recent work suggests a strong correlation between stock market development and long-term growth (see the May 1996 issue of the *World Bank Economic Review*).

About the data

The level of stock market development in an economy is closely related to its overall level of development. At low levels of development, commercial banks tend to dominate the financial system. As economies grow, specialized financial intermediaries and equity markets develop.

Stock market size can be measured in a variety of ways, each of which may produce a different ranking among countries. Market capitalization in U.S. dollars gives the overall size, and the ratio to GDP the size relative to the economy. Market size is positively correlated with the ability to mobilize capital and diversify risk.

Market liquidity is measured by dividing the total value traded by GDP. This indicator complements the market capitalization ratio by showing whether market size is matched by trading. The turnover ratio—shares traded as a percentage of market capitalization—is also a measure of liquidity as well as of transactions costs. (High turnover is an indication of low transactions costs.) This indicator also complements the ratio of value traded to GDP, since turnover is related to the size of the market, and the value traded ratio to the size of the economy. A small, liquid market will have a high turnover ratio but a small value traded ratio. The number of domestic companies listed is also a useful indicator of the size of stock markets.

The price-earnings (P/E) ratio measures the current price or value of a stock divided by its latest earnings distribution. The average P/E ratios in the table are based on the International Finance Corporation's (IFC) Global Index for each market, and represent the market capitalization of the index divided by the earnings of companies in the index. (Average P/E ratios are unavailable for many countries.) If the P/E ratio of a stock is at a historic high, investors may believe that the price of the stock is likely to move downward, and the opposite if the P/E ratio is low. Thus the average P/E ratio is sometimes used as a leading indicator of the direction in which an economy is likely to turn.

Definitions

● **Market capitalization,** or market value, is the share price times the number of shares outstanding. ● **Value traded** refers to the total value of shares traded during the period. ● **Turnover ratio** is the total value of shares traded during the period divided by the average market capitalization for the period. Average market capitalization is calculated as the average of the end-of-period values for the current period and the previous period. ● **Listed domestic companies** are the domestically incorporated companies listed on the country's stock exchanges at the end of the year. Investment companies, mutual funds, and other collective investment vehicles are excluded. ● **IFC Global Index price-earnings ratio** is the total market capitalization divided by the total earnings of listed companies on a trailing 12-month basis. The ratios in the table reflect only the companies included in the IFC Global Index for each market.

Data sources

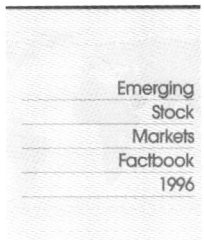

Data are from the IFC's *Emerging Stock Markets Factbook 1996*. The IFC collects data through an annual survey of the world's stock exchanges, supplemented by information provided by Reuters and the IFC's network of correspondents. GDP data are from the World Bank's national accounts data files. The feature text is based on Demirgüç-Kunt and Levine (1996b).

5.4 | State-owned enterprises

	Economic activity	Investment	Credit	Net financial flows from government	External debt	Overall balance before transfers	Employment	Proceeds from privatization
	% of GDP 1986–91	% of gross domestic investment 1986–91	% of gross domestic credit 1986–91	% of GDP 1986–91	% of GDP 1986–91	% of total 1986–91	% of total 1986–91	millions of 1995 $ 1989–95
Albania	..	..	..	..	..	..	..	22
Algeria	57.6	30.7	..	..	33.9	..	7.2 [a]	..
Angola	..	..	..	..	..	..	..	..
Argentina	4.7	8.5	..	2.7	7.3	–2.6	2.5	20,644
Armenia	..	..	..	..	..	..	..	..
Australia	..	14.7 [b]	..	..	..	..	..	..
Austria	13.9	..	..	..	..	..	..	..
Azerbaijan	..	..	..	..	..	..	..	..
Bangladesh	3.0 [a]	29.8	16.4	..	0.3	–3.0	..	55
Belarus	..	..	..	..	..	..	..	..
Belgium	2.8 [a]	7.0	..	..	..	..	..	..
Benin	..	15.8	..	..	21.5	..	..	63
Bolivia	13.7 [a]	26.9	..	–8.5 [a]	10.5	6.8 [a]	2.1 [a]	813
Bosnia and Herzegovina	..	..	..	..	..	..	..	..
Botswana	5.9	20.6	8.5	–12.7	26.0	–4.5	5.9	..
Brazil	8.6	15.2	20.5	–0.8 [b]	21.5	1.7 [b]	..	10,724
Bulgaria	..	..	..	..	..	..	..	321
Burkina Faso	..	..	..	–0.5	6.3	..	..	0
Burundi	7.3	40.3	22.1	2.1	0.3	..	32.5 [b,c]	5
Cambodia	..	..	..	..	..	..	..	..
Cameroon	18.0	..	..	1.2	17.4	..	10.0 [c]	..
Canada	..	..	..	..	..	..	..	..
Central African Republic	3.9	17.0	..	..	11.5	–3.5	..	..
Chad	..	..	..	..	..	..	..	..
Chile	12.9	19.1	2.2	–9.9	9.8	9.8	1.1 [a]	1,550
China	..	..	..	..	..	..	..	7,720
Colombia	6.7	12.0	4.4	–1.0	29.4	1.2	1.9	826
Congo	16.1 [a]	..	..	..	5.4	..	18.9 [a]	..
Costa Rica	8.2	8.4	..	–1.8	11.6	2.2	..	64
Côte d'Ivoire	..	21.0 [b]	..	..	7.1	..	20.8 [b,c]	168
Croatia	..	..	..	..	..	..	..	97
Cuba	..	..	..	..	..	..	..	..
Czech Republic	..	..	..	..	..	..	..	1,645
Denmark	5.1	13.5	..	..	..	..	..	..
Dominican Republic	..	10.6 [b]	14.2	..	7.9	..	..	..
Ecuador	10.5	13.4	0.0	0.2	8.5	–1.2	..	178
Egypt, Arab Rep.	30.0 [b]	63.3	21.3	0.2	16.5	–3.3	13.6	735
El Salvador	1.6 [a]	7.7	2.5	0.3 [a]	6.0	–0.5 [a]	..	..
Eritrea	..	..	..	..	..	..	..	..
Estonia	..	..	..	..	..	..	..	267
Ethiopia	..	..	..	..	15.4	..	..	..
Finland	..	..	..	..	..	..	..	..
France	..	11.6	..	..	..	..	..	..
Gabon	..	..	..	..	6.0	..	24.9	..
Gambia, The	3.8	..	..	3.4 [a]	3.7	–2.2	25.0 [c]	..
Georgia	..	..	..	..	..	..	..	..
Germany	..	..	..	..	..	..	..	..
Ghana	8.4	25.0	10.9	0.4 [a]	7.6	0.1	36.1 [c]	667
Greece	11.5	19.6	..	..	..	..	..	1,231
Guatemala	2.0	7.8	..	0.1 [a]	16.7	0.0	..	17
Guinea	8.7	..	..	..	0.8	..	..	..
Guinea-Bissau	..	..	..	..	0.7	..	..	..
Haiti	..	9.8	7.2	..	4.5	0.5	..	..
Honduras	5.5	12.6	..	0.0	13.0	–0.6	..	114
Hong Kong	..	..	..	..	..	..	..	..

	Economic activity	Investment	Credit	Net financial flows from government	External debt	Overall balance before transfers	Employment	Proceeds from privatization
	% of GDP 1986–91	% of gross domestic investment 1986–91	% of gross domestic credit 1986–91	% of GDP 1986–91	% of GDP 1986–91	% of total 1986–91	% of total 1986–91	millions of 1995 $ 1989–95
Hungary	..	..	..	..	..	..	..	8,648
India	13.8	39.0	..	–0.5	13.6	–2.5	8.5	5,744
Indonesia	14.1	10.3	..	1.1	0.9	–1.0	1.0	4,199
Iran, Islamic Rep.	..	..	..	..	..	..	..	7
Iraq	..	..	..	..	..	..	..	..
Ireland	..	..	..	..	..	..	..	..
Israel	..	..	..	..	..	..	..	..
Italy	..	12.9	..	..	..	..	..	..
Jamaica	..	21.3	2.4	..	7.6	–1.4	..	546
Japan	..	5.5	..	..	..	..	..	..
Jordan	..	..	..	..	..	..	..	15
Kazakstan	..	..	..	..	..	..	..	341
Kenya	11.5	20.8	5.6	0.0	13.3	..	8.0	77
Korea, Dem. Rep.	..	..	..	..	..	..	..	..
Korea, Rep.	10.3	15.3	..	–0.3	13.6	0.7	1.9	4,717
Kuwait	..	..	..	..	..	..	..	951
Kyrgyz Republic	..	..	..	..	..	..	..	..
Lao PDR	..	..	..	..	..	..	..	35
Latvia	..	..	..	..	..	..	..	173
Lebanon	..	..	..	..	..	..	..	..
Lesotho	..	..	..	..	..	..	..	..
Libya	..	..	..	..	..	..	..	..
Lithuania	..	..	..	..	..	..	..	114
Macedonia, FYR	..	..	..	..	..	..	..	685
Madagascar	..	..	..	..	13.4	..	..	..
Malawi	4.1 [a]	10.3	..	0.8 [a]	4.3	–1.5 [a]	12.0	..
Malaysia	17.0	15.8	..	..	17.5	0.0	..	9,981
Mali	..	..	..	–0.8	0.8	–1.1	..	..
Mauritania	..	19.3	..	1.3	18.5	..	..	1
Mauritius	1.8	..	..	–0.5	11.7	..	..	..
Mexico	11.0	14.3	5.4	–2.6	9.2	2.5	3.4	31,717
Moldova	..	..	..	..	..	..	..	..
Mongolia	..	..	..	..	..	..	..	..
Morocco	17.2 [b]	18.7	..	0.2 [a]	9.9	–2.9	..	922
Mozambique	..	..	..	..	..	..	..	66
Myanmar	..	30.8 [b]	..	–3.4	..	–1.1	..	..
Namibia	..	10.8	..	2.5 [a]	..	–0.7	2.7	..
Nepal	..	53.3	6.6	–0.5	7.2	–9.0	..	14
Netherlands	..	6.0	..	..	..	..	..	..
New Zealand	..	..	..	..	..	..	..	..
Nicaragua	..	..	..	..	2.4	..	..	146
Niger	5.2	14.5	..	..	4.8	–0.2	..	..
Nigeria	14.8	15.1	..	..	9.4	1.0	..	862
Norway	..	26.8 [b]	..	..	..	..	..	..
Oman	..	..	..	..	..	..	..	67
Pakistan	11.4 [b]	28.6	..	..	3.8	..	..	1,726
Panama	8.4	8.9	..	–1.0	12.6	2.1	..	111
Papua New Guinea	..	7.1	..	..	8.8	..	..	..
Paraguay	4.1	10.7	..	0.0	30.1	–1.4	..	20
Peru	5.3	7.7	..	–2.6	16.2	1.0	2.5	4,735
Philippines	2.4	6.7	7.8	1.8	16.8	–1.6	0.8	3,760
Poland	..	..	..	..	..	..	..	3,234
Portugal	14.2	15.3	..	..	..	..	..	..
Puerto Rico	..	..	..	..	..	..	..	..
Romania	..	..	..	..	..	..	..	125
Russian Federation	..	..	..	..	..	..	..	1,226

	Economic activity	Investment	Credit	Net financial flows from government	External debt	Overall balance before transfers	Employment	Proceeds from privatization
	% of GDP 1986–91	% of gross domestic investment 1986–91	% of gross domestic credit 1986–91	% of GDP 1986–91	% of GDP 1986–91	% of total 1986–91	% of total 1986–91	millions of 1995 $ 1989–95
Rwanda	10.0	..	..	0.3	..	1.0	..	..
Saudi Arabia	..	..	..	..	..	..	..	..
Senegal	6.2	22.0	..	5.0	6.2	–0.6	20.3[c]	..
Sierra Leone	..	..	..	0.0[b]	4.6	..	..	..
Singapore	..	..	..	..	..	..	..	..
Slovak Republic	..	..	..	..	..	..	..	1,525
Slovenia	..	..	..	..	..	..	..	565
South Africa	14.7	15.5	..	..	..	..	..	796
Spain	..	8.6	..	..	..	..	..	..
Sri Lanka	10.4	25.5	..	2.2	6.7	..	13.6[b]	316
Sudan	48.2[b]	..	33.3	..	1.0	..	..	..
Sweden	..	10.1	..	..	..	..	..	..
Switzerland	..	..	..	..	..	..	..	..
Syrian Arab Republic	..	..	..	..	..	..	..	..
Tajikistan	..	..	..	..	..	..	..	..
Tanzania	13.7	30.0	..	..	5.6	–9.9	22.3	113
Thailand	5.4	13.5	1.6	–0.3	31.2	–0.3	0.9[b]	1,171
Togo	11.8	11.4	..	1.6	4.5	0.0	..	32
Trinidad and Tobago	9.1[a]	16.4	10.4	–2.0	25.3	0.7[a]	..	492
Tunisia	30.2	30.4	..	7.6	22.3	..	..	148
Turkey	9.1	31.9	..	2.6	14.8	–5.5	3.6	3,434
Turkmenistan	..	..	..	..	..	..	..	..
Uganda	..	..	..	..	3.6	..	..	107
Ukraine	..	..	..	..	..	..	..	264
United Arab Emirates	..	..	..	..	..	..	..	190
United Kingdom	3.0	5.6[b]	..	..	..	..	..	..
United States	1.0	3.7	..	..	..	..	..	..
Uruguay	5.4	14.7	12.3	–3.4	5.5	3.7	..	20
Uzbekistan	..	..	..	..	..	..	..	30
Venezuela	23.0	53.6	1.7	–11.9	8.0	9.7	..	2,918
Vietnam	..	..	..	..	..	..	..	..
West Bank and Gaza	..	..	..	..	..	..	..	..
Yemen, Rep.	..	..	..	..	..	..	..	..
Yugoslavia, Fed. Rep.	..	..	..	..	..	..	..	..
Zaire	..	19.0	0.8	..	14.6	2.9	10.0[c]	..
Zambia	29.8	..	..	–3.1	15.0	..	..	72
Zimbabwe	..	..	24.0	..	16.4	..	..	290

a. Selected major state-owned enterprises only. b. Includes financial state-owned enterprises. c. As a percentage of formal sector employment.

State-owned enterprises—still important

Despite more than a decade of divestiture efforts and the growing consensus that the private sector should play a larger role, state-owned enterprises account for nearly as large a share of developing economies today as they did 20 years ago. Indeed, as data compiled for the World Bank's *Bureaucrats in Business: The Economics and Politics of Government Ownership* (1995b) show, the size of the state enterprise sector has diminished significantly only in the formerly socialist economies and a few middle-income countries. In most developing countries, particularly the poorest, bureaucrats run as much of the economy as ever.

Are state enterprises a problem? The answer people give depends on where they sit on the ideological spectrum. But consider how these enterprises influence the economies of developing countries:

• In many developing economies state enterprises absorb large amounts of money that could be better spent on basic social services. In Tanzania the central government provides them with subsidies equal to 72 percent of its spending on education and 150 percent of its spending on health.

• State enterprises often capture a disproportionate share of credit, squeezing out private borrowing. In Bangladesh they take about one-sixth of domestic credit, but account for less than 3 percent of GDP.

• A modest improvement in the efficiency of state-owned enterprises would substantially reduce the fiscal deficit in most developing countries and eliminate it in some. Reducing their operating costs by a mere 5 percent in Egypt, Peru, Senegal, and Turkey would reduce the fiscal deficit by about one-third.

Although governments are selling more and bigger enterprises, the state enterprise sector has remained stubbornly large outside Eastern Europe, the former Soviet Union, and a handful of countries in other regions. These large sectors can hinder growth—in part because state enterprises are often less efficient than private firms and in part because the resulting deficits are typically financed in ways that undermine macroeconomic stability. And because these sectors tend to be larger in low-income countries, state enterprises are likely to be most costly in the countries that can least afford them.

About the data

State-owned enterprises are defined as government-owned or -controlled economic entities that generate the bulk of their revenue from selling goods and services. This definition limits such enterprises to commercial activities in which government controls management decisions by virtue of its ownership stake. But it encompasses enterprises directly operated by a government department or those in which the government holds a majority of shares directly or indirectly through other state enterprises. It also encompasses enterprises in which the state holds a minority of shares, if the distribution of the remaining shares leaves the government with effective control. It excludes much public sector activity—such as education, health services, and road construction and maintenance—that is financed in other ways, usually from the government's general revenue. The focus is on nonfinancial state enterprises.

Data for state enterprises do not always correspond to this definition. What is considered a state enterprise varies not only among countries but also within countries over time. In exceptional cases governments include in their data on state enterprises activities that are not commercial, such as agricultural research institutes. But more frequently they omit activities that clearly are state enterprises. The most frequent omissions occur when governments define state enterprises narrowly—for example, by excluding those with a particular legal form (such as departmental enterprises), those owned by local governments (typically utilities), or those considered unimportant in terms of size or need for fiscal resources. Accordingly, data on state enterprises tend to underestimate their relative importance in economic activity.

Privatization is the transfer of productive assets from the public to the private sector. Direct sales are the most commonly used method of privatization, accounting for 79 percent of all transactions in 1995. Through this method, governments can attract strategic investors who are able to transfer technological and management know-how (and capital) to newly privatized enterprises. Selling equity, however, may not change effective control. It may result only in revenue effects, with no gains in efficiency. The second most commonly used method is share issues in domestic and international capital markets, accounting for 32 percent of all sales and 9 percent of transactions in 1995.

Definitions

• **Economic activity** is the value added of state enterprises, estimated as their sales revenue minus the cost of their intermediate inputs, or as the sum of their operating surplus (balance) and wage payments. • **Investment** refers to fixed capital formation by state enterprises. • **Credit** is credit extended to state enterprises by domestic financial institutions. • **Net financial flows from government** is the difference between total financial flows from the government to state enterprises (including government loans, equity, and subsidies) and total flows from state enterprises to the government (including dividends and taxes). Taxes paid by state enterprises are treated as a transfer of financial resources to the government. • **External debt** is the debt outstanding and disbursed as a result of the direct external borrowing of state enterprises, whether or not government guaranteed. It generally does not include debt that may have been assumed or incurred by the government on behalf of state enterprises. • **Overall balance before transfers** (current account or savings) is the sum of net operating and net nonoperating revenues. Unless otherwise noted, net operating revenues (or operating surplus or balance) refer to gross operating profits, or operating revenues minus the costs of intermediate inputs, wages, factor rentals, and depreciation. • **Employment** for many countries refers to the share of full-time state enterprise employees in total formal sector employment only, but for some it refers to employment in all state enterprises, including financial ones. Thus the data for state enterprise employment are not directly comparable. • **Proceeds from privatization** include all sales of public assets to private entities through public offers, direct sale, management and employee buyouts, concessions or licensing agreements, and joint venture arrangements.

Data sources

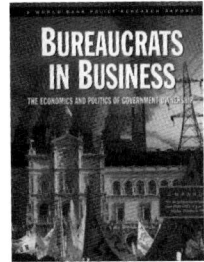

Data on state enterprises were collected mainly from World Bank member country central banks, finance ministries, enterprises, and World Bank and International Monetary Fund reports. These data were then collated into a single database for the World Bank Policy Research Report *Bureaucrats in Business: The Economics and Politics of Government Ownership* (1995b). The feature text also draws from this source. Data on privatization are from the World Bank's *Global Development Finance 1997*.

	Official exchange rate	Ratio of official to parallel exchange rate	Real effective exchange rate	Purchasing power parity conversion factor		Interest rates			Key agricultural producer prices	
	local currency units to $		1990 = 100	local currency units to international $		Deposit %	Lending %	Real %	$ per metric ton	
									Wheat	Maize
	1995	1995	1995	1990	1995	1995	1995	1995	1993	1993
Albania	92.7	0.9	..	..	..	15.3	19.7	4.8	..	..
Algeria	47.7	0.4	..	4.0	12.3	..	..	..	_456_	_523_
Angola	_59,515.0_	..	..	18.4	749,629.2	..	..	..	..	..
Argentina	1.0	1.0	..	0.3	0.9	11.9	17.8	9.2	..	..
Armenia	405.9	..	..	..	77.7	..	..	..	..	..
Australia	1.3	1.0	84.9	1.4	1.3	..	..	..	121	136
Austria	10.1	1.0	91.7	13.3	13.5	2.2	..	0.0	287	250
Azerbaijan	4,413.5	..	..	0.1	1,109.7	..	162.5	..	..	..
Bangladesh	40.3	0.8	..	6.3	6.9	6.0	14.0	−2.5	136	..
Belarus	..	..	..	0.7	2,672.1	100.8	175.0	−73.6	..	..
Belgium	29.5	1.0	105.9	36.1	35.6	4.0	8.4	1.9	..	..
Benin	499.1	..	..	74.3	101.5	..	..	..	..	187
Bolivia	4.8	1.0	90.2	1.0	1.4	18.9	51.0	6.6	178	148
Bosnia and Herzegovina	..	..	..	..	..	..	..	..	..	..
Botswana	2.8	1.0	..	1.1	1.4	10.0	14.2	0.6	..	153
Brazil	0.9	1.0	..	0.0	0.7	52.2	..	−12.1	..	..
Bulgaria	67.2	0.8	..	1.1	20.8	..	..	..	..	..
Burkina Faso	499.1	..	..	120.1	134.8	..	..	..	..	..
Burundi	249.8	0.7	97.9	48.9	62.1	..	15.3	..	..	..
Cambodia	2,450.8	1.0	..	..	..	8.7	18.7	−0.3	..	..
Cameroon	499.1	..	66.4	111.7	147.3	5.5	16.0	−5.7	..	..
Canada	1.4	1.0	78.8	1.3	1.2	7.1	8.6	4.0	110	102
Central African Republic	499.1	1.0	63.2	112.3	152.5	5.5	16.0	−5.6	..	..
Chad	499.1	..	..	91.2	118.2	5.5	16.0	−1.0	318	127
Chile	396.8	0.9	119.6	107.4	170.4	13.7	18.2	8.3	183	143
China	8.4	0.9	..	1.1	1.6	11.0	12.1	0.0	..	..
Colombia	912.8	1.0	134.5	122.1	298.7	32.3	42.7	9.2	219	181
Congo	499.1	..	..	112.2	148.0	5.5	16.0	2.8	..	353
Costa Rica	179.7	1.0	101.4	36.5	78.3	23.9	36.7	0.2	..	176
Côte d'Ivoire	499.1	..	69.9	150.0	205.8	..	..	..	..	..
Croatia	5.2	0.6	..	..	..	5.5	20.2	_−46.6_	..	..
Cuba	..	..	..	..	..	..	..	..	..	..
Czech Republic	26.5	1.0	..	5.5	11.5	7.0	12.8	−1.9	101	114
Denmark	5.6	1.0	107.0	8.9	8.3	3.9	10.3	2.4	182	..
Dominican Republic	13.6	1.0	113.7	2.9	5.0	..	..	..	..	_220_
Ecuador	2,564.5	1.0	129.5	209.3	850.8	43.3	55.7	16.3	174	_117_
Egypt, Arab Rep.	3.4	1.0	..	0.4	0.7	10.9	16.5	2.4	_161_	_142_
El Salvador	8.8	0.9	..	3.9	5.5	14.4	19.1	4.3	..	164
Eritrea	..	..	..	..	..	..	..	..	..	..
Estonia	11.5	0.8	..	0.1	6.1	8.7	16.0	−12.3	..	..
Ethiopia	6.2	0.6	..	0.9	1.3	11.5	15.1	−4.5	_393_	_254_
Finland	4.4	1.0	74.1	6.0	5.7	3.2	7.7	0.1	386	..
France	5.0	1.0	100.2	6.5	6.1	4.5	8.1	2.8	157	152
Gabon	499.1	..	62.5	..	..	5.5	16.0	−0.4	..	..
Gambia, The	9.5	0.9	94.7	2.8	..	12.5	25.0	_7.2_	..	_211_
Georgia	..	..	..	0.6	418,462.4	..	..	..	..	..
Germany	1.4	1.0	121.4	..	..	3.9	10.9	1.8	165	164
Ghana	1,200.4	1.0	..	84.1	215.4	28.7	..	−8.0	..	144
Greece	231.7	1.0	100.7	109.1	169.8	15.8	23.1	6.2	254	198
Guatemala	5.8	1.0	..	1.3	2.3	7.9	21.2	−1.9	204	177
Guinea	991.4	1.0	..	..	..	17.5	21.5	11.6	..	..
Guinea-Bissau	18,072.5	..	..	812.1	5,209.6	26.5	32.9	−13.4	..	73
Haiti	15.1	0.5	..	1.9	4.5	..	..	..	..	..
Honduras	9.5	1.0	..	1.4	3.0	12.0	27.0	−10.8	..	168
Hong Kong	7.7	1.0	..	6.1	7.6	..	..	..	..	..

	Official exchange rate	Ratio of official to parallel exchange rate	Real effective exchange rate	Purchasing power parity conversion factor		Interest rates			Key agricultural producer prices	
	local currency units to $		1990 = 100	local currency units to international $		Deposit %	Lending %	Real %	\$ per metric ton	
									Wheat	Maize
	1995	1995	1995	1990	1995	1995	1995	1995	1993	1993
Hungary	125.7	1.0	125.9	31.3	81.3	26.1	32.6	–0.7	102	111
India	32.4	1.0	..	5.8	8.0	..	*16.3*	..	*137*	*102*
Indonesia	2,248.6	1.0	..	452.4	561.5	..	*17.1*	..	..	132
Iran, Islamic Rep.	1,747.9	0.3	..	147.0	457.5	..	..	..	..	..
Iraq	0.3	0.0	..	..	..	..	..	..	..	..
Ireland	0.6	1.0	76.4	0.6	0.6	0.4	6.6	–0.9	..	..
Israel	3.0	1.0	..	1.9	2.9	14.1	20.2	4.1	..	..
Italy	1,628.9	1.0	71.6	1,396.2	1,515.5	6.4	12.5	1.6	234	202
Jamaica	35.1	1.0	..	4.1	13.6	23.2	43.6	0.7	..	384
Japan	94.1	1.0	154.6	189.9	168.1	0.7	3.4	1.3	..	..
Jordan	0.7	1.1	..	0.2	0.3	3.3	9.0	*–0.5*	210	136
Kazakstan	61.0	..	..	..	20.8	..	..	..	..	..
Kenya	51.4	1.0	..	6.3	10.2	13.6	28.8	12.7	97	140
Korea, Dem. Rep.	..	..	..	..	..	..	..	..	..	..
Korea, Rep.	771.3	1.0	..	566.6	660.7	8.8	9.0	3.2	..	325
Kuwait	0.3	1.0	..	0.2	0.2	6.5	8.4	..	..	..
Kyrgyz Republic	..	..	..	..	1.9	..	..	..	..	..
Lao PDR	804.7	1.0	..	..	..	14.0	25.7	–4.9	..	..
Latvia	0.5	..	..	..	0.3	14.8	34.6	–8.2	70	..
Lebanon	1,621.4	1.0	..	..	..	16.3	24.7	7.2	..	..
Lesotho	3.6	1.0	108.9	1.1	1.5	13.3	16.4	4.0	..	..
Libya	0.3	0.2	..	..	..	*5.5*	*7.0*	..	..	..
Lithuania	4.0	..	..	..	1.4	8.4	27.1	–25.5	..	..
Macedonia, FYR	37.9	..	..	..	..	..	..	..	..	..
Madagascar	4,265.6	1.0	..	557.6	1,410.4	..	..	..	*245*	*139*
Malawi	15.3	0.9	59.6	0.8	2.6	37.3	47.3	–18.1	227	107
Malaysia	2.5	1.0	102.7	1.0	1.1	5.9	7.6	0.9	..	..
Mali	499.1	..	..	158.3	217.8	..	..	..	..	*132*
Mauritania	129.8	..	..	30.7	36.4	..	..	..	..	..
Mauritius	17.4	1.0	..	3.6	4.4	12.2	20.8	5.9	..	284
Mexico	6.4	1.0	..	1.3	2.5	39.2	..	2.8	215	251
Moldova	4.5	..	..	..	..	..	..	..	..	..
Mongolia	448.6	..	..	2.0	78.9	60.1	114.9	23.3	..	..
Morocco	8.5	1.0	112.5	2.8	3.0	..	*10.0*	..	*375*	*296*
Mozambique	9,024.3	..	..	133.1	859.8	..	..	..	..	..
Myanmar	5.7	0.1	..	4.6	..	*9.0*	..	*–6.3*	..	..
Namibia	3.6	..	..	1.3	1.7	10.8	18.5	5.8	215	184
Nepal	51.9	0.8	..	6.2	8.7	..	..	..	..	..
Netherlands	1.6	0.9	101.6	2.1	2.0	4.4	7.2	2.3	..	..
New Zealand	1.5	1.0	99.9	1.6	1.4	8.5	12.2	10.4	..	..
Nicaragua	7.5	1.0	81.4	..	..	11.1	19.9	–0.1	..	155
Niger	499.1	..	..	114.4	..	..	..	..	..	..
Nigeria	21.9	0.3	122.2	2.3	14.9	13.5	20.2	–54.4	538	338
Norway	6.3	1.0	103.5	9.2	8.3	5.0	7.8	2.5	394	..
Oman	0.4	1.0	..	0.3	0.2	6.5	9.4	4.5	..	..
Pakistan	31.6	1.0	..	4.3	6.4	..	..	..	*118*	..
Panama	1.0	..	..	0.5	0.4	7.2	11.1	4.4	..	258
Papua New Guinea	1.3	1.0	84.9	0.5	0.5	*5.1*	*9.2*	*0.4*	..	..
Paraguay	1,970.4	0.9	113.4	486.7	946.9	21.2	31.0	10.0	119	130
Peru	2.3	1.0	..	0.1	1.4	16.0	36.6	5.7	250	198
Philippines	25.7	1.0	120.4	7.3	9.8	8.4	14.7	1.0	..	171
Poland	2.4	1.0	193.3	0.3	1.4	26.8	33.5	–0.2	..	..
Portugal	151.1	1.0	114.7	92.3	119.4	8.4	13.8	4.4	218	201
Puerto Rico	..	..	..	0.7	..	..	..	..	..	..
Romania	2,033.3	0.8	..	9.1	696.3	..	..	..	132	125
Russian Federation	*4,559.2*	1.0	..	0.7	2,419.8	102.0	319.5	–30.5	..	..

	Official exchange rate	Ratio of official to parallel exchange rate	Real effective exchange rate	Purchasing power parity conversion factor		Interest rates			Key agricultural producer prices	
	local currency units to $		1990 = 100	local currency units to international $		Deposit %	Lending %	Real %	$ per metric ton	
									Wheat	Maize
	1995	1995	1995	1990	1995	1995	1995	1995	1993	1993
Rwanda	144.3	..	..	42.2	95.0	5.0	15.0	-8.5	..	..
Saudi Arabia	3.7	1.0	91.0	3.0	2.8	..	..	..	..	..
Senegal	499.1	..	..	130.1	168.9	..	..	..	..	..
Sierra Leone	755.2	1.0	105.6	46.2	232.3	7.0	28.8	-9.3	..	..
Singapore	1.4	1.0	..	1.7	1.7	3.5	6.4	0.9	..	..
Slovak Republic	29.7	0.9	..	5.2	58.5	9.0	15.6	-0.3	..	..
Slovenia	118.5	0.8	..	..	..	15.3	24.8	4.8	..	..
South Africa	3.6	1.0	98.2	1.6	2.2	13.5	17.9	3.0	226	126
Spain	124.7	1.0	86.9	106.5	117.9	7.7	10.0	2.9	212	224
Sri Lanka	51.3	1.0	..	7.8	10.5	16.1	14.7	6.0	..	148
Sudan	289.6	..	..	2.7	..	..	..	..	209	..
Sweden	7.1	1.0	72.4	9.2	8.8	6.2	11.1	9.0	146	..
Switzerland	1.2	1.0	115.6	2.1	2.0	1.3	5.5	1.0	709	480
Syrian Arab Republic	11.2	0.2	..	5.5	7.1	..	..	..	759	..
Tajikistan	2,204.3	..	..	..	9.4	..	..	..	..	..
Tanzania	574.8	1.0	..	46.5	109.2	24.6	42.8	-8.4	..	..
Thailand	24.9	1.0	..	8.3	9.0	11.6	14.4	4.8	..	109
Togo	499.1	..	71.9	104.2	128.0	..	..	..	..	..
Trinidad and Tobago	5.9	1.0	83.8	2.2	2.5	6.9	15.2	-5.0	..	407
Tunisia	0.9	0.9	..	0.3	..	..	..	..	272	..
Turkey	45,845.1	1.0	..	1,567.8	21,965.0	76.1	..	-2.3	167	201
Turkmenistan	404.4	..	..	..	..	..	..	..	..	..
Uganda	968.9	0.9	91.7	75.7	182.5	7.6	20.2	-1.6	..	198
Ukraine	1.5	0.4	..	0.7	40,072.6	70.3	122.7	-66.7	..	..
United Arab Emirates	3.7	..	..	3.8	3.9	..	..	..	..	..
United Kingdom	0.6	0.9	86.4	0.6	0.6	4.1	6.7	1.3	177	..
United States	1.0	..	92.1	1.0	1.0	..	8.8	..	120	100
Uruguay	6.3	1.0	157.4	0.6	4.9	38.2	99.1	-0.6	132	133
Uzbekistan	..	..	..	..	4.7	..	..	..	..	..
Venezuela	176.8	0.8	139.9	17.2	73.3	24.7	32.2	-18.6	..	164
Vietnam	10,962.1	..	..	..	..	..	..	..	..	..
West Bank and Gaza	..	..	..	..	..	..	..	..	..	..
Yemen, Rep.	40.8	0.3	..	..	..	..	..	..	749	875
Yugoslavia, Fed. Rep.	..	..	..	..	..	..	..	..	..	..
Zaire	7,024.4	0.9	83.5	188.5	1,648.1	..	..	..	..	..
Zambia	857.2	0.9	107.4	14.3	366.0	..	113.3	..	134	86
Zimbabwe	8.7	1.0	..	0.8	2.4	25.9	34.7	2.0	223	..

About the data

Prices measured relative to the overall price level or in relation to other prices in the economy provide vital information to the three main economic agents: households, producers, and the government. In a market-based economy the decisions of these agents about the allocation of resources are influenced by relative prices, and relative prices reflect, to a large extent, the choices of these agents. Thus relative prices—the real exchange rate, real wages, real interest rates, and relative commodity prices—convey vital information about the interaction of economic agents in an economy and in relation to the rest of the world, at a given point in time as well as over time.

The exchange rate is the relative price of a currency in terms of another currency. Official exchange rates are established by governments. Parallel, or "black market," exchange rates reflect rates negotiated by traders and are by their nature difficult to measure reliably. Parallel exchange rate markets often account for only a small share of transactions and may therefore be both thin and volatile. The parallel rates reported here are collected by Currency Data & Intelligence, Inc. from a variety of sources, some within the country and some outside but doing business with entities based in the country. The sources include import-export firms, banknote collectors trading with local partners, and other business travelers. For currencies that are heavily restricted from free trade and transferability, the "black market" rate is used. For currencies with little or no exchange restrictions but which trade at rates that differ slightly from the rates fixed by government banking institutions or rates observed in official interbank channels, "free market" rates are used. For currencies for which multiple rates exist, the rates are averaged to derive an estimate applicable to unofficial transfers.

Real effective exchange rates are derived by deflating a trade-weighted average of the nominal exchange rates that apply between trading partners. For most industrial countries the weights are based on trade in manufactured goods with other industrial countries and an index of relative, normalized unit labor costs is used as the deflator. For other countries the weights take into account trade in manufactured and primary products during 1980–82 and an index of relative changes in consumer prices is used as the deflator. An increase in the real effective exchange rate represents an appreciation of the local currency. Because of conceptual and data limitations, movements in real effective exchange rates should be interpreted with considerable caution.

Purchasing power parity (PPP) conversion factors are based on surveys of the comparative purchasing power of currencies by the United Nations International Comparison Programme (ICP). The conversion factors can be treated as an exchange rate relative to the "international dollar," a common currency or unit of account that equalizes price levels in all economies. It has the same purchasing power over total GNP as the U.S. dollar in a given year. (For further discussion of the PPP conversion factor see the notes to table 4.14.)

Many interest rates exist in an economy, reflecting differences in creditors, debtors, the terms governing loans and deposits, and competitive conditions. In some economies interest rates may be set by administrative action or regulation. In economies with imperfect markets or where reported nominal rates are not indicative of the effective rates, it may be difficult to obtain data on interest rates that reflect actual market transactions. The deposit and lending rates in the table are collected by the International Monetary Fund (IMF) as representative interest rates offered by banks to resident customers; however, the terms and conditions attached to these rates differ from country to country. Real interest rates are calculated by adjusting nominal rates by an estimate of the rate of inflation in the economy. A negative real interest rate indicates a loss in the purchasing power of the principal. The real interest rates in the table are calculated as $(i - P)/(1 + P)$, where i is the nominal interest rate and P is the rate of inflation.

Domestic prices for two key agricultural commodities, wheat and maize, show that prices often are not equalized across international markets (even after adjusting for freight, transport, insurance, and differences in quality). Market imperfections, such as taxes, subsidies, and trade barriers, drive a wedge between domestic and international prices. Commodity prices in local currency are converted into U.S. dollars using official, period average exchange rates.

Definitions

● **Official exchange rate** is an annual average based on exchange rates (local currency units to U.S. dollars) determined by country authorities, or rates determined largely by market forces in the legally sanctioned exchange market. ● **Ratio of official to parallel exchange rate** measures the premium people must pay to exchange the domestic currency for dollars in the black market relative to the official exchange rate. ● **Real effective exchange rate** is the nominal effective exchange rate (a measure of the value of a currency against a weighted average of several foreign currencies) divided by a price deflator or index of costs. ● **Purchasing power parity conversion factor** is the number of units of a country's currency required to buy the same amounts of goods and services in the domestic market as one dollar would buy in the United States. ● **Deposit interest rate** is the rate paid by commercial or similar banks for demand, time, or savings deposits. ● **Lending interest rate** is the rate charged by banks on loans to prime customers. ● **Real interest rate** is the deposit interest rate adjusted for inflation as measured by the GDP deflator. ● **Key agricultural producer prices** are the domestic producer prices per metric ton for wheat and maize converted to U.S. dollars using the official exchange rate.

Data sources

Official and real effective exchange rates are from the IMF's *International Financial Statistics*. Estimates of parallel market exchange rates are from Currency Data & Intelligence, Inc.'s *Global Currency Report*. PPP conversion factors are from ICP and World Bank staff estimates. Deposit and lending interest rates are from the IMF's *International Financial Statistics*. Real interest rates are calculated using World Bank data on the GDP deflator. Agricultural price data are compiled by the Food and Agriculture Organization (FAO) and published in its *Production Yearbook*. The IMF and the FAO provide the World Bank with electronic data files that are usually more up-to-date than the print publications cited here.

5.6 | Trade policies

	All products			Primary products			Manufactured products		
	Mean tariff % 1990–93	Standard deviation of tariff rates 1990–93	Covered by nontariff barriers % 1990–93	Mean tariff % 1990–93	Standard deviation of tariff rates 1990–93	Covered by nontariff barriers % 1990–93	Mean tariff % 1990–93	Standard deviation of tariff rates 1990–93	Covered by nontariff barriers % 1990–93
Albania	..	..	..	..		..	..		..
Algeria	24.8	19.6	9.5	21.6	20.5	26.8	26.2	19.4	2.8
Angola[a]	11.6	..	0.7	10.6	..	0.0	11.9	..	0.9
Argentina	9.9	6.9	0.2	8.3	5.4	0.1	10.2	7.1	0.3
Armenia	..	..	..	..	..	..	..	..	..
Australia	9.8	11.9	8.1	2.2	4.6	0.0	11.7	12.4	9.4
Austria	..	..	3.5	..	..	12.1	..	..	1.4
Azerbaijan	..	..	..	..	..	..	..	..	..
Bangladesh	84.1	26.1	..	79.6	37.4	..	85.6	22.3	..
Belarus	..	..	..	..	..	..	..	..	..
Belgium	6.7	5.8	13.4	9.2	10.2	22.0	6.1	4.0	11.5
Benin[a]	37.4	..	17.0	35.0	..	24.3	38.3	..	14.2
Bolivia	9.7	1.2	2.0	10.0	0.1	1.6	9.6	1.2	1.8
Bosnia and Herzegovina	..	..	..	..	..	..	..	..	..
Botswana	..	..	..	..	..	..	..	..	..
Brazil	11.1	6.3	1.5	8.2	5.5	4.1	11.7	6.3	0.4
Bulgaria	..	..	..	..	..	..	..	..	..
Burkina Faso	..	..	..	..	..	..	..	..	..
Burundi	..	..	0.3	..	..	0.2	..	..	0.4
Cambodia	..	..	..	..	..	..	..	..	..
Cameroon	18.7	12.0	..	21.3	9.6	..	18.0	12.6	..
Canada	10.5	26.6	4.0	19.3	60.6	2.3	8.8	6.6	4.4
Central African Republic[a]	32.0	..	5.1	28.9	..	9.3	33.0	..	3.1
Chad	..	..	..	..	..	..	..	..	..
Chile	11.0	0.7	0.1	11.0	0.0	0.3	10.9	0.8	0.0
China	36.3	28.0	11.3	34.4	25.1	11.5	37.6	29.0	11.3
Colombia	13.3	4.9	1.7	12.8	6.0	1.0	13.5	4.6	1.6
Congo	18.6	9.5	..	21.6	9.3	..	17.7	9.4	..
Costa Rica[a]	21.1	..	0.8	20.4	..	0.0	21.5	..	1.0
Côte d'Ivoire	4.9	1.5	..	4.8	1.0	..	4.9	1.6	..
Croatia	..	..	..	..	..	..	..	..	..
Cuba	..	..	..	..	..	..	..	..	..
Czech Republic	6.7	6.4	..	8.0	10.5	..	6.4	3.9	..
Denmark	6.7	5.8	13.4	9.2	10.2	22.0	6.1	4.0	11.5
Dominican Republic	..	..	..	..	..	..	..	..	..
Ecuador	12.3	5.5	63.6	12.5	6.4	67.5	12.4	5.5	61.8
Egypt, Arab Rep.	28.3	28.9	45.2	26.6	45.0	43.8	29.5	24.2	45.6
El Salvador[a]	21.1	..	19.2	19.9	..	17.7	21.5	..	19.7
Eritrea	..	..	..	..	..	..	..	..	..
Estonia	..	..	..	..	..	..	..	..	..
Ethiopia	28.8	23.9	22.5	32.6	21.8	42.9	28.2	24.3	14.7
Finland	..	..	3.7	..	..	25.2	..	..	0.1
France	6.7	5.8	13.4	9.2	10.2	22.0	6.1	4.0	11.5
Gabon	..	..	..	..	..	..	..	..	..
Gambia, The	..	..	..	..	..	..	..	..	..
Georgia	..	..	..	..	..	..	..	..	..
Germany	6.7	5.8	13.4	9.2	10.2	22.0	6.1	4.0	11.5
Ghana	15.0	8.3	..	18.5	8.1	..	14.1	8.0	..
Greece	6.7	5.8	13.4	9.2	10.2	22.0	6.1	4.0	11.5
Guatemala[a]	22.8	..	7.4	20.9	..	12.5	23.5	..	5.0
Guinea a	8.9	..	38.2	9.2	..	46.9	8.8	..	35.1
Guinea-Bissau	..	..	..	..	..	..	..	..	..
Haiti[a]	11.6	..	30.8	14.5	..	34.5	10.5	..	29.7
Honduras	10.1	6.5	..	12.2	6.2	..	9.7	6.5	..
Hong Kong	0.0	0.0	0.5	0.0	0.0	0.8	0.0	0.0	0.3

	All products			Primary products			Manufactured products		
	Mean tariff % 1990–93	Standard deviation of tariff rates 1990–93	Covered by nontariff barriers % 1990–93	Mean tariff % 1990–93	Standard deviation of tariff rates 1990–93	Covered by nontariff barriers % 1990–93	Mean tariff % 1990–93	Standard deviation of tariff rates 1990–93	Covered by nontariff barriers % 1990–93
Hungary	11.0	9.7	..	15.8	17.1	..	10.1	6.8	..
India	56.3	23.6	62.6	43.5	39.2	71.7	59.4	16.6	58.9
Indonesia	19.4	16.1	2.7	17.4	12.5	4.6	20.3	17.1	2.0
Iran, Islamic Rep.[a]	20.7	..	99.3	16.8	..	99.0	22.2	..	99.4
Iraq	..	..	..	..	..	..	..	..	..
Ireland	6.7	5.8	13.4	9.2	10.2	22.0	6.1	4.0	11.5
Israel	8.3	10.8	..	5.7	8.8	..	9.0	11.2	..
Italy	6.7	5.8	13.4	9.2	10.2	22.0	6.1	4.0	11.5
Jamaica[a]	17.3	..	6.6	11.6	..	10.3	19.3	..	4.8
Japan	6.3	8.4	3.9	10.2	11.4	9.2	5.1	6.8	2.4
Jordan[a]	13.8	..	12.9	7.2	..	37.0	16.2	..	3.6
Kazakstan	..	..	..	..	..	..	..	..	..
Kenya	35.1	13.3	37.8	38.0	14.1	37.0	34.6	13.5	38.3
Korea, Dem. Rep.	..	..	..	..	..	..	..	..	..
Korea, Rep.	9.0	6.6	..	13.9	13.1	..	7.8	1.3	..
Kuwait	..	..	3.5	..	..	6.8	..	..	1.8
Kyrgyz Republic	..	..	..	..	..	..	..	..	..
Lao PDR	..	..	..	..	..	..	..	..	..
Latvia	..	..	..	..	..	..	..	..	..
Lebanon	..	..	..	..	..	..	..	..	..
Lesotho	..	..	..	..	..	..	..	..	..
Libya[a]	18.3	..	10.3	14.2	..	15.0	19.7	..	8.4
Lithuania	..	..	..	..	..	..	..	..	..
Macedonia, FYR	..	..	..	..	..	..	..	..	..
Madagascar	..	..	1.7	..	..	0.8	..	..	1.6
Malawi	..	..	91.3	..	..	84.8	..	..	93.8
Malaysia	14.3	14.0	2.1	11.9	13.2	1.2	15.2	14.3	2.4
Mali	3.0	2.4	..	3.9	2.1	..	2.8	2.5	..
Mauritania	..	..	..	..	..	..	..	..	..
Mauritius	..	..	35.2	..	..	30.8	..	..	36.9
Mexico	12.6	5.4	3.9	12.4	6.3	8.5	12.6	5.3	1.8
Moldova	..	..	..	..	..	..	..	..	..
Mongolia	..	..	..	..	..	..	..	..	..
Morocco	24.5	13.2	..	23.7	15.4	..	25.3	12.4	..
Mozambique	5.0	0.0	..	5.0	0.0	..	5.0	0.0	..
Myanmar	..	..	..	..	..	..	..	..	..
Namibia	..	..	..	..	..	..	..	..	..
Nepal	16.7	15.9	0.7	8.5	13.9	1.0	19.0	16.0	0.5
Netherlands	6.7	5.8	13.4	9.2	10.2	22.0	6.1	4.0	11.5
New Zealand	8.5	10.4	0.0	4.3	5.9	0.1	9.7	11.1	0.0
Nicaragua	10.7	17.8	..	15.6	37.3	..	9.5	6.0	..
Niger	..	..	..	..	..	..	..	..	..
Nigeria	34.3	25.0	8.8	32.2	22.5	22.7	35.1	25.6	3.1
Norway	5.7	6.6	5.4	0.8	3.9	7.9	6.7	6.7	5.0
Oman	5.7	9.2	..	8.1	19.5	..	5.1	3.3	..
Pakistan	51.0	21.9	14.5	44.4	23.1	6.8	53.0	21.2	17.3
Panama	..	..	..	..	..	..	..	..	..
Papua New Guinea[a]	7.0	..	2.6	4.5	..	9.4	7.7	..	0.0
Paraguay	9.3	6.9	1.8	8.2	5.4	6.4	9.5	7.2	0.0
Peru	17.6	4.4	..	17.6	4.4	..	17.7	4.4	..
Philippines	20.0	11.0	..	21.8	13.1	..	19.5	10.3	..
Poland	12.0	7.8	..	12.9	9.9	..	11.7	6.9	..
Portugal	6.7	5.8	13.4	9.2	10.2	22.0	6.1	4.0	11.5
Puerto Rico	..	..	..	..	..	..	..	..	..
Romania[a]	16.7	..	0.0	13.8	..	0.0	18.0	..	0.0
Russian Federation	..	..	..	..	..	..	..	..	..

5.6 | Trade policies

	All products			Primary products			Manufactured products		
	Mean tariff % 1990–93	Standard deviation of tariff rates 1990–93	Covered by nontariff barriers % 1990–93	Mean tariff % 1990–93	Standard deviation of tariff rates 1990–93	Covered by nontariff barriers % 1990–93	Mean tariff % 1990–93	Standard deviation of tariff rates 1990–93	Covered by nontariff barriers % 1990–93
Rwanda	34.8	33.1	..	47.1	41.0	..	32.1	30.5	..
Saudi Arabia	12.1	3.3	3.9	12.0	3.6	4.4	12.2	3.2	3.4
Senegal[a]	34.2	..	7.2	38.9	..	8.4	32.3	..	6.1
Sierra Leone[a]	25.8	..	100.0	19.4	..	100.0	28.0	..	100.0
Singapore	0.5	2.7	0.3	0.2	2.5	1.2	0.6	2.8	0.0
Slovak Republic	..	..	..	..	..	..	..	..	..
Slovenia	..	..	..	..	..	..	..	..	..
South Africa	19.7	21.9	..	9.0	12.0	..	21.2	22.7	..
Spain	6.7	5.8	13.4	9.2	10.2	22.0	6.1	4.0	11.5
Sri Lanka	24.1	18.1	3.8	28.5	22.8	2.8	23.5	16.9	4.0
Sudan[a]	56.6	..	10.0	56.6	..	12.0	56.4	..	9.4
Sweden	..	..	5.7	..	..	23.7	..	..	1.6
Switzerland	..	..	8.8	..	..	25.3	..	..	4.8
Syrian Arab Republic[a]	14.8	..	36.6	13.1	..	30.7	15.5	..	38.7
Tajikistan	..	..	..	..	..	..	..	..	..
Tanzania	19.5	12.3	79.7	25.3	12.7	64.3	18.1	11.9	85.9
Thailand	23.1	16.9	5.5	32.2	23.2	8.8	21.6	14.9	4.2
Togo	..	..	..	..	..	..	..	..	..
Trinidad and Tobago	18.7	15.3	23.4	24.6	18.0	30.8	17.4	14.1	20.5
Tunisia	30.0	11.7	32.7	30.3	13.0	37.3	30.2	11.2	30.5
Turkey	9.5	5.7	96.4	9.9	9.1	93.9	9.5	4.4	97.3
Turkmenistan	..	..	..	..	..	..	..	..	..
Uganda	17.1	9.1	..	20.9	10.5	..	16.3	8.5	..
Ukraine	..	..	..	..	..	..	..	..	..
United Arab Emirates[a]	4.5	..	1.0	3.2	..	2.9	4.9	..	0.3
United Kingdom	6.7	5.8	13.4	9.2	10.2	22.0	6.1	4.0	11.5
United States	5.9	7.1	4.3	5.9	11.7	4.0	6.0	6.0	4.3
Uruguay	9.3	7.1	..	8.2	5.4	..	9.5	7.4	..
Uzbekistan	..	..	..	..	..	..	..	..	..
Venezuela	13.4	4.8	2.4	12.9	5.8	3.0	13.5	4.5	1.7
Vietnam	12.0	15.5	..	13.6	18.2	..	12.0	14.9	..
West Bank and Gaza	..	..	..	..	..	..	..	..	..
Yemen, Rep.[a]	16.2	..	28.7	17.9	..	25.2	15.6	..	30.2
Yugoslavia, Fed. Rep.	..	..	..	..	..	..	..	..	..
Zaire	..	..	100.0	..	..	100.0	..	..	100.0
Zambia	25.9	10.6	..	30.2	10.3	..	25.1	10.5	..
Zimbabwe	..	..	93.6	..	..	99.7	..	..	91.2

a. Data are for the mid-1980s.

Trade and tariffs

Economies regulate their imports through a combination of tariff and nontariff measures. The most common form of tariff is an ad valorem duty, but tariffs may also be levied on a specific, or per unit, basis. Tariffs may be used to raise fiscal revenues or to protect domestic industries from foreign competition—or both. Nontariff barriers, which limit the quantity of imports of a particular good, take many forms. Some common ones are licensing schemes, quotas, prohibitions, and export restraint arrangements.

Some countries set fairly uniform tariff rates across all imports. Others are more selective, setting high tariffs to protect favored domestic industries and setting low tariffs on goods that have few domestic suppliers or that are necessary inputs for domestic industry.

The standard deviation of tariffs is a measure of the dispersion of tariff rates around their mean value. Highly dispersed rates are evidence of discriminatory tariffs that may distort production and consumption decisions. But this tells only part of the story. The effective rate of protection—the degree to which the value added in an industry is protected—may exceed the nominal rate if the tariff system systematically differentiates among imports of raw materials, intermediate products, and finished goods.

Nontariff barriers are generally considered more detrimental to economic efficiency than tariffs because efficient foreign producers cannot undercut the barrier by reducing their costs and thus their prices. A high percentage of products subject to nontariff barriers indicates a protectionist trade regime, but the frequency of nontariff barriers does not measure their restrictiveness. Moreover, a wide range of domestic policies and regulations (such as health regulations) may act as nontariff barriers but are not measured by this indicator. A full evaluation would require careful analysis of the individual measures.

One of the goals of the Uruguay Round negotiations was the "tariffication" of agricultural nontariff barriers. Many others, such as the Multifibre Arrangement, will be phased out over a period of years. Although many nontariff barriers were replaced by ad valorem tariffs, the reduction of nontariff barriers on the imports of high-income countries should offer new opportunities for competitive exporters in developing countries (table 5.6a).

About the data

The data show the average applied tariff rates before the conclusion of the Uruguay Round of the General Agreement on Tariffs and Trade (GATT) in 1994. Tariff and nontariff measures may be applied generally, against imports from all sources, or selectively, against imports from specific trading partners. Countries typically maintain a hierarchy of trade preferences applicable to different trading partners. The applied rates in the table are ad valorem equivalents of the most-favored-nation duties charged on imports not covered by preferential trade arrangements such as the North American Free Trade Agreement or the European Union. The mean tariff is the simple average across all tariff lines. Simple averages are a better indicator of tariff protection than averages weighted by import values, which are biased downward, especially when tariffs are set so high as to discourage trade.

The tariffs bound under the Uruguay Round will be phased in over five years beginning in 1995. So, the rates shown here are generally representative of current levels of protection. Nontariff barriers are being phased out slowly; in some cases their conversion to tariffs may result in higher rates of tariff protection. See table 6.4 for estimates of the tariff concessions made during the Uruguay Round.

For some developing countries data on mean tariffs and nontariff barriers are for years before 1987; many of these countries maintain their tariff data in the old Customs Cooperation Council Nomenclature (CCCN) classification system, which is no longer compatible with the six-digit Harmonized System codes used to maintain the UNCTAD Database on Trade Control Measures. The CCCN had fewer tariff lines, and the definitions of these lines were not uniform across countries. For other countries data on tariffs and nontariff barriers are for 1990–93. Data on nontariff barriers for high-income OECD members are for 1993.

The commodity groupings are based on the Standard International Trade Classification (SITC). To construct aggregates based on tariff lines, the SITC classification was mapped into equivalent tariff lines of the Harmonized System.

Definitions

● **Primary products** are commodities classified in SITC sections 0, 1, 2, 3, and 4 plus division 68 (non-ferrous metals). ● **Manufactured products** are commodities classified in SITC sections 5, 6, 7, 8, and 9, excluding division 68. ● **Mean tariff** is the simple average of the applied rates for all products subject to tariffs. ● **Standard deviation of tariff rates** measures the average dispersion of tariff rates around the mean; it is also calculated using unweighted tariff data. ● **Products covered by nontariff barriers** is the percentage of tariff lines to which nontariff barriers are applied. No attempt is made to estimate their tariff equivalent.

Data sources

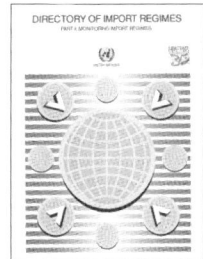

Mean tariff rates and their standard deviations were calculated by World Bank staff using the Trade Analysis and Information System (TRAINS) database maintained by UNCTAD. Estimates from TRAINS were supplemented by data from UNCTAD's *Directory of Import Regimes, Part I* and *A Statistical Analysis of Trade Control Measures of Developing Countries*. Data on nontariff barriers of developing countries come from the UNCTAD Database on Trade Control Measures, published in these same UNCTAD sources. Data on nontariff barriers of high-income countries come from special compilations by World Bank staff using data provided by UNCTAD.

Table 5.6a OECD imports covered by nontariff barriers before and after the Uruguay Round

| | From developing countries | | From other OECD countries | |
| | Pre–Uruguay Round | Post–Uruguay Round | Pre–Uruguay Round | Post–Uruguay Round |
Sector	%	%	%	%
Agriculture	13.3	1.7	22.0	1.8
Other primary	5.6	3.6	6.2	1.2
Manufacturing	17.0	1.5	8.3	3.5
Total imports	15.0	5.0	8.3	3.4

Note: Post–Uruguay Round nontariff barriers are based on World Bank staff estimates.
Source: Low and Yeats 1994.

5.7 | Export competitiveness

	Nominal export growth 1983–84 to 1988–89				Nominal export growth 1988–89 to 1993–94			
	Annual average %	From world demand %	From market share %	From export diversifi- cation %	Annual average %	From world demand %	From market share %	From export diversifi- cation %
Albania	6.4	6.5	–3.0	3.0	–4.5	5.8	–18.3	10.4
Algeria	–6.5	–1.8	–5.2	0.5	2.2	5.5	–2.8	–0.2
Angola	8.7	–4.1	11.3	1.8	3.3	5.6	–1.3	–0.8
Argentina	8.8	9.1	–4.6	4.6	8.6	5.6	0.9	1.9
Armenia	..	..	..	..	..	..	..	..
Australia	10.4	–0.4	9.7	1.1	4.6	4.5	–2.3	2.6
Austria	17.2	15.9	1.5	–0.4	5.7	8.0	–1.7	–0.5
Azerbaijan	..	..	..	..	..	..	..	..
Bangladesh	14.5	8.0	6.2	–0.2	16.4	7.0	8.8	0.0
Belarus	..	..	..	..	..	..	..	..
Belgium	14.8	14.3	0.7	–0.2	3.0	7.4	–4.0	–0.1
Benin	–4.8	–3.4	–4.9	3.6	10.6	4.9	7.3	–1.7
Bolivia	–6.5	–4.8	–4.0	2.3	3.8	4.3	–8.5	8.9
Bosnia and Herzegovina	..	..	..	..	..	..	..	..
Botswana	..	..	..	..	..	..	..	..
Brazil	9.4	11.7	–3.2	1.2	3.1	5.8	–3.8	1.3
Bulgaria	1.7	13.1	–12.7	3.0	13.2	7.9	0.6	4.3
Burkina Faso	6.8	10.4	–4.0	0.7	–2.5	5.4	–7.6	0.1
Burundi	3.5	13.4	–9.4	0.7	–6.3	5.5	–12.5	1.5
Cambodia	28.7	17.1	–12.5	25.6	82.0	8.2	84.9	–9.1
Cameroon	–3.4	–3.1	–1.0	0.7	–0.4	4.2	–4.2	–0.2
Canada	8.6	8.5	–0.5	0.6	6.2	7.1	–1.1	0.3
Central African Republic	–0.3	8.4	–8.8	0.8	–1.7	3.0	–4.1	–0.4
Chad	–13.0	5.2	–18.6	1.7	–2.3	5.5	–11.3	4.3
Chile	15.7	12.8	2.0	0.6	7.7	3.1	1.6	2.8
China	22.8	4.3	14.1	3.2	21.9	6.3	12.4	2.0
Colombia	10.9	6.5	–1.9	6.1	7.4	5.5	–1.1	3.0
Congo	–2.8	–3.2	0.2	0.2	4.4	4.1	0.2	0.1
Costa Rica	9.9	14.0	–2.9	–0.7	12.2	9.0	1.5	1.3
Côte d'Ivoire	0.6	–4.0	3.0	1.7	2.6	4.7	–1.2	–0.8
Croatia	..	..	..	..	..	..	..	..
Cuba	9.5	–3.6	14.5	–0.8	–5.6	4.5	–10.2	0.6
Czech Republic	..	..	..	..	..	..	..	..
Denmark	12.2	10.4	1.2	0.4	3.7	7.9	–3.1	–0.8
Dominican Republic	12.6	14.5	–3.6	2.0	12.4	8.5	3.1	0.5
Ecuador	–0.5	–3.6	2.7	0.5	9.2	4.5	3.0	1.5
Egypt, Arab Rep.	–3.6	–0.7	–4.6	1.8	7.5	5.2	–1.7	4.0
El Salvador	–4.6	14.5	–17.9	1.4	11.7	9.9	0.4	1.2
Eritrea	..	..	..	..	..	..	..	..
Estonia	..	..	..	..	..	..	..	..
Ethiopia	0.8	3.6	–3.9	1.3	–6.1	4.2	–9.8	–0.1
Finland	14.4	13.3	0.6	0.3	4.9	7.2	–2.9	0.8
France	..	..	..	..	..	..	..	..
Gabon	–5.8	–3.5	–2.6	0.3	11.2	4.1	6.9	–0.2
Gambia, The	24.4	13.6	9.1	0.4	2.4	8.8	–8.0	2.3
Georgia	..	..	..	..	..	..	..	..
Germany	15.4	14.3	1.3	–0.4	2.7	7.5	–4.6	0.1
Ghana	13.7	6.7	6.0	0.5	5.8	3.1	1.6	1.0
Greece	9.4	0.6	7.1	1.5	–2.2	5.3	–8.7	1.7
Guatemala	1.3	–0.3	–0.6	2.3	12.7	6.4	–0.5	6.6
Guinea–Bissau	5.1	11.3	–6.1	0.6	3.6	4.5	–2.0	1.1
Guinea	3.1	13.0	–9.5	0.8	31.2	6.0	24.8	–0.8
Haiti	0.0	16.1	–13.7	–0.2	–21.4	11.2	–29.9	0.8
Honduras	4.4	13.0	–7.2	–0.4	10.6	7.0	2.6	0.8
Hong Kong	19.2	17.7	–1.5	2.8	2.2	10.8	–7.6	–0.2

Export dynamics

Thirty years ago the research staff of the General Agreement on Tariffs and Trade (GATT), the predecessor to the World Trade Organization, examined broad patterns of export growth among developing countries. Their work addressed three issues: To what extent are differences in the patterns of merchandise export growth across countries explained by growth in the markets for their traditional exports? Had some countries succeeded in expanding their market share of their traditional exports? And how important was trade diversification in determining the export performance of countries? (See GATT 1966, pp. 23–32.)

The GATT analysis decomposed the growth of nominal exports over the period 1959–65 into three multiplicative factors. The first, f_1, measured the growth due to expansion of the world market for the country's traditional exports. The second, f_2, measured the growth due to expansion of its market share for its traditional exports. The third, f_3, measured as a residual, captured the growth in exports due to diversification into nontraditional exports. By construction, nominal export growth is equal to the product of the three factors: $f_1 \cdot f_2 \cdot f_3$.

The indicators in the table update the GATT results for 1983–84 through 1988–89 and 1988–89 through 1993–94. (Two-year averages were used as starting and ending points to reduce the influence of a single-year outlier.) The growth in total nominal exports and the three growth factors are shown as compound annual growth rates over the two periods.

In 1966 the GATT concluded that during the period 1959–61 to 1964–65 "above average total export performances were, in the majority of cases, associated with gains in market shares" (p. 30). Irving Kravis, in his well-known article "Trade as a Handmaiden to Growth," reviewed the same data and concluded that "the successful performers among [developing countries] were differentiated from the less successful primarily by increases in their shares in world markets for their traditional exports rather than by good fortune in world demand for their particular exports" (1970, p. 868). The data in the table encompass a wide range of export per-

	Nominal export growth 1983–84 to 1988–89				Nominal export growth 1988–89 to 1993–94			
	Annual average %	From world demand %	From market share %	From export diversifi-cation %	Annual average %	From world demand %	From market share %	From export diversifi-cation %
Hungary	10.8	13.1	−2.8	0.7	8.5	7.1	0.1	1.3
India	9.8	1.5	6.4	1.6	12.8	5.6	4.0	2.6
Indonesia	1.1	−4.7	1.0	5.0	12.1	4.3	0.3	7.1
Iran, Islamic Rep.	−10.9	−2.7	−8.8	0.4	10.0	4.6	4.3	0.8
Iraq	5.5	−2.7	8.2	0.2	−47.3	5.4	−49.9	−0.1
Ireland	17.2	14.2	2.6	0.0	9.0	8.3	2.1	−1.4
Israel	15.9	13.3	1.6	0.7	7.5	8.2	−1.0	0.3
Italy	14.9	14.1	1.0	−0.2	4.4	7.7	−3.2	0.1
Jamaica	7.9	6.4	1.7	−0.2	7.4	5.8	1.7	−0.1
Japan	14.1	15.7	−0.7	−0.7	7.5	8.2	−0.7	0.1
Jordan	7.8	3.4	5.5	−1.2	−2.8	5.3	−8.4	0.8
Kazakstan	..	..	..	..	..	..	..	..
Kenya	2.3	1.4	−0.4	1.3	4.2	4.0	−1.3	1.5
Korea, Dem. Rep.	22.0	14.3	2.6	4.1	11.1	7.5	−7.4	11.6
Korea, Rep.	22.1	13.4	7.0	0.6	6.5	8.8	−3.0	0.9
Kuwait	−1.0	−3.5	2.3	0.3	1.7	5.5	−3.5	−0.1
Kyrgyz Republic	..	..	..	..	..	..	..	..
Lao PDR	31.8	13.6	8.1	7.3	21.7	8.9	8.6	2.9
Latvia	..	..	..	..	..	..	..	..
Lebanon	1.2	15.0	−13.5	1.8	1.2	6.6	−6.6	1.7
Lesotho	..	..	..	..	..	..	..	..
Libya	−8.2	0.5	−8.9	0.2	2.9	5.4	−2.6	0.2
Lithuania	..	..	..	..	..	..	..	..
Macedonia, FYR	..	..	..	..	..	..	..	..
Madagascar	0.5	10.1	−9.6	1.0	7.2	2.3	−2.5	7.5
Malawi	3.9	11.1	−7.3	0.8	4.0	6.4	−2.0	−0.3
Malaysia	10.2	0.8	5.4	3.7	17.0	8.7	1.9	5.6
Mali	7.2	11.7	−5.6	1.6	7.6	4.3	1.5	1.7
Mauritania	10.4	−1.6	12.0	0.2	−2.0	6.1	−7.6	0.0
Mauritius	21.8	16.5	3.7	0.8	4.8	8.4	−3.1	−0.3
Mexico	4.1	6.0	−7.6	6.2	10.6	7.9	2.3	0.2
Moldova	..	..	..	..	..	..	..	..
Mongolia	22.9	14.5	4.3	2.9	19.9	7.5	7.4	3.9
Morocco	13.2	14.1	−1.1	0.3	7.1	6.4	0.0	0.6
Mozambique	14.8	5.1	2.7	6.4	−13.0	4.0	−14.4	−2.3
Myanmar	0.5	5.2	−6.8	2.5	16.5	3.6	12.6	−0.1
Namibia	..	..	..	..	..	..	..	..
Nepal	17.1	6.1	11.7	−1.2	14.9	6.8	8.5	−0.8
Netherlands	11.4	13.5	−2.5	0.7	2.8	7.7	−5.3	0.8
New Zealand	11.3	14.2	−3.1	0.6	4.8	4.0	−1.9	2.8
Nicaragua	−8.3	10.8	−19.5	2.8	3.3	4.7	−4.0	2.7
Niger	8.6	−2.2	8.9	2.0	−17.2	3.1	−20.4	0.9
Nigeria	−6.2	−5.1	−1.4	0.3	5.1	4.2	0.6	0.3
Norway	8.1	2.3	3.6	2.0	5.2	5.2	1.4	−1.4
Oman	−3.1	3.5	−6.9	0.7	6.3	8.0	−2.4	0.9
Pakistan	18.3	7.5	11.5	−1.3	8.4	6.4	1.2	0.7
Panama	7.5	8.9	−1.8	0.5	2.9	6.7	−7.3	4.1
Papua New Guinea	9.3	8.6	0.6	0.1	11.2	2.8	0.1	8.1
Paraguay	14.6	6.6	6.7	0.8	−2.1	3.8	−9.1	3.8
Peru	1.9	−3.5	4.8	0.8	3.4	3.6	−1.6	1.4
Philippines	6.9	9.5	−5.5	3.4	10.4	8.0	−0.8	3.0
Poland	10.1	12.5	−5.2	3.3	14.2	6.3	6.6	0.8
Portugal	20.9	13.6	5.9	0.5	6.0	7.9	−2.9	1.1
Puerto Rico	..	..	..	..	..	..	..	..
Romania	3.9	12.2	−7.4	0.1	−5.3	6.3	−12.7	2.1
Russian Federation	..	..	..	..	..	..	..	..

formance—from Iraq's loss of 47 percent a year during the second period to Yemen's increase of 85 percent a year during the first. Some of these extreme changes were caused by unusual events, such as wars, or by the fact that the economy started from a very low level.

Among large exporters and particularly among high-income countries, the data reveal a pattern of declining market shares for traditional exports and relatively small growth through export diversification. However, these data do not reflect complementary data on the expansion of service exports, which have become a leading factor in the growth of world trade. Thus high-income economies may be losing shares in their traditional markets for manufactured goods by diversifying their export regimes into

For many economies the largest factor in export growth has been the general expansion of world trade

services. A similar pattern can be seen among the rapidly growing economies of Asia—Hong Kong, the Republic of Korea, and Singapore. In contrast, the less mature economies of Indonesia, Malaysia, and Thailand still show evidence of rapid diversification of their trade in goods.

Table 5.7a summarizes the average growth of total exports and each of the three growth factors for two groups of countries: those that suffered a loss in nominal exports in both periods and those that increased their exports in both periods. The data suggest that most economies that gain in exports do so by expanding their traditional markets (world demand), while those who lose do so by losing their share of traditional markets. This holds true in both periods, but in the second period even gainers show losses in market share, while losers make a greater effort to diversify their exports.

The correlation between export growth and growth in each of the three factors is shown in table 5.7b. The correlation coefficients suggest a different story than the simple averages.

	Nominal export growth 1983–84 to 1988–89				Nominal export growth 1988–89 to 1993–94			
	Annual average %	From world demand %	From market share %	From export diversifi- cation %	Annual average %	From world demand %	From market share %	From export diversifi- cation %
Rwanda	4.3	13.9	–10.5	2.4	–14.1	10.2	–21.7	–0.4
South Africa	6.3	11.6	–5.5	0.8	3.4	1.0	–1.8	4.3
Saudi Arabia	–8.4	4.0	–13.0	1.2	8.9	6.3	2.5	0.0
Senegal	9.1	9.4	–1.4	1.1	–8.3	3.4	–11.5	0.2
Sierra Leone	8.2	3.1	4.2	0.7	0.1	3.1	–4.1	1.2
Singapore	12.1	13.2	–2.5	1.6	15.2	9.4	6.7	–1.3
Slovak Republic	..	..	..	..	..	..	..	..
Slovenia	..	..	..	..	..	..	..	..
Spain	14.7	13.5	0.0	1.0	9.4	7.4	2.4	–0.5
Sri Lanka	9.4	7.5	0.8	1.0	13.7	6.1	5.6	1.5
Sudan	–2.5	6.7	–9.6	1.1	–5.4	2.9	–9.6	1.8
Sweden	13.0	13.7	–0.5	–0.1	2.2	7.5	–4.8	–0.1
Switzerland	16.5	16.4	0.6	–0.5	5.3	8.2	–3.0	0.3
Syrian Arab Republic	–2.6	–0.4	–3.2	1.0	23.0	6.2	16.2	–0.4
Tajikistan	..	..	..	..	..	..	..	..
Tanzania	1.7	1.1	–4.0	4.7	0.3	3.2	–3.3	0.5
Thailand	21.9	14.0	1.1	5.8	17.4	8.7	1.0	6.8
Togo	7.5	9.6	–3.9	2.1	–9.4	4.6	–13.3	–0.1
Trinidad and Tobago	–7.8	–0.4	–8.9	1.6	5.6	5.3	–0.6	0.9
Tunisia	10.9	–0.7	9.3	2.1	9.8	5.8	3.4	0.3
Turkey	19.9	–0.1	15.6	3.8	7.4	5.9	–1.2	2.7
Turkmenistan	..	..	..	..	..	..	..	..
Uganda	–4.3	9.4	–12.6	0.1	–2.6	3.8	–7.9	1.9
Ukraine	..	..	..	..	..	..	..	..
United Arab Emirates	–4.4	–1.7	–4.0	1.3	8.5	5.4	1.4	1.5
United Kingdom	9.8	10.1	–1.2	0.9	5.7	7.6	–1.2	–0.6
United States	10.0	13.3	–3.6	0.8	8.6	7.6	0.9	0.1
Uruguay	13.2	13.9	–1.5	0.9	8.4	6.9	–4.1	5.7
Uzbekistan	..	..	..	..	..	..	..	..
Venezuela	–4.3	1.2	–6.8	1.5	7.2	4.9	0.4	1.7
Vietnam	26.2	9.0	3.0	12.4	39.4	4.2	14.9	16.5
West Bank and Gaza	..	..	..	..	..	..	..	..
Yemen, Rep.	85.4	7.1	3.0	67.9	9.7	7.7	26.8	–19.7
Yugoslavia, Fed. Rep.	..	..	..	..	..	..	..	..
Zaire	5.0	–0.9	6.0	–0.1	–10.7	5.2	–16.1	1.3
Zambia	8.2	12.9	–4.5	0.3	–3.1	2.9	–6.1	0.3
Zimbabwe	12.6	8.6	1.6	2.0	–1.4	2.1	–5.0	1.7

Table 5.7a Average annual growth of exports and export growth factors, 1983–94

	1983–84 to 1988–89			
Country group	Total exports	World demand	Market share	Diversifi- cation
Positive growth	12.8	10.0	1.9	0.6
Negative growth	–6.7	1.9	–9.4	1.0
All economies	11.2	8.3	1.6	1.0

	1988–89 to 1993–94			
Positive growth	6.9	7.1	–0.8	0.6
Negative growth	–9.9	6.4	–17.3	2.5
All economies	6.7	7.0	–0.9	0.6

Source: World Bank staff estimates.

In the first period the diversification factor has the strongest correlation with export growth. Thus countries that diversified tended to be the most successful in expanding total exports. Growth in world demand for traditional exports is also positively correlated with export growth, but there is virtually no correlation for countries with a loss in exports. The negative sign on the diversification factor suggests that the greater the loss in trade, the more economies tried to diversify. In the second period, growth in market share is strongly associated with total export growth, but diversification is relatively unimportant.

Care must be used in drawing conclusions about development strategies from these data. While successful exporters have diversified their commodity mix, diversification does not guarantee growth. For many economies the largest factor in export growth has been the general expansion of world trade, which has allowed their export markets to grow. World trade patterns continue to change. In seeking new opportunities, some economies will enter new markets while other will seek to increase their share of existing markets. And for some the new frontier lies in services, giving up their hold on traditional markets to the newly indus- trializing economies.

Table 5.7b Correlation of export growth factors with export growth, 1983–94

	1983–84 to 1988–89		
Country group	World demand	Market share	Diversifi-cation
Positive growth	0.232	0.250	0.703
Negative growth	0.009	0.677	–0.366
All economies	0.408	0.511	0.644
	1988–89 to 1993–94		
Positive growth	0.116	0.784	0.145
Negative growth	–0.043	0.854	0.169
All economies	0.219	0.943	–0.012

Source: World Bank staff estimates.

About the data

Data on commodity exports were taken from the United Nations COMTRADE database, using partner country reports of imports at the three-digit Standard International Trade Classification (SITC) level. The use of partner trade minimizes the effects of nonreporting among developing countries. Because most large importers report trade on a timely basis, the trade included is estimated to cover 95 percent of world trade in a given year. Two-year averages are computed to reduce the effect of a single unusual year. No trade data were reported for China in 1983, so 1984 data are used for the base year. The results for Germany for 1983–84 to 1988–89 refer only to the former Federal Republic of Germany.

Traditional exports for a country are defined as the three-digit commodity groups that made up at least 75 percent of the value of the country's exports in 1983–84 and included at least the 10 largest commodity groups. The same export bundle is used to calculate the indexes in 1988–89 to 1993–94.

Trade growth due to world demand for traditional exports is computed as

$$f_1 = Xmt/Xm_0$$

where Xmt is the value of total world trade in the country's traditional exports at the end of the period and Xm_0 is the corresponding value at the beginning of the period.

The growth due to an increase (or decrease) in market share is computed as

$$f_2 = (xmt/xm_0)/(Xmt/Xm_0)$$

where xmt and xm_0 are the country's exports of traditional goods at the end and the beginning of the period. Thus factor f_2 is the ratio of the country's share of world trade in traditional exports at the end of the period to its share at the beginning of the period.

The third factor, trade diversification, is determined as the residual export growth over the period. It can be shown that

$$f_3 = (xm_0/x_0)/(xmt/xt)$$

where xt and x_0 represent the country's total traditional and nontraditional exports. Thus the trade diversification factor represents the reciprocal of the change in shares of traditional exports from the beginning to the end of the period. In other words, it shows the room made available in the county's export bundle for nontraditional exports.

While GATT (1966) stated the factors in index form relative to their base year level, the table shows them as compound annual growth rates.

Definitions

- **Total export growth** is the compound annual rate of growth in the value of merchandise exports.
- **Export growth from world demand** measures the compound annual growth in exports due to growth of the world market for the country's traditional exports. Traditional exports are defined as the 10 largest three-digit commodity groups, or the groups that made up at least 75 percent of the country's trade in the base year, whichever is greater. ● **Export growth from market share** measures the compound annual growth in exports due to growth in the country's share of the world market in its traditional exports.
- **Export growth from export diversification** measures the compound annual growth in exports due to growth of nontraditional exports.

Data sources

Raw data come from the United Nations COMTRADE database. Computations were carried out by staff of the World Bank's International Economics Department, Development Data Group.

5.8 Tax policies

	Tax revenue	Taxes on income, profits, and capital gains		Domestic taxes on goods and services		Export duties		Import duties		Highest marginal tax rate		
	% of GDP	% of total taxes		% of value added of industry and services		% of exports		% of imports		Individual rate %	rate on income exceeding $	Corporate rate %
	1995	1980	1995	1980	1995	1980	1995	1980	1995	1996	1996	1996
Albania	18.3	..	10.7	..	21.1	..	..	..	..	..	..	..
Algeria	..	..	..	..	..	..	..	..	..	..	..	..
Angola	..	..	..	..	..	..	..	..	..	..	..	..
Argentina	..	0.0	..	..	..	..	..	..	..	30	120,060	30
Armenia	..	..	..	..	..	..	..	..	..	..	..	..
Australia	22.3	67.6	70.4	5.2	4.9	0.5	0.0	8.3	4.7	47	38,841	36
Austria	32.9	22.8	21.1	9.3	9.3	0.2	0.0	1.6	1.7	50	63,091	34
Azerbaijan	..	..	..	..	..	..	..	..	..	..	..	..
Bangladesh	..	14.9	..	5.7	..	3.5	..	16.5	..	..	..	..
Belarus	..	..	..	..	..	..	..	..	..	..	..	..
Belgium	43.7	40.3	36.0	10.8	..	..	..	..	..	55	76,011	39
Benin	..	..	..	..	..	2.2	..	..	..	..	..	..
Bolivia	11.8	..	3.8	..	..	..	0.0	..	5.9	13	..	25
Bosnia and Herzegovina	..	..	..	..	..	..	..	..	..	..	..	..
Botswana	28.1	45.5	59.4	0.3	1.6	0.1	0.0	21.2	23.6	30	22,080	25
Brazil	18.6	13.6	21.0	..	..	..	..	..	..	20	..	25
Bulgaria	29.0	..	21.7	..	12.0	..	..	..	..	50	4,847	40
Burkina Faso	..	20.1	..	2.9	..	..	..	..	..	..	..	..
Burundi	..	20.4	..	10.1	..	..	..	..	..	..	..	..
Cambodia	..	..	..	..	..	..	..	..	..	..	..	..
Cameroon	9.5	23.7	29.7	4.1	3.6	6.5	1.0	19.0	29.3	60	14,029	39
Canada	..	60.8	..	3.9	..	1.0	..	4.5	..	29	43,387	38
Central African Republic	..	17.7	..	6.0	..	9.3	..	23.9	..	..	..	..
Chad	..	..	..	..	..	..	..	..	..	..	..	..
Chile	17.8	22.1	21.0	12.3	..	..	..	7.0	..	45	6,523	15
China	5.7	..	9.1	..	5.8	..	..	..	..	45	11,840	30
Colombia	14.0	28.9	40.9	3.4	6.5	7.2	0.0	12.3	8.7	35	48,360	35
Congo	..	63.7	..	3.1	..	0.1	..	14.0	..	50	14,964	49
Costa Rica	22.0	14.6	12.9	6.6	10.1	6.6	1.3	6.9	8.9	25	27,661	30
Côte d'Ivoire	..	14.1	..	8.0	..	8.0	..	28.8	..	10	4,489	35
Croatia	43.0	..	11.1	..	27.1	..	..	..	..	..	..	..
Cuba	..	..	..	..	..	..	..	..	..	..	..	..
Czech Republic	37.5	..	16.1	..	13.9	..	..	..	..	40	20,108	39
Denmark	35.4	40.7	45.3	23.2	20.7	..	..	0.1	0.1	65	..	38
Dominican Republic	14.9	24.8	15.5	3.9	6.2	6.2	0.0	14.9	12.1	26	11,482	25
Ecuador	13.9	46.5	56.5	2.5	4.6	3.0	0.0	16.3	8.3	25	64,519	25
Egypt, Arab Rep.	26.3	29.5	32.2	5.5	7.4	5.3	0.0	26.0	16.1	48	..	40
El Salvador	12.1	23.8	27.7	5.4	7.4	10.3	0.0	4.4	6.1	30	22,857	25
Eritrea	..	..	..	..	..	..	..	..	..	..	..	..
Estonia	33.2	..	22.3	..	11.1	..	..	..	..	26	..	26
Ethiopia	11.9	25.3	28.8	9.1	..	33.7	2.6	17.2	12.6	..	..	..
Finland	29.3	30.8	31.6	21.0	19.2	..	..	1.9	1.3	39	61,140	28
France	38.1	19.1	18.7	12.9	11.5	..	..	0.1	0.0	..	..	33
Gabon	..	60.1	..	1.8	..	1.7	..	38.3	..	55	..	40
Gambia, The	21.8	18.1	15.5	1.3	12.9	12.7	0.1	22.1	17.0	..	..	..
Georgia	..	..	..	..	..	..	..	..	..	..	..	..
Germany	30.0	19.4	17.0	..	..	..	..	0.0	0.0	53	77,506	30
Ghana	12.9	22.0	21.6	15.9	10.8	30.0	5.2	14.2	11.9	35	15,200	35
Greece	26.0	19.4	31.4	23.3	38.1	..	..	6.3	0.1	45	62,474	40
Guatemala	6.8	14.4	16.8	..	4.9	9.9	0.0	7.6	8.2	30	31,867	30
Guinea	..	..	..	..	..	..	..	..	..	..	..	..
Guinea-Bissau	..	..	..	..	..	..	..	..	..	..	..	..
Haiti	..	15.9	..	..	..	10.2	..	12.3	..	..	..	..
Honduras	..	32.9	..	5.1	..	7.4	..	7.9	..	40	106,382	35
Hong Kong	..	..	..	..	..	..	..	..	..	20	10,339	17

	Tax revenue	Taxes on income, profits, and capital gains		Domestic taxes on goods and services		Export duties		Import duties		Highest marginal tax rate		
				% of value added of industry and services						Individual		Corporate
										rate %	rate on income exceeding $	rate %
	% of GDP 1995	% of total taxes 1980	1995	1980	1995	% of exports 1980	1995	% of imports 1980	1995	1996	1996	1996
Hungary	..	22.1	..	..	..	..	..	..	..	48	8,131	18
India	9.6	21.9	28.8	8.9	6.6	1.8	..	29.9	..	40	3,824	40
Indonesia	16.4	82.0	52.8	2.4	7.5	0.9	0.2	5.1	5.9	30	22,727	30
Iran, Islamic Rep.	8.2	12.2	26.5	1.0	..	..	..	20.8	13.6	54	173,851	10
Iraq	..	..	..	..	..	..	..	..	..	..	..	..
Ireland	35.1	38.4	41.9	..	..	..	..	6.0	4.2	48	14,246	40
Israel	33.4	47.3	45.0	..	..	..	..	..	0.6	50	57,256	36
Italy	38.4	32.1	37.7	..	..	..	..	..	..	51	184,078	37
Jamaica	..	35.0	..	15.4	..	..	..	2.3	..	25	1,270	33
Japan	17.6	74.6	43.1	2.5	3.1	..	..	2.3	4.1	50	300,782	38
Jordan	20.4	17.0	15.7	..	8.4	..	..	15.8	15.4	..	..	..
Kazakstan	..	..	..	..	..	..	..	..	..	40	..	30
Kenya	19.6	33.4	30.7	14.8	17.2	1.3	0.0	11.8	8.2	35	348	35
Korea, Dem. Rep.	..	..	..	..	..	..	..	..	..	..	..	..
Korea, Rep.	17.7	25.4	35.9	9.3	7.0	..	..	7.7	4.7	40	103,133	28
Kuwait	1.2	63.6	24.7	0.2	0.0	..	..	2.7	3.0	0	..	55
Kyrgyz Republic	..	..	..	..	..	..	..	..	..	..	..	..
Lao PDR	..	..	..	..	..	..	..	..	..	..	..	..
Latvia	23.1	..	8.4	..	11.4	..	..	..	..	35	109,489	25
Lebanon	10.8	..	15.1	..	1.3	..	..	..	..	..	..	..
Lesotho	44.4	15.5	14.9	5.3	10.2	3.4	0.1	..	..	..	..	..
Libya	..	..	..	..	..	..	..	..	..	..	..	..
Lithuania	24.4	..	13.0	..	12.9	..	..	..	..	..	..	29
Macedonia, FYR	..	..	..	..	..	..	..	..	..	..	..	..
Madagascar	8.2	17.1	15.0	8.4	3.6	..	..	..	..	..	..	..
Malawi	..	38.9	..	10.6	..	..	..	..	..	38	2,745	38
Malaysia	20.6	42.1	45.6	5.6	7.5	9.0	0.9	8.9	3.9	30	58,594	30
Mali	..	20.5	..	10.7	..	..	..	..	..	..	..	..
Mauritania	..	..	..	..	..	..	..	..	..	..	..	..
Mauritius	18.2	17.3	14.3	4.8	6.9	..	..	..	..	30	3,079	35
Mexico	14.8	38.8	39.3	2.7	8.6	17.6	0.0	4.6	4.7	35	22,283	34
Moldova	..	..	..	..	..	..	..	..	..	..	..	..
Mongolia	20.3	..	43.5	..	..	..	..	..	..	..	..	..
Morocco	..	22.0	..	10.0	..	..	..	..	..	44	6,697	35
Mozambique	..	..	..	..	..	..	..	..	..	..	..	..
Myanmar	4.6	4.9	33.5	..	..	..	..	17.6	..	..	..	..
Namibia	31.4	..	32.2	..	13.2	..	..	..	..	35	22,577	35
Nepal	9.1	6.6	13.6	8.0	7.9	5.1	1.9	13.8	9.7	..	..	..
Netherlands	42.9	33.1	27.0	10.6	10.9	..	..	..	..	60	53,468	37
New Zealand	34.4	75.1	64.5	7.1	..	0.1	0.0	4.5	3.9	33	19,837	33
Nicaragua	23.6	8.9	11.8	..	16.2	..	0.0	..	11.8	30	25,310	30
Niger	..	28.1	..	4.5	..	..	..	..	..	..	..	..
Nigeria	..	..	..	..	..	..	..	..	..	30	2,728	30
Norway	31.6	30.2	20.7	15.4	..	0.0	0.0	0.9	1.0	28	6,891	28
Oman	8.5	92.8	77.7	0.2	..	..	..	1.6	2.7	0	..	50
Pakistan	15.3	16.8	20.3	8.6	10.6	1.8	0.0	22.4	23.9	35	9,740	46
Panama	20.1	29.0	25.0	..	5.7	0.5	0.2	3.0	3.0	30	200,000	34
Papua New Guinea	18.9	67.5	58.2	4.0	3.2	..	..	..	..	35	16,969	25
Paraguay	9.1	16.6	16.0	2.7	6.7	0.8	0.0	13.2	4.4	0	..	30
Peru	14.4	28.1	18.6	..	8.2	..	0.0	..	13.0	30	54,495	30
Philippines	16.0	23.6	33.9	7.8	6.3	1.0	0.0	13.4	13.6	35	20,477	35
Poland	36.7	..	30.9	..	12.5	..	..	..	..	45	13,442	40
Portugal	30.9	20.9	26.7	..	..	0.0	0.0	4.4	0.0	40	37,714	36
Puerto Rico	..	..	..	..	..	..	..	..	..	33	..	20
Romania	26.3	0.0	34.0	..	9.0	..	..	..	..	60	6,875	38
Russian Federation	16.1	..	15.8	..	5.8	..	..	..	..	35	13,521	35

	Tax revenue	Taxes on income, profits, and capital gains		Domestic taxes on goods and services		Export duties		Import duties		Highest marginal tax rate		
	% of GDP	% of total taxes		% of value added of industry and services		% of exports		% of imports		Individual rate %	on income exceeding $	Corporate rate %
	1995	1980	1995	1980	1995	1980	1995	1980	1995	1996	1996	1996
Rwanda	..	20.6	..	5.3	..	..	..	..	..	..	..	..
Saudi Arabia	..	..	..	..	..	..	..	..	..	0	..	45
Senegal	..	21.4	..	7.7	..	..	..	..	..	..	..	..
Sierra Leone	12.5	24.9	23.0	4.3	8.2	..	..	..	..	..	..	..
Singapore	17.2	47.0	45.6	4.2	4.7	..	..	0.9	0.3	30	273,841	27
Slovak Republic	..	..	..	..	..	..	..	..	..	..	..	..
Slovenia	..	..	..	..	..	..	..	..	..	..	..	..
South Africa	25.2	63.8	52.8	6.2	11.7	0.1	0.0	3.0	1.1	45	22,577	35
Spain	28.7	25.2	33.7	..	..	..	..	6.0	0.1	56	77,593	35
Sri Lanka	18.0	16.5	14.5	8.0	15.6	22.0	0.0	9.6	11.2	35	2,101	35
Sudan	..	17.2	..	7.0	..	..	..	..	..	..	..	..
Sweden	32.8	21.1	16.9	12.8	15.5	..	..	1.5	1.2	30	28,024	28
Switzerland	21.5	15.0	16.0	..	..	..	..	4.0	5.0	13	424,247	46
Syrian Arab Republic	17.8	24.6	27.5	1.8	..	1.7	6.7	11.6	23.9	..	..	..
Tajikistan	..	..	..	..	..	..	..	..	..	..	..	..
Tanzania	..	35.3	..	19.1	..	..	..	..	..	30	2,808	35
Thailand	17.1	19.3	34.1	8.6	8.3	4.4	0.1	11.1	9.4	37	159,426	30
Togo	..	38.6	..	6.4	..	..	..	..	..	..	..	..
Trinidad and Tobago	..	86.7	..	1.6	..	..	..	9.8	..	35	6,742	35
Tunisia	..	19.1	..	8.8	..	..	..	..	..	..	..	..
Turkey	14.3	61.9	40.4	5.1	9.6	..	..	8.9	3.2	55	247,895	25
Turkmenistan	..	..	..	..	..	..	..	..	..	..	..	..
Uganda	..	11.8	..	46.4	..	..	..	..	..	30	5,309	30
Ukraine	..	..	..	..	..	..	..	..	..	..	..	..
United Arab Emirates	0.6	..	0.0	0.0	0.5	..	..	..	..	..	..	..
United Kingdom	33.5	43.4	38.9	12.7	13.0	0.0	0.0	0.1	0.1	40	39,844	33
United States	19.0	61.7	56.6	0.9	0.8	..	..	3.0	2.6	40	263,750	35
Uruguay	27.6	11.5	10.3	..	10.6	..	0.2	..	7.7	0	..	30
Uzbekistan	..	..	..	..	..	..	..	..	..	..	..	..
Venezuela	14.8	79.4	47.5	1.0	4.2	..	..	9.6	9.9	34	..	34
Vietnam	..	..	..	..	..	..	..	..	..	50	6,335	25
West Bank and Gaza	..	..	..	..	..	..	..	..	..	..	..	..
Yemen, Rep.	13.0	..	37.8	..	11.3	..	..	..	30.1	..	..	..
Yugoslavia, Fed. Rep.	..	..	..	..	..	..	..	..	..	..	..	..
Zaire	..	..	..	..	..	..	..	..	..	..	..	50
Zambia	13.4	41.2	37.4	12.4	9.1	..	..	..	..	35	1,764	35
Zimbabwe	..	57.9	..	9.0	..	..	..	..	..	40	6,451	38
World	**23.3 w**	**48.4 w**	**41.3 w**	**4.5 w**	..							
Low income	8.1 w	..	18.1 w	..	6.6 w							
Excl. China & India	..	..	..	..	..							
Middle income	..	..	..	..	..							
Lower middle income	17.7 w	..	27.0 w	..	..							
Upper middle income	20.1 w	25.9 w	31.3 w	..	..							
Low & middle income	..	..	..	..	..							
East Asia & Pacific	10.0 w	..	22.3 w	..	6.5 w							
Europe & Central Asia	22.8 w	..	21.1 w	..	..							
Latin America & Carib.	16.5 w	26.0 w	31.1 w	..	..							
Middle East & N. Africa	..	..	..	..	..							
South Asia	10.5 w	20.6 w	27.3 w	8.7 w	7.1 w							
Sub-Saharan Africa	..	42.3 w	..	8.2 w	..							
High income	25.3 w	51.5 w	45.6 w	4.3 w	..							

About the data

Taxes are compulsory, unrequited payments made to governments by individuals, businesses, or institutions. They are described as unrequited because governments provide nothing specifically in return for them, although they may use the funds received to provide goods or services to individuals or communities. The sources of the revenue received by governments and the relative contributions of these sources are determined by policy choices about where and how to impose taxes and by changes in the structure of the economy. Tax policy may reflect concerns about distributional effects, economic efficiency (including corrections for externalities), and the practical problems of administering a tax system. There is no single correct model for distributing tax revenues among sources, nor is any distribution likely to remain constant over time.

The definitions used here are those used by the International Monetary Fund (IMF) in its *Manual on Government Finance Statistics.* Taxes traditionally have been classified either as direct—taxes levied directly on the income, profits, or property of individuals and corporations—or indirect—sales and excise taxes and duties. Indirect taxes have been construed as those that could be passed on by increasing the prices of goods or services sold to intermediate or final purchasers. But it is extremely difficult to determine the incidence of taxes, so the distinction has been dropped both from the United Nations System of National Accounts and by the IMF, although it remains useful for general discussion.

The level of taxation is typically measured by tax revenue as a share of GDP. Comparing levels of taxation across countries provides a quick overview of the structure of fiscal incentives facing the private sector. In this table tax data measured in local currencies are normalized by scale variables in the same units to ease cross-country comparisons. Data for 1980 are included to give a quick impression of changes over time. The table relies on central government data, which may considerably understate the total tax burden, particularly in countries where provincial and municipal governments are important.

Ratios of tax to GDP may reflect weak administration and large-scale tax avoidance or tax evasion. They also may reflect the presence of a substantial parallel economy with unrecorded and undisclosed incomes. These ratios tend to rise with level of income, with more developed countries relying on taxes to finance a much broader range of social services and social security than less developed countries are able to provide. Many of the poorest countries have low tax revenues relative to GDP, and so must rely heavily on external assistance.

As countries develop, they typically expand their capacity to tax residents directly, and indirect taxes become less important as a revenue source. Thus the share of taxes on income, profits, and capital gains is one measure of a tax system's level of development. In the early stages of development governments tend to rely on indirect taxes because the administrative costs of collection are relatively low. There are two principal sources of indirect taxes: customs revenues and domestic taxes on goods and services. The table shows these domestic taxes as a percentage of value added in industry and services. Agriculture and mining are excluded from the denominator because indirect taxation of these sectors is usually negligible. What is missing here is a measure of the uniformity of these taxes across industries and along the value added chain of production. Without such data no clear inferences can be drawn about how neutral a tax system is between subsectors with respect to incentives. Revenues raised by some governments by charging higher prices for goods produced by state-owned enterprises are not counted as tax revenues.

Export and import duties are shown separately because their burden on growth is likely to be high. Export duties, typically levied on primary (particularly agricultural) products, reduce the incentive to export and encourage a shift to other crops. High import tariffs penalize consumers, promote inefficient production, and implicitly tax exports. By contrast, lowering trade taxes enhances openness—to foreign competition, foreign knowledge, and foreign resources—energizing the development process in many ways. The economies growing fastest over the past 15 years have not relied on tax revenues from exports and, seeing this pattern, many other countries have reduced their export duties. For some countries, such as members of the European Union, most customs duties are collected by the supranational authority; these revenues are not reported in the individual countries' accounts.

The revenues collected by governments are the outcomes of tax systems that are often complex, containing many exceptions, exemptions, penalties, and other inducements that affect tax incidence and thus influence the decisions of workers, managers, and entrepreneurs. A potentially important influence on both domestic and international investors is the progressivity of a tax system, as measured roughly by the highest marginal tax rate on individual and corporate income.

Definitions

● **Tax revenue** comprises compulsory, unrequited, nonrepayable receipts for public purposes collected by central governments. It includes interest collected on tax arrears and penalties collected on nonpayment or late payment of taxes and is shown net of refunds and other corrective transactions. ● **Taxes on income, profits, and capital gains** include taxes levied by central governments on the actual or presumptive net income of individuals and profits of enterprises. Also included are taxes levied on capital gains, whether realized on sales of land, securities, or other assets. Social security contributions based on gross pay, payroll, or number of employees are not included, but social security contributions based on personal income after deductions and personal exemptions are included. ● **Domestic taxes on goods and services** include all taxes and duties levied by central governments on the production, extraction, sale, transfer, leasing, or delivery of goods and rendering of services, or in respect of the use of goods or permission to use goods or to perform activities. Such taxes include general sales taxes, turnover or value added taxes, excises, and motor vehicle taxes. ● **Export duties** include all levies collected on goods at the point of export from the country. Rebates on exported goods comprising repayments of previously paid general consumption taxes, excises, or import duties should be deducted from the gross receipts of the appropriate taxes, not from export duty receipts. ● **Import duties** comprise all levies collected on goods at the point of entry into the country. They include levies for revenue purposes or import protection, whether on a specific or ad valorem basis, as long as they are restricted by law to imported products. ● **Highest marginal tax rate** is the highest rate shown on the schedule of tax rates applied to the taxable income of individuals and corporations. For some countries the highest marginal tax rate is also the basic or flat rate, and other surtaxes, deductions, and the like may apply. Also presented are the income levels above which the highest marginal tax rates apply for individuals.

Data sources

Data on tax revenues are from print and electronic editions of the IMF's *Government Finance Statistics Yearbook.* Data on individual and corporate tax rates are from Price Waterhouse, *Individual Taxes: A Worldwide Summary* (1996) and *Corporate Taxes: A Worldwide Summary* (1996).

5.9 Portfolio investment regulation and risk

	Entry and exit regulations			Composite ICRG risk rating	Institutional Investor credit rating	Euromoney country credit-worthiness rating	Moody's sovereign long-term debt rating		Standard & Poor's sovereign long-term debt rating	
	Entry 1995	Repatriation of income 1995	Repatriation of capital 1995	December 1996	September 1996	September 1996	Foreign currency November 1996	Domestic currency November 1996	Foreign currency November 1996	Domestic currency November 1996
Albania	..	..	..	64.5	14.1	34.2	..	..	..	..
Algeria	..	..	..	59.0	22.8	37.7	..	..	..	..
Angola	..	..	..	48.5	12.4	17.7	..	..	..	..
Argentina	Free	Free	Free	73.5	38.9	57.3	B1	..	BB–	BBB–
Armenia	..	..	..	..	..	28.5	..	..	..	..
Australia	..	..	..	85.5	71.7	91.4	Aa2	Aaa	AA	AAA
Austria	..	..	..	89.5	86.0	95.2	Aaa	..	AAA	AAA
Azerbaijan	..	..	..	..	..	16.9	..	..	..	..
Bangladesh	Free	Free	Free	65.0	26.9	40.3	..	..	..	..
Belarus	..	..	..	..	14.6	27.7	..	..	..	..
Belgium	..	..	..	87.5	79.6	93.4	Aa1	..	AA+	AAA
Benin	..	..	..	..	17.2	30.2	..	..	..	..
Bolivia	..	..	..	65.5	25.4	40.7	..	..	..	..
Bosnia and Herzegovina	..	..	..	..	..	..	..	..	..	..
Botswana	Free	Free	Free	79.0	49.8	51.1	..	..	..	..
Brazil	Free	Free	Free	67.0	38.3	56.8	B1	..	B+	BB
Bulgaria	..	..	..	64.5	23.5	40.4	B3	..	..	..
Burkina Faso	..	..	..	61.0	17.5	34.2	..	..	..	..
Burundi	..	..	..	..	..	..	..	..	..	..
Cambodia	..	..	..	..	..	35.3	..	..	..	..
Cameroon	..	..	..	57.0	18.8	32.1	..	..	..	..
Canada	..	..	..	85.0	79.4	91.8	Aa2	Aa1	AA+	AAA
Central African Republic	..	..	..	..	..	33.0	..	..	..	..
Chad	..	..	..	..	..	30.0	..	..	..	..
Chile	Rel. free[a]	Free	Delayed[b]	82.0	61.2	77.4	..	..	A–	AA
China	Special	Free	Free	74.5	57.2	71.3	A3	..	BBB	..
Colombia	Auth. only[c]	Free	Free	62.0	46.7	62.4	Baa3	..	BBB–	A+
Congo	..	..	..	60.5	14.7	22.7	..	..	..	..
Costa Rica	Free	Free	Free	73.0	33.9	41.2	..	..	..	..
Côte d'Ivoire	Free	Free	Free	64.0	18.5	39.8	..	..	..	..
Croatia	Free	Free	Free	..	26.0	47.2	..	..	..	..
Cuba	..	..	..	62.0	10.8	11.5	..	..	..	..
Czech Republic	Free	Free	Free	83.5	62.0	73.7	Baa1	..	A	..
Denmark	..	..	..	89.5	80.7	94.8	Aa1	Aaa	AA+	AAA
Dominican Republic	..	..	..	69.0	23.1	35.4	..	..	..	..
Ecuador	Free	Free	Free	59.5	26.4	45.0	..	..	..	..
Egypt, Arab Rep.	Free	Free	Free	67.5	35.1	45.7	Ba2	..	..	..
El Salvador	..	..	..	68.5	21.6	40.7	..	..	BB	BBB+
Eritrea	..	..	..	..	..	..	..	..	..	..
Estonia	..	..	..	..	31.1	48.0	..	..	..	..
Ethiopia	..	..	..	63.5	15.9	28.1	..	..	..	..
Finland	..	..	..	85.0	73.1	91.5	Aa2	..	AA–	AAA
France	..	..	..	82.5	87.1	95.7	Aaa	Aaa	AAA	AAA
Gabon	..	..	..	64.5	25.7	37.7	..	..	..	..
Gambia, The	..	..	..	64.5	..	35.1	..	..	..	..
Georgia	..	..	..	..	9.4	24.1	..	..	..	..
Germany	..	..	..	85.0	90.9	95.7	..	Aaa	AAA	AAA
Ghana	Free	Free	Free	62.0	29.6	44.6	..	..	..	..
Greece	Free	Free	Free	77.5	50.3	72.8	Baa3	..	BBB–	..
Guatemala	..	..	..	65.5	22.7	35.4	..	..	..	..
Guinea-Bissau	..	..	..	44.0	..	21.3	..	..	..	..
Guinea	..	..	..	53.0	14.5	30.0	..	..	..	..
Haiti	..	..	..	49.0	10.4	27.3	..	..	..	..
Honduras	..	..	..	55.5	18.7	33.1	..	..	..	..
Hong Kong	..	..	..	85.0	65.3	82.4	..	..	A	A+

	Entry and exit regulations			Composite ICRG risk rating	Institutional Investor credit rating	Euromoney country credit-worthiness rating	Moody's sovereign long-term debt rating		Standard & Poor's sovereign long-term debt rating	
	Entry 1995	Repatriation of income 1995	Repatriation of capital 1995	December 1996	September 1996	September 1996	Foreign currency November 1996	Domestic currency November 1996	Foreign currency November 1996	Domestic currency November 1996
Hungary	Free	Free	Free	77.5	44.7	67.2	Ba1	..	BBB–	A–
India	Auth. only[c]	Free	Free	69.0	46.3	63.7	..	..	BB+	BBB+
Indonesia	Rel. free[a]	Restricted	Restricted	70.0	52.2	70.8	Baa3	..	BBB	A+
Iran, Islamic Rep.	..	..	..	72.0	24.7	35.6	..	..	..	..
Iraq	..	..	..	35.0	9.1	9.4	..	..	..	..
Ireland	..	..	..	88.5	74.5	92.3	Aa2	Aaa	AA	AAA
Israel	..	..	..	68.5	52.2	75.5	..	..	A–	AA–
Italy	..	..	..	82.5	72.4	87.8	Aa3	Aa3	AA	AAA
Jamaica	Rel. free[a]	Free	Free	71.0	27.5	36.8	..	..	..	..
Japan	..	..	..	89.5	91.1	94.0	..	Aaa	AAA	AAA
Jordan	Free	Free	Free	73.0	33.1	47.8	Ba3	..	BB–	BBB–
Kazakstan	..	..	..	..	19.6	30.6	..	..	BB–	BB+
Kenya	Rel. free[a]	Free	Free	67.5	27.9	42.3	..	..	..	..
Korea, Dem. Rep.	..	..	..	45.5	..	5.4	..	..	..	..
Korea, Rep.	Rel. free[a]	Free	Free	85.0	72.1	84.3	..	..	AA–	..
Kuwait	..	..	..	80.5	54.7	74.8	..	..	..	..
Kyrgyz Republic	..	..	..	..	..	23.6	..	..	..	..
Lao PDR	..	..	..	..	..	30.5	..	..	..	..
Latvia	..	..	..	..	25.7	47.1	..	..	..	..
Lebanon	..	..	..	62.5	27.2	44.3	..	..	..	..
Lesotho	..	..	..	..	..	31.6	..	..	..	..
Libya	..	..	..	63.5	27.9	17.1	..	..	..	..
Lithuania	Rel. free[a]	Free	Free	..	25.3	55.2	Ba2	..	..	..
Macedonia, FYR	..	..	..	..	..	36.3	..	..	..	..
Madagascar	..	..	..	54.5	..	30.8	..	..	..	..
Malawi	..	..	..	59.5	19.7	33.7	..	..	..	..
Malaysia	Free	Free	Free	81.5	67.7	80.2	A1	..	A+	AA+
Mali	..	..	..	56.0	16.7	33.6	..	..	..	..
Mauritania	..	..	..	..	..	32.3	..	..	..	..
Mauritius	Auth. only[c]	Free	Free	..	50.8	51.3	Baa2	..	..	..
Mexico	Free	Free	Free	70.0	41.6	60.3	Ba2	Baa3	BB	BBB+
Moldova	..	..	..	..	..	31.5	..	..	..	..
Mongolia	..	..	..	68.0	..	26.4	..	..	..	..
Morocco	..	..	..	71.5	39.3	..	..	..	..	..
Mozambique	..	..	..	49.0	14.0	21.7	..	..	..	..
Myanmar	..	..	..	56.0	21.4	43.8	..	..	..	..
Namibia	Free	Free	Free	79.0	..	30.8	..	..	..	..
Nepal	..	..	..	..	25.7	40.3	..	..	..	..
Netherlands	..	..	..	89.5	89.2	97.9	..	..	AAA	AAA
New Zealand	..	..	..	85.0	71.6	92.0	Aa1	Aaa	AA+	AAA
Nicaragua	..	..	..	56.5	11.4	24.7	..	..	..	..
Niger	..	..	..	52.5	..	32.0	..	..	..	..
Nigeria	Closed	Restricted	Restricted	50.5	15.2	31.1	..	..	..	..
Norway	..	..	..	92.5	83.1	95.0	Aa1	Aaa	AAA	AAA
Oman	Free	Free	Free	77.5	52.7	64.4	..	..	BBB–	..
Pakistan	Free	Free	Free	62.0	29.2	49.8	B1	..	B+	..
Panama	Free	Free	Free	68.0	28.5	49.0	..	..	..	..
Papua New Guinea	..	..	..	68.5	32.9	45.3	..	..	..	..
Paraguay	..	..	..	74.0	32.1	49.0	..	..	BB–	BBB–
Peru	Free	Free	Free	66.0	30.0	47.6	..	..	..	..
Philippines	Special[d]	Free	Free	71.5	40.5	61.5	Ba2	..	BB	BBB+
Poland	Free	Free	Free	80.0	44.0	57.1	Baa3	..	BBB–	A–
Portugal	Free	Free	Free	85.5	69.2	80.2	A1	..	AA–	AAA
Puerto Rico	..	..	..	..	..	..	..	..	..	..
Romania	..	..	..	65.0	31.0	53.1	Ba3	..	BB–	BBB–
Russian Federation	..	..	..	62.5	21.4	42.6	Ba2	..	BB–	..

	Entry and exit regulations			Composite ICRG risk rating	Institutional Investor credit rating	Euromoney country credit-worthiness rating	Moody's sovereign long-term debt rating		Standard & Poor's sovereign long-term debt rating	
	Entry 1995	Repatriation of income 1995	Repatriation of capital 1995	December 1996	September 1996	September 1996	Foreign currency November 1996	Domestic currency November 1996	Foreign currency November 1996	Domestic currency November 1996
Rwanda	..	..	..	..	..	23.9	..	..	..	..
Saudi Arabia	..	..	..	73.0	55.1	72.6	..	..	..	..
Senegal	..	..	..	61.5	21.2	35.9	..	..	..	..
Sierra Leone	..	..	..	45.0	7.3	..	..	..	..	..
Singapore	..	..	..	91.0	83.7	95.7	..	..	AAA	AAA
Slovak Republic	..	..	..	78.5	41.2	62.2	Baa3	..	BBB–	A
Slovenia	..	..	..	..	49.9	73.8	A3	..	A	AA
South Africa	Free	Free	Free	72.5	46.3	62.3	Baa3	Baa1	BB+	BBB+
Spain	..	..	..	80.5	73.6	83.7	Aa2	..	AA	AAA
Sri Lanka	Rel. free[a]	Restricted	Restricted	62.5	33.7	43.0	..	..	..	..
Sudan	..	..	..	32.5	7.5	22.7	..	..	..	..
Sweden	..	..	..	84.0	74.2	90.0	Aa3	Aa1	AA+	AAA
Switzerland	..	..	..	89.5	91.9	98.8	..	..	AAA	AAA
Syrian Arab Republic	..	..	..	66.5	24.5	25.7	..	..	..	..
Tajikistan	..	..	..	..	..	14.5	..	..	..	..
Tanzania	..	..	..	62.5	18.1	29.5	..	..	..	..
Thailand	Rel. free[a]	Free	Free	81.0	63.2	77.2	A2	..	A	AA
Togo	..	..	..	58.0	16.7	34.4	..	..	..	..
Trinidad and Tobago	Rel. free[a]	Free	Free	71.0	38.0	50.6	Ba1	..	BB+	BBB+
Tunisia	..	..	..	73.0	45.5	61.6	Baa3	..	..	..
Turkey	Free	Free	Free	57.0	41.1	57.5	Ba3	..	B+	..
Turkmenistan	..	..	..	..	..	22.9	..	..	..	..
Uganda	..	..	..	58.5	16.1	37.7	..	..	..	..
Ukraine	..	..	..	..	16.6	29.5	..	..	..	..
United Arab Emirates	..	..	..	76.0	61.2	75.8	..	..	..	..
United Kingdom	..	..	..	83.0	88.1	96.1	Aaa	Aaa	AAA	AAA
United States	..	..	..	86.0	90.7	98.4	..	Aaa	AAA	AAA
Uruguay	..	..	..	70.5	40.1	56.9	Ba1	..	BB+	BBB
Uzbekistan	..	..	..	..	16.1	26.4	..	..	..	..
Venezuela	Rel. free[a]	Restricted	Restricted	63.5	32.0	45.4	Ba2	..	B	..
Vietnam	..	..	..	70.5	32.8	52.0	..	..	..	..
West Bank and Gaza	..	..	..	..	..	..	..	..	..	..
Yemen, Rep.	..	..	..	64.0	..	27.9	..	..	..	..
Yugoslavia, Fed. Rep.	..	..	..	53.5	9.1	..	..	..	..	..
Zaire	..	..	..	32.0	8.0	20.2	..	..	..	..
Zambia	Free	Free	Free	56.0	16.5	32.8	..	..	..	..
Zimbabwe	Rel. free[a]	Free	Free	56.0	32.5	46.1	..	..	..	..

a. Relatively free entry. b. Repatriation allowed after one year. c. Authorized investors only. d. Special classes of shares.

As investment portfolios become increasingly global, both investors and governments seeking to attract foreign investment must have a good understanding of country risk. This table presents information on country risk and creditworthiness from several major international rating services.

The information on the regulation of entry to and exit from stock markets is reported by the International Finance Corporation (IFC) for emerging markets only. In many economies certain industries are considered strategic and are not open to foreign or nonresident investors. Or the level of foreign investment in a company or in certain classes of stocks may be limited by national law or corporate policy. The regulations summarized in the table refer to "new money" investment by foreign institutions; other regulations may apply to capital invested through debt conversion schemes or to capital from other sources. The regulations shown here are formal ones. But even formal regulations may have quite different effects in different countries because of the prevailing bureaucratic culture, the speed with which applications are processed, and the density of red tape. The effect of entry and exit regulations may also be influenced by graft and corruption, which are impossible to quantify.

Risk ratings may be highly subjective, reflecting external perceptions that do not always capture the actual situation in a country. But these subjective perceptions are the reality that policymakers face in the climate they create for foreign private inflows.

Risk ratings are usually numerical or alphabetical. For numerical ratings, the higher the number, the lower the risk. For alphabetical ratings, the closer to the beginning of the alphabet, the lower the risk. Readers should refer to the original sources for more details on the rating processes of the rating agencies. Countries not rated by credit risk rating agencies typically do not attract private flows.

The International Country Risk Guide (ICRG) collects information on 24 components of risk and converts it into numerical risk assessments. The ratings represent a very broad measure of political, economic, and financial risk. Ratings below 50 are considered very high risk, and those above 85 very low risk.

Institutional Investor country credit ratings are based on information provided by leading international banks. Responses are weighted using a formula that gives more importance to those from banks with greater worldwide exposure and more sophisticated country analysis systems. Countries are graded on a scale of zero to 100, and ratings are updated every six months.

Euromoney country creditworthiness ratings are based on analytical, credit, and market indicators. The ratings are based on polls of economists and political

analysts supplemented by quantitative data such as debt ratios and access to capital markets. The ratings are on a scale of zero to 100.

Ratings of sovereign foreign and domestic currency debt by Moody's Investors Service are presented for obligations that extend longer than one year. These long-term ratings measure total expected credit loss over the life of the security; they are not intended to measure other risks in fixed income investment, such as market risk. Moody's uses a multidisciplinary, or "universal," approach to risk analysis, designed to take into account all relevant risk factors and viewpoints.

The ratings by Standard & Poor's of sovereign long-term foreign and domestic currency are based on current information furnished by the issuer or obtained by Standard & Poor's from other sources it considers reliable. The ratings are based on several risk factors such as the likelihood of default and the capacity and willingness of the debtor to make timely payments of interest and repayments of principal in accordance with the terms of the obligation. The ratings measure the creditworthiness of the debtor and do not take into account exchange-related uncertainties for foreign currency debt.

● **Regulations on entry** into emerging stock markets are evaluated using the following terms: free (no significant restrictions), relatively free (some registration procedures required to ensure repatriation rights), special classes (foreigners restricted to certain classes of stocks designated for foreign investors), authorized investors only (only approved foreign investors may buy stocks), closed (closed or access severely restricted, as for nonresident nationals only). ● **Regulations on repatriation of income** (dividends, interest, and realized capital gains) and **repatriation of capital** from emerging markets are evaluated as free (repatriation done routinely) or restricted (requires registration with or permission of a government agency that may restrict the timing of exchange release). ● **Composite International Country Risk Guide (ICRG) risk rating** is an overall index based on 24 components of risk grouped into three major categories: political, financial, and economic. ● **Institutional Investor credit rating** ranks the chances of a country's default from zero to 100. ● **Euromoney country creditworthiness rating** is a measure of the riskiness of investing in an economy. Ratings are on a scale of zero to 100; the higher the number, the lower the risk. ● **Moody's sovereign foreign and domestic currency long-term debt rating** assesses the risk of lending to governments. Aaa bonds are judged to be of the best quality, Aa bonds of high quality, and C bonds of the lowest quality. Numerical modifiers 1–3 are applied to classifications from Aa to B, with 1 indicating that the obligation ranks at the higher end of its generic rating category. ● **Standard & Poor's foreign and domestic currency sovereign long-term debt ratings** are categorized as investment grade (AAA through BBB) and speculative grade (BB through C). Ratings from AA to CCC may be modified by the addition of a plus (+) or minus (–) sign to show relative standing within the rating category.

Data covering emerging stock markets' entry and exit regulations are from the IFC's *Emerging Stock Markets Factbook 1996*. Information on country risk and creditworthiness are from several sources: Political Risk Services' monthly *International Country Risk Guide;* the monthly publication *Institutional Investor;* the monthly publication *Euromoney;* Moody's Investors Service's *Sovereign, Subnational and Sovereign-Guaranteed Issuers;* and Standard & Poor's Sovereign List in *Credit Week.*

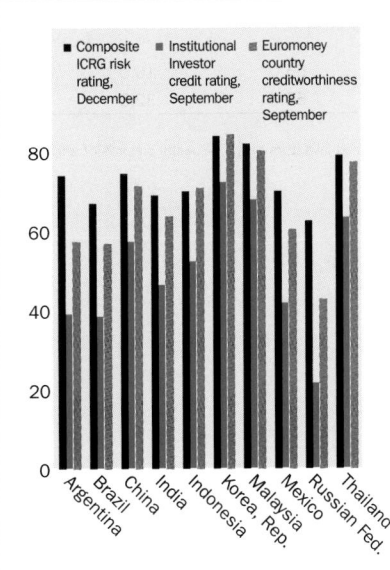

Figure 5.9a Country rating of top 10 developing economy recipients of private capital flows, 1996

■ Composite ICRG risk rating, December
■ Institutional Investor credit rating, September
■ Euromoney country creditworthiness rating, September

Argentina, Brazil, China, India, Indonesia, Korea, Rep., Malaysia, Mexico, Russian Fed., Thailand

Note: The higher the rating, the lower the risk.

| | Domestic credit provided by banking sector | | Liquid liabilities | | Quasi-liquid liabilities | | Interest rate spread | | Spread over LIBOR | |
| | % of GDP | | % of GDP | | % of GDP | | Lending minus deposit rate percentage points | | Lending rate minus LIBOR percentage points | |
	1990	1995	1990	1995	1990	1995	1990	1995	1990	1995
Albania	..	41.8	..	52.5	..	23.6	2.1	4.4	*16.7*	13.7
Algeria	74.7	49.1	73.6	40.4	24.8	14.1	..	..	..	..
Angola	..	..	..	..	..	..				
Argentina	32.4	25.6	11.5	18.6	7.1	12.7	..	5.9	..	11.8
Armenia	*62.2*	9.1	..	..	..	..				
Australia	104.4	85.3	63.6	63.8	51.3	46.0	6.8	..	12.2	..
Austria	123.9	127.3	89.4	91.7	75.7	75.3	..	..		
Azerbaijan	*63.3*	10.8	*37.1*	10.5	*12.9*	3.5	..	..	..	156.5
Bangladesh	32.5	30.5	31.8	37.7	22.8	26.1	3.8	8.0	7.7	8.0
Belarus	..	15.4	..	15.1	..	6.7	..	74.2	..	169.0
Belgium	77.9	154.2	48.6	82.2	29.6	62.2	6.9	4.4	4.7	2.4
Benin	22.4	*11.5*	26.7	*30.0*	5.9	*7.8*	9.0	..	7.7	..
Bolivia	33.3	57.5	26.6	46.6	19.5	33.3	18.0	32.1	33.5	45.0
Bosnia and Herzegovina	..	..	..	..	..	..				
Botswana	−53.0	−40.2	25.2	27.0	15.7	20.0	1.8	4.2	−0.4	8.2
Brazil	87.2	39.5	25.6	31.2	17.9	26.1	..	..		
Bulgaria	95.0	..	109.2	..	61.5	..	3.4	..	−2.2	..
Burkina Faso	13.7	5.7	21.3	24.5	7.5	6.1	9.0	..	7.7	..
Burundi	24.5	*23.8*	18.2	*22.7*	6.5	*6.3*	..	..	4.0	9.3
Cambodia	..	6.2	..	9.0	..	5.2	..	10.0	..	12.7
Cameroon	31.2	19.2	22.6	15.7	10.1	8.0	11.0	10.5	10.2	10.0
Canada	86.5	95.5	74.8	78.3	60.3	61.1	1.3	1.5	5.8	2.6
Central African Republic	14.7	11.2	17.5	21.3	2.1	1.6	11.0	10.5	10.2	10.0
Chad	14.5	12.6	20.9	16.4	0.8	1.4	11.0	10.5	10.2	10.0
Chile	72.9	58.4	40.6	38.9	32.6	30.3	8.5	4.5	40.5	12.2
China	90.0	90.9	79.2	104.3	41.4	60.3	0.8	1.1	1.1	6.1
Colombia	36.3	45.0	29.8	38.8	19.3	27.6	8.8	10.4	36.9	36.7
Congo	29.1	16.9	22.0	14.7	6.1	2.3	11.0	10.5	10.2	10.0
Costa Rica	29.9	20.3	42.6	32.9	29.9	23.8	11.4	12.8	24.3	30.7
Côte d'Ivoire	44.5	30.6	28.8	28.4	10.9	9.6	9.0	..	7.7	..
Croatia	..	52.1	..	25.8	..	17.1	499.3	14.7	*1,153.9*	14.2
Cuba	..	..	..	..	..	..	..	..	..	..
Czech Republic	..	93.4	..	91.4	..	55.1	..	5.8	..	6.8
Denmark	65.1	56.5	60.9	59.6	30.3	29.3	6.2	6.4	5.8	4.3
Dominican Republic	29.1	28.8	23.9	28.8	12.2	18.1	..	..		
Ecuador	17.2	32.3	23.3	33.3	12.8	24.2	−6.0	12.4	29.2	49.7
Egypt, Arab Rep.	130.1	103.9	107.1	105.3	73.9	79.4	7.0	5.6	10.7	10.5
El Salvador	32.0	40.6	30.6	42.4	19.6	32.2	3.2	4.7	12.9	13.1
Eritrea	..	..	..	..	..	..				
Estonia	*65.0*	12.8	136.2	25.2	*93.5*	5.4	..	7.3	26.6	10.0
Ethiopia	67.3	43.1	42.0	43.9	12.5	16.0	3.6	3.6	−2.3	9.1
Finland	84.3	68.2	55.3	58.6	46.7	26.5	4.1	4.5	3.3	1.7
France	107.0	102.4	64.6	67.7	38.7	43.9	6.0	3.6	2.2	2.1
Gabon	21.9	19.4	19.4	15.3	7.2	6.0	11.0	10.5	10.2	10.0
Gambia, The	3.2	7.6	19.7	24.6	8.4	11.9	15.2	12.5	18.2	19.0
Georgia	..	..	..	..	..	..	..	..		
Germany	*110.0*	129.9	*64.5*	68.2	*44.3*	45.5	*4.5*	7.0	3.3	4.9
Ghana	12.4	24.4	13.4	17.6	3.2	5.3	..	..		
Greece	129.3	113.5	90.0	*80.0*	72.5	*62.1*	8.1	*7.3*	19.3	17.1
Guatemala	17.4	19.4	21.2	25.2	11.8	16.0	5.1	13.3	15.0	15.2
Guinea	*5.5*	*7.7*	*9.3*	9.3	*1.2*	1.8	*0.2*	4.0	12.9	15.5
Guinea-Bissau	43.5	8.0	17.0	16.3	4.5	6.2	13.1	6.4	37.5	26.9
Haiti	32.9	33.7	31.4	48.0	15.9	26.2	..	..		
Honduras	40.9	26.3	33.6	30.8	18.8	18.3	8.3	15.0	8.8	21.0
Hong Kong	..	..	..	..	..	..	..	..	..	..

	Domestic credit provided by banking sector		Liquid liabilities		Quasi-liquid liabilities		Interest rate spread		Spread over LIBOR	
	% of GDP		% of GDP		% of GDP		Lending minus deposit rate percentage points		Lending rate minus LIBOR percentage points	
	1990	1995	1990	1995	1990	1995	1990	1995	1990	1995
Hungary	82.6	*64.1*	43.8	*45.7*	20.8	*25.2*	4.1	*6.5*	20.5	26.6
India	54.7	48.5	45.7	48.4	29.8	31.1	..	..	8.2	13.0
Indonesia	45.5	..	40.4	..	29.1	..	3.3	..	12.3	12.4
Iran, Islamic Rep.	71.0	45.8	57.6	39.1	31.0	20.4	..	..	..	..
Iraq	..	..	..	..	..	..	..	..	..	..
Ireland	58.8	61.3	45.2	57.5	32.9	43.3	5.0	6.2	3.0	0.6
Israel	101.3	79.4	67.0	73.9	60.6	67.8	12.0	6.1	18.1	14.2
Italy	75.8	..	74.4	*64.7*	37.6	27.4	7.3	*6.1*	5.8	6.5
Jamaica	34.8	30.7	51.1	53.4	38.0	36.4	6.6	20.4	22.2	37.6
Japan	266.8	295.9	187.4	203.3	159.6	167.6	3.4	2.7	–1.3	–2.6
Jordan	117.9	*93.9*	131.2	*105.9*	77.8	*65.1*	3.2	*5.7*	1.7	3.0
Kazakstan	..	9.5	..	..	..	..	..	..	..	..
Kenya	52.7	51.3	43.2	40.4	29.2	25.6	5.1	15.2	10.5	22.8
Korea, Dem. Rep.	..	..	..	..	..	..	..	..	..	..
Korea, Rep.	65.4	69.9	54.4	79.1	45.5	68.1	0.0	0.2	1.7	3.0
Kuwait	*216.6*	58.7	174.5	80.8	*135.2*	66.1	*0.4*	1.9	*4.1*	2.4
Kyrgyz Republic	..	..	..	..	..	..	..	..	..	..
Lao PDR	5.1	11.1	7.2	13.6	3.1	8.9	2.5	11.7	*20.0*	19.7
Latvia	..	13.7	..	22.0	..	7.8	..	19.8	..	28.6
Lebanon	132.6	87.0	193.7	126.6	170.9	118.0	23.0	8.4	31.6	18.7
Lesotho	30.7	–8.6	39.9	30.1	23.0	16.1	7.4	3.1	12.1	10.4
Libya	..	..	..	..	..	..	1.5	1.5	–1.3	*3.7*
Lithuania	..	17.1	..	25.5	..	9.8	..	18.7	..	21.1
Macedonia, FYR	..	..	..	..	..	..	..	..	..	..
Madagascar	26.2	18.4	17.8	21.2	5.3	7.6	..	..	..	..
Malawi	19.9	14.0	21.3	20.2	11.8	10.4	8.9	10.0	12.7	41.3
Malaysia	77.9	131.9	66.3	121.7	44.3	91.9	1.3	1.7	–1.1	1.6
Mali	13.4	11.1	20.0	20.8	5.4	4.6	9.0	..	7.7	..
Mauritania	54.7	23.7	28.5	18.8	7.0	5.6	5.0	..	1.7	..
Mauritius	45.1	68.1	63.4	80.1	49.2	66.1	5.4	8.6	9.7	14.8
Mexico	43.9	53.1	25.0	37.9	18.2	28.5	..	..	..	..
Moldova	*66.7*	17.8	*74.6*	14.4	*37.6*	4.6	..	..	..	..
Mongolia	*68.5*	11.0	*54.3*	29.1	*13.8*	15.2	..	54.8	..	108.9
Morocco	60.1	81.0	61.1	77.7	18.5	28.6	0.5	..	0.7	5.3
Mozambique	37.5	..	38.9	..	..	..	..	..	..	..
Myanmar	32.7	..	27.9	..	7.8	..	2.1	..	–0.3	..
Namibia	20.7	64.1	24.8	43.2	14.5	26.6	10.6	7.7	*17.4*	12.5
Nepal	28.9	*29.9*	32.2	*36.5*	18.5	*21.2*	..	..	6.1	..
Netherlands	107.5	117.8	84.1	84.3	60.1	57.1	8.5	2.8	3.5	1.2
New Zealand	73.5	90.1	65.4	79.5	32.2	41.3	4.3	3.7	7.7	6.2
Nicaragua	206.6	189.4	56.9	34.1	23.2	24.9	12.5	8.8	13.7	13.9
Niger	16.2	8.8	19.8	14.5	8.3	3.6	9.0	..	7.7	..
Nigeria	23.7	18.7	23.6	*28.9*	10.3	*9.9*	5.5	*6.7*	17.0	14.2
Norway	89.6	77.0	59.9	56.6	27.0	17.8	4.6	2.8	6.0	1.8
Oman	16.6	29.2	28.9	32.5	19.3	22.4	1.4	2.9	1.4	3.4
Pakistan	50.9	50.5	39.7	44.2	10.0	17.9	..	..	..	..
Panama	55.9	71.8	43.6	70.5	35.0	59.5	3.6	3.9	3.7	5.1
Papua New Guinea	35.8	28.8	35.2	*30.0*	24.0	*19.0*	6.8	*4.1*	7.2	*4.5*
Paraguay	14.9	22.7	21.5	28.9	12.8	18.7	8.1	9.8	22.7	25.0
Peru	16.2	11.4	19.9	19.2	9.4	13.4	2,334.9	20.6	4,766.2	30.6
Philippines	26.9	62.9	36.8	55.1	28.1	44.9	4.6	6.3	15.8	8.7
Poland	19.5	34.6	34.0	36.5	17.2	23.4	462.5	6.7	495.9	27.5
Portugal	73.8	92.9	65.1	81.7	39.7	53.4	7.8	5.4	13.5	7.8
Puerto Rico	..	..	..	..	..	..	..	..	..	..
Romania	79.7	23.6	60.4	25.1	32.7	15.7	..	..	..	..
Russian Federation	..	20.7	..	15.8	..	7.2	..	217.5	..	313.5

	Domestic credit provided by banking sector		Liquid liabilities		Quasi-liquid liabilities		Interest rate spread		Spread over LIBOR	
							Lending minus deposit rate percentage points		Lending rate minus LIBOR percentage points	
	% of GDP		% of GDP		% of GDP					
	1990	1995	1990	1995	1990	1995	1990	1995	1990	1995
Rwanda	17.0	13.5	14.8	19.7	7.0	7.2	6.3	10.0	4.9	*11.7*
Saudi Arabia	58.7	37.9	47.9	51.1	21.9	24.6	..	..	..	..
Senegal	33.7	22.1	22.9	20.6	9.7	7.6	9.0	..	7.7	..
Sierra Leone	11.1	68.5	14.5	10.7	4.0	2.6	12.0	21.8	44.2	22.8
Singapore	76.0	76.2	123.9	115.5	100.9	94.1	2.7	2.9	−0.9	0.4
Slovak Republic	..	52.3	..	68.2	..	39.3	..	6.6		9.6
Slovenia	*36.8*	36.6	*34.2*	36.7	*25.8*	28.6	*179.9*	9.5	*847.5*	18.8
South Africa	102.7	153.5	47.1	44.4	28.8	21.7	2.1	4.4	12.7	11.9
Spain	109.0	105.7	76.6	80.5	45.3	53.0	5.3	2.3	7.7	4.0
Sri Lanka	43.0	36.7	35.1	43.4	22.8	32.0	−6.4	−1.4	4.7	8.7
Sudan	29.9	*18.9*	29.4	*24.0*	4.2	*9.4*	..	..	..	..
Sweden	145.5	123.9	46.6	45.5	..	..	6.8	4.9	8.4	5.1
Switzerland	180.9	187.6	146.8	147.2	120.0	118.9	−0.9	4.2	−0.9	−0.5
Syrian Arab Republic	56.6	*64.2*	54.7	*69.1*	10.5	13.9	..	..	..	..
Tajikistan	..	..	..	..	..	..	..	..	..	..
Tanzania	42.8	30.9	24.6	*35.3*	7.8	14.7	..	18.2	..	36.8
Thailand	90.7	136.5	74.8	79.5	65.9	70.2	4.2	5.9	8.2	9.7
Togo	21.2	26.9	35.9	31.8	19.0	*10.9*	9.0	..	7.7	..
Trinidad and Tobago	58.5	54.1	54.8	50.4	42.8	38.0	6.9	9.1	4.6	*9.2*
Tunisia	62.5	71.2	51.5	48.4	26.7	27.1	..	..	..	..
Turkey	25.9	29.6	24.1	32.3	16.4	27.2	..	..	..	..
Turkmenistan	..	..	..	..	..	..	..	..	..	..
Uganda	*17.8*	3.9	7.6	10.8	*1.4*	2.8	7.4	12.6	30.4	14.2
Ukraine	*0.0*	0.0	*0.0*	0.0	*0.0*	0.0	..	52.4	..	116.7
United Arab Emirates	35.2	48.6	47.0	56.7	38.2	42.2	..	..	..	..
United Kingdom	123.0	125.7	..	..	..	..	2.3	2.6	6.5	0.7
United States	115.6	132.1	68.7	61.1	51.8	43.6	..	..	1.7	2.8
Uruguay	60.8	38.9	61.2	39.2	53.3	32.5	76.7	60.9	166.2	93.1
Uzbekistan	..	..	..	..	..	..	..	..	..	..
Venezuela	37.4	37.0	42.3	30.8	29.4	19.9	0.4	7.5	19.9	26.2
Vietnam	..	..	..	..	..	..	..	..	..	..
West Bank and Gaza	..		..		..		..		..	
Yemen, Rep.	79.6	50.0	72.3	56.5	13.7	18.7	..	..	..	..
Yugoslavia, Fed. Rep.										
Zaire	..		..		..		..		..	
Zambia	68.4	50.3	21.7	15.3	10.5	8.9	9.4	..	26.8	110.0
Zimbabwe	53.8	54.8	54.2	48.7	39.3	28.9	2.9	8.8	..	..

The financial system—intermediating

Households and institutions save and invest in isolation. The role of the financial system is to intermediate between them. Savers accumulate claims on the financial institutions, which pass the funds they obtain this way to the final users. Gradually, as an economy develops, this indirect lending by savers to investors results in greater financial assets relative to GDP. This wealth allows increased saving and investment, enhancing the economy's rate of growth.

The financial system develops with the economy. As more specialized savings and financial institutions emerge, a greater diversity of instruments becomes available, helping to reduce risk for liability holders. And as securities markets mature, savers are able to invest their resources directly in financial assets issued by firms.

No less important than the size and structure of the financial sector is its efficiency, indicated by the margin between the cost of

Borrowers in developing economies have to pay 1.6 to 313.5 percentage points over LIBOR for their local currency loans ●

mobilizing liabilities and the earnings on assets. Small margins are crucial for economic growth, since they reduce interest rates and thus the overall cost of investment. Interest rates reflect the responsiveness of financial institutions to competition and price incentives.

Selective credit controls and controls on deposit and lending rates distort financial markets in some countries. In addition, interest rates may reflect the diversion of resources to finance the public sector deficit through direct borrowing from the banking system and statutory reserve requirements. Moreover, in economies where the financial sector is dominated by state-owned banks, credit allocation decisions may be excessively influenced by noncommercial considerations.

About the data

There are several reasons for caution in using the indicators in the table. These indicators are quantitative assessments, but qualitative assessments of policy actions, laws, and regulations are needed in analyzing overall financial conditions. In addition, the accuracy of financial data is dependent on the quality of accounting systems, which are weak in some developing economies. Some of these indicators are highly correlated, particularly the ratios of liquid liabilities, quasi-liquid liabilities, and bank credit to GDP, because changes in liquid and quasi-liquid liabilities flow directly from changes in bank credit. The precise definition of the financial aggregates on which data are presented varies from one economy to another. Monetary data are end-of-year levels.

The ratio of domestic credit provided by the banking sector to GDP is used as a measure of the growth of the banking system because it reflects the extent to which savings are financial. Liquid liabilities include bank deposits of generally less than one year plus currency. The ratio of these assets to GDP indicates the ease with which their owners can use them to buy goods and services without incurring any cost. Quasi-liquid liabilities are long-term deposits and assets, such as certificates of deposit, commercial paper, and bonds, that can be converted into currency or demand deposits but at a cost.

The interest rate spread is a summary measure of the efficiency of the banking system, known as the intermediation margin. This measure may not be reliable to the extent that information about interest rates is inaccurate, banks do not monitor firm managers, or the government intervenes to fix deposit and lending rates. The spread over LIBOR reflects the interest rate differential between a country's lending rate and the London Interbank Offer Rate (ignoring expected changes in the exchange rate). Interest rates are annual averages.

The indicators here do not capture the activities of the informal sector, which remains important, especially in developing economies. Because financial arrangements based on personal contacts inspire more confidence among owners and users of funds, personal credit or credit extended through community-based pooling of assets may be the only source of credit available to small farmers, small businesses, or home-based producers. In economies characterized by financial repression, the rationing of formal credit forces many borrowers and lenders to turn to the informal market.

Definitions

● **Domestic credit provided by banking sector** includes all credit to various sectors on a gross basis, with the exception of credit to the central government, which is net. The banking sector includes monetary authorities and deposit money banks, as well as other banking institutions where data are available (including institutions that do not accept transferable deposits but do incur such liabilities as time and savings deposits). Examples of other banking institutions are savings and mortgage loan institutions and building and loan associations. ● **Liquid liabilities** are also known as broad money, or M3. They are the sum of currency and deposits in the central bank (M0), plus transferable deposits and electronic currency (M1), plus time and savings deposits, foreign currency transferable deposits, certificates of deposit, and securities repurchase agreements (M2), plus travelers checks, foreign currency time deposits, commercial paper, and shares of mutual funds or market funds held by residents. ● **Quasi-liquid liabilities** are the M3 money supply less M1. ● **Interest rate spread** is the interest rate charged by banks on loans to prime customers minus the interest rate paid by commercial or similar banks for demand, time, or savings deposits. ● **Spread over LIBOR** (London Interbank Offer Rate) is the interest rate charged by banks on loans to prime customers minus LIBOR. LIBOR is the most commonly recognized international interest rate and is quoted in several currencies. The average three-month LIBOR on U.S. dollar deposits is used here.

Data sources

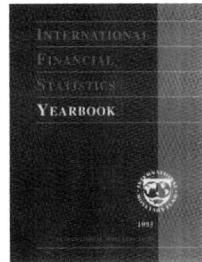

Data on money and interest rates are collected from central banks and finance ministries and are reported in the print and electronic versions of the International Monetary Fund's *International Financial Statistics*.

5.11 | Power and communications

	Electric power		Telephone mainlines			International telecommunications	
	Production million kwh 1994	Transmission and distribution losses % of output 1994	per 1,000 people 1995	% of total in largest city 1995	Waiting time years 1995	Outgoing traffic minutes per subscriber 1995	Average price per call $ per three minutes 1995
Albania	3,903	13	12	29	..	548	9.51
Algeria	19,883	16	42	18	9.5	67	9.45
Angola	955	28	6	66	..	300	1.45
Argentina	65,962	18	160	49	0.2	27	7.37
Armenia	5,658	40	156	44	..	92	..
Australia	167,155	6	510	20	0.0	103	3.00
Austria	53,259	4	465	27	0.1	240	3.77
Azerbaijan	17,600	20	85	45	..	109	..
Bangladesh	9,891	32	2	96	..	82	5.97
Belarus	31,397	12	190	80	9.1	67	8.09
Belgium	72,236	5	457	18	0.0	239	3.05
Benin	6	17	5	68	1.7	212	8.65
Bolivia	2,824	13	35	38	..	71	6.10
Bosnia and Herzegovina	1,921	21	71	..	..	26	..
Botswana	..	..	40	46	1.5	499	..
Brazil	260,682	16	75	17	0.7	24	4.99
Bulgaria	38,133	12	335	18	..	34	5.98
Burkina Faso	..	..	3	67	..	203	12.22
Burundi	..	..	3	89	3.5	163	16.39
Cambodia	..	..	1	82	20.9	959	..
Cameroon	2,740	4	4	50	25.3	399	12.02
Canada	554,227	6	590	..	..	154	1.16
Central African Republic	..	..	2	91	1.0	303	24.04
Chad	..	..	1	82	9.2	307	14.42
Chile	25,276	11	132	56	0.3	72	2.79
China	928,083	6	34	5	0.2	33	..
Colombia	43,354	21	100	38	2.2	33	4.12
Congo	435	0	8	60	0.6	190	..
Costa Rica	4,772	8	164	64	0.8	95	5.06
Côte d'Ivoire	2,305	4	8	75	5.6	250	..
Croatia	8,275	19	269	24	0.5	164	7.34
Cuba	10,982	13	32	45	..	32	..
Czech Republic	58,705	8	236	26	3.3	75	5.65
Denmark	40,097	4	613	..	0.0	165	3.35
Dominican Republic	6,182	25	79	60	..	105	..
Ecuador	8,256	20	61	52	1.1	53	8.21
Egypt, Arab Rep.	51,947	0	46	34	5.7	37	6.19
El Salvador	3,211	13	53	73	5.0	233	6.46
Eritrea	..	..	5	77	28.7	70	10.27
Estonia	9,151	17	277	41	4.1	129	5.23
Ethiopia	1,293	3	2	66	34.8	74	..
Finland	65,546	5	550	25	0.0	112	3.88
France	476,200	6	558	..	0.0	87	3.03
Gabon	933	9	30	83	..	504	..
Gambia, The	..	..	18	38	10.1	244	6.34
Georgia	6,803	25	96	49	..	3	..
Germany	528,221	4	493	5	..	130	4.17
Ghana	6,115	4	4	65	7.0	279	4.70
Greece	40,623	8	493	42	0.6	90	3.82
Guatemala	3,161	13	27	79	4.0	126	..
Guinea	..	..	2	57	95.0	278	8.88
Guinea-Bissau	..	..	9	96	1.4	240	21.72
Haiti	362	32	8	41	8.0	422	6.62
Honduras	2,672	28	29	53	12.3	211	8.57
Hong Kong	26,743	15	530	100	0.0	516	2.65

	Electric power		Telephone mainlines			International telecommunications	
	Production million kwh 1994	Transmission and distribution losses % of output 1994	per 1,000 people 1995	% of total in largest city 1995	Waiting time years 1995	Outgoing traffic minutes per subscriber 1995	Average price per call $ per three minutes 1995
Hungary	33,486	13	185	39	2.1	131	4.77
India	386,500	17	13	13	1.3	29	6.94
Indonesia	53,414	12	17	36	0.2	63	6.07
Iran, Islamic Rep.	79,128	14	79	29	1.4	41	6.02
Iraq	27,060	0	33	..	..	..	..
Ireland	17,105	9	365	41	0.0	311	3.32
Israel	32,781	3	418	34	0.1	108	3.43
Italy	231,804	7	434	..	0.1	77	3.36
Jamaica	2,336	19	116	51	4.1	189	..
Japan	964,328	4	487	0	0.0	27	5.10
Jordan	5,076	9	73	73	9.9	226	9.44
Kazakstan	66,397	14	118	76	4.2	8	..
Kenya	3,539	16	9	59	6.6	87	11.17
Korea, Dem. Rep.	38,000	84	47	18	..	3	..
Korea, Rep.	164,993	5	415	34	0.0	30	4.88
Kuwait	22,798	0	230	12	0.2	329	5.53
Kyrgyz Republic	12,932	17	73	53	..	4	..
Lao PDR	..	..	4	68	..	107	..
Latvia	4,440	29	280	40	6.3	62	11.40
Lebanon	5,184	16	82	66	..	103	..
Lesotho	..	..	9	62	3.9	945	..
Libya	17,800	..	59	29	8.5	147	..
Lithuania	10,055	20	254	21	4.4	59	7.88
Macedonia, FYR	5,511	12	165	36	1.5	129	..
Madagascar	..	..	2	57	..	134	30.83
Malawi	..	..	4	57	18.4	230	9.81
Malaysia	39,093	10	166	9	0.3	111	5.99
Mali	..	..	2	70	..	413	18.03
Mauritania	..	..	4	82	1.8	529	5.21
Mauritius	..	..	131	20	2.0	135	6.04
Mexico	147,926	14	96	36	0.3	107	3.01
Moldova	8,228	19	131	33	11.1	117	6.54
Mongolia	..	..	32	55	13.8	25	15.05
Morocco	11,100	4	43	30	0.6	112	8.36
Mozambique	490	0	3	61	5.0	274	19.38
Myanmar	3,500	35	3	46	..	75	25.82
Namibia	..	..	51	47	1.3	622	6.76
Nepal	927	25	4	66	..	173	8.75
Netherlands	79,647	4	525	..	0.0	180	3.18
New Zealand	35,135	13	479	27	0.0	179	4.78
Nicaragua	1,688	27	23	62	..	304	8.46
Niger	..	..	1	68	1.4	265	9.73
Nigeria	15,530	28	4	35	3.5	233	3.41
Norway	113,488	8	556	15	0.1	177	2.36
Oman	6,187	0	77	49	0.2	318	7.80
Pakistan	58,529	19	16	28	0.7	31	5.86
Panama	3,380	24	114	67	0.9	130	..
Papua New Guinea	..	..	10	86	..	521	10.38
Paraguay	36,415	1	31	75	..	106	8.34
Peru	15,563	18	47	71	0.8	56	5.76
Philippines	27,062	16	21	71	3.6	122	6.22
Poland	135,347	13	148	11	3.8	67	4.58
Portugal	31,380	11	361	32	0.0	84	4.60
Puerto Rico	..	..	332	16	2.8	689	..
Romania	55,136	9	131	22	9.6	30	5.31
Russian Federation	875,914	9	170	16	15.0	9	9.67

	Electric power		Telephone mainlines			International telecommunications	
	Production million kwh 1994	Transmission and distribution losses % of output 1994	per 1,000 people 1995	% of total in largest city 1995	Waiting time years 1995	Outgoing traffic minutes per subscriber 1995	Average price per call $ per three minutes 1995
Rwanda	..	..	2	66	..	89	..
Saudi Arabia	91,019	10	96	22	..	312	6.41
Senegal	1,002	13	10	69	1.8	247	7.93
Sierra Leone	..	..	4	87	7.0	138	8.05
Singapore	20,046	5	478	100	0.0	541	4.02
Slovak Republic	24,740	6	208	21	1.7	53	5.45
Slovenia	12,630	4	309	33	1.4	164	6.35
South Africa	189,316	7	95	29	1.0	78	5.04
Spain	161,654	9	385	15	0.0	70	3.49
Sri Lanka	4,387	18	11	68	8.1	132	7.35
Sudan	1,333	19	3	16	20.5	102	15.78
Sweden	142,895	6	681	22	0.0	159	2.65
Switzerland	65,724	5	613	7	0.0	403	3.25
Syrian Arab Republic	15,182	0	63	27	17.2	65	14.10
Tajikistan	17,000	13	45	44	..	1	..
Tanzania	1,913	12	3	44	39.5	63	18.39
Thailand	71,177	10	59	55	1.9	64	7.30
Togo	..	..	5	76	2.5	391	13.52
Trinidad and Tobago	4,069	11	160	18	0.8	280	3.48
Tunisia	6,714	11	58	26	2.6	150	6.66
Turkey	78,322	15	212	23	0.6	29	3.93
Turkmenistan	10,496	9	76	85	..	17	..
Uganda	..	..	2	71	1.1	111	9.29
Ukraine	202,995	10	157	10	..	..	..
United Arab Emirates	18,870	0	283	37	0.0	749	4.45
United Kingdom	325,383	8	502	..	0.0	139	1.86
United States	3,473,620	7	627	..	0.0	95	..
Uruguay	7,617	16	196	64	1.8	83	6.17
Uzbekistan	47,000	10	76	29	3.3	78	..
Venezuela	73,116	15	111	32	3.1	52	6.62
Vietnam	12,270	22	11	36	0.7	54	..
West Bank and Gaza	..	..	..	..	..	..	..
Yemen, Rep.	2,159	23	12	37	5.2	123	13.44
Yugoslavia, Fed. Rep.	33,171	10	191	25	4.3	105	2.10
Zaire	5,545	4	1	54	..	36	..
Zambia	7,785	11	8	40	116.0	157	5.12
Zimbabwe	7,334	7	14	51	11.1	359	8.20
World	**12,906,649 t**	**8 w**	**130 w**	**23 w**	**2.9 w**	**73 w**	..
Low income	1,602,412 t	14 w	21 w	23 w	3.3 w	67 w	..
Excl. China & India	252,163 t	20 w	..	54 w	..	139 w	9.66 w
Middle income	3,321,146 t	13 w	98 w	33 w	3.8 w	69 w	6.19 w
Lower middle income	2,276,120 t	13 w	88 w	35 w	4.7 w	62 w	6.79 w
Upper middle income	1,042,489 t	13 w	119 w	28 w	1.8 w	85 w	4.84 w
Low & middle income	4,914,025 t	13 w	47 w	27 w	3.5 w	67 w	..
East Asia & Pacific	1,194,322 t	13 w	34 w	16 w	0.6 w	51 w	..
Europe & Central Asia	1,858,386 t	11 w	177 w	25 w	7.9 w	45 w	6.91 w
Latin America & Carib.	752,725 t	16 w	91 w	37 w	1.3 w	74 w	5.02 w
Middle East & N. Africa	342,989 t	10 w	51 w	28 w	6.5 w	92 w	7.79 w
South Asia	468,843 t	18 w	13 w	26 w	1.3 w	38 w	6.77 w
Sub-Saharan Africa	289,949 t	12 w	11 w	51 w	15.2 w	181 w	9.74 w
High income	8,030,951 t	6 w	524 w	7 w	0.0 w	104 w	3.69 w

About the data

An adequate and reliable supply of electrical power is an essential ingredient for modern economic development. Expanding the supply of electricity to meet the growing demand of increasingly urbanized and industrialized economies is one of the great challenges facing developing countries. To meet this challenge without incurring unacceptable social, economic, and environmental costs often requires institutional, regulatory, and financial reforms to improve the power sector's performance.

An economy's production of electricity is a basic indicator of its size and level of development. Although some countries export electrical power, most production is for domestic consumption. Power production data do not reflect power distribution losses through faulty equipment and poorly designed systems and illegal diversions of power by consumers. Nor do they capture the reliability of supplies, including frequency of outages, breakdowns, and load factors.

Data on electrical power production are collected from national energy agencies by the International Energy Agency (IEA) and adjusted by the IEA to meet international definitions. Adjustments are made, for example, to account for electricity production by self-producers (establishments that, in addition to their main activities, generate electricity wholly or partly for their own use). Self-generation by small entrepreneurs and households can be substantial in some countries because of unreliable public power sources or remoteness, however, and in these cases may not be adequately reflected in these adjustments.

Telecommunications is at the center of an information economy. Governments that realize this have integrated telecommunications policies with their macroeconomic strategies. National performance indicators for the telecommunications sector can include measures of supply and demand, quality of service, productivity, economic and financial performance, capital investment, and tariffs.

Until a decade ago the number of mainlines accurately reflected the full capacity of the telephone system. But the advent—and rapid spread—of cellular telephones has changed the picture. (See table 5.14 for estimates of cellular, mobile phone subscribers.) Demand in the telecommunications sector is measured by the sum of mainlines and the number of registered applicants for new connections. But in some countries the list of registered applicants does not indicate the real current pending demand. There is often hidden or suppressed demand, reflecting a situation of acute short supply in which many potential applicants have been discouraged from applying for telephone service. And in some cases waiting

lists may overstate demand as a result of applicants placing their names on the list several times to improve their chances.

International telecommunications is a fundamental link to the global economy. As telecommunications tariffs have declined with new technical advances, an oversupply of international lines, and increased competition, international telephone traffic has rapidly expanded. Worldwide, telephone traffic has grown 16 percent a year for the past 10 years—about four times faster than global GDP.

Definitions

● **Electric power production** refers to gross production in kilowatt-hours by private companies, cooperative organizations, local or regional authorities, government organizations, and self-producers. It includes consumption by station auxiliaries, any losses in the transformers that are considered integral parts of the station, and electric energy produced by pumping installations. It covers electricity generated from all primary sources of energy—coal, oil, gas, nuclear, hydro, geothermal, wind, tide and wave, and combustible renewables—where data are available. ● **Electric power transmission and distribution losses** include losses in transmission between sources of supply and points of distribution and in the distribution to consumers, including pilferage. Production less transmission and distribution losses, own-use, and transformation losses is equal to end-use electricity consumption. ● **Telephone mainlines** refer to telephone lines connecting a customer's equipment (such as a telephone or facsimile machine) to the public switched telephone network. A mainline is normally identified by a unique number that is the one billed. Data are presented here as mainlines per 1,000 people; this is a measure of telephone density or penetration. ● **Waiting time** shows the approximate number of years applicants must wait for a telephone line. It is calculated by dividing the number of applicants on the waiting list by the average number of mainlines added per year over the past three years. ● **Outgoing traffic** refers to the telephone traffic, measured in minutes per subscriber, that originated in the country with a destination outside the country. ● **Average price per call** is the cost of a three-minute peak rate call from any country to the United States.

Data sources

Data on electricity production and losses are from the IEA's *Energy Statistics and Balances of Non-OECD Countries 1993–94,* the IEA's *Energy Statistics of OECD Countries 1993–94,* and the United Nations *Energy Statistics Yearbook.* Telecommunications data come from the International Telecommunication Union's *World Telecommunication Development Report* and Direction of Traffic database.

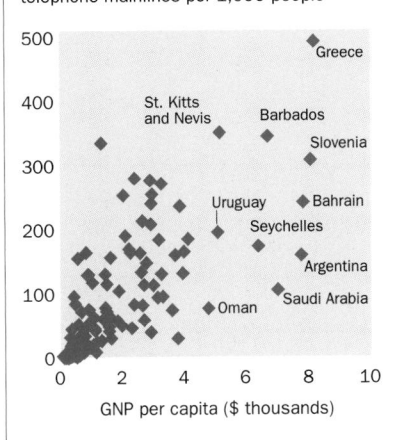

Figure 5.11a GNP per capita and telephone density in developing economies, 1995

telephone mainlines per 1,000 people

Source: International Telecommunication Union data.

5.12 Transport infrastructure

	Roads			Railways		Air		
	Paved roads % 1995	Normalized road index 1995	Goods transported million ton-km 1995	Rail traffic km per million $ GDP 1995	Goods transported million ton-km 1995	Aircraft departures thousands 1995	Passengers carried thousands 1995	Air freight ton-km 1995
Albania	30.0	28	3	11	1	1	13	0
Algeria	68.9	161	..	*11*	..	47	3,478	21
Angola	25.0	..	..	..	..	8	545	58
Argentina	28.5	117	..	..	..	112	6,532	178
Armenia	97.1	89	..	..	..	..	..	..
Australia	38.6	107	..	..	..	407	28,690	1,771
Austria	100.0	123	*64,368*	10	68,474	113	4,369	173
Azerbaijan	93.8	..	..	..	..	20	1,156	34
Bangladesh	9.3	29	..	..	..	13	1,261	165
Belarus	98.6	113	350	185	47	35	805	2
Belgium	..	109	*428*	5	*63*	141	5,001	595
Benin	31.4	55	..	..	..	1	74	15
Bolivia	4.8	40	..	*18*	1	17	1,224	49
Bosnia and Herzegovina	..	..	..	..	..	..	..	..
Botswana	14.2	256	..	..	..	4	100	0
Brazil	9.2	120	..	8	..	435	19,510	1,577
Bulgaria	91.9	98	45	..	30	15	863	30
Burkina Faso	..	74	..	..	..	3	137	15
Burundi	7.1	121	..	..	..	1	9	0
Cambodia	7.5	..	..	..	..	..	..	..
Cameroon	12.5	56	..	*14*	..	4	345	39
Canada	35.1	76	..	*30*	..	283	20,291	1,637
Central African Republic	1.8	31	..	..	..	..	..	..
Chad	0.8	21	..	..	..	2	92	15
Chile	13.8	58	..	5	..	79	3,197	775
China	89.7	..	438,000	231	1,310,000	398	47,565	1,501
Colombia	11.9	46	..	..	..	149	6,227	491
Congo	9.7	68	..	*26*	..	5	245	16
Costa Rica	16.7	211	..	..	..	27	870	44
Côte d'Ivoire	9.6	90	..	5	..	4	175	15
Croatia	81.5	..	4	16	3	13	644	2
Cuba	55.8	..	..	..	..	13	824	33
Czech Republic	..	..	566	68	55	26	1,285	26
Denmark	100.0	103	..	4	..	101	5,652	134
Dominican Republic	49.3	63	..	..	..	3	316	3
Ecuador	18.4	73	51,900	..	..	33	1,166	38
Egypt, Arab Rep.	78.0	111	..	*118*	..	39	3,897	164
El Salvador	13.9	75	..	..	..	20	1,698	15
Eritrea	..	..	..	..	..	..	..	..
Estonia	54.0	61	10	100	41	7	169	0
Ethiopia	15.0	60	..	..	..	26	750	115
Finland	63.0	77	..	10	..	97	5,212	212
France	..	122	*1,275*	7	..	447	34,057	4,578
Gabon	8.2	35	..	*11*	..	12	505	32
Gambia, The	35.3	239	..	..	..	..	19	..
Georgia	..	..	7	..	3	1	177	2
Germany	99.0	..	*211,600*	5	69,800	513	33,960	5,834
Ghana	24.9	96	..	..	..	3	186	24
Greece	91.7	154	..	2	..	89	6,006	117
Guatemala	27.5	59	..	..	..	5	300	25
Guinea	16.4	45	..	..	..	1	15	1
Guinea-Bissau	10.2	..	..	..	..	1	21	0
Haiti	24.2	..	..	..	..	..	..	..
Honduras	20.2	115	..	..	..	12	474	2
Hong Kong	100.0	..	14	..	1	..	..	..

	Roads			Railways		Air		
	Paved roads % 1995	Normalized road index 1995	Goods transported million ton-km 1995	Rail traffic km per million $ GDP 1995	Goods transported million ton-km 1995	Aircraft departures thousands 1995	Passengers carried thousands 1995	Air freight ton-km 1995
Hungary	44.1	171	35	32	18	22	1,311	29
India	50.1	462	..	190	..	150	13,214	650
Indonesia	45.5	38	..	10	8,851	241	15,194	778
Iran, Islamic Rep.	59.1	..	..	..	..	49	6,291	108
Iraq	86.0	..	..	..	..	..	31	..
Ireland	94.0	279	..	3	..	84	6,587	107
Israel	100.0	98	..	2	9	48	3,453	1,071
Italy	100.0	57	..	7	..	271	23,482	1,470
Jamaica	70.6	283	..	..	..	17	1,126	22
Japan	74.0	72	..	6	..	536	91,797	6,538
Jordan	100.0	113	..	11	..	17	1,274	266
Kazakstan	68.4	170	..	714	..	13	709	16
Kenya	13.8	117	..	23	..	13	740	53
Korea, Dem. Rep.	..	..	..	..	..	..	254	..
Korea, Rep.	6.3	118	410	12	57	..	29,345	..
Kuwait	80.5	..	..	..	..	18	1,951	330
Kyrgyz Republic	91.0	..	74	..	40	12	439	1
Lao PDR	13.8	277	..	..	..	4	125	1
Latvia	38.3	78	21	184	29	5	183	1
Lebanon	95.0	..	..	..	..	11	770	129
Lesotho	17.9	144	..	..	..	3	28	0
Libya	57.1	..	..	..	..	6	623	0
Lithuania	86.4	271	138	118	26	7	210	2
Macedonia, FYR	..	71	3	..	2	..	..	..
Madagascar	11.5	168	..	..	..	18	497	32
Malawi	18.4	177	..	8	..	4	149	4
Malaysia	75.0	..	..	4	..	178	15,418	1,199
Mali	12.0	154	..	..	..	1	74	15
Mauritania	11.2	117	..	..	..	5	228	16
Mauritius	93.0	111	..	..	..	9	676	116
Mexico	37.3	107	..	11	..	225	14,969	156
Moldova	..	105	41	..	13	..	170	..
Mongolia	11.0	..	147	566	1,850	10	662	3
Morocco	50.3	23	12	21	27	33	2,147	58
Mozambique	18.6	143	..	..	..	3	168	6
Myanmar	..	..	..	..	..	15	334	1
Namibia	13.1	199	..	37	..	7	225	27
Nepal	41.4	69	..	..	..	27	717	17
Netherlands	90.0	60	..	5	..	192	14,463	3,672
New Zealand	58.0	106	..	6	..	128	7,677	580
Nicaragua	10.0	66	..	..	..	1	49	9
Niger	7.9	127	..	..	..	1	74	15
Nigeria	82.6	126	..	..	..	7	548	2
Norway	73.5	103	250	..	4	266	11,659	140
Oman	..	211	..	..	..	16	1,453	133
Pakistan	54.0	242	..	43	..	69	5,343	446
Panama	33.5	123	..	..	..	12	661	7
Papua New Guinea	3.4	34	..	..	..	..	..	..
Paraguay	9.4	..	..	..	..	1	105	7
Peru	10.9	45	..	1	..	38	2,584	27
Philippines	..	47	..	..	..	64	7,180	374
Poland	65.3	150	1,630	76	226	32	1,657	66
Portugal	..	99	280	7	..	72	4,590	194
Puerto Rico	100.0	..	..	..	..	..	..	..
Romania	51.0	108	616,044	121	105,131	22	1,245	18
Russian Federation	78.8	..	31,000	420	1,213,000	586	26,525	890

	Roads			Railways		Air		
	Paved roads % 1995	Normalized road index 1995	Goods transported million ton-km 1995	Rail traffic km per million $ GDP 1995	Goods transported million ton-km 1995	Aircraft departures thousands 1995	Passengers carried thousands 1995	Air freight ton-km 1995
Rwanda	9.9	97	..	..	..	..	9	..
Saudi Arabia	42.7	143	..	1	..	98	11,525	895
Senegal	28.9	116	..	15	..	4	150	15
Sierra Leone	11.0	105	..	..	..	0	15	0
Singapore	97.3	..	..	..	..	52	10,779	3,687
Slovak Republic	..	..	32,043	103	60,776	2	41	0
Slovenia	..	85	4	20	2	8	371	4
South Africa	32.8	115	..	71	..	74	6,396	263
Spain	99.0	102	582	4	10	279	23,298	690
Sri Lanka	..	116	..	29	..	9	1,156	156
Sudan	36.2	..	..	..	..	9	497	53
Sweden	76.0	84	..	11	..	170	9,572	191
Switzerland	..	72	405,150	..	46	191	9,859	1,510
Syrian Arab Republic	71.0	..	..	12	..	..	563	..
Tajikistan	82.7	..	..	..	..	3	783	3
Tanzania	4.2	82	..	11	..	6	236	3
Thailand	97.4	140	..	14	..	87	12,771	1,308
Togo	31.6	150	..	..	..	1	74	15
Trinidad and Tobago	51.0	114	..	..	..	..	1,727	..
Tunisia	78.8	183	..	21	..	15	1,417	18
Turkey	23.0	192	112,515	9	8,632	79	7,749	215
Turkmenistan	81.2	..	..	..	..	12	748	2
Uganda	7.7	55	..	6	..	1	95	1
Ukraine	94.8	92	..	324	..	20	864	19
United Arab Emirates	100.0	44	..	..	..	34	3,551	557
United Kingdom	100.0	63	1,689	4	97	713	59,129	6,831
United States	59.9	109	..	27	..	7,469	527,414	19,615
Uruguay	13.7	148	..	1	..	9	477	4
Uzbekistan	87.2	..	..	..	..	16	2,217	9
Venezuela	39.3	726	..	..	..	80	4,446	120
Vietnam	25.9	..	..	16	..	27	2,290	2
West Bank and Gaza	..	..	..	..	..	..	..	..
Yemen, Rep.	7.9	..	..	..	..	5	375	4
Yugoslavia, Fed. Rep.	..	..	..	..	..	..	..	..
Zaire	..	..	..	..	..	..	178	..
Zambia	18.3	191	..	16	..	..	235	..
Zimbabwe	19.0	263	..	..	..	10	626	144

About the data

Transport infrastructure—highways, railways, ports and waterways, airports and air traffic control systems—and the services that flow from it are crucial to the activities of households, producers, and governments. Taken together, the services associated with the use of infrastructure (measured in terms of value added) account for 7–11 percent of GDP, with transport being the largest sector. Transport alone commonly absorbs 5–8 percent of total paid employment. Providing the infrastructure for transportation to meet the demands of a modern economy is one of the major challenges of economic development.

Internationally comparable data are not available for most transport subsectors. Unlike for demographic statistics, national income accounts, and international trade, the collection of infrastructure data has not been "internationalized." Even when data are available, they are often of limited value because of definitional incompatibilities, inappropriate geographical units of observation, or lack of timeliness. Serious efforts need to be made to create internationally comparable databases whose comparability and accuracy can be gradually improved. Because performance characteristics vary significantly by mode of transport and according to whether the focus is measuring the infrastructure or measuring the services flowing from the infrastructure, highly specialized and carefully specified indicators are required.

The table includes selected indicators of the size and extent of roads, railways, and air transport systems and the volume of freight and passengers carried. In addition to quantity, the quality of transport service is important in assessing an economy's transport infrastructure. The shipping sector (including port operations) is important for many economies, but internationally comparable data in this area are available for only a few countries and so are not presented here.

To measure the relative size of an indicator over time or across countries, some form of normalization is required. The table presents two normalized indicators: rail traffic per million dollars of GDP and the normalized road index. While the rail traffic indicator is normalized by a single indicator—the size of the economy—the normalized road index uses a multidimensional regression function to estimate the "normal," or expected, stock of roads in a country (Armington and Dikhanov 1996). The "normalizing" variables include population, population density, per capita income, urbanization, and regional differences. The value of the normalized road index shows whether the stock of roads in a country exceeds or falls short of the average for a country of similar characteristics.

Definitions

- **Paved roads** are roads that have been sealed with asphalt or similar road-building materials.
- **Normalized road index** is the total length of roads in a country compared with the expected length of roads, where the expectation is conditioned on population, population density, per capita income, urbanization, and regional-specific dummy variables. A value of 100 is "normal." If the index is more than 100, the country's stock of roads exceeds the average. ● **Goods transported** by road are the volume of goods transported by road vehicles, measured in millions of metric tons times kilometers traveled. ● **Rail traffic** is the number of rail traffic units (the sum of passenger-kilometers and ton-kilometers) per million U.S. dollars of GDP.
- **Goods transported** by rail are the tonnage of goods transported times kilometers traveled.
- **Aircraft departures** are the number of domestic and international takeoffs of aircraft. ● **Passengers carried** include both domestic and international aircraft passengers. ● **Air freight** is the sum of the tons of freight, express, and diplomatic bags carried on each flight stage (the operation of an aircraft from takeoff to its next landing) multiplied by the stage distance.

Data sources

Data on roads are from the International Road Federation's *World Road Statistics*. The normalized road index is based on World Bank staff estimates. Railway data are from a database maintained by the World Bank's Transportation, Water, and Urban Development Department, Transport Division. Air transport data are from the International Civil Aviation Organization.

5.13 Science and technology

	Scientists and engineers in research and development	Technicians in research and development	Expenditures for research and development	High-technology exports		Royalty and license fees			
					% of manufactured exports	Receipts $ millions		Payments $ millions	
	per million people 1981–92[a]	per million people 1981–92[a]	% of GNP 1981–92[a]	$ millions 1995	1995	1990	1995	1990	1995
Albania	..	..	..	..	..	0	0	0	0
Algeria	..	..	..	29	12	0	..	1	..
Angola	..	..	..	..	..	0	14	0	0
Argentina	350	197	0.3	1,126	16	4	2	409	206
Armenia	..	..	..	..	..	..	..	..	..
Australia	2,477	943	1.4	5,802	41	162	240	827	1,015
Austria	1,146	1,101	1.4	11,407	25	91	132	287	521
Azerbaijan	..	..	..	..	..	..	..	..	..
Bangladesh	..	..	..	4	0	0	0	0	0
Belarus	3,300	515	0.9	..	..	..	..	..	..
Belgium	1,856	2,041	1.7	..	..	..	..	..	..
Benin	177	54	0.7	..	..	0	0	0	0
Bolivia	250	154	1.7	30	15	0	0	3	4
Bosnia and Herzegovina	..	..	..	..	..	..	..	..	..
Botswana	..	..	..	..	..	0	0	8	6
Brazil	391	..	0.4	4,021	16	12	32	54	529
Bulgaria	4,240	1,205	1.7	..	..	0	0	0	0
Burkina Faso	..	..	..	..	..	0	0	0	0
Burundi	32	31	0.3	..	..	0	0	0	0
Cambodia	..	..	..	..	..	..	..	..	..
Cameroon	..	..	..	..	..	1	0	0	2
Canada	2,322	978	1.6	27,648	23	..	..	..	..
Central African Republic	55	31	0.2	..	..	0	..	0	..
Chad	..	..	..	..	..	0	0	0	0
Chile	364	231	0.7	339	16	0	1	37	50
China	..	..	..	24,393	19	0	0	0	0
Colombia	39	37	0.1	815	21	21	44	13	32
Congo	461	788	0.0	2	12	0	0	0	0
Costa Rica	539	..	0.3	94	14	1	3	9	12
Côte d'Ivoire	..	..	..	..	..	0	0	0	0
Croatia	1,977	845	..	723	21	..	..	..	..
Cuba	1,369	878	0.9	..	..	..	..	..	..
Czech Republic	3,248	1,298	1.8	2,241	13	..	13	..	53
Denmark	2,341	2,663	1.8	6,912	24	0	0	0	0
Dominican Republic	..	..	..	295	19	0	..	0	4
Ecuador	169	215	0.1	24	8	0	0	37	53
Egypt, Arab Rep.	458	340	1.0	89	6	0	47	0	97
El Salvador	19	299	0.0	59	16	0	0	1	3
Eritrea	..	..	..	..	..	..	..	..	..
Estonia	..	..	..	..	..	..	1	..	1
Ethiopia	..	..	..	..	..	0	0	0	0
Finland	2,282	2,093	2.1	7,151	21	50	58	317	389
France	2,267	2,972	2.4	67,152	31	1,295	1,850	1,629	2,320
Gabon	189	17	0.0	11	42	0	0	0	0
Gambia, The	..	..	..	..	..	0	0	0	0
Georgia	..	..	..	..	..	..	..	..	..
Germany	..	..	..	..	..	1,987	2,778	3,797	5,439
Ghana	..	..	..	..	..	0	0	0	1
Greece	53	49	0.3	497	10	0	0	15	58
Guatemala	99	107	0.2	93	17	0	0	0	0
Guinea	264	126	..	..	..	..	..	..	..
Guinea-Bissau	..	..	..	..	..	0	0	0	0
Haiti	..	..	..	..	..	0	0	0	0
Honduras	..	..	..	3	5	0	0	3	9
Hong Kong	..	..	..	8,112	29	..	..	..	..

	Scientists and engineers in research and development	Technicians in research and development	Expenditures for research and development	High-technology exports		Royalty and license fees			
					% of manufactured exports	Receipts $ millions		Payments $ millions	
	per million people 1981–92[a]	per million people 1981–92[a]	% of GNP 1981–92[a]	$ millions 1995	1995	1990	1995	1990	1995
Hungary	1,200	697	1.1	..	..	49	32	36	70
India	..	..	..	..	..	1	..	72	..
Indonesia	..	..	..	3,615	16	0	0	0	0
Iran, Islamic Rep.	..	..	..	..	..	0	0	0	0
Iraq	..	..	..	..	..	..	..	..	..
Ireland	1,801	366	0.9	19,811	63	38	114	591	2,554
Israel	..	..	..	4,722	28	63	124	73	152
Italy	1,366	742	1.3	32,496	16	1,040	462	1,959	1,166
Jamaica	8	6	0.0	..	..	3	4	7	19
Japan	..	..	..	165,972	39	2,490	6,010	6,040	9,363
Jordan	..	..	..	183	26	0	0	0	0
Kazakstan	..	..	..	..	..	..	..	..	..
Kenya	..	..	..	20	5	9	6	6	0
Korea, Dem. Rep.	..	..	..	..	..	..	..	..	..
Korea, Rep.	..	..	..	47,805	42	37	299	136	2,385
Kuwait	..	..	..	77	13	0	0	0	0
Kyrgyz Republic	..	..	..	..	..	..	..	..	..
Lao PDR	..	..	..	..	..	0	0	0	0
Latvia	3,387	..	0.3	126	17	0	0	0	0
Lebanon	..	..	..	..	..	..	..	..	..
Lesotho	..	..	..	..	..	0	0	1	0
Libya	361	493	0.2	..	..	0	..	0	..
Lithuania	1,278	..	..	246	23	..	0	..	1
Macedonia, FYR	1,258	334	..	..	..	..	..	..	..
Madagascar	22	79	0.5	2	3	0	1	0	9
Malawi	..	..	..	..	..	0	0	0	0
Malaysia	..	..	..	37,072	67	0	0	0	0
Mali	..	..	..	..	..	0	0	0	0
Mauritania	..	..	..	..	..	0	0	0	0
Mauritius	361	158	0.0	24	2	0	0	0	0
Mexico	226	399	0.2	21,438	35	73	114	380	484
Moldova	..	..	..	15	9	..	..	..	..
Mongolia	..	..	..	..	..	0	..	0	..
Morocco	..	..	..	619	25	4	3	60	125
Mozambique	..	..	..	1	5	0	..	0	..
Myanmar	..	..	..	..	..	0	..	0	..
Namibia	..	..	..	..	..	1	0	3	3
Nepal	..	..	..	0	0	0	0	0	0
Netherlands	2,656	1,774	1.9	44,729	40	1,086	2,350	1,751	3,050
New Zealand	1,555	785	0.9	405	11	0	0	0	0
Nicaragua	214	89	..	39	38	0	0	0	0
Niger	..	..	..	..	..	..	..	0	1
Nigeria	15	69	0.1	..	..	0	0	0	0
Norway	3,159	1,594	1.9	2,525	23	133	287	148	231
Oman	..	..	..	65	8	0	0	0	0
Pakistan	..	..	..	..	..	0	2	0	12
Panama	..	..	..	..	..	..	..	9	11
Papua New Guinea	..	..	..	29	35	0	0	0	0
Paraguay	..	..	..	3	3	0	..	0	..
Peru	273	..	0.2	69	9	..	1	5	60
Philippines	..	..	..	2,986	42	1	2	38	99
Poland	1,083	1,380	0.9	1,688	10	0	4	0	44
Portugal	599	381	0.6	2,581	14	14	20	117	217
Puerto Rico	..	..	..	..	..	..	..	..	..
Romania	1,220	492	0.7	355	8	0	3	0	8
Russian Federation	5,930	1,354	1.8	..	..	..	..	..	..

	Scientists and engineers in research and development	Technicians in research and development	Expenditures for research and development	High-technology exports		Royalty and license fees			
	per million people 1981–92[a]	per million people 1981–92[a]	% of GNP 1981–92[a]	$ millions 1995	% of manufactured exports 1995	Receipts $ millions 1990	Receipts $ millions 1995	Payments $ millions 1990	Payments $ millions 1995
Rwanda	12	11	0.5	..	..	0	0	0	0
Saudi Arabia	..	..	..	935	34	0	0	0	0
Senegal	342	467	..	79	39	1	1	0	0
Sierra Leone	..	..	..	..	..	0	0	0	0
Singapore	1,284	583	0.9	69,249	70	0	0	0	0
Slovak Republic	..	..	..	908	17	..	11	..	79
Slovenia	2,998	2,390	1.5	1,123	15	4	4	5	23
South Africa	319	132	1.0	1,879	15	54	66	130	102
Spain	956	299	0.9	11,834	17	90	196	1,022	1,269
Sri Lanka	173	43	0.2	59	3	0	0	0	0
Sudan	..	..	..	..	..	0	..	0	..
Sweden	3,081	3,148	2.9	17,731	26	563	876	743	999
Switzerland	2,409	1,374	1.8	19,755	26	..	..	..	..
Syrian Arab Republic	..	..	..	..	..	0	..	0	..
Tajikistan	..	..	..	..	..	..	..	..	..
Tanzania	..	..	..	..	..	0	0	0	0
Thailand	173	51	0.2	14,826	36	0	1	170	630
Togo	..	..	..	..	..	0	0	0	0
Trinidad and Tobago	240	222	0.8	304	28	0	0	7	0
Tunisia	388	71	0.3	429	10	1	1	1	2
Turkey	209	23	0.8	1,289	8	..	..	..	..
Turkmenistan	..	..	..	..	..	..	..	..	..
Uganda	..	..	..	..	..	0	0	0	0
Ukraine	6,761	..	..	..	..	..	..	..	..
United Arab Emirates	..	..	..	15	3	..	..	..	..
United Kingdom	..	..	2.1	79,256	41	2,540	4,566	2,992	2,855
United States	3,873	..	2.9	181,233	43	16,635	26,960	3,138	6,300
Uruguay	..	..	..	82	10	0	1	0	5
Uzbekistan	1,760	313	..	..	..	..	..	..	..
Venezuela	..	..	..	377	14	..	0	..	0
Vietnam	334	..	0.4	..	..	..	..	..	..
West Bank and Gaza	..	..	..	..	..	..	..	..	..
Yemen, Rep.	..	..	..	..	..	..	..	..	..
Yugoslavia, Fed. Rep.	1,476	400	..	..	..	..	..	..	..
Zaire	..	..	..	..	..	..	..	..	..
Zambia	..	..	..	..	..	0	..	0	..
Zimbabwe	..	..	..	27	..	1	1	..	..
World	..	..	..	..	..	**35,477 t**	**59,369 t**	**33,193 t**	**52,889 t**
Low income	..	..	..	..	..	14 t	23 t	99 t	..
Excl. China & India	..	..	..	..	..	14 t	24 t	23 t	48 t
Middle income	..	..	..	..	..	345 t	389 t	..	..
Lower middle income	..	..	..	..	..	..	..	..	..
Upper middle income	..	..	..	..	..	193 t	258 t	1,069 t	1,534 t
Low & middle income	..	..	..	..	..	341 t	582 t	2,097 t	4,038 t
East Asia & Pacific	..	..	..	..	..	4 t	18 t	219 t	764 t
Europe & Central Asia	..	..	..	..	..	..	..	..	..
Latin America & Carib.	..	..	..	..	..	130 t	220 t	1,090 t	1,653 t
Middle East & N. Africa	..	..	..	..	..	6 t	58 t	72 t	261 t
South Asia	..	..	..	..	..	1 t	..	73 t	..
Sub-Saharan Africa	..	..	..	..	..	70 t	95 t	154 t	118 t
High income	..	..	..	..	..	34,159 t	57,155 t	30,422 t	47,926 t

a. See *Primary data documentation* for survey year.

Rapid progress in science and technology is changing the global economy and increasing the importance of knowledge as a factor of production. It is also driving the rapid shifts in comparative advantage between countries. The table shows a few key indicators that provide a very partial picture of the "technological base" in countries: the availability of skilled human resources (the scientists, engineers, and technicians employed in research and development, or R&D), the competitive edge countries enjoy in high-technology exports, and their purchases of technology through royalties and licenses.

An indication of a country's skilled human resources is obtained either from the total stock of scientists, engineers, and technicians or the number of economically active persons with the necessary qualifications to be scientists, engineers, or technicians. Missing data on potential scientists and engineers have been estimated by the United Nations Educational, Scientific, and Cultural Organization (UNESCO) using the number of people who have completed education at ISCED (International Standard Classification of Education) levels 6 and 7; for technicians, missing data are estimated using the number of people who have completed education at ISCED level 5. These data are normally calculated in terms of full-time equivalent staff. Such data cannot take account of variation in the quality of the training or education received, which is considerable.

R&D expenditures may reflect different tax treatment of such expenditures. And in some countries they may reflect a large and possibly unproductive outlay by governments or state-owned research establishments.

High-technology exports are those produced by the top 10 industries (based on U.S. industries) according to R&D intensity. The rankings used in preparing the data on high-technology exports in the table are based on a methodology developed by Davis (1982). Using input-output techniques, Davis estimated the technology intensity for any given industry in the United States in terms of the R&D expenditures required to produce a certain manufactured good. This methodology takes into account not only the direct R&D investments made by final producers, but also the indirect R&D expenditures made by suppliers of intermediate goods used in producing the final good. Industries classified on the basis of the U.S. Standard Industrial Classification (SIC) were ranked according to their R&D intensity, with the top 10 SIC groups (three-digit classification) designated as high-technology industries. The industry ranked tenth had an R&D index 30 percent greater than the industry in eleventh place and more than 100 percent greater than the average for the manufacturing sector.

To translate Davis's industry classification into a definition of high-technology trade, Braga and Yeats (1992) used the concordance between the SIC grouping and the SITC (Standard International Trade Classification), revision 1 classification proposed by Hatter (1985). Given the imperfect match between SIC and SITC codes, Hatter estimated high-technology weights (the proportion of U.S. high-technology imports and exports in each SITC group, based on 1975–77 U.S. trade data) as a way to highlight the relative importance of high-technology products in any given SITC grouping. In preparing the data on high-technology trade, Braga and Yeats considered only those SITC groups (at a four-digit level) that presented a high-technology weight greater or equal to 50 percent. Examples of high-technology exports include aircraft, office machinery, scientific instruments, and pharmaceutical goods (see Braga and Yeats 1992).

Note that the appropriateness of this methodology relies on the somewhat unrealistic assumption that the use of the U.S. input-output relations and trade patterns for high-technology production does not introduce a bias in the classification.

● **Scientists and engineers in research and development** are people trained to work in those capacities (usually requires completion of tertiary education) in any field of science who are engaged in professional work in R&D activities (including administrators). ● **Technicians in research and development** are people engaged in R&D activities who have received vocational or technical training in any branch of knowledge or technology of a specified standard (usually three years beyond the first stage of secondary education). ● **Expenditures for research and development** are expenditures on any creative, systematic activity undertaken to increase the stock of knowledge (including knowledge of people, culture, and society) and the use of this knowledge to devise new applications. Included are fundamental research, applied research, and experimental development work leading to new devices, products, or processes. Total expenditure for R&D comprises current expenditure, including overhead, and capital expenditure. ● **High-technology exports** are goods produced by industries (based on U.S. industries) that rank in the top 10 according to R&D expenditures. Manufactured exports are the commodities in the SITC, revision 1, sections 5–9 (chemicals and related products, basic manufactures, manufactured articles, machinery and transport equipment, and other manufactured articles and goods not elsewhere classified), excluding division 68 (nonferrous metals). ● **Royalty and license fees** are payments and receipts between residents and nonresidents for the authorized use of intangible, nonproduced, nonfinancial assets and proprietary rights (such as patents, copyrights, trademarks, industrial processes, and franchises) and for the use, through licensing agreements, of produced originals of prototypes (such as manuscripts and films).

Data on technical personnel and R&D expenditures are collected by UNESCO from member states, mainly from official replies to UNESCO questionnaires and special surveys, as well as from official reports and publications, supplemented by information from other national and international sources. These data are published in UNESCO's *Statistical Yearbook*. Information on high-technology exports are from the United Nations COMTRADE database, and data on royalty payments are from the International Monetary Fund's *Balance of Payments Statistics Yearbook*.

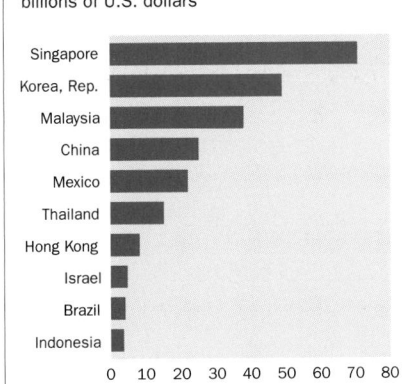

Figure 5.13a High-technology exports from the top 10 high-technology exporters among developing economies, 1995

billions of U.S. dollars

Note: The economies here are drawn from those for which data are shown in table 5.13. High-technology exports are those produced in the top 10 industries ranked by R&D expenditures.
Source: United Nations COMTRADE database.

	Daily newspapers	Radios	Television sets	Mobile phones	Fax machines	Personal computers	Internet hosts
	per 1,000 people 1992	per 1,000 people 1995	per 1,000 people 1995	per 1,000 people 1995	per 1,000 people 1995	per 1,000 people 1995	per 10,000 people July 1996
Albania	49	..	*89*	0.0	..	..	0.24
Algeria	38	..	*71*	0.2	0.2	3.0	0.01
Angola	12	*59*	51	0.2	..	..	0.00
Argentina	143	..	347	9.9	1.4	24.6	2.72
Armenia	24	..	*241*	*0.0*	*0.1*	..	0.28
Australia	265	..	641	127.7	26.3	275.8	220.15
Austria	398	*348*	497	47.6	31.0	124.2	88.27
Azerbaijan	59	..	*214*	*0.1*	*0.3*	..	0.02
Bangladesh	6	*48*	7	*0.0*	*0.0*	..	..
Belarus	186	320	*265*	0.6	0.9	..	0.10
Belgium	310	..	464	23.2	*16.4*	138.3	42.78
Benin	2	*1,127*	*57*	0.2	0.1	..	0.01
Bolivia	57	..	202	1.0	..	..	0.21
Bosnia and Herzegovina	131	..	*94*	0.0	..	..	..
Botswana	29	821	23	0.0	2.1	..	0.00
Brazil	55	..	278	8.0	*1.3*	13.0	2.90
Bulgaria	164	..	*260*	..	*1.1*	21.4	2.68
Burkina Faso	0	*30*	6	0.0	..	0.0	0.00
Burundi	3	65	7	*0.1*	*0.0*	..	0.00
Cambodia	..	*124*	8	1.5	0.1	..	0.00
Cameroon	4	*325*	75	0.2	..	..	0.00
Canada	215	..	*647*	86.5	*18.1*	192.5	143.33
Central African Republic	1	*94*	5	0.0	0.1	..	0.02
Chad	0	620	2	0.0	0.0	0.0	..
Chile	147	..	280	13.8	*1.1*	37.8	9.27
China	43	*163*	250	3.0	0.2	2.2	0.09
Colombia	63	..	188	7.1	2.6	16.2	1.43
Congo	8	*312*	*17*	0.0	..	..	..
Costa Rica	101	..	220	5.5	*0.7*	..	7.58
Côte d'Ivoire	7	..	*59*	0.0	..	..	0.00
Croatia	..	..	*230*	7.1	8.0	20.9	5.19
Cuba	122	..	200	*0.1*	..	..	0.00
Czech Republic	583	..	406	4.7	7.1	53.2	31.17
Denmark	332	..	536	157.3	47.8	270.5	147.20
Dominican Republic	36	..	87	..	..	..	0.18
Ecuador	64	..	148	4.6	*2.7*	3.9	0.53
Egypt, Arab Rep.	41	..	126	0.1	*0.4*	*3.4*	0.14
El Salvador	90	..	241	2.5	..	..	0.07
Eritrea	..	..	6	0.0	0.2	..	..
Estonia	..	..	410	20.5	8.7	6.7	44.42
Ethiopia	1	*200*	4	0.0	0.0	..	0.00
Finland	512	..	519	199.2	25.8	182.1	542.69
France	..	..	579	23.8	32.7	134.3	32.69
Gabon	16	..	*49*	*2.5*	..	4.5	..
Gambia, The	2	*158*	..	1.3	*0.6*	..	..
Georgia	..	*62*	*220*	*0.0*	*0.1*	..	0.22
Germany	0	..	550	42.8	*17.8*	164.9	66.96
Ghana	18	..	*16*	0.4	*0.3*	1.2	0.00
Greece	135	..	442	26.1	*1.5*	33.4	12.12
Guatemala	18	..	54	2.8	*1.0*	2.8	0.15
Guinea	..	76	76	0.1	0.0	0.2	0.00
Guinea-Bissau	6	*40*	0	0.0	0.5	..	..
Haiti	7	*60*	5	0.0	..	..	..
Honduras	31	102	80	0.0	..	..	0.15
Hong Kong	822	..	*359*	129.0	46.0	116.3	38.99

	Daily newspapers	Radios	Television sets	Mobile phones	Fax machines	Personal computers	Internet hosts
	per 1,000 people 1992	per 1,000 people 1995	per 1,000 people 1995	per 1,000 people 1995	per 1,000 people 1995	per 1,000 people 1995	per 10,000 people July 1996
Hungary	282	..	444	25.9	*2.5*	39.2	24.58
India	31	*120*	61	0.1	*0.1*	1.3	0.02
Indonesia	24	..	*147*	1.1	0.4	3.7	0.27
Iran, Islamic Rep.	20	250	140	*0.1*	*0.5*	..	0.05
Iraq	35	..	*74*	0.0	..	..	..
Ireland	186	..	382	44.1	*22.4*	145.0	59.86
Israel	246	..	*295*	53.5	25.0	99.8	71.75
Italy	106	*102*	436	67.4	*3.5*	83.7	19.97
Jamaica	67	*750*	285	17.9	..	..	0.77
Japan	577	..	619	81.5	*48.1*	152.5	39.65
Jordan	53	*340*	*175*	2.6	7.3	8.0	0.18
Kazakstan	..	..	266	0.3	0.2	..	0.33
Kenya	14	..	*18*	0.1	0.1	0.7	0.05
Korea, Dem. Rep.	221	*163*	*323*	0.0	*0.1*	..	..
Korea, Rep.	412	..	*115*	*36.6*	8.4	120.8	10.70
Kuwait	248	..	379	70.7	21.0	57.1	11.80
Kyrgyz Republic	..	..	*238*	*0.0*	..	..	..
Lao PDR	3	*126*	7	*0.1*	0.1	..	0.00
Latvia	98	..	*470*	6.0	*0.3*	7.9	11.65
Lebanon	185	..	268	30.0	..	12.5	0.90
Lesotho	7	*79*	7	0.0	0.3	..	0.00
Libya	15	..	*115*	0.0	..	..	..
Lithuania	225	404	364	4.0	1.0	6.5	3.60
Macedonia, FYR	..	..	*169*	0.0	0.8	..	0.44
Madagascar	4	*211*	*24*	0.0	..	..	0.02
Malawi	2	*250*	..	0.0	*0.1*	..	..
Malaysia	117	*469*	*231*	43.4	*3.0*	39.7	4.24
Mali	4	*168*	*12*	0.0	..	..	0.00
Mauritania	1	*187*	58	0.0	0.1	..	0.00
Mauritius	74	..	192	10.4	17.7	31.9	0.42
Mexico	116	..	192	7.0	*2.1*	26.1	2.21
Moldova	..	209	300	0.0	0.1	2.1	0.02
Mongolia	92	74	59	0.0	0.9	*0.2*	0.04
Morocco	13	..	*145*	1.1	*0.3*	1.7	0.13
Mozambique	5	*49*	*3*	0.0	*0.4*	..	0.01
Myanmar	7	*89*	*76*	0.0	0.0	..	..
Namibia	147	..	29	2.3	..	..	0.54
Nepal	7	*36*	*3*	0.0	*0.0*	..	0.03
Netherlands	303	..	495	33.2	32.3	200.5	138.88
New Zealand	305	..	*508*	108.0	18.1	222.7	216.81
Nicaragua	23	..	170	1.1	..	..	0.69
Niger	1	*62*	*23*	0.0	0.0	..	0.00
Nigeria	18	..	*38*	0.1	..	*4.1*	0.00
Norway	607	..	561	224.4	*30.1*	273.0	277.46
Oman	41	..	*654*	3.7	..	..	0.00
Pakistan	6	..	*22*	0.3	1.2	1.2	0.03
Panama	90	..	169	0.0	..	..	0.78
Papua New Guinea	16	..	*166*	*0.0*	*0.2*	..	0.00
Paraguay	37	..	73	3.2	..	..	0.17
Peru	71	..	100	3.1	0.6	5.9	0.96
Philippines	50	*166*	*121*	7.3	*0.5*	11.4	0.46
Poland	159	..	408	1.9	*0.8*	28.5	9.95
Portugal	47	..	332	34.3	*3.4*	60.4	17.70
Puerto Rico	..	787	322	47.6	*150.2*	..	0.20
Romania	324	..	*201*	0.4	0.9	5.3	1.20
Russian Federation	386	*341*	*379*	0.6	*0.2*	17.7	2.17

	Daily newspapers	Radios	Television sets	Mobile phones	Fax machines	Personal computers	Internet hosts
	per 1,000 people 1992	per 1,000 people 1995	per 1,000 people 1995	per 1,000 people 1995	per 1,000 people 1995	per 1,000 people 1995	per 10,000 people July 1996
Rwanda	0	95	1	0.0	..	..	..
Saudi Arabia	43	..	255	0.9	4.4	25.1	0.15
Senegal	6	..	37	0.0	..	7.2	0.05
Sierra Leone	2	72	16	0.0	0.2	..	..
Singapore	336	..	362	97.7	19.9	172.4	128.50
Slovak Republic	317	170	216	2.3	8.3	41.0	10.24
Slovenia	160	..	374	13.6	7.8	47.7	49.97
South Africa	32	..	101	12.9	1.8	26.5	20.10
Spain	104	1,022	490	24.1	5.5	81.6	15.93
Sri Lanka	27	207	66	2.8	0.6	1.1	0.13
Sudan	24	328	80	0.0	0.2	..	..
Sweden	511	..	476	229.4	37.3	192.5	211.02
Switzerland	377	..	461	63.5	28.0	348.0	145.87
Syrian Arab Republic	22	..	89	0.0	0.3	0.1	0.00
Tajikistan	21	171	258	0.0	0.2	..	..
Tanzania	8	398	16	0.1	..	..	0.00
Thailand	85	208	221	18.5	1.0	15.3	1.08
Togo	3	367	12	0.0	2.4	0.0	..
Trinidad and Tobago	138	..	318	4.3	1.6	19.2	0.51
Tunisia	49	175	156	0.4	2.8	6.7	0.04
Turkey	71	128	240	7.0	1.6	12.5	1.25
Turkmenistan	..	..	217	0.2	..	..	..
Uganda	4	124	26	0.1	0.1	0.5	0.03
Ukraine	118	..	233	0.3	..	5.6	0.87
United Arab Emirates	189	..	263	54.2	10.5	48.4	1.97
United Kingdom	383	..	612	98.0	30.8	186.2	99.01
United States	236	..	776	128.4	53.9	328.0	313.16
Uruguay	240	..	305	12.6	3.5	22.0	2.76
Uzbekistan	21	..	183	..	0.1	..	0.03
Venezuela	205	..	180	18.0	0.8	16.7	..
Vietnam	8	..	110	0.2	0.1	..	..
West Bank and Gaza	..	..	..	..	..	..	..
Yemen, Rep.	19	44	254	0.5	0.1	..	..
Yugoslavia, Fed. Rep.	0	..	170	0.0	1.4	11.8	..
Zaire	3	102	41	0.2	0.1	..	..
Zambia	8	118	64	0.2	0.1	..	..
Zimbabwe	19	..	27	0.0	0.9	3.0	..
World	**91 w**	..	**227 w**	**15.7 w**	**6.3 w**	**43.1 w**	..
Low income	29 w	..	127 w	1.2 w	0.2 w	1.8 w	..
Excl. China & India	10 w	..	43 w	0.2 w	0.3 w	..	..
Middle income	112 w	..	216 w	5.4 w	1.5 w	14.4 w	..
Lower middle income	116 w	..	201 w	3.2 w	0.8 w	10.3 w	..
Upper middle income	101 w	..	256 w	11.0 w	3.4 w	23.3 w	..
Low & middle income	57 w	..	157 w	2.6 w	0.6 w	6.2 w	..
East Asia & Pacific	43 w	..	217 w	3.7 w	0.3 w	3.8 w	..
Europe & Central Asia	227 w	..	303 w	3.0 w	1.1 w	17.7 w	..
Latin America & Carib.	86 w	..	223 w	7.7 w	2.9 w	17.4 w	..
Middle East & N. Africa	33 w	..	145 w	0.9 w	0.9 w	..	..
South Asia	25 w	..	50 w	0.1 w	0.2 w	1.3 w	..
Sub-Saharan Africa	11 w	..	36 w	1.0 w	..	..	..
High income	284 w	..	597 w	84.2 w	33.7 w	201.0 w	..

The global economy is undergoing an information revolution that will be as significant in effect as the industrial revolution of the nineteenth century. A sign of the importance of this revolution is the size of the global information sector, estimated at $1,425 billion in 1994.

This estimate, drawn from a number of data sources, covers:

- Telecommunications services and equipment.
- Computer software, services, and equipment.
- Sound and television broadcasting and equipment.
- Audiovisual entertainment.

The global information sector thus defined is growing faster than the global economy. It also appears to be immune to economic downswings. While the global economy contracted by 3.3 percent in 1991, the information industry grew by 6 percent. The sector's contribution to global output is growing apace and stood at 5.9 percent in 1994.

These estimates notwithstanding, the economic impact of the information sector is difficult to measure. In statistical reporting the major industries involved in processing and distributing information—telecommunications, broadcasting, and computing—have traditionally been categorized under different subsectors. These classification differences can be overcome, but a far greater problem is that most national and international statistical agencies fail to adequately cover these subsectors. Statistical yearbooks have profuse data on agriculture, industry, and trade, but few data on services, let alone the information industry.

A further complication is that there are no agreed definitions on what constitutes the information industry. Should it include both services and equipment? Should it include industries that create and distribute nonelectronic information—such as publishing and postal services?

Some countries have taken steps toward measuring the impact of information industries more effectively. Industry Canada, Statistics Canada, and Canadian Heritage are undertaking a major revision of the classification system for industries. A new information technologies and telecommunications classification is proposed that combines telecommunications, broadcasting, and computer services as well as the consumer electronic, telecommunications equipment, and computer hardware industries. The reason for the revision is that, under current classifications, it is difficult to analyze the information technologies and telecommunications industry or to understand it clearly enough to develop programs and policies. Furthermore, the current classification system does not reflect the technological and regulatory changes that have taken place in information technologies and telecommunications

industries. The proposed revisions are being coordinated with U.S. and Mexican statisticians to enhance comparability within the North American Free Trade Area.

In the absence of economic indicators, the table uses a number of proxy indicators to measure progress in the information age. Data covering radios are estimates of receivers in use and are obtained from statistical surveys carried out by UNESCO. They vary widely in reliability from country to country and should be used with caution. Estimates of television sets also vary in reliability. Some countries require that television sets be registered. To the extent that households do not register their television sets or do not register all of their television sets, the number of licensed sets may understate the true number.

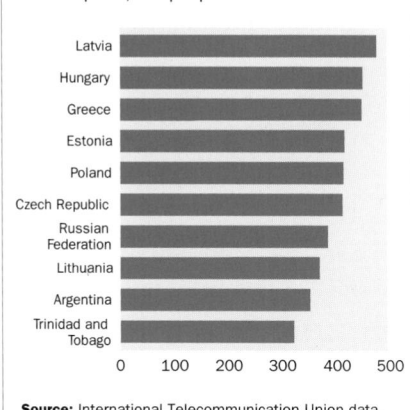

Figure 5.14a The 10 developing economies with the most TV sets per capita, 1995

TV sets per 1,000 people

Source: International Telecommunication Union data.

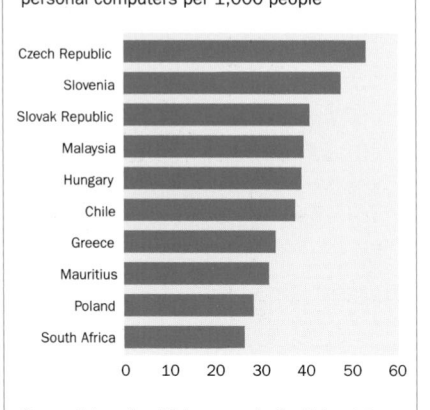

Figure 5.14b The 10 developing economies with the most personal computers per capita, 1995

personal computers per 1,000 people

Source: International Telecommunication Union data.

- **Daily newspapers** is the number of newspapers published at least four times a week, per 1,000 people. ● **Radios** is the estimated number of radio receivers in use for broadcasts to the general public, per 1,000 people. ● **Television sets** represent the estimated number of television sets in use, per 1,000 people. ● **Mobile phones** refers to users of portable telephones subscribing to an automatic public mobile telephone service using cellular technology that provides access to the public switched telephone network, per 1,000 people. ● **Fax machines** is the estimated number of facsimile machines connected to the public switched telephone network, per 1,000 people. ● **Personal computers** is of the estimated number of self-contained computers designed to be used by a single individual, per 1,000 people. ● **Internet hosts** is the number of computers directly connected to the worldwide network of interconnected computer systems, per 1,000 people. All hosts without a country identification are assumed to be located in the United States

Data covering newspapers and radios are from UNESCO, which compiles data mainly from official replies by member states to UNESCO questionnaires and special surveys, but also from official reports and publications, supplemented by information from national and international sources.

Data for the other indicators are from the annual questionnaire sent to member countries by the International Telecommunication Union (ITU). These data are reported in the *World Telecommunication Development Report* or the Telecommunications Indicators database. The text also draws on ITU sources. Data on Internet hosts are from Network Wizards (http://www.nw.com).

Global links

The network of economic links binding nations has become stronger in the past four decades. World trade has grown faster than GDP. Foreign investment has increased rapidly. International financial markets have expanded enormously in their scale and in the diversity of their instruments. And new technologies have revolutionized international communications and altered long-standing patterns of production and employment. All a striking contrast to the first half of the century, when wars, autarky, and depression impeded the growth of trade and international finance.

In some ways the past four decades can be viewed as a return to the pre-1913 era—when goods, labor, and capital moved around the world relatively freely. But there also are striking differences. Compared with the reign of commodities before 1913, trade now has a higher share of manufactures and services, in part a reflection of the declining price of commodities relative to manufactures. Other differences between the current period of financial integration and that of the late 19th century are the greater global scope and depth of integration and the speed with which the market can now react.

Global economic integration—the widening and intensifying of links between the economies of industrial and developing countries—has accelerated rapidly. Underpinning the intensification of these links—which include trade, finance, investment, technology, and migration—are several structural factors. The progressive liberalization of trade policies negotiated during consecutive rounds of trade talks—culminating in the Uruguay Round—has lowered tariffs and stimulated trade. The integration of the world economy through trade has been reinforced by increases in private capital flows, particularly in the 1990s. And technological advances in transport and communications have lowered the cost of operating globally and provided developing countries with new opportunities to benefit from the growing world economy.

Despite a brief reversal in the mid-1970s and early 1980s, the global economic environment has become increasingly favorable, with expanding opportunities for developing countries that have adopted an outward orientation. This environment has been characterized by buoyant growth in industrial countries, low world inflation and energy prices, and modest real interest rates (table 6a).

The principal beneficiaries of economic integration have been a few larger and more rapidly growing developing economies, while the poorer and more slowly developing economies remain heavily dependent on official aid flows from high-income countries. These poorer economies typically are also less diversified and more dependent on exports of primary commodities to high-income economies—and vulnerable to price fluctuations in global markets.

This section provides information on the links between the high-income, industrial economies of the Organization for Economic Cooperation and Development (OECD) and low- and middle-income economies—focusing on trade, private and official capital flows, and labor migration.

Disparities in global integration

Over the past decade the ratio of trade to GDP, a common measure of integration, has risen—strongly in such regions as East Asia and Europe and Central Asia (table 6.1). The amount of foreign direct investment flowing to developing and transition economies has increased fourfold, raising the ratio of FDI to GDP in some regions. But there are wide disparities: the ratio of trade to GDP fell in many economies, especially in Africa, and rose only slightly in South Asia. The distribution of FDI across developing economies is also highly skewed: eight developing countries accounted for two-thirds of FDI flows during 1990–93.

Growing trade links . . .

Trade has been the main engine driving global integration in the second half of the 20th century. Since 1950 trade has grown faster than output, and the trade links between high-income OECD members and other countries have strengthened significantly, particularly for manufactured goods (tables 6.2 and 6.3). The importance of trade for all economies derives from its impact on production efficiencies—through economies of scale and scope as production expands beyond the size limits of the domestic market and through increases in competitiveness as exposure to global learning spreads technological innovation.

Spurred by the success of the newly industrializing economies in Asia and a growing body of evidence supporting the growth-enhancing effects of integration, more developing countries are seeking to use trade, particularly manufactured exports, as a vehicle for growth and diversification. The share of manufactured exports, an important indicator of integration, has risen most significantly in dynamic, fast-growing regions.

While OECD import growth will continue to be healthy, developing country import demand will be even more buoyant—particularly in East and South Asia, as capital and intermediate goods are imported to support their large infrastructure needs and their fast-growing export sectors. International trade is expected to continue to grow rapidly, spurred by reductions in trade barriers agreed to in the Uruguay Round (table 6.4). It is bolstered by regional trade arrangements—such as the North American Free Trade Agreement, the European Union–Mediterranean Initiative, the Asia-Pacific Economic Cooperation Forum, and the Southern Cone common market, Mercosur—and by unilateral trade liberalization in many developing countries. Over the next decade world trade is projected to grow in volume by an average of 6.4 percent a year—almost twice the pace of world output growth.

The relative decline of primary exports from the developing world is a striking trend—real commodity prices fell by more than half in 1980–93 (table 6.5). Production and trade of primary commodities have not grown as fast as world income because of the low elasticity of demand for most commodities, especially food, and the declining intensity of metals and agricultural raw materials in industrial economies. Although prices are expected to be flat in the longer term, this trend will be better than the large price declines suffered during the 1980s and early 1990s—and will provide a more stable environment for primary goods exporters to pursue long-term economic restructuring.

The terms of trade remain a major issue for Sub-Saharan Africa, however, which is still the least diversified region in primary exports. Failure to obtain higher export prices hampers the ability of Sub-Saharan countries to reduce their debt burdens and to channel other resources into priority sectors.

. . . as barriers to trade fall

The progressive liberalization of trade policies agreed to during consecutive rounds of negotiations of the General Agreement on Tariffs and Trade (GATT) has culminated in the reduction of tariffs from about 40 percent in the immediate postwar era to about 6 percent today for OECD countries. From the mid-1970s onward, support for trade liberalization weakened as industrial and developing countries began to establish new nontariff barriers to trade, such as voluntary export restraints and quotas. But the latest round of negotiations—the Uruguay Round—resulted in an agreement by the OECD countries to lower tariffs even further—to 3.8 percent on manufactured goods by the second half of the 1990s.

The full impact of the Uruguay Round on the strength of the global trading system is difficult to gauge. Several studies have estimated the global income gains at up to $200 billion a year. Between a quarter and a half of these gains—which come from the reduction and binding of tariffs and the elimination of nontariff barriers and voluntary export restraints—are expected to go to developing countries. High-income economies reduced tar-

---

Table 6a Global environment for developing economies, 1974–2006

average annual percentage change (except for LIBOR)

	1974–80	1981–90	1991–93	1994	1995	1996[a]	1997–2006[a]
Real GDP in G-7 countries[b]	3.0	3.1	1.4	2.9	1.9	2.2	2.7
G-7 inflation (consumer prices, weighted by GDP)[b]	10.0	4.3	3.2	2.2	2.3	2.1	2.7
World trade volume[c]	4.8	4.2	4.1	9.6	8.1	6.1	6.4
Nominal LIBOR (six-month rate, $)[d]	9.5	10.0	4.6	5.1	6.1	5.6	6.1
Real six-month LIBOR[e]	0.2	5.2	1.0	2.4	3.2	2.5	3.1
Price indexes ($)							
G-5 export unit value of manufactures (MUV)[f]	11.6	3.3	2.1	3.6	8.3	–2.5	2.3
Oil prices[g]	26.7	–5.3	–11.5	–5.7	8.2	17.8	–0.4
World Bank nonfuel commodity price index	–1.5	–5.4	–4.8	22.2	9.5	–6.0	1.3

Note: Data are as of October 1996. a. Estimates and projections. b. The G-7 countries are Canada, France, Germany, Italy, Japan, the United Kingdom, and the United States. c. Trade data refer to exports through 1993 and to the average of exports and imports from 1994 onward. d. London Interbank Offer Rate. e. Nominal LIBOR, adjusted for inflation. f. The G-5 countries are France, Germany, Japan, the United Kingdom, and the United States. g. Oil prices refer to the average of OPEC crude oil prices through 1995 and to the average of Brent, Dubai, and West Texas Intermediate, equally weighted, from 1996 onward.
Source: World Bank data and staff estimates.

iffs by an average 39 percent on imports from developing countries, giving an overall trade-weighted tariff on manufactured imports of 2.5 percent, down from 4.1 percent—with the reductions to be phased in over five years. Developing countries reduced tariff rates by an average 21.3 percent on manufactured products from all sources, giving an overall trade-weighted tariff of 13.3 percent.

The effects of the Round on real incomes and real wages will differ depending on the efficiency gains from each country's liberalization, terms of trade effects, and the implications of abolishing the Multifibre Arrangement (MFA) quotas on textiles and clothing. Liberalizations that translate into large reductions in the domestic prices of imports will lead to larger gains in real income. The reason? Reduced trade barriers mean that consumers can buy from the most efficient source and producers can reorient production toward items in which they have a comparative advantage.

Further gains can come from greater exploitation of scale economies in production—and from improvements in the range and quality of specialized products available to producers and consumers. In addition, countries can gain from reductions in protection by their trading partners, particularly if reduced protection increases the demand for their exports and improves their terms of trade. The phasing out of the MFA (over 10 years) is expected to generate considerable benefits for exporting and importing countries alike. In South Asia, for example, its abolition could mean a substantial increase (200 percent in one estimate) in the output of textiles and apparel exports.

Private flows grow . . .

Aggregate net resource flows to the "part I" developing countries from the countries of the OECD's Development Assistance Committee (DAC) reached $166 billion in 1994, of which private capital flows accounted for 55 percent (table 6.6). Despite a slowdown in portfolio equity flows following Mexico's crisis in December 1994, total private capital flows from high-income OECD countries to developing countries are expected to remain buoyant—particularly as foreign direct investment continues to grow robustly.

Two factors are driving the growing interest of industrial country investors in developing country markets. One is the improvement in long-term expected rates of return following policy reforms and strengthening creditworthiness. The other is the opportunity for risk diversification due to the low correlations between returns in developing and industrial countries. On the supply side institutional investors, especially through mutual and pension funds, are allocating more of their rapidly growing portfolios to international assets.

. . . while official aid declines

Official development assistance (ODA) from DAC countries constituted more than one-third of net resource flows to developing countries and nearly two-thirds of net resource flows to low-income countries. Although many developing countries experienced a surge of private capital flows as creditworthiness improved, for many of the poorest countries ODA is almost the only source of external financing—and it accounts for a large share of their income.

Although aid accounts for a tiny fraction of donor countries' central government budgets, aid nevertheless comes under pressure in many countries whenever budgets are being cut. Net official development assistance fell to 0.3 percent of DAC countries' GNP in 1994, the lowest level since 1973 (table 6.7). At the same time, the composition of aid has shifted in the 1990s, as a bigger share of ODA is diverted to disaster relief and peacekeeping operations and less is spent to support long-term development. Thus even the declining share of ODA in DAC countries' GNP overstates the amount being spent on long-term development. With aid budgets on the decline, aid effectiveness—in reaching the poor and improving their quality of life—is becoming a major concern for DAC donors, and they are pursuing a partnership approach in directing more of their aid to poverty reduction and to countries pursuing sound policies.

The terms of ODA loans have improved considerably, with grants accounting for 80 percent of all ODA flows and for a higher share for all DAC countries except Austria, Japan, and Spain (table 6.8). The grant element of concessional loans also has risen, to an average of 62 percent. But untied aid is still less than one-half of all ODA.

Low-income countries receive 47 percent of aid flows (table 6.10). On a per capita basis Sub-Saharan Africa, which has little access to private flows, remains the largest recipient of ODA among developing regions.

The most significant increase in aid has been in Europe and Central Asia—the result of the large net inflow of official aid to the transition economies of Eastern Europe and the former Soviet Union.

International labor flows—benefits and costs

Like trade and capital flows, international labor flows offer great potential for benefit for both home and host countries (table 6.13). Migrants are often more productive in the host country, reducing labor costs there, while sending remittances back home, boosting incomes in the usually poorer home countries. But migration causes concern among unskilled workers in host countries—where there is a perception that immigration puts downward pressure on wages. As a result international migration remains much more politically charged than trade and capital flows, with public opposition to unskilled migrants rising sharply in many countries and often exacerbated by high unemployment.

	Real trade as a share of GDP		Institutional Investor credit rating		Net foreign direct investment as a share of PPP GDP		Manufactured exports as a share of total exports	
	Initial level % 1981–83	Annual average difference 1980–83 to 1990–93[a]	Initial level 1981–83	Annual average difference 1983–85 to 1993–95[a]	Initial level % 1981–83	Annual average difference 1980–82 to 1990–92[a]	Initial level % 1981–83	Annual average difference 1981–83 to 1991–93[a]
Albania	..	..			..	..	..	..
Algeria	18.8	–0.97	54.1	–2.81	0.0	0.00	0.5	0.18
Angola	34.1	0.02	13.7	–0.19	1.5	–0.05	12.7	–0.21
Argentina	9.0	0.37	25.7	0.93	0.3	0.14	22.4	0.56
Armenia	..	..			..	..	..	..
Australia	15.7	1.02	85.2	–1.59	1.7	–0.03	23.8	1.24
Austria	31.8	1.95	81.6	0.41	0.3	0.01	83.8	0.48
Azerbaijan	..	..			..	..	..	..
Bangladesh	12.2	0.06	13.6	0.78	0.0	0.00	66.3	1.04
Belarus	..	..			..	..	..	..
Belgium[b]	60.0	3.00	73.0	0.62	1.3	0.38	73.9	0.71
Benin	47.5	–4.53			0.0	0.00	23.2	0.70
Bolivia	16.2	0.69	10.0	1.00	0.4	0.01	3.1	0.58
Bosnia and Herzegovina	..	..			..	..	..	..
Botswana	106.9	–2.69	35.5	0.96	2.4	–0.17	..	..
Brazil	7.7	0.50	36.6	–0.66	0.6	–0.04	39.6	1.61
Bulgaria	37.6	–6.02	41.8	–2.16	0.0	0.01	..	..
Burkina Faso	..	..			..	..	..	..
Burundi	18.1	–0.37			0.0	0.00	2.3	0.00
Cambodia	..	..			..	..	..	..
Cameroon	16.4	1.81	35.7	–1.55	0.8	–0.10	5.3	1.16
Canada	22.1	1.81	86.9	–0.56	–0.3	0.09	51.5	1.26
Central African Republic	33.0	–2.38			0.3	–0.03	32.0	1.16
Chad	27.4	0.83			0.0	0.01	5.3	0.00
Chile	31.0	0.97	32.1	2.06	0.8	–0.01	8.4	0.59
China	16.7	0.58	63.9	–0.66	0.1	0.04	70.4	0.61
Colombia	13.1	0.77	48.5	–0.62	0.5	–0.01	24.4	0.59
Congo	57.9	–2.83	17.1	–0.19	1.2	–0.12	6.9	–0.38
Costa Rica	28.1	2.82	13.8	1.39	0.8	0.03	31.5	–0.01
Côte d'Ivoire	35.4	–0.75	32.1	–1.52	0.3	0.01	9.6	0.12
Croatia	..	..	..	..	..	..	..	..
Cuba	..	..	..	..	..	..	..	..
Czech Republic	..	..			..	..	..	..
Denmark	29.1	1.13	70.2	0.73	0.2	0.13	56.5	0.88
Dominican Republic	37.2	–0.34	15.2	0.57	0.3	0.04	19.6	0.00
Ecuador	27.2	0.28	27.7	–0.49	0.2	0.03	3.1	–0.02
Egypt, Arab Rep.	33.6	–1.88	33.7	–0.37	0.6	–0.04	9.2	2.70
El Salvador	25.3	–0.26	6.6	1.04	0.1	0.01	37.4	0.22
Eritrea	..	..	..	..	..	..	..	..
Estonia	..	..			..	..	..	..
Ethiopia	13.3	–0.11	8.8	0.21	0.0	0.01	0.8	0.32
Finland	25.5	0.43	75.5	–0.56	0.1	0.02	72.7	0.98
France	19.3	0.91	79.9	0.84	0.3	0.15	73.6	0.42
Gabon	44.3	–0.20	36.0	–0.89	1.1	–0.08	4.2	0.00
Gambia, The	..	..	..	..	..	..	..	..
Georgia	..	..			..	..	..	..
Germany	24.5	1.30	92.9	–0.28	0.2	0.01	86.5	0.35
Ghana	21.0	4.49	20.3	0.65	0.1	0.00	0.7	0.04
Greece	19.9	3.14	53.2	–0.45	0.9	0.03	50.3	0.29
Guatemala	23.2	–0.32	13.1	0.72	0.5	–0.02	26.6	0.08
Guinea-Bissau	28.5	0.19	..	..	0.0	0.02	..	..
Guinea	..	..			0.0	0.02	..	..
Haiti	19.4	0.42	9.9	–0.19	0.1	–0.01	41.8	0.10
Honduras	25.8	–0.52	10.8	0.50	0.2	0.02	11.0	0.04
Hong Kong	87.9	19.10	68.1	–0.19	0.0	0.00	96.8	–0.12

	Real trade as a share of GDP		Institutional Investor credit rating		Net foreign direct investment as a share of PPP GDP		Manufactured exports as a share of total exports	
	Initial level % 1981–83	Annual average difference 1980–83 to 1990–93ª	Initial level 1981–83	Annual average difference 1983–85 to 1993–95ª	Initial level % 1981–83	Annual average difference 1980–82 to 1990–92ª	Initial level % 1981–83	Annual average difference 1981–83 to 1991–93ª
Hungary	35.6	1.06	45.7	–0.01	0.0	0.29	64.6	0.05
India	7.4	0.09	46.6	–0.57	0.0	0.00	56.0	1.61
Indonesia	26.9	–1.40	51.0	0.06	0.1	0.02	3.2	3.81
Iran, Islamic Rep.	5.5	0.04	17.0	1.14	0.0	0.00	3.6	0.00
Iraq	35.0	–4.85	23.6	–1.61	0.0	0.00	20.4	0.00
Ireland	42.0	3.30	62.3	0.85	0.9	–0.07	61.6	1.21
Israel	32.2	0.73	29.8	1.38	0.3	0.04	81.2	0.67
Italy	17.3	1.05	71.7	0.16	0.2	0.01	83.9	0.54
Jamaica	36.4	3.31	15.9	0.77	–0.3	0.18	62.6	0.06
Japan	9.0	0.24	95.1	–0.38	0.0	0.00	96.4	0.12
Jordan	48.2	2.39	36.5	–1.33	0.3	–0.02	39.9	0.88
Kazakstan	..	..	..	..	..	..	..	..
Kenya	27.1	–0.27	28.0	–0.39	0.1	–0.01	11.9	1.46
Korea, Dem. Rep.	..	..	..	..	..	..	..	..
Korea, Rep.	31.9	1.37	56.3	1.35	0.1	0.01	90.6	0.26
Kuwait	56.0	3.51	65.3	–1.43	0.0	0.00	16.0	0.50
Kyrgyz Republic	..	..	..	..	..	..	..	..
Lao PDR	..	..	..	..	..	..	..	..
Latvia	..	..	..	..	..	..	..	..
Lebanon	..	..	..	..	..	..	..	..
Lesotho	83.3	–3.28	..	..	0.3	0.00	..	..
Libya	..	..	..	..	..	..	..	..
Lithuania	..	..	..	..	..	..	..	..
Macedonia, FYR	..	..	..	..	..	..	..	..
Madagascar	28.3	–1.43	..	..	0.0	0.03	7.1	1.11
Malawi	33.3	–0.35	15.9	0.16	0.0	0.01	6.7	–0.29
Malaysia	51.3	5.74	67.9	–0.15	2.6	0.05	20.8	3.80
Mali	18.4	1.53	..	..	0.1	–0.01	3.5	0.39
Mauritania	57.1	–1.44	..	..	0.5	–0.03	4.6	0.12
Mauritius	50.1	3.82	19.0	2.34	0.0	0.01	31.6	3.48
Mexico	16.5	1.62	37.3	0.90	0.7	0.01	10.5	3.85
Moldova	..	..	..	..	..	..	..	..
Mongolia	..	..	..	..	..	..	..	..
Morocco	24.8	0.39	26.3	0.93	0.2	0.03	28.7	2.52
Mozambique	..	..	..	..	..	..	..	..
Myanmar	6.6	..	..	–0.09	0.0	..	4.5	–0.05
Namibia	..	..	..	..	..	..	..	..
Nepal	14.0	0.00	24.1	–0.10	0.0	0.00	40.8	5.11
Netherlands	43.4	2.07	86.1	0.27	1.1	0.15	49.9	1.36
New Zealand	22.8	1.43	71.3	–0.52	0.8	–0.08	20.4	0.56
Nicaragua	17.7	–0.05	5.6	0.36	0.0	0.01	10.5	–0.22
Niger	26.2	–1.70	..	..	0.2	–0.02	1.9	–0.05
Nigeria	55.5	–5.59	34.0	–1.52	0.6	0.00	0.8	0.03
Norway	36.3	1.37	86.1	–0.73	1.2	–0.02	31.5	0.12
Oman	45.7	–1.61	48.9	0.29	2.5	–0.14	4.2	0.06
Pakistan	17.5	0.05	22.9	0.63	0.1	0.01	53.5	2.56
Panama	36.6	0.45	35.1	–1.23	0.3	–0.03	10.4	1.11
Papua New Guinea	48.5	–1.11	40.8	–0.82	2.6	0.06	6.7	0.64
Paraguay	31.3	2.36	36.2	–0.72	0.3	0.03	10.7	0.14
Peru	16.2	–1.41	26.7	–0.83	0.1	0.01	15.8	0.32
Philippines	24.6	1.84	26.9	0.41	0.1	0.02	43.7	2.69
Poland	19.2	2.10	10.9	2.01	0.0	0.05	68.2	–1.05
Portugal	30.0	3.61	49.6	1.73	0.3	0.15	72.6	0.94
Puerto Rico	..	..	..	..	..	..	..	..
Romania	34.8	0.63	19.9	0.60	0.0	0.01	72.8	0.24
Russian Federation	..	..	..	..	..	..	..	..

	Real trade as a share of GDP		Institutional Investor credit rating		Net foreign direct investment as a share of PPP GDP		Manufactured exports as a share of total exports	
	Initial level % 1981–83	Annual average difference 1980–83 to 1990–93ª	Initial level 1981–83	Annual average difference 1983–85 to 1993–95ª	Initial level % 1981–83	Annual average difference 1980–82 to 1990–92ª	Initial level % 1981–83	Annual average difference 1981–83 to 1991–93ª
Rwanda	12.1	0.45	..	..	0.5	–0.04	..	..
Saudi Arabia	49.5	1.31	71.5	–1.40	6.2	–0.62	0.8	0.01
Senegal	28.8	–0.46	16.5	0.43	0.1	–0.01	14.1	0.79
Sierra Leone	30.8	–3.53	8.2	–0.09	0.2	0.03	62.9	–3.06
Singapore	158.0	11.11	78.3	0.32	8.8	0.37	55.6	1.93
Slovak Republic	..	..	..	..	..	..	..	..
Slovenia	..	..	..	..	..	..	..	..
South Africa	28.3	0.16	56.9	–1.65	0.1	–0.01	75.1	–2.79
Spain	15.7	1.54	63.3	1.14	0.7	0.10	71.3	0.52
Sri Lanka	32.0	–0.33	27.8	0.07	0.2	0.00	22.1	4.27
Sudan	9.4	–1.01	7.9	–0.15	0.0	0.00	0.8	–0.01
Sweden	28.0	1.07	77.3	–0.26	0.3	0.17	79.4	0.54
Switzerland	31.8	0.94	95.2	–0.29	0.2	0.08	91.9	0.17
Syrian Arab Republic	21.5	–1.05	19.0	0.44	0.0	0.00	8.9	2.36
Tajikistan	..	..	..	..	..	..	..	..
Tanzania	26.2	–0.65	9.0	0.51	0.0	0.01	13.5	0.22
Thailand	24.6	3.25	51.9	0.97	0.3	0.05	27.7	3.83
Togo	42.3	1.28	..	..	0.4	–0.04	10.9	–0.15
Trinidad and Tobago	22.2	3.12	50.9	–1.97	2.5	–0.01	8.0	2.05
Tunisia	42.3	–0.27	45.1	–0.35	1.5	–0.08	36.9	3.34
Turkey	10.0	1.65	27.8	1.60	0.1	0.03	35.7	3.27
Turkmenistan	..	..	..	..	..	..	..	..
Uganda	9.4	0.24	4.6	0.55	0.0	0.00	0.3	0.00
Ukraine	..	..	..	..	..	..	..	..
United Arab Emirates	41.0	1.97	60.7	–0.13	0.0	0.00	3.7	0.00
United Kingdom	23.5	1.02	88.7	–0.26	1.1	0.05	70.0	1.17
United States	8.1	0.78	95.9	–0.63	0.5	–0.02	69.1	1.04
Uruguay	19.9	1.06	31.2	0.48	0.9	–0.12	33.5	0.67
Uzbekistan	..	..	..	..	..	..	..	..
Venezuela	22.4	0.26	44.0	–0.76	0.2	0.04	2.1	0.82
Vietnam	..	..	..	..	..	..	..	..
West Bank and Gaza	..	..	..	..	..	..	..	..
Yemen, Rep.	..	..	..	..	0.3	–0.01	0.0	0.00
Yugoslavia, Fed. Rep.	..	..	..	..	..	..	..	..
Zaire	14.9	1.82	6.0	0.15	0.0	0.00	5.9	0.04
Zambia	46.1	–2.29	10.0	0.31	0.2	0.01	0.7	0.00
Zimbabwe	29.3	0.31	20.5	0.83	0.0	0.01	34.4	–0.29
World	**27.3 m**	**0.39 m**	**35.9 m**	**–0.14 m**	**0.19 m**	**0.01 m**	**23.2 m**	**0.42 m**
Low income	25.8 m	–0.21 m	16.2 m	–0.14 m	–0.14 m	0.00 m	10.0 m	0.10 m
Excl. China & India	26.2 m	–0.27 m	16.2 m	–0.14 m	–0.14 m	0.00 m	7.1 m	0.10 m
Middle income	28.1 m	0.39 m	35.1 m	–0.05 m	–0.05 m	0.01 m	21.6 m	0.59 m
Lower middle income	27.0 m	0.15 m	27.7 m	0.04 m	0.04 m	0.01 m	20.4 m	0.59 m
Upper middle income	30.1 m	1.06 m	41.5 m	–0.18 m	–0.18 m	–0.01 m	22.4 m	0.59 m
Low & middle income	26.6 m	0.03 m	26.9 m	–0.14 m	–0.14 m	0.00 m	12.3 m	0.30 m
East Asia & Pacific	24.6 m	1.40 m	67.9 m	–0.22 m	–0.22 m	0.02 m	35.7 m	0.63 m
Europe and Central Asia	34.8 m	0.63 m	30.8 m	0.57 m	0.57 m	0.05 m	70.5 m	0.24 m
Latin America & Carib.	22.4 m	0.45 m	26.7 m	0.21 m	0.21 m	0.01 m	15.8 m	0.32 m
Middle East & N. Africa	34.3 m	–0.12 m	36.5 m	–0.45 m	–0.45 m	0.00 m	9.2 m	0.25 m
South Asia	14.0 m	0.05 m	24.1 m	–0.08 m	–0.08 m	0.00 m	53.5 m	2.56 m
Sub-Saharan Africa	28.8 m	–0.35 m	17.1 m	–0.14 m	–0.14 m	0.00 m	5.9 m	0.04 m
High income	29.5 m	1.37 m	75.5 m	–0.04 m	–0.04 m	0.02 m	72.6 m	0.54 m

a. Computed as the difference between the endpoints of the period shown, averaged over 10 years. b. Includes Luxembourg.

Growth and integration

The pace of global economic integration continues to accelerate dramatically. Between 1985 and 1994 the ratio of world trade to GDP rose three times faster than during the previous decade. During the same 10-year period foreign direct investment (FDI) doubled as a share of global GDP. Developing countries have participated extensively in the acceleration of global integration. Over the past decade their ratio of trade to GDP has increased, and their share of global FDI has risen to more than one-third.

A closer look, however, reveals sharp differences among countries. Although developing countries as a group kept pace with the growth of world trade, the ratio of trade to GDP fell in 44 of 93 developing countries over the past 10 years. There were similar disparities in the distribution of FDI: two-thirds of FDI to developing countries went to just eight countries, and half the countries received little or none. These disparities are likely to continue.

Countries that integrate faster tend to grow faster ●

Integration matters because there is an association between integration and growth. Fast growth tends to promote a more open economy, and policies that promote an open economy also promote faster growth. Thus lagging integration is a sign of underlying policy deficiencies. In addition, integration can lead to higher growth through better resource allocation, greater competition, transfer of technology, and access to foreign savings. Many of the countries lagging in global integration are among the world's poorest.

For many developing countries successful integration depends on fundamental economic reform, requiring difficult policy decisions that often lead to real short-term dislocation. These costs must be acknowledged from the outset, and the effects carefully taken into account in the design of reform programs. But the costs are manageable. In fact, openness to external trade and investment is often the necessary first step to solid, sustainable economic development.

About the data

Indicators of the speed of integration were developed for the World Bank's *Global Economic Prospects and the Developing Countries 1996*. The concept underlying the indicators is that the change in variables associated with integration gives an indication of how rapidly an economy is integrating with the global economy. The changes in the integration variables are computed between three-year averages to reduce the effect of a single year. But the results must be interpreted with care. For example, a decline in Switzerland's credit rating, already one of the highest in the world, probably should not be given the same weight as a similar decline for a developing country. (Selected country risk indicators are shown in table 5.9.)

Definitions

● **Real trade** is the sum of exports and imports of goods and services measured in constant prices. The data here differ from those in the World Bank's *Global Economic Prospects 1996*, where they were adjusted for population size. ● **Institutional Investor credit rating** ranks the chances of a country's default from zero to 100, with 100 representing the least chance of default. For further discussion of these ratings see Shapiro (1996). ● **Net foreign direct investment** is investment to acquire a lasting management interest (at least 10 percent of voting stock) in an enterprise operating in a country other than that of the investor. It includes equity capital, reinvestment of earnings, other long-term capital, and short-term capital. The indicator is computed as a ratio to GDP converted to international dollars using purchasing power parities (PPPs). ● **Manufactured exports** are commodities in the Standard International Trade Classification (SITC), revision 1, sections 5–9 (chemical and related products, basic manufactures, manufactured articles, machinery and transport equipment, and other manufactured articles and goods not elsewhere classified), excluding division 68 (nonferrous metals).

Data sources

These data first appeared in the World Bank's *Global Economic Prospects and the Developing Countries 1996*. Data on real trade, net foreign direct investment, total exports, and gross domestic product come from the World Bank's national accounts and balance of payments files. Data on manufactured exports come from the United Nations COMTRADE database. Credit ratings prepared by Institutional Investor appear in the monthly publication *Institutional Investor*.

6.2 | Direction of OECD trade

Exports from high-income OECD countries	High-income OECD countries		European Union		United States		Japan	
	1985	1995	1985	1995	1985	1995	1985	1995
$ billions								
Low- and middle-income economies	245.8	680.5	119.0	316.0	58.8	176.6	50.2	145.3
East Asia & Pacific	57.5	237.1	13.4	56.6	12.6	52.6	25.7	106.4
Europe & Central Asia	29.3	146.9	23.5	128.4	2.8	10.0	1.5	3.7
Latin America & Carib.	55.0	162.4	14.9	45.3	28.8	91.4	7.6	18.4
Middle East & N. Africa	62.1	68.7	41.0	45.9	8.2	12.5	9.3	6.1
South Asia	14.0	25.1	6.7	13.0	2.7	4.7	3.1	4.7
Sub-Saharan Africa	27.9	40.3	19.5	26.8	3.7	5.3	3.0	6.0
High-income economies	996.7	2,416.7	585.9	1,434.3	146.4	364.9	125.7	297.3
Non-OECD	74.5	298.3	21.6	80.4	20.4	78.7	26.1	115.3
OECD	922.2	2,118.4	564.3	1,353.9	126.0	286.2	99.6	182.0
World	**1,242.6**	**3,097.2**	**704.9**	**1,750.2**	**205.2**	**541.4**	**175.9**	**442.6**
% of total exports								
Low- and middle-income economies	19.8	22.0	16.9	18.1	28.6	32.6	28.5	32.8
East Asia & Pacific	4.6	7.7	1.9	3.2	6.1	9.7	14.6	24.0
Europe & Central Asia	2.4	4.7	3.3	7.3	1.4	1.9	0.8	0.8
Latin America & Carib.	4.4	5.2	2.1	2.6	14.0	16.9	4.3	4.2
Middle East & N. Africa	5.0	2.2	5.8	2.6	4.0	2.3	5.3	1.4
South Asia	1.1	0.8	0.9	0.7	1.3	0.9	1.8	1.1
Sub-Saharan Africa	2.2	1.3	2.8	1.5	1.8	1.0	1.7	1.3
High-income economies	80.2	78.0	83.1	81.9	71.3	67.4	71.5	67.2
Non-OECD	6.0	9.6	3.1	4.6	9.9	14.5	14.8	26.1
OECD	74.2	68.4	80.1	77.4	61.4	52.9	56.6	41.1
World	**100.0**	**100.0**	**100.0**	**100.0**	**100.0**	**100.0**	**100.0**	**100.0**

Strengthening trade links

International trade links between OECD and developing countries have strengthened considerably during the past three decades. The share of exports from high-income OECD countries going to developing countries has increased—and so has the share of developing country exports going to OECD countries. The increase in trade is most pronounced in the rapidly integrating regions of East Asia and the Pacific and Latin America. The freeing of trade regimes in the transition economies of Europe and Central Asia has begun to have an impact on their trade, especially with the European Union. South Asia, starting from a much smaller base, has made large relative gains. But the Middle East and North Africa and Sub-Saharan Africa continue to lose share in trade with the OECD.

Particularly important for developing countries, because of employment-creating effects, has been the strong growth of the OECD's market for their manufactured exports. In 1964 only about 7 percent of OECD imports of manufactures originated in non-OECD countries (based on 1995 OECD membership); by 1995 this share had risen to about 25 percent.

Just as there are differences in the export performance of developing countries, there are those in the import performance of OECD countries. Links between North America and non-OECD countries have expanded at an above-average pace—U.S. and Canadian manufactured imports originating in non-OECD countries grew fourfold between 1964 and 1995, from 9 percent to 37 percent. Partly as a result of European integration initiatives, trade in manufactures between the European Union (EU) and developing countries grew at a below-average pace. In 1995 only about 18 percent of EU imports of manufactures originated in non-OECD countries. Labor-intensive products have been among the most dynamic categories of manufactured trade for developing countries, which roughly doubled their market share in high-income economies for these products during the past two decades.

	High-income OECD countries		European Union		United States		Japan	
Imports by high-income OECD countries	1985	1995	1985	1995	1985	1995	1985	1995
$ billions								
Low- and middle-income economies	302.9	744.7	133.9	299.1	103.3	277.4	55.5	132.6
East Asia & Pacific	78.5	306.3	14.0	69.7	33.3	124.4	27.2	92.2
Europe & Central Asia	23.2	125.8	19.0	107.2	3.2	10.5	0.4	5.7
Latin America & Carib.	84.0	163.9	26.2	37.3	47.4	106.5	6.1	11.3
Middle East & N. Africa	67.3	75.3	43.8	46.4	6.1	12.3	17.6	15.7
South Asia	9.5	28.8	3.9	12.9	3.4	10.2	1.7	3.9
Sub-Saharan Africa	40.4	44.5	27.0	25.5	9.9	13.4	2.5	3.7
High-income economies	1,047.2	2,301.3	588.6	1,322.4	255.4	491.3	72.0	200.3
Non-OECD	100.2	227.4	22.3	55.5	46.9	94.6	24.3	59.1
OECD	947.0	2,073.9	566.3	1,267.0	208.5	396.7	47.6	141.1
World	**1,350.1**	**3,046.0**	**722.4**	**1,621.5**	**358.7**	**768.7**	**127.5**	**332.8**
% of total imports								
Low- and middle-income economies	22.4	24.4	18.5	18.4	28.8	36.1	43.5	39.8
East Asia & Pacific	5.8	10.1	1.9	4.3	9.3	16.2	21.3	27.7
Europe & Central Asia	1.7	4.1	2.6	6.6	0.9	1.4	0.3	1.7
Latin America & Carib.	6.2	5.4	3.6	2.3	13.2	13.9	4.8	3.4
Middle East & N. Africa	5.0	2.5	6.1	2.9	1.7	1.6	13.8	4.7
South Asia	0.7	0.9	0.5	0.8	0.9	1.3	1.4	1.2
Sub-Saharan Africa	3.0	1.5	3.7	1.6	2.8	1.7	2.0	1.1
High-income economies	77.6	75.6	81.5	81.6	71.2	63.9	56.4	60.2
Non-OECD	7.4	7.5	3.1	3.4	13.1	12.3	19.1	17.8
OECD	70.1	68.1	78.4	78.1	58.1	51.6	37.3	42.4
World	**100.0**	**100.0**	**100.0**	**100.0**	**100.0**	**100.0**	**100.0**	**100.0**

About the data

Data on merchandise trade are compiled from customs reports by the United Nations Statistical Office in the Commodity Trade (COMTRADE) database. COMTRADE contains data on the imports and exports of more than 150 countries or economic areas classified by product and by country of origin and destination. For many countries records tabulated according to revision 1 of the Standard International Trade Classification (SITC) system extend back to 1962. In the mid-1970s COMTRADE also began reporting more detailed SITC revision 2 data, and in the late 1980s it began compiling records in the still more detailed revision 3 system. At its lowest level the revision 3 system differentiates among more than 2,000 items.

Various statistical problems may affect the quality of COMTRADE statistics. Because COMTRADE expresses all trade values in U.S. dollars, exchange rates are used to convert data originally expressed in local currencies. In some countries, particularly those in which there are black market rates that differ from official rates, the selection of an inappropriate conversion factor may produce important statistical biases. At more detailed levels of product classification countries may inadvertently classify goods in different SITC groups, resulting in discrepancies in matched partner country statistics. An even more serious problem may be traders' incentives to falsify customs invoices (to reduce tariff charges or to effect capital flight). Smuggling, which is not reflected in COMTRADE, also may affect data quality, particularly for trade between countries with shared borders. And information on trade is missing or unreliable for many African countries that have not yet developed the capacity to compile accurate statistics.

Definitions

● **Exports** are all merchandise exports by high-income OECD countries to low- and middle-income economies as recorded in the United Nations COMTRADE database. ● **Imports** are all merchandise imports by high-income OECD countries from low- and middle-income economies as recorded in the United Nations COMTRADE database. ● **High-income OECD countries** in 1995 were Australia, Austria, Belgium, Canada, Denmark, Finland, France, Germany, Iceland, Ireland, Italy, Japan, Luxembourg, the Netherlands, New Zealand, Norway, Portugal, Spain, Sweden, Switzerland, the United Kingdom, and the United States. ● **High-income, non-OECD economies** in 1995 included Hong Kong, Israel, the Republic of Korea, Kuwait, Singapore, United Arab Emirates, and Taiwan, China. ● **European Union** comprises Austria, Belgium, Denmark, Finland, France, Germany, Greece, Italy, Ireland, Luxembourg, the Netherlands, Portugal, Spain, Sweden, and the United Kingdom.

Data sources

COMTRADE statistics are available in machine-readable form from the United Nations Statistical Office. Although not as comprehensive as the underlying COMTRADE records, detailed statistics on international trade are published annually in the United Nations Conference on Trade and Development's *Handbook of International Trade and Development Statistics* and the United Nations *International Trade Statistics Yearbook*.

6.3 OECD trade with low- and middle-income economies

Exports to low- and middle-income economies	High-income OECD countries		European Union		United States		Japan	
	1985	1995	1985	1995	1985	1995	1985	1995
$ billions								
Food	27.5	60.0	12.1	31.1	9.9	20.7	0.5	0.7
Cereals	11.1	17.6	3.0	5.6	5.1	9.6	0.0	0.1
Agricultural raw materials	6.9	16.6	2.4	4.6	2.5	7.2	0.6	1.5
Ores and nonferrous metals	5.6	14.1	2.0	4.8	1.3	3.7	0.6	2.3
Fuels	6.6	11.8	2.8	4.9	2.5	3.9	0.3	1.0
Crude petroleum	0.2	0.7	0.1	0.0	..	0.0	0.0	..
Petroleum products	4.0	8.1	2.4	4.7	1.3	2.6	0.1	0.9
Manufactured goods	194.7	559.7	97.1	265.8	41.1	133.0	47.8	138.0
Chemical products	29.3	74.5	17.1	36.8	7.2	20.9	2.9	11.3
Machinery and transport equipment	109.3	332.1	48.9	145.8	26.5	79.9	29.6	95.2
Other	56.1	153.1	31.1	83.1	7.3	32.1	15.2	31.5
Miscellaneous goods	4.6	18.2	2.5	4.8	1.5	8.1	0.4	1.8
Total	**245.8**	**680.5**	**119.0**	**316.0**	**58.8**	**176.6**	**50.2**	**145.3**
% of total exports								
Food	11.2	8.8	10.2	9.8	16.8	11.7	1.0	0.5
Cereals	4.5	2.6	2.5	1.8	8.7	5.4	0.1	0.1
Agricultural raw materials	2.8	2.4	2.0	1.4	4.3	4.1	1.3	1.0
Ores and nonferrous metals	2.3	2.1	1.7	1.5	2.2	2.1	1.1	1.6
Fuels	2.7	1.7	2.3	1.6	4.3	2.2	0.6	0.7
Crude petroleum	0.1	0.1	0.1	0.0	..	0.0	0.0	..
Petroleum products	1.6	1.2	2.0	1.5	2.2	1.5	0.3	0.6
Manufactured goods	79.2	82.3	81.6	84.1	69.9	75.3	95.3	94.9
Chemical products	11.9	11.0	14.4	11.7	12.3	11.9	5.8	7.8
Machinery and transport equipment	44.5	48.8	41.1	46.2	45.2	45.3	59.1	65.5
Other	22.8	22.5	26.1	26.3	12.4	18.2	30.4	21.7
Miscellaneous goods	1.9	2.7	2.1	1.5	2.5	4.6	0.8	1.3
Total	**100.0**	**100.0**	**100.0**	**100.0**	**100.0**	**100.0**	**100.0**	**100.0**

Developing countries diversify exports

In recent years many developing countries have attempted to increase the share of processed and manufactured goods in their exports and decrease the share of primary products. They have pursued this strategy for several reasons:

• The deterioration in the terms of trade for many primary commodities.

• The substitution of synthetics for some primary products (for example, plastics for metals, artificial fibers for natural, and chemical sweeteners for sugar), which has dampened prospects for commodity exports.

• The instability of primary product prices in international markets and thus of export revenues, which makes development planning difficult.

• The observed long-term tendency for the share of primary commodities in world trade to diminish.

• The increased employment opportunities associated with producing and exporting processed goods and manufactures.

• The potential for realizing economy wide linkages and learning effects through more local processing.

Are developing countries achieving their goal of export diversification? A look at the import patterns of high-income OECD countries, which have been both the best markets for the exports of developing countries and the main

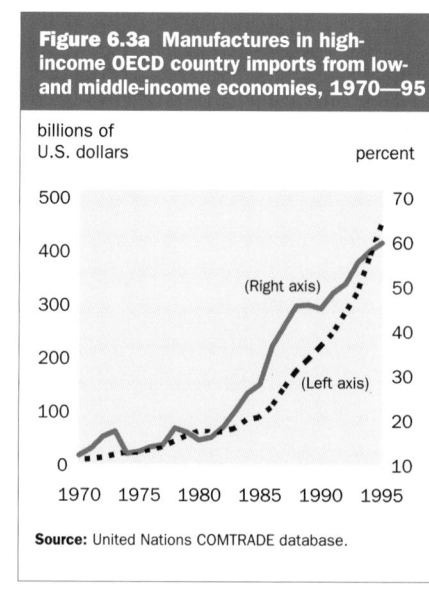

Figure 6.3a Manufactures in high-income OECD country imports from low- and middle-income economies, 1970—95

Source: United Nations COMTRADE database.

Imports from low- and middle-income economies	High-income OECD countries		European Union		United States		Japan	
	1985	1995	1985	1995	1985	1995	1985	1995
$ billions								
Food	47.8	89.6	25.4	43.1	13.9	20.0	6.2	21.9
Cereals	1.6	1.6	0.8	0.8	0.1	0.4	0.6	0.3
Agricultural raw materials	12.2	26.1	6.6	13.8	1.7	4.7	3.6	6.8
Ores and nonferrous metals	19.2	43.8	9.3	20.5	3.8	8.4	5.6	13.1
Fuels	136.0	128.6	64.3	58.1	36.6	40.0	33.6	28.0
Crude petroleum	98.9	91.7	49.7	39.1	25.1	33.2	23.2	17.2
Petroleum products	23.9	16.7	9.1	8.0	11.1	6.0	3.1	2.6
Manufactured goods	84.9	445.4	27.7	159.4	45.8	199.1	6.0	61.2
Chemical products	7.9	27.0	3.7	14.1	2.6	7.2	1.1	3.9
Machinery and transport equipment	23.8	157.1	6.0	43.4	15.7	87.2	0.8	17.1
Other	53.1	261.3	18.0	101.9	27.5	104.7	4.1	40.2
Miscellaneous goods	2.8	11.3	0.6	4.2	1.5	5.2	0.6	1.5
Total	**302.9**	**744.7**	**133.9**	**299.1**	**103.3**	**277.4**	**55.6**	**132.6**
% of total imports								
Food	15.8	12.0	19.0	14.4	13.4	7.2	11.2	16.5
Cereals	0.5	0.2	0.6	0.3	0.1	0.1	1.2	0.2
Agricultural raw materials	4.0	3.5	4.9	4.6	1.7	1.7	6.5	5.1
Ores and nonferrous metals	6.3	5.9	7.0	6.8	3.7	3.0	10.1	9.9
Fuels	44.9	17.3	48.0	19.4	35.4	14.4	60.4	21.2
Crude petroleum	32.6	12.3	37.1	13.1	24.3	12.0	41.7	13.0
Petroleum products	7.9	2.2	6.8	2.7	10.7	2.2	5.5	1.9
Manufactured goods	28.0	59.8	20.7	53.3	44.3	71.8	10.8	46.1
Chemical products	2.6	3.6	2.7	4.7	2.5	2.6	2.0	2.9
Machinery and transport equipment	7.9	21.1	4.4	14.5	15.2	31.5	1.4	12.9
Other	17.5	35.1	13.5	34.1	26.6	37.7	7.4	30.3
Miscellaneous goods	0.9	1.5	0.5	1.4	1.4	1.9	1.1	1.1
Total	**100.0**	**100.0**	**100.0**	**100.0**	**100.0**	**100.0**	**100.0**	**100.0**

source of their imports, suggests that the answer is yes. Food and primary commodities have fallen as a share of OECD imports, while the share of manufactures has grown substantially (figure 6.3a). Developing countries have become competitive suppliers for a wide range of manufactured goods, though they continue to lag in some highly capital-intensive products (such as chemicals).

Developing countries also have concerns relating to the level and structure of their imports. A key part of industrialization is expanding the available stock of capital goods—goods in which OECD countries have a comparative advantage. Thus the level and share of manufactures (particularly such capital goods as machinery and transport equipment) in OECD exports to developing countries indicate these countries' progress in expanding their industrial base. The level and structure of imports may also bear on other policy concerns. For example, many developing countries place a high priority on improving food self-sufficiency or food security. Trends in the level and share of food imports may show whether these objectives are being achieved.

About the data

The table was compiled from detailed trade flows data in the United Nations Statistical Office's Commodity Trade (COMTRADE) database. For more information on commodity trade data, see the notes to tables 4.7–4.9 and table 6.2.

Definitions

The product groups in the table are defined in accordance with the Standard International Trade Classification (SITC revision 1): **food** (0, 1,22,4), **cereals** (04), **agricultural raw materials** (2 excluding 22, 27, and 28), **ores and nonferrous metals** (27, 28, and 68), **fuels** (3), **crude petroleum** (331), **petroleum products** (332), **manufactured goods** (5–8 excluding 68), **chemical products** (5), **machinery and transport equipment** (7), **other manufactured goods** (6 and 8 excluding 68), and **miscellaneous goods** (9). • **Exports** are all merchandise exports by high-income OECD countries to low- and middle-income economies as recorded in the United Nations COMTRADE database. • **Imports** are all merchandise imports by high-

income OECD countries from low- and middle-income economies as recorded in the United Nations COMTRADE database. • **High-income OECD countries** in 1995 were Australia, Austria, Belgium, Canada, Denmark, Finland, France, Germany, Iceland, Ireland, Italy, Japan, Luxembourg, the Netherlands, New Zealand, Norway, Portugal, Spain, Sweden, Switzerland, the United Kingdom, and the United States. • **European Union** comprises Austria, Belgium, Denmark, Finland, France, Germany, Greece, Italy, Ireland, Luxembourg, the Netherlands, Portugal, Spain, Sweden, and the United Kingdom.

Data sources

COMTRADE statistics are available in machine-readable form from the United Nations Statistical Office. Although not as comprehensive as the underlying COMTRADE records, detailed statistics on international trade are published annually in the United Nations Conference on Trade and Development's *Handbook of International Trade and Development Statistics* and the United Nations *International Trade Statistics Yearbook*.

	Imports bound under the GATT					Imports from low- and middle-income economies			Imports from world		
	Before the Round %	After the Round %	Above applied rates %	At applied rates %	Below applied rates %	Applied rate before the Round %	Applied rate after the Round %	Tariff reduction %	Applied rate before the Round %	Applied rate after the Round %	Tariff reduction %
Selected high-income economies											
Agriculture	71.0	99.9	7.8	39.6	34.9	9.6	8.7	9.4	7.7	5.2	32.5
Fish and fish products	79.5	98.4	10.5	44.7	43.0	8.0	6.4	20.0	5.5	4.2	23.6
Petroleum oils	45.8	47.0	8.4	36.7	0.9	0.9	0.8	11.1	0.8	0.7	12.5
Industrial goods	84.7	91.7	21.7	37.7	32.3	5.9	4.4	25.4	4.1	2.5	39.0
Wood, pulp, paper, and furniture	84.9	94.5	7.6	69.3	17.5	4.1	2.9	29.3	1.8	0.5	72.2
Textiles and clothing	73.7	79.9	17.0	9.8	53.0	11.7	10.0	14.5	10.3	8.4	18.4
Leather, rubber, and footwear	79.1	89.7	16.5	41.8	31.4	7.0	6.1	12.9	6.5	5.5	15.4
Metals	90.8	97.5	19.2	47.4	30.8	3.7	2.2	40.5	2.5	0.9	64.0
Chemical and photographic supplies	82.7	91.4	27.5	30.8	33.0	6.7	4.6	31.3	4.2	2.2	47.6
Transport equipment	93.8	95.5	39.9	42.0	13.7	4.3	3.7	14.0	4.9	4.2	14.3
Nonelectrical machinery	88.7	94.9	24.4	26.5	44.1	3.9	3.0	23.1	3.2	1.1	65.6
Electrical machinery	77.5	88.5	25.3	26.8	36.4	5.2	3.5	32.7	3.9	2.3	41.0
Mineral products, precious stones, and metals	86.6	92.1	12.6	61.9	17.6	1.3	0.9	30.8	1.1	0.7	36.4
Other manufactured goods	81.3	89.7	12.1	36.5	40.8	5.2	3.1	40.4	3.3	1.4	57.6
All merchandise imports	**80.2**	**88.5**	**19.3**	**37.9**	**29.9**	**5.9**	**4.3**	**27.1**	**4.1**	**2.6**	**36.6**

	Imports bound under the GATT					Imports from low- and middle-income economies			Imports from world		
	Before the Round %	After the Round %	Above applied rates %	At applied rates %	Below applied rates %	Applied rate before the Round %	Applied rate after the Round %	Tariff reduction %	Applied rate before the Round %	Applied rate after the Round %	Tariff reduction %
Selected low- and middle-income economies											
Agriculture	36.6	99.9	66.8	12.8	17.4	20.6	19.9	3.4	20.3	18.6	8.4
Fish and fish products	9.7	77.3	14.8	9.2	53.3	38.5	25.9	32.7	32.0	8.6	73.1
Petroleum oils	11.4	42.8	15.7	10.6	0.6	9.0	8.4	6.7	7.9	7.9	0
Industrial goods	31.8	83.6	36.4	13.0	33.4	16.2	13.3	17.9	16.9	13.3	21.3
Wood, pulp, paper, and furniture	42.6	83.2	41.7	13.4	26.7	12.6	10.3	18.3	11.7	8.9	23.9
Textiles and clothing	24.0	84.7	29.6	6.2	48.6	30.7	25.5	16.9	27.0	21.2	21.5
Leather, rubber, and footwear	30.8	89.9	38.4	8.2	43.1	19.9	15.4	22.6	19.0	14.9	21.6
Metals	25.7	76.8	34.5	13.5	25.5	12.7	10.4	18.1	14.1	10.8	23.4
Chemical and photographic supplies	27.2	87.5	43.6	9.5	33.8	21.1	16.8	20.4	16.8	12.4	26.2
Transport equipment	41.5	72.6	33.4	22.6	16.3	14.0	13.2	5.7	23.3	19.9	14.6
Nonelectrical machinery	39.3	91.0	40.7	9.8	40.3	16.6	14.5	12.7	16.9	13.5	20.1
Electrical machinery	31.4	81.5	26.5	12.5	42.5	19.6	17.2	12.2	18.7	14.6	21.9
Mineral products, precious stones, and metals	29.6	73.7	36.4	23.2	12.6	9.2	8.1	12.0	9.1	7.8	14.3
Other manufactured goods	28.1	89.1	34.3	15.1	39.4	11.1	9.2	17.1	15.8	12.1	23.4
All merchandise imports	**30.1**	**80.8**	**36.8**	**12.7**	**28.7**	**15.8**	**13.0**	**17.7**	**16.7**	**13.3**	**20.4**

About the data

Countries participating in the Uruguay Round negotiations of the General Agreement on Tariffs and Trade (GATT) negotiated a new set of tariff rates covering most trade not governed by preferential trade agreements. In most cases the new tariff rates are lower than the old ones, creating new incentives for global trade. The table provides a profile of the effect of the Uruguay Round agreements on trade between high-income and developing economies.

Each country participating in the Uruguay Round agreed to bind its tariff rates at its final offer rates and to maintain its rates at or below these bound levels. The rates actually applied by countries may differ from their bound rates. Some countries bound rates at higher levels than the rates they actually applied before or after the Round. Some countries introduced unilateral tariff reductions during the Uruguay Round. And other countries entered into free trade agreements during the Round. To give a better picture of the results from the Round, the data in the table are based on applied rates and exclude reductions not conditioned on reciprocal reductions by trade partners. Trade covered by free trade agreements is also excluded.

Data on tariffs are available from the Integrated Database maintained by the GATT's successor, the World Trade Organization (WTO), for all industrial and transition economies that participated in the Uruguay Round and 26 of the 94 developing economies that participated. The database covers 100 percent of the nonpetroleum imports of North America, Western Europe, and Central and Eastern European GATT members; 90 percent of Asia's nonpetroleum imports; 80 percent of Latin America's nonpetroleum imports; and 30 percent of Africa's nonpetroleum imports.

Countries participating in the Integrated Database submitted ad valorem equivalents for most specific, compound, and mixed duties on manufactures. For agriculture and petroleum oils there are relatively few ad valorem equivalents, so caution should be used in interpreting the statistics. In addition, for some countries average tariffs and reductions may be based on a few product categories with a relatively small weight in trade.

The first two columns of the table show the percentage of imports for which tariffs were bound under the GATT before and after the Uruguay Round. The next three columns separate imports into three categories according to whether the post–Uruguay Round bindings were above, at, or below the rates applied before the Round. The share of imports for which the bound rate is below the pre–Uruguay Round applied rate is the percentage of imports for which there were tariff cuts.

Tariff bindings above applied rates cover imports under the GATT as well as under free trade agreements. For imports covered by free trade agreements the applied rate, before and after the Round, is zero, so a binding is above the applied rate for all product categories for which the bound rate is greater than zero. Similarly, a binding is at the applied rate when the bound rate is zero. The trade arrangements covered by the data are Australia–New Zealand, the North American Free Trade Agreement (NAFTA), the European Free Trade Area (EFTA), and the European Union (EU). The EU-EFTA trade arrangement does not cover agricultural goods, so agricultural imports by one EU-EFTA partner from another are treated as imports not covered by a free trade agreement.

The last six columns give weighted average tariffs and tariff reductions on imports from trade partners with which the importing country has not entered into a free trade agreement. Averages are weighted by the value of imports assessed at these rates from low- and middle-income economies and from the world.

Definitions

• **High-income economies** included in the data set are Australia, Canada, Hong Kong, Iceland, Japan, New Zealand, Norway, Singapore, Switzerland, the United States, and the countries of the European Union. • **Low- and middle-income economies** included in the data set are Argentina, Brazil, Chile, Colombia, the Czech Republic, El Salvador, Hungary, India, Indonesia, Jamaica, the Republic of Korea, Macao, Malaysia, Mexico, Peru, the Philippines, Poland, Romania, Senegal, the Slovak Republic, Sri Lanka, Thailand, Tunisia, Turkey, Uruguay, Venezuela, and Zimbabwe. • **Imports bound under the GATT** are the proportion of product categories for which tariff rates were agreed and bound, before and after the conclusion of the Uruguay Round negotiations. • **Applied rates** are stated as ad valorem equivalents of the most-favored-nation duty that countries charge on imports that do not receive any form of preference. Product category averages are weighted by the value of imports. • **Tariff reductions** are the change in the trade-weighted applied tariff rate for the product category shown.

Data sources

Data are drawn from the WTO Integrated Database, the most comprehensive source of trade and tariff statistics on the Uruguay Round. Pre– and post–Uruguay Round applied rates were calculated by J. Michael Finger, Merlinda Ingco, and Ulrich Reincke of the World Bank. See *The Uruguay Round: Statistics on Tariff Concessions Given and Received* (Finger, Ingco, and Reincke 1996) for detailed results for all reporting countries.

6.5 | Commodity prices

	1980	1985	1991	1992	1993	1994	1995
Commodity price index							
(1990 = 100)							
Nonfuel commodities	174	133	93	86	86	101	102
Agriculture	191	145	96	88	93	112	110
Beverages	253	239	91	73	79	135	127
Fertilizers	179	130	100	90	79	85	87
Food	191	124	97	94	93	97	98
Metals and minerals	132	102	87	81	70	77	85
Raw materials	145	103	97	92	104	114	113
Petroleum	224	173	83	78	69	63	63
Steel products[a]	110	88	96	83	86	84	89
MUV G-5 index	72	69	102	107	106	110	119
Commodity prices							
(1990 $)							
Agricultural raw materials							
Cotton (cents/kg)	284.3	192.1	164.1	119.9	120.4	160.0	178.2
Logs, Cameroon ($/cu. m)[a]	349.4	253.5	309.2	310.8	291.9	299.7	284.3
Logs, Malaysian ($/cu. m)	271.5	177.5	187.4	196.5	366.7	279.1	214.1
Rubber (cents/kg)	197.9	110.6	80.8	80.8	78.2	102.2	132.3
Sawnwood, Malaysian ($/cu. m)	550.3	447.7	540.6	569.6	713.3	745.0	619.7
Tobacco ($/mt)	3,160.9	3,807.3	3,424.7	3,226.6	2,535.6	2,399.0	2,210.6
Beverages (cents/kg)							
Cocoa	361.6	328.6	116.9	103.2	105.1	126.7	120.0
Coffee, robustas	450.4	386.1	104.9	88.2	108.9	237.8	232.1
Coffee, other milds	481.4	471.0	183.3	132.4	146.8	300.2	279.1
Tea, auctions, avg.	250.3	263.6	167.9	159.8	157.8	143.1	128.1
Tea, London, all	309.9	289.1	180.3	187.6	175.3	166.2	137.6
Energy							
Coal, Australian ($/mt)	55.9	49.2	38.8	36.2	29.5	29.3	33.0
Coal, U.S. ($/mt)	..	68.0	40.6	38.1	35.7	33.1	32.8
Natural gas, Europe ($/mmbtu)	..	..	3.0	2.4	2.5	2.2	2.3
Natural gas, U.S. ($/mmbtu)	..	..	1.5	1.7	2.0	1.7	1.4
Petroleum ($/bbl)	51.2	39.6	19.0	17.8	15.8	14.4	14.4
Fertilizers ($/mt)							
Phosphate rock	64.9	49.4	41.6	39.2	31.0	29.9	29.3
TSP	250.3	176.9	130.3	113.3	105.3	119.9	125.3
Food							
Fats and oils ($/mt)							
Coconut oil	935.8	860.1	423.7	541.8	423.6	551.3	561.1
Groundnut oil	1,193.1	1,319.2	875.5	572.1	695.3	928.1	830.0
Palm oil	810.4	730.3	331.7	369.1	355.4	479.5	526.0
Soybeans	411.4	326.5	234.4	220.9	240.0	228.5	216.9
Soybean meal	363.9	228.9	192.9	191.7	195.8	174.6	165.0
Soybean oil	830.0	833.8	444.4	402.4	451.9	558.6	523.5
Grains ($/mt)							
Grain sorghum	179.0	150.1	102.8	96.4	93.2	94.3	99.7
Maize	174.0	163.6	105.1	97.8	96.0	97.6	103.4
Rice	570.5	287.1	287.0	251.6	221.5	242.8	268.7
Wheat	239.9	198.0	125.9	141.8	131.9	135.9	148.2

Falling commodity prices

Commodity prices were subject to severe downward pressure during 1980–93 (figure 6.5a). The terms of trade for many developing countries declined as primary commodity prices fell relative to the prices of manufactures (see the notes to table 4.7). More than three-quarters of the decline in nonfuel commodity prices was due to the fall in the prices of agricultural commodities. Part of the explanation for falling commodity prices lies with sluggish demand in industrial countries, especially during the 1980s. But even more important was the sharp increase in the supply of commodities on world markets, which grew four times faster than in the 1970s. Most of this supply increase came from upper-middle-income and high-income countries. Metals prices, for example, were depressed by large exports from countries of the former Soviet Union and Eastern Europe following the collapse of the Soviet bloc.

There is still debate about whether the relative decline in commodity prices is permanent or transitory—or merely the result of mismeasuring quality shifts in manufactured goods. Still, countries that depend on primary commodity exports suffered badly during the 1980s. The declining terms of trade reduced the resources available for investment, slowing

Figure 6.5a Weighted index of primary commodity prices for low- and middle-income economies, 1970—95

index (1990 = 100)

Source: World Bank, *Commodity Markets and the Developing Countries*, various issues.

	1980	1985	1991	1992	1993	1994	1995
Other food							
Bananas ($/mt)	526.4	554.4	547.5	443.8	416.8	398.8	372.8
Beef (cents/kg)	383.3	314.0	260.6	230.3	246.3	211.5	159.7
Oranges ($/mt)	542.5	580.8	509.8	458.9	406.9	373.1	445.1
Sugar, EU domestic (cents/kg)	48.7	35.0	61.2	62.8	61.9	62.2	68.8
Sugar, U.S. domestic (cents/kg)	66.2	44.9	47.5	47.0	47.6	48.6	50.8
Sugar, world (cents/kg)	87.7	13.1	19.3	18.7	20.7	24.2	24.5
Metals and minerals							
Aluminum ($/mt)	2,022.2	1,517.5	1,274.2	1,176.6	1,071.5	1,340.1	1,512.3
Copper ($/mt)	3,030.6	2,066.2	2,288.5	2,139.9	1,799.7	2,093.8	2,458.6
Iron ore (cents/DMTU)	39.0	38.7	32.5	29.6	26.5	23.1	22.6
Lead (cents/kg)	125.8	57.0	54.6	50.8	38.2	49.7	52.8
Nickel ($/mt)	9,053.8	7,141.5	7,980.0	6,567.8	4,979.7	5,753.0	6,891.2
Tin (cents/kg)	2,329.8	1,682.1	547.5	572.3	485.5	495.8	520.4
Zinc (cents/kg)	105.7	114.1	109.3	116.3	90.5	90.5	86.4

a. Series not included in the nonfuel index.

growth in real output and per capita income and in many cases complicating already severe adjustment problems. But some developing countries have substantially increased their production and exports of manufactures in the past 30 years, and for these countries the terms of trade have deteriorated less rapidly. Other countries have increased their exports of high-value commodities—cut flowers, shrimp, fruits and vegetables—commodities that have not experienced price declines relative to manufactures over the past 15 years.

About the data

Data on primary commodity prices are collected from a variety of sources, including international study groups, trade journals, newspaper and wire service reports, government market surveys, and commodity exchange spot and near-term forward prices. The most reliable and frequently updated price reports are used. When export prices are unavailable, import prices are used. Annual price series are generally simple averages based on higher-frequency data. The constant price series in the table are deflated using the MUV G-5 index (see below).

The commodity price indexes are calculated as Laspeyres index numbers in which the fixed weights are the 1987–89 export values for low- and middle-income economies, rebased to 1990. Each index represents a fixed basket of commodity exports. The nonfuel commodity price index contains 37 price series for 31 nonfuel commodities. Indexes are compiled separately for petroleum and steel products, which are not included in the nonfuel commodity price index.

The manufactures unit value (MUV) index is a composite index of prices for manufactured exports from the five major (G-5) industrial countries (France, Germany, Japan, the United Kingdom, and the United States) to low- and middle-income economies, valued in U.S. dollars. The index covers products in Standard International Trade Classification (SITC) groups 5–8. To construct the MUV G-5 index, unit value indexes for each country are combined using weights determined by the export share of each country.

Definitions

● **Nonfuel commodities** price index covers the 31 nonfuel commodities that make up the agriculture, fertilizer, and metals and minerals indexes; **agriculture,** in addition to food, beverages, and agricultural raw materials, includes sugar, bananas, beef, and oranges; **beverages** include cocoa, coffee, and tea; **fertilizers** include phosphate rock and triple superphosphate (TSP); **food** includes rice, wheat, maize, sorghum, soybeans, soybean oil, soybean meal, palm oil, coconut oil, and groundnut oil; **metals and minerals** include aluminum, copper, iron ore, lead, nickel, tin, and zinc; **agricultural raw materials** include timber (logs and sawnwood), cotton, natural rubber, and tobacco. ● **Petroleum** price index refers to the average spot price of Brent, Dubai, and West Texas Intermediate crude oil, equally weighted. **Steel products** price index is the composite price index for eight selected steel products based on quotations f.o.b. (free on board) Japan excluding shipments to China and the United States, weighted by product shares of apparent combined consumption (volume of deliveries) at Germany, Japan, and the United States. **MUV G-5** index is the manufactures unit value index for the G-5 country exports to developing countries. ● **Commodity prices—** for definitions and sources see the World Bank's *Commodity Markets and the Developing Countries* or its World Wide Web site on commodities at http://www.worldbank.org/html/ieccp/ieccp.html.

Data sources

Commodity price data are compiled by the Commodity Policy and Analysis Unit of the World Bank's International Economics Department. More information can be obtained from the unit's quarterly publication *Commodity Markets and the Developing Countries*. The MUV index is constructed by the International Economic Analysis and Prospects Division of the International Economics Department. Monthly updates of commodity prices are available on the Internet at http://www. worldbank.org /html/ieccp/ieccp.html.

Net flows to part I countries	Official development assistance				Other official flows	Private flows						Total net flows
	Total	Bilateral grants	Bilateral loans	Contributions to multilateral institutions		Total	Foreign direct investment	Bilateral portfolio investment	Multilateral portfolio investment	Private export credits	Net grants by NGOs	
$ millions, 1994												
Australia	1,091	824	0	267	170	800	1,283	−484	0	0	75	2,136
Austria	655	354	182	120	65	273	66	0	0	206	36	1,029
Belgium	726	431	4	291	334	1,117	−204	1,329	0	−76	52	2,230
Canada	2,250	1,431	−9	827	740	2,373	2,720	−137	0	−209	273	5,637
Denmark	1,446	881	−78	643	−74	−92	−4	0	0	−46	39	1,319
Finland	290	213	0	77	67	192	49	24	0	119	3	552
France	8,466	5,991	620	1,855	134	3,837	1,677	1,231	−63	712	280	12,717
Germany	6,818	3,549	595	2,674	3,540	12,602	2,944	6,500	182	2,977	981	23,941
Ireland	109	56	0	53	0	37	0	0	0	37	52	198
Italy	2,705	665	1,169	870	690	−31	143	279	0	−905	57	3,421
Japan	13,239	5,299	4,259	3,681	3,229	11,807	7,358	5,644	−2,870	1,675	213	28,487
Luxembourg	60	40	0	19	0	0	0	0	0	0	5	64
Netherlands	2,517	1,932	−232	816	49	1,823	1,872	384	−340	−93	266	4,654
New Zealand	110	85	0	25	0	0	0	0	0	0	16	126
Norway	1,137	822	6	309	−1	217	62	0	0	155	127	1,479
Portugal	308	147	68	93	428	−531	−32	0	0	−499	0	205
Spain	1,305	257	597	450	−214	2,315	2,315	0	0	0	127	3,532
Sweden	1,819	1,372	1	446	0	420	6	0	−1	497	130	2,369
Switzerland	982	729	−4	258	0	−1,006	538	0	0	−1,012	167	143
United Kingdom	3,197	1,809	−46	1,435	34	8,199	6,258	1,900	0	−156	535	11,965
United States	9,927	8,301	−1,017	2,643	867	46,330	21,407	19,838	606	4,479	2,614	59,738
Total	**59,156**	**35,190**	**6,115**	**17,851**	**10,057**	**90,682**	**48,457**	**36,507**	**−2,486**	**7,859**	**6,046**	**165,941**

Net flows to part II countries	Official aid				Other official flows	Private flows						Total net flows
	Total	Bilateral grants	Bilateral loans	Contributions to multilateral institutions		Total	Foreign direct investment	Bilateral portfolio investment	Multilateral portfolio investment	Private export credits	Net grants by NGOs	
$ millions, 1994												
Australia	4	1	0	4	0	0	0	0	0	0	0	4
Austria	261	231	0	30	64	381	381	0	0	0	5	710
Belgium	86	1	9	76	0	236	51	155	0	30	0	322
Canada	73	46	0	27	33	26	0	0	0	26	0	132
Denmark	37	0	0	37	0	0	0	0	0	0	0	37
Finland	51	32	0	19	109	−127	64	−122	0	−69	0	33
France	650	333	11	305	0	−2,964	234	−1,220	−1,233	−745	0	−2,315
Germany	2,527	2,031	−64	560	2,711	4,604	1,667	1,641	0	1,297	72	9,913
Ireland	16	0	0	15	0	0	0	0	0	0	0	16
Italy	196	13	0	183	1,066	−2,200	0	103	0	−2,303	0	−939
Japan	247	129	5	114	417	−1,422	86	−1,370	0	−138	0	−758
Luxembourg	7	2	0	5	0	0	0	0	0	0	0	7
Netherlands	118	0	0	118	0	0	0	0	0	0	0	118
New Zealand	1	0	0	1	0	0	0	0	0	0	0	1
Norway	79	63	0	16	2	0	0	0	0	0	0	81
Portugal	29	0	0	29	0	−5	0	0	0	−5	0	23
Spain	157	0	0	157	0	0	0	0	0	0	0	157
Sweden	91	72	6	13	0	41	44	0	0	−3	0	132
Switzerland	124	98	0	26	11	−204	0	0	0	−204	10	−68
United Kingdom	293	101	0	191	0	353	153	200	0	0	30	676
United States	2,422	2,220	133	69	87	146	443	1,183	0	−1,480	294	2,949
Total	**7,468**	**5,373**	**100**	**1,993**	**4,498**	**−1,135**	**3,122**	**569**	**−1,233**	**−3,592**	**411**	**11,231**

Private flows overtake official

The high-income countries of the Organization for Economic Cooperation and Development (OECD) are the principal source of external finance for developing countries. Until recently a large share of these financial resources came in the form of grants and bilateral loans from one government to another. Now private resources—particularly direct and portfolio investment—have far surpassed those from official sources. This table gives an overview of the flow of financial resources from members of the OECD Development Assistance Committee (DAC) to developing countries.

DAC exists to help its member countries coordinate their development assistance policies and to encourage the expansion and improve the effectiveness of the aggregate resources made available to developing and transition economies. In this capacity it monitors the flow of all financial resources, but its principal concern is official development assistance (ODA). DAC has three criteria for ODA:

• It is undertaken by the official sector.
• It promotes economic development or welfare as a main objective.
• It is provided on concessional terms, with a grant element of at least 25 percent on loans.

This definition excludes nonconcessional flows from official creditors and assistance for military purposes. It includes capital projects food aid, emergency relief, peacekeeping efforts, and technical cooperation. Also included are contributions to multilateral institutions, such as the United Nations and its specialized agencies and concessional funding to the multilateral development banks.

DAC maintains a list of countries and territories that are aid recipients. Part I of the list comprises countries and territories considered collectively by DAC members to be eligible for ODA. Part II of the list, created after the collapse of the Soviet Union, monitors the flow of concessional assistance to transition economies, that were not considered eligible for ODA but that nevertheless receive ODA-like flows. Under a procedure agreed to in 1993, countries with relatively higher incomes are moving from part I to part II status.

About the data

The data here measure the flow of resources from DAC members to countries on the DAC list of aid recipients and to multilateral institutions such as the United Nations, the World Bank, and the regional development banks. The data were compiled from replies by DAC member countries to questionnaires issued by the DAC Secretariat. Net flows of resources are defined as gross disbursements of grants and loans minus repayments on earlier loans.

Because they are based on donor country reports, the data do not provide a complete picture of the resources received by developing countries, for three reasons. First, flows from DAC members are only part of the aggregate resource flows to developing countries. Second, the data that record contributions to multilateral institutions measure the flow of resources made available to them by DAC countries, not the flow of resources from these institutions to developing countries. Third, because some of the countries and territories on the DAC recipient list are normally classified as high income, the reported flows may overstate the resources available to low- and middle-income countries. However, high-income countries receive only a small fraction of all development assistance.

Data sources

Data on financial flows are compiled by DAC and published in its annual statistical report, *Geographical Distribution of Financial Flows to Aid Recipients*, and the DAC chairman's annual report, *Development Cooperation*. The OECD also makes its data available on diskette and magnetic tape and the Internet.

Definitions

• **Official development assistance** (ODA) comprises grants and loans that meet the DAC definition of ODA and are made to countries and territories in part I of the DAC list of aid recipients. • **Official aid** comprises grants and ODA-like loans to countries and territories in part II of the DAC list of aid recipients. • **Bilateral grants** are transfers in money or in kind for which no repayment is required. • **Bilateral loans** are loans extended by governments or official agencies that have a grant element of at least 25 percent and for which repayment is required in convertible currencies or in kind. • **Contributions to multilateral agencies** are concessional funding received by multilateral institutions from DAC countries in the form of grants or capital subscriptions. A contribution by a DAC member country is defined as multilateral if it is pooled with other contributions and disbursed at the discretion of the multilateral agency. • **Other official flows** are transactions by the official sector whose main objective is other than development or whose grant element is less than 25 percent, such as official export credits, official sector equity and portfolio investment, and debt reorganization undertaken by the official sector on nonconcessional terms. • **Private flows** consist of flows at market terms financed from private sector resources. They include changes in holdings of private long-term assets by residents of the reporting country and private grants by nongovernmental organizations, net of subsidies from the official sector. • **Foreign direct investment** is investment by residents of DAC countries to acquire a lasting management interest (at least 10 percent of voting stock) in an enterprise operating in the recipient country. The data in the table reflect the changes in net worth of subsidiaries in recipient countries whose parent company is in the DAC source country. • **Bilateral portfolio investment** covers bank lending and the purchase of bonds, shares, and real estate by residents of DAC countries in recipient countries. • **Multilateral portfolio investment** records the transactions of private banks and the nonbank sector in DAC countries in the securities issued by multilateral institutions. • **Private export credits** are loans that are extended to recipient countries by the private sector in DAC countries for the purpose of promoting trade and are supported by an official guarantee. • **Net grants by NGOs** are grants by nongovernmental organizations, net of subsidies from the official sector. • **Total net flows** comprise ODA or official aid flows, other official flows, private flows, and net grants by NGOs.

Aid flows from Development Assistance
6.7 Committee countries

	Net official development assistance								Aid appropriations	
Net flows to part I countries	$ millions		% of GNP		annual average % change in volume 1989–90 to 1994–95[a,b]	Per capita of donor country[b] $	$		% of central government budget	
	1990[a]	1994	1990[a]	1994		1990[a]	1994		1990[a]	1994
Australia	955	1,091	0.34	0.34	2.5	56	61		1.3	1.2
Austria	394	655	0.25	0.33	9.3	51	82		0.5	..
Belgium	889	726	0.46	0.32	−3.9	89	72		1.2	..
Canada	2,470	2,250	0.44	0.43	−0.6	93	77		2.0	1.4
Denmark	1,171	1,446	0.94	1.03	3.3	228	277		2.9	2.3
Finland	846	290	0.65	0.31	−14.5	170	57		2.6	1.0
France	7,164	8,466	0.60	0.64	0.8	126	146		2.2	
Germany	6,320	6,818	0.42	0.34	−0.9	79	83		2.4	1.9
Ireland	57	109	0.16	0.25	17.4	16	30		..	0.6
Italy	3,395	2,705	0.31	0.27	−9.7	59	47		0.8	0.5
Japan	9,069	13,239	0.31	0.29	0.2	73	106		1.2	1.3
Luxembourg	25	60	0.21	0.40	14.4	67	153		..	1.2
Netherlands	2,538	2,517	0.92	0.76	−0.8	170	165		2.7	3.1
New Zealand	95	110	0.23	0.24	2.7	28	31		..	..
Norway	1,205	1,137	1.17	1.05	1.1	284	261		2.2	1.9
Portugal	148	308	0.25	0.35	8.3	15	31		..	..
Spain	965	1,305	0.20	0.28	10.1	25	32		0.5	0.9
Sweden	2,007	1,819	0.91	0.96	−1.8	235	207		2.8	2.6
Switzerland	750	982	0.32	0.36	3.0	110	140		3.3	3.0
United Kingdom	2,638	3,197	0.27	0.31	1.8	46	55		1.2	1.2
United States	11,394	9,927	0.21	0.14	−4.4	46	38		0.7	1.4
Total or average	**52,961**	**59,156**	**0.33**	**0.30**	**−0.9**	**69**	**73**		**..**	**..**

	Net official aid								Aid appropriations	
Net flows to part II countries	$ millions		% of GNP		annual average % change in volume 1989–90 to 1994–95[b]	Per capita of donor country[b] $	$		% of central government budget	
	1990	1994	1990	1994		1990	1994		1990	1994
Australia	6	4	0.00	0.00	−6.1	0	0		..	..
Austria	84	261	0.05	0.13	22.0	11	33		..	..
Belgium	21	86	0.01	0.04	29.7	2	9		..	..
Canada	11	73	0.00	0.01	47.9	0	3		..	..
Denmark	15	37	0.01	0.03	18.8	3	7		..	..
Finland	17	51	0.01	0.05	30.9	3	10		..	..
France	76	650	0.01	0.05	51.6	1	11		..	..
Germany	1,014	2,527	0.07	0.12	17.0	13	31		..	..
Ireland	5	16	0.01	0.04	27.5	1	4		..	..
Italy	128	196	0.01	0.02	11.1	2	3		..	..
Japan	153	247	0.01	0.01	1.8	1	2		..	..
Luxembourg	1	7	0.01	0.05	51.3	2	18		..	..
Netherlands	62	118	0.02	0.04	11.7	4	8		..	..
New Zealand	0	1	0.00	0.00	..	0	0		..	..
Norway	21	79	0.02	0.07	32.0	5	18		..	..
Portugal	4	29	0.01	0.03	44.5	0	3		..	..
Spain	24	157	0.00	0.03	47.2	1	4		..	..
Sweden	2	91	0.00	0.05	112.3	3	10		..	..
Switzerland	9	124	0.00	0.05	64.4	1	18		..	..
United Kingdom	259	293	0.03	0.03	2.4	5	5		..	..
United States	338	2,422	0.01	0.03	45.4	1	9		..	..
Total or average	**2,248**	**7,468**	**0.01**	**0.04**	**24.4**	**3**	**9**		**..**	**..**

a. Data for 1990 include forgiveness of non-ODA debt by the following countries: France ($294 million), Japan ($15 million), the Netherlands ($12 million), Sweden ($5 million), the United Kingdom ($8 million), and the United States ($1.2 billion). Debt forgiveness is not reflected in the total. b. At 1994 exchange rates and prices.

Budgetary problems depress aid

Net aid to developing countries has stagnated or declined over the past decade. Measured in constant 1994 dollars, net official development assistance (ODA) received by developing countries remained in the range of $54–$61 billion during 1986–94. During the same period the share of net ODA in Development Assistance Committee (DAC) members' combined GNP dropped from 0.33 percent to 0.29 percent, the lowest level since 1973 (figure 6.7a). This is expected to decline further in 1995 to about 0.27 percent on average. This overall decline conceals a change in burden sharing among DAC members, with some, including the United States and Italy, reducing their contributions, while Japan has become the largest donor (figure 6.7b).

Among the factors contributing to the decline in aid, the most significant is the budgetary problems facing DAC countries. This factor can be best seen in aid appropriations, for which most DAC countries reported a decline in 1994. But some countries have increased their contributions of official aid to part II countries at the same time that their ODA contributions for part I countries have declined. By 1994 net official aid accounted for 11.7 percent of DAC members' concessional assistance, with the largest increases going to Central and Eastern European countries. The increase in official aid still does not offset the decline in ODA, however.

About the data

As part of its work, DAC assesses the aid performance of member countries relative to the size of their economies. As measured here, aid comprises bilateral disbursements of concessional financing to recipient countries plus the provision by donor governments of concessional financing to multilateral institutions. Volume measures, in constant prices and exchange rates, are used to measure the change in real resources provided over time. Aid flows to part I recipients—ODA—are tabulated separately from official aid to part II recipients.

Measures of aid flows from the perspective of donors will differ from aid receipts by the recipient countries. This is because the concessional funding received by multilateral institutions from donor countries is recorded as an aid disbursement by the donor when the funds are deposited with the multilateral institution and recorded as a resource receipt by the recipient country when the multilateral institution makes a disbursement.

Aid to GNP ratios, aid per capita, and aid appropriations as a percentage of donor government budgets are calculated by the OECD. The denominators used in calculating these ratios may differ from corresponding values elsewhere in this book because of differences in timing or definition.

Definitions

● **Net official development assistance** and **net official aid** record the actual international transfer by the donor of financial resources or of goods or services valued at the cost to the donor, less any repayments of loan principal during the same period. Data are shown at current prices and dollar exchange rates. ● **Aid as percentage of GNP** shows the donor's contributions of ODA or official aid as a percentage of its GNP. ● **Annual average percentage change in volume** and **aid per capita of donor country** are calculated using 1994 exchange rates and prices. ● **Aid appropriations** are the percentage share of ODA or official aid appropriations in national budgets.

Data sources

Data in this table appear in the DAC chairman's report, *Development Co-operation*. The OECD also makes its data available on diskette and magnetic tape and the Internet.

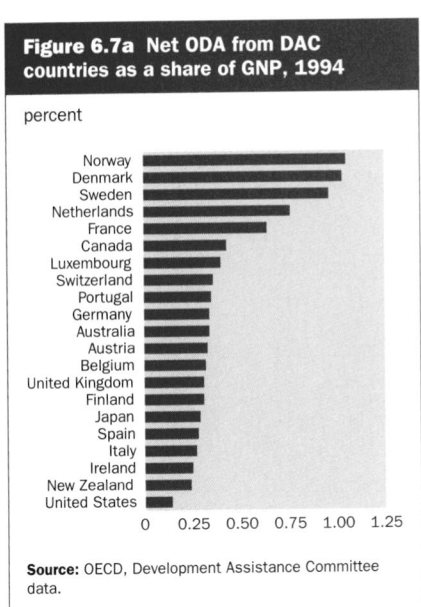

Figure 6.7a Net ODA from DAC countries as a share of GNP, 1994

Source: OECD, Development Assistance Committee data.

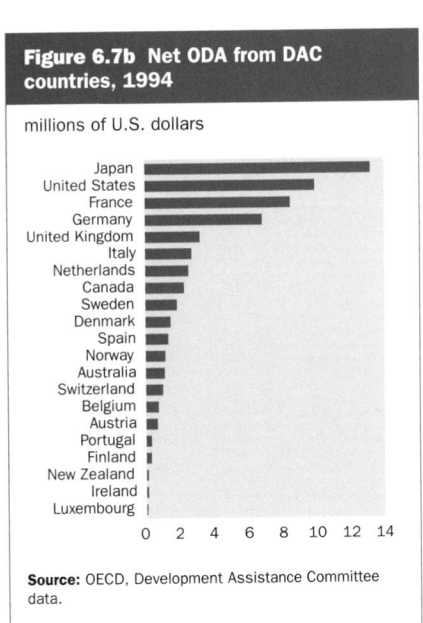

Figure 6.7b Net ODA from DAC countries, 1994

Source: OECD, Development Assistance Committee data.

Financial terms of official development
6.8 | assistance commitments

	Grants		Loans										Untied aid	
	% of total ODA		Grant element		Maturity		Grace period		Interest rate				% of total ODA	
			%	%	years	years	years	years	%	%				
	1980	1994	1980	1994	1980	1994	1980	1994	1980	1994			1980	1994
Australia	100	100	..	..	..	..	..	..	..	..			45.5	35.8
Austria	57	73	33.1	52.7	15	24	5	8	5.1	2.9			0.4	..
Belgium	89	95	83.1	84.0	30	30	11	11	..	..			14.7	..
Canada	87	95	80.8	90.3	44	40	9	16	0.7	..			6.0	27.3
Denmark	81	100	83.7	..	38	..	9	..	..	..			29.5	..
Finland	95	99	52.2	28.7	18	37	7	1	2.1	6.4			13.2	24.6
France	70	82	47.3	54.3	24	24	8	9	3.6	2.9			50.8	40.7
Germany	67	80	61.7	57.9	33	29	9	9	2.4	2.6			45.9	29.7
Ireland	100	100	..	..	..	..	..	..	..	..			..	..
Italy	98	91	30.6	72.2	13	27	4	11	3.8	1.1			2.3	35.9
Japan	40	51	56.2	64.0	28	29	9	9	2.9	2.0			13.2	65.3
Luxembourg	..	100	..	..	..	..	..	..	..	..			..	..
Netherlands	79	100	59.6	48.9	30	25	8	7	2.4	3.5			34.1	80.0
New Zealand	99	100	..	..	..	..	..	..	..	..			31.7	..
Norway	100	99	..	34.6	..	8	..	2	..	0.3			41.6	56.7
Portugal	..	100	..	..	..	..	..	..	..	..			..	63.6
Spain	..	..	..	74.8	..	31	..	11	..	1.0			..	..
Sweden	99	100	29.5	..	14	..	7	..	5.5	..			65.8	19.2
Switzerland	92	100	75.5	..	20	..	10	..	..	..			55.4	71.3
United Kingdom	94	100	47.4	..	23	..	6	..	4.2	..			15.3	22.5
United States	73	99	66.4	58.0	37	27	10	7	2.7	2.7			20.8	..
Total	**73**	**80**	**59.2**	**62.4**	**31**	**28**	**9**	**9**	**2.8**	**2.1**			**..**	**47.3**[a]

a. Estimated average of figures reported above.

Changing patterns of aid

By definition, official development assistance (ODA) must have a grant element of at least 25 percent. In recent years many bilateral donors have shifted their aid programs away from loans and now award all their ODA in the form of grants (figure 6.8a). Belgium, Denmark, the Netherlands, and the United Kingdom have either phased out or greatly reduced their loan programs over the past decade, while others, such as Australia, have maintained an all-grant program. One reason for the increasing share of grants has been the rising expenditures reported by Development Assistance Committee (DAC) members on emergency and humanitarian aid and refugee relief. Loans remain important, however, because such countries as France, Japan, and Spain, which have large concessional loan programs, have been rapidly increasing their aid in recent years.

The pattern of aid has also been changing in other ways. Among these changes is the decline in the share of ODA going to multilateral organizations. Almost 35 percent in the early 1980s, when the regional development banks were rapidly expanding their operations, this share had fallen to about 30 percent of ODA commitments by DAC donors in 1993–94. Because contributions to multilateral organizations take the form of capital subscriptions or outright grants, the decline in these contributions has affected the distribution of ODA commitments between loans and grants.

The proportion of untied aid has increased. Aid that is tied obliges recipients to purchase goods and services from the donor country or from a specified group of countries. Partially untied aid allows procurement from the donor country and most developing countries. Untied aid has no such restrictions. Tying arrangements may be justified on the grounds that they prevent a recipient from misappropriating or mismanaging aid receipts—they may help to keep targeted aid on target. But to the extent that they prevent recipients from obtaining the best value for their money, they reduce the value—and thus the efficiency—of the aid received.

Like other data on ODA in this section, information on the financial terms of ODA commitments is furnished by DAC members. The loans and grants reported here are part of bilateral aid programs and do not include contributions by donors to multilateral institutions. Nor do they include the grants and loans to aid recipients made by the multilateral institutions from these contributions.

The terms of ODA loans are used to determine their grant element, which, according to the DAC definition of ODA, must be at least 25 percent. The grant element measures the concessionality of the loan: the difference between the face value of a loan and its present value when discounted at an interest rate below the market rate over the life of the loan. The market rate is conventionally taken as 10 percent in DAC statistics. Thus the grant element is nil for a loan carrying an interest rate of 10 percent, 100 percent for a grant, and somewhere in between for a soft loan made at less than 10 percent interest. Longer grace periods and longer maturities increase the grant element of loans.

Definitions

● **Grants** are the share in total ODA of transfers made in cash, goods, or services for which no repayment is required. ● **Grant element** reflects the concessionality of a commitment's financial terms: its maturity, grace period, and interest rate. ● **Maturity** is the date on which the final repayment of a loan is due and, by extension, a measure of the scheduled life of the loan. ● **Grace period** is the interval between the time a loan is made and the first repayment of principal. ● **Interest rate** is the cost of borrowing funds, expressed as an annual percentage. ● **Untied aid** is the share of ODA under which associated goods and services may be fully and freely procured.

Data sources

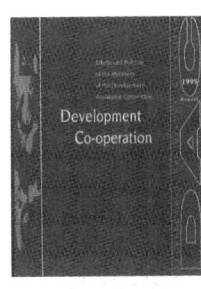

Data on aid are compiled by DAC and published in the DAC chairman's report, *Development Co-operation*. The OECD also makes its data available on diskette and magnetic tape and on the Internet.

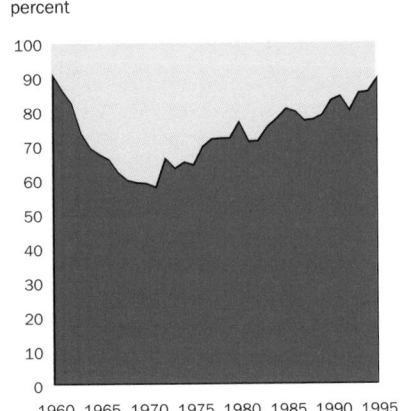

Figure 6.8a Share of grants in net bilateral ODA from DAC countries, 1960—95

Source: OECD, Development Assistance Committee data.

$ millions, 1994	Total	Canada	France	Germany	Italy	Japan	Netherlands	Norway	Sweden	United Kingdom	United States	Others
Albania	69.1	0.0	5.5	16.8	9.5	8.9	6.8	0.4	0.2	1.7	10.0	9.4
Algeria	373.5	0.9	209.3	11.0	22.6	–0.9	0.1	0.1	1.4	0.2	1.0	127.8
Angola	225.9	6.0	27.4	18.2	19.2	0.1	5.9	14.9	32.0	25.1	34.0	43.1
Argentina	145.1	1.4	7.4	31.5	51.5	18.0	1.6	0.0	1.4	0.2	2.0	30.1
Armenia	99.8	0.4	1.6	2.4	0.0	0.0	0.8	0.3	5.6	1.9	86.0	0.8
Australia												
Austria												
Azerbaijan	26.0	0.5	0.6	2.1	0.0	0.0	1.4	2.0	2.6	2.9	13.0	0.9
Bangladesh	843.7	53.7	29.6	104.9	5.7	227.6	54.5	36.7	25.2	65.7	152.0	88.1
Belarus	108.4	0.2	0.5	77.7	0.0	0.2	0.0	0.0	0.0	0.9	27.0	1.9
Belgium												
Benin	142.0	2.2	56.4	31.1	0.0	11.4	8.3	0.0	0.0	0.0	16.0	16.6
Bolivia	385.3	9.6	14.4	68.2	4.8	80.4	33.1	2.2	17.0	7.6	89.0	58.9
Bosnia and Herzegovina	..	..	..	..	..	..	..	..	..	..	..	..
Botswana	56.7	1.5	0.7	9.4	0.0	3.0	5.4	7.7	9.5	4.2	12.0	3.4
Brazil	202.1	2.7	20.0	34.7	16.8	89.4	16.4	1.8	1.3	8.6	–2.0	12.5
Bulgaria	51.4	0.1	5.0	20.2	0.3	7.7	0.0	0.0	0.0	2.9	10.0	5.1
Burkina Faso	264.7	9.1	99.3	37.4	24.4	11.8	28.6	0.1	0.2	0.2	13.0	40.6
Burundi	108.5	3.3	23.0	27.7	1.8	7.4	1.6	1.3	1.5	4.6	10.0	26.2
Cambodia	181.0	3.2	28.4	12.2	0.3	64.5	11.0	5.0	10.1	7.0	16.0	23.3
Cameroon	397.0	12.4	308.6	33.0	2.7	10.1	8.8	0.5	0.0	3.6	8.0	9.4
Canada												
Central African Republic	94.2	0.4	62.0	10.2	0.5	10.4	0.4	0.0	0.0	0.0	10.0	0.3
Chad	103.5	0.3	65.5	19.1	0.1	0.2	1.5	0.1	0.0	0.5	8.0	8.3
Chile	132.1	2.6	18.8	42.1	9.1	31.4	15.9	3.1	17.8	2.3	–27.0	16.1
China	2,393.9	68.6	97.7	300.0	69.6	1,479.4	10.1	22.6	17.5	47.0	0.0	281.5
Colombia	66.0	4.4	17.8	17.2	12.4	18.7	11.6	0.5	1.2	4.1	–33.0	11.0
Congo	252.9	0.2	227.2	12.5	0.3	0.4	0.1	0.1	0.0	0.0	10.0	2.2
Costa Rica	71.2	3.2	3.8	14.0	0.0	17.1	13.1	0.8	7.1	6.0	–4.0	10.0
Côte d'Ivoire	820.2	6.0	649.7	45.9	0.1	20.4	0.2	0.4	0.0	0.1	23.0	74.4
Croatia	..	..	..	..	..	..	..	..	..	..	..	..
Cuba	18.7	0.2	1.4	1.4	3.4	1.0	1.0	0.4	6.4	0.3	0.0	3.3
Czech Republic	56.0	1.4	6.1	15.1	0.2	3.3	0.0	1.3	0.3	3.9	2.0	22.3
Denmark												
Dominican Republic	35.8	0.3	2.2	4.0	5.9	10.4	2.3	0.3	0.5	0.0	6.0	3.9
Ecuador	173.0	7.0	12.0	21.7	2.9	33.1	6.6	0.5	2.4	3.0	21.0	63.0
Egypt, Arab Rep.	2,310.7	26.9	409.6	291.6	616.7	189.0	19.5	3.1	2.9	7.3	685.0	59.2
El Salvador	237.0	1.0	1.7	29.6	4.7	21.0	7.7	2.0	5.3	0.5	142.0	21.4
Eritrea	95.7	4.5	2.5	20.0	14.9	0.1	5.6	9.1	8.9	7.7	9.0	13.4
Estonia	33.0	1.1	0.5	6.4	0.1	0.1	0.0	2.3	11.3	1.0	0.0	10.2
Ethiopia	566.9	15.0	17.6	165.6	41.1	43.3	32.5	29.1	25.6	43.2	122.0	31.8
Finland												
France												
Gabon	161.2	1.9	150.3	4.0	0.0	0.2	0.0	0.0	0.0	0.0	2.0	2.8
Gambia, The	38.2	0.2	2.6	5.6	1.1	11.5	2.9	0.7	0.0	3.3	8.0	2.4
Georgia	67.3	1.5	0.3	2.1	0.0	0.0	1.8	0.5	2.6	4.0	53.0	1.6
Germany												
Ghana	331.8	16.7	27.0	23.9	5.7	134.8	21.8	0.6	0.4	28.9	53.0	19.0
Greece	0.0	0.0	0.0	0.0	0.0	0.0	0.0	0.0	0.0	0.0	0.0	0.0
Guatemala	157.3	3.7	1.9	17.7	6.5	43.0	6.6	8.0	2.0	0.2	54.0	13.9
Guinea–Bissau	125.4	0.5	7.0	2.7	0.5	3.7	4.2	0.1	11.4	0.0	6.0	89.4
Guinea	186.3	6.6	55.6	23.4	21.8	33.8	2.2	0.0	0.4	0.4	33.0	9.2
Haiti	597.1	14.9	14.9	1.5	0.0	0.4	4.9	1.4	1.9	0.5	541.0	15.7
Honduras	178.2	7.7	5.0	15.0	14.6	45.6	7.8	1.0	0.6	2.3	42.0	36.7
Hong Kong	9.8	0.0	2.2	1.4	0.0	4.9	0.1	0.0	0.0	0.5	0.0	0.8

$ millions, 1994	Total	Ten major DAC donors										Others
		Canada	France	Germany	Italy	Japan	Netherlands	Norway	Sweden	United Kingdom	United States	
Hungary	68.3	2.9	7.9	24.2	1.1	7.8	0.0	0.5	0.2	9.1	3.0	11.6
India	1,378.0	34.6	4.1	123.1	0.9	886.5	48.6	12.5	91.1	100.4	6.0	70.1
Indonesia	1,557.0	23.9	107.7	265.8	39.5	886.2	−49.0	1.3	0.6	34.1	−17.0	264.0
Iran, Islamic Rep.	87.2	0.0	8.7	61.1	0.5	−4.2	3.3	0.8	2.1	0.1	0.0	14.6
Iraq	187.3	1.8	1.9	13.1	0.4	0.1	19.6	2.0	17.5	14.0	112.0	5.0
Ireland												
Israel	1,218.0	0.1	9.6	−57.9	0.4	1.2	15.9	0.0	0.0	0.0	1,245.0	3.8
Italy												
Jamaica	74.3	11.0	0.5	3.8	2.5	2.2	7.7	1.1	0.6	1.9	43.0	0.2
Japan												
Jordan	229.3	8.6	19.4	33.3	17.0	106.7	0.1	0.0	1.0	6.4	34.0	2.8
Kazakstan	30.0	0.4	0.8	7.2	0.2	1.6	0.0	0.0	0.0	2.3	12.0	5.6
Kenya	400.5	7.8	16.1	46.7	22.1	128.9	42.0	2.9	17.4	44.3	29.0	43.4
Korea, Dem. Rep.	0.9	0.0	0.0	0.5	0.0	0.0	0.3	0.0	0.0	0.0	0.0	0.1
Korea, Rep.	−107.0	0.0	7.2	18.9	0.1	−95.2	0.0	0.0	0.0	0.0	−43.0	5.0
Kuwait	1.7	0.0	1.2	0.1	0.0	0.4	0.0	0.0	0.0	0.0	0.0	0.0
Kyrgyz Republic	87.0	0.1	0.1	2.0	1.2	44.5	0.1	0.1	0.0	0.3	22.0	16.4
Lao PDR	123.8	0.6	14.3	9.0	0.0	60.7	1.9	5.6	13.2	0.3	0.0	18.3
Latvia	36.8	1.3	0.4	10.9	0.0	0.1	0.0	2.8	11.8	1.3	2.0	6.2
Lebanon	79.9	1.7	36.4	6.8	7.2	0.6	0.4	1.5	2.1	0.5	20.0	2.8
Lesotho	45.5	0.7	1.2	12.1	0.0	1.4	0.8	2.7	3.3	7.4	5.0	10.9
Libya	1.8	0.0	0.6	0.5	0.3	0.1	0.0	0.0	0.0	0.0	0.0	0.2
Lithuania	52.0	1.3	1.7	11.1	1.4	0.1	0.0	3.3	11.3	1.7	15.0	5.3
Macedonia, FYR	..	..	..	..	..	..	..	..	..	..	..	..
Madagascar	189.9	1.1	92.3	15.8	2.0	34.3	0.8	3.9	0.2	1.2	22.0	16.4
Malawi	251.1	8.0	1.2	36.8	0.0	100.3	3.7	7.4	0.1	55.9	28.0	9.7
Malaysia	64.8	5.7	5.9	6.5	0.3	5.3	1.2	0.1	2.4	15.1	0.0	22.3
Mali	243.0	20.3	90.7	25.7	6.3	21.9	20.9	7.7	0.0	1.5	29.0	19.0
Mauritania	128.1	0.8	66.2	18.9	1.0	34.1	0.3	0.1	0.0	0.8	2.0	4.0
Mauritius	7.7	0.3	7.4	−3.1	0.0	0.0	0.0	0.0	0.3	0.4	−1.0	3.3
Mexico	396.8	4.5	35.8	14.6	0.5	183.1	3.9	0.4	0.4	5.2	1.0	147.5
Moldova	22.4	0.0	0.2	0.7	0.1	0.1	0.0	0.0	0.0	0.2	21.0	0.0
Mongolia	108.1	0.0	0.1	11.0	1.3	71.1	1.3	0.0	1.7	1.4	14.0	6.2
Morocco	317.9	6.5	151.9	11.0	39.3	59.6	0.0	0.0	0.9	15.2	4.0	29.4
Mozambique	733.4	17.4	33.2	101.3	93.9	43.3	41.7	72.2	73.5	38.7	73.0	145.2
Myanmar	142.8	2.6	2.0	1.4	0.0	133.8	0.8	0.7	0.0	0.6	0.0	0.8
Namibia	112.5	1.8	7.5	27.6	0.9	9.8	6.7	11.4	15.0	5.0	5.0	21.9
Nepal	267.7	4.1	3.9	22.6	1.5	118.8	8.3	5.2	0.5	24.0	20.0	58.8
Netherlands												
New Zealand												
Nicaragua	417.6	9.1	7.8	43.9	101.0	54.7	26.6	20.3	30.7	0.9	60.0	62.7
Niger	261.5	3.9	136.1	27.3	9.4	41.5	7.0	1.6	0.0	0.9	19.0	14.7
Nigeria	47.3	1.0	10.2	12.6	1.6	−9.4	1.9	0.1	0.2	10.8	12.0	6.1
Norway												
Oman	79.3	0.0	0.6	0.7	0.0	7.8	0.0	0.0	0.0	0.2	70.0	0.0
Pakistan	508.5	4.6	105.7	86.5	−4.0	271.0	19.3	10.3	3.4	36.5	−53.0	28.2
Panama	31.2	0.2	0.5	3.1	0.0	18.6	0.6	0.0	0.1	1.0	6.0	1.1
Papua New Guinea	276.0	0.0	0.3	9.8	0.1	21.8	0.8	0.0	0.0	1.5	3.0	238.6
Paraguay	84.5	0.5	−0.1	6.2	0.1	70.3	0.8	0.5	1.3	0.4	2.0	2.7
Peru	293.8	13.7	12.5	51.7	21.7	54.6	25.8	1.9	3.9	5.2	85.0	17.9
Philippines	942.6	24.1	15.4	56.4	4.5	591.6	17.9	3.8	25.3	12.9	116.0	74.8
Poland	1,548.3	2.2	267.0	92.7	1.2	92.9	0.0	25.8	6.3	18.3	841.0	200.9
Portugal												
Puerto Rico	0.0	0.0	0.0	0.0	0.0	0.0	0.0	0.0	0.0	0.0	0.0	0.0
Romania	62.8	2.4	11.7	15.6	0.6	6.6	0.0	0.1	0.1	5.6	15.0	5.1
Russian Federation	1,754.8	15.5	15.0	1,444.2	7.2	12.0	0.0	20.0	6.0	37.5	174.0	23.4

$ millions, 1994	Total	Ten major DAC donors										Others
		Canada	France	Germany	Italy	Japan	Netherlands	Norway	Sweden	United Kingdom	United States	
Rwanda	487.4	18.2	24.3	46.6	12.4	16.5	32.2	8.8	12.1	44.6	194.0	77.7
Saudi Arabia	14.0	0.0	3.9	1.7	0.0	8.1	0.0	0.0	0.0	0.0	0.0	0.1
Senegal	475.1	17.0	280.8	18.3	17.0	76.9	7.0	1.2	0.3	1.7	30.0	25.1
Sierra Leone	53.8	0.1	9.7	7.4	0.8	10.3	1.8	0.7	0.1	6.2	10.0	6.6
Singapore	14.9	0.8	3.6	−2.3	0.0	13.6	0.0	0.0	0.0	−1.3	0.0	0.5
Slovak Republic	31.4	0.7	2.4	6.0	0.3	1.9	0.0	0.7	0.1	3.4	1.0	14.9
Slovenia	..	..	..	..	..	..	..	..	..	..	..	..
South Africa	214.4	10.8	1.9	19.7	0.3	3.1	12.6	17.9	29.7	23.9	71.0	23.5
Spain												
Sri Lanka	334.0	4.9	−0.2	7.0	5.4	213.8	14.7	15.0	8.5	12.4	37.0	15.6
Sudan	174.5	8.3	5.2	24.5	5.7	20.6	29.1	7.8	5.2	25.7	32.0	10.5
Sweden												
Switzerland												
Syrian Arab Republic	361.4	0.6	11.7	16.5	0.9	330.0	0.3	0.1	0.0	0.1	0.0	1.1
Tajikistan	28.3	0.0	0.1	0.6	0.0	0.2	1.3	0.8	3.2	2.3	18.0	1.9
Tanzania	570.3	10.7	10.0	64.4	10.6	104.8	57.8	50.3	51.3	43.8	24.0	142.7
Thailand	543.2	14.2	11.3	44.4	0.4	382.6	4.8	1.7	3.6	14.2	9.0	57.2
Togo	63.5	0.3	36.5	14.0	0.0	1.7	0.8	0.0	1.1	0.9	6.0	2.0
Trinidad and Tobago	−0.9	0.2	0.5	−4.6	0.0	2.2	0.1	0.0	0.1	0.6	0.0	0.1
Tunisia	72.7	2.9	76.7	−10.9	3.2	−5.9	5.0	0.1	7.4	0.2	−15.0	9.0
Turkey	41.8	0.3	43.1	25.8	−3.0	9.1	−1.2	0.1	2.4	20.7	−71.0	15.6
Turkmenistan	13.5	0.0	0.0	0.0	0.0	0.2	0.0	0.0	0.0	0.2	13.0	0.1
Uganda	344.5	4.7	3.0	29.5	3.1	48.7	25.5	19.3	25.4	52.0	51.0	82.3
Ukraine	262.4	10.5	3.6	138.6	0.6	0.0	0.0	0.2	0.0	7.7	99.0	2.2
United Arab Emirates	−9.2	0.0	1.6	−13.2	0.0	2.4	0.0	0.0	0.0	0.0	0.0	0.0
United Kingdom												
United States												
Uruguay	67.8	1.0	4.9	8.7	3.5	11.4	1.8	0.1	1.4	0.2	1.0	33.7
Uzbekistan	11.7	0.0	1.1	1.0	0.0	2.6	0.0	0.1	0.9	0.8	4.0	1.4
Venezuela	21.8	1.4	4.7	5.2	0.9	6.3	0.5	0.0	0.4	0.3	0.0	2.1
Vietnam	585.6	7.1	179.8	52.7	92.3	79.5	16.1	6.1	21.1	16.1	10.0	105.1
West Bank and Gaza	..	..	..	..	..	..	..	..	..	..	..	..
Yemen, Rep.	106.0	0.6	14.2	29.9	1.3	22.5	25.3	0.0	0.2	8.0	1.0	3.2
Yugoslavia, Fed. Rep[a]	956.8	9.7	5.4	302.5	35.6	0.4	102.6	94.6	102.1	97.4	19.0	187.8
Zaire	97.3	0.8	12.3	27.8	0.6	4.5	5.2	1.3	4.1	4.3	1.0	35.5
Zambia	434.0	10.1	11.5	54.5	2.4	106.3	28.2	51.2	35.5	68.9	13.0	52.4
Zimbabwe	280.3	13.4	9.9	25.9	11.1	25.7	28.1	17.3	34.0	37.8	34.0	43.2
World[b]	**46,664 t**	**1,469 t**	**6,955 t**	**6,111 t**	**1,847 t**	**9,691 t**	**1,701 t**	**891 t**	**1,451 t**	**1,756 t**	**9,637 t**	**5,154 t**
Low income	18,161 t	463 t	3,029 t	1,957 t	668 t	4,926 t	748 t	474 t	596 t	919 t	2,442 t	1,938 t
Excl. China & India	14,389 t	360 t	2,927 t	1,534 t	598 t	2,560 t	690 t	439 t	488 t	772 t	2,436 t	1,586 t
Middle income	16,656 t	264 t	1,959 t	3,481 t	1,006 t	3,603 t	372 t	231 t	358 t	458 t	2,845 t	2,077 t
Lower middle income	14,870 t	221 t	1,583 t	3,286 t	879 t	3,227 t	313 t	206 t	302 t	381 t	2,722 t	1,750 t
Upper middle income	1,786 t	42 t	376 t	196 t	127 t	377 t	59 t	25 t	55 t	77 t	123 t	327 t
Low & middle income	35,222 t	729 t	5,390 t	5,438 t	1,675 t	8,530 t	1,121 t	705 t	954 t	1,378 t	5,287 t	4,017 t
East Asia & Pacific	7,502 t	155 t	477 t	774 t	208 t	3,917 t	19 t	47 t	97 t	167 t	424 t	1,217 t
Europe & Central Asia	6,956 t	59 t	407 t	2,331 t	101 t	206 t	114 t	162 t	198 t	235 t	2,533 t	611 t
Latin America & Carib.	4,474 t	137 t	210 t	454 t	299 t	832 t	264 t	55 t	128 t	90 t	1,355 t	649 t
Middle East & N. Africa	4,931 t	53 t	965 t	480 t	722 t	716 t	76 t	22 t	45 t	62 t	1,499 t	290 t
South Asia	3,542 t	110 t	148 t	370 t	10 t	1,758 t	162 t	90 t	141 t	246 t	215 t	292 t
Sub-Saharan Africa	10,737 t	260 t	3,120 t	1,179 t	389 t	1,160 t	519 t	359 t	425 t	614 t	1,448 t	1,266 t
High income	1,983 t	3 t	797 t	−56 t	1 t	−67 t	69 t	0 t	0 t	3 t	1,217 t	14 t

a. Includes net flows to states of the former Yugoslavia: Bosnia and Herzegovina, Croatia, Macedonia FYR, and Slovenia. b. Includes data for economies not specified elsewhere.

Figure 6.9a Distribution of net bilateral ODA and official aid from the five largest donors, 1994

Japan

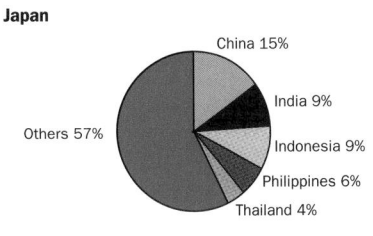

China 15%
India 9%
Indonesia 9%
Philippines 6%
Thailand 4%
Others 57%

United States

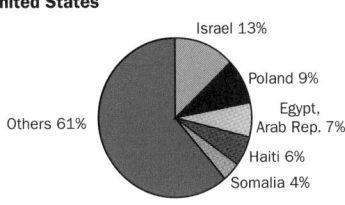

Israel 13%
Poland 9%
Egypt, Arab Rep. 7%
Haiti 6%
Somalia 4%
Others 61%

France

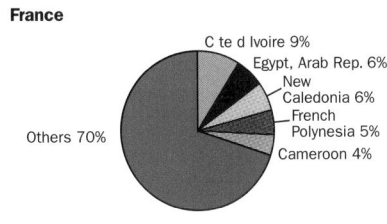

C te d Ivoire 9%
Egypt, Arab Rep. 6%
New Caledonia 6%
French Polynesia 5%
Cameroon 4%
Others 70%

Germany

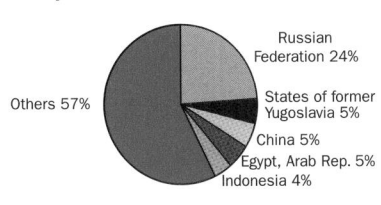

Russian Federation 24%
States of former Yugoslavia 5%
China 5%
Egypt, Arab Rep. 5%
Indonesia 4%
Others 57%

Italy

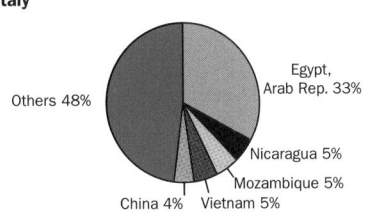

Egypt, Arab Rep. 33%
Nicaragua 5%
Mozambique 5%
Vietnam 5%
China 4%
Others 48%

Source: OECD, Development Assistance Committee data.

About the data

The data here show net bilateral aid to low- and middle-income economies from members of the Development Assistance Committee (DAC). Aid to countries and territories not shown in the table has been assigned to regional totals based on the World Bank's regional classification system. Aid to unspecified economies within a region has been included in regional totals, but not in totals for income groups. Aid not allocated by country or region (including administrative costs, research into development issues, and aid to non-governmental organizations) is included in the world total; regional and income group totals therefore do not add up to the world total.

Because these data are based on donor country reports of bilateral programs, they cannot be reconciled with recipient country reports, nor do they reflect the full extent of aid flows from the reporting donor country or to recipient countries. A full accounting would include donor country contributions to multilateral institutions and the flow of resources from multilateral institutions to recipient countries as well as flows from countries that are not members of DAC. In addition, the expenditures countries report as official development assistance (ODA) have changed. Recently, for example, some DAC countries providing aid to refugees within their own borders have reported these expenditures as ODA.

Definitions

● **Net aid** comprises net bilateral ODA to part I recipients and net bilateral official aid to part II recipients.
● **Other DAC donors** are Australia, Austria, Belgium, Denmark, Finland, Ireland, Luxembourg, New Zealand, Portugal, Spain, and Switzerland.

Data sources

Data on aid are compiled by DAC and published in its annual statistical report, *Geographical Distribution of Financial Flows to Aid Recipients,* and in the DAC chairman's report, *Development Co-operation.* The OECD also makes its data available on diskette and magnetic tape and on the Internet.

6.10 | Aid dependency

	Official development assistance and official aid ($ millions)		Aid per capita ($)		Aid dependency ratios							
					Aid as % of GNP		Aid as % of gross domestic investment		Aid as % of imports of goods and services		Aid as % of central government expenditures	
	1990	1994	1990	1994	1990	1994	1990	1994	1990	1994	1990	1994
Albania	11	165	3	52	0.5	9.1	2.8	67.8	2.3	21.3	..	..
Algeria	263	420	11	15	0.4	1.0	1.6	3.1	2.1	3.7	..	..
Angola	270	453	29	43	3.7	11.0	25.3	46.6	6.5	10.5	..	..
Argentina	184	225	6	7	0.1	0.1	0.9	0.4	1.4	0.7	1.2	..
Armenia	0	191	0	51	0.0	9.8	0.0	96.2	..	41.3	..	..
Australia												
Austria												
Azerbaijan	0	147	0	20	0.0	3.8	0.0	20.1	..	..	..	..
Bangladesh	2,100	1,758	19	15	9.4	6.8	73.3	44.2	48.3	36.1	..	..
Belarus	0	119	0	11	0.0	0.5	0.0	1.8	..	3.6	..	..
Belgium												
Benin	269	257	57	48	14.9	17.4	102.4	86.1	44.7	49.7	..	..
Bolivia	554	578	84	80	13.0	10.9	92.9	71.6	40.9	34.6	69.4	41.7
Bosnia and Herzegovina	..	..	..	..	..	..	..	..	..	..	..	..
Botswana	148	89	116	63	5.0	2.2	11.5	9.0	5.9	4.2	11.7	..
Brazil	167	337	1	2	0.0	0.1	0.2	0.3	0.4	0.6	0.1	..
Bulgaria	15	158	2	19	0.1	1.6	0.3	7.5	0.2	2.9	0.1	3.6
Burkina Faso	335	436	37	43	12.2	23.7	58.9	106.1	43.2	83.7	80.7	..
Burundi	265	313	48	51	23.8	31.6	161.3	336.3	77.8	109.0	..	..
Cambodia	42	339	5	35	3.7	14.3	45.4	73.4	..	36.3	..	..
Cameroon	447	731	39	57	4.3	10.0	22.5	60.6	16.0	34.6	17.1	..
Canada												
Central African Republic	251	166	86	52	19.6	19.4	189.4	139.1	58.1	62.3	..	..
Chad	316	215	56	34	27.1	23.9	279.0	..	61.9	50.7	83.6	..
Chile	108	158	8	11	0.4	0.3	1.4	1.1	1.0	1.0	1.8	1.5
China	2,093	3,238	2	3	0.6	0.6	1.7	1.5	4.3	2.7	5.3	6.3
Colombia	96	128	3	4	0.3	0.2	1.3	1.0	1.0	0.8	2.1	..
Congo	218	362	96	141	9.3	24.9	45.3	41.9	12.4	19.1	..	..
Costa Rica	230	76	76	23	4.2	0.9	14.7	0.9	8.5	2.0	15.7	3.0
Côte d'Ivoire	689	1,594	58	117	7.1	24.8	75.5	178.2	15.0	48.1	..	..
Croatia	..	..	..	..	..	..	..	..	..	..	..	..
Cuba	51	48	5	4	..	..	..	..	..	..	..	..
Czech Republic	3	143	0	14	0.0	0.4	0.0	2.0	..	0.7	..	0.9
Denmark												
Dominican Republic	101	68	14	9	1.5	0.7	6.7	3.2	3.9	1.1	12.3	3.8
Ecuador	163	217	16	19	1.7	1.4	8.7	6.9	4.3	4.0	10.5	8.3
Egypt, Arab Rep.	5,438	2,695	104	47	15.8	6.4	70.2	35.8	35.3	16.7	31.6	..
El Salvador	347	318	69	58	7.4	3.9	52.2	21.0	19.4	10.7	59.7	26.9
Eritrea	0	158	0	45	..	..	..	..	..	39.3	..	..
Estonia	0	43	0	29	0.0	1.1	0.0	3.9	..	2.0	..	5.9
Ethiopia	1,020	1,074	20	20	11.9	22.7	133.1	106.3	89.4	90.4	43.7	76.7
Finland												
France												
Gabon	132	182	142	171	2.7	5.6	9.9	18.2	5.4	8.5	11.0	..
Gambia, The	100	71	108	66	31.4	19.8	153.1	93.1	48.7	27.9	143.6	..
Georgia	0	176	0	33	0.0	7.5	0.0	2,449.3	..	..	..	..
Germany												
Ghana	563	546	38	33	9.2	8.5	62.7	52.4	34.7	25.7	72.3	..
Greece	37	0	4	0	0.1	0.0	0.3	0.0	0.2	0.0	0.1	..
Guatemala	203	224	22	22	2.7	1.7	19.6	10.5	10.0	6.6	26.5	19.4
Guinea	296	360	51	56	11.3	11.0	59.8	77.8	26.5	31.8	45.7	..
Guinea-Bissau	132	177	137	170	53.1	74.3	227.5	370.3	127.5	169.6	..	..
Haiti	172	601	27	86	5.8	37.3	47.5	2,179.9	31.9	278.0	..	..
Honduras	451	298	88	52	16.3	9.5	64.5	34.2	32.6	15.7	..	..
Hong Kong	38	27	7	4	0.1	0.0	0.2	0.1	0.0	0.0	..	..

	Official development assistance and official aid ($ millions)		Aid per capita ($)		Aid dependency ratios							
					Aid as % of GNP		Aid as % of gross domestic investment		Aid as % of imports of goods and services		Aid as % of central government expenditures	
	1990	1994	1990	1994	1990	1994	1990	1994	1990	1994	1990	1994
Hungary	67	200	6	20	0.2	0.5	0.8	2.3	0.5	1.2	0.4	..
India	1,407	2,325	2	3	0.5	0.8	1.9	3.3	3.9	5.4	2.7	4.7
Indonesia	1,747	1,642	10	9	1.6	1.0	5.0	2.7	5.3	3.3	8.3	5.7
Iran, Islamic Rep.	105	131	2	2	0.1	..	0.3	..	0.5	0.8	0.1	0.7
Iraq	64	259	4	13	0.1	..	..	..	..	..	..	..
Ireland												
Israel	1,372	1,237	295	230	2.5	1.6	13.1	6.8	5.8	3.6	5.2	3.7
Italy												
Jamaica	273	114	113	45	7.3	2.9	32.6	12.2	9.3	3.4		
Japan												
Jordan	888	370	280	92	24.6	6.5	69.3	23.0	22.0	8.0	61.7	19.8
Kazakstan	0	48	0	3	0.0	0.2	..	1.3	..	0.9		
Kenya	1,187	677	51	26	14.6	9.7	57.3	49.1	38.0	23.8	50.6	33.3
Korea, Dem. Rep.	8	6	0	0	..	..	..	..	..	..	..	..
Korea, Rep.	52	–114	1	–3	0.0	0.0	0.1	–0.1	0.1	–0.1	0.1	–0.2
Kuwait	7	6	3	4	0.0	0.0	0.2	0.1	0.1	0.0	0.1	0.0
Kyrgyz Republic	0	172	0	38	0.0	5.5	0.0	30.1	..	35.1		
Lao PDR	151	218	36	46	17.4	14.2	141.7	..	70.3	34.4	..	..
Latvia	0	52	0	20	0.0	0.9	0.0	4.6	..	3.1		5.1
Lebanon	259	235	71	60	7.3	2.5	51.4	9.0	8.9	4.3	..	7.4
Lesotho	143	117	80	60	13.7	8.9	32.5	15.3	18.4	12.8	44.8	..
Libya	20	7	4	1	..	..	..	..	..	0.2	..	..
Lithuania	0	71	0	19	0.0	1.1	0.0	6.1	..	2.7		6.6
Macedonia, FYR	..	..	..	..	..	..	..	..	..	..		
Madagascar	399	289	34	22	13.6	10.2	76.4	89.1	40.6	28.0	80.7	51.4
Malawi	505	470	59	49	27.8	38.0	142.2	227.6	79.2	48.9	105.3	..
Malaysia	469	68	26	3	1.1	0.1	3.3	0.2	1.3	0.1	3.7	0.4
Mali	487	443	58	47	20.0	24.5	87.7	..	54.9	56.2	..	..
Mauritania	240	269	120	121	25.0	27.7	117.9	162.5	42.1	46.3	..	..
Mauritius	89	14	84	13	3.4	0.4	10.9	1.3	4.5	0.6	14.9	1.8
Mexico	160	431	2	5	0.1	0.1	0.3	0.5	0.3	0.4	0.3	0.7
Moldova	0	54	0	12	0.0	1.5	..	18.7	..	7.0		
Mongolia	13	184	6	76	0.6	27.6	1.4	..	1.1	41.2	..	..
Morocco	1,051	631	44	24	4.2	2.2	16.2	9.8	11.9	5.9	14.1	..
Mozambique	1,008	1,232	71	79	82.1	101.0	152.3	139.4	86.6	83.4	..	..
Myanmar	164	162	4	4	..	..	..	..	12.9	9.1	4.3	2.0
Namibia	123	138	91	92	5.3	4.7	21.3	24.0	7.5	7.4	15.7	..
Nepal	429	448	23	21	12.0	10.9	64.4	49.6	56.0	34.0	70.9	75.6
Netherlands												
New Zealand												
Nicaragua	335	602	89	142	33.8	46.1	169.7	176.7	36.7	42.1	41.7	..
Niger	398	377	52	43	16.4	25.0	198.3	..	49.6	81.1	..	..
Nigeria	250	190	3	2	0.9	0.6	5.2	3.3	2.5	1.5	..	..
Norway												
Oman	66	95	41	45	0.7	1.0	4.8	5.0	1.7	1.8	1.6	1.9
Pakistan	1,130	1,606	10	13	2.7	3.1	14.9	15.8	10.8	12.6	12.8	12.9
Panama	99	40	41	15	2.1	0.6	11.5	2.3	1.8	0.4	7.8	2.0
Papua New Guinea	413	326	108	78	13.3	6.4	52.5	38.9	24.1	13.8	36.9	20.2
Paraguay	57	103	13	22	1.1	1.3	4.7	5.7	..	..	11.4	..
Peru	401	417	19	18	1.3	0.8	8.3	3.9	7.0	4.5	7.2	4.9
Philippines	1,277	1,058	21	16	2.9	1.6	11.9	6.9	7.8	3.8	14.7	..
Poland	1,322	1,801	35	47	2.4	2.0	8.8	12.3	6.9	7.0	..	4.4
Portugal												
Puerto Rico	..	..	..	..	..	..	..	..	..	..	..	..
Romania	243	145	10	6	0.6	0.5	2.1	1.8	2.5	1.8	1.9	1.5
Russian Federation	254	1,844	2	12	0.0	0.6	0.1	2.0	0.3	2.7	..	2.4

	Official development assistance and official aid		Aid per capita		Aid dependency ratios								
							Aid as % of gross domestic investment		Aid as % of imports of goods and services		Aid as % of central government expenditures	
	$ millions		$		Aid as % of GNP							
	1990	1994	1990	1994	1990	1994	1990	1994	1990	1994	1990	1994
Rwanda	293	715	42	115	11.4	95.9	105.3	1,048.0	77.2	144.2	60.0	..
Saudi Arabia	44	20	3	1	0.0	0.0	0.2	0.1	0.1	0.0	..	..
Senegal	823	645	111	78	14.9	17.2	106.5	121.7	40.1	38.4	..	..
Sierra Leone	63	277	16	66	8.0	36.0	60.3	377.0	21.9	78.3	115.8	..
Singapore	–3	17	–1	6	0.0	0.0	0.0	0.1	0.0	0.0	0.0	..
Slovak Republic	2	78	0	15	0.0	0.6	0.0	2.5	..	0.9	..	..
Slovenia	..	..	..	..	..	..	..	..	..	..	..	..
South Africa	0	295	0	7	0.0	0.2	0.0	1.4	0.0	1.0	0.0	0.7
Spain												
Sri Lanka	730	595	43	33	9.2	5.1	40.9	18.8	22.6	10.9	32.1	18.7
Sudan	827	413	34	16	9.5	..	67.3	..	40.2	18.7	..	..
Sweden												
Switzerland												
Syrian Arab Republic	684	745	56	54	5.9	5.3	36.1	..	18.1	10.5	13.1	6.3
Tajikistan	0	67	0	12	0.0	3.1	0.0	13.5	..	8.8	..	..
Tanzania	1,174	969	46	34	32.0	29.9	83.4	91.5	70.5	48.4	..	..
Thailand	797	578	14	10	0.9	0.4	2.3	1.0	2.1	0.9	6.6	2.5
Togo	261	126	74	32	16.3	13.8	64.2	118.3	28.6	25.5	..	..
Trinidad and Tobago	18	21	15	17	0.4	0.5	2.8	3.2	1.0	1.1	..	..
Tunisia	393	107	48	12	3.3	0.7	11.8	61.3	6.0	1.3	9.2	..
Turkey	1,220	163	22	3	0.8	0.1	3.2	0.6	4.2	0.5	4.7	0.5
Turkmenistan	0	25	0	6	0.0	0.6	0.0	..	..	1.2	..	..
Uganda	671	753	41	41	15.9	19.2	122.7	128.4	89.1	78.1	..	..
Ukraine	289	290	6	6	0.2	0.3	..	..	..	1.6	..	..
United Arab Emirates	5	–7	3	–3	0.0	0.0	0.1	–0.1	..	..	0.1	–0.2
United Kingdom												
United States												
Uruguay	54	86	17	27	0.7	0.5	5.9	4.2	2.4	2.1	2.5	1.5
Uzbekistan	0	28	0	1	0.0	0.1	0.0	0.6	..	0.8	..	..
Venezuela	80	31	4	1	0.2	0.1	1.6	0.4	0.6	0.2	0.8	0.3
Vietnam	190	897	3	12	..	5.9	22.6	22.6	8.1	13.0	..	..
West Bank and Gaza	..	..	..	..	..	..	..	..	..	..	..	..
Yemen, Rep.	406	172	34	12	6.4	4.6	52.6	31.9	15.3	6.3	..	..
Yugoslavia, Fed. Rep.[a]	47	1,718	..	..	..	..	..	..	..	..	..	..
Zaire	898	245	24	6	11.0	4.6	..	..	29.1	..	51.1	88.2
Zambia	481	719	62	82	16.0	20.7	84.6	282.0	20.6	43.3	56.5	..
Zimbabwe	340	562	35	52	5.2	10.2	20.8	..	14.9	19.8	14.2	..
World[b]	**60,274 t**	**68,010 t**										
Low income	26,427 t	31,754 t	9 w	10 w	3.6 w	4.3 w	9.9 w	8.6 w	15.3 w	11.7 w	..	..
Excl. China & India	22,928 t	26,191 t	25 w	26 w	11.2 w	12.6 w	39.4 w	49.9 w	26.6 w	25.5 w	..	..
Middle income	22,546 t	22,394 t	15 w	14 w	1.6 w	1.0 w	2.9 w	2.3 w	3.2 w	2.1 w	..	..
Lower middle income	20,662 t	19,873 t	19 w	18 w	2.2 w	1.4 w	4.3 w	4.0 w	5.4 w	3.4 w	..	..
Upper middle income	1,884 t	2,521 t	5 w	6 w	0.2 w	0.1 w	0.6 w	0.6 w	0.6 w	0.6 w	..	..
Low & middle income	48,973 t	54,148 t	11 w	12 w	2.9 w	3.3 w	4.7 w	4.2 w	5.7 w	4.2 w	..	..
East Asia & Pacific	7,765 t	9,358 t	5 w	5 w	0.9 w	1.1 w	3.4 w	2.1 w	4.2 w	2.6 w	..	..
Europe & Central Asia	3,631 t	8,071 t	8 w	17 w	0.4 w	0.9 w	1.0 w	3.0 w	1.8 w	2.4 w	..	..
Latin America & Carib.	5,191 t	6,061 t	11 w	12 w	1.4 w	1.7 w	2.1 w	1.6 w	2.3 w	1.7 w	..	..
Middle East & N. Africa	10,559 t	7,539 t	41 w	24 w	5.3 w	..	10.1 w	8.0 w	6.8 w	4.2 w	..	..
South Asia	6,003 t	7,068 t	5 w	6 w	1.9 w	1.9 w	6.6 w	7.7 w	10.6 w	10.1 w	..	..
Sub-Saharan Africa	17,906 t	18,903 t	34 w	32 w	13.3 w	16.3 w	33.8 w	34.1 w	18.6 w	18.4 w	..	..
High income	2,251 t	2,045 t										

a. Includes net flows to the states of the former Yugoslavia: Bosnia and Herzegovina, Croatia, Macedonia FYR, and Slovenia. b. Includes data for economies not specified elsewhere.

What aid dependency ratios show

Poor countries, like poor people, tend to consume most of their income, leaving little for savings. Thus they depend on aid to raise investment, to purchase essential imports, and to maintain a minimum level of expenditure on education and health services. As countries develop, they become less reliant on aid. Many East Asian economies were once large recipients, but today receive little or no aid. Exceptions to this pattern are the large, poor countries (such as India and China) that by virtue of their size have had relatively low levels of aid relative to their economies.

Aid dependency ratios measure inflows of aid relative to the recipient country's GNP, investment, imports, or public spending. They are a better measure of the contribution of aid than absolute levels because they compare these flows to key macroeconomic variables. Nevertheless, care must be taken in drawing policy conclusions. In general, aid dependency ratios are much higher in Sub-Saharan Africa

ODA finances nearly half of the investment in low-income economies other than China and India ●

than in other regions, and they increased during the 1980s. These high ratios are due only in part to the volume of aid flows. Many of these countries experienced a severe erosion in their terms of trade in the 1980s, which, along with weak policies, contributed to falling income, imports, and investment. Thus the increase in aid dependency ratios reflects events affecting both the numerator and the denominator.

Comparisons of official development assistance (ODA) flows with domestic investment may lead to misleading conclusions about the domestic savings effort. In many countries, particularly poorer ones, lack of information prevents independent estimates of domestic savings, which are calculated as a residual in the national accounts based on estimates of investment and public savings. An increase in foreign savings through an increase in aid results in lower domestic savings for any level of investment.

For foreign policy reasons some countries have traditionally received large amounts of assistance. Aid dependency ratios may therefore reveal as much about the interests of donors as they do about the need of recipients.

About the data

As defined here, aid includes ODA flows to recipients listed as developing countries and territories by the Development Assistance Committee (DAC) of the OECD, and ODA-like flows of official aid provided to the transition economies of Eastern Europe and the former Soviet Union and to some advanced developing countries and territories. The data cover bilateral loans and grants from DAC countries, multilateral organizations, and certain Arab countries.

The data in the table do not distinguish among different types of aid (program, project, or food aid, emergency assistance, peacekeeping assistance, and technical cooperation), each of which may have a very different impact on the economy. Technical cooperation expenditures do not always directly benefit the economy to the extent that they defray costs incurred outside the country on the salaries and benefits of technical experts and the overhead costs of firms supplying technical services.

Because the table relies on information from donors, it is not consistent with information recorded by recipients in the balance of payments. Such information often excludes all or some technical assistance, particularly payments to expatriates made directly by the donor. Similarly, grant commodity aid may not always be recorded in trade data or in the balance of payments. Although ODA estimates in balance of payments statistics are meant to exclude purely military assistance, the distinction is sometimes blurred. The definition used by the country of origin usually prevails.

The nominal values used here tend to overestimate the amount of resources transferred. Changes in international prices and in exchange rates reduce the purchasing power of aid. The practice of tying aid, still prevalent though declining in importance, also reduces the purchasing power of aid (see the notes to table 6.8). The same volume of aid may represent different purchasing power, depending on the relative costs of suppliers in different countries to which the aid is tied and the degree to which each recipient's aid basket is untied.

Aid not allocated by country or region (including administrative costs, research into development issues, and aid to nongovernmental organizations) is included in the world total; regional and income group totals therefore do not add up to the world total.

Definitions

● **Official development assistance** consists of net disbursements of loans and grants made on concessional terms by official agencies of the members of DAC and certain Arab countries to promote economic development and welfare in recipient economies listed as developing by DAC. Loans with a grant element of more than 25 percent are included in ODA. ODA also includes technical cooperation and assistance. ● **Official aid** refers to aid flows from official donors to the transition economies of Eastern Europe and the former Soviet Union and to certain advanced developing countries and territories as determined by DAC. Official aid is provided under terms and conditions similar to those for ODA. ● **Aid per capita** includes both ODA and official aid. ● **Aid dependency ratios** are computed using values in U.S. dollars converted at official exchange rates. For definitions of GNP, gross domestic investment, imports of goods and services, and central government expenditures, see the notes to tables 1.1, 4.12, and 4.18.

Data sources

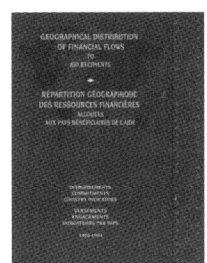

Data on aid are compiled by DAC and published in its annual statistical report, *Geographical Distribution of Financial Flows to Aid Recipients,* and in the DAC chairman's report, *Development Co-operation.* The OECD also makes its data available on diskette and magnetic tape and on the Internet.

$ millions, 1994	International financial institutions							United Nations					Total
	IDA	IMF	AfDB	ADB	IDB	CEC	Others	WFP	UNDP	UNFPA	UNICEF	Others	
Albania	35.0	22.2				31.4	1.8	0.0	1.5	0.7	0.9	2.0	95
Algeria			0.0			37.1	−1.7	7.1	0.6	1.2	0.7	9.0	54
Angola	33.3	0.0	0.1			56.5	0.0	106.9	2.0	0.9	18.4	8.9	227
Argentina					−14.1	5.2	−12.2	0.0	79.4	0.0	2.1	5.1	79
Armenia	5.5	0.0				71.3	0.5	7.3	0.1	0.0	2.1	4.7	91
Australia													
Austria													
Azerbaijan	0.0	0.0				102.8	0.2	8.6	0.0	0.5	1.9	6.5	121
Bangladesh	379.5	−55.0		358.1		56.3	3.2	67.0	23.4	6.1	37.1	31.1	907
Belarus						8.4	1.6	0.0	0.2	0.0	0.0	0.5	11
Belgium													
Benin	25.9	25.1	30.9			10.4	1.5	2.5	4.9	0.8	2.8	5.7	110
Bolivia	77.4	28.6			23.1	28.0	24.9	2.1	12.9	2.1	6.4	9.0	191
Bosnia and Herzegovina													
Botswana	−0.5		0.4			10.3	−0.3	3.3	4.4	0.9	1.3	1.9	22
Brazil					−0.9	24.3	−2.0	7.2	84.6	2.9	12.2	5.4	135
Bulgaria						102.8	1.5	0.0	1.1	0.0	0.0	1.6	107
Burkina Faso	76.1	25.3	7.6			47.0	−1.0	3.0	9.7	1.9	4.5	2.7	177
Burundi	25.5	−6.2	12.5			36.5	0.5	64.2	2.7	0.9	5.0	68.5	210
Cambodia	38.2	20.0		16.4		11.4	0.0	10.0	30.0	0.6	10.9	18.0	156
Cameroon	176.1	0.0	34.6			114.1	0.0	2.4	1.9	1.0	1.9	2.2	334
Canada													
Central African Republic	38.9	−4.2	−0.5			25.2	2.1	3.1	2.8	1.0	1.6	4.2	74
Chad	36.1	−1.7	19.7			37.1	0.0	4.9	7.4	0.8	2.8	2.3	109
Chile	−0.7				−4.8	16.9	−4.8	0.0	9.7	0.1	1.1	3.3	26
China	671.0	0.0		16.7		14.1	10.8	24.9	38.4	6.7	22.5	13.2	818
Colombia	−0.7				−16.4	12.1	−17.0	5.0	56.3	0.5	1.4	5.0	62
Congo	97.1	0.0	3.0			5.9	−1.2	0.5	0.8	0.4	0.9	1.9	109
Costa Rica	−0.2				−11.5	4.0	−11.6	1.1	3.8	0.6	0.8	6.7	5
Côte d'Ivoire	447.8	170.5	2.7			134.1	0.3	4.5	2.1	0.9	2.4	8.6	774
Croatia[a]													
Cuba						17.7	0.0	3.6	2.4	0.7	1.8	2.6	29
Czech Republic						84.2	1.5	0.0	0.5	0.0	0.0	0.9	87
Denmark													
Dominican Republic	−0.7				3.2	16.9	2.5	0.5	9.2	1.6	1.1	2.2	33
Ecuador	−1.1				18.9	8.9	19.8	0.5	6.6	1.0	3.3	4.8	44
Egypt, Arab Rep.	37.7	0.0	6.5			136.5	0.7	14.0	11.7	2.7	5.6	8.3	224
El Salvador	−0.6				31.7	24.8	34.1	1.3	15.5	1.1	1.5	3.2	81
Eritrea	0.0	0.0	0.0			1.5	0.0	30.7	4.1	0.1	6.8	7.2	50
Estonia						8.0	1.8	0.0	0.3	0.0	0.0	0.3	10
Ethiopia	156.2	20.2	60.6			181.9	−0.4	26.3	13.2	4.2	21.0	26.8	510
Finland													
France													
Gabon			0.9			17.8	0.0	0.0	0.9	0.1	0.6	1.2	21
Gambia, The	8.6	−3.9	6.8			10.6	0.1	3.0	3.3	0.6	1.2	2.4	33
Georgia	1.0	0.0				91.9	0.0	7.6	0.2	0.0	1.6	6.9	109
Germany													
Ghana	171.8	−43.7	19.9			42.4	2.4	9.3	4.8	2.3	4.3	6.5	220
Greece						0.0	0.0	0.0	0.0	0.0	0.0	0.0	0
Guatemala					22.2	17.7	24.5	5.2	8.5	0.3	1.7	8.1	66
Guinea	61.0	6.6	21.8			47.5	3.5	2.3	4.5	0.8	3.5	18.3	170
Guinea-Bissau	10.4	−0.4	0.6			24.8	0.0	2.2	7.2	0.5	1.6	2.2	49
Haiti	0.0	−7.6			−15.5	13.6	−15.5	2.1	2.3	1.4	4.7	3.2	4
Honduras	62.1				36.5	6.8	36.2	5.6	5.7	1.2	1.1	3.3	122
Hong Kong						2.3	0.0	0.0	0.0	0.0	0.0	14.7	17

$ millions, 1994	IDA	IMF	AfDB	ADB	IDB	CEC	Others	WFP	UNDP	UNFPA	UNICEF	Others	Total
			International financial institutions						United Nations				Total
Hungary						125.3	1.3	0.0	0.1	0.1	0.0	5.5	132
India	772.5	0.0		3.4		56.8	3.0	28.3	27.6	11.9	68.1	13.8	985
Indonesia	−19.9			44.7		14.2	−1.0	5.6	15.1	5.3	11.8	9.8	85
Iran, Islamic Rep.						12.2	0.0	2.9	2.1	1.8	1.3	19.0	39
Iraq						17.7	0.0	14.7	1.0	0.0	29.2	9.4	72
Ireland													
Israel						19.1	0.0	0.0	0.0	0.0	0.0	0.1	19
Italy													
Jamaica					−5.7	39.3	−10.2	1.3	5.4	0.5	2.1	1.1	40
Japan													
Jordan	−1.8					52.0	−1.3	3.7	2.4	1.0	1.0	73.8	131
Kazakstan				0.8		13.0	2.6	0.0	0.1	0.6	0.9	0.3	18
Kenya	88.9	18.5	15.5			36.3	0.2	48.7	10.8	4.9	16.6	45.4	286
Korea, Dem. Rep.						0.0	0.0	0.0	2.9	0.4	0.6	1.1	5
Korea, Rep.	−3.5			0.0		0.0	0.0	0.0	1.6	0.5	0.0	0.9	0
Kuwait						0.0	0.0	0.0	3.9	0.0	0.0	0.2	4
Kyrgyz Republic	35.7	13.6		2.4		27.2	1.2	1.8	1.2	0.4	1.4	0.1	85
Lao PDR	26.2	8.5		24.0		6.5	2.8	3.2	6.9	1.1	3.6	7.6	90
Latvia						12.3	2.1	0.0	0.1	0.0	0.0	0.2	15
Lebanon						13.9	0.6	1.1	3.2	0.6	2.5	38.4	60
Lesotho	5.2	3.9	18.2			30.6	0.2	5.9	2.7	0.5	1.8	2.0	71
Libya			0.0			0.0	0.0	0.0	2.8	0.0	0.0	1.9	5
Lithuania						16.2	2.2	0.0	0.4	0.0	0.0	0.3	19
Macedonia, FYR[a]													
Madagascar	53.6	−5.3	4.8			24.5	1.8	1.4	7.1	1.1	8.0	2.5	99
Malawi	53.0	4.0	40.5			35.4	1.3	45.5	11.9	1.5	4.3	20.9	218
Malaysia				0.5		1.3	0.0	0.0	3.3	0.3	0.7	4.5	10
Mali	87.4	39.4	10.3			52.7	−0.6	1.8	7.2	0.9	7.1	4.2	210
Mauritania	33.3	18.3	10.6			44.9	−0.3	7.3	4.0	1.2	2.0	9.2	130
Mauritius	−0.6		0.2			6.9	−0.5	0.1	0.5	0.6	0.7	0.9	9
Mexico					−19.1	14.9	−17.4	8.4	6.9	4.2	3.5	13.7	34
Moldova						30.6	0.5	0.0	0.4	0.0	0.0	0.2	32
Mongolia	17.4	21.2		26.7		1.4	0.0	0.7	2.9	1.5	1.1	3.0	76
Morocco	−1.2		4.2			199.0	−1.3	8.9	3.2	3.8	1.8	4.0	222
Mozambique	176.3	10.6	32.3			101.4	0.0	47.7	49.0	1.9	19.7	57.7	497
Myanmar	−1.7	0.0		−10.1		0.1	0.0	0.0	10.9	0.1	6.5	11.3	17
Namibia			5.1			8.8	0.0	0.0	3.6	0.7	4.0	3.1	25
Nepal	70.4	2.7		62.5		4.1	−0.1	7.7	9.8	3.9	9.8	12.2	183
Netherlands													
New Zealand													
Nicaragua	51.0	28.6			55.7	22.3	55.4	7.6	11.9	1.5	3.4	4.8	187
Niger	41.5	−7.3	6.0			43.8	0.7	7.1	6.8	1.0	4.6	6.1	110
Nigeria	58.9	0.0	22.7			26.8	4.1	0.0	7.3	4.2	14.9	4.0	143
Norway						0.0	0.0	0.0	0.0	0.0	0.0	0.0	0
Oman						0.1	0.0	0.0	0.1	0.1	0.8	0.6	2
Pakistan	292.8	273.9		420.5		18.7	1.4	35.2	12.6	3.4	15.6	27.5	1,102
Panama					−6.2	3.8	−7.2	0.0	9.4	0.5	0.8	1.3	9
Papua New Guinea	−1.7			25.2		18.4	−0.2	0.0	4.7	0.4	1.1	2.7	51
Paraguay	−1.1				4.8	4.1	4.6	0.2	9.1	0.8	1.6	0.9	20
Peru					−12.3	40.7	−12.0	6.1	74.4	2.2	6.7	4.7	123
Philippines	2.9			55.0		22.8	1.5	1.0	4.0	4.1	8.8	11.6	112
Poland						248.0	1.8	0.0	0.5	0.1	0.0	2.8	253
Portugal													
Puerto Rico						0.0	0.0	0.0	0.0	0.0	0.0	0.0	0
Romania						74.2	3.0	0.0	1.3	0.1	0.9	2.4	82
Russian Federation						61.2	16.9	0.0	0.4	0.0	1.7	8.9	89

$ millions, 1994	International financial institutions							United Nations					Total
	IDA	IMF	AfDB	ADB	IDB	CEC	Others	WFP	UNDP	UNFPA	UNICEF	Others	
Rwanda	11.1	0.0	3.5			45.6	0.2	47.7	3.6	0.6	32.3	81.6	226
Saudi Arabia						0.1	0.0	0.0	5.9	0.0	0.0	0.7	7
Senegal	48.7	−1.0	14.1			69.6	0.1	3.0	7.9	1.6	7.7	9.3	161
Sierra Leone	36.6	117.1	16.0			35.8	1.5	0.9	6.9	0.3	3.3	4.6	223
Singapore						1.1	0.0	0.0	0.0	0.0	0.0	0.8	2
Slovak Republic						44.5	1.7	0.0	0.1	0.0	0.0	0.8	47
Slovenia[a]													
South Africa						69.4	0.0	0.0	0.0	0.2	2.4	8.3	80
Spain													
Sri Lanka	70.6	67.5		89.2		6.3	1.6	5.6	6.2	1.2	3.2	8.0	259
Sudan	7.6	0.0	12.5			33.1	3.5	110.7	10.0	1.0	40.2	21.2	240
Sweden													
Switzerland													
Syrian Arab Republic						11.4	0.2	14.1	2.2	2.3	0.9	25.6	57
Tajikistan	0.0	0.0				28.7	0.2	6.1	0.0	0.4	2.7	0.3	38
Tanzania	172.3	−15.3	23.7			87.3	4.6	43.5	7.8	2.2	11.6	57.8	395
Thailand	−1.7		0.0	0.7		20.7	−2.3	1.5	3.2	0.9	3.6	17.1	44
Togo	25.0	12.3	8.3			9.4	−0.2	1.7	2.4	0.3	1.4	1.8	62
Trinidad and Tobago					1.0	19.7	1.0	0.0	0.5	0.0	0.0	1.2	22
Tunisia	−2.1		0.0			38.0	0.9	3.7	1.2	1.5	1.2	1.7	46
Turkey	−5.9					−23.3	−0.4	0.4	1.8	0.8	1.8	6.1	−19
Turkmenistan						9.5	0.6	0.0	0.0	0.4	1.0	0.1	12
Uganda	215.5	28.1	26.4			59.0	2.0	18.4	11.8	4.5	16.3	19.3	401
Ukraine						23.6	2.1	0.0	0.4	0.0	0.9	0.4	27
United Arab Emirates						0.1	0.0	0.0	2.1	0.0	0.0	0.3	3
United Kingdom													
United States													
Uruguay				−1.7		3.0	−1.2	0.0	12.8	0.1	0.9	2.6	18
Uzbekistan				0.0		11.2	1.3	0.0	0.8	1.0	1.6	0.1	
Venezuela				−1.3		2.1	−1.7	0.0	4.9	0.2	1.1	2.9	10
Vietnam	125.2	86.5		8.8		20.7	1.2	15.1	15.1	8.9	15.1	16.3	313
West Bank and Gaza													
Yemen, Rep.	29.8	0.0				3.7	2.7	2.2	4.3	1.0	4.0	6.8	54
Yugoslavia, Fed. Rep[a]	40.0					285.0	3.0	151.0	1.0	0.0	21.0	244.0	744
Zaire	1.4	0.0	1.3			8.4	0.0	53.8	7.3	0.1	7.7	68.3	148
Zambia	185.0	0.0	19.3			45.7	4.9	6.0	4.3	0.5	7.2	9.8	283
Zimbabwe	101.0	47.8	1.9			96.8	4.0	4.4	4.9	2.9	5.2	13.3	282

World[b]	**5,756 t**	**1,006 t**	**655 t**	**1,216 t**	**94 t**	**6,436 t**	**231 t**	**1,611 t**	**1,336 t**	**209 t**	**871 t**	**2,781 t**	**22,106 t**
Low income	5,473 t	953 t	501 t	1,021 t	35 t	2,327 t	157 t	1,015 t	500 t	103 t	543 t	841 t	13,434 t
Excl. China & India	4,030 t	953 t	502 t	1,001 t	35 t	2,256 t	143 t	962 t	434 t	84 t	453 t	814 t	11,631 t
Middle income	136 t	32 t	68 t	148 t	9 t	2,350 t	54 t	291 t	535 t	56 t	169 t	818 t	4,658 t
Lower middle income	137 t	32 t	67 t	148 t	50 t	1,944 t	92 t	258 t	326 t	47 t	144 t	760 t	3,972 t
Upper middle income	−1 t	0 t	1 t	0 t	−41 t	406 t	−38 t	16 t	209 t	9 t	25 t	58 t	685 t
Low & middle income	5,609 t	984 t	569 t	1,169 t	44 t	5,782 t	211 t	1,306 t	1,035 t	159 t	712 t	1,659 t	18,097 t
East Asia & Pacific	857 t	136 t	0 t	227 t	0 t	152 t	15 t	62 t	141 t	33 t	87 t	120 t	1,832 t
Europe & Central Asia	111 t	36 t	0 t	3 t	0 t	1,890 t	55 t	183 t	18 t	6 t	40 t	337 t	2,679 t
Latin America & Carib.	198 t	62 t	0 t	0 t	44 t	467 t	92 t	59 t	462 t	29 t	69 t	152 t	1,589 t
Middle East & N. Africa	62 t	0 t	11 t	0 t	0 t	664 t	1 t	72 t	62 t	17 t	52 t	415 t	1,355 t
South Asia	1,593 t	290 t	0 t	939 t	0 t	169 t	11 t	169 t	104 t	28 t	145 t	109 t	3,557 t
Sub-Saharan Africa	2,788 t	462 t	559 t	0 t	0 t	2,069 t	38 t	761 t	278 t	53 t	329 t	657 t	7,994 t
High income	0 t	0 t	0 t	0 t	0 t	41 t	0 t	0 t	11 t	0 t	1 t	31 t	84 t

a. Includes net flows to the states of the former Yugoslavia: Bosnia and Herzegovina, Croatia, Macedonia FYR, and Slovenia. b. Includes data for economies not specified elsewhere. See *About the data* in the notes to the table.

About the data

Complementing table 6.9, this table shows concessional aid flows to developing countries from multilateral institutions as reported by the Development Assistance Committee (DAC) of the OECD. These institutions include multilateral development banks (for example, the World Bank and regional development banks), United Nations agencies, and regional groups such as the Commission of the European Communities (CEC).

Concessional flows from multilateral institutions can take the form of loans or grants. The data here cover resources provided through designated "soft loan windows," such as the World Bank Group's International Development Association (IDA) and the development funds of the regional development banks. IDA provides long-term, interest-free loans to the poorest countries to promote economic development; in 1996, 79 countries were eligible for IDA assistance.

The International Monetary Fund (IMF) provides concessional loans through the IMF Trust Fund, its Structural Adjustment Facility (SAF), and its Enhanced Structural Adjustment Facility (ESAF). ESAF, the successor to SAF (no SAF commitments have been made since 1994) provides assistance to help strengthen a country's balance of payments position and to foster economic growth in low-income member countries facing protracted balance of payments problems. ESAF loans cover a three-year period and carry an annual interest rate of 0.5 percent with a five-year grace period and 10-year maturity.

Resources for concessional lending come from contributions by member countries and retained earnings from the multilateral institutions' nonconcessional business. (Although some loans provided through the nonconcessional arms of the development banks may meet the DAC definition of concessional, they are not reported here. They are, however, included in table 6.12). Funding for United Nations agencies is provided by DAC member countries and other members of the United Nations to support a range of development and humanitarian activities, including support for refugees and peacekeeping operations in war-torn countries.

Aid not allocated by country or region (including administrative costs, research into development issues, and aid to nongovernmental organizations) is included in the world total; regional and income group totals therefore do not add up to the world total.

Definitions

- **Multilateral institutions** are organizations with governmental membership that conduct all or a significant part of their activities to promote development.
- **IDA** is the International Development Association, the soft loan window of the World Bank Group. ● **IMF** is the International Monetary Fund, which provides concessional loans through the Structural Adjustment Facility (SAF), the Enhanced Structural Adjustment Facility (ESAF), and the IMF Trust Fund. ● **AfDB** is the African Development Bank, which provides concessional loans through the African Development Fund.
- **ADB** is the Asian Development Bank, which provides concessional loans through the Asian Development Fund. ● **IDB** is the Inter-American Development Bank, which provides concessional loans through the Inter-American Development Fund for Special Operations. ● **CEC** is the Commission of the European Communities. Its development fund, the European Development Fund, provides assistance to developing countries that are signatories to the Lomé Convention. ● **Other international financial institutions** include the International Fund for Agricultural Development and the European Bank for Reconstruction and Development. ● **WFP** is the World Food Programme. ● **UNDP** is the United Nations Development Programme. ● **UNFPA** is the United Nations Population Fund. ● **UNICEF** is the United Nations Children's Fund. ● **Other United Nations agencies** include the United Nations High Commissioner for Refugees, the United Nations Relief and Works Agency for Palestine Refugees in the Near East, and the United Nations Regular Program for Technical Assistance.

Data sources

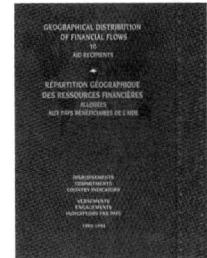

Data on aid are compiled by DAC and published in its annual statistical report, *Geographical Distribution of Financial Flows to Aid Recipients*, and in the DAC chairman's report, *Development Co-operation*. The OECD also makes its data available on diskette and magnetic tape and on the Internet.

$ millions, 1995	World Bank		IMF		African Development Bank		Asian Development Bank		Inter-American Development Bank		Others	
	IBRD	IDA	Nonconcessional	Concessional	Nonconcessional	Concessional	Nonconcessional	Concessional	Nonconcessional	Concessional	Nonconcessional	Concessional
Albania		43	−1	11							0	0
Algeria	294		304		25	0					−20	43
Angola		30	0	0	−1	0					0	0
Argentina	682		1,881						747	−5	0	0
Armenia	3	88	46	0							0	11
Australia			0									
Austria			0									
Azerbaijan	0	30	103	0							59	0
Bangladesh	−5	155	0	−61			0	244			0	−8
Belarus	11		182								−4	0
Belgium			0									
Benin		27	0	12	−1	20					1	13
Bolivia	−26	110	0	−1					44	34	99	4
Bosnia and Herzegovina	0	0	18	0							0	0
Botswana	−23		0		−9	−1					−3	9
Brazil	−539		−49						121	−7	0	0
Bulgaria	15		−246								−80	0
Burkina Faso		81	0	27	−3	10					−3	−4
Burundi		24	0	−9	−2	11					−1	−4
Cambodia		25	0	42			0	36			0	0
Cameroon	−85	31	7	0	2	0					−21	22
Canada			0									
Central African Republic		28	0	−7	0	0					0	1
Chad		41	0	6	0	13					0	0
Chile	−621	−1	−303						−1,115	−1	0	0
China	1,107	798	0	0			496	15			−4	6
Colombia	−176	−1	0						−63	−10	0	0
Congo	−17	−1	−2	0	0	0					0	0
Costa Rica	−39		−44						108	−11	−71	4
Côte d'Ivoire	−180	226	−86	181	6	16					2	−16
Croatia	29		93								−35	−12
Cuba												
Czech Republic	57		0								−52	38
Denmark			0									
Dominican Republic	−4	−1	−34						63	16	−5	−4
Ecuador	221	−1	−29						103	42	−16	−2
Egypt, Arab Rep.	−156	69	−95	0	−25	6					−23	84
El Salvador	5	−1	0						80	19	−19	−1
Eritrea		0	0	0	0	0					..	..
Estonia	18		30								43	0
Ethiopia[a]	−4	77	0	0	22	84					0	−3
Finland			0									
France			0									
Gabon	−8		5		121	76					−11	5
Gambia, The		11	0	−6	−2	3					0	2
Georgia	0	85	76	0							0	0
Germany			0									
Ghana	−15	234	−20	−46	−5	17	0	0	0	0	−5	−10
Greece			0									
Guatemala	−26		0						−1	6	−9	1
Guinea		8	0	1	−4	6					−1	−3
Guinea-Bissau		57	0	22	20	8					2	44
Haiti	.	39	2	−9					0	38	0	−3
Honduras	−51	76	−44	31					16	29	−14	5
Hong Kong												

$ millions, 1995	World Bank		IMF		African Development Bank		Asian Development Bank		Inter-American Development Bank		Others	
	IBRD	IDA	Nonconcessional	Concessional	Nonconcessional	Concessional	Nonconcessional	Concessional	Nonconcessional	Concessional	Nonconcessional	Concessional
Hungary	−63		−793								−342	76
India	−354	503	−1,719	0			233	17			−9	−11
Indonesia	90	−20	0				212	189			3	13
Iran, Islamic Rep.	79		0								−11	0
Iraq			0									
Ireland			0									
Israel			−99.6									
Italy			0									
Jamaica	−24		−85						13	−5	−2	10
Japan			0									
Jordan	81	−2	107								32	40
Kazakstan	107		141				24	40			0	0
Kenya	−100	150	0	−39	7	12					−3	4
Korea, Dem. Rep.												
Korea, Rep.	−317	−3	0									
Kuwait			0									
Kyrgyz Republic	0	81	0	46			0	34			−21	0
Lao PDR		27	0	16			0	56			0	5
Latvia	9		−3								7	5
Lebanon	47		0								5	18
Lesotho	11	7	0	−3	−2	7					0	3
Libya			0									
Lithuania	12		63								29	0
Macedonia, FYR	1	42	37	0							16	0
Madagascar	−4	69	−1	−14	0	−1					−2	−2
Malawi	−12	66	0	2	−5	17					−1	−1
Malaysia	−106		0				−15	0			−2	−1
Mali		80	−1	39	−1	46					−1	−3
Mauritania	−2	29	0	13	1	5					−4	24
Mauritius	−13	−1	0		−2	1					0	−1
Mexico	321		12,144						642	−8	0	0
Moldova	50		64								−30	26
Mongolia		8	−9	0			0	50			0	0
Morocco	78	−1	−100		−4	144					−13	118
Mozambique		160	0	−14	−3	42					0	7
Myanmar		−9	0	0			−1	−10			0	−4
Namibia	0		0		0	0						
Nepal		74	0	−8			0	46			0	4
Netherlands			0									
New Zealand			0									
Nicaragua	−15	17	−13	0					24	71	15	3
Niger		21	0	−10	−1	−3					0	2
Nigeria	−202	85	0	0	68	12					0	0
Norway			0									
Oman	−9		0								−5	27
Pakistan	52	218	109	−82			−6	321			−9	17
Panama	−40		−26						53	−4	0	0
Papua New Guinea	7	−2	34				−7	11			0	−1
Paraguay	−15	−1	0						42	19	−2	10
Peru	116		0						191	−8	107	23
Philippines	−21	8	−363				−26	7			0	−2
Poland	191		−1,394								−139	0
Portugal	−18		0									
Puerto Rico												
Romania	128		−316								185	0
Russian Federation	824		5,453								−244	−151

$ millions, 1995	World Bank		IMF		African Development Bank		Asian Development Bank		Inter-American Development Bank		Others	
	IBRD	IDA	Nonconcessional	Concessional	Nonconcessional	Concessional	Nonconcessional	Concessional	Nonconcessional	Concessional	Nonconcessional	Concessional
Rwanda		29	14	0	0	14					0	0
Saudi Arabia			0									
Senegal	−12	101	−41	42	−7	2					−7	−14
Sierra Leone	−1	42	0	16	0	28					0	17
Singapore			0									
Slovak Republic	8		−201								66	80
Slovenia	14		−3								−4	1
South Africa	0		0									
Spain			0									
Sri Lanka	−7	98	0	−34			0	79			0	0
Sudan		0	−35	−5	18	18					0	0
Sweden			0									
Switzerland			0									
Syrian Arab Republic	−13		0								−9	103
Tajikistan		0	0	0								
Tanzania	−34	148	0	−19	−13	47					1	1
Thailand	−55	−2	0				14	−1			22	20
Togo		17	−3	25	0	5					0	−3
Trinidad and Tobago	9		−44						92	0	−4	16
Tunisia	−65	−2	−15		132	0					7	32
Turkey	−460	−6	341								−225	−66
Turkmenistan	1		0								0	0
Uganda	−12	152	0	27	−4	29					−6	2
Ukraine	401		1,196								−3	0
United Arab Emirates			0									
United Kingdom			0									
United States			0									
Uruguay	−46		−10						12	14	6	0
Uzbekistan	162		161								84	0
Venezuela	−69		−462						143	2	−11	0
Vietnam		46	0	92			0	46			0	−1
West Bank and Gaza												
Yemen, Rep.		34	0	0							16	5
Yugoslavia, Fed. Rep.											..	..
Zaire		0	−1	0	0	0					0	0
Zambia	−50	207	−826	1,254	10	13					−31	2
Zimbabwe	−16	15	29	51	3	1					6	43
World	**1,099 t**	**4,929 t**	**15,080 t**	**1,600 t**								
Low income	−21 t	4,719 t	−2,423 t	1,604 t	108 t	481 t	723 t	937 t	30 t	157 t	−41 t	148 t
Excl. China & India	−774 t	3,418 t	−704 t	1,604 t	105 t	487 t	−6 t	905 t	30 t	157 t	−28 t	153 t
Middle income	1,455 t	213 t	17,604 t	−4 t	240 t	249 t	201 t	263 t	1,277 t	91 t	−712 t	571 t
Lower middle income	1,748 t	215 t	4,683 t	−4 t	121 t	172 t	216 t	263 t	778 t	98 t	−263 t	422 t
Upper middle income	−293 t	−2 t	12,921 t	0 t	119 t	77 t	−15 t	0 t	499 t	−7 t	−449 t	149 t
Low & middle income	1,434 t	4,932 t	15,181 t	1,600 t	348 t	730 t	924 t	1,200 t	1,307 t	248 t	−752 t	719 t
East Asia & Pacific	1,016 t	884 t	−338 t	150 t	0 t	0 t	672 t	411 t	0 t	0 t	13 t	32 t
Europe & Central Asia	1,519 t	364 t	5,047 t	57 t	0 t	0 t	24 t	74 t	0 t	0 t	−717 t	7 t
Latin America & Carib.	−342 t	257 t	12,844 t	34 t	0 t	0 t	0 t	0 t	1,307 t	248 t	79 t	61 t
Middle East & N. Africa	337 t	98 t	199 t	0 t	128 t	150 t	0 t	0 t	0 t	0 t	−21 t	470 t
South Asia	−314 t	1,054 t	−1,610 t	−184 t	0 t	0 t	228 t	715 t	0 t	0 t	−18 t	12 t
Sub-Saharan Africa	−782 t	2,275 t	−962 t	1,543 t	218 t	580 t	0 t	0 t	0 t	0 t	−88 t	137 t
High income	−335 t	−3 t	−100 t	0 t								

a. Includes Eritrea.

Figure 6.12a Net IBRD and IDA lending,
1970–95

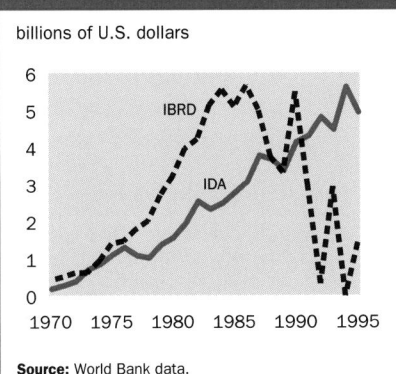

billions of U.S. dollars

Source: World Bank data.

About the data

The table shows concessional and nonconcessional lending by the major multilateral financial institutions—the World Bank, the International Monetary Fund (IMF), and the regional development banks—for the calendar year 1995. Unlike the data in the preceding tables, the data here come from the World Bank's Debtor Reporting System (DRS) and, except for the data for the World Bank, the IMF, the Asian Development Bank, and the African Development Bank, are based on debtor reports.

The multilateral development banks fund their nonconcessional lending operations primarily by selling low-interest, highly rated bonds (the World Bank, for example, has a AAA rating) backed by prudent lending and financial policies and the strong financial backing of their members. These funds are then on-lent at slightly higher interest rates, and with relatively long maturities (15–20 years), to developing countries. Lending terms vary with market conditions and the policies of the banks.

Concessional lending by the World Bank Group is carried out primarily through the International Development Association (IDA), although some loans by the International Bank for Reconstruction and Development (IBRD) are made on terms that qualify as concessional. Eligibility for IDA lending is based on estimates of average GNP per capita, which are revised annually. In 1995 countries with GNP per capita of $865 or less were eligible for IDA lending. The IMF makes concessional funds available through its Enhanced Structural Adjustment Facility (ESAF), the successor to the Structural Adjustment Facility, and through the IMF Trust Fund. Low-income countries that face protracted balance of payments problems are eligible for ESAF funds.

The regional development banks also maintain concessional, or soft loan, windows for funds. But the identity of these funds is not consistently recorded in the DRS. The tabulation of flows from these institutions as concessional and nonconcessional is therefore based on the Development Assistance Committee (DAC) definition. Under the DAC definition, concessional flows contain a grant element of at least 25 percent. The grant element of loans is evaluated assuming a nominal, market interest rate of 10 percent. The grant element of a loan carrying a 10 percent interest rate is nil, and for a grant, which requires no repayment, it is 100 percent. (See the notes to table 6.8 for further discussion of lending terms and the calculation of the grant element.) In some cases nonconcessional loans by these institutions may be on terms that meet the DAC definition of concessional; thus the figures here may not match tabulations based on other definitions.

Definitions

• **World Bank** consists of the IBRD and IDA. • **IMF nonconcessional lending** is the credit provided by the IMF to its members, principally to meet their balance of payments needs. • **IMF concessional assistance** is provided through the Enhanced Structural Adjustment Facility. • **African Development Bank,** based in Abidjan, Côte d'Ivoire, lends to all of Africa, including North Africa. • **Asian Development Bank,** based in Manila, Philippines, serves countries in South Asia and East Asia and the Pacific. • **Inter-American Development Bank,** based in Washington, D.C., is the principal development bank of the Americas. • **Others** is a residual category in the World Bank's Debtor Reporting System. It includes such institutions as the Caribbean Development Bank, European Investment Bank, and European Development Fund. • **Concessional** includes all grants and loans with a grant element of at least 25 percent according to DAC criteria. • **Nonconcessional** covers all other disbursements.

Data sources

Unlike tables 6.6–6.11, which are based on OECD DAC data, this table draws on data from the World Bank's Debtor Reporting System. These data are published annually in the World Bank's *Global Development Finance* (formerly *World Debt Tables*).

6.13 | Foreign labor and population in OECD countries

	Foreign population[a]				Foreign labor force			
	thousands		% of total population		% of total labor force		Participation rate %	%
	1990	1994	1990	1994	1990	1994	1990	1994
Austria	456 [b]	714 [b]	5.9	8.9	..	9.6	..	..
Belgium	905	922	9.1	9.1	7.5	8.1	49.7	55.1
Denmark	161	197	3.1	3.8	2.0	1.7	69.9	64.9
Finland	26	62	0.5	1.2	..	..	..	..
France	3,597	..	6.3	..	6.4	6.4	62.8	62.2
Germany	5,343 [c]	6,991	8.4 [c]	8.6	8.4	9.0	67.1	67.9
Ireland	80 [d]	..	2.3 [d]	..	2.6	2.9	56.4	60.9
Italy	781 [e]	923 [e]	1.4	1.6	..	..	..	..
Japan	1,075 [f]	1,354 [f]	0.9 [f]	1.1 [f]	..	..	..	..
Luxembourg	110	130 [g]	28.6	32.0 [g]	33.4	41.8	66.1	70.2
Netherlands	692	774	4.6	5.0	3.7	4.0	56.4	54.0
Norway	143 [h]	164 [h]	3.4 [h]	3.8 [h]	..	4.5	..	..
Portugal	108 [i]	157 [i]	1.1 [i]	1.6 [i]	..	..	..	..
Spain	279 [j]	461 [j]	0.7 [j]	1.2 [j]	..	0.6	..	..
Sweden	484	537	5.6	6.1	5.6	5.1 [k]	74.5	61.6 [k]
Switzerland	1,100 [l]	1,300 [l]	16.3	18.6	..	22.5	..	..
United Kingdom	1,723 [d]	1,946 [d]	3.2 [d]	3.4 [d]	3.5	3.6	70.6	66.4

	Foreign-born population[m]				Foreign-born labor force[n]			
	thousands		% of total population		% of total labor force		Participation rate %	%
	1990	1994	1990	1994	1990	1994	1990	1994
Australia	4,125 [o]	..	22.7 [o]	..	25.8	25.3 [k]	55.4	53.4 [k]
Canada	4,343 [o]	..	15.6 [o]	..	18.4 [p]	19.5 [o]	77.3 [p]	78.2 [o]
United States	19,767	24,557 [q]	7.9	9.3 [q]	9.4	..	73.7	..

a. Except for France, Japan, Portugal, and the United Kingdom, data are from population registers and refer to the population on December 31 of the years indicated. b. Annual average. c. Data refer to the Federal Republic of Germany before unification. d. Estimated from the annual labor force survey. e. Data are adjusted to take account of the regularizations in 1987–88 and 1990. f. Data refer to registered foreign nationals, who include foreigners staying in Japan for more than 90 days. g. Provisional data. h. Includes asylum seekers whose requests are being processed. i. Includes all foreigners who hold a valid residence permit. j. Data refer to foreigners with a residence permit. k. Data refer to 1993. l. Data refer to foreigners with an annual residence permit or with a settlement permit (permanent permit). m. Data are from the latest population census. n. Data are from labor force surveys except for Canada and the United States, for which data are from the latest population census. o. Data refer to 1991. p. Data refer to 1986. q. Data are from the U.S. Census Bureau March 1996 population survey and refer to 1996.

Migration's benefits—and costs

Today at least 125 million people live outside their country of origin. Each year 2–3 million new migrants—legal and illegal—leave developing countries. About half go to industrial countries. The foreign population in OECD countries has reached more than 60 million (legal), and the share of immigrants originating in developing countries is increasing.

In Australia, Canada, and the United States inflows from developing countries have risen slowly, reaching about 900,000 a year by 1993. In Western Europe a period of large-scale labor migration due to labor shortages in such countries as Germany and Switzerland was followed by a period of restricted migration after the oil shock of 1976, as the fear of recession induced return migration. A dip in the growth of the foreign population in the late 1970s and early 1980s was soon followed by a rise—to about 180,000 a year (Zimmermann 1995).

Today population growth in OECD countries is being driven by an increase in net migration and the natural increase of the population (excess of births over deaths), fostered by higher fertility rates among immigrants. Since 1987 more than 60 percent of the population increase in Western Europe has been due to migration. In North America migration accounted for about a quarter of the increase between 1982 and 1991.

International labor often benefits both the home country of the migrant, which receives remittances that boost the country's foreign exchange earnings, and the host country, which receives productive and less expensive labor. Remittances can be as much as 25–50 percent of export revenues, as in Bangladesh, Egypt, Greece, Pakistan, and Turkey. As many as 70 percent of recent migrants from developing countries perform unskilled labor that native workers prefer to avoid. Unskilled migrants, mainly from North Africa and Turkey, make up 60 percent and 80 percent of total migrant flows in France, and 80 percent in Germany. But inflows of unskilled migrants are regarded unfavorably when jobs are lost to immigrants or wages fall. In a period of economic downturn foreign workers are more vulnerable to unemployment than are native workers. Labor force participation is lower

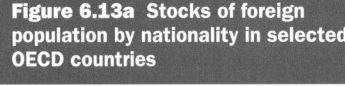

Figure 6.13a Stocks of foreign population by nationality in selected OECD countries

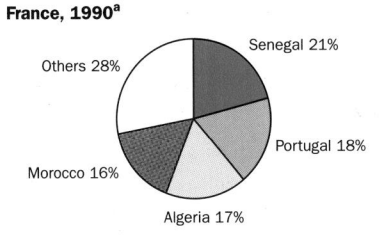

France, 1990[a]

- Senegal 21%
- Others 28%
- Portugal 18%
- Morocco 16%
- Algeria 17%

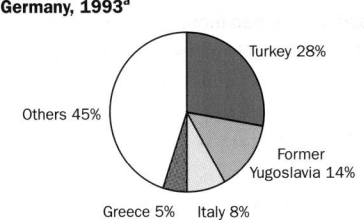

Germany, 1993[a]

- Turkey 28%
- Others 45%
- Former Yugoslavia 14%
- Greece 5%
- Italy 8%

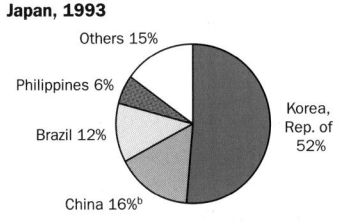

Japan, 1993

- Others 15%
- Philippines 6%
- Brazil 12%
- Korea, Rep. of 52%
- China 16%[b]

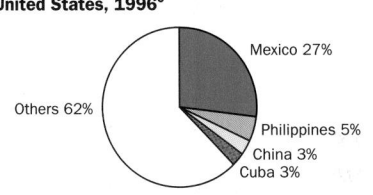

United States, 1996[c]

- Mexico 27%
- Others 62%
- Philippines 5%
- China 3%
- Cuba 3%

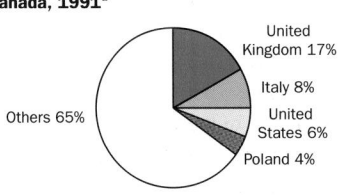

Canada, 1991[d]

- United Kingdom 17%
- Italy 8%
- Others 65%
- United States 6%
- Poland 4%

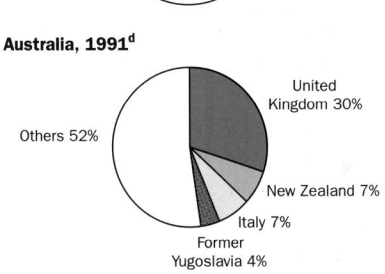

Australia, 1991[d]

- United Kingdom 30%
- Others 52%
- New Zealand 7%
- Italy 7%
- Former Yugoslavia 4%

a. Data are from population censuses.
b. Includes Taiwan, China.
c. Data refer to immigrant population by place of birth, according to census results of 1996.
d. Data refer to immigrant population by place of birth, according to census results of 1991.
Source: OECD 1995.

among foreign workers than among native workers, and notably lower among foreign women than among native women. In an attempt to control the quality as well as the quantity of foreign workers, OECD countries are increasingly issuing temporary work permits that require workers to return home when the permits expire.

Compared with immigrants in earlier periods, recent immigrants have more diversified cultural, economic, and social backgrounds, requiring OECD countries to adopt policies to help them integrate with the society and the labor market. In parallel, these countries are adopting policies aimed at strictly controlling legal and illegal flows, tightening border controls, and restricting entry by asylum seekers. In 1995 the number of asylum seekers dropped to 460,000 from the 1992 peak of 825,000, as a result of policy changes to curb the inflow of those whose sole purpose in seeking asylum may be economic.

About the data

The data here are based on national definitions and data collection practices and are not fully comparable across countries. Japan and the European members of the OECD traditionally have defined foreigners by nationality of descent. Australia, Canada, and the United States use the criterion of place of birth, which is closer to the concept of the immigrant stock as defined by the United Nations. However, very few countries apply only one criterion in all circumstances. For this and other reasons, data based on the concept of foreign nationality and data based on the concept of foreign-born cannot be completely reconciled.

Statistics on the stock and flow of the foreign labor force are also problematic. Countries use different permit systems to gather information on immigrants. Some countries issue a single permit for both residence and work, while others issue separate residence and work permits. Differences in immigration laws across countries, particularly with respect to immigrants' access to the labor market, greatly affect the recording and measurement of migration and reduce the comparability of raw data at the international level.

Definitions

- **Foreign population** is the stock of foreign national or foreign-born residents in a country. ● **Foreign labor force as a percentage of total labor force** is the percentage of foreign or foreign-born workers in a country's workforce. ● **Foreign labor force participation rate** is the percentage of foreign population of working age that is economically active.

Data sources

International migration data are collected by the OECD through information provided by national correspondents to the Continuous Reporting System on Migration (SOPEMI) network, which provides an annual overview of trends and policies. Data appear in the OECD's *Trends in International Migration* (1995).

Credits

This book has drawn on a wide range of World Bank reports and numerous external sources. These are listed in the bibliography that follows this note. Many people inside and outside the World Bank helped in redesigning and in writing and producing the *World Development Indicators*. This note identifies those who made specific contributions. Numerous others, too many to acknowledge here, helped in many ways for which the team is extremely grateful.

Section 1—World view was prepared by K. M. Vijayalakshmi with help from Sulekha Patel. The content of the section owes much to T. N. Srinivasan's suggestions on table topics and indicators. The introductory text was drafted by K. Sarwar Lateef. The charts and text that follow in *Our changing world* were conceptualized by Bruce Ross-Larson.

Section 2—People was prepared by Sulekha Patel in partnership with the World Bank's Human Development Network and in collaboration with the former Poverty and Social Policy Department and the Poverty and Human Resources Division of the Policy and Research Department. We would particularly like to acknowledge the encouragement and support we received from Jane Armitage, Ishrat Husain, Emmanuel Jimenez, Oey Astra Meesook, and Minh Chau Nguyen at all stages of the production. Aelim Chi helped to prepare the data for this section. Extensive consultations were held with counterparts from the ILO, the WHO, UNICEF, and UNESCO at various stages of production. The introduction to the section was written by Sulekha Patel. Substantial inputs to the section were provided by Eduard Bos (demography), Zafiris Tzannatos (labor force and employment), Martin Ravallion and Shaohua Chen (poverty and income distribution), Bertha Namfua (education), and M. Subramanian of WHO in Geneva and Alexander Preker (health). Vivian Hon was instrumental in the smooth transfer of health data from the Human Development Network, and Farhad Mehran of the ILO in Geneva and Mildred Weiss in the smooth transfer of labor force and employment data. David de Ferranti of the Human Development Council facilitated the data review by the Bank's regional staff. Extensive comments and suggestions were received from Eduard Bos, Mariam Claeson, Jeffrey Hammer, Elizabeth King, Marlaine Lockheed, Andrew Mason, Harry Patrinos, Alexander Preker, Lant Pritchett, George Psacharopoulos, Martin Rama, Martin Ravallion, Eluned Roberts-Schweitzer, T. Sverrir Sigurdsson, Jee-Peng Tan, Tara Vishwanath, and Michael Ward at various stages from design to production.

Section 3—Environment was prepared by Saeed Ordoubadi in partnership with the World Bank's Environmentally and Socially Sustainable Development Network and in collaboration with the Policy and Research Department's Environment, Infrastructure, and Agriculture Division. The World Resources Institute was consulted in the initial phases of the design and made helpful contri-

butions. Jihee Kim assisted with the data preparation. John Dixon, Jan Bakkes, Kirk Hamilton, Arundhati Kunte, and Michael Ward provided invaluable comments and guidance in all stages of the work, from design to final production. Andrew Steer provided considerable encouragement and support and helped ensure the substantial ownership the World Bank's Environment Department feels for this section. The Environment Department devoted substantial staff resources to the book, for which we are very grateful. John Dixon wrote the introduction to the section, and inputs were provided by Stefano Pagiola (biodiversity); Arundhati Kunte (water); Michael Corbin, Kirk Hamilton, and Shane Streifel (energy); Gordon Hughes and David Shaman (air pollution); and Sergio Margulis (government commitment). The team received valuable comments at various stages from Jean Aden, Charles Di Leva, Lev Freinkman, Jeffrey Gutman, Rafik Hirji, Todd Johnson, Victor Loksha, Hughes Ravenel, Colin Rees, Jitu Shah, David Wheeler, Tony Whitten, and John Williamson.

Section 4—Economy was prepared by K. M. Vijayalakshmi and Eric Swanson in close collaboration with the Macroeconomic Data Team of the Development Data Group, led by Robin Lynch, and with the Macroeconomics and Growth Division of the Policy Research Department. The introduction to this section was written by K. Sarwar Lateef. Substantial inputs to the section were provided by Michael Ward (national accounts); Hans Binswanger and Chandra Hardy (agriculture); Alexander Yeats (trade); Caroline Farah (service exports); Sultan Ahmad and Yonas Biru (structure of consumption in PPP terms); Amar Bhattacharya, William Easterly, and Chandra Hardy (macroeconomic indicators); Deena Khatkhate (monetary indicators); Jim McKee and Jong-goo Park (balance of payments); and Punam Chuhan and Robert Powell (external debt). The national accounts and balance of payments data for low- and middle-income economies are gathered from the World Bank's regional staff through the annual Unified Survey. Boris Blazic-Metzner, Maja Bresslauer, Raquel Fok, Olga Ivanova, Taranjit Kaur, Jong-goo Park, Bessie Smith, and Vilay Soulatha worked on updating, estimating, and validating the databases for national accounts, trade, and the balance of payments. The national accounts data for OECD countries were processed by Abdel Stambouli and reviewed by Robert King, Robert Lynn, and Mick Riordan. Betty Dow helped with the data from the FAO. The external debt tables were prepared by the Financial Data Team, led by Punam Chuhan, and were reviewed by Nevin Fahmy and Shelley Fu. Systems support was provided by Shelley Fu, John Herring, Sup Lee, and Ibrahim Levent.

Section 5—States and markets was prepared by David Cieslikowski in partnership with the World Bank's Finance, Private Sector, and Infrastructure Network, the International Finance Corporation, and the Multilateral Investment Guarantee Agency and in close collaboration with the Finance and Private Sector Development and Public Economics Divisions of the Policy Research Department. Mildred Weiss contributed substantially to the overall preparation of this section. Shantayanan Devarajan, William Easterly, Andrew Ewing, Fred Jasperson, Catherine Kleynhoff, Guy Pfeffermann, and Mary Shirley contributed substantially to the design and commented on the execution. The introduction to this section was drafted by Bruce Ross-Larson. Substantial inputs were made by Punam Chuhan, Nevin Fahmy, Shelley Fu, John Herring, Ibrahim Levent, and Malvina Pollock (private capital flows and external debt); Robert Shakotko and Peter Wall (stock markets); Luke Haggerty (state enterprises); Sarath Rajapatirana (relative prices); Azita Amjadi, Ulrich Reincke, Bessie Smith, Eric Swanson, and Alexander Yeats (trade); Deena Khatkhate, Asli Demirgüç-Kunt, and Ross Levine (financial sector); Carlos Braga and Michael Minges of the ITU (communications and information); and Christine Kessides (transport).

Section 6—Global links was prepared by Aelim Chi and Eric Swanson in collaboration with other staff in the International Economics Department and with special assistance from the OECD's Development Cooperation Directorate. Takamasa Akiyama, Betty Dow, Malvina Pollock, Alan Winters, and Alexander Yeats helped considerably in the design of this section and advised on its content. The introduction to the section was drafted by Kim Murrell. Substantial inputs were provided by Milan Brahmbhatt and William Marcus (integration); Azita Amjadi and Alexander Yeats (trade); Ulrich Reinke (Uruguay Round tariff reductions); Don Mitchell (commodity prices); Nevin Fahmy, Jean-Louis Grolleau of the OECD, Weili Gu, Chandra Hardy, Ibrahim Levent, and Malvina Pollock (aid); and Cecile Thoreau of the OECD (migration). Extensive comments and suggestions were received from Takamasa Akiyama, Richard Carey of the OECD, Punam Chuhan, Alma Conty, Brian Hammond of the OECD, and Alexander Shakow.

Other parts—The maps on the inside covers were prepared by Jeff Lecksell. The section on *Partners* was coordinated and edited by Eric Swanson. *Acronyms and abbreviations* was prepared by Estela Zamora. The *Users guide* was prepared by David Cieslikowski. *Primary data documentation* was coordinated and written by David Cieslikowski. *Statistical methods* was written by Eric Swanson. The bibliography was prepared by Mila Divino. The index of indicators was laboriously collated by Eric Swanson.

Systems support—Mehdi Akhlaghi was responsible for database management and programming and overall systems support. In this he drew on the Development Data Group's Systems Upgrade Team, led by Henry Burt, and in particular on Reza Farivari.

Administrative assistance and office technology support—Estela Zamora provided excellent administrative assistance. She was supported by Karen Adams, Moira Coleridge-Taylor, Elfrida O'Reilly-Campbell, Funke Orimoloye, and Premi Rathan Raj. Office technology support was provided by Yusri Harun, Nacer Megherbi, Shahin Outadi, and Paulette Shelton.

Design, production, and editing—David Cieslikowski coordinated all aspects of the production of the book with the American Writing Corporation team, led by Laurel Morais. Bruce Ross-Larson of American Writing contributed much to both the content and the visual design for the *World Development Indicators* and the *Atlas*. Bruce and the other staff at American Writing did the editing, layout, and design. In particular, we would like to thank their design team of Peter Grundy and Kim Bieler, the editing team of Alison Strong and Paul Holtz, the desktopping team of Laurel Morais, Damon Iacovelli, and Christian Perez, and the production team of Sandra Cutshall, Kelli Ashley, Erika Schelble, and Wendy Guyette.

Client services—The Development Data Group's Client Services Team, led by Elizabeth Crayford, contributed to the design and planning of the book and helped coordinate with the Office of the Publisher.

External Affairs—Connie Eysenck, Stephanie Gerard, and Carol Rosen in the Office of the Publisher helped with the design and publication of the *World Development Indicators*, the *Atlas*, and the related CD-ROM. Caroline Anstey, Anthony Gaeta, Brett Kitchen, and Carlos Rossel of the External Affairs Vice Presidency assisted with the development of a communications strategy.

The Atlas—Production was managed by K. M. Vijayalakshmi. The preparation of data benefited from the work on corresponding sections in the *World Development Indicators*. William Prince assisted with systems support and production of tables and graphs. Jeff Lecksell produced the maps.

World Development Indicators CD-ROM—Design, programming, and production were carried out by Reza Farivari (the project leader) and his team: Mehdi Akhlaghi, Azita Amjadi, Elizabeth Crayford, Asieh Kehyari, Angelo Kostopoulos, and William Prince.

A number of people outside the Bank reviewed early outlines of the book. We particularly wish to acknowledge comments and suggestions from Stephen Commins, Ashok V. Desai, Michael A. Edwards, and Tagi Sagafi-nejad.

Bibliography

Ahmad, Sultan. 1992. "Regression Estimates of Per Capita GDP Based on Purchasing Power Parities." Policy Research Working Paper 956. World Bank, International Economics Department, Washington, D.C.

———. 1994. "Improving Inter-Spatial and Inter-Temporal Comparability of National Accounts." *Journal of Development Economics* 44:53–75.

American Automobile Manufacturers Association. 1995. *World Motor Vehicle Data.* Detroit.

Armington, Paul, and Yuri Dikhanov. 1996. "Multivariate Normalization of Infrastructure (e.g. Roads) for Comparative Purposes." World Bank, International Economics Department, Washington, D.C.

Berhrman, Jere R., and Mark R. Rosenzweig. 1994. "Caveat Emptor: Cross-Country Data on Education and the Labor Force." *Journal of Development Economics* 44:147–71.

Bobadilla, José Luis, Peter Cowley, Philip Musgrove, and Helen Saxenian. 1994. "Design, Content and Financing of an Essential Package of Health Services." In Christopher Murray and others, eds., *Global Comparative Assessments in the Health Sector: Disease Burden, Expenditures and Intervention Packages.* Geneva: World Health Organization.

Bos, Eduard, My T. Vu, Ernest Massiah, and Rodolfo Bulatao. 1994. *World Population Projections 1994–95.* Baltimore: Johns Hopkins University Press.

Braga, C.A. Primo, and Alexander Yeats. 1992. "How Minilateral Trading Arrangements May Affect the Post–Uruguay Round World." World Bank, International Economics Department, Washington, D.C.

Caiola, Marcello. 1995. *A Manual for Country Economists.* Training Series 1, vol. 1. Washington, D.C.: International Monetary Fund.

Cassen, Robert, and associates. 1986. *Does Aid Work?* Report to an Intergovernmental Task Force on Concessional Flows. Oxford: Clarendon Press.

Chamie, Joseph. 1994. "Demography: Population Databases in Development Analysis." *Journal of Development Economics* 44:131–46.

Chellaraj, Gnanaraj, Olusoji Adeyi, Alexander S. Preker, and Ellen Goldstein. 1996. *Trends in Health Status, Services, and Finance: The Transition in Central and Eastern Europe.* Vol. 2, *Statistical Annex.* World Bank Technical Paper 348. Washington, D.C.

Council of Europe. 1995. *Recent Demographic Developments in Europe and North America.* Strasbourg: Council of Europe Press.

Currency Data & Intelligence, Inc. Various issues. *Global Currency Report* (monthly). Brooklyn, N.Y.

Dasgupta, Partha. 1993. *An Inquiry into Well-Being and Destitution.* Oxford: Clarendon Press.

Dasgupta, Partha, and Martin Weale. 1992. "On Measuring the Quality of Life." *World Development* 20:119–31.

Davis, Lester. 1982. *Technology Intensity of U.S. Output and Trade.* Washington, D.C.: U.S. Department of Commerce.

Deininger, Klaus, and Lyn Squire. 1996. "A New Data Set Measuring Income Inequality." *World Bank Economic Review* 10(3):565–91.

Demirgüç-Kunt, Asli, and Ross Levine. 1996a. "Stock Market Development and Financial Intermediaries: Stylized Facts." *World Bank Economic Review* 10(2):291–321.

——— 1996b. "Stock Markets, Corporate Finance, and Economic Growth: An Overview." *World Bank Economic Review* 10(2):223–39.

Drucker, Peter F. 1994. "The Age of Social Transformation." *Atlantic Monthly* 274 (November).

Euromoney. 1996. "Asia's economies start to slip." September, pp. 200–03.

EUROSTAT (Statistical Office of the European Communities). Various years. *Demographic Statistics.* Luxembourg.

———. Various years. *Statistical Yearbook.* Luxembourg.

Evenson, Robert E., and Carl E. Pray. 1994. "Measuring Food Production (with reference to South Asia)." *Journal of Development Economics* 44:173–97.

Faiz, Asif, Christopher S. Weaver, and Michael P. Walsh. 1996. *Air Pollution from Motor Vehicles: Standards and Technologies for Controlling Emissions.* Washington, D.C.: World Bank.

FAO (Food and Agriculture Organization). 1986. "Inter-Country Comparisons of Agricultural Production Aggregates." Economic and Social Development Paper 61. Rome.

———. 1990. "Tobacco: Supply, Demand and Trade Projections 1995 and 2000." Economic and Social Development Paper 86. Rome.

———. 1996. *Food Aid in Figures 1994.* Vol. 12. Rome.

———. Various years. *Fertilizer Yearbook.* FAO Statistics Series. Rome.

———. Various years. *Production Yearbook.* FAO Statistics Series. Rome.

———. Various years. *Trade Yearbook.* FAO Statistics Series. Rome.

Finger, J. Michael, Merlinda Ingco, and Ulrich Reincke. 1996. *The Uruguay Round: Statistics on Tariff Concessions Given and Received.* Washington, D.C.: World Bank.

Fischer, Stanley. 1993. "The Role of Macroeconomic Factors in Growth." *Journal of Monetary Economics* 32:485–512.

Fischer, Stanley, and William Easterly. 1990. "The Economics of the Government Budget Constraint." *World Bank Research Observer* 5(2):127–42.

Fredriksen, Birger. 1991. "An Introduction to the Analysis of Student Enrollment and Flows Statistics." PHREE Background Paper Series 91/39. World Bank, Washington, D.C.

Gannon, Colin, and Zmarak Shalizi. 1995. "The Use of Sectoral and Project Performance Indicators in Bank-Financed Transport Operations." TWU Discussion Paper 21. World Bank, Transportation, Water, and Urban Development Department, Washington, D.C.

GATT (General Agreement on Tariffs and Trade). 1966. *International Trade 1965.* Geneva.

———. 1989. *International Trade 1988–89.* Geneva.

Goldfinger, Charles. 1994. *L'utile et le futile: L'économie de l'immatériel.* Paris: Editions Odile Jacob.

Goldstein, Ellen, Alexander S. Preker, Olusoji Adeyi, and Gnanaraj Chellaraj. 1996. *Trends in Health Status, Services, and Finance: The Transition in Central and Eastern Europe.* Vol. 1. World Bank Technical Paper 341. Washington, D.C.

Hatter, Victoria L. 1985. *U.S. High-Technology Trade and Competitiveness.* Washington, D.C.: U.S. Department of Commerce.

Heck, W.W. 1989. "Assessment of Crop Losses from Air Pollutants in the U.S." In J.J. McKenzie and M.T. El Ashry, eds., *Air Pollution's Toll on Forests and Crops.* New Haven, Conn.: Yale University Press.

Heston, Alan. 1994. "A Brief Review of Some Problems in Using National Accounts Data in Level of Output Comparisons and Growth Studies." *Journal of Development Economics* 44:29–52.

Heyneman, Stephen P. 1996. "The Quality of Education in the Middle East and North Africa." EMT Working Paper Series No. 3. World Bank, Europe and Central Asia, and Middle East and North Africa Regions Technical Department, Washington, D.C.

Hill, M. Anne, and Elizabeth M. King. 1993. "Women's Education in Developing Countries: An Overview." In Elizabeth M. King and M. Anne Hill, eds., *Women's Education in Developing Countries.* Baltimore: Johns Hopkins University Press.

ICAO (International Civil Aviation Organization). 1996. "Civil Aviation Statistics of the World: 1995." *ICAO Statistical Yearbook.* 21st ed. Montreal.

IEA (International Energy Agency). 1996a. *Energy Statistics and Balances of Non-OECD Countries 1993–94.* Paris.

———. 1996b. *Energy Statistics of OECD Countries 1993–94.* Paris.

IFC (International Finance Corporation). 1996a. *Emerging Stock Markets Factbook 1996.* Washington, D.C.

———. 1996b. *Trends in Private Investment in Developing Countries 1996.* Washington, D.C.

ILO (International Labour Organisation). 1990a. *ILO Manual on Concepts and Methods.* Geneva: International Labour Office.

———. 1990b. *Yearbook of Labour Statistics: Retrospective Edition of Population Censuses 1945–89.* Geneva: International Labour Office.

———. Various years. *Sources and Methods: Labour Statistics.* (Formerly *Statistical Sources and Methods.*) Geneva: International Labour Office.

———. Various years. *Yearbook of Labour Statistics.* Geneva: International Labour Office.

IMF (International Monetary Fund). 1977. *Balance of Payments Manual.* 4th ed. Washington, D.C.

———. 1986. *A Manual on Government Finance Statistics.* Washington, D.C.

———. 1993. *Balance of Payments Manual.* 5th ed. Washington, D.C.

———. 1995. *Balance of Payments Compilation Guide.* Washington, D.C.

———. 1996a. *Balance of Payments Textbook.* Washington, D.C.

———. 1996b. "Manual on Monetary and Financial Statistics." Washington, D.C.

———. Various years. *Balance of Payments Statistics Yearbook.* Parts 1 and 2. Washington, D. C.

———. Various years. *Direction of Trade Statistics Yearbook.* Washington, D.C.

———. Various years. *Government Finance Statistics Yearbook.* Washington, D.C.

———. Various issues. *International Financial Statistics* (monthly). Washington, D.C.

———. Various years. *International Financial Statistics Yearbook.* Washington, D.C.

Institutional Investor. 1996. September. New York.

International Road Federation. 1995. *World Road Statistics 1990–1994.* Geneva.

International Telecommunication Union. 1995. *World Telecommunication Development Report.* Geneva.

International Working Group of External Debt Compilers (Bank for International Settlements, International Monetary Fund, Organization for Economic Cooperation and Development, and World Bank). 1987. *External Debt Definitions.* Washington, D.C.

Inter-Secretariat Working Group on National Accounts (Commission of the European Communities, International Monetary Fund, Organization for Economic Cooperation and Development, United Nations, and World Bank). 1993. *System of National Accounts.* Brussels, Luxembourg, New York, and Washington, D.C.

IUCN (World Conservation Union). 1993. *Red List of Threatened Animals 1994.* Edited by B. Groombridge. Gland, Switzerland.

Journal of Development Economics. 1994. Special issue on database for development analysis. Edited by T.N. Srinivasan. Vol. 44, no. 1.

Klugman, Jeni, and George Schieber. 1996. *A Survey of Health Reform in Central Asia.* World Bank Technical Paper 344. Washington, D.C.

Kravis, Irving B. 1970. "Trade as a Handmaiden of Growth." *Economic Journal* (December).

Krueger, Anne O., Constantine Michalopoulos, and Vernon W. Ruttan. 1989. *Aid and Development.* Baltimore: Johns Hopkins University Press.

Levine, Ross, and Sara Zervos. 1996. "Stock Market Development and Long-Run Growth." *World Bank Economic Review* 10(2):323–40.

Lewis, Stephen R., Jr. 1989. "Primary Exporting Countries." In Hollis Chenery and T.N. Srinivasan, eds., *Handbook of Development Economics.* Vol. 2. Amsterdam: North Holland.

Lim, Lin Lean. 1996. *More and Better Jobs for Women: An Action Guide.* An ILO follow-up to the fourth World Conference on Women and the World Summit for Social Development. Geneva: International Labour Office.

Lockheed, Marlaine E., Adriaan M. Verspoor, and associates. 1991. *Improving Primary Education in Developing Countries.* New York: Oxford University Press.

Low, Patrick, and Alexander Yeats. 1994. "Nontariff Measures and Developing Countries: Has the Uruguay Round Leveled the Playing Field?" Policy Research Working Paper 1353. World Bank, International Economics Department, Washington, D.C.

Midgley, Peter. 1994. *Urban Transport in Asia: An Operational Agenda for the 1990s.* World Bank Technical Paper 224. Washington, D.C.

Moody's Investors Service. 1996. *Sovereign, Subnational and Sovereign-Guaranteed Issuers.* November. New York.

Morgenstern, O. 1963. *On the Accuracy of Economic Observations.* Princeton, N.J.: Princeton University Press.

Murray, Christopher, Ramesh Govindaraj, and Gnanaraj Chellaraj. 1994. "Global Domestic Expenditures in Health." Background paper 13 to *World Development Report 1993.* World Bank, Washington, D.C.

OECD (Organization for Economic Cooperation and Development). 1985. "Measuring Health Care 1960–1983: Expenditure, Costs, Performance." OECD Social Policy Studies 2. Paris.

———. 1989. "Health Care Expenditure and Other Data: An International Compendium from the OECD." *Health Care Financing Review.* Annual supplement. Paris.

———. 1995. *Trends in International Migration: Continuous Reporting System on Migration.* 1994 Annual Report. Paris.

———. 1996a. *Development Assistance: Efforts and Policies of the Members of the Development Assistance Committee.* Paris.

———. 1996b. *Development Co-operation: 1995 Report.* Paris.

———. 1996c. *Geographical Distribution of Financial Flows to Aid Recipients: Disbursements, Commitments, Country Indicators, 1990–1994.* Paris.

———. 1996d. *National Accounts 1960–1994.* Vol. 1, *Main Aggregates.* Paris.

———. 1996e. *National Accounts 1960–1994.* Vol. 2, *Detailed Tables.* Paris.

———. 1996f. "Shaping the 21st Century: The Contribution of Development Cooperation." Paris.

Political Risk Services. 1996. *International Country Risk Guide.* December. East Syracuse, N.Y.

Price Waterhouse. 1996a. *Corporate Taxes: A Worldwide Summary.* New York.

———. 1996b. *Individual Taxes: A Worldwide Summary.* New York.

Psacharopoulos, George. 1994. "Returns to Investment in Education: A Global Update." *World Development* 22(9):1325–43.

———. 1995. *Building Human Capital for Better Lives.* Washington, D.C.: World Bank.

Ravallion, Martin. 1996. "Poverty and Growth: Lessons from 40 Years of Data on India's Poor." DEC Notes No. 20. World Bank, Development Economics Vice Presidency, Washington, D.C.

Ravallion, Martin, and Shaohua Chen. 1996. "What Can New Survey Data Tell Us about the Recent Changes in Living Standards in Developing and Transitional Economies?" World Bank, Policy Research Department, Washington, D.C.

———. Forthcoming. "What Can New Survey Data Tell Us about Recent Changes in Distribution and Poverty?" *World Bank Economic Review.*

Ruggles, R. 1994. "Issues Relating to the UN System of National Accounts and Developing Countries." *Journal of Development Economics* 44(1):87–102.

Schultz, T. Paul. 1993. "Returns to Women's Education." In Elizabeth M. King and M. Anne Hill, eds, *Women's Education in Developing Countries.* Baltimore: Johns Hopkins University Press.

Sen, A. 1988. "The Concept of Development." In Hollis Chenery and T.N. Srinivasan, eds., *Handbook of Development Economics.* Vol. 1. Amsterdam: North Holland.

Shapiro, Harvey. 1996. "Restoration Drama." *Institutional Investor* 21 (September):9.

Shiklovanov, Igor. 1993. "World Fresh Water Resources." In Peter H. Gleick, ed., *Water in Crisis: A Guide to Fresh Water Resources.* New York: Oxford University Press.

Srinivasan, T.N. 1991. "Development Thought, Policy, and Strategy, Then and Now." Background paper to *World Development Report 1991.* World Bank, Washington, D.C.

———. 1994. "Database for Development Analysis: An Overview." *Journal of Development Economics* 44(1):3–28.

Standard & Poor's. 1996. *Credit Week.* November. New York.

Syrquin, Moshe. 1988. "Patterns of Structural Change." In Hollis Chenery and T.N. Srinivasan, eds., *Handbook of Development Economics.* Vol. 1. Amsterdam: North Holland.

Tanzi, Vito, and Ludger Schuknecht. 1995. "The Growth of Government and the Reform of the State in Industrial Countries." International Monetary Fund Working Paper 95/130. Washington, D.C.

UNAIDS. 1996. "The HIV/AIDS Situation in Mid-1996." Fact Sheet. July 1. Geneva.

UNCTAD (United Nations Conference on Trade and Development). 1987. *A Statistical Analysis of Trade Control Measures of Developing Countries.* Supplement to *Handbook of Trade Control Measures of Developing Countries.* Geneva.

———. 1994. *Directory of Import Regimes.* 2 vols. Geneva.

———. Various years. *Handbook of International Trade and Development Statistics.* Geneva.

UNEP (United Nations Environment Programme). 1991. *Urban Air Pollution.* Nairobi.

UNEP (United Nations Environment Programme) and WHO (World Health Organization). 1992. *Urban Air Pollution in Megacities of the World.* Cambridge, Mass.: Blackwell.

———. 1995. *City Air Quality Trends.* Nairobi, Kenya.

UNESCO (United Nations Educational, Scientific, and Cultural Organization). 1995a. *Statistical Yearbook.* Paris: UNESCO and Oxford University Press.

———. 1995b. *World Education Report*. Paris: UNESCO and Oxford University Press.

UNICEF (United Nations Children's Fund). 1997. *The State of the World's Children 1997*. New York: Oxford University Press.

UNIDO (United Nations Industrial Development Organization). 1996. *International Yearbook of Industrial Statistics 1996*. Vienna.

United Nations. 1947. *Measurement of National Income and the Construction of Social Accounts*. New York.

———. 1968. *A System of National Accounts: Studies and Methods*. Series F. No. 2. Rev. 3. New York.

———. 1985. *National Accounts Statistics: Compendium of Income Distribution Statistics*. New York.

———. 1990. *Assessing the Nutritional Status of Young Children*. National Household Survey Capability Programme. New York.

———. 1993. *International Trade Statistics Yearbook*. Vol. 1. New York.

———. 1995. *World Urbanization Prospects: The 1994 Revision*. New York.

———. Various years. *Energy Statistics Yearbook*. New York.

———. Various issues. *Monthly Bulletin of Statistics*. New York.

———. Various years. *National Income Accounts*. Statistics Division. New York.

———. Various years. *Statistical Yearbook*. New York.

———. Various years. *Update on the Nutrition Situation*. Administrative Committee on Coordination, Subcommittee on Nutrition. Geneva.

United Nations Department of Economic and Social Information and Policy Analysis. 1996. *World Population Prospects: The 1996 Edition*. New York.

———. Various years. *Levels and Trends of Contraceptive Use*. New York.

———. Various years. *Population and Vital Statistics Report*. New York.

UNRISD (United Nations Research Institute for Social Development). 1977. *Research Data Bank of Development Indicators*. Vol. 4, *Notes on the Indicators*. Report no. 77.2. Geneva.

U.S. Bureau of the Census. 1996. *World Population Profile 1996*. Washington, D.C.: U.S. Government Printing Office.

Walsh, Michael P. 1994. "Motor Vehicle Pollution Control: An Increasingly Critical Issue for Developing Countries." World Bank, Washington, D.C.

WHO (World Health Organization). 1977. *International Classification of Diseases, Ninth Revision*. Geneva.

———. 1990. *World Health Statistics Quarterly* 43(4).

———. 1991. *Maternal Mortality: A Global Factbook*. Geneva.

———. 1994. *Progress towards Health for All: Statistics of Member States*. Geneva.

———. 1995. *World Health Statistics Quarterly* 48(3/4).

———. 1996a. "HIV/AIDS Data." February 1. Geneva.

———. 1996b. *World Health Report 1996*. Geneva.

———. Various years. *World Health Statistics Annual*. Geneva.

WHO (World Health Organization) and UNICEF (United Nations Children's Fund). 1996. *Revised 1990 Estimates on Maternal Mortality: A New Approach*. Geneva.

Windham, Douglas M. 1988. *Indicators of Educational Effectiveness and Efficiency*. Tallahassee, Fla.: Florida State University, Educational Efficiency Clearinghouse.

World Bank. 1988. *World Development Report 1988: Public Finance in Development*. New York: Oxford University Press.

———. 1990. *World Development Report 1990: Poverty*. New York: Oxford University Press.

———. 1991a. *Developing the Private Sector: The World Bank's Experience and Approach*. Washington, D.C.

———. 1991b. *World Development Report 1991: The Challenge of Development*. New York: Oxford University Press.

———. 1992. *World Development Report 1992: Development and the Environment*. New York: Oxford University Press.

———. 1993a. *The Environmental Data Book: A Guide to Statistics on the Environment and Development*. Washington, D.C.

———. 1993b. *Purchasing Power of Currencies: Comparing National Incomes Using ICP Data*. International Economics Department. Washington, D.C.

———. 1993c. *World Development Report 1993: Investing in Health*. New York: Oxford University Press.

———. 1994a. *Global Economic Prospects and the Developing Countries 1994*. Washington, D.C.

———. 1994b. *World Development Report 1994: Infrastructure for Development*. New York: Oxford University Press.

———. 1995a. *Advancing Social Development: A World Bank Contribution to the Social Summit*. Washington, D.C.

———. 1995b. *Bureaucrats in Business: The Economics and Politics of Government Ownership*. Washington, D.C.

———. 1995c. *Global Economic Prospects and the Developing Countries 1995*. Washington, D.C.

———. 1995d. *Priorities and Strategies for Education: A Review*. Washington, D.C.

———. 1995e. *Private Sector Development in Low-Income Countries*. Washington, D.C.

———. 1995f. *Toward Gender Equality: The Role of Public Policy—An Overview*. Washington, D.C.

———. 1995g. *World Development Report 1995: Workers in an Integrating World*. New York: Oxford University Press.

———. 1996a. *Environment Matters* (summer). Environment Department. Washington, D.C.

———. 1996b. *From Vision to Action in the Rural Sector*. Agriculture Department. Washington, D.C.

———. 1996c. *Global Economic Prospects and the Developing Countries 1996*. Washington, D.C.

———. 1996d. *Livable Cities for the 21st Century*. Washington, D.C.

———. 1996e. *National Environmental Strategies: Learning from Experience*. Environment Department. Washington, D.C.

———. 1996f. *Poverty Reduction and the World Bank: Progress and Challenges in the 1990s*. Washington, D.C.

———. 1997. *Global Development Finance 1997.* Washington, D.C.

———. Various issues. *Commodity Markets and the Developing Countries* (quarterly). Washington, D.C.

———. Various years. *World Debt Tables.* Washington, D.C.

World Conservation Monitoring Centre (WCMC). 1992. *Global Biodiversity Status of the Earth's Living Resources.* London: Chapman and Hall.

———. 1994. *Biodiversity Data Sourcebook.* Cambridge, U.K.: World Conservation Press.

World Resources Institute in collaboration with UNEP (United Nations Environment Programme) and UNDP (United Nations Development Programme). 1994. *World Resources 1994–95: A Guide to the Global Environment.* New York: Oxford University Press.

World Resources Institute, UNEP (United Nations Environment Programme), UNDP (United Nations Development Programme), and World Bank. 1996. *World Resources 1996–97: A Guide to the Global Environment.* New York: Oxford University Press.

World Resources Institute, International Institute for Environment and Development, and IUCN (World Conservation Union). 1992. *1993 Directory of Country Environmental Studies.* Washington, D.C.

Zimmermann, Klaus F. 1995. "European Migration: Push and Pull." In *Proceedings of the World Bank Annual Conference on Development Economics 1994.* Washington, D.C.: World Bank.

Index of indicators

References are to table numbers.

Index of indicators

World Development Indicators 1997

new publication! Formerly the statistical appendix to the *World Development Report*, these comprehensive data have been enlarged to include more than 75 tables with some 600 indicators. This major new publication provides an expanded view of the world economy for nearly 150 countries—with chapters focusing on people, economy, environment, states and markets, and global links. Concise, insightful commentary tells the story of how people live and work, and how countries are expanding and changing.

April 1997 376 Pages Stock no. 13701 (ISBN 0-8213-3701-7) $60.00

World Development Indicators on CD-ROM

This comprehensive database, which replaces *World Data*, contains most of the underlying time-series data for the *World Development Indicators* and *World Bank Atlas*. We've added powerful new features—now you can generate maps and charts, and download your results to other software programs. Requires Windows 3.1.™

April 1997   Individual Version: Stock no. 13703 (ISBN 0-8213-3703-3) $275.00
Network Version: Stock no. 13702 (ISBN 0-8213-3702-5) $550.00

more features!

World Bank Atlas 1997

One of the Bank's most popular offerings, the *Atlas* has been redesigned as a companion to the *World Development Indicators*. Tables, charts, and 21 colorful maps address the development themes of people, economy, environment, and states and markets. This easy-to-use, inexpensive book is an international standard in statistical compilations and an ideal reference for office or classroom. Text, maps, and references appear in English, French, and Spanish.

April 1997 48 Pages Stock no. 13576 (ISBN 0-8213-3 576-6) $15.00

expanded data!

World Bank Publications

In the USA, contact The World Bank (order form below), P.O. Box 7247-8619, Philadelphia, PA 19170-8619 or phone: (703) 661-1580, Fax: (703) 661-1501. Shipping and handling: US$5.00. For airmail delivery outside the USA, add US$13.00 for one item plus US$6.00 for each additional item. Payment by US$ check to the World Bank or by VISA, MasterCard, or American Express. Customers outside the USA, please contact your World Bank distributor. To find the distributor in your country, please contact the World Bank Office of the Publisher by fax: 202-522-2631 or check the World Bank website www.worldbank.org/. Click on Publications.

Quantity	Title	Stock #	Price	Total Price

❑ Bank check   ❑ VISA   ❑ MasterCard   ❑ American Express

_____
credit card account number

Subtotal cost US$ _____
Shipping and handling US$ _____
Total US$ _____

Expiration Date _____   Signature (required to validate all orders) _____

PLEASE PRINT CLEARLY

Name_____

Address _____

City_____ State _____ Postal Code _____

Country _____ Telephone _____

World Development Indicators

1997

Readers survey

Special offer

If you complete and return this questionnaire before 30 June 1997, we will send you a free copy of next year's World Bank Atlas when it is published in early 1998. Please be sure to complete the mailing information on the reverse side and mail or fax a copy of the questionnaire to us immediately. If you can't make the deadline, we would still like to hear from you.

We need your help!

We would like to know what you think about the new World Development Indicators book and how it compares with other sources of information you use. Your response will help us continue to improve the family of World Development Indicators products.

---

1. How do you use the World Development Indicators?
   (Check as many as apply)
- ○ Analysis and research
- ○ Background information for my work
- ○ Policy formulation
- ○ Supplement to the WDI CD-ROM
- ○ Reference source
- ○ Teaching or training tool
- ○ Update on world issues
- ○ Other

2. How did you obtain the WDI?
- ○ Own purchase
- ○ Employer purchase
- ○ Borrowed
- ○ Library
- ○ Gift

3. How do you rate the overall usefulness of the World Development Indicators? (Check one)
- ○ Very useful
- ○ Useful
- ○ Marginally useful
- ○ Not at all useful

4. What does the World Development Indicators offer that is not provided by other sources?
- ○ Information and statistics
- ○ Background for topical economic events and trends
- ○ Insights into the development process
- ○ Analysis of statistical issues
- ○ Other

6. What sections do you refer to most?
- ○ World view
- ○ People
- ○ Environment
- ○ Economy
- ○ States and markets
- ○ Global links

7. Should we add/subtract tables or indicators to/from any of the sections? Please list against each section.
- ○ World view
- ○ People
- ○ Environment
- ○ Economy
- ○ States and markets
- ○ Global links

8. What do you like most about the WDI's design?
- ○ Section introductions
- ○ Tabular design
- ○ Commentary
- ○ About the data
- ○ Definitions and sources
- ○ Other design features

9. What aspects of the WDI do you least like? What should be changed or improved?
- ○ Section introductions
- ○ Tabular design
- ○ Commentary
- ○ About the data
- ○ Definitions and sources
- ○ Other design features

---

5. How do you rate World Development Indicators?
   (Check one box in each case)

	Excellent	Good	Adequate	Poor
Accuracy	○	○	○	○
Coverage	○	○	○	○
Objectivity	○	○	○	○
Presentation and readability	○	○	○	○
Technical information	○	○	○	○
Usefulness of indicators	○	○	○	○

10. When seeking information on economic development and related subjects how useful do you find the following sources?

	Slightly	Moderately	Very
Books	○	○	○
CD-ROM or diskette products	○	○	○
Colleagues	○	○	○
Courses & seminars	○	○	○
Internet or online services	○	○	○
Journals	○	○	○
Newspapers	○	○	○
Other:	○	○	○

11. Please name one other source of information on economic development that you regularly use:

12. How do you classify the organization where you work?
- ○ Central bank
- ○ Finance ministry
- ○ Planning agency
- ○ Other government agency or public enterprise
- ○ International or regional organization
- ○ Commercial bank or financial organization
- ○ News media outlet
- ○ Other private enterprise
- ○ Nongovernmental organization
- ○ Policy/research institution
- ○ University or college
- ○ Primary or secondary school
- ○ Library
- ○ Other

13. What are your areas of specialization?
- ○ Administration/management
- ○ Economics
- ○ Engineering
- ○ Environmental sciences
- ○ Finance/banking
- ○ Health
- ○ Information management
- ○ Law
- ○ Natural sciences
- ○ Politics
- ○ Public affairs
- ○ Other social sciences
- ○ Teaching
- ○ Other (please state)

14. How large is your organization worldwide?
- ○ 100 or fewer employees
- ○ 100–999 employees
- ○ 1,000–9,999 employees
- ○ 10,000 or more employees

15. How would you categorize your position in the organization where you work?
- ○ Senior management
- ○ Middle management
- ○ Professional staff or faculty
- ○ Consultant
- ○ Student
- ○ Other

16. What is your age?
- ○ Under 25 years
- ○ 25–34 years
- ○ 35–44 years
- ○ 45–54 years
- ○ 55–64 years
- ○ 65 years or older

17. What is your highest level of educational attainment?
- ○ Secondary education or upper level
- ○ University level
- ○ Postgraduate work
- ○ Other

18. Last, please tell us the country in which you are currently residing.

Thank you for completing this survey. Please use the space below or a separate sheet of paper to add any comments about this survey or to elaborate on any of your responses.

Your information:
(should you wish to provide it)

Name

Organization

Street address

City

State/Province

Country, Postal code

Return a copy of this form to:

Information Center, Development Data Group
The World Bank
1818 H Street, NW, Washington, DC 20433 USA
Fax: 202 522 1498

For further information, contact DD Information Center
Tel: 800 590 1906 or 202 473 7824
Fax: 202 522 1498
Email: info@worldbank.org